An Atlas of Interpersonal Situations

An Atlas of Interpersonal Situations provides a systematic theoretical account for understanding the impact of situations on patterns of social interaction. Through descriptions of 21 of the most common situations that people encounter in everyday life, the authors aim to give readers the tools needed to understand how those situations influence interpersonal behavior. These descriptions are intended to be freestanding, each one offering analysis, research examples, and descriptions of the prototypical situation. The authors build upon the tools of interdependence theory, which stresses the manner in which people's outcomes are determined by the structure of their interaction with each other. This analysis makes clear exactly what is "social" about "social psychology."

Harold H. Kelley has won numerous scientific awards, including the American Psychological Association's Distinguished Scientific Contribution Award, the American Sociological Association's Cooley-Mead Award, the Society for Experimental Social Psychology's Distinguished Career Contribution Award, and the International Society for the Study of Personal Relationships' Distinguished Career Contribution Award. He is the coauthor of *The Social Psychology of Groups* and of *Interpersonal Relations: A Theory of Interdependence.* **John G. Holmes** is a three-time winner of the International Society for the Study of Personal Relationships' Distinguished New Contribution Award, former Executive Committee Chair of the Society for Experimental Social Psychology, and former Associate Editor of the *Journal of Personality and Social Psychology.* **Norbert L. Kerr** is the coauthor of *Group Process, Group Decision, and Group Action,* former Associate Editor of the *Journal of Personality and Social Psychology* and of the *Personality and Social Psychology Review,* and a former Executive Committee Chair of the Society for Experimental Social Psychology. **Harry T. Reis** is the President of the International Society for the Study of Personal Relationships, executive officer of the Society for Personality and Social Psychology, former Editor of the *Journal of Personality and Social Psychology,* and coeditor of the *Handbook of Research Methods in Personality and Social Psychology.* **Caryl E. Rusbult** is winner of the National Conference on Family Relations' Reuben Hill Award and the International Society for the Study of Personal Relationships' Distinguished New Contribution Award, and former Associate Editor of the *Journal of Personality and Social Psychology;* she holds the William Friday Professorship, an endowed professorship, at the University of North Carolina director of the Kurt Lewin Institute, an Inte Psychology and Its Applications in The *Journal of Personality and Social Psychology European Journal of Social Psychology.*

T0204826

An Atlas of Interpersonal Situations

HAROLD H. KELLEY
University of California, Los Angeles

JOHN G. HOLMES
University of Waterloo

NORBERT L. KERR
Michigan State University

HARRY T. REIS
University of Rochester

CARYL E. RUSBULT
University of North Carolina

PAUL A. M. VAN LANGE
Vrije Universiteit

CAMBRIDGE
UNIVERSITY PRESS

PUBLISHED BY THE PRESS SYNDICATE OF THE UNIVERSITY OF CAMBRIDGE
The Pitt Building, Trumpington Street, Cambridge, United Kingdom

CAMBRIDGE UNIVERSITY PRESS
The Edinburgh Building, Cambridge CB2 2RU, UK
40 West 20th Street, New York, NY 10011-4211, USA
477 Williamstown Road, Port Melbourne, VIC 3207, Australia
Ruiz de Alarcón 13, 28014 Madrid, Spain
Dock House, The Waterfront, Cape Town 8001, South Africa

http://www.cambridge.org

First published 2003

Printed in the United States of America

Typeface Palatino 10/13 pt.   *System* LATEX 2_ε [TB]

A catalog record for this book is available from the British Library.

Library of Congress Cataloging in Publication Data
An atlas of interpersonal situations / Harold H. Kelley . . . [et al.].
    p.   cm.
Includes bibliographical references and index.
ISBN 0-521-81252-6 – ISBN 0-521-01180-9 (pbk.)
1. Interpersonal relations.   2. Social interaction.   I. Kelley, Harold H.

HM 1106. A85   2002
302 – dc21

                                                    2002067686

ISBN 0 521 81252 6 hardback
ISBN 0 521 01180 9 paperback

This book is dedicated to John W. Thibaut ... friend, colleague, mentor, and admired exemplar of the best in social psychology. Whatever the merits of interdependence theory may be, it is doubtful whether its perspective on interpersonal relations would have existed without his contributions.

Contents

Preface

This preface is a sketch of the "history" of this Atlas, an acknowledgment of the support we had in its preparation, and a characterization of the social process involved in working together. Perhaps we may be forgiven if, in this preface, we pat ourselves on the back for the effort and goodwill we have managed to put into the enterprise. The reader will be left to judge whether those were "worth our whiles."

It all began one fall evening on the corner of 24th and M Streets in Washington, D.C. Earlier that day, in an address to the joint meeting of the Society for Experimental Social Psychology (SESP) and the European Association of Experimental Social Psychology (EAESP), Kelley had described the notion of distinguishing all possible "2 × 2" situations and their implications for personal motivation and social interaction and cognition. The meeting participants had enjoyed a dinner reception at the French Embassy, with dancing and champagne. Holmes, Kelley, and Rusbult had returned to the hotel and were standing on the corner when Reis leapt off a later bus and ran up to them saying, "Why don't we get a grant from the Rockefeller Foundation to go to the Bellagio Center on Lake Como and think and write about all those situations?" We quickly planned to discuss the suggestion at breakfast the next morning, at which time we and another colleague, Van Lange, agreed to pursue it.

Subsequently, Kelley prepared a grant application for the Rockefeller Foundation which, unfortunately, did not draw a favorable response. Meantime, however, Van Lange solicited support from the Kurt Lewin Institute at the Free University of Amsterdam, which enabled Kelley, Rusbult, and Van Lange to meet there for two weeks in the spring of 1996. The concept of "atlas" was already in their thinking, so they took it as their mission to map out the "terrain" of possible situations and how they variously could be distinguished. They had intense discussions about the properties of interdependence and developed an extensive and detailed outline of headings under which each different situation and its implications would be described. In e-mail consultation with Holmes and Reis, the three also decided to invite Kerr and Eddy Van Avermaet to join the enterprise, and they met with Eddy in Amsterdam.

In the summer of 1996, the original five, all of whom are active members of the International Society for the Study of Personal Relationships, met for an afternoon and evening discussion immediately after its Biennial Conference, held that year at the Banff Conference Center in Alberta. Dismay was expressed at the technical detail and complexity of the entry format developed from the Amsterdam discussions. Reis, in particular, argued for an approach that would produce shorter descriptions of each situation, would be more accessible to readers unfamiliar with the technical ideas, and would resonate more strongly with their existing knowledge of interpersonal phenomena. Thus, there developed a mild tension between the favorite technical pirouettes of some of the interdependence theory aficionados and the vision of an audience of readers unfamiliar with interdependence thinking advanced by the "newcomers" to the theory. The resolution of that tension is reflected in the format to be found in this Atlas.

Several members volunteered to prepare some sample "entries" according to suggestions growing out of the Banff meeting. Those were discussed at the next meeting of the group, which followed the 1997 meeting of SESP in Sturbridge, Massachusetts. Kerr joined the group at that meeting and provided an additional "outsider" perspective. Further entries were planned.

Meantime, the absence of outside support for our meetings began to concern us. It became clear that we should ask ourselves about the feasibility of pursuing a project of this magnitude without such support. A crucial unscheduled meeting took place one evening in the front room of Kelley's home in Malibu. He, Van Avermaet, and Van Lange were discussing the matter when the same thought occurred to Kelley and Van Lange: "Let's just do it ourselves, without outside support," or in Paul's colorful phrase, "Let's go for the banana!" That was the point at which we (or at least some of us) gave up the idea of an exotic working trip and replaced it with an implicit plan to continue our ad hoc sessions, piggybacked on conferences, and rely primarily on independent individual work interspersed with group feedback. It goes without saying that the feasibility of that process depended heavily on the fact that we all tended to go to the same conferences and, during the interim periods, had access to e-mail and could rapidly exchange ideas, rough drafts, and comments.

All seven of us met next at the 1998 SESP meetings in Lexington, Kentucky. (Van Avermaet later found it necessary to withdraw because of the growing demands of his university duties in Louvain.) At that time we each volunteered to prepare specific entries according to the emerging format. At our next meeting, in July of 1999 in the charming courtyard of the Old Parsonage in Oxford (in connection with the EAESP meetings), both Holmes (by e-mail) and Reis felt able to announce, "We have the makings of a book here."

Two later piggyback meetings were held in conjunction with the new independent meetings of the Society for Personality and Social Psychology (Nashville, 2000; San Antonio, 2001). And we are greatly indebted to SSCI (Social Sciences Conferences Incorporated), and to Bibb Latané and Deborah Richardson, for their generous support of a very productive five-day working session in late May 2000, at their Nags Head Conference facility at Sea Frolic, Highland Beach, Florida.

In retrospect, an important component of the project's initial appeal was to have a trip to Bellagio and the Italian Lake region, with good friends. Later, as we slowly got under way with the Atlas and began to produce entries, we realized how intrinsically interesting the enterprise itself was. We learned a good deal from each other about how to distinguish and represent situations and how to conceptualize their different implications. That learning was bidirectional, with the "newcomers" becoming familiar with the interdependence perspective and language, but also with the "card-carrying" interdependence people being encouraged to simplify and clarify that language (while still adding conceptual curlicues necessary for richer situational analysis). And it was not unusual for a simple idea innocently advanced by one person in preparing a particular entry to lead to an unanticipated and useful conceptual advance proposed by another member of the group. We also learned to work together, sweetening criticism with humor and making jokes out of each other's foibles. So, increasingly, the meetings became welcome occasions of pleasurable intellectual exchange. Perhaps the reader will also realize that the joint product presented here was accomplished by a group of senior people in their various specialties and departments – people who have had and continue to have heavy responsibilities of instructing graduates, chairing departments or areas, officiating at conferences, gaining grant support, and supervising assistants in research programs.

So we present here, with considerable pride, the product of that rather extended and messy, but ultimately enjoyable, process. Perhaps we may be forgiven for some minor variations in style and voice among the various sections of the Atlas. The person(s) indicated as primarily responsible for each portion produced the first draft and made subsequent revisions, but every section was read closely by each of the six of us and was almost always subject to several cycles of revision. So we feel that the designation of the six of us as "authors" is entirely justified by that process. In the list of authors that appears on the cover and title page, Kelley drew the first position in recognition of the other authors' gratitude for his contributions to the development of interdependence theory. The rest of the list is in alphabetical order.

The Authors, May 2002

PART ONE

INTRODUCTION AND THEORY

1

Interpersonal Situations

The Context of Social Behavior

Our goal in writing this Atlas was to provide behavioral scientists with a tool for analyzing and understanding the influence of interpersonal situations on social interaction. We believe that there are important insights about human social behavior to be gained from systematic investigation of the properties of situations. To be sure, "the situation" has long been the object of considerable attention in several of the behavioral sciences, notably social psychology (the discipline that we six authors all call home). Nonetheless, our impression is that this scrutiny has been more intuitive than theoretical, more haphazard than systematic. Furthermore, existing research has tended to emphasize the relatively impersonal aspects of situations even though interpersonal factors are often likely to dominate the individual's attention and behavior. We maintain that a more comprehensive theoretical approach to the description and analysis of situations, and especially to their interpersonal properties, will do much to advance our understanding of social interaction.

Interdependence theory forms the conceptual skeleton for our analysis. First proposed by Thibaut and Kelley (1959) and later extended by Kelley and Thibaut (1978), interdependence theory provides a systematic account of certain key interpersonal properties of situations, as well as the individual's response to those properties, as the causal determinants of social interaction. The term "interdependence" refers to the manner in which two individuals influence each other's outcomes in the course of their interaction. This Atlas, however, is only incidentally a primer on interdependence

Harry Reis had primary responsibility for preparation of this chapter.

theory; our foremost goal is to apply this theory to the description and analysis of certain common social situations. Each of these situations receives detailed examination in a series of "entries," as we refer to them throughout this Atlas, which will illustrate to the reader the benefits of considering social situations in terms of the abstract and characteristic properties of interdependence that exist between the interacting partners. Readers will encounter in these entries many important questions that have engaged the curiosity of behavioral scientists for decades. By identifying each situation's basic properties of interdependence, as well as the elements shared with, and differentiated from, other situations, our analysis sheds new (or as we see it, conceptually clearer) light on these questions. In so doing, we hope to provide readers with a set of conceptual tools for analyzing these and other situations.

1.1 The Concept of Situation in Social Psychology

The American Heritage Dictionary defines situation as "a position or status with regard to conditions and attendant circumstances" and as "a combination of circumstances at a given moment; state of affairs." As nearly all textbooks show, social psychology takes pride in ascribing to itself the study of "situationism" and "the power of the situation" – that is, to demonstrate that the situational context is a potent force in shaping behavior. In this regard, social psychologists trace their roots to the E in Kurt Lewin's (1936/1966) paradigmatic equation, $B = f(P, E)$ – *Behavior* depends on the *Person* and the *Environment*. Solomon Asch, for example, stipulated that "most social acts have to be understood in their setting, and lose meaning if isolated. . . . No error in thinking about social facts is more serious than the failure to see their place and function" (1952, p. 61). Similarly, in their classic review of some of the field's most influential studies, Nisbett and Ross (1991) provide compelling testimony to the explanatory power of situational explanations of behavior.

Current practice in social psychology treats situationism as an exceedingly broad concept, encompassing, for example, the impact of information about a new acquaintance or hypothetical other on thoughts, feelings, and behavior toward that person; the interplay of stylistic and substantive factors on the appeal of persuasive messages; and the degree of deliberateness with which bits of social information are processed. Despite this diversity, or perhaps because of it, the field has been criticized for its failure to develop a comprehensive theoretical model of situations and their structure or impact. For example, Kenny, Mohr, and Levesque (2001) echoed a widespread opinion in stating that

Although social psychologists have emphasized the importance of the situation, they have been less successful in its conceptualization. . . . [T]here is no universally accepted scheme for understanding what is meant by situation. It does not even appear that there are major competing schemes, and all too often the situation is undefined. (p. 129)

The absence of such a conceptual framework, as Rozin (2001) has observed, may not be problematic in the short term, but it seems certain to inhibit the long-term conceptual development of a discipline that takes "the situation" as a central conceptual focus (see also Zajonc, 1999).

This Atlas provides such a conceptualization of situations, beginning in chapter 2. However, the theoretical framework that we favor differs from the field's more colloquial use of the term in two key respects. First, whereas existing studies of situational influences on behavior often focus on impersonal features of the situation, *we emphasize its interpersonal core* – the degree and kind of interdependence between people, the information they have about each other and the situation, and the behavioral options open to them as they interact. We do so for a variety of conceptual and practical reasons, all of which amount to an appreciation for the fundamental importance of social relations in understanding human behavior. These reasons may be evident in a cardinal observation: That from the actor's perspective, interpersonal factors – who one is with, one's history with that person and similar others in related situations, what one is trying to accomplish with that person, and how one's personal outcomes link to the other's outcomes – are fundamental to differentiating one situation from another and, therefore, to understanding the impact of situations on behavior (Reis, Collins, & Berscheid, 2000). For example, a critical comment from a dinner companion has very different implications for cognition, emotion, and behavior coming from one's adolescent daughter, well-meaning best friend, boss, maternal grandfather, dissertation advisor, insurance agent, therapist, or a stranger.

A second distinction intrinsic to our meaning of the term situation involves *a focus on its objective properties*. Social psychologists in large part subscribe to Nisbett and Ross's (1991) principle of construal: that causal analysis should concentrate on the personal and subjective meaning of the situation to the actor. Although we do not deny the significance of personal construals – indeed, throughout this Atlas, readers will see that "what the

individual makes of the situation" is a central ingredient of our analysis –
we suggest that the analysis of social interaction must begin at an earlier
causal step, namely, with description of the situation's objective elements
(see chapter 2). In this regard, we concur with Gottman and Notarius (2000)
who, in a slightly different context, observed that to understand a spouse's
interpretation of an interaction, one must first know what actually took
place in that interaction. (For example, to understand an adolescent's complaint that her parents are unsupportive, it would be useful to observe a
support-seeking interaction between them.) To be somewhat more specific,
our analysis focuses on a small set of key properties that define situations
with interdependence between individuals and that serve as the basis for
the interactions that emerge between those individuals. We maintain that
the interaction patterns that we commonly observe in everyday life, in fact,
may be better understood by clearly differentiating the situation from the
interpersonal motives and attitudes that operate on or transform that situation and together shape those interaction patterns. We further maintain
that to diagnose the reality of a situation and to understand the behaviors that partners exhibit, it is necessary to determine the interdependent
structure of their goals. In other words, as discussed below, the study of
interaction can help researchers uncover the person factors that shape the
individual's response to situations.

Although this analysis begins with an objective assessment of situations, it is not inconsistent with theories that emphasize the individual's
personal construal of those situations. As an illustration, one may consider the well-known Milgram obedience experiments, in which an insis-
tent authority figure (the experimenter) repeatedly demanded that subjects
administer increasingly painful, and eventually seemingly lethal, electric
shocks to a peer who, unbeknownst to the subjects, was an experimental
confederate and who in actuality received no shocks. The fact that a large
percentage of the subjects complied with those instructions is often cited
as evidence of "the power of the situation" – in other words, that the experimenter's demands somehow "caused" the subjects' obedient behavior.
We propose instead that the situation created in this experiment, defined
in terms of the subjects' relationship with the authoritative domineering
experimenter and the putative dependent peer, afforded subjects with an
opportunity to select one of two interaction patterns: to obediently shock
the peer or to resist the experimenter's entreaties and thereby act in accord with more humane principles. The choice reflects "what the subject
makes of the situation"; that is, the subject's considered response to the
objective conditions inherent in this situation, as it has been devised by the

researchers. Indeed, part of what fascinates us about this classic work is that in the base situation, the experimenter has little if any objective means to compel the subject to comply with his demands – the subject must transform an objectively harmless refusal to comply into an act of disobedience to authority, or an act of compliance that is objectively harmless to the self into an act of seeming violence toward another human being. As we show in chapter 3, a full situational analysis involves explicit differentiation of the objective properties of the situation (e.g., a source of social influence with some degree of social status or authority; acts that clearly will inflict pain on another person) from the interpersonal motives and attitudes that shape the individual's response to those properties. Thus, rather than demonstrating "the power of the situation," to our way of thinking, this research demonstrates "the power of what the person makes of the situation."

Our analysis of the situation focuses on three aspects of interdependence: the ways in which partners affect each other's outcomes, how they share information with each other, and the serial ordering of their responses. Of course, there are other ways in which situations may be described, involving various other interpersonal and impersonal attributes. We emphasize these particular properties because of their fundamental and pervasive impact on social interaction. Social interaction is for many researchers the central topic of social psychology (e.g., Hinde, 1997; Holmes, 2000; Kelley et al., 1983; Reis et al., 2000). Kelley (2000), for example, asserted that "the proper study of social psychology is the study of interaction and its immediate determinants and consequences" (p. 11). Nevertheless, over many years interaction has drifted from the center of the field to its periphery (Barone, 1999), reflecting the field's growing emphasis on individualistic, intrapsychic processes (Steiner, 1986). Zajonc (1998) critically highlighted this trend in observing that social psychologists "need to look less at the mind and more at interactions." The infrastructure needed for such redirection includes a more comprehensive and differentiated description than currently exists of the basic patterns of social interdependence that arise regularly in common everyday situations.

We find the absence of a systematic map of interpersonal situations somewhat ironic. We have been repeatedly struck by people's intuitive ability to recognize situations in their own lives without any sort of formal training in interdependence analysis and, moreover, usually without the ability to articulate the abstract properties that underlie such recognition. For example, most people readily appreciate that situations with shared interests are more likely to foster cooperative interaction than are situations with conflicting interests. And, most people intuitively grasp that when one partner's outcomes depend strongly on the other's behavior, the more dependent individual must take pains to avoid offending the more powerful other. The ability to distinguish situations from one another has functional value for the individual because it facilitates effective social interaction; that is, if one is aware that such interdependencies exist, one may adjust one's behavior accordingly. On the other hand, misrecognizing the structure of an existing situation may result in interactions that are awkward, uncomfortable, poorly coordinated, quarrelsome, or dangerous. The presentation in this Atlas is organized around prototypes of common situations in order to capitalize on people's implicit ability to recognize patterns of interdependence.

We speculate that an ability to recognize certain interpersonal situations might have evolutionary roots. Cosmides and Tooby (1992) instruct us that

> the mind consists of a set of adaptations, designed to solve the longstanding adaptive problems humans encountered as hunter-gatherers. Such a view is not controversial to most behavioral scientists when applied to topics such as vision or balance. Yet adaptationist approaches to human psychology are considered radical – or even transparently false – when applied to most other areas of human thought and action, especially social behavior. Our ancestors ... needed to construct ... a social map of the persons, relationships, motives, interactions, emotions, and intentions that made up their social world. (p. 163)

What could be more central to such a map, we submit, than understanding precisely how one is interdependent with others in the social environment? Coping effectively with this interdependence is, after all, central to successful resolution of such adaptive concerns as mate selection, reproduction, child rearing, monitoring and besting sexual rivals, resource and food acquisition, forming and maintaining reliable alliances while fending off competitors, and protection against predators, to name some of the more significant examples. (See Kenrick & Trost, 1997, for a more general discussion of the role of social relations in evolutionary adaptation.)

If there is adaptive significance in recognizing the abstract patterns of interdependence that are present in everyday social relations, then learning to recognize them becomes an important developmental task. Certain socialization practices and experiences are designed to teach children how to distinguish among situations and to behave accordingly once identified. Bugental (2000) has described some of these practices in proposing a typology of fundamental and distinct relationship domains, each one of which is linked to specialized neural "modules." Clearly, the ability to understand abstract patterns of interaction, as well as their likely determinants and consequences, involves many complex cognitive judgments and insights. For instance (and as the entries in this Atlas will illustrate), the individual must be able to discern which situation she is in and which she is not in; must appreciate the values, norms, dispositions, and motives relevant to the existing situation; must be able to predict the likely behavior of interaction partners in this situation; must anticipate potential unfoldings of events over time; and must also imagine each of these from the partner's perspective. Perhaps it is no wonder, then, that the complexity of analyzing interpersonal situations has given theorists more than their share of intellectual headaches!

In short, as with its intellectual parent, interdependence theory, this Atlas takes as its guiding premise the idea that the systematic analysis of interpersonal situations offers a potentially fruitful tool for understanding the patterns of social interaction that both behavioral scientists and lay persons observe in everyday life.

1.1.1 The Situation and the Person

The analysis of situations is sometimes thought to contradict, or at least to be independent of, the analysis of person factors. Even the oft-cited P $\times$ S (Person $\times$ Situation) interactionist perspective implies that the characteristics of situations and of person factors are somehow separable and distinct. Throughout this volume, we take a different approach. We suggest that situations and person factors are inextricably linked such that each cannot be understood in isolation from the other.

The term "person factors," as is more fully explained in chapter 3, refers to any properties of the individual that come into play when he/she is aware of and responsive to the situation. Thus this rather broad term includes motives, values, personality traits, habits, attitudes, goals, preferences, and defenses, both in regard to the individual's general orientation to the social world and to his or her orientation to a specific role, partner, or relationship. Person factors are a necessary component of the study of social interaction because they determine the individual's perception of and response to the objective properties of the situation. That is, because situations present the individual with behavioral options, each of which has tangible consequences for the self and the other, they make possible (or "afford," to use terminology proposed by Gibson, 1979) the expression of relevant person factors in behavior – for example, an existing vulnerability of one's partner to oneself affords possible responses of exploitation or support, the choice between which will depend on relevant person factors. On the other hand, our analysis suggests that the influence of "person factors" is difficult to diagnose when the situation compels a particular behavior. Thus, for example, we would describe a person as cooperative only when he or she pursued prosocial goals in situations that do not demand such behavior. "Person factors," in other words, serve to determine "what the actor makes" of the existing interdependent situation, and their impact is reflected directly in the interaction that ensues.

The idea that situations provide a context in which person factors may be revealed is central to the personality theory of Mischel and Shoda (1995). They theorize that the features of situations activate particular and relevant individual difference variables, which in turn trigger the cognitions and emotions that lead to a behavioral response. This process is idiographic at several levels: the selection of certain situations from among myriad possibilities; the situational features that are most salient to a given person; the "cognitive-affective mediating units" that are activated for that person; and the dynamic way in which these levels interact. Central to our analysis is their notion that personality be conceptualized as a predictable pattern of variability across situations; that is, as a series of *if X exists, then response Y is more likely* contingencies. For example, Shoda, Mischel, and Wright (1994) examined children's behavior as a function of certain eliciting conditions – for example, *if* "peer teased, provoked, or threatened," *then* "child was verbally aggressive." Our analysis also uses the logic of *if...then* contingencies, but we define the antecedents and consequents somewhat more narrowly: the X refers to the objective properties of situations, whereas the Y refers to interpersonal behavior.

This model of person factors emphasizes the manner in which individual differences are fundamentally and inextricably rooted in situations. Interestingly, it resembles the East Asian, collectivist conception of the person as being situated in a broad social context. As Choi, Nisbett, and Norenzayan (1999) discuss, whereas in the Western world causal accounts tend to locate responsibility primarily in the attributes of the individual, Eastern explanations of behavior tend to stress the individual's response to the social environment. This difference can be seen, for example, in the fact that whereas we in Western psychology have an extensive, highly articulate, and well-differentiated vocabulary for describing individual differences (especially personality), our language for describing situations is vague and poorly developed (Snyder & Cantor, 1998). In fact, the authors of this Atlas came squarely face-to-face with this inadequacy in our rather protracted discussions about the names for the various entries. As readers may guess, we struggled to find names that would be descriptive and accurate, and that would evoke unambiguous referents in the reader's mind. It is far easier to find names for individual attributes, as terms like "extraversion," "conscientiousness," and "self-esteem" plainly reveal. Another hope for this Atlas is that it will contribute to a lexicon of situations.

1.2 Why an "Atlas"?

Readers may wonder why we refer to this volume as an atlas. The name is intended to be more than an evocative allusion. An atlas is a collection of maps or charts that systematically illustrates its subject by representing one or more of its properties in relation to the same properties of neighboring or otherwise similar subjects. Thus there are atlases that depict particular places by describing their geography – longitude and latitude, rivers and lakes, roadways, boundaries, and so forth – and their localized segments – states, cities, and census tracts. There are also atlases that display variation along specific dimensions – for example, elevation maps, rainfall maps, population density maps, and maps that display the distribution of ethnicities or religions within an area. Each map or chart portrays its subject in sharp detail; the collection thereof provides a multidimensional space in which each individual entry can be located in relation to every other entry. In so doing, the collection demonstrates the nearness or distance (i.e., similarities and differences) among the various components.

Much as a geographical atlas may sharpen its reader's working knowledge of a place, an atlas of interpersonal situations may sharpen our perceptions by providing detailed descriptions of each situation, while simultaneously indicating its location with reference to other situations. Thus our discussion of each situation includes a detailed account of its defining properties and an analysis of its relationship to neighboring (i.e., conceptually similar) situations. Each entry provides a representation (like a map) intended to facilitate the reader's identification and delineation of that situation. In combination, the collective Atlas organizes its topical domain – interpersonal situations – into a conceptually bounded series of distinct and basic situations that we hope will illuminate some of the basic dimensions of all interpersonal situations. The entries, in short, are specialized maps of particular interpersonal situations; the full Atlas displays the structure of the social world, a mosaic of such situations.

In making each situation the centerpiece of scrutiny, our analysis borrows loosely from a Roschian approach to learning. Rosch's work on object categorization demonstrates that people tend to learn and think about objects at intermediate (or, as she put it, "basic") levels of abstraction – for example, chairs (Rosch, Mervis, Gray, Johnson, & Boyes-Braem, 1976;

Rosch, 1988). Gradually, people learn to infer upward in a hierarchy of classification to the superordinate categories of which the basic levels are elements – furniture – and downward, to the more specific examples that are subordinate to the basic level – desk chairs, beach chairs, high chairs, and so on. In our usage, the basic-level phenomena are the set of fundamental situations themselves. As readers acquire familiarity with them, we expect their conceptual grasp to extend upward to a more superordinate level – here, the basic dimensions of interdependence – and downward to the various more specific manifestations of each situation.

It bears mention that this Atlas is in many ways more like the primitive atlases of the Age of Exploration than the computer-generated, space-age atlases of today. In large part, we have elected to focus on the well-explored terrain of existing research and theory, bypassing the treacheries of "terra incognita" phenomena. Our rationale is likely similar to that of the early cartographers: We have depicted what we know with the conviction that even an incomplete and occasionally inaccurate map will be useful, and with the hope that our guide will point more intrepid explorers into uncharted areas.

We intend this Atlas to be used in many of the ways that atlases of the physical world are used. For example, a visitor from outside the United States might be aware that there is a city named Denver, but know little about it. And so she might consult an atlas to determine its location with regard to known sites, to obtain travel itineraries from other places, and to acquire useful information about Denver's principle features – for example, its topography, population, and landmarks. In an analogous fashion, a researcher might know that there is a situation called Hero, but know little about it. This Atlas can help her scout Hero's terrain by describing its location with regard to other situations, its defining properties of interdependence, and its characteristic patterns of social interaction. Both cases allow the investigator to know a place better by identifying the place in detail and by locating it within a larger perspective.

Finally, we also designed this Atlas to help scholars explore situations from within. Much as a pioneer standing on a plot of land is likely to have little idea how that land looks on a map, researchers sometimes have difficulty situating their particular research problem within the larger universe of interpersonal situations. Discovering one's particular location can be invaluable. By pinpointing the situation to which a given process applies, researchers may recognize heretofore obscure commonalities with neighboring situations, thereby highlighting potential generalizations of existing findings and suggesting fruitful extensions in new directions. For example, a developmental psychologist might gain new and valuable insights about delay of gratification by recognizing and considering its conceptual situational neighbor, the Investment situation. Similarly, in more applied settings, possible solutions to seemingly intractable interactional dilemmas may be suggested by considering methods adapted from situations with shared conceptual features.

Readers, then, will find our use of the term "Atlas" to be more than metaphorical. We invite readers to begin their reading much as they would enter a road atlas: to select a map of current interest. As they explore that map, they will discover branches that lead their journey to other maps and into unexpected and perhaps uncharted regions as well. Traversing back and forth across the full domain of interpersonal situations represented in this Atlas will, we hope, produce the same appreciation for the larger entity and its organizational structure as would a road trip that repeatedly crisscrosses a geographical entity.

1.3 What This Atlas Is

Our foremost goal in writing this Atlas was to foster the reader's awareness and understanding of the regularities in social behavior that originate in the interdependent properties of interpersonal situations. As noted above, and as we more fully explicate in chapter 2, the causal roots of social interaction are a product of the objective properties of situations and the interpersonal dispositions and motives of the actors involved. Besides their most immediate and direct impact on behavior, situations make certain interaction processes more salient (and hence more likely to be evident in overt behavior) and other processes less salient. Thus, to account for the expression of particular interaction processes, it is necessary to have a systematic theory of the structure and interactional implications of interpersonal situations.

We speculate that researchers often have in mind implicit notions of this sort as they design and conduct research. (For example, an investigator seeking to study the impact of spousal attitudes on marital interaction may recognize the need to create a situation with diverging interests, to distinguish feelings for one's spouse from general approval for the activity under consideration.) Making such notions explicit and grounding them in formal theory is one of our main aims.

In preparing this Atlas, we also sought to create a sort of "traveler's guide" to an intrinsically interesting set of common and distinctive situations, each of which illuminates a recognizable and well-defined pattern of interaction. The 21 situations selected are neither exhaustive nor necessarily ideal from the perspective of theoretical completeness. But they do serve two purposes: one, they illustrate basic principles of the interdependence analysis of interpersonal situations; and two, they depict some of the more familiar and frequent situations that arise in ordinary life. Our approach is taxonomic only in the sense that the situations can be discriminated and classified according to conceptually defined properties; we do not claim to have parsed the domain of interpersonal situations in the best or most thorough manner. In fact, we anticipate that future atlases will improve on our scheme.

We also hope that this volume will spur interaction researchers to further explore the impact of situational factors in structuring interactional possibilities. As readers will see, we argue that interaction process cannot be fully comprehended without describing and understanding the role of the situation in shaping that process. In its central thesis, our position is reminiscent of Steiner's (1972) observation that understanding of the task is fundamental to any and all analyses of group performance, because distinct tasks by their very nature require that group members interact in different ways. (For example, tasks that can be subdivided into relatively independent parts tend to engender different forms of interaction than tasks that compel joint activity.) We similarly suggest that delineation of the interpersonal situation is central to the analysis of social interaction. Appreciation of this principle is likely to encourage more situation-focused research, another end toward which this Atlas is dedicated.

1.4 What This Atlas Is Not

Readers may find their travels through this Atlas simplified by knowing some of the goals we did not intend this Atlas to achieve. First, we did not write a textbook on interdependence theory. Reflecting the Roschian metaphor described earlier, our presentation is situation-centered, not theory-centered. Although we do use interdependence theory as our basic analytic tool (hence chapters 2 through 4, which provide just enough theory for readers to comprehend our expedition through the situations), readers well grounded in the theory will find in these pages a somewhat different presentation than that to which they are accustomed.

Second, we neither advance nor advocate a game theoretic analysis of social interaction as preferable to other forms of conceptual scrutiny. To be sure, there is a superficial resemblance in our use of certain tools commonly employed by game theorists – notably, matrix representations and numerical outcomes – but these are in most instances not essential for readers to follow our analysis of the situations. (The advantage of these tools rests in their ability to describe properties of situations in abstract, precise, and universal terms, and that is why we use them to present the basic theory. Chapter 2 discusses the oft-asked question: "Where do the numbers come from?") Nonetheless, the analysis can at times become technically complex. We recommend that readers committed to mastering the full potential of the combinatorial approach we develop begin their reading with some of the Atlas's early, less technically demanding entries.

Third, we cannot emphasize too strongly that this is not an economically grounded theory of self-interest, that is, of the sort that begins (and ends) with the premise that people seek to "maximize rewards and minimize costs." Instead, our analysis follows Kelley and Thibaut (1985) in rejecting that narrow assumption. Self-interest is but one of a number of motives applicable to the analysis of interpersonal situations. Although we rely on terms familiar to self-interested economic models – for example, "reward," "cost," and "investment" – we use them to describe objective properties of situations or their corresponding patterns of interaction in abstract but readily accessible language. In fact, as readers will see, in many instances our analysis begins with the observation that people often forsake immediate self-interest in favor of other interpersonal motives – altruism, justice, loyalty, accommodation, heroism, self-destruction, and the willingness to sacrifice, to name but a few of the examples that readers will encounter in the entries. The tendency to take one's social partners into account is an essential condition of social life – as Miller (1999, p. 1059) put it, "Homo economicus, it should not be forgotten, inhabits a social world" – and therefore that tendency should not and cannot be ignored, dismissed, or reduced to naked self-interest. A major advantage of the situational analysis that we perform is its ability to consider, within a single theoretical model, the varieties of behavior displayed when self-interest and other social motives conflict.

Finally, it should be noted that this Atlas is not intended to replace existing theories of social cognition, interpersonal relationships, or group processes. Rather, wherever feasible we integrate the principles and findings of those theories with our own schematic approach to interdependence. Of course we hope researchers in all those areas of inquiry will choose to include the constructs of this Atlas in their own theoretical toolboxes.

1.5 Organization of the Atlas

The Atlas begins with four chapters (including this one) that describe our theoretical approach and the key principles of interdependence theory, as it informs our analysis of the situations. Chapters 2 and 3 present the rudiments of the theory, highlighting the three basic features of our analysis (outcome interdependence, response conditions, and information conditions), and discussing the role of person factors. Chapter 4 provides a somewhat more intricate "geography" that illustrates how complex situations may be explained as particular combinations of more basic components. Readers who are less comfortable with the technical dictates of the matrix approach may wish to skip this chapter and move directly to the entries.

The main body of the Atlas follows, consisting of 21 entries, preceded by an introduction that provides a general discussion of the rationale for including each of them in the Atlas. Each entry examines in some detail the properties and interactional consequences of a distinctive interpersonal situation. Each entry also includes clear everyday examples, a formal analysis of the situation, discussion of similarities and differences from neighboring situations, and description of some relevant research, chiefly drawn from the social and psychological sciences and focusing on patterns of social interaction likely to arise in that situation. Readers are advised to begin with the earlier simple situations (simple, because they represent relatively straightforward combinations of the basic components), and then to progress to the later, more complex situations. The entries have been written to be freestanding, to permit readers to move among them in more or less any order according to the dictates of scholarly curiosity or passing fancy.

The Atlas concludes with an epilogue that reexamines the Atlas's goals and likely accomplishments, and identifies some fruitful directions for further theoretical and empirical work on the questions raised by the Atlas.

2

Outcome Interdependence

A "situation" is defined in the dictionary as "a position with respect to conditions and circumstances," or, more generally, as a "site" or "problem." These introductory chapters describe how, in keeping with that definition, we describe and distinguish among situations involving several persons, that is, interpersonal situations. In this chapter, we give concrete examples of a simple yet useful method for characterizing such situations, namely, the "outcome matrix," and explain the rationale for its use. We then show the implications of that method as well as some of its limitations. Chapter 3 describes our remedies for those limitations.

This Atlas is based on a particular theory known as "interdependence theory." It was first presented by Thibaut and Kelley (1959) and then elaborated in Kelley and Thibaut (1978) and Kelley (1984b). It derives from Kurt Lewin's emphasis on interdependence as "the essence of a group" (1948, p. 84), and it implements that view by borrowing payoff matrices from game theory (Luce & Raiffa, 1957) and adapting them to the broader purposes of an interpersonal psychology. Other, newer elaborations of the theory, concerning situational conditions affecting the timing and sequencing of behavior and the availability of information, are less well developed but deserve and receive attention in our Atlas.

The theory aspires to provide a means for drawing systematic and logical distinctions among situations which make it possible to imagine laying them out on a "map" or "globe" of the situational "world" – hence our metaphor of an "atlas." In its pursuit of that goal, the theory succeeds

Harold Kelley had primary responsibility for preparation of this chapter.

fairly well in its analysis of the central phenomena of interdependence which is how persons control each other's *outcomes*, that is, their rewards and costs, well-being, satisfaction-dissatisfaction. (The fruits of that analysis are described in some detail in chapter 4.) The theory makes certain assumptions about control (e.g., it focuses on dyadic patterns of outcome interdependence), but within the limits set by those assumptions, it permits us to specify many theoretically possible situations. Moreover, it draws our attention to certain "landmark" patterns which, by virtue of their location in the domain, are prototypes of the problems that interdependent persons may encounter.

2.1 The Matrix Representation of Outcome Interdependence: Some Examples

Let us consider first what it means to focus on *outcome* interdependence. We select some simple examples from a weekend in the life of two young people. Eamon and Kyoko are driving through Sacramento on Interstate 80 at 3:30 A.M. one spring Saturday morning, on their way to the lower reaches of the Sierra Nevadas above Auburn. After some heated argument about how long it would take them to reach their destination, they had left San Jose around 2:00 A.M. Part of the problem was that Eamon tends to be a "night person" and likes his sleep in the morning. Kyoko does her "best" sleeping early in the night and doesn't mind getting up early. So she is doing the driving and Eamon is sporadically nodding off.

These two young people, in their early 30s, had met at their work in a small computer software company and have shared an apartment in San Jose for 8 months. Kyoko, a third-generation Japanese American, is an expert programmer. Eamon arrived in the United States several years ago, on a special entry permit based on his talents and engineering experience gained with a computer manufacturer in Ireland.

They are driving north on their way to record bird songs in a meadow along a branch of the Holmes River. They had made this same trip 3 weeks before in order to join members of the Nature Sounds Society in recording the wrens, red-winged blackbirds, bullfrogs, cicadas, and so on, that are plentiful in that particular meadow. They both had found it an exhilarating experience. Eamon was especially taken with the technology of the parabolic and shotgun microphones and the high fidelity recordings. For her part, Kyoko treasured the bird songs themselves, which reminded her of her childhood on the farm her father had leased near the small Swedish enclave of Langeburg in the Central San Joaquin Valley. On the earlier trip, they had learned from the Society members that the best sounds can be heard while the sky is still dark but just before dawn. After sunrise, the birds quiet down, and with daylight the bird-listeners' activities are often defeated by the noisy chatter and movements of bird-watchers.

2.1.1 Coordination Problems

As they leave the highway and finally reach the dirt road leading into the meadow, they encounter two problems. The first is an unexpected fork in the road and neither is sure which way to take. As they discuss the problem, they are still a bit miffed with each other from the argument about their departure time. Eamon is sure that they should take the left turn and cross the bridge over the small creek that runs out of the meadow. Kyoko angrily reminds him that he was asleep the last time they came up this road. She remembers taking the right road at the fork and, over his objections, simply proceeds to do so.

After several miles, they encounter a second problem. Along the swampy roadside a birch tree, weakened near its roots, has been blown over by the night's wind and now lies in the road, blocking their way. The tree is too large for Eamon to move out of the way by himself. However, they see that if he lifts one end and Kyoko lifts the other, the two of them can move it off to one side.

Our matrix representation of this situation is shown by the upper matrix in Table 2.1. The log has an east end and a west end, so we label Kyoko's and Eamon's behavioral options according to the two ends each might lift. The matrix shows that, depending on what each person does, any one of four distinctive events may occur, namely, both lift the east end, Eamon lifts the east end while Kyoko lifts the west end, and so forth. The consequences of each of the four events – the outcomes each person experiences as a result of their two actions – are shown in each cell of the matrix. Kyoko's outcomes are shown in the upper right portion of each cell and Eamon's, in the lower left portion. The positive outcomes represent their benefits to be gained from moving the log. Their outcomes are shown to be equal but that need not be the case, because the outcomes to each one depend on many factors, including the strength of their respective desires to continue to the meadow and other possible differences between them. For example, if Kyoko suffers from a "trick back," it may give her great pain or it may even become dislocated by the heavy lifting. In that event, her outcomes from any lifting include very negative ones. Under other circumstances, the prospect of negative outcomes for both of them provide the impetus to their coordination. For example, if they are already somewhat late in arriving at

TABLE 2.1. *Outcome Matrices for Two Coordination Problems (Corresponding versus Conflicting Interests)*

Kyoko

	East	West
East	0 0	+5 +5
West	+5 +5	0 0

Eamon (East / West rows)

Matrix 3*
Corresponding Interests

Kyoko

	Knoll	Reeds
Knoll	+5 −5	0 +5
Reeds	0 +5	+5 −5

Eamon (Knoll / Reeds rows)

Matrix 4*
Conflicting Interests

* The matrix number indicates the relevant entry in the body of the Atlas.

the meadow, both will want to avoid the loss of valuable recording time through failing quickly to move the log and continue on their way.

In the situation shown, the positive covariance (correlation) between their respective outcomes from the four possible events shows that the log's removal is an event they both desire. (We describe the situation as one with "corresponding interests.") The most important feature of the outcome pattern is that it shows that they are required to coordinate their actions in a way that enables them to lift opposite ends. Their situation is obviously one of interdependence inasmuch as their actions affect each other's outcomes. The interdependence problem can be solved by their joint efforts and they have a common interest in creating an interaction that includes such efforts.

In the course of their interaction, one person's initial action may more or less dictate what the other must then do. If Kyoko goes to pick up one end, it becomes apparent that Eamon should go to the other end. And an important temporal aspect of the problem is that it requires them to do their lifting at the same time. Communication will be useful in facilitating that simultaneity of their actions. To get the two properly positioned, she may go to one end while pointing to the other end, or she may say, "I'll take this end and you take that one." If the two ends of the tree are not equally heavy and Kyoko's back poses a problem, their anticipated outcomes from taking one end or the other may not be the same for the two. In that case, a suggestion made by Eamon in ignorance of Kyoko's side of the problem may be quite inappropriate. To solve the simultaneity problem, one of them is likely to say, "On three, we'll both lift. One, two, ... " Those examples illustrate the important roles that the timing of behavior, possession of information, and communication of intentions play in solving interdependence problems. The matrix representation of a situation does not specify its temporal and informational features. Our suggestions for how those features can be represented are left for chapter 3.

In the example above, as in many of life's situations, coordination is achieved by the two persons' doing different but *complementary* things. However, in many other situations, coordination is achieved by taking *similar* actions. For example, if they go to separate listening posts but want then to meet after the morning wears on and the birds quiet down, it will be necessary for them to coordinate their actions in a way that will take them to the *same* one of the several possible meeting spots.

In some circumstances, Eamon and Kyoko may have different preferences about how a coordination problem should be solved. For example, on their earlier trip, they learned the location of the two best listening spots, so the question arises of whether this time they should go together to one of them or should separate. Eamon strongly prefers that they separate, arguing that separating will enable them to capture the sounds of a wider range of birds and frogs on their recordings. On the other hand, Kyoko is unsure about how to use her parabolic microphone to its optimal advantage and would like to be with Eamon for the advice he can give. The matrix for this situation is shown as matrix 4 in Table 2.1. The two best locations are on a small grassy knoll at the edge of the meadow and, further down at the edge of the stream, in a clump of reeds. These are designated in matrix 4 in Table 2.1 as "Knoll" and "Reeds," and the four possibilities include both persons on the knoll, both in the reeds, and Eamon at one and Kyoko at the other. Again there is a coordination problem, but here there is a conflict of interest about how it is to be dealt with, reflected in the negative covariance (over the four possible events) between their outcomes. We describe the situation as one with "conflicting interests." The ranges of outcomes for the two (from −5 to +5 for Eamon and from 0 to +5 for Kyoko) show that Eamon feels more strongly about going to separate locations than Kyoko feels about going to the same place as he. It is appropriate to describe him as being more dependent in this situation – more affected by their decisions – than she is. We also see that Eamon experiences negative outcomes if Kyoko accompanies him, perhaps because he anticipates her seeking his advice at inappropriate moments. The negative outcomes probably reflect his expectations of the benefits of being on his own, which expectations provide him with a "comparison level" (Thibaut & Kelley, 1959) with respect to which he will find Kyoko's presence unpleasant.

Among the many other examples of this kind of situation is the game of "hide and seek." In a sense, the person who prefers to be alone is the one who hides and the person who prefers to be together is the one who seeks. Like all situations with a strong conflict of interest, this one has strong implications for restraints on the communication of information. For example, a "hider" often tries to mislead the other about where he or she will go, and the "seeker" may try to conceal his or her strategy of search.

2.1.2 *Exchange Problems*

In sharp contrast to the coordination problems above are problems of exchange. An example is provided by a circumstance in which, when Eamon and Kyoko unpack their recording gear, he finds that in his hurried packing that morning, he has failed to include recording tape. Fortunately, Kyoko packed extra tape. On the other hand, in the rush of her work the day before, she failed to purchase backup batteries for her equipment. But again, fortunately, Eamon always carries some extra batteries. These circumstances, of one person's needs mirrored by what the other can provide, create an occasion for "exchange." Each can supply what the other needs in exchange for receiving what he or she needs.

The matrix representation of the situation, in Table 2.2, shows that each can benefit the other by giving something the other lacks without losing much or anything by doing so. This is called an "exchange" problem because a process of exchanging or trading provides a mutually satisfactory interaction. The covariance (correlation) between the two sets of outcomes

TABLE 2.2. *Outcome Matrix for an Exchange Problem*

	Kyoko	
	Give (Tape)	Keep
Give (Batteries)	+10 / +10	+10 / 0
Keep	0 / +10	0 / 0

Eamon

Matrix 2*

* The matrix number indicates the relevant entry in the body of the Atlas.

is zero, reflecting the fact that although some of the events yield similar outcomes to the two (when both give or both keep), other possible events yield different outcomes (when one gives and the other keeps).

2.2 Some Questions and Answers

We will have more to say about our representation of situations, but now, let us answer some questions that the above examples raise.

1. What is meant by "outcomes" and aren't people interdependent in other ways? In any "situation," at any particular place and on any occasion, the persons involved obviously affect each other in many ways – in what they do, what they say, how they feel, what they think, and so forth. In their effects on each other, they are "interdependent," that is, each one's actions, comments, feelings, thoughts, and so on, depend, in some way and to some degree, upon the other's. Their "interaction" consists of this interplay in which they each affect and are affected by one another.

In order to simplify the complexities of these phenomena, it is useful to focus on a broad class of effects, defined as *outcomes*. "Outcomes" refer to the positive and/or negative consequences of their interaction for each person. Many different terms are used to describe these consequences, such as rewards and costs, positive and negative reinforcement, and benefit versus harm. Positive outcomes are consequences that people seek to attain, increase, or maximize, and negative outcomes are consequences they seek to avoid, reduce, or minimize. Using that meaning of "outcomes," we distinguish situations in terms of the extent to which and the ways in which they make it possible for persons, by varying their behavior, to control each other's outcomes. Hence, our Atlas of "situations" is a compendium of patterns of *outcome interdependence*.

Of course, in their interaction people affect each other in ways only indirectly related to "outcomes." For example, they may have access to different sources of information and, hence, be able to influence each other through sharing and assembling that information – that is, they may be *informationally interdependent*. Informational interdependence would include the ways in which people provide helpful cues to each other about such matters as the likely consequences of their actions or the proper sequence in which they should do things. People are also *behaviorally interdependent*, in the ways one person's behavior directly affects the other's behavioral options. For example, one person's quickly taking a seat on a crowded bus precludes another person's taking it. In the game of "Simon Says," the leader instructs the followers quickly to imitate his actions but only when they are preceded by his phrase, "Simon says." With a proper training schedule and emphasis on speed, the followers often become so intent on quickly carrying out the instructions that they fail to pay attention to what the leader says and their actions come under the control of his actions, that is, become "conditioned" to them.

In what follows, we will consider all three of these kinds of interdependence – in outcomes, in information, and in behavior. We do not deny the importance of the latter two kinds of interdependence. Indeed, we give considerable attention to them. However, we begin with and continue to emphasize outcome interdependence as defining the "core problem" of any situation. It is the primary feature that we use to define the dimensions of our geography – the poles, axes, and equators of our "situational globe" (described more fully in chapter 4). Our argument for emphasizing outcome interdependence is that *it is basic to the other kinds of interdependence*. People exchange information primarily to exercise better control over their outcomes. In their affective expressions, of joy, sadness, pride, pity, and such, they provide information about their evaluative reactions to interaction events, that is, about their outcomes. They act to limit or encourage others' behavior out of concern for its outcome consequences. Taking account of those various facts, we believe that "outcomes" provide the best initial focus for the analysis of interdependence, providing the most useful foundation for the analysis of interaction events.

2. What are the purposes of being abstract in the representation of a situation? In characterizing interdependence in terms of outcomes, we identify *abstract* categories of situations each of which includes large numbers of diverse *concrete* situations. This is reflected in the variety of concrete examples we offer in each Atlas entry as illustrations of the abstract pattern of that situation. Thus, our analysis leaves behind the multitude of concrete everyday situations and problems – the various coordination problems of sharing limited seating, taking turns in conversation, avoiding collisions at four-way stop signs, and arriving when "dinner is served," and the various exchange problems of giving Christmas presents, loaning tools to a neighbor who later gives helpful computer advice, trading compliments about personal appearance, and paying money for goods. From the great variety of phenomena at the concrete level, the analysis distills abstract categories based on a limited number of themes, such as coordination and exchange, dependence and power, cooperation and conflict, pursuit of immediate versus distant goals, and so on.

Chapter 1 emphasized that our broad purpose in analyzing situations is to use them to understand patterns of interaction that we observe in daily life. And on the assumption that interaction is jointly determined by situations and the "personalities" of the actors, the situation analysis provides a systematic way to distinguish the interpersonal motives and attitudes that people display through their interaction. In short, the abstract analysis of situations has the consequence that interaction and personality are also viewed in abstract terms. We move beyond the details of particular interactions (e.g., coordination in assembling the child's bicycle on Christmas morning, coordination in moving heavy furniture, and coordination in meeting for lunch) to the problems of coordination in their general form. Similarly, we examine the personal factors often revealed in coordination situations, such as "readiness to take initiative" or "alertness in following others' leads," as a general phenomenon rather than as one linked to the contents of particular everyday coordination problems. (These theoretical interconnections among situations, interaction, and persons are discussed in sections 3.5 and 3.6 of chapter 3.)

3. Where do the numbers in the matrix come from? The numbers have several theoretical justifications. They are essential to our abstract representations which are made possible by reducing a wide variety of kinds of rewards, costs, benefits, and harms to simple numerical scales. Also, as we will show in this chapter, numbers are necessary for our *theoretical* analysis of various situations, enabling us to distinguish contrasting patterns of outcome interdependence. In short, numbers are a tool for cleanly describing and differentiating situational patterns using an abstract, precise, and universal language. For the reader who worries about our scaling assumptions, we may note that for most purposes, the most important patterns can be distinguished by using only ordinal numbers, ranking the four outcomes in a 2 × 2 matrix from largest to smallest, or by simply categorizing them as "large" or "small." However, we usually use a larger range of numbers and our manipulation of those numbers for theoretical purposes, to define and distinguish their patterns, implicitly assumes that they come from ratio scales.

The numbers also serve several important *practical* purposes. They have been very useful, indeed essential, in experimental "game research," where particular patterns of numerical outcomes are presented to subjects who are assumed or instructed to try to gain high outcomes rather than lower ones. As we will illustrate below, researchers can also distinguish among the natural situations people find themselves in by asking them to rate, using simple numerical scales, various events that occur in interpersonal settings. Such ratings receive validation through their consistency between people for a particular situation and/or through the consistency in an individual's ratings on repeated occasions. Research on the Semantic Differential has shown there to be considerable within-person consistency and between-person agreement as to how "good" or "bad" many different objects, persons, and events are (e.g., Osgood, Suci, & Tannenbaum, 1957).

Finally, numbers have proven useful in designing items for scales that assess persons' social value orientations – the value criteria that guide their behavior in interdependence situations. A person's choices among several allocations of numerical outcomes between self and some "other" has been shown to provide reliable and valid measures of that person's tendency to be cooperative, competitive, or individualistic (focused on own outcomes) in interdependence situations (McClintock & Liebrand, 1988).

4. Why do we focus on the 2 × 2 matrix? As the above "Eamon and Kyoko" examples imply, much of our analysis focuses on situations that involve two people, each of whom has only two behavioral options. It is obvious that any number of people can be interdependent and that each person often faces three or more alternative courses of action. The reasons for our limiting ourselves to the minimal number of persons and each with the minimal number of behavioral options are as follows.

As many economists and environmentalists emphasize, everyone in the world is interdependent, in some way and to some degree, with everyone else. Recognizing that fact, other branches of social science, such as economics, political science, and sociology, study interdependence among large numbers of people. However, as social psychologists, and having special interests in interpersonal phenomena, we focus mainly on the various forms of interdependence in the smallest unit in which it can exist – the dyad. (Exceptions are made in Entry #19, where we consider the effects on the dyad of a third person, Entry #20, the Prisoner's Dilemma for multiple persons, and to a limited extent, in Entries #9 and #10 on conjunctive and disjunctive interdependence.) This focus greatly simplifies our problems of conceptual analysis in ways that make it possible to provide a detailed understanding of interpersonal processes. It also provides a basis for close analysis of the role that situations play in the basic dyadic units of social life, such as dating and mating pairs, relatives, friends, neighbors, and co-workers.

If empirical warrant is needed for our focus on the dyad, it exists in at least two forms. If one observes the size of informal groupings in public places (as James did, 1953), the vast majority are dyads. If one asks people to keep track of what they are doing at various times of the day, of the occasions on which they are with other people, about half the time they are with only one other person (Sorokin & Berger, 1939; Tidwell, Reis, & Shaver, 1996; Wheeler & Nezlek, 1977). Demographically, the dyad is a very important part of human life.

Perhaps our most important reason for emphasizing the dyad is our desire to be both *thorough* and *precise* in laying out the major patterns of interdependence. It would be impossible to satisfy those criteria if we tried to include three, four, and more persons.

The desire to be thorough and precise also enters into our emphasis on the simplest dyadic situations in which each person has two behavioral options. It is obvious that people usually have more than two things they might do in any situation, but it is also plausible to assume that they can often narrow their decision down to a pair of alternative actions. Those are the possible actions that most strongly contend for one's attention by virtue of their consequences. We occasionally relax this restriction, as for Negotiation situations (Entry #15) in which each person is able to make several different offers to the other. In Entry #21, on selection between situations, we include special behavioral options that enable a person to leave a situation rather than deal with the problems it poses.

It is difficult to judge what we lose by imposing those limitations on our analysis. Perhaps the proper question concerns what our simplified analysis yields. That is best left to the reader to judge – after examining the analysis in these chapters and the applications of its distinctions to the situations of everyday life and social psychological research described in the entries that follow.

   5. Is the outcome matrix too limited as a representation of situations? If we recall the example of Eamon and Kyoko coordinating their efforts in moving the birch tree that blocked the road, their interaction included certain events that are not inherent to the outcome matrix. That matrix, in Table 2.1, has no implications regarding the possibility that one of the two might direct the coordination process, as by taking the initiative in moving to one end of the log or by telling the other person which end to grasp. Those are, indeed, limitations of the matrix representation of the situation. In chapter 3, we explain how we deal with these limitations by representations of two further important aspects of a situation, namely, its response conditions and its information conditions.

   However, throughout this Atlas we emphasize that the outcome matrix describes the essential *problem* that a situation poses for its occupants. The outcomes represent the possible *consequences* of their interaction, and it is those consequences – those incentives or disincentives – that provide the ultimate impetus for that interaction. The behavioral options of an outcome matrix specify the *means* the two persons have for achieving, through individual or joint efforts, the desired consequences and for avoiding undesired ones. In a sense, the options provide the paths they may take in pursuit of their outcome goals.

   This chapter focuses on patterns of interdependence as specified by outcome matrices and the problems they pose. As noted above, chapter 3 will describe two conditions that affect interaction about those problems. The *response conditions* are the circumstances in a situation that limit or expand the opportunities for *responding* to the situation. They are the sequential-temporal constraints that determine *when* and in *what order* the behavioral options may or must be exercised. *Information conditions* consist of the information about the situation and each other that each person may possess and their means of sharing that information with or withholding it from each other.

2.3 The Two Properties of Outcome Matrices

As described above, an outcome matrix specifies a set of possible consequences for the pair of persons. These can be summarized by the *outcome distribution* of the four pairs of outcomes in a 2×2 matrix. The matrix also specifies the means by which the two persons, through their individual and/or joint behavior, might gain or arrive at any one of those consequences. Those means are summarized by the *outcome controls* that the matrix shows the two persons to possess. Here, we describe those two properties of an outcome matrix – its outcome distribution and its outcome controls – and illustrate them by examples from Eamon and Kyoko's adventures.

2.3.1 *The Outcome Distribution*

This describes (a) the *ranges and levels of outcomes*, defined by the average outcome and variability in outcomes for each person, over the four events possible in the situation, and (b) the *covariation* between their two sets of outcomes. These are the two characteristics of the scatterplot of the relationship between the persons' outcomes in a 2 × 2 matrix, plotted for each of the four possible events. That scatterplot shows the location of each person's outcomes relative to the axis representing those outcomes *and* the covariation (correlation) between the two person's sets of outcomes. Examples are shown in Figure 2.1.

The *range* of each person's outcomes may cover a broad scale from large positive to large negative outcomes, or it may cover a narrower scale – being largely in the positive values, in the mid-range, or in the negative values.

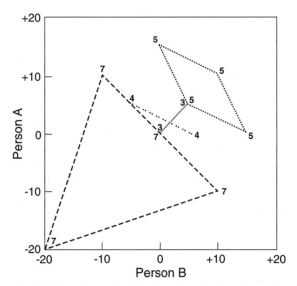

FIGURE 2.1. Scatterplots of the outcome distributions of several situations, illustrating variations in ranges, levels, and covariation. Legend: 3: see Table 2.1 and Entry #3; 4: see Table 2.1 and Entry #4; 5: see Table 3.1 and Entry #5; 7: see Table 3.8 and Entry #7.

The neutral point on the scale represents outcomes about which people are indifferent. In some cases, that indifference reflects a person's expectations or "comparison level" (Thibaut & Kelley, 1959) for a particular situation. For example, "the movie was just about what I expected – neither better nor worse." Better-than-expected outcomes are experienced as pleasant, and worse-than-expected, as disappointing. In other cases, the neutral outcome is defined by what a person can get in an alternative situation or with an alternative partner – the concept of "comparison level for alternatives" (Thibaut & Kelley, 1959). ("The other movie would have been better.")

In the log removal example above, Kyoko's trick back may yield her largely negative outcomes when the two lift, especially if she tries to lift the heavier end of the tree trunk. If the imminent sunrise threatens to spoil their day's recording effort, an essential feature of the situation is the extremely negative outcomes for both persons that will result from failure to coordinate their efforts quickly. Eamon's negative outcomes, if Kyoko joins him at the same listening post, are probably relative to his expectations for what the pair would do that morning.

Figure 2.1 presents the scatterplots for four of the situations included in the Atlas, which illustrate variations in ranges and covariation. To indicate the possible pairs of outcomes for each situation, their entry numbers are located in the plot in relation to the A and B axes representing the two persons' outcomes. (The legend of the figure lists the tables in this chapter and the next in which those four situations are represented.) It can be seen that Entries #3 and #4 (illustrated by Eamon and Kyoko's examples in Table 2.1, with her outcomes plotted on the vertical or A axis) have perfect correlations between the two sets of outcomes, the first covariation being positive (referred to as *"corresponding interests"*) and the second, negative (referred to as *"conflicting interests"*). The distribution for Entry #5 shows a moderate negative covariation and the one for Entry #7, very little covariation. Situations with these latter types of distribution are sometimes described as posing "mixed motive" problems: The two persons have a common interest in avoiding the poorer outcomes (especially, in the case of Entry #7) but conflicting interests in regard to their divergent best outcomes.

In this Atlas, we have generally limited ourselves to moderate ranges of positive outcomes. As a consequence, our discussion has focused primarily on the attainment or maximization of gains and less on the avoidance or minimization of costs. This decision does not stem from a belief that the scope and level of the ranges are not important. However, to give ranges and levels extensive attention here would complicate our presentation more than seems useful.

We may also note that limiting the analysis to positive outcomes enables us to avoid some thorny problems relating to the commensurability of positive and negative values from subjective scales. Those problems come to the fore when we combine positive and negative outcomes by simply adding them. There are good reasons to believe (and, indeed, it is a part of everyday experience) that the positive and negative aspects of an experience do not simply cancel each other out. (See, e.g., Cacioppo & Berntson, 1999; Kahneman & Tversky, 1979.) Rather, they often put the person in a strong conflict about what to do. So when an actor considers an action that may yield both a positive and a negative outcome, a simple sum of the two values may not provide an adequate characterization of the "outcome" associated with that action. Here, we usually avoid this problem by limiting our analysis to outcome ranges on the positive side of the neutral point. We make an occasional exception when an essential characteristic of a situation requires describing both the positive and negative consequences it can generate, as in the case of Chicken in which the positive outcomes gained from showing one's self to be more courageous than an opponent are pitted against the negative consequences of a head-on collision. (Cf. the plot for Entry #7, which is shown as matrix 7 in Figure 3.8 and is discussed in section 3.6.2.)

The other aspect of the distribution of outcomes – the *covariation* between the two persons' outcomes over the situation's possible events – figures importantly in our distinctions among situations. In the log-removal situation, Eamon's and Kyoko's interests are perfectly correlated (cf. the plot for matrix 3 in Figure 2.1). If the threat of the sunrise is great enough to outweigh more minor considerations of effort and back pains, this positive covariation between their outcomes would be extended into the negative values, as they began to worry about failing to successfully coordinate their removing the tree.

The ranges and covariation specify the outcomes that each person may experience and whether they have corresponding or conflicting concerns about what may happen. Those facts define the possible consequences the situation has for the interdependent pair – consequences that may include both opportunities (for example, good outcomes for both persons) and potential difficulties (for example, conflict and disappointment for one or both). For the task of moving the log, the opportunities lie in moving along the road toward their goal. The potential difficulties lie in their possible failure effectively and quickly to coordinate their efforts. We state the obvious by saying that the situation is a "cooperative" one, meaning that the positive covariance between their outcomes is likely to promote their cooperative thoughts and behavior. Other situations, such as those with negative covariance, have the opposite effect, promoting noncooperative thoughts and behavior. That would be true in the log-removal example if Kyoko were a reluctant companion on the bird-recording expedition and really wished to give up the enterprise and turn around and drive back down the road to a comfortable lodge in Kerrville. There would no longer be corresponding interests but conflicting ones and, possibly, interaction reflecting that conflict.

2.3.2 The Outcome Controls

While the ranges and covariance of outcomes define a situation's possible consequences for the pair, their means of attaining or avoiding those consequences are provided by its *outcome controls*. Those controls are specified in the matrix by how each person's available behavioral options affect their own and their partner's outcomes.

Identifying the Outcome Controls for an Observed Matrix: "Cleaning the Apartment." How do we determine the outcome controls specified in a particular outcome matrix? Kelley and Thibaut (1978) found that an efficient way to identify the outcome controls in any matrix is to employ the logic of analysis of variance. That logic tells us that any rectangular matrix of numbers can be analyzed into three components, a main between-columns effect, a main between-rows effect, and a column-by-row, or interaction, effect.

This procedure can be illustrated by an example from Eamon and Kyoko. Let us assume that their apartment badly needs to be cleaned up. Both have been under heavy pressure at work and have often found it necessary to bring their work home and, therefore, have not found time to keep their quarters tidy. Getting ready for the "bird songs" expedition has also interfered with their usual household routine. When they return late Sunday afternoon, the cleaning job requires their attention. Their problem involves who should do the cleaning, one or the other or both.

We can estimate the structure of that situation by drawing on data collected and reported by Kelley (1979, p. 27). The matrix of observed data in the upper portion of Table 2.3 is based on ratings obtained at UCLA from 100 heterosexual pairs of undergraduates who had relationships of 3 months or more and were sharing an apartment. They were asked to imagine that their apartment needs cleaning but that each of them has other

TABLE 2.3. *The Scatterplot and Analysis of Variance (Control Components) for "Cleaning the Apartment"*

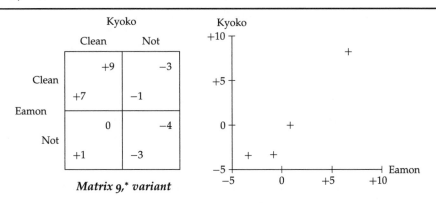

Matrix 9,* variant

The Analysis of Variance

Sources of Control	Ky's Outcomes	Eam's Outcomes	[2 × 2 Component]
Actor (AC)	+8	+4	[BAC]
Partner (PC)	+5	+6	[MPC]
Act.-by-Part. (JC)	+4	+2	[MJC]

The Three Components

Ky

	Clean	Not
Clean	+4 / +2	−4 / +2
Not	+4 / −2	−4 / −2

Bilateral Actor Control (BAC)

Ky

	Clean	Not
Clean	+2.5 / +3	+2.5 / −3
Not	−2.5 / +3	−2.5 / −3

Mutual Partner Control (MPC)

Ky

	Clean	Not
Clean	+2 / +1	−2 / −1
Not	−2 / −1	+2 / +1

Mutual Joint Control (MJC)

* The matrix number indicates the relevant entry in the body of the Atlas.

things to do – work or study. On scales ranging from +10 (very satisfied) to −10 (very dissatisfied), they rated each of the four possible events: both clean, one cleans and the other not, and neither cleans. The observed averages have been rounded a bit to facilitate the calculations of the components.

The scatterplot to the right of the matrix shows that there is a high degree of common interest between the two. (We refer to them as having "corresponding outcomes" rather than "conflicting" ones.)

The analysis of variance table below the matrix shows the three sources of variance in each person's outcomes, that is, the three sources of control over each one's outcomes:

(1) the person's own actions (Actor Control or AC),
(2) the partner's actions (Partner Control or PC), and
(3) the interaction between their two actions (Actor-by-Partner Control, or Joint Control – JC).

The values assigned those components are derived from calculations (described below) of the average degree to which the outcomes in a particular column, row, or diagonal are greater than those in the opposite column, row, or diagonal. As a convention, a difference is assigned a positive value if the outcomes are highest in the upper left cell ("Clean" and "Clean" in the example). Otherwise, a difference is assigned a negative value. So the AC values of +8 and +4 for Kyoko and Eamon, respectively, mean that both gain better outcomes when they themselves decide to clean than when they do not.

The component matrices at the bottom of Table 2.3 show the three types of control as they exist for both persons. The Bilateral Actor Control (BAC) component shows how each person affects his or her own outcomes. "Bilateral" refers to the fact that the AC may exist on both sides of the dyad. The Mutual Partner Control (MPC) component shows how each person is affected by the partner and the Mutual Joint Control (MJC) component shows how each is affected by their joint actions. "Mutual" refers to how their control may be mutual, exercised by each (in whole or in part) over the other's outcomes. It can be seen that the control values in the analysis of variance table correspond to certain differences between rows, columns, and diagonals described in the component matrices. So the analysis of variance table and the three components are alternative ways of describing the controls in the initial matrix.

We may use the example in Table 2.3 to illustrate how the three sources of control are calculated. Let us first focus on Kyoko's outcomes. A formal analysis of variance procedure would require us first to convert all of her outcomes into *deviations* from her average or mean value for the entire matrix (in this example, her mean value over the four cells is +0.5) and then sort out the components of variance in those deviations. However, we can avoid that step by calculating the sources of variance from the "raw" outcome values and then reproducing the original matrix by adding in her mean value. In this way, we initially set aside the matter of her average level of outcomes until after we determine the sources of their variance.

We first determine that Kyoko's outcomes in the "Clean" column are, on the average, eight units larger than in the "Not" column. To show that fact, we might simply enter a +8 for Kyoko in her "Clean" column and a 0 in the "Not" column. However, for "bookkeeping" purposes when we eventually add in her mean value, it is convenient to divide that difference between the two columns. This is shown in the BAC component at the bottom of Table 2.3, where she gains 8 more outcome units when she cleans (+4) than when she does not (−4). For her outcomes in the MPC component, her outcomes are five units higher when Eamon cleans than when he does not. This fact is represented in the component matrix by +2.5 for the upper row and −2.5 for the lower row. We calculate the third component for Kyoko (the MJC component) by comparing her outcomes in the major diagonal of the matrix – from upper left to lower right – with those in the minor diagonal – from upper right to lower left. (This is a simple calculation of what is known in statistics as the "interaction effect" between the two causal variables constituted by their respective actions. It describes the degree to which Kyoko and Eamon *jointly* control her outcomes.) We find that she gains four more units of outcome when she and Eamon do the same thing (both clean or both do not) than when one cleans and the other not. This is represented in the MJC component matrix by +2 as her outcomes on the major diagonal and −2 as her outcomes on the minor one. At this point, we can check our arithmetic by taking account of her average level of outcomes (+0.5) in this situation. If we add her outcomes in each of the four separate cells across the three components, and then add her average, our totals should reproduce her outcomes in the original matrix. In Table 2.3, our calculations are shown to be accurate by the fact that (e.g., in the upper left cell and reading across the three components) $4.0 + 2.5 + 2.0 + 0.5 = +9$. The same check can be made for her outcomes in the other three cells.

Similar calculations for Eamon's outcomes yield the values shown in the three component matrices in Table 2.3. In those calculations, care must be taken to shift from how, in contrast to Kyoko, his BAC and MPC are determined and represented. Her Actor Control (AC) is determined by comparing the two columns, but his AC is determined by comparing the two rows, and her Partner Control (PC) is determined by comparing the two rows where his PC is determined by comparing the two columns. However, the JC terms for the two are calculated by the same comparisons between the major and minor diagonals of the original matrix. Again, as for Kyoko's outcomes, we can check our arithmetic for Eamon by adding across the components for a particular cell and adding the average of his outcomes (+1.0) to obtain the outcome for that cell in the original matrix. For example, in the "Clean-Clean" cell, Eamon's component values plus his mean yields the original value of +7 (2.0 + 3.0 + 1.0 plus his average, +1.0).

The analysis of variance table in Table 2.3 summarizes the ways in which Kyoko's and Eamon's outcomes are controlled. The numerical values summarize the degree of each type of control and the algebraic signs indicate the direction of that control. In this example, every source of control favors an action that includes the upper left cell, so all the signs are positive. That suggests that there is considerable agreement between the two in what they want to happen – a fact also shown in the scatterplot. A closer examination of the results suggests that there may be some gender-role based division of labor here. She gains more from doing the cleaning herself than from having him do it, whereas the opposite is true for his outcomes. His outcomes increase more when she does the cleaning than when he does it. And she has a stronger interest than he in having them do the same thing, that either both pitch in and do the work or that neither does.

Some readers will find that our use of the analysis of variance is somewhat unusual. There are, of course, no error terms, inasmuch as there is only one observation for each value. The most unique aspect of the procedure is that the two independent variables (Kyoko's and Eamon's behavioral options) have different psychological implications for the two persons affected. For example, the column effect for his outcomes reflects her control over him, but the column effect for her outcomes reflects her control over herself. This is reflected in our labeling of the effects from the perspective of the person affected. That is, we refer to them as "actor" or "partner" effects rather than in terms of the independent variable responsible for the effect. This enables us to see the implications of the situation for each individual person.

The analysis of variance table in the middle of Table 2.3 is a simple "recipe" for the Cleaning the Apartment situation. It indicates the proportions and orientations (directions) of the various controls that one would have to bring together in order to create that situation. But while it indicates the possible sources of each person's outcomes, the analysis of variance table by itself makes it difficult to see the total pattern of the situation. That pattern is more apparent if, following Kelley and Thibaut's lead, we view each matrix as composed of the three component matrices. Those components correspond to the three rows of the ANOVA table, and are separately represented by the three matrices at the bottom of Table 2.3.

This example illustrates a point made earlier, that numerical ratings made by partners can help us understand the situations they are in. The components allow us to examine the situation as to the two persons' relative dependence on their partners. This involves a comparison of the magnitude of the Actor Control (AC) terms, which reflect each person's control over his or her own outcomes, with the other two, both of which involve the partner's control. For the problem of cleaning the apartment, the typical man in the sample is somewhat more dependent on the woman's efforts than she is on his. Our attention is also drawn to the combined effect of the three components of the matrix. Both have a strong preference for doing the cleaning together, which reflects a convergence of all three sources of control on the upper left cell of the matrix.

In its broad configuration, the "cleaning the apartment" pattern is much like Entry #9, the Conjunctive situation. This is shown in Table 2.4 which represents the simplest way to construct a conjunctive pattern, by merely superimposing three equally important components in the proper orientations to each other. In this example, we represent the three sources of variance as contrasts between positive values and zero, rather than as contrasts between positive and negative values, as in Table 2.3. We will use this simpler method in all our subsequent examples where we combine components to form theoretical patterns. The use of positive and negative values will be reserved for the analysis of "natural" patterns – those observed in empirical work.

The property of "conjunctivity" means that *both* persons must take particular actions if they are to gain their highest outcomes. The three components in Table 2.4 show that this is accomplished because all three control effects converge on the a_1b_1 cell. If and only if the pair selects that pair of options, do they manage to combine the potential beneficial effects of all three types of controls. (The contrasting case, of disjunctivity, means that only one person, either one, needs to take the proper action in order for them to gain their best outcomes. It consists of the same three component matrices but they are superimposed in different orientations to each other, as described in Entry #10.)

In comparing the "cleaning the apartment" matrix with that of the Conjunctive situation, we juxtapose a particular *concrete* situation and one

TABLE 2.4. *The Combination of Symmetrical Components That Combine to Form a Conjunctive Situation*

	A: a1	A: a2			A: a1	A: a2			A: a1	A: a2	
b1	2 / 2	2		b1	2 / 2	2		b1	2 / 2		
B b2	2		+	B	2		+	B	2	2	=
				b2	2			b2		2	
BAC				**MPC**				**MJC**			

	A: a1	A: a2
b1	6 / 6	2 / 2
B b2	2 / 2	2 / 2

Matrix 9*
Conjunctive Situation

* The matrix number indicates the relevant entry in the body of the Atlas.

of our *abstract* patterns. The latter are derived theoretically, by constructing outcome patterns through combining certain patterns of the simple components. As explained below and in chapter 4, the theoretical patterns both define and are located in our "geography" of the domain of outcome matrices. Each such abstract pattern is assumed to describe a paradigmatic pattern for which there is a large number of (more or less) similar concrete patterns. This is well illustrated by the present case. There are undoubtedly many concrete outcome matrices that resemble the abstract pattern of the Conjunctive situation. That fact implies that the abstract pattern contributes to a wide-ranging understanding of many concrete problems. Our Atlas is designed precisely to illustrate and take advantage of that point.

The abstract pattern in Table 2.4 and the concrete one in Table 2.3 result from the way the three components (BAC, MPC, and MJC) converge on, or contribute to, the upper left cell of the matrix. (That convergence is also reflected in the signs of the sources of control in the analysis of variance table.) We describe that convergence in terms of how the three component matrices are oriented to one another. In this case, they are "concordant" with each other. In other patterns, they are said to be "discordant," to suggest that they clash with or interfere with one another. That can be illustrated by another example from Kyoko and Eamon's adventures.

Identifying the Outcome Controls for an Observed Matrix: "Going to the Movies." In the evening following their sound recording efforts and after resting a bit after their strenuous day, they have time to go to a movie in the small theater in Kerrville, a nearby village. Like many such establishments, it is divided into two separate, small auditoriums. This particular night, it is showing an old Western movie in one and a recent X-rated import in the other. So Eamon and Kyoko had a clear choice between the behavioral options described in Table 2.5. Again, we can assign them a pattern of outcomes adapted from ratings made on a +10 to −10 scale by students at UCLA (cf. Kelley, 1979, pp. 63–64). These were 96 assorted undergraduates who rated their satisfaction-dissatisfaction with common events occurring in their relationships with opposite sex partners.[1]

The situation's matrix, in Table 2.5, shows a clear conflict of interest. Kyoko obviously prefers that they go together to movie X and Eamon prefers the same for movie W. Each will be quite dissatisfied if they go separately to their preferred movies (she to X and he to W) and, of course, they will be even more dissatisfied if they go separately to their respective nonpreferred movies. The scatterplot in Table 2.5 suggests that they might easily agree not to go separately, but will have a fairly sharp disagreement about where to go together.

The values in the analysis of variance table as well as the values in the three component matrices were derived in the manner described for the "cleaning the apartment" example in Table 2.3. Both persons' average values are −0.5 outcome units, so the reader can check the accuracy of the values in the component matrices by adding across the three values in each

---

[1] For reasons explained in Entry #8, the averages in Table 2.5 are from ratings made on the assumption that the partner has no preference between the two movies. The ratings were made by only one member of a pair, so they describe outcomes in only that member's "half" of the matrix. For present purposes, we have assumed that those in the other half have the same pattern. The numbers have been rounded and adjusted somewhat in order to simplify the calculations.

TABLE 2.5. *The Scatterplot and Analysis of Variance (Control Components) for "Going to the Movies"*

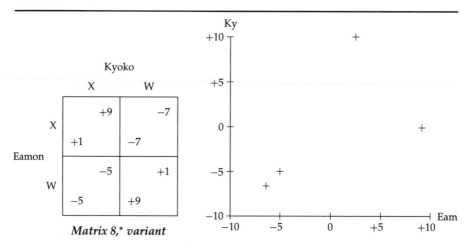

Matrix 8,* variant

The Analysis of Variance

Source of Control	Ky's Outcomes	Eam's Outcomes	[2 × 2 Component]
Actor (AC)	+5	−5	[BAC]
Partner (PC)	+3	−3	[MPC]
Act.-by-Part. (JC)	+11	+11	[MJC]

The Three Components

Ky

	X	W
X	+2.5 / −2.5	−2.5 / −2.5
W	+2.5 / +2.5	−2.5 / +2.5

Bilateral Actor Control (BAC)

Ky

	X	W
X	+1.5 / −1.5	+1.5 / +1.5
W	−1.5 / −1.5	−1.5 / +1.5

Mutual Partner Control (MPC)

Ky

	X	W
X	+5.5 / +5.5	−5.5 / −5.5
W	−5.5 / −5.5	+5.5 / +5.5

Mutual Joint Control (MJC)

* The matrix number indicates the relevant entry in the body of the Atlas.

position, adding the constant of −0.5 in each case, and checking that the values in the original matrix are reproduced.

The source of the conflict between Kyoko and Eamon is revealed by the component analysis. The signs in the analysis of variance table, as well as the relative orientations of the three control components at the bottom of the table, show how the "pull" of each one's movie preferences interferes with doing what would benefit the partner. We describe this as a discordant relation between the BAC and MPC components. An even more important source of "discordance" is found between the MJC and BAC components. The MJC component shows their strong shared desire to stay together, at one movie or the other, but the BAC component shows how their control over their own outcomes tends to pull them apart. The pattern is one in which a mild difference in preferences about what to do is pitted against a shared and strong desire to do something together.

Again, as for the "cleaning the apartment" example, this concrete situation is quite similar to one of our paradigmatic abstract patterns, namely, "Hero." Shown in Table 2.6 (and described in Entry #8) is a pattern often referred to as "Hero." As Table 2.6 shows, in its simplest form "Hero" involves only the two components of BAC and MJC, oriented to each other so that the BAC component interferes with the coordination required by the MJC component. The name derives from an assumed episode in which both persons are about to select their most preferred options, but one, seeing that their doing so will result in needlessly poor outcomes for both, acts as a "hero" and volunteers to go along with what the partner most desires. It can be seen that the "going to the movies" example departs from the Hero paradigm in having a small MPC component. That does not change the possibilities for "heroism," but it suggests that on the average, the UCLA respondents would derive some small pleasure from knowing that their partners are seeing the movie they themselves regard as the better one. Or, perhaps they are imagining that the partner will be "educated" by exposure to the "better" movie and is simply not perceptive enough to realize that in advance.

The above examples illustrate the important idea that any 2 × 2 outcome matrix can be decomposed into the three components – the BAC, MPC, and MJC matrices. The simplest situations, such as those we described for Eamon and Kyoko in Tables 2.1 and 2.2, have entries for only one of the three components. Their coordination problem of clearing the log from the road is entirely defined by its MJC component. It has corresponding interests, so the matrix is referred to as "*Corr MJC.*" Their problem of going to the same or different listening posts is well defined by a MJC pattern with

TABLE 2.6. *The Combination of Symmetrical Components That Combine to Form the "Hero" Situation*

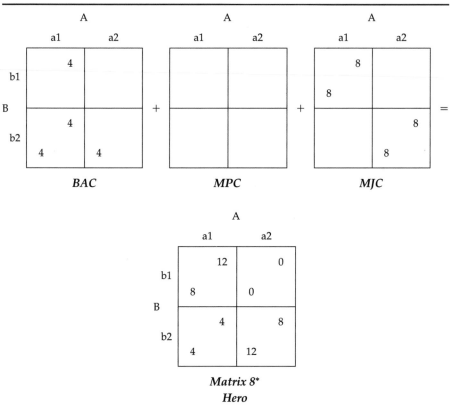

Matrix 8*
Hero

* The matrix number indicates the relevant entry in the body of the Atlas.

conflicting interests, referred to as *"Conf MJC."* In the Conf MJC pattern, there is greater variance in Eamon's outcomes than in Kyoko's, so he is more dependent on their joint action. The situation that made possible a trade of recording tape for batteries, in Table 2.2, consists entirely of an MPC component. In our later discussion of asymmetrical dependence, we examine situations in which, for example, person A has values in only the BAC component, and person B has entries only in one or both of the MPC and MJC components.

Our Terms for the Control Components. The foregoing examples illustrate the terms we use to distinguish the control sources and control components. The concepts bear repeating and require a bit of explanation. We have noted that Actor Control (AC for short) refers to each person's effect on his or her own outcomes and Partner Control (PC for short) refers to the other person's control over the actor's outcomes. We use the term "partner" despite the fact that in some situations, for example, those with considerable conflict of interest, the persons involved may not regard each other as "partners." Actor-by-Partner Control (Joint Control or JC for short) refers to their joint effect on a person's outcomes. As we have seen, the three terms may be different in magnitude as between the two persons, as in instances of asymmetrical or, in the extreme case, unilateral dependence.

Our terms for the three *components*, shown at the bottom on the several preceding tables, purposely make a distinction between "mutual" and "bilateral." We use the term "mutual" for "Mutual Partner Control" and "Mutual Joint Control" to make it clear that we are describing a property of the *situation* and not something about either person. The term "mutual" emphasizes the fact that being subject to the kind of control the matrix shows is a circumstance the two persons may share – a circumstance in which PC control is (per the dictionary definition of "mutual") "directed by each toward the other" or in which the jointly generated control (JC) is directed by both to each. In contrast, the term "bilateral" for the Bilateral Actor Control component serves to highlight a different property of the situation, in which the control exists on the "two sides."

In previous writings (e.g., Thibaut & Kelley, 1959; Kelley & Thibaut, 1978), the terms Bilateral Reflexive Control, Mutual Fate Control, and Mutual Behavior Control were used instead of the terms used here, respectively, Bilateral Actor Control, Mutual Partner Control, and Mutual Joint Control. In adopting new terms, our hope is that they will add simplicity and clarity. We recognize and regret the possibility of confusion for those already familiar with the older terminology. As we see them, the problems with the older terms were that they were unnecessarily vague as to sources of control (in the use of "reflexive" and "fate") and required an explanation in terms of a brief bit of possible interaction (e.g., "A is subject to Behavior Control if, when B changes his or her behavior, A will have reason to change his"). The terms proposed here seem more clearly focused on the phenomena to which they are intended to apply, namely, the *situational* patterns of outcome control.

Using Component Analysis to Construct Theoretical Outcome Matrices. The analysis of an outcome matrix into its three components can be used in two ways: (1) to break apart the elements that underlie a particular observed matrix, as in two of the preceding examples, and (2) to combine elements to create theoretical matrices, as in two other examples. We can consider the components as elements into which any initial matrix can be broken, but we can also think of them as "building blocks" that can be superimposed for theoretical purposes to create possibly "new" situations. An outcome matrix constructed for the latter purpose can be used as an hypothesis about a kind of interdependence problem that exists in some nook or cranny of interpersonal life. It can be examined for the kinds of issues and interactions it is likely to generate, and we can speculate about what concrete circumstances might give rise to it. The theoretical use of the component analysis serves an important purpose in chapter 4. There, assembling the components in various combinations is used as a means of exploring the domain of 2×2 patterns, identifying "all possible" combinations of symmetric components.

2.4 The Dimensions of Outcome Interdependence

The now familiar control components of interdependence are shown in Table 2.7. Each is shown in abstract form, the two persons being labeled A and B and their behavioral options, a_1 and a_2 for A, and b_1 and b_2 for B. The outcome values are selected merely to illustrate contrasting patterns of covariation and control. Two versions of Mutual Joint Control are given, one for corresponding interests and another for conflicting interests.

Because it describes mutual *in*dependence rather than any degree of interdependence, matrix 1, of Bilateral Actor Control, may not seem to belong in our Atlas of *inter*dependence situations. However, Bilateral Actor Control plays several very important roles in our theory. In the examples in Tables 2.4 and 2.5, we have already seen that BAC is important in how, through its concordance or discordance with the other components, it affects the total pattern of interdependence. The importance of BAC also derives from the fact that in some situations or for some relationships, it is possible for people to completely withdraw from their partner and become independent. Hence it is important to discuss BAC, because it may sometimes serve as a viable alternative to the other situations. And we will now see the further role that BAC serves in anchoring the dimensions of the situational "space."

The four patterns in Table 2.7 define a three-dimensional space in which all the *symmetric* 2×2 patterns of outcome interdependence are located. ("Symmetric" patterns are those in which both persons are subject to the same controls and to the same degree – though not necessarily with the same "signs" or orientations.) This is explained more fully in chapter 4, but here we can identify the theoretical dimensions that are shown in Figure 2.2.

TABLE 2.7. *The Four Basic Patterns of Interdependence*

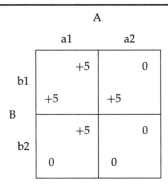

Matrix 1*
Bilateral Actor Control (BAC)

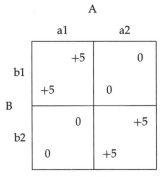

	Matrix 3*		*Matrix 4**
	Corresponding		*Conflicting*
	Mutual Joint Control		*Mutual Joint Control*
	(Corr MJC)		*(Conf MJC)*

Matrix 2*
Mutual Partner Control (MPC)

---

* The matrix number indicates the relevant entry in the body of the Atlas.

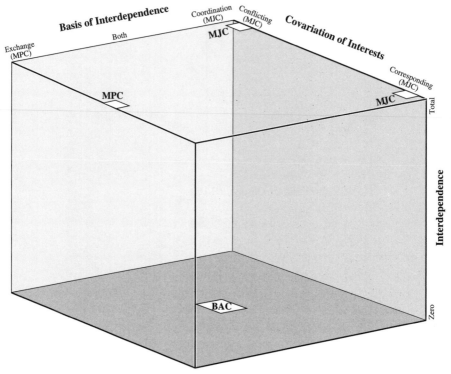

FIGURE 2.2. The three dimensions defined by the basic components of symmetric interdependence. *Legend*: BAC: Bilateral Actor Control; MJC: Mutual Joint Control; MPC: Mutual Partner Control.

The theoretical dimensions may be identified by comparing various subsets of the four patterns in Table 2.7. We see first that as compared with the other three, matrix 1 defines a dimension of *degree of interdependence*, with Bilateral Actor Control representing zero interdependence and the other three, total interdependence. The term "interdependence" is appropriate here because with symmetric components, the two person's individual dependencies are the same. Mutuality of dependence being total, it is not reflected in the three dimensions.

The contrast between matrices 3 and 4 defines a second dimension of *covariation of interests*, ranging from matrix 3, in which the two have *corresponding* interests, to matrix 4, in which the two have *conflicting* interests. As the figure shows, matrix 1 (Bilateral Actor Control) and matrix 2 (Mutual Partner Control) are intermediate on this dimension. In each case, there is no covariation between the two sets of outcomes.

The contrast between matrix 2, on the one hand, and the 3 and 4 pair, on the other hand, defines a third dimension that distinguishes the particular *basis of interdependence* involved in the situation, whether it is control by each other (Mutual Partner Control) or by their joint actions (Mutual Joint Control). We have referred to Mutual Partner Control as *"exchange"* inasmuch as the beneficial use of the control by one person can be traded or exchanged for the partner's similar use of their control. We have described the Mutual Joint Control extreme of the dimension as *"coordination"* because the effects of MJC depend on how the two persons' coordinate their actions. Both aspects of control can be combined and they define mixtures of exchange and coordination, located in the middle of that dimension.

Figure 2.2 defines the space in which we can expect to locate the various theoretical patterns of interdependence that can be constructed by combining the four symmetric patterns on the corners and surface of the figure. Many of the situations included in the Atlas's entries can be found in that space. Figure 4.4 in chapter 4 shows where various situations are located in that "geography," as well as the inverted pyramidal shape of their distribution (narrow at bottom and broad at the top), a shape that is vaguely suggested by the locations of the situations in Figure 2.2.

2.5 Asymmetric (Unilateral) Dependence

The situations shown above all involve the special condition that each particular type of control is symmetrical between the two persons. This was true for the four basic patterns in Table 2.7, but not for the problem of cleaning the apartment (Table 2.3). The equalities in controls between the two persons are not necessary theoretically, and from our practical experience, we know that one person often has more control over the other's outcomes than vice versa.

Among the patterns of interdependence in which the components are not symmetrical, the most extreme cases (the most asymmetrical ones) are those of total or *unilateral* dependence of one person on the other one. Person B is dependent on A but A is not dependent on B. Logically, there are three basic types of total dependence, depending on whether the dependent person is subject to Partner Control, Joint Control, or both. The three types are shown in Table 2.8. In each case, the dependent person is B and, for case I where B is dependent on A's Partner Control, A's preferences are shown to be either concordant or discordant with B's outcomes.

As explained in Entry #11, Asymmetric Dependence, the several patterns of dependence have quite different implications for the dependent

TABLE 2.8. *Three Cases of Unilateral Dependence: Person B Is Totally Dependent on Person A, Who Is Totally Independent*

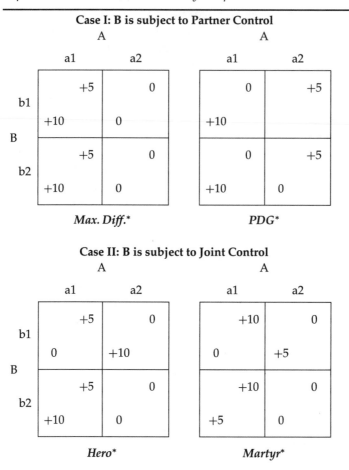

Case I: B is subject to Partner Control

	A				A	
	a1	a2		a1	a2
b1	+5	0		0	+5
	+10	0		+10	
b2	+5	0		0	+5
	+10	0		+10	0

       Max. Diff.*   *PDG**

Case II: B is subject to Joint Control

	A				A	
	a1	a2		a1	a2
b1	+5	0		+10	0
	0	+10		0	+5
b2	+5	0		+10	0
	+10	0		+5	0

       Hero*   *Martyr**

Case III: B is subject to both Partner Control and Joint Control

	A				A	
	a1	a2		a1	a2
b1	0	0		0	0
	+10	+5		+5	+10
b2	0	0		0	0
	+15	0		+15	0

       Chicken*   *Turn Taking**

* The matrix shown is an asymmetric variant of the symmetric pattern named. See section 4.2.4, chapter 4.

person. If subject to Partner Control, the dependent person is helpless – at the mercy of the partner and only able to hope that the partner will want to do what is good for the person. In contrast, if subject to Joint Control, the dependent person's problem is to discern what the controlling person is likely to do and then make a behavioral adjustment that coordinates with it. An example is the pupil at school who learns to anticipate his teacher's preferences and behaviors (e.g., when the teacher becomes really angry) and to act accordingly (e.g., when to be quiet and not whisper to the friend sitting at the next desk).

Interdependence (or mutual dependence) versus asymmetric (including unilateral) dependence constitutes a fourth "dimension" of our situations. It is difficult to show that dimension in Figure 2.2. As explained in chapter 4, the three contrasting kinds of dependence described above consist of sets of patterns that extend off in different directions because of their relation to the three distinct regions of the situational space.

2.6 Summary

We have described the use of outcome matrices to represent situations of interdependence. Circumstances encountered during the course of an adventurous day by a fictional couple, Eamon and Kyoko, have been used to illustrate matrices and their implications. We have shown how an outcome matrix is a convenient way to describe the core problem that a particular situation poses for its occupants. The various pairs of entries in a matrix can be summarized by its *outcome distribution*. The ranges and covariance of that distribution describe the likely goals they will have in the situation, for example, whether they will be concerned about avoiding negative outcomes or trying to reach positive ones, and whether they have corresponding or conflicting interests in the outcomes they may achieve. Their primary means of working on that problem are provided by the situation's *outcome controls*. Those specify how the two persons individually or jointly control the outcomes that each one experiences. We have shown that any combination of three types of outcome control may exist in a situation and may be identified by applying the logic of analysis of variance. Those three types of control are shown to define a three-dimensional space in which the many possible 2 × 2 outcome patterns based on symmetrical components are located. Thus, kinds of interdependence situation can be characterized in terms of (1) degree of interdependence, (2) corresponding versus conflicting interests, and (3) type of interdependence problem – whether coordination, exchange, or both. In addition, there is a "fourth dimension" that reflects the symmetry or asymmetry between the two persons in their dependence on each other.

Exactly how a pair is able to go about exercising the outcome controls in a situation is determined by two further features, the response conditions and the information conditions, which are explained in the next chapter. There we also consider how interaction between any particular pair of persons depends not only on the situations they encounter but also on the attitudes and values they bring to bear in their decisions in those situations. Finally, chapter 4 uses the three-dimensional space of situations developed here to plot the location of various particular patterns and to note the parts of that domain that the entries in this Atlas explore.

3

Interaction Conditions and Person Factors

This chapter continues our discussion of the properties of interdependence situations. It first considers the two conditions that affect how people can go about using their outcome controls to select among the various pairs of outcomes made possible in a situation. These are the *response conditions* – the sequential-temporal structure that governs when and in what order the behavioral responses possible in a situation can be exercised, and *information conditions*, which affect what the persons know and can communicate to each other. This chapter describes how we distinguish and represent those conditions.

Then we briefly consider the determinants of a situation and the question of its "reality." Finally, we turn our attention to the "person factors" that enter into the interaction in particular situations. These are the interpersonal attitudes and values that people bring to and express through their interdependence. It will be recalled that our overarching model is that interaction is jointly determined by the situation and by the "person factors" of the two persons. In the Atlas's entries describing various important kinds of situation, we consider both the "person factors" relevant to each one and some of the patterns of interaction generated by partners for whom those particular factors are operative.

3.1 Some Examples of Response Conditions and Information Conditions

Recalling Eamon and Kyoko, we know that to accomplish their coordination task of removing the log that blocked their way, it was necessary

Harold Kelley had primary responsibility for preparation of this chapter.

for them to lift their respective ends at the same time. This *simultaneity* requirement is to be contrasted with other possible sequential-temporal requirements for action. For example, there may be an *order* requirement, one person being required to act first in order to create the conditions that make possible the other person's necessary actions. Eamon may have to hold back some stray branches before Kyoko finally drives past the fallen tree. *Ad lib* conditions permit one or both persons to abstain from action rather than select one of the behavioral options. Thus, they are able to act at liberty, being free at any given time to act or not. And situations differ in the *revocability* of actions, that is, whether an action, once taken, can be "taken back" or revoked. Those examples illustrate various factors that determine the sequential-temporal constraints on interdependent action, defined here as the situation's *response conditions*. Just as situations can be distinguished by their outcome distributions and outcome controls, they also involve various types of these constraints. Below, we discuss the major types of response conditions that occur in interdependent life.

The other important factor that shapes interaction in a situation is the *information conditions* associated with it. In the log-removal example, both persons probably have access to all the relevant information about their problem (unless Eamon is not aware of Kyoko's trick back and its implications for her possible pain). If one had been blind, much of the necessary information would have been available only to the sighted partner. We saw that communication of intentions, by signals or words, was useful in promoting Eamon and Kyoko's efficient coordination. Under other conditions, as in pitch black darkness, hand signals would not have been a useful means of communicating information. Similarly, with a totally deaf partner, speech would not have been useful. Those are simple examples of the various facets of the information conditions, which may be summarized by two questions: (1) What information about the situation (i.e., about behavioral options and their consequences) is available to whom? (2) What means of communicating information are available to whom? Formal examples of variations in amount and communication are given in a later section.

The phenomena of information and communication are extremely complex and we can only touch on them in this Atlas. That is not to deny their crucial role in guiding and constraining the selections of actions, but we cannot give them systematic and thorough attention.

The response conditions and information conditions are logically independent of the other two aspects of a situation – its outcome distribution and pattern of outcome controls. A circumstance at any location in the situational domain (e.g., in Figure 2.2) may have any of the kinds of response and information features we distinguish here. Although we will find those two types of conditions to be related in several ways, we will consider them separately, beginning here with the response conditions and then, in a subsequent section, sketching the information conditions.

3.2 Varieties of Response Conditions

Over the range of possible natural circumstances, there are several possible interaction routes to any of the pairs of outcomes provided by a situation. These routes are determined by factors that determine when the two persons can take the actions specified in the matrix. We have indicated the major kinds of these response conditions by the examples above. Whereas the outcome matrix specifies *what* responses a situation makes it possible for each person to make, its sequential-temporal structure specifies *when* they can or must take any of those responses. These structures also describe situations in which a certain *sequence* of actions must be taken to reach some end state. Thus, the particular sequence and timing of behaviors by which a pair deals with a situation's problems and opportunities reflect its response conditions.

When we view the outcome matrix for a particular situation and try to imagine what will or might happen, we almost invariably think of a certain sequence of events. In doing so, we implicitly assume that the interaction is occurring under particular response conditions. From our experience in natural interaction, we are most familiar with *ad lib* conditions. Under these, each person is able to act when they wish, or to not act at all. We usually assume ad lib conditions when we observe people working together on informal tasks or talking together in casual conversation.

We also know that in many circumstances, people do not have freedom to act when they want to. In playing many games (e.g., chess, poker), when it comes their turn, players must (within some time limit) act one way or another. In everyday exchange transactions, the buyer is often required to make a payment before the seller is required to deliver the goods. Thus, the rules of games and social customs impose a certain order on responses. We also observe certain sequences of activities, for example, in organized work interactions, such as those among the workers at a fast food restaurant. Those sequences depend largely on the nature of the tasks, for example, that an order must be placed before the food is prepared and that the food must be prepared before it is served.

The "A, then B" or *order* requirement, illustrated above, is contrasted to the "both A and B" or *simultaneity* requirement. In this case, the two persons are required to act simultaneously (or functionally so, by the requirement that their actions be chosen and taken independently, that is, without knowledge of each other's choice). The simultaneity requirement has often been imposed on subjects in experimental "game" research for such situations as the Prisoner's Dilemma and Chicken. This usage reflects the origins of game theory in the study of military strategies for situations of perfect conflict of interest (usually, "zero-sum" games). The warring opponents are assumed to conceal their strategies from each other so completely that they have to make independent choices based only on analyses of the likely outcomes from various combinations of their and their partner's likely strategies. Simultaneity of responses also occurs in everyday life. For example, in their busy lives, Kyoko and Eamon will sometimes be out of contact with each other and have to make independent and, for practical purposes, simultaneous decisions about a matter they forgot to discuss, for example, who is to pick up the take-out dinner on the way home. This is one of many instances in which the sequential-temporal structure affects the information conditions. By definition, simultaneous actions leave each person ignorant of the other's choice and, perhaps, exposed to risks created by the other's independently deployed outcome control.

Ignorance of the partner's action is particularly important if, once taken, a selected behavior selection cannot be changed or revoked before it has its consequences. The mobilizations involved in military operations often involve actions that are so complex and cumbersome that, once underway, they are essentially irrevocable. In everyday life, Eamon and Kyoko find that the unnecessary, duplicate take-out order cannot be returned. Conditions relating to *revocability* are commonly imposed by the rules of various games. For example, once a chess player's hand is lifted from a piece after a move, that move cannot be changed. Revocability as a natural condition (rather than a social convention) assumes that there is a time gap between the taking of an action and its consequences or completion. Of course, in some interaction, no such gap exists. One person's negative comment about another or a physical slap in the face can rarely be undone. Adults may demand apologies for such acts and children may apply physical threats to "take that back!" but the consequences usually follow immediately and irreversibly on the heels of the hurtful remark or action. A gap between an action and its consequences is sometimes created by environmental conditions that generate a time-extended chain of causality between the "taking" of an action and its effect. This is illustrated by the chain of events intervening between one's payment by check and its being presented for collection to one's bank. That chain enables us to stop payment on – to revoke – the check.

The several types of response conditions described above may occur in various combinations and patterns. The combination permitting the greatest flexibility is that of ad lib and revocability. Each person can take an action at any time, but then "take it back" if the partner's response is not acceptable. For example, in buying a souvenir at a bazaar in a country where neither you nor the merchant understands the other's language, he may hold out some curio for which, in return, you hold out some of the local currency. If the trade is not satisfactory to him, the merchant may present a different item he's willing to sell for the money you offer, and you may then either insist on the original object and offer more money, or reduce the amount you will pay for the lesser one. This sort of bargaining through tentative (i.e., revocable) and successively adjusted actions can continue until the two of you either agree on a transaction or one of you shrugs your shoulders and gives up. A briefer adjustment and counteradjustment process often occurs at a narrow doorway when two persons reach it at the same time and, as sometimes happens, both try to pass through or wait for the other to do so. The incipient moves toward the door can be started, then undone, then started again, and so on, until an "agreement" is reached on the order of using the door.

The freedom to act or not, and to revoke actions once taken, provides for flexible interaction in which people can communicate their desires to each other simply by their actions. Those conditions permit the pair to cycle through a problem repeatedly, indicating preferences among the options and dissatisfaction with each other's "proposals." This is another case in which response conditions and information conditions overlap: The tentative actions could easily be replaced by verbal "offers." (In either case, there arise questions of "good faith": An "offer," whether made by a tentative action or stated verbally, should be made seriously and not merely to "test the waters." And if "accepted" by an appropriate response, an offer should not be reneged.) Even without verbal communication, the ad lib, revocable conditions make possible a degree of information exchange relevant to their final actions that is in sharp contrast to the minimal information available in a more constrained sequential-temporal structure, such as one with a simultaneity requirement.

Associated with each outcome pattern, such as those shown in chapter 2, there are several possible interaction sequences, depending on the various sequential temporal structures within which the outcome control pattern is embedded. Certain structures are particularly useful for exercising certain controls. For example, the ad lib revocability condition permits one person to take the lead in solving common interest coordination (Mutual Joint Control) problems. Doing so requires being firmly assertive, by acting quickly and persisting with the chosen action so that the partner may coordinate with it.

3.2.1 *Transition Lists: The Schematic Representation of Sequential-Temporal Structures*

The various possible response conditions can be represented by *transition lists* (Kelley, 1984b). In our entries we will have several occasions to use them so a brief description is appropriate here. More forbidding in appearance than they actually are, they may more readily be understood if the reader thinks of them as similar to simple computer programs. They specify *when* and *in what order* various actions may be taken and the consequences of those actions in moving the pair through a series of stages ("junctures") to the ultimate attainment of the possible outcomes.

Let us examine transitions lists for the outcome pattern known as the Prisoner's Dilemma (Entry #5). But first, we must explain the matrix for that situation along with its control components. Table 3.1 shows that the situation consists of a combination of Bilateral Actor Control and Mutual Partner Control, with the latter being the larger. The ratio in this example is 2:1 with the MPC component contributing twice as much variance to the resultant pattern. Most important is the fact that the BAC and MPC are combined in a "discordant" orientation to each other, meaning that for each person, the action (Keep) that benefits the self is opposite the action (Give) that benefits the partner. Because of the ratio of the effects, each person can, at some sacrifice, benefit the partner to a degree that outweighs that sacrifice. It is easy to imagine this as representing the standard situation in which people trade commodities whose values to their receivers outweigh the costs to their givers. Both can gain if they make the exchange, hence, the situation might be described as "Exchange for Mutual Profit."[1] (Entry #5 explains

---

[1] The reader may notice that the matrix in Table 3.1 is probably an improved rendition of Eamon and Kyoko's situation of exchanging recording tape for batteries (shown in Table 2.2). It is plausible to assume that Eamon has some preference for keeping his extra batteries (for future use) rather than giving them to Kyoko, and that she has a similar preference for keeping her extra tapes. If so, a trade requires each person to override the Actor Control component in order to induce the other to employ his or her Partner Control in a helpful manner.

TABLE 3.1. *The Combination of Symmetrical Components That Combine to Form the "Exchange for Mutual Profit" Situation (The Prisoner's Dilemma)*

BAC

	A	
	Give a1	Keep a2
Give b1	0 / 0	+5 / 0
Keep b2	0 / +5	+5 / +5

(B at left)

$+$

MPC

	A	
	a1	a2
b1	+10 / +10	+10 / 0
b2	0 / +10	0 / 0

$+$

MJC

	A	
	a1	a2
(b1)	0 / 0	0 / 0
(b2)	0 / 0	0 / 0

$=$

Matrix 5*

	A	
	a1	a2
b1	+10 / +10	+15 / 0
b2	0 / +15	+5 / +5

Exchange for Mutual Profit
(The Prisoner's Dilema)

* The matrix number corresponds to the entry in the body of the Atlas.

why this simple situation, illustrating the interdependence structure that promotes "doing business" by buying and selling at mutual profit, is usually referred to as the "Prisoner's Dilemma." Here, we will refer to it as the "Exchange for Mutual Profit" situation.)

Tables 3.2A and 3.2B present transition lists that describe two contrasting sets of response conditions as they might exist for the "Exchange for Mutual Profit" situation. The list in Table 3.2A describes a situation in which the two persons are required to make simultaneous and irrevocable selections between their two options. The conventions for writing transition lists specify that selections among the options listed at each juncture in

TABLE 3.2A. *The "Exchange for Mutual Profit" Situation with Response Conditions Requiring Simultaneous Irrevocable Selections*

Junctures	Options	Possible Selections	Outcomes for A and B		Transition to Next Juncture
[J	(a1, a2)	a1b1	+10,	+10	X]
[	(b1, b2)	a1b2	0,	+15	X]
[		a2b1	+15,	0	X]
[		a2b2	+5,	+5	X]

TABLE 3.2B. *The "Exchange for Mutual Profit" Situation with Response Conditions Permitting Revocability until Agreement*

Junctures	Options	Possible Selections	Outcomes for A and B		Transition to Next Juncture
[J	(a1, a2)	a1b1	−,	−	K]
[	(b1, b2)	a1b2	−,	−	L]
[		a2b1	−,	−	M]
[		a2b2	−,	−	N]
[K	(a1, a2)	a1b1	+10,	+10	X]
[	(b1, b2)	a1b2	−,	−	J]
[		a2b1	−,	−	J]
[		a2b2	−,	−	J]
[L	(a1, a2)	a1b1	−,	−	J]
[	(b1, b2)	a1b2	0,	+15	X]
[		a2b1	−,	−	J]
[		a2b2	−,	−	J]
[M	(a1, a2)	a1b1	−,	−	J]
[	(b1, b2)	a1b2	−,	−	J]
[		a2b1	+15,	0	X]
[		a2b2	−,	−	J]
[N	(a1, a2)	a1b1	−,	−	J]
[	(b1, b2)	a1b2	−,	−	J]
[		a2b1	−,	−	J]
[		a2b2	+5,	+5	X]

a list are assumed to be made simultaneously and independently.[2] Moreover, in the list in Table 3.2A, the selections at juncture J result directly

---

[2] However, the set of options at a particular juncture may include the "null" response, meaning that a person's "selection" at that juncture may be to do nothing. None of the examples in this chapter include that possibility. For more details, see Kelley (1984b).

in the outcomes for A and B shown there. Those selections are irrevocable because, as the list shows, after one of the pair of outcomes occurs, the pair is moved directly to a next juncture, in this case, "X," which is the "exit" from (or conclusion of) this situation. (When they leave this situation, they move on to some unspecified different situation.) In brief, in a simultaneous, irrevocable condition, they make their independent selections, experience the consequences, and that ends that particular episode of their interaction.

It can be seen that the set of outcomes and their associated options in the list in Table 3.2A are the same as those for matrix 5 in Table 3.1. The transition list describes the same possible pairings of A's and B's response options and the same outcome consequences for each pairing. That is true for *all* transition lists, that they include, at some location in the list, *all* the information about the outcome matrix to which the particular sequential-temporal structure applies.

Before proceeding to examine the transition list in Table 3.2B, let us recall the interaction we often observe in everyday instances of the "Exchange for Mutual Profit" situation, as illustrated by the encounter with the souvenir merchant in the bazaar. One person, A, tentatively offers something to B and then, if B seems willing to reciprocate appropriately, A gives it to B. But, if B fails to reciprocate, A withdraws the offer. It should be clear that the simultaneous, irrevocable conditions represented in the list in Table 3.2A do not permit that sequence to occur because each person has to decide independently and irrevocably whether to give or keep. Among the several other possible response conditions, the one we implicitly assume in imagining the exchange scenario is one that permits an offer to be made tentatively, but revoked unless met with an appropriate response. Such conditions are shown in Table 3.2B. When the two persons make their choices at the initial juncture, they then have an opportunity either to persist in them (in a sense, "confirming" them) or to change them. And they gain the situation's outcomes only after mutually confirming their most recent choices.

For example, if, at the initial juncture, A selects a2 and B selects b2, the transitions move them to juncture N. At that point, each has an opportunity either to change their selection or to persist in it. If either one changes, not repeating the #2 selection, they are returned to juncture J and have an opportunity to make new "offers." Only if *both* persons persist with (in a sense, "insist on") a particular pair of options do they gain its outcomes. And once they "agree," they leave the situation. The series of successive opportunities to "propose" and then "change" or "persist" enables them to follow any one of several possible "routes" through the transition list and, in principle, they may arrive at any one of the four possible pairs of outcomes. As a consequence, their agreement need not be "fair" nor meet any other standard. But the structure, enabling revocability until agreement is reached, provides each person with considerable control over the final transaction. A problem, of course, is that the process might proceed endlessly, so people can usually exit from this sort of situation without agreement. That possibility can easily be represented in the transition list by simply adding a third option for each person at juncture J, which, if used by either person, takes them directly to the exit.

3.2.2 *Extended and Repeated Situations*

Transition lists also permit us to describe situations that are extended in time. The problem is solved – the "goal" of the situation is reached – only at the end of a required sequence of intermediate junctures. (Thus, the extension is required by the situation and not merely a phenomenon the persons may generate, as above.) At each of the junctures, an exit from the situation is available. Taking that exit amounts to leaving the situation before it is "completed," that is, before its potential outcomes are achieved. Extended situations provide the settings in which various important person factors are displayed, having to do with what we might describe (following Leonard Doob, 1971) as temporal motives: persistence in the face of costs, resistance to the temptations offered by attractive byways, patience in waiting for one's partner, time perspective, and the broad set of factors summarized by the term "commitment."

In Kyoko and Eamon's lives, being a "morning" person, Kyoko frequently becomes impatient when she has to wait for Eamon to get ready for an early joint activity. The situation is an extended one because she must cycle repeatedly through the initial juncture before being able to move on with him to the subsequent ones where they do things together. The waiting cycles are usually frustrating because they do not make it possible to move on to rewarding activities in the meantime – thus, the source of the negative effect associated with "losing one's patience."

The transition list for the "extended situation" known as the Investment situation (Entry #13) is shown in Table 3.3. At each of the initial junctures, each person can make an "investment" of two units (by a1 and b1, respectively), or not (a2 and b2, respectively). Only if both make their contributions at each of those times do they move toward the goal of mutually high outcomes. At any juncture along the way, if either fails to meet the necessary payment, they are dropped out of the situation. They then lose their payments made up to that point and lose the possibility of the final payoffs from the investments. If they continue to the final point (when the "investment

TABLE 3.3. *Mutual Investment Situation: Investments by Both Persons Move the Pair toward the Goal of Mutually Desirable Payoffs*

Junctures	Options	Possible Selections	Outcomes for A and B		Transition to Next Juncture
[J	(a1, a2)	a1b1	−2,	−2	K]
[	(b1, b2)	a1b2	−2,	0	X]
[		a2b1	0,	−2	X]
[		a2b2	−,	−	X]
[K	(a1, a2)	a1b1	−2,	−2	L]
[	(b1, b2)	a1b2	−2,	0	X]
[		a2b1	0,	−2	X]
[		a2b2	−,	−	X]
[L	(a1, a2)	a1b1	−2,	−2	M]
[	(b1, b2)	a1b2	−2,	0	X]
[		a2b1	0,	−2	X]
[		a2b2	−,	−	X]
[M	(a1, a2)	a1b1	−2,	−2	N]
[	(b1, b2)	a1b2	−2,	0	X]
[		a2b1	0,	−2	X]
[		a2b2	−,	−	X]
[N	(a3, a3)	a3b3	+14,	+14	X]

matures"), they simply collect their shares of the dividends (by their a3 and b3 options). The situation obviously encourages persistence in the effort which, in turn, is promoted by confidence in the "investment" and trust in one's partner to continue making their contributions.

Some situations are *repeated* in close succession, with the pair's completion of one problem leading directly and necessarily to their being confronted again with the same problem. Repetition is common in work settings where a pair of workers have to repeat a particular assembly task over and over again during the work day. Friends may have a regular schedule of going to movies on Friday night and may think of the successive occasions as repetitions of the same sort of joint decision problem. In game research, these are illustrated by the *iterated* situations frequently employed. For example, experimental subjects may repeatedly "play" the Prisoner's Dilemma Game, making simultaneous and independent selections on, say, 20 consecutive occasions. Research on this situation is described in Entry #12.

The matrix and transition list for an iterated "turn-taking" game are shown in Tables 3.4A and 3.4B. This situation arose for Kyoko and Eamon when they went to the small cabin in which they planned to spend the night. It had a bare wood floor and only one cot. The matrix for their situation is shown in Table 3.4A. The large outcomes are obtained when one of them, either one, sleeps in the cot (+15) and the other sleeps in a sleeping bag on the floor (+10). The worst outcomes occur (obviously) when both try to use the cot. Joint use of the sleeping bag is tolerable but not as good as when one person uses it and the other uses the cot. Eamon, raised by his mother always to be helpful to a woman, gallantly volunteers to take the floor. Kyoko, raised in a family that gave precedence to the men in the house, objects and suggests that she take the floor. In order to resolve that conflict, it is plausible for them to change the situation into an iterated one, with the night being divided into successive periods, allowing each to have one or more turns occupying the more desirable location.

The iteration of the situation is shown in the transition list in Table 3.4B. The temporal structure of the problem is obvious from the sequence of "junctures" and "next junctures" in the list. The pair makes the same set of decisions on five successive occasions and then leaves the iteration process. At each juncture, the complete set of options and outcomes is available to the pair and whatever they do, the same set is presented to them at the next juncture (except after the final iteration).

The situation is appropriately dubbed a "turn-taking" game because over the repeated junctures, it permits the pair to take turns in who gets the better outcomes and, therefore, to more or less even out their respective total outcomes. (For reasons that are somewhat obscure, this situation is sometimes referred to as the "Battle of the Sexes.")

Do the persons in the "turn-taking" game find it necessary to explicitly discuss their decisions at each occasion if they are to develop the turn-taking process? Explicit communication would surely speed up that development, but the iteration conditions also make possible an implicit process, much like the "offer, then counteroffer" process in reaching "agreement" on exchanges, or the "adjustment, then counteradjustment" process that enables two persons to proceed through a narrow doorway. The transition list in Table 3.4B does not permit tentative actions that indicate one's initial desires but that then may be revoked. However, somewhat the same effect can be achieved (though less efficiently) in iterated interaction. Early choices reveal both what each person desires and what each expects from the partner. With that information, both the desires and expectations can

TABLE 3.4A. *The Turn-Taking Situation in Matrix Format*

Eamon

		Floor a1	Cot a2
Kyoko	Floor b1	+5 / +5	+15 / +10
	Cot b2	+10 / +15	0 / 0

TABLE 3.4B. *The Turn-Taking Situation in a Transition List Format Requiring Iteration*

Junctures	Options	Possible Selections	Outcomes for A and B	Transition to Next Juncture
[J	(a1, a2)	a1b1	+5, +5	K]
[	(b1, b2)	a1b2	+10, +15	K]
[		a2b1	+15, +10	K]
[		a2b2	0, 0	K]
[K	(a1, a2)	a1b1	+5, +5	L]
[	(b1, b2)	a1b2	+10, +15	L]
[		a2b1	+15, +10	L]
[		a2b2	0, 0	L]
[L	(a1, a2)	a1b1	+5, +5	M]
[	(b1, b2)	a1b2	+10, +15	M]
[		a2b1	+15, +10	M]
[		a2b2	0, 0	M]
[M	(a1, a2)	a1b1	+5, +5	N]
[	(b1, b2)	a1b2	+10, +15	N]
[		a2b1	+15, +10	N]
[		a2b2	0, 0	N]
[N	(a1, a2)	a1b1	+5, +5	X]
[	(b1, b2)	a1b2	+10, +15	X]
[		a2b1	+15, +10	X]
[		a2b2	0, 0	X]

be adjusted or persisted in, creating the possibility of an eventual tacit agreement on a mutually acceptable pair or sequence of pairs of outcomes. In other words, the flexibility possible with the ad lib and revocability sequential-temporal structures can, to some degree, be simulated by the succession of simultaneous but irrevocable choices made over a series of iterations. This phenomenon has been investigated by Axelrod (1984) and others in the iterated Prisoner's Dilemma game. As explained below in section 3.4, a "tit-for-tat" strategy of making successive decisions serves implicitly but effectively to communicate an attitude of willingness to cooperate with a partner but unwillingness to accept their selfish or competitive behavior. This is yet another instance of the implications of various response conditions for the communication of information.

3.3 Selection between Situations

In the repetition conditions described above, the persons are "carried" through the successive stages of a particular situation, being required to move from one iteration to the next. Often, the succession of different situations that A and B enter is under their own control. Transitions lists are useful in distinguishing different ways in which a pair might exercise such control. Consider the example represented by the transition list in Table 3.5A. At juncture J, the two persons make choices that determine whether they move to situation K, to L, or to neither. For any move to K or L to occur, their selections at J must agree, so the movement is jointly controlled. The list there offers a choice between K, an "Exchange with Mutual Profit" situation which offers good and equal outcomes if they cooperate but also provides temptations to each individual to try to gain even higher outcomes, and L, a simple common interest coordination problem with modest outcomes.

That example illustrates the two questions to be raised about situation selection problems: (1) How is the choice controlled? (2) What are the alternatives they are choosing among?

With respect to the *first* question, a 2×2 set of behavioral options at a selection juncture that offers only two situational options affords only three patterns of control over intersituational movement. These are similar to several patterns of outcome control: (1) *Unilateral control*, that is, absolute control by one of the pair, similar to an outcome pattern of unilateral dependence. (2) *Joint control*, that is, the two persons together control the movement. Similar to Mutual Joint Control of outcomes, this is illustrated in Table 3.5A which offers choices between situation K, situation L,

TABLE 3.5A. *Juncture at Which the Pair Has Joint Control over Which of Two Situations to Enter (or Whether to Enter Neither)*

Junctures	Options	Possible Selections	Outcomes for A and B		Transition to Next Juncture
[J	(a1, a2)	a1b1	−,	−	K]
[	(b1, b2)	a1b2	−,	−	X]
[		a2b1	−,	−	X]
[		a2b2	−,	−	L]
[K	(a1, a2)	a1b1	+10,	+10	X]
[	(b1, b2)	a1b2	0,	+20	X]
[		a2b1	+20,	0	X]
[		a2b2	+1,	+1	X]
[L	(a1, a2)	a1b1	+2,	+2	X]
[	(b1, b2)	a1b2	0,	0	X]
[		a2b1	0,	0	X]
[		a2b2	+2,	+2	X]

TABLE 3.5B. *Juncture at Which Either Can Veto the Selection of Situation K in Favor of L ("Conjunctive" for K and "Disjunctive" for L)*

Junctures	Options	Possible Selections	Outcomes for A and B		Transition to Next Juncture
[J	(a1, a2)	a1b1	−,	−	K]
[	(b1, b2)	a1b2	−,	−	L]
[		a2b1	−,	−	L]
[		a2b2	−,	−	L]

or making no choice. Both persons must elect to go to K or L and, in the event of disagreement, they do neither but simply leave the choice juncture. (3) *Conjunctive/disjunctive control*, that is, both must agree if they are to move to one of two options (the conjunctive requirement) and, the opposite side of the coin, either can unilaterally move them to the other option. This is shown in Table 3.5B in which either person can veto a move to situation K. (The pattern is similar to the conjunctive or disjunctive outcome patterns, in Entries #9 and #10, being conjunctive for moving to K but disjunctive for moving to L.)

It goes without saying that at a selection juncture with more options and more alternative situations, there are many more patterns of control. However, the main varieties of control over the process of selecting among situations contrast ones where one person can completely control the process with those in which the control is divided between the two in one of several ways.

The *second* question, about the alternative situations available at the choice point, concerns the criteria that underlie individuals' preferences among situations. That, of course, is an extremely complex matter. It can be approached systematically by reference to the four dimensions identified in chapter 2 as distinguishing aspects of interdependence situations. That is, we can inquire into what various individuals prefer among the various kinds of situations located in the space shown in Figure 2.2 and various kinds of asymmetric dependence. Do they like closeness, that is, high interdependence, or does that make them uncomfortable, as Eidelson (1980) shows to be true of some people and as attachment theory proposes to be characteristic of persons with avoidant attachment tendencies (Shaver, Belsky, & Brennan, 2000). Do they enjoy the give and take of negotiation and, therefore, seek the challenges of situations with conflicting interests? Or do they prefer tasks with corresponding interests and, in the list in Table 3.5A, perhaps sacrifice opportunities for high outcomes in order to avoid conflict?

Answers to questions such as these are complicated by the common necessity of moving within the domain of interdependence with a particular partner. So the preferences a person expresses among situations will undoubtedly depend on the partner likely to be involved. For example, the commitment and trust required for success in an Investment situation (e.g., Table 3.3) may exist with one potential partner but not another. Some of these issues are discussed in Entry #21, Movement among Situations.

The kinds of situations in which a pair tends repeatedly to find or locate themselves begin to define their "relationship." As we observe the particular sample of locations to which their excursions in the situational geography take them, we can characterize their relationship as one of closeness or distance, corresponding or conflicting interests, exchange or coordination, and equality or inequality of control. And we observe them when, as they leave the upper reaches of interdependence with its potentials for both frustrating conflict and richly rewarding interaction and move toward *in*dependence, their relationship may be said to undergo deterioration. All of which is to emphasize that the notion of dyadic shifts among situations expands the scope of our analysis and moves us from the situation-by-situation level of analysis toward a basic understanding of *relationships*. The analysis of control over intersituational movement calls our attention to how a relationship reflects (1) the situations *available* to a pair and external constraints on their movement, (2) the expression, through their patterns of movement control, of their individual and negotiated preferences *among* various available situations, and, affecting their subsequent selections, (3) their selections *within* those situations (per their "person factors").

3.4 The Representation of Information Conditions

Associated with each outcome matrix and transition list we have described, there may be any one of a number of information conditions. These conditions have two aspects: (1) the amount of information (who knows what) and (2) communication (who can convey information to whom and by what means).

The information pertaining to any situation is very complex, relating to all the facts schematically represented in the matrix or transition list. Thus, the relevant information concerns the person's behavioral options and the outcomes those options, singly and jointly, yield. And although it is not our concern in the present focus on the *situation*, it is also very important for each person to have information about the other *person*. For example, how generous will the partner be in exercising Partner Control over the self and how assertive and skillful will the partner be in the synchronization of the pair's efforts on coordination problems? Those questions are usually answered on the basis of the person's prior knowledge of and *expectations* about particular partners. In addition, the information conditions include the communication options the two persons have – options that enable them to transmit explicit information from one to the other, without relying on the implicit communication conveyed by their behavioral choices.

We do not have a means of representing all the possible variations in information conditions. And we recognize that the eventual systematic and complete representation of the information conditions will be an extremely complicated matter. Incomplete information might exist for any of the situations we distinguish in this Atlas, but we have chosen to include only certain situations where incomplete information is an essential feature of the situation as it occurs in social life. These include Negotiation (Entry #15), Encounters with Strangers (Entry #16), Joint Decisions under Uncertainty (Entry #17), and Twists of Fate (Entry #18). In such cases, our simple method of representing the incomplete information is to place question marks in the transition list format to indicate where outcome values are not known by one or both partners.

That method is illustrated for the Joint Decisions under Uncertainty situation in Table 3.6. This situation is one of *symmetric partial* information, inasmuch as (at juncture J) both persons lack access to the *same* important

TABLE 3.6. *Joint Decisions under Uncertainty: Lack of Information about Outcomes at Juncture K (See Entry #17)*

Junctures	Options	Possible Selections	Outcomes for A and B		Transition to Next Juncture
[J	(a1, a2)	a1b1	+5,	+6	X]
[	(b1, b2)	a1b2	+5,	+6	X]
[		a2b1	+5,	+6	X]
[		a2b2	−,	−	K]
[K	(a3, a4)	a3b3	?,	?	X]
[	(b3, b4)	a3b4	?,	?	X]
[		a4b3	?,	?	X]
[		a4b4	?,	?	X]

data (the outcomes available at juncture K). The problem involves whether the pair should take the outcomes known to be available at the initial juncture or should move to the next juncture on the chance that the unknown outcomes there will be better. Discussed in Entry #17, examples include whether a couple should stay at the first motel they come to along the highway or proceed to some further (presently out-of-sight) motel down the road. In Table 3.6, the pattern of control over stopping versus moving on is such that both persons have to agree to give up the known quantity in favor of the unknown one. (Other control patterns might exist for this problem.) An important feature of the situation is that the choice at J is irrevocable – there is no path from K back to J.

The decision situation in Table 3.6 is a simplified representation of a common fact of life – that we face a sequence of decision points ("junctures" in transition lists) that extend into the uncertain future. In a sense, the future course of life often has "corners" around which one cannot see and, therefore, beyond which nothing is directly (through one's immediate observation) knowable. And it is often impossible to turn back – to retrace one's steps. Once passed up, earlier opportunities may no longer be available. Taking an early, known opportunity entails remaining ignorant of what later ones *might* have been. Of course, the pair may draw on their past experiences in similar environments to generate *expectations* about the likely outcomes to be gained at the presently out-of-sight locations. In doing so, they fill in the gaps in the directly knowable information and, in a sense, modify the information parameters of the situation.

Eamon and Kyoko faced an incomplete information situation when, as they hurried toward the meadow, they came to a fork in the road, with no signs indicating the direction of the meadow. Their situation was somewhat

TABLE 3.7. *Simple Negotiation with Lack of Information about Each Other's Outcomes*

Junctures	Options	Possible Selections	Outcomes known to A	B	Transition to Next Juncture
[J	(a1 to a7)	a1b1	10, ?	?, 2	X]
[	(b1 to b7)	a2b2	9, ?	?, 4	X]
[		a3b3	9, ?	?, 6	X]
[		a4b4	8, ?	?, 8	X]
[		a5b5	7, ?	?, 5	X]
[		a6b6	4, ?	?, 10	X]
[		a7, any b	5, ?	?, 3	X]
[		any a, b7	5, ?	?, 3	X]
[		all other pairs	–, –	–, –	J]

similar to the situation selection situation in Tables 3.5A and 3.5B, except that, in the absence of signs, the situation they faced had question marks entered for all the possibilities at junctures K and L. It is also apparent that because she was driving, Kyoko had unilateral control over the direction in which they would move. That was a fortunate circumstance because her memory provided the missing information and she was not afraid to take responsibility for the decision. Her assertiveness in the matter enabled them to arrive before sunrise, as they both desired.

In contrast to the examples above, the situation represented in Table 3.7 is one in which each person's *partial* information pertains to *different* aspects of the total picture. In this simple negotiation problem, as is commonly true in natural negotiations, both persons have information about their own outcomes but lack information about the partner's. Of the seven behavioral options, the first six represent "offers" – say, proposals about the price the buyer will pay the seller for various quantities of goods. If the two agree on one of the six deals, they receive their respective outcomes (e.g., the "profit" that the exchange yields to each) and leave the situation. However, A knows only his own outcomes from each of the six possible agreements, and the same is true for B who knows his own outcomes but not those of A. If they fail to agree on one of the six "deals," they are returned to juncture J and may repeat their offers. The seventh options are special, representing breaking off the bargaining and "taking your business elsewhere." Breaking off can be done unilaterally by either bargainer: Option a7 combined with any of the "b" options, or b7 combined with any of the "a" options, terminates the negotiation. Each person also derives certain outcomes from doing so and, again, each knows only his own consequences of doing business elsewhere. So the interaction proceeds, with offers and counteroffers, until they agree on a particular deal or one or both break off the process.

In the negotiation situation, as in most natural situations, the interdependent persons are able to provide information to each other by explicit means or by implicit means, the latter by their successive offers, facial expressions, gestures, and so forth. If the negotiators could assume that their interests coincide perfectly, they could simply reach agreement by explicitly sharing their sets of information and seeing what settlement fulfills their common interests. However, as is typical in negotiation situations, their interests are strongly though not entirely in conflict. Each seeks to cooperate to get some deal but each also pursues his or her own interests by seeking to get the best deal possible. From our complete knowledge of their outcomes, we can see in Table 3.7 that what A most prefers is what B least prefers, and vice versa. But we can also see that there are several possible agreements that are better for both than what they can get by going to alternative businesses.

In short, similar to the plot of Entry #5 in Figure 2.1, this situation combines elements of corresponding and conflicting interests. Logically, the reconciliation of those elements requires a delicate blend of the communication behaviors characteristic of situations with corresponding interests (openness, honesty, and trust) and the communication behaviors characteristic of situations with conflicting interests (secrecy, deceit, and distrust). Assuming that the persons involved are experienced in negotiation situations of this sort, they are likely to have generalized expectations about this situation that enable them to think of it as a "mixed motive" situation and motivate them to walk a fine line between cooperative and competitive communication procedures. The communication opportunities in the situation permit them to do this, by mixing words (not all of which will be either totally honest or dishonest) with actions (quick vs. slow, intransigent vs. concessive, etc.) in a way that permits exploring the possible agreements without prematurely breaking off the process. (See Entry #15 for details.)

Experimental research on various situations has examined several information conditions. Negotiation studies have typically provided the type of "incomplete" information just described, but have permitted unrestricted communication. In contrast, Prisoner's Dilemma research has usually provided both persons with complete information about the outcome matrix but has required them to make independent decisions, without any communication. As noted earlier, when subjects are required to play the Prisoner's Dilemma repeatedly (the Iterated PD, Entry #12), their pattern of successive selections can serve tacitly to communicate their intentions as well as their desires for what the partner should do. The "tit-for-tat" strategy of iterated play (which begins with a cooperative choice but on subsequent iterations always does what the other person did on the last iteration) can be described as implicitly saying to the partner, "I will be cooperative if you will, but if not, I will not let you exploit me and will reciprocate your competitiveness." (Axelrod describes tit-for-tat as a "combination of being nice, retaliatory, forgiving, and clear," 1984, p. 54.) That behavior strategy with its implicit message results in more frequent cooperative interaction than other sequences of action. Tit-for-tat has an interesting parallel in a set of explicit, written messages devised by Deutsch (1958) to convey the same ideas: the person's intention to cooperate, the desire for the partner to cooperate, the intention to punish the partner's competition by reciprocating it, but the willingness then to cooperate if the partner decides to do so. Deutsch found that those messages also promoted cooperation. An interesting point here is that the comparison of the tit-for-tat behavioral strategy with the verbal messages illustrates the close parallels between communication made possible (implicitly) by actions and (explicitly) by words.

3.5 The Determinants of Situational Properties

Readers of interdependence theory sometimes ask "Are situations real?" By that question, they mean something like "Are situations objective or subjective? Are they simply what people perceive or expect them to be? Or, do situations have some more 'objective' status?" These questions can be answered by considering the determinants of a situation. What factors underlie its outcome distribution and controls, its response conditions, and its information conditions? For each of those features, the answer is the same: It is determined jointly by environmental and psychological factors.

To consider this matter, we must first return to the broad principle that underlies our work: "Interaction is a function of the Situation, Person A, and Person B." That statement might be taken to imply that the "situation" and the "persons" (both understood in their common meaning) are *independent* factors. That implication is not intended. As we now explain, we use "person" in two different senses, only one of which is intended for use in the above formulation. Specifically, in that statement we refer to the *particular set of properties of the person* (habits, motives, thoughts, etc.) *that come into play when an actor is cognizant of and responsive to the entire pattern of interdependence, including the partner's outcomes and controls.* Perhaps those particular properties are more properly labeled as *"social person factors."*

Returning to the questions about the "situation," it is determined by the interplay between environmental or task factors and the basic abilities and needs of the actors. In other words, S = f (E, A′ B′) where E refers to the environment (broadly speaking) and A′ and B′ refer to sets of person factors we will describe as *"basic person factors."*

To illustrate the point: The facts summarized in the outcome matrix (or what we often refer to as the "given" matrix) are jointly determined by the physical world and by certain basic properties of the persons in it. The actions they may take are governed by the tools and means in their physical surroundings *relative to* the persons' abilities in their use. The outcomes that may result from various combinations of their actions depend upon the physical consequences of those actions (food, music, shelter, etc.) *relative to* the persons' needs and states of deprivation regarding such "incentives," and their resulting simple personal preferences.

The response conditions reflect that same interplay between environmental circumstances and basic personal factors. Simultaneous (independent) selections are imposed by physical separation relative to a pair's communication abilities. Order conditions are created, for example, by the width of passageways relative to the girths of two persons moving in opposite directions. Repetitions of a particular situation, perhaps providing opportunities for turn taking, are imposed on a couple by their recurrent environmental conditions (including their varying supply of hot water available for showers, or the current television schedules of their preferred programs) relative to their respective needs and preferences. Certain successions of situations are imposed by the structural logic of the physical world relative to their skills. For example, on a moonless night, a couple on a hiking trip may find it necessary first to build a fire so that they can then have the light necessary for pitching their tent. The information conditions similarly depend on the interplay between the environment and the persons' needs and abilities. The circumstances include the fences, corners, and illumination which, relative to their heights and sensory acuities, determine what each can know about the situation.

In general, we may say that the situation in which a pair finds themselves is "real," *but it is real is a special sense.* We do *not* mean a set of factors defined in purely physical or geographical terms. Rather, we mean features that are defined by the *interplay* between environmental factors (implements, objects, physical stimuli) and basic person factors (size, strength, abilities, needs).

This point can be clarified by an analogy. A situation is "objective" for the two persons in the same sense that a maze is real for the rat exploring it. The "environment" of the maze is defined by its pattern of walls, corners, and doors and its "incentives" in the form of food or shocks. Those physical facts define the "situation" for the rat *only in relation to* the "basic" psychological facts of its hunger and aversions (pertinent to its outcomes) and its sensory and motor skills (pertinent to its gaining information and taking action). Being a joint product of the psychological and the physical, it is appropriate to say that the maze constitutes a "psychophysical" reality for the rat.

The analogy is useful in making a further important point. Why do we place rats in mazes and observe their behavior? The obvious reason is that we are interested in how they adapt to that kind of situation – how they differ in their exploratory behavior (freezing up vs. showing "curiosity"), what patterns they most easily learn, and how they are revealed to be bright or dull animals. In short, our understanding of the situation permits us to focus our attention on various *"higher level"* abilities and tendencies that are revealed in the situation we have created – factors that only become apparent when we observe the rats in that situation. We use the term "higher level" to contrast those abilities and tendencies with the more "basic" factors that enter into the specification of the situation itself. We cannot study maze learning and the associated "higher level" motivational and cognitive processes without specifying the more basic "rodent" factors that, together with the pattern of alleys, goal boxes, and food, define the "reality" of the maze for the rat.

Another example: In research on human concept formation (a higher level process), the investigator must first make sure that the shapes, sizes, colors, and illumination of his stimulus materials are well suited to his subjects' (more basic) perceptual skills, including visual acuity and color perception. Those examples remind us that distinguishing between higher and lower levels of functioning is not unique to our present approach but is and has been necessary in all domains of psychological thought and research. The investigation of higher levels requires us first to distinguish and specify the lower levels.

In analogy to those examples, when we observe people in various interdependence situations (partially specified relative to their simple, "basic" abilities and needs), we learn about certain more complex or "higher level" properties that are only apparent in those situations. For example, we learn about their cooperativeness, assertiveness, and patience. The latter depend on the former for their very existence. The higher level factors can be put into play only by virtue of how the basic ones, along with environmental factors, have generated a situation appropriate for their expression.

That idea is expressed by the concept of "affordance," as advanced by Gibson (1979). Situations afford (make possible) the manifestation of the higher-level "social person factors." This follows from the "Interaction is a function of the Situation, Person A, and Person B" formulation, $I = f$ (S, A, B), described earlier. That statement implies that A and B, the "social persons," can be known from observing interaction and taking account of the situation. We may say that each situation opens a window on various interpersonal aspects of the "social" personality – the "bad" antisocial aspects as well as the "good" prosocial ones. The outcomes and their controls afford the expression of such dispositions as altruism, competitiveness, and fairness. The response conditions afford the expression of tendencies relating to control, dominance, and passivity. The information conditions afford the expression of various communication tendencies (honesty, deceit, secretiveness) and expectations (misanthropy, optimism, trust). In short, each situation affords the expression of particular "social" tendencies, skills, and knowledge, and each situation enables us to observe individual differences in those "person factors." On the other hand, a particular situation does not permit the expression of certain such factors. We fully know a "social" person only when we have observed him or her in a variety of interdependence contexts.

3.6 Person Factors: The "Social Person"

We go into considerable detail about the determinants and affordances of the "situation" because their understanding is also essential to understanding the "person" terms in the $I = f$ (S, A, B) formula. As described above, those terms refer to the higher level processes that constitute the "social person." The formula implies that they can be known from observing interaction in interdependence situations, which, as emphasized above, are themselves partially determined by more basic processes.

Earlier, we described the "social person factors" as the particular set of properties of the person (values, motives, thoughts, etc.) that come into play when an actor is cognizant of and responsive to the interdependence situation. These factors entail recognizing and taking account of the situation, including the partner's outcomes, its affordances, and, in general, its implications for expressing or fulfilling various personal and social values, such as fairness, competitiveness, and taking initiative.

The operations of the "social person factors" are known by the ways in which a person's behavior "departs" from the situation as defined by the basic personal factors, that is, as "given." The person acts not in a way indicated by his or her immediate self-interests but rather in a way that reveals taking account of the partner's outcomes. In general, the person does something that the "given" situation does not strongly indicate or require – something that departs from it. The separateness of the "social person" and the actor governed by more basic processes is revealed in such departures. From an attributional perspective, the behavior cannot be explained simply by the "psychophysical" or given situation, but requires an attribution to a "social person." Such attributions are exceedingly common in everyday life, which shows us that observers, partners, and actors themselves regularly make the distinction made here, *between* the "basic" person, operating at the "gut level" and solely concerned about immediate self-interest, *and* a more "social" person, motivated by social motives and values. Some years ago, Gallo expressed this distinction in terms of "two classes of payoffs . . . the tangible payoffs and the intangible, or symbolic payoffs" (1972, p. 44). The "basic" person is interested only in the tangible outcomes but the "social" person is also concerned with the symbolic ones, gained (in ways that depend on the situation) through showing generosity and being fair, but perhaps also through sacrificing one's own tangible outcomes simply to beat another person (as in the Chicken situation, discussed below).

3.6.1 *Transforming the Situation: "Making Something" out of the Situation As "Given"*

When a "social person" departs from what his or her own immediate interests in the situation indicate, they are essentially "playing a different game" from the one before them. They may be said to "transform" the given situation. As shown in everyday conversation, the phenomenon of "transformation" is widely recognized and understood. For example, we hear it said that "She's making a mountain out of a molehill," "He makes every game into a competitive contest," or "He treats her with more consideration than she deserves." In the corner bar or on the football field, we hear one male say to another, "So you think you're tough. Wanna make sumpin of it?" In this Atlas, we do not treat this phenomenon, of "making something" out of a situation, as an aberrant event but as an important, universal process. To describe it, we will refer to "transforming" the situation. What we mean is that when people express their "social personalities" in situations, they in effect change those situations from the "psychophysical" form in which they exist for (are "given" to) the pair. They modify that given situation in different ways and those different "transformations" enable us to understand differences among them as "social persons." Recalling the distinction above between tangible and symbolic payoffs, we can understand these transformations are reflecting the symbolic outcomes that the "social person" essentially adds to or uses to replace the tangible outcomes provided by the "given" situation.

Rather than "social person factors," we use the less awkward term *"person factors"* to refer to the variety of motives, attitudes, behavioral tendencies, and informational dispositions that underlie and cause those differences. These include factors that transform or modify each of the various situational features. For example, cooperative versus competitive motives tend to create a strongly corresponding or conflicting outcome distribution for a "given" situation that is intermediate on that dimension (e.g., the Prisoner's Dilemma situation). An initiative-taking behavioral tendency modifies the response conditions of a "given" situation, for example, creating an "A, then B" order structure for a situation that itself, permitting ad lib and revocable responding, imposes no necessary order. Expectations, like other person factors brought to a situation, serve to transform an incomplete information situation into one with more information, by supplying "information" to fill the gaps in the situation as given. Thus, an optimistic orientation to uncertainty tends to fill such gaps in a different way than does a pessimistic orientation: The optimist "makes something" different out of the situation than does the pessimist.

What the actors "make out of" a given situation often depends on their agreement with a partner about how to "transform" or change it. A pair's agreement to iterate a particular kind of situation and take turns in who benefits the most changes a haphazard sequence of events and outcomes into a regular sequence that fulfills their shared value of fairness and maximizes their joint outcomes. That kind of agreement modifies both the outcome pattern they experience and the transition list in which they act. For example, when Eamon and Kyoko both offered to let the other use the cot (see Table 3.4A), to some degree the outcomes in their transformed matrix reflect their awareness of the total situation including each other's given outcomes. In other words, that awareness introduces the operation of the "social person factors," which add an outcome component reflecting the satisfaction they each gain from helping the other. Furthermore, when they recognized the possibility of dividing the use of the cot into time segments, they transformed the response conditions of the situation, shifting it from actions at a single choice point (i.e., juncture) to an iterated situation with successive junctures (as in the transition list in Table 3.4B). In doing so, they were able to satisfy a mutually held value criterion of "share and share alike."

That example highlights the fact that the "social person factors" may not be simply individual-level interpersonal "traits." They may also reflect relationship-specific factors (e.g., commitment to each other, mutual caring) and broad social norms (e.g., reciprocity, justice). The gap between the "given" situation and the observed behavior always indicates that "person factors" are at work, but those factors may be traced to various more distal factors such as socialization experiences, pair agreements, and cultural influences.

3.6.2 *The Example of Chicken*

The distinction between a "given" situation and the one produced by its transformation can be illustrated by analyzing the outcome transformations in the "Game of Chicken." (This situation is discussed in Entry #7. The analysis here suggests that some of the situations we implicitly treat as "given" may actually be transformations of some simpler situation.)

This situation takes its name from the "game" said to be played on a deserted country road by two young men who drive their hot rods directly toward each other at a high speed, in order to see which one, if either, turns to one side to avoid the head-on collision. The first one to do so is said to be a "chicken." An adequate representation of this situation would require a transition list, but because we wish to focus on the outcome matrix of the "game," we simply collapse the extended nature of the game into the more compact story of a "challenge to fight."

This situation developed for Eamon during the evening he and Kyoko spent in the Kerrville Tavern after the movie. They were sitting at a table near the bar when a large fellow standing at the bar looked at them and, noting Eamon's red hair, remarked, "Hey, Mick. Where'd you get that beautiful Jap girl?" Angered by the remark, Eamon replied sharply, "Mind your own business!" The man approached their table and said, "Think you're tough, huh? Want to go outside and fight?" Eamon was about to get up, but Kyoko restrained him: "Sit down and don't get involved with that guy. It's stupid to brawl with a guy you don't even know. And get all messed up for what we've planned to do tomorrow."[3]

---

[3] One might object that it is unreasonable for Kyoko to ask Eamon to forgo the symbolic rewards he can gain from at least trying to "defend her honor." One might think that she is showing an insensitivity to how he has transformed the situation. And is it really "stupid" to at least try to stand up to a bully? Relevant to this question are results presented by Van Lange and Kuhlman (1994) from research on a single-play Prisoner's Dilemma Game. They found that cooperative people associate noncooperative behavior with lower levels of intelligence and rationality. In contrast, individualists (who make the noncooperative choice) make similar judgments of the low intelligence revealed by cooperative behavior. So what is "stupid" for some persons may be the opposite of what others regard as "stupid."

TABLE 3.8. *The Game of Chicken as a Transformation of a "Given" Matrix That Is Conjunctive for Negative Outcomes*

A

	Not	Fight	
Not	0 / 0	0 / 0	
B			**Given**
Fight	0 / 0	0 / −20 −20	

Conjunctive for Negative Outcomes

A

	Not	Fight	
Not	0 / 0	*+10* / *−10*	
B			**Transformed***
Fight	*−10* / *+10*	*−20* / *−20*	

Matrix 7[†]
Chicken

---

* The outcomes in *italics* are symbolic ones.
[†] The matrix number indicates the relevant entry in the body of the Atlas.

The matrix representation of this "fight" situation is shown in the lower portion of Table 3.8. The options for the two persons are to "fight" or not. A mutual decision not to fight is shown to result in neutral outcomes for both, and a similar decision to fight, in large negative outcomes for both. Unilateral willingness to fight is rewarding for the one who is willing but negative for the one who is not.

Our problem is to see where that pattern of outcomes comes from. The upper left and lower right outcomes are easy to understand – no outcomes if they don't fight and mutually negative ones if they do (assuming they can do considerable harm to each other). Those are plausibly aspects of the situation as "given," that is, outcomes relating to each one's immediate self interests. But where do the other outcomes come from? For example, why is one's unwillingness to fight in the face of the other's willingness a source of negative outcomes for one's self but positive outcomes for the other? The obvious answer is suggested by the name of the game, "Chicken." Refusal to fight when challenged to do so, is (for many men at least) a reason to be ashamed and, thus, a basis for negative outcomes. In contrast, the other person's willingness to fight displays courage in facing the risks of fighting. Courage is often a source of positive outcomes, from pride in meeting one's own standards and, possibly, from the approval of onlookers. If met with a refusal to fight, the challenger may also experience a "competitive" pride from having been braver than the other. These latter outcomes reveal the operation of "social person factors", that is, higher level processes that take account of the total pattern of the situation, including both person's outcomes and controls. The "challenger" recognizes both (1) the "bind" in which the challenge places the other and the risk he himself is taking by putting himself under the other's control, and (2) the interpersonal significance (as a display of their relative bravery) of their respective choices.

That analysis suggests that the Chicken pattern, as shown in the lower part of Table 3.8, reflects "person factors" that transform an underlying given situation into "Chicken." The only *tangible* payoffs in the situation related to the two persons' "basic processes" (i.e., the only part of the pattern *not* interpretable as consequences of the higher level processes of the "social person") are the mutually negative consequences of fighting. This suggests that the "given" situation is the one in the upper part of Table 3.8. That is a situation that is "conjunctive for negative outcomes," meaning that *both* persons have to fight to produce them. One person's challenge (willingness) to fight transforms the upper "given" situation into the lower "chicken" situation. By offering to put his "fate" in the hands of the other, the "challenger" makes the situation into a test of the relative courage of the two men. The challenge is an attempt to gain the *symbolic* satisfaction of gaining status or maintaining face and self-respect by winning the zero-sum game of courage.[4] Kyoko's admonishment encouraged Eamon to disregard the symbolic outcomes and, in a sense, to avoid being drawn

---

[4] The situation's usefulness as a site for such a test depends on the partner's characteristics, *both* the *basic* ones (e.g., if a small or physically handicapped man, the other's negative outcomes from fighting may be far greater than the challenger's, so a refusal will show "rationality" rather than cowardice) and the *"higher level"* ones (e.g., if the other person does not share the value the challenger places on a display of courage, the other's outcomes will not be the ones shown in the lower left and upper right cells). To satisfy his interpersonal

into the proposed mutual transformation of the situation. Her reference to the "stupidity" of the fight recognizes the basic, "given" situation (in the upper part of Table 3.8) and expresses how deciding to fight in that situation should, by the criterion of "rationality," be judged.

This analysis reveals that the situation presented as being the stage on which is played out one of the classic stories in the game literature is not a "given" situation but reflects transformations. Are there "given" situations with outcomes that conform to the "chicken" pattern in the lower portion of Table 3.8? Yes. Some examples are given in Entry #7.[5]

3.7 Summary

In this chapter and chapter 2, we have distinguished and described the major properties of situations as they are defined in interdependence theory. We have described how the various properties are represented schematically and how such representations enable us to distinguish varieties of each one. The outcome matrix was described in chapter 2 as our basic representational device inasmuch as it summarizes both the outcome distribution and the outcome controls. The present chapter has described how we distinguish and represent varieties of the remaining two properties, the response conditions and the information conditions. The former are particularly important in providing systematic tools for representing constraints or freedoms in the timing of behavior, and for describing situations that extend over time. This chapter has also discussed the important questions, delayed until now, of the determinants of "situations" and of the "person factors" that are expressed through interaction in situations. A major portion of each of our entries is devoted to research that documents the interaction patterns and person factors observed in that particular situation.

The next chapter, chapter 4, carries further this chapter's analysis of varieties of outcome patterns and their location in the 3-D space. We

---

goal of competitiveness in courage, a challenger must pick his "opponent" with some care, so as not to appear to be a mere "bully" who creates spurious displays of "bravery" or who only "picks on pacifists."

[5] The example also shows that both given and transformed outcome patterns can be located in our multidimensional space of such patterns. That implies, further, that the transformation process can be conceptualized as a vector in that space. In Table 3.8, if both A and B make the transformations of the "conjunctive for negative outcomes" pattern necessary to create the "chicken" pattern, their pair of transformations can be described as a vector originating at the first pattern and terminating at the latter one. This suggests a theoretical linkage between the varieties of situations and of "person factors." The domain of the latter, at least in their pairings, must stand in some rough isomorphic relation to the domain of the former. This logical but very abstract notion has not yet been pursued.

might say that chapter 4 continues our exploration of the "geography" of interdependence situations. It zeroes in on the problems distinguished by symmetric-component outcome matrices and found at different locations in the 3-D space. Thus, it enables us to gain a differentiated view of the major regions of the "situational map." The chapter becomes a bit technical, so the casual reader may wish to skip over it and go directly to some of the Atlas entries. Or, to gain an overview of the coverage of the "geography" provided by the 21 entries included in the Atlas, the reader may wish to consult the brief "Introduction to the Entries" chapter which provides what is essentially a "table of contents" of the entries.

4

Exploring the Geography of the Outcome Patterns

In this chapter, we examine in some detail the 2×2 outcome matrices which, as explained in chapter 2, define the problems that interdependent persons may encounter. This requires further explanation of how the basic patterns of interdependence (see Table 2.7) may be combined to produce more complex patterns. Our general point is that many complex situations can be understood more clearly when considered as a combination of certain basic elements. We then take a closer look at the three dimensions of symmetric interdependence shown in chapter 2 (Figure 2.2) and see how various common patterns are distributed through those dimensions. The distribution enables us to gain further understanding of each situation by examining its location relative to other situations. For example, as will be explained in this chapter, the distribution of the situations has implications for the developmental course of a dyadic relationship as, through changes in the individuals and the problems they encounter, a pair moves from one kind of situation to another. Readers who are less interested in the full implications of our combinatorial system may prefer to skip this chapter and go directly to the following "Introduction to the Entries" and to the entries themselves.

4.1 Exploring the Possible 2 × 2 Matrices by Combining the Basic Components

All possible patterns of 2 × 2 interdependence can be constructed by combining the patterns of control represented in Table 2.7: Bilateral Actor

Harold Kelley had primary responsibility for preparation of this chapter.

TABLE 4.1. *Examples of the Three Possible Two-Component Patterns*

Maximizing Difference: **BAC and MPC, in Ratio of 4:8, Combined Concordantly**

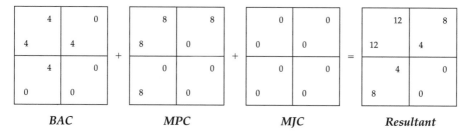

| | BAC | | MPC | | MJC | | Resultant |

Hero: **BAC and MJC, in Ratio of 4:8, Combined Discordantly**

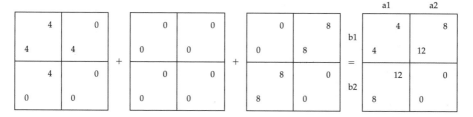

Trust: **MPC and MJC, in Ratio of 8:4, Combined Concordantly**

Control (BAC), Mutual Partner Control (MPC), and Corresponding or Conflicting Mutual Joint Control (MJC). The combination is performed by simply superimposing two or more of the three components and varying their relative magnitudes (or importance) and, as we will explain, their concordant or discordant orientations to each other.

The operation of combining the simple components, two at a time, is illustrated in Table 4.1. The first pattern there is known as the Maximizing Difference Game, or MDG. It may be seen that it is created by superimposing a BAC component on an MPC one and orienting them so that the BAC component supports or is compatible – concordant with – with the MPC component. That implies that the action by which each person benefits him or her self is also the action that benefits his or her partner. This game has been identified as a useful supplement to the Prisoner's Dilemma Game (Entry #5) in distinguishing the motives a person may have for selecting the "noncooperative" option (Messick and McClintock, 1968). As shown for the PD in Table 3.1, if A chooses option a2, we cannot tell whether A is simply maximizing A's own outcomes *or* is being "competitive," seeking higher outcomes than B's. The MDG permits those two motives to be distinguished inasmuch as the a2 option unambiguously reveals a competitive motive, since it makes possible "maximizing the difference" without also maximizing the joint outcome.[1] The difference between the two situations lies solely in the concordance between the BAC and MPC components in the case of the MDG as contrasted with the discordance between those components for the PDG.

The second pattern in Table 4.1 is known as Hero. It results from a combination of BAC and MJC in which the latter is larger and is discordant with the BAC component: The actions by which each person benefits him or her self prevent the pair from fulfilling the MJC coordination requirement. The name, Hero, reflects a scenario possible within the situation, in which (1) both persons are inclined to take their first options, which threatens to yield both outcomes of only 4, and then, (2) one of them volunteers to take the second option (e.g., A is willing to take a2). That makes A a "hero" in the sense that the proposed shift benefits both persons but the partner more than A. (Below, in the discussion of Figure 4.2, this pattern is compared with that of Martyr, with its implication of a subtly different event.)

The third pattern in Table 4.1 is referred to as the Trust Game. The MPC and MJC components are combined concordantly, so that the ways they benefit each other also satisfy the coordination requirement specified by their MJC component. The pattern provides an obvious point of agreement – on the a1b1 cell. However, if one of the persons, say A, brings a competitive interest to this setting, that person would choose the a2 option. If the partner, B, distrusts A's intentions and suspects that A may be

---

[1] However, that interpretational benefit merely introduces a different attributional ambiguity. In the Maximizing Difference Game, the choice of a1 may be motivated by self-interest (maximizing own outcomes) *or* it may reflect a cooperative concern about the total benefits to the pair. The problem, of course, is that to distinguish among those three motives (e.g., self-interest, competitiveness, and cooperativeness), it is necessary for a situation to have more than two options. In the development of measures of these social orientations, e.g., in the work of Kuhlman and Marshello (1975), it has been found useful to offer at least three alternatives for the person to choose among.

out to gain the higher outcomes, B's course of action is to protect him or her self. The outcomes in the a2b2 cell at least satisfy a "maximin" choice criterion for B, providing the maximum smallest outcome that B can insure for him or her self.

By the combination method illustrated in Table 4.1 (and earlier in Table 3.1), it is possible to construct a great many 2 × 2 patterns of inter-dependence. We may think of the three components, BAC, MPC, and MJC (the last with either corresponding or conflicting interests) as the build-ing blocks of outcome matrices. They can be combined two or three at a time, with varying relative weights or importance, and placed in different (concordant or discordant) orientations to each other.

The contrasting orientations in which patterns may be combined are further illustrated in Table 4.2. The "discordant" combination in the upper part of Table 4.2 orients the two components in opposition to each other, and thereby serves to generate a pattern of conflicting interests. This game is sometimes described as a constant sum game because the total outcomes are the same for all four cells. A special case, a pattern in which the sum is zero in each cell, is the oft-mentioned "zero-sum game." In the lower

TABLE 4.2. *Conflicting and Corresponding Interest Combinations of BAC and MPC*

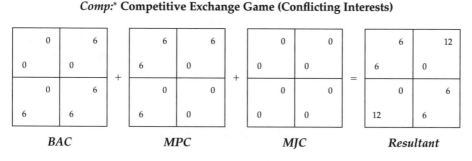

*Comp:** **Competitive Exchange Game (Conflicting Interests)**

| BAC | MPC | MJC | Resultant |

*Coop:** **Cooperative Exchange Game (Corresponding Interests)**

* These abbreviations are used in Figure 4.4 to show the locations there of these patterns.

combination, the BAC and MPC components converge on the a1b1 pair of actions and that "concordance" creates a resultant situation with perfectly corresponding interests. It can be referred to as the Constant Difference Game, for obvious reasons. The examples in Table 4.2 make it clear that we use the terms "corresponding" versus "conflicting" interests to describe a property of a matrix, but the terms "concordant" versus "discordant" to describe the way the components of a matrix are oriented to each other.

These examples show what was noted in chapter 2, that the separate representation of the several components makes it easy to pinpoint the sources of a situation's possible problems and opportunities, locating them in the relations among the three kinds of outcome control as to their relative importance and concordant or discordant orientations.

By using the combination process, we can imagine building all possible 2 × 2 patterns of interdependence. That would generate an unmanageably large number of patterns, but the effort can be considerably simplified by combining only "symmetrical" components. Those are components in which the particular type of control (whether AC, PC, or JC) acts on both persons to the same degree. The patterns in Tables 4.1 and 4.2 are based on symmetrical components. (Patterns composed of asymmetric components are described in section 4.2.4 below. Asymmetry was illustrated in the analysis of the "cleaning the apartment" example, in Table 2.3.)

Kelley and Thibaut (1978) used the combination procedure to make an extensive analysis of the interdependence patterns generated by the *pairs* of symmetric components. They also examined many patterns comprised of all three components. We rely here on their analysis to provide us with our "geography" of 2 × 2 situations.

4.2 The Location of Selected Situations within the Domain of Interdependence

4.2.1 *Two-Component Patterns: The Three "Continents"*
Possible patterns generated by combining each pair of the three components are illustrated in Tables 4.1 and 4.2. It can be seen that each pattern is created by combining two symmetric components, that is, ones in which one person's controls are identical with those of the other person. More complete pictures of each type of pair are presented in Figures 4.1, 4.2, and 4.3.[2] Following the geographical metaphor of this Atlas, we may

---

[2] Figures 4.1, 4.2, 4.3, and 4.4 are adapted from chapter 4 in Kelley and Thibaut (1978).

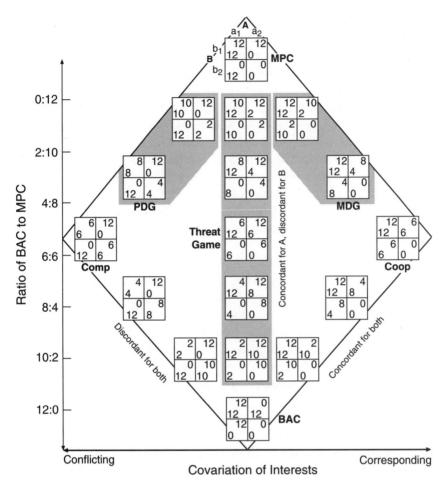

FIGURE 4.1. Combinations of BAC and MPC (adapted from Kelley & Thibaut, 1978). *Legend*: BAC: Bilateral Actor Control; Comp: Competitive Exchange; Coop: Cooperative Exchange; MDG: Maximizing Difference Game; MPC: Mutual Partner Control; PDG: Prisoner's Dilemma Game

describe these as the three major "continents" of situations characterized by symmetric outcome interdependence.

Figure 4.1 describes the "exchange" region inasmuch as it includes the various possible combinations of BAC and MPC, that is, the region of situations where people can provide benefits for each other but, to varying degrees, have effects on their own outcomes that promote doing so (concordant combinations) or that interfere with doing so (discordant combinations). The vertical scale in Figure 4.1 represents different ratios of the BAC component to the MPC component. At the bottom, each person affects only his or her own outcomes and at the top, each person affects only the partner's outcomes. Thus, the situations range from zero interdependence at the bottom to total interdependence at the top. At each intermediate level of interdependence (i.e., at each ratio of BAC to MPC) are shown three matrices, generated by placing the two components in different concordant-discordant orientations to each other, either concordant for both persons, discordant for both, or concordant for one and discordant for the other. At the middle degree of interdependence, when the BAC and MPC components are of equal weight, the left corner of the area is defined by a pattern of conflicting interests (which we describe as "Competitive Exchange" – "Comp" for short) and the right corner is defined by a pattern of corresponding interests (which we describe as "Cooperative Exchange" – "Coop" for short). Those patterns and their components were shown in Table 4.2.

Also on this continent are the Prisoner's Dilemma (Entry #5), its location reflecting its exchange possibilities but its considerable conflict of interest, and the symmetrically located Maximizing Difference Game (MDG), shown in Table 4.1.

The Threat Game (Entry #6) is located in the center of the area, where its position indicates both its moderate degree of interdependence and its mixture of corresponding and conflicting interests. The unique scenario from which it takes its name reflects the fact that its equal components of Bilateral Actor Control and Mutual Partner Control are oriented in a concordant manner for A but in a discordant manner for B. Thus, B's providing benefits to A is consistent with B's providing benefits to B's self, but the opposite is true for A. Those facts create B's dependency for good outcomes on a partner who may be tempted to serve his or her own interests rather than help B. If adequate outcomes are not forthcoming, B's only sanction is to reduce the outcomes for both of them. The game takes its name from a scenario in which B is treated unfairly and threatens to use that sanction.

One fact shown in Figure 4.1 is that the patterns to which we attach names have areas around them that include variants of the named pattern. The shaded areas around the three named patterns in Figure 4.1 include the variants of each one. For example, each of the patterns in the shaded area extending up and down from the Threat Game provides an opportunity for person A to exploit B by favoring A's own outcomes as well as the opportunity for B to retaliate by reducing both person's outcomes. The advantage of both exploitation and use of threat increases in magnitude as the degree of MPC is increased, in the situation at the top of the shaded area. The game we label as "Threat" is intermediate, posing an intermediate degree of temptation to A and an intermediate degree of threat capability to B. Is that, in some sense, an "optimal" Threat Game? We consider that question in a later section below devoted to "paradigmatic representations."

Although Figure 4.1 does not show it clearly, there are also variants of the PDG and MDG not only above their matrices but also below. These would be apparent if we used a more finely differentiated scale of the ratios. For example, a BAC:MPC ratio of 5:7 would produce a variant of the PDG below and to the left of the named matrix. Again, there is the question of whether the named matrix is the "best" of its kind.

Figure 4.2 describes the "coordination" region of the symmetric-component 2 × 2 domain. It is defined by the two contrasting coordination problems (Mutual Joint Control with corresponding vs. conflicting interests) and is anchored at the lower end by simple BAC. Like those

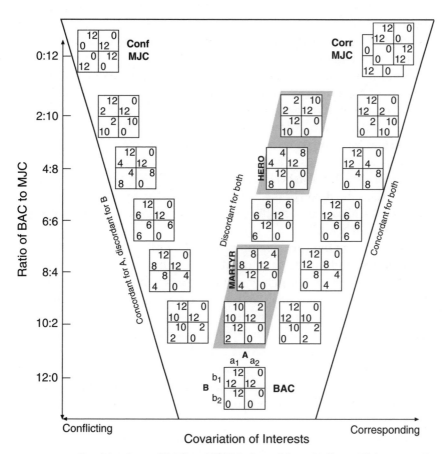

FIGURE 4.2. Combinations of BAC and MJC (adapted from Kelley & Thibaut, 1978). *Legend*: BAC: Bilateral Actor Control; MJC: Mutual Joint Control

in Figure 4.1, the situations on the coordination plane vary in degree of interdependence and in degree of corresponding versus conflicting interests. Located there is the situation known as Hero (Entry #8) and the neighboring pattern known as Martyr. Those patterns take their names from a scenario in which the two persons are about to follow their individual interests and select the a1b1 combination. However, one person, for example, A, volunteers to take the other option, that is, a2. In the case of Hero, this is an act of "heroism" because, although it benefits both, it benefits B more. In the case of Martyr, this is an act of "martyrdom" because it benefits B at the *expense* of A's own outcomes. Note that the names for the situations are based on distinctive dispositional qualities that may be revealed by a person's actions in a particular scenario possible within them.

Here, as in Figure 4.1, there is an area of variants for each of the named patterns (indicated by the shaded area around each one), extending both above and below it (if finer gradations of the ratio of BAC to MJC were used in the figure.) And again there are questions of what is the optimal version of each pattern.

Figure 4.3 shows the "total interdependence" region of the symmetric-component 2 × 2 domain, so-called because none of the patterns have a BAC component. In none of these does either person have direct control over his or her own outcomes. Because the region includes combinations of MPC and MJC, the patterns represent coordination problems, exchange problems, and mixtures of both. In that region are located the Chicken situation (Entry #7), the Trust Game, and the Turn-Taking pattern (sometimes referred to as the Battle of the Sexes). It can be seen that, for example, the location of Chicken reflects the fact that the MPC factor is the stronger component, by a ratio of 2:1.

The location of the Turn-Taking pattern shows that its principal component is corresponding interest Mutual Joint Control. The minor component of MPC is superimposed in a way that creates a mild conflict of interest about the persons' coordination, but creates an opportunity for them to take turns in gaining their best outcomes (assuming they enter the situation on multiple occasions). The transition list format for this situation in Table 3.4B represents response conditions that would enable them to do so.

The shaded areas in Figure 4.3 again show regions in which variants of the three named patterns are located. Our prior discussions of the extent of these regions and the question of optimal versions of the named patterns apply here.

One further point deserves mention: In all three figures, there are regions in which there are no "named" patterns. For example, in Figure 4.3 we do

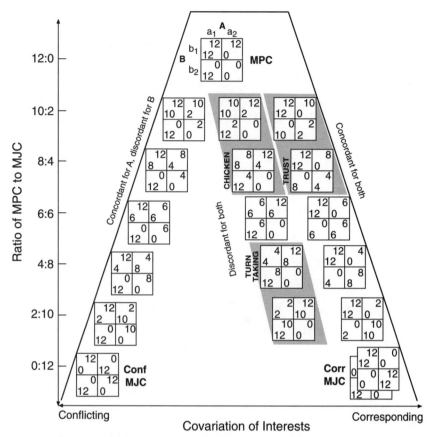

FIGURE 4.3. Combinations of MPC and MJC (adapted from Kelley & Thibaut, 1978). *Legend*: MJC: Mutual Joint Control; MPC: Mutual Partner Control

not name any matrix in the left, conflicting-interest string of patterns, nor is there a named pattern in the lower right string of corresponding interests and strong MJC. The patterns in those regions may deserve closer attention than we are able to give them here.

4.2.2 *Two-Component Patterns: The Three Dimensional "World"*

In Figure 2.2 in chapter 2, we showed that the locations of the four simple (single-component) patterns define the extremes of three dimensions. We now locate the three "continents" distinguished above within the cube-shaped framework of those three dimensions. The result is the 3-D view of our "world" of symmetric-component 2 × 2 patterns, shown in Figure 4.4.

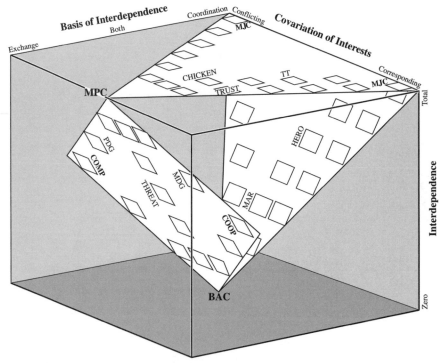

FIGURE 4.4. The distribution of symmetric dyadic situations in the three-dimensional space shown in Figure 2.2 (adapted from Kelley & Thibaut, 1978). *Legend*: BAC: Bilateral Actor Control; Comp: Competitive Exchange; Coop: Cooperative Exchange; MAR: Martyr; MDG: Maximizing Difference Game; MJC: Mutual Joint Control; MPC: Mutual Partner Control; PDG: Prisoner's Dilemma Game; TT: Turn Taking

The figure is constructed by first locating within the cube the plane in Figure 4.1, placing its bottom apex at the BAC point at the center of the bottom of the cube, its top apex at the MPC point at center of the upper left edge of the cube, and the extremes of its horizontal axis at the near and far sides of the cube. In the last instance, the corner of Figure 4.1 having the Cooperative Exchange pattern ("Coop," with corresponding outcomes) is located on the near side of the cube, and the Competitive Exchange pattern ("Comp," with conflicting outcomes), on the far side.

Next, the triangular plane in Figure 4.2 is also anchored within the cube, with its lower apex at the BAC point and its upper side along the far upper edge. The conflicting-interests version of MJC is located, of course, at the far upper corner of the cube, and the corresponding-interests version of MJC, at the near upper right corner of the cube. Finally, the triangular plane in

Figure 4.3 forms a sort of lid for the odd shape in Figure 4.4, with the MPC apex at the center of the upper left side and the two MJC patterns attached to their respective conflicting- and corresponding-interests corners at the top right edge of the cube. It can be seen that the three "continents" are joined at points where they share one of the component patterns or a side.

Figure 4.4 shows the locations in the 3-D space of the first eight situations discussed in our entries, along with several other patterns described above. Below, we consider some of the implications of the inverted pyramidal shape formed by the three two-component planes of Figure 4.4, particularly as that shape relates to the consequences of increasing or decreasing interdependence.

4.2.3 Three-Component Patterns

Kelley and Thibaut (1978) also explored patterns created by combining three components. However, because there is an enormous number of possible such patterns, the analysis was more selective. Inasmuch as those patterns consist of all three of the basic components (BAC, MPC, and MJC), these patterns may be thought of as lying in "strings" (similar to the strings of patterns in Figures 4.1, 4.2, and 4.3) that extend between two-component patterns on one of the three planes and a pattern on another plane that includes the third component. For example, we may construct a string of matrices stretching from the PDG to one of the simple MJC patterns. This string would include variously weighted and oriented combinations of BAC, MPC, and MJC. Kelley and Thibaut observed that the essential property of the PD is destroyed when the MJC component is equal to or larger than the smaller of the two components that makes up the PD, namely, BAC. And this is true for other patterns as well. This fact implies, incidentally, that the area encompassed by variants of a two-component pattern extends a short distance into the interior of the 3-D figure. So the shaded areas in Figures 4.1, 4.2, and 4.3 have "depth," reaching to some degree into the 3-D "solid" represented in Figure 4.4.

The possible three-component patterns have not been thoroughly explored, but Table 4.3 shows a pair of important patterns not among the two-component ones. When we construct a string of three-component combinations extending between the Corr MJC and the Cooperative Exchange patterns (both on the right side of the cube nearest to us), all of the new combinations also have perfectly corresponding interests. However, two particular patterns, each having equal proportions of the three components and differing only in the orientations of those components (concordance vs. discordance) to one another, are of particular interest. These are shown

TABLE 4.3. *Four Patterns, Each Based on Combinations of the Three Components*

		A				A	
		a1	a2			a1	a2
b1		+12	+4			+8	+8
B	+12		+4		+8		+8
b2		+4	+4			+8	0
	+4		+4		+8		0

| | | Matrix 9* Conjunctive Control | | | | Matrix 10* Disjunctive Control | |

		a1	a2			a1	a2
b1		+5	+15			+5	+15
B	+5		+5		+15		+5
b2		+5	+5			+5	+5
	+15		+5		+5		+5

| | | Schematic Turn Taking | | | | Schematic Threat | |

* The matrix number indicates the relevant entry in the body of the Atlas.

in the upper portion of Table 4.3. In the *Con*junctive situation (Entry #9) *both persons* must take a particular action in order for both to gain maximum benefit. The conjunctivity property reflects the way in which what each person prefers to do (BAC) converges with what each wants the partner to do (MPC) and those, in turn, converge with one of the optimal ways to coordinate their actions (MJC). Both must make a particular coordination selection if they are to gain the benefits of the three converging effects. (The convergence of the three components of this situation was shown in Table 2.4.) In the *Dis*junctive situation (Entry #10) it is only necessary for one person – *either one* – to take a particular action in order for both to get their best outcomes. In this case, the MJC component is incompatible with the other two components, favoring the a1b2 and a2b1 corners of the matrix where the other two favor the a1b1 corner. As a consequence, the MJC component compensates for either person's failure to generate the benefits provided by the other components. However, relative to the conjunctive pattern, that effect reduces the maximum level of outcomes the pair can gain from the situation.

From their equal components, we might expect both these patterns to represent an intermediate degree of interdependence. However, the different ways in which their MJC maps onto the other components create sharply different patterns. Because the MPC and MJC components supplement each other in a way that renders the BAC component irrelevant, the Conjunctive Control pattern is essentially one of *total* interdependence. In contrast, in the Disjunctive Control pattern, the MPC and MJC patterns neutralize each other so the pair is left with what is essentially a BAC pattern of *zero* interdependence. So though formally located inside the solid, the Conjunctive Control pattern is functionally in the upper plane with other situations of total interdependence, and the Disjunctive Control is functionally at the bottom of the solid, with the BAC pattern of zero interdependence.

4.2.4 Asymmetric (Unilateral) Dependence

The situations shown above all involve the special condition described earlier, that each particular type of control is *symmetrical* between the two persons. Thus, in all the patterns located in Figure 4.4, the Actor Control for A is equal to that for B, the Partner Control acting on A is equal to the Partner Control acting on B, and the Joint Control acting on A is equal to that acting on B. We have assumed those equalities in order to simplify our analysis of the "geography" of the 2 × 2 situational space. However, to provide a full mapping of that space, it is also necessary to include asymmetric components and to examine their various combinations. Because there are many, many degrees and patterns of asymmetry, that is a very complex undertaking. However, the task can be simplified by examining the most extreme instances of asymmetry (those of *unilateral* dependence) and seeing if and how they can be linked to the situations of symmetric dependence. In chapter 2 (and illustrated in Table 2.8), we described the three basic types of unilateral dependence, that is, those in which person B is totally dependent on person A who, in turn, is totally independent of B. The three types are distinguished by whether B is subject to Partner Control, to Joint Control, or to both. (In all three cases, A is subject only to

Actor Control.) We now consider how those patterns are related to the various types of symmetric dependence. Where do we visualize the unilateral patterns as being located relative to the 3-D solid in Figure 4.4? Where are they to be found in our "geography"?

It is reasonable to assume, first, that the three types of unilateral dependence are systematically related to the three surfaces ("continents") of Figure 4.4. If B, but not A, is subject to Partner Control, that dependence must be related to one or more of the symmetric patterns involving *Mutual* Partner Control. It must be a variant of some MPC pattern – a variant in which the Partner Control acting on A is no longer present. In the same way, a unilateral pattern in which B but not A is subject to Joint Control must be related to some symmetric pattern involving *Mutual* Joint Control. It must be a variant of some MJC pattern – a variant in which the Joint Control acting on A is no longer present. And the same can be said for the unilateral case in which B is subject to both PC and JC and A is subject to neither.

That idea can be tested by adopting the procedure used in constructing Figures 4.1, 4.2, and 4.3. There we showed how shifting the ratios of the symmetric components modifies a situation, even to the extent of changing it into a different one. Employing that principle, let us consider how a symmetric situation is changed if we introduce inequalities into its components in a way that leaves one person in total control of the outcome variance there. This is easily accomplished by simply eliminating one person's (A's) outcomes from both of the "dependence" components (MPC and/or MJC) and eliminating the other's (B's) outcomes from the "independence" component (BAC). Those changes will make A totally independent of B and B totally dependent on A. Or, better yet, we might *gradually reduce* the MPC and MJC components for A and the BAC component for B. If we perform those operations for the components of any particular pattern in Figure 4.4, we create a series of "dependency variants" of that pattern, that is, variations of the symmetric, equal dependence pattern as it is gradually shifted toward an inequality between the two persons in their dependence on each other. And if we were to perform those operations for all the patterns on one of the three planes of Figure 4.4, we would create the collection of dependency variants for that plane.

That process is illustrated in Table 4.4. We begin at the bottom of the table with a situation from each of the three planes shown in Figure 4.4: the Prisoner's Dilemma from the BAC and MPC plane (Figure 4.1), Hero from the BAC and MJC plane (Figure 4.2), and Chicken from the MPC and MJC plane (Figure 4.3). For each, as we move up the column, person B is made increasingly dependent on A and A is made increasingly

TABLE 4.4. *Dependence Variants of Matrices from the Three Planes of Figure 4.4*

	BAC and MPC	BAC and MJC	MPC and MJC
Total Asymmetry (Unilateral dependence)	0 · 4 / 8 · 0	4 · 0 / 0 · 8	0 · 0 / 8 · 4
(B's total dependence on A, who is independent)	0 · 4 / 8 · 0	4 · 0 / 8 · 0	0 · 0 / 12 · 0

	BAC and MPC	BAC and MJC	MPC and MJC
Moderate Asymmetry	3 · 7 / 8 · 0 (top) 0 · 4 / 10 · 2 (bottom)	4 · 3 / 2 · 10 (top) 7 · 0 / 8 · 0 (bottom)	3 · 4 / 8 · 4 (top) 2 · 0 / 12 · 0 (bottom)

	BAC and MPC	BAC and MJC	MPC and MJC
Slight Asymmetry	6 · 10 / 8 · 0 (top) 0 · 4 / 11 · 3 (bottom)	4 · 6 / 3 · 11 (top) 10 · 0 / 8 · 0 (bottom)	6 · 8 / 8 · 4 (top) 3 · 0 / 12 · 0 (bottom)

	BAC and MPC	BAC and MJC	MPC and MJC
Interdependence (Equal & mutual dependence)	8 · 12 / 8 · 0 (top) 0 · 4 / 12 · 4 (bottom)	4 · 8 / 4 · 12 (top) 12 · 0 / 8 · 0 (bottom)	8 · 12 / 8 · 4 (top) 4 · 0 / 12 · 0 (bottom)

| | PDG | Hero | Chicken |

independent of B. Person B's control over his or her own outcomes (AC) and B's control over A's outcomes, whether through Partner Control and/or Joint Control, are gradually reduced, but A's similar controls, over his or her own outcomes and over B's outcomes, remain constant.

We may visualize the three columns of patterns in Table 4.4 as columns of increasingly asymmetric patterns erected perpendicularly to each plane. (These "columns" are obviously similar to the "strings" by which, in Tables 4.1, 4.2, and 4.3, we explored various combinations of symmetric components.) Thus, the column on the right would rise straight up from Chicken on the upper plane, the column on the left would project downward and outward to the left from the PDG on the diamond-shaped plane, and the center column would project downward and outward toward the right from Hero on the plane on the far right of the figure.

Now, imagine that we construct and erect similar columns for *every* pattern on each plane. The result would resemble a colonnade (per *Webster's*: a series of columns set at regular intervals) rising out of each plane. And at the top level of that colonnade would be a layer of situations of unilateral dependence. Those three colonnades constitute the domain of 2 × 2 patterns of *asymmetric* dependence and, taken together, the top layers of the three define all possible patterns of *unilateral* dependence.

In short, our method of identifying and distinguishing among the patterns of asymmetric and unilateral dependence derives them systematically from the various patterns of symmetric dependence. This method leads us to visualize the asymmetric patterns as a colonnade rising perpendicularly to each plane in Figure 4.4, that is, extending outward from the center of the 3-D solid. The set of patterns at the outermost level of each colonnade defines a surface of unilateral patterns roughly parallel to the underlying symmetric surface and, being variants of the underlying patterns, bearing some resemblance to them. We now consider that "resemblance."

Each column obviously includes patterns that share properties of the "root" patterns located below. Table 4.4 shows how the properties of the root patterns are carried up into the total dependence patterns at the top of the colonnade. For example, Table 4.4 shows that the *mutual* coordination problem present in symmetric patterns that include MJC (such as Hero and Chicken) is left as a *unilateral* coordination problem that the dependent person faces in the dependence variants. The concordance or discordance in the root pattern is also preserved in the dependence patterns. For example, the left column of Table 4.4 shows that the discordance between the BAC and MPC components of the PDG is reflected in the pattern of B's total dependence, where what A prefers to do is opposite what B prefers A to do. In contrast, as shown in Table 2.8, the concordance between the same two components in the Maximizing Difference Game is reflected in its dependency variant, where A prefers to do the thing that benefits B.

However, with increasing asymmetry some of the root-pattern properties disappear. For example, as we go up the column based on the PDG, with moderate or total asymmetry the pattern no longer has the ordering of outcomes necessary for the situation to qualify as the "Prisoner's Dilemma." (The necessary order is the one shown in the PDG, in which the series of inequalities, $12 > 8 > 4 > 0$, follows a particular zigzag path for each person through the four cells of the matrix.) Table 4.4 shows that this order is maintained with the slight degree of asymmetry but not for more extreme degrees. As we later discuss, this fact reveals that the region in which the variants of the PDG are located extends slightly "upward" into the domain of asymmetric patterns.

The implications of our visualization of the three colonnades of dependence variants rising over each of the three surfaces in Figure 4.4 remain to be explored, but the imagery gives rise to some interesting ideas. We might think of those colonnades as defining the situational regions *from* which pairs of people grow or develop into symmetrical dependence, or *toward* which pairs move as, over time, they become differentially dependent. For example, the patterns of total dependence may be useful in distinguishing among the kinds of situations in which children begin their interpersonal lives. Case I in Table 2.8 shows that in her relation with a parent, a daughter may be subject to "absolute" Partner Control, either in the conflictual (noncorrespondent) dependence variant of the PDG (as in Table 2.8 as well as Table 4.4) or in the benign, corresponding dependence variant of the MDG (as also in Table 2.8). If she experiences the PDG variant, might we infer that as she develops means of control over her own outcomes and of control over the parent's outcomes, the former are likely to have a discordant relation with the latter. In other words, if the typical parent-child situation is the dependence variant of the PDG (in which the parent has self-interest that conflicts with doing what is best for the child), will the child's developing independence and control involve a similar conflict between own and partners' outcomes, and take the pair toward the PDG location in the symmetrical patterns?

Similarly, the dependence variants may be used to distinguish the kinds of situations toward which a pair moves when one member, through illness, injury, or aging, becomes dependent. For this purpose, the several dependence variants suggest problems that may arise. For example, in the Hero dependence variant (Table 4.4 or Case II in Table 2.8), the diminished cognitive competencies of a dependent husband may make it difficult for him to identify which actions his wife prefers (her preferences being rather small) and, therefore, make it difficult for him to make the necessary, important behavioral adjustments to her actions. The same problem for B exists in a more vexing form in the dependence variant of Chicken in Table 4.4 in which A has no preference between the options. In this case, the dependent husband faces the problem of guessing what his wife will do or, if the response conditions permit, of always having to wait and see what she does before adjusting his own behavior. If he resorts to guessing, he faces a classic choice between an option that is guaranteed to yield some outcome whatever the wife does, and an all-or-nothing option with great variance in its possible results.

One further brief point: Recalling the notion of areas extending around the named situations that include variants of those situations (illustrated by the shaded areas in Figures 4.1, 4.2, and 4.3), we see in Table 4.4 that similar areas extend into the lower levels of the colonnades of asymmetric patterns. At the level of "slight asymmetry," the outcome orders characteristic of each of the three "root" patterns are preserved, though weakened for person A. Thus, we visualize the region of variants of the PDG as extending not only horizontally in the plane shown in Figure 4.1, but also as "bulging" both "inward" toward the center of the solid figure in Figure 4.4 (per the earlier discussion of three-component patterns) and "outward," into the colonnade of asymmetric patterns.

In sum, the analysis of dependence variants of the situations in Figure 4.4 provides a way of understanding how the situational domain of asymmetric dependence relates to the domain of symmetric dependence. In principle, all possible 2 × 2 *asymmetric* patterns can be derived from the set of symmetric patterns distinguished earlier. Those patterns can be visualized as colonnades (series of columns) of asymmetric patterns that rise over each region of the symmetric domain and together constitute a set of successive layers of increasingly asymmetric situations that cover those regions. At their extremes and depending on the underlying region, those many columns culminate in one of the handful of extreme patterns shown in Table 2.8 and at the top of Table 4.4. In each such extreme pattern one person is totally dependent on the other. (See section 2.5 in chapter 2 for further descriptions of the extreme patterns and their implications.)

In section 4.3.2, below, we briefly consider what it means for a pair of persons to increase or decrease their *inter*dependence. Those changes can be viewed as shifts in the location of the situations they experience in their daily life, as they move upward in Figure 4.4 toward the region of total interdependence at the top, or downward toward mutual "freedom." Now we can understand that the overlying colonnades of asymmetrical dependence patterns enable us to envision what it may mean for a pair to shift the symmetry of their interdependence, as, in some cases, they move inward through a colonnade toward increasing symmetry, or, in other cases, outward toward increasing asymmetry.[3]

4.3 The Distribution of Situations and Its Implications

4.3.1 *Paradigmatic Representations*
Figure 4.4 shows the locations of the first eight situations that we have included in this Atlas. The shaded areas in Figures 4.1, 4.2, and 4.3 suggest the range of variants of the several named patterns, so the blank areas between the patterns in Figure 4.4 are not vacant but are occupied by those variants. We have also seen in our analyses of three-component patterns and patterns of asymmetric dependence that a pattern located on one of the planes of Figure 4.4, as is the PDG, also has variants when mild degrees of the third component or of asymmetry are introduced. Those observations raise the question of how best to represent a particular situation. When we examine matrix patterns that resemble the Prisoner's Dilemma, which among them is the "paradigm" or "prototype" for that situation?

In the case of the Prisoner's Dilemma, students of "games" have come to agree that the ultimate criterion of that matrix is that the four outcome values must be arranged in the *order* shown for the PDG in Figure 4.1. That is, A's values must be ordered from largest to smallest as we follow a zigzag path through the matrix, from the a2b1 cell, to the a1b1 cell, to the a2b2 cell, and finally, to the a1b2 cell, and symmetrically for B's outcomes. It turns out that this criterion requires only that the MPC component be larger than the BAC component and that the two be overlaid in the "discordant" way shown in Table 3.1. Furthermore, if there is an MJC component, it must be less important, that is, contribute less variance, than the BAC component. So there are many variations on the theme of the "Prisoner's Dilemma." However, when we vary the relative weights of the two necessary components (BAC and MPC), we see that those variations do not pose the same degree of "dilemma" to the actors. With a very strong BAC

---

[3] There is one other type of pattern that is "asymmetrical," but in a different sense than discussed above in the text. In it, one person is subject *only* to PC and the other, *only* to JC. This pattern is one of *inter*dependence, but does not appear among the patterns summarized in Figure 4.4 because, for simplicity of analysis, they are limited to ones comprised of symmetric components. The pattern just described is obviously a variant of patterns located on the MPC and MJC surface of Figure 4.4 – a variant created by eliminating the PC for one person and the JC for the other.

component, an actor has little reason not to benefit self. With a very strong MPC component, it is reasonable to set aside self-interest and act to benefit the partner.

Kelley and Thibaut (1978, pp. 133–36) present arguments to the effect that the type of pattern labeled PDG in Figure 4.1, with its equal spacing between the successive rank-ordered values (of $12 > 8 > 4 > 0$), is the optimal pattern. One argument is that with the equal spacing, the gain from mutual cooperation as opposed to mutual self-interest (8 minus 4) is equal to (and exactly counterbalances) either of the two motives a person may have for making the self-interested choice, whether that of greed (12 minus 8) or fear (4 minus 0). Thus, the pattern should produce a sharp conflict for both the greedy person and the fearful one.

Kelley and Thibaut (1978, pp. 134–36) use similar reasoning from counterbalanced forces for the Chicken pattern with a 2:1 ratio of MPC to MJC (as in Figure 4.3). However, the conflict does not exist for each of the actors, but rather is the conflict one of them is able to create for the other. The argument is that the 2:1 ratio enables a challenger to place the other person in the most acute conflict between fighting and refusing to fight. As a consequence, the challenger makes his dare with maximum uncertainty about how the other will respond and, therefore, creates an optimum setting for displaying brave risk taking "in the face of the unknown."

The argument to be made for the paradigmatic quality of the particular Threat Game pattern in the middle of Figure 4.1 focuses on the balance of factors most likely to produce the exploitation-threat scenario. Examining the shaded area of variants, we see that in the upper matrices, A can create more inequality but because helping B is less costly and B's sanction can be quite great, A has less incentive to be exploitative. In the lower matrices, A has strong motivation to exploit B, but the possible exploitation is less and B's ability to punish A is less, so B is likely to accept it. In the middle, those two features are balanced out: A's temptation to be exploitative is plausible (helping B is moderately costly) and A's ability to punish exploitation is sufficient to make it a plausible reaction to exploitation. The incentive structure promotes both the exploitation and a threat reaction to it.

Each of the arguments above comes to focus on "balanced forces," which create sharp conflict, either within an actor, for an actor's partner, or between the two persons. In general, by arguments like those, it seems possible to identify a prototypical instance of each kind of situation, that is, a pattern that most clearly presents its problems and opportunities to the participants.

In general, a matrix we give a name in our various figures can probably be considered to be a pattern that presents in distinctive and clear-cut terms a particular kind of problem to the interdependent pair. In the shaded regions around a named pattern are fuzzy examples of it – patterns that possess but do not sharply define its unique properties. With major modifications of a situation's components, we move outside its shaded area and identify other situations that are closely related "neighbors" but have their own distinctive features.

As a qualification to the above, we should note that the problems posed by two of the situations located on the surface of the 3-D solid in Figure 4.4 are dramatically represented by a pair of the three-component patterns. These are shown as "schematic" patterns in the lower portion of Table 4.3: The schematic turn-taking pattern and threat game are both simpler than their two-component versions and seem to provide appropriate settings for the respective scenarios envisioned for them. Are there other such simple patterns to be found in the interior regions of the solid? And are there other interesting situations waiting to be identified along the strings lacking in named matrices in Figures 4.1, 4.2, and 4.3, or along strings that can be traced within the solid from one side to another? We leave those as questions for others to explore.

It is worth noting that the above-described properties of the situational domain may have important implications for how people might, in their everyday experience, learn to discriminate among the various patterns that we distinguish here. One would think that they might form concepts around the paradigmatic patterns and employ discriminative labels related to those patterns. It seems likely, further, that in their roles as actors rather than observers of interdependent life, the exigencies of action tend to focus people on the implications of the patterns for interaction process and, thereby, to encourage their use of process labels – turn taking, threats, challenges, coordinating efforts, avoiding collisions, helping partner in the face of selfish interests, debates over fairness, and so forth. On this point, the reader is referred to section 4.4 below which indicates some of the distinctions among situations reflected in everyday language.

4.3.2 *The Names of Situations*
The phenomenon of naming situations is interesting in its own right. In this Atlas, except for the extreme situations to which we have attached theoretical monikers, the others have names relating either to the *roles* of the occupants (Prisoner's Dilemma, "Battle of the Sexes" for the Turn-Taking

Game), to a *personal characteristic* or motive that may be revealed in inter-action (Hero, Martyr, Chicken, Maximizing Difference), or to an *interaction process* the situation supports (Threat, Conjunctive and Disjunctive cooper-ation). It appears that our language is not very responsive to talking about situations per se. This apparent limitation of language may reflect what we pay attention to in describing interpersonal events. It has been said in social psychology that the language of situations is not nearly as extensive as the language of persons (e.g., Snyder and Cantor, 1998, p. 643). A plau-sible explanation for this, suggested by Jones and Nisbett (1971), is that situations provide the *background* against which persons and their actions are *figures*. We usually watch the actors and don't pay much attention to the "scenery," with the result that we don't have occasion to develop a rich lexicon for distinguishing among situations.

This question of "names" must be considered in the context of our theo-retical emphasis on moving from the concrete to the abstract. Everyday lan-guage certainly provides names for recurrent common situations, such as "going to the movies," "meeting for lunch," "sharing the work on a task," "driving in heavy traffic," and so on. But our abstract analysis removes those concrete details and leaves us with notions of *patterns* of control, de-pendence, conflict, exchange, and so on. It is not clear how well subjects unfamiliar with the distinctions drawn in this Atlas could sort into our categories the concrete examples we provide for each Atlas entry. On the other hand, the ideas of "control," "dependence," "mutual helping," and so forth, are in common usage. So perhaps it is our abstract "skeletons" of the various situations, each with their articulation of various "bones" (of control, conflict, etc.), that are missing from common thought. The ele-ments or parts are well understood but their possible *patterns* may not be, or may be understood only in their concrete manifestations.

4.3.3 *The Implications of the Distribution*

The overall shape of the solid in Figure 4.4 deserves comment. Its most prominent feature is that the diversity of patterns increases as interde-pendence increases, that is, as we move upward in the space, from the zero interdependence pattern (simple BAC) toward the upper plane of the region of total interdependence. If we consider that upward movement to be the direction in which dyadic relationships may be said to "grow" or "develop" (i.e., as two persons become increasingly interdependent), then we see that with relationship growth, there is (1) increasing potential for both conflict and commonality of interest and (2) increasing diversity in the variety of problems likely to be encountered, that is, in whether they be exchange problems, coordination problems, or a combination of those.

Figure 4.4 also shows that although the extremes of corresponding versus conflicting interests occur at maximum interdependence for coordination problems, they occur only at intermediate degrees of interdependence for the exchange problems. The implications of that difference are not clear. Perhaps the extremes of the coordination problems at the highest level of interdependence tell us something about two kinds of dyadic interactions that many of us find entertaining to watch but not desirable to participate in. At both extremes, there are great risks. With conflicting interests, the MJC situation affords a setting for interaction in which one person will inevitably win and the other will suffer a loss. When the stakes are high and cover the range from positive to negatives (and when the situation permits ad lib, repetitive but irrevocable actions), this is the situation in which we watch the performance of boxers, wrestlers, duelists, and toreadors. At the other extreme, where there is a coordination problem with high stakes but common interests, there are the risks of failures of coordination. We enjoy watching interaction in which those risks occur, for example, trapeze or high wire teams performing without their nets, or ice-skating duos trying to perform unusual feats.

4.4 Empirical Studies of the Psychological Dimensions of Situations

There have been many proposals for taxonomies of interpersonal situations and some dozen or so empirical studies of how people distinguish among them. Pervin (1978) and Forgas (1983b) have provided useful overviews of the ideas and results. For our present purposes, it is useful to see whether the taxonomy our theory generates is reflected in the data that research subjects generate in their ratings or judgments of various natural situations.

A simple summary of the empirical data is not easy to prepare, inasmuch as the relevant studies vary in (1) the stimulus materials used to elicit the judgments, (2) the terms in which subjects are required to express their judgments, and (3) the statistical methods used to extract order from the data sets. For example, on the first and second points, the items being judged (sometimes "interpersonal relations," "roles," or "interaction episodes," and seldom "situations" per se) have been evaluated as to the behaviors they elicit, the likely feelings people experience in them, and "situation traits" – threatening, friendly, ambiguous, and so forth.

Yet, as we have examined the numerous factors, dimensions, and item loadings, we can detect some common themes in the results.[4] The list of situational factors or dimensions they suggest reads something like the following:

(1) Positive versus negative: pleasant, friendly, and cooperative *versus* their opposites.

(2) Involvement or intensity: seriousness, feeling involved, interaction with each other, activity *versus* their opposites.

(3) Feelings of self-confidence: feeling one knows how to behave, feeling relaxed; the situation is routine or informal *versus* feeling ill-at-ease, anxious; the situation is formal, intermittent, unpredictable.

(4) (Less clear than the above): Equality *versus* unequal power, dominance.

Lining those up against our theoretical dimensions, it seems reasonable to assume that (1) reflects covariation in outcomes (corresponding vs. conflicting interests) and that (2) reflects degree of interdependence (high vs. low). Number (4) seems to have to do with the distinction we make between symmetry versus asymmetry in dependence.

Number (3) seems to have to do with familiarity with the situation resulting from its recurrence in the person's interactions. Thus, this factor may reflect a broad distinction among situations in regard to (1) how much *information* they provide about the concrete situation and the persons involved and (2) the extent of the actors' experience-based *expectations* that enable them to supply missing information. It is understandable that with

---

[4] The following sources are reflected in this summary: Forgas, 1976, 1983a, & 1983b; King & Sorrentino, 1983; Magnusson, 1971; Murtha, Kanfer, & Ackerman, 1996; Pervin, 1976; Wish, Deutsch, & Kaplan, 1976; and Wish & Kaplan, 1977. Other studies that relate in some way to "situations" were not included on various grounds. The work of Walter Mischel and his colleagues deals explicitly with "situations" but tends to stay at a very concrete level in its analysis, dealing with everyday categories of interpersonal settings (e.g., "being at a cocktail party" and "being on a tour of Roman ruins" are examples from Cantor, Mischel, and Schwartz, 1982) or of "person factors" relevant to performance in various situations (e.g., "ability to speak in front of others" and "physical strength, stamina" are examples from Shoda, Mischel, and Wright, 1993). Haslam's (1994) work, deriving from Alan Fiske's elementary forms of social relationship (1991), is indirectly related to the present situation analysis insofar as it deals with a mixture of what this Atlas refers to as "person factors" (e.g., taking initiative, concern about another person's needs) and the resulting interactions (e.g., turn taking, sharing). To some degree, those imply different broad classes of situation, but the focus seems be on the various normative patterns by which interdependent behavior is regulated. In any case, Haslam rejects dimensional representation of relationship phenomena in favor of Fiske's four broad categories.

a lack of information and of relevant expectations (as in interacting with new people in new situations vs. with family and friends in old, familiar situations), a person sometimes literally "doesn't know how to behave."

Although it is not alone in this respect, the third factor is also interesting in its focus on the *feelings* elicited by the contrasting features (apparently, in this case, informational features) of various situations – "relaxed" and "at ease" versus "anxiety" and "uncertainty." Pervin notes the importance of affects in these factors and suggests that "we may organize situations not so much in terms of cognitively perceived similar attributes but in terms of bodily experiences associated with them" (1976, p. 471). He observes that Mehrabian and Russell (1974) made a similar proposal, that environments are distinguished in terms of their emotion-eliciting properties. This is an interesting idea and surely not without merit. But we would hasten to point out that affective experiences must depend on what happens in a situation, that is, on the interaction. We have repeatedly emphasized (e.g., in chapter 3) that interaction is a joint function of the situation and the two persons. So each situation makes possible several patterns of interaction, depending not only on its features but on the persons involved – their attitudes, motives, values, and so forth. Various pairs will have different experiences in a particular situation and each person's feelings (anxiety, uncertainty, confidence, pleasure, seriousness, involvement, etc.) will depend on such variations. Affect is undoubtedly an important determinant of reactions to situations (and to partners within situations) and, when opportunities present themselves, of subsequent selections among further situations and partners. However, from our theoretical perspective, affect per se is not a useful distinguishing mark of a situation. The *pattern* of possible affects or, perhaps, some typical or modal affect (for the kind of pairs most "typical" in that situation) may be useful, but not a particular affect.

The reader will notice that the exchange versus coordination distinction, which figures importantly in our theoretical analysis, is not apparent in the various studies of people's intersituational distinctions. However, we know that people can take account of the implications of these two patterns of control. As explained in Kelley (1997b), within the broad class of "dominant" behaviors, college students can distinguish those that employ partner control (threat and promise) from those, such as taking the initiative, that are based on joint control, that is, corresponding MJC patterns. And Nucci and Turiel's research (1978) suggests that school children readily draw distinctions between misbehaviors related to partner control ("moral" transgressions) and those related to joint control ("conventional" incoordinations). However, people do not seem to use these distinctions in their characterizations of situations. Perhaps the response conditions customary in daily life, namely, ad lib and revocability, permit the behavioral patterns associated with exchange versus coordination situations to become so blurred that particular examples and prompts are required to reveal their presence in common understanding.

The reports of both Wish (Wish, Deutsch, & Kaplan, 1976; Wish & Kaplan, 1977) and Forgas (1983a) present evidence about what we interpret to be judgments of (a) corresponding versus conflicting interests and (b) degree of interdependence. Those data enable us to test one implication of the distribution of situations shown in Figure 4.4, namely, that there is a broad range of variation in corresponding versus conflicting interests at the intermediate and higher levels of interdependence, but a narrow range of such variation at low levels of interdependence. All three sets of data are consistent with that pattern. Low interdependence situations (e.g., "episodes" of low "involvement") are never characterized as "competitive." If anything, they tend to be judged as slightly "cooperative." But situations of higher involvement or intensity range over the entire spectrum of characterizations as to "cooperation versus competition."

We must be careful in how we interpret this result. Does it reflect the fact that situations with little interdependence cannot, *structurally*, exhibit much variation in covariation between the two persons' outcomes – as our situational analysis in Figure 4.4 implies? Or is it rather a matter of *process* – that is, for whatever reasons (situational and/or personal) a pair generates competitiveness and conflict, in doing so they change the terms of their interaction? Put simply, conflict in interaction may generally escalate in ways that increase the interdependence – as the actors introduce new options that bring increasing degrees of outcome control to bear upon each other.

4.5 Summary

We have examined various 2 × 2 outcome matrices that are formed by combining two or three of the components identified in chapter 2. As described in the earlier chapter, those matrices define the kinds of problems that interdependent persons face and the outcome controls that constitute the primary means of dealing with those problems. We have shown the location of those matrices in the three-dimensional space defined by degree of interdependence, corresponding versus conflicting interests, and the nature of the problem defined by the interdependence (whether coordination, exchange, or both). We have also shown how situations of asymmetric and unilateral dependence are located in the space, relative to the patterns of symmetric interdependence, and in a sense, provide a fourth dimension of "equal versus unequal." That space and the distribution of outcome patterns within it constitute the basic (though admittedly somewhat primitive and overly simple) map of the "world" of interdependence situations that underlies our characterization of this book as an "atlas" and that, to a degree, has guided our exploration of the broad domain of such situations. Brief final comments in the chapter concern implications of the spatial distribution of situations in that map.

The brief "Introduction to the Entries" that follows describes the properties of the situations included in this Atlas and explains our reasons for their inclusion.

PART TWO

THE SITUATIONS

Introduction to the Entries for the Situations

The following section of the Atlas devotes a chapter to each of 21 abstract interpersonal situations that we have chosen to describe in detail. We will use the term "entry" for each of these situations, parallel to usage in listings for maps in a geographical atlas, topics in an encyclopedia, or locations in a table of basic elements. In this introduction, we first describe the structure and contents of each entry. Then we describe our reasons for selecting these particular situations, the criteria used for including or excluding potential entries. Finally, we discuss the issue of the adequacy of our coverage of situations and the potential strengths and weaknesses of our reasoning.

The Structure of Individual Entries

Each situation is first described through concrete, everyday examples from interpersonal life, with the goal of illustrating the more abstract features of each entry in a nontechnical fashion. A conceptual description follows, using the various analytical tools developed in the earlier chapters. Each situation is characterized in terms of the basic control components that influence individuals' outcomes in the situation, as well as the response and informational conditions that are typically part of the social problem. Then, the relation of this entry to other "family" members or "neighbors" is discussed, in order to help the reader gain perspective on the conceptual "location" of the situation, the region of the interpersonal situation map that it occupies.

John Holmes had primary responsibility for preparation of this chapter.

Next, each entry focuses on interaction patterns and person factors associated with the situation, the processes and mechanisms relevant to finding solutions to the particular interdependence problem. Our discussion of these topics is necessarily selective rather than exhaustive, with the purpose of representing and illustrating the basic ideas. As will become apparent, each situation "affords" or permits a limited number of specific interaction possibilities. In fact, as noted in chapter 4, many situations become known by the prototypical interaction pattern for which they provide the opportunity, rather than by the features of the situations themselves. Further, the opportunities to act in a certain way in a situation allow the person to express aspects of his or her "social personality," to exhibit motivations and goals that go beyond what the situation calls for in terms of immediate self-interests. For each situation, we discuss social person factors relevant to the particular social dilemma, including interpersonal dispositions, relationship-specific orientations, and social norms. Finally, each entry ends with a more technical description of the situation, where appropriate, in the form of either a matrix representation or transition list.

Each entry has been designed to stand alone and the entry chapters need not be read in the order in which they are presented and numbered. Nevertheless, there is something to be gained by starting with the simpler situations, especially the "basic" situations, Entries #1–#4, that describe the control components. Our analysis of situations starts with combinations of these components, goes on to add complexity in terms of time-extended patterns, and then considers situations with incomplete information and uncertainty about the future. Finally, several important and basic patterns of interdependence involving more than two persons in a dyad are discussed, as is the critical issue of "movement" among situations. The convention we have adopted in naming the situations is to have a two-part title in which the more technical name we have chosen is followed by a brief description that captures an aspect of the dynamics of the situation in everyday language.

Selecting the Set of Prototypical Situations

2 × 2 Interdependence Patterns

As a first criterion, situations were selected on the theoretical grounds developed in the taxonomy derived from interdependence theory described in chapter 4. In that logical scheme, all possible patterns of 2×2 interdependence can be constructed from the basic patterns of *control* or influence on outcomes, Bilateral Actor Control (BAC), Mutual Partner Control (MPC), and Mutual Joint Control (MJC). That is, the three components, BAC, MPC, and MJC (the last with either corresponding or conflicting interests), are the building blocks of outcome matrices. They may be combined two or three at a time, with varying relative weights or importance, and placed in different (concordant or discordant) orientations to each other.

Single Component Patterns. In Figure 4.4, we saw that the locations of the four simple patterns corresponding to these building blocks define the extremes of three *dimensions*, which together describe the three different planes in the space depicted in the figure. The dimensions of the taxonomy include the degree of interdependence, the extent of corresponding or conflicting interests, and the distinction involving exchange versus co-ordination problems. These three dimensions, as well as the response and information conditions, can be used to classify the situations we have chosen for inclusion in the Atlas (see Introduction Table). Note that the four basic patterns are included as the initial Entries #1 through #4. In the logical scheme represented by a dimensional taxonomy, it is particularly important to pay attention to the situations that are located at the extremes of a given dimension. These situations are Independence (#1), Mutual Partner Control (#2), Corresponding Mutual Joint Control (#3), and Conflicting Mutual Joint Control (#4).

Figure 4.4 in chapter 4 showed the location of the first eight situations derived from our 2×2 matrix analysis that we have included in this Atlas. Here we briefly consider why they were selected and, then, the coverage they seem to provide for understanding interpersonal phenomena.

Two- and Three-Component Patterns. Using the logic developed in chapter 4, we first identified "families" or clusters of situations located on the three planes or "continents" defined by the three different dimensions. First, the *"exchange" region* of the space included various combinations of Bilateral Actor Control (BAC) and Mutual Partner Control (MPC), such that both individuals' personal preferences vary in the extent to which they either encourage or inhibit helping the partner. (The corners of the plane are thus defined by a purely corresponding interests pattern or a purely conflicting interests pattern, known as a constant sum game, of which the well-known zero-sum game is a special case.) Within this region, we focus first on the classic exchange situation where personal gain is in conflict with collective, joint profit, known as the Prisoner's Dilemma (#5: "Me versus we"). Then we describe the Threat situation (#6: "Trading loyalty for justice"), where personal preferences (AC) and helping the partner (PC) are concordant for one person but discordant for the other, resulting in the important scenario in which issues of justice versus loyalty are raised.

Quite apart from their theoretical importance in representing significant problems in the exchange region, these two entries (and later ones) were selected because they have drawn much attention in research. That attention is reflected in the fact that the situations have names, as discussed in chapter 4. Over the early years of "game" research, investigators attached names to particular situations in order to suggest that a game is relevant to some natural phenomena and also, of course, to enable their work to be associated with that of others working on the same patterns. So the selective coverage provided by our "named" situations reflects the portions of the domain that various investigators have found to be interesting and potentially important – worth thinking about and studying. For our purposes, those are important criteria for inclusion. They imply that a particular pattern has many implications for everyday phenomena, and they also point to the existence of a research literature that may be usefully drawn upon through our efforts. (See Allison, Beggan, & Midgley, 1996, for a discussion of metaphors in social dilemma research and their ability to draw together similar instances and give insight into practical applications.)

However, these same arguments might raise the issue of why the Maximizing Difference Game (MDG; see Figure 4.1 and chapter 4), given the attention it has received in the research literature, is not included in the Atlas. Our response is that the MDG received attention largely because of its usefulness in distinguishing individualistic (i.e., own gain) versus competitive (i.e., relative gain) motives in the Prisoner's Dilemma (PDG), rather than because its structure represented a classic and unique problem in its own right. Thus we regard it as a member of the same "family" as the PDG prototype and discuss it within that entry as a relevant "neighbor." Further, as noted in chapter 4, section 4.3.1, some structures such as the PDG seem more paradigmatic, while others could be viewed as "fuzzy" examples that do not have a truly distinctive pattern. Thus, for example, if the component weights in the PDG are changed somewhat, the dilemma in it is not as sharp as it might be. Of course, these judgments are open to debate, and some readers might conclude that situations we include as "variants" or "neighbors" deserve separate entries.

Next, the upper, triangular plane of Figure 4.4 can be characterized as a *"total interdependence" region*, in that the patterns there reflect situations where each person has no independent, personal preference for which action to pursue (i.e., no control over own outcomes, or BAC). Thus these situations are a mixture of exchange (MPC) and coordination (MJC) problems. For instance, the Turn-Taking pattern involves a corresponding interest Mutual Joint Control structure, where (weaker) motivations to receive help from the partner create a mild conflict of interest about how to coordinate (see Entry #3 for a fuller discussion). A strategy where individuals take turns in gaining their best outcomes solves this common dilemma. Chicken (#7: "Death before dishonor") is also seen as a prototype of the type of problems in this region. However, in this case, the MPC factor, the desire *not* to have the opponent gain at your expense, is stronger than incentives to coordinate (MJC). A "mixed motive" situation results, where both cooperative and competitive motivations are aroused.

The triangular plane on the far right side of Figure 4.4 has been described as the *"coordination" region* of the 2 × 2 domains. It is defined by the two contrasting coordination problems (#3: "Getting in sync" and #4: "Match or mismatch") and is anchored at the lower end by a location involving independent personal preferences (BAC, #1). Hero (#8: "Let's do it your way") is perhaps the most interesting exemplar of patterns showcasing the internal conflict that can result from opposing forces involving personal preferences versus the desire for coordinated endeavors: Taking the initiative in pursuing joint interests favors the partner's choice of activity. The Martyr pattern is an important neighbor with similar dynamics, though in this case stronger individual preferences must be sacrificed in order to take the initiative in coordinating activities with the partner.

Whereas the previous four entries involve only two components of control, Entries #9 and #10 involve all three. The cases where the components are weighted equally are discussed. In the Conjunctive Problem (#9), *both persons* must take a particular action in order for both to gain maximum benefit. In this case, what each individual wants to do converges with preferences for the partner's actions and coordination: "Together we can do it." In the Disjunctive Problem (#10), it is only necessary for *one* person to take a particular action in order for both to get their best outcomes: "Either of us can do it." The coordination component thereby does not contribute to the convergence created by the other two components.

Finally, the above situations represent problems that are basically symmetric in nature in terms of how each person is affected by the various types of influence. This assumption was made in order to simplify our analysis, though such patterns are very common in everyday life and probably reflect the majority of interpersonal situations that people encounter. Of course, various forms of asymmetrical dependence can occur (see Table 2.8 and section 4.2.3). The Asymmetric Dependence entry (#11: "You're the boss") illustrates these variations, discusses the impact of the different structures on interaction patterns, and suggests person factors most relevant to coping with the roles of the controlling and the dependent persons in such situations.

Time-Extended Patterns

Other situations were selected for inclusion in the Atlas on the basis of their representing problems that illustrate crucial sequential and temporal aspects of response conditions. As described in chapter 3, these types of response conditions can be represented schematically by transition lists, specifying when and in what order various actions must to be taken to achieve a certain goal.

Sometimes the temporal aspect of joint decision making simply involves the experience of encountering the same sort of problem on *repeated* occasions. The most obvious such situation is the classic PDG, where personal profit conflicts with collective gain. Considerable research explores this situation, in which previous joint decisions provide an important context for further decisions. This situation is known in the literature as the Iterated PDG (#12: "United we stand, divided we fall"). Of course, other situations where turn taking is a prominent possible solution to a problem are also of interest when they are repeatedly encountered, such as the Threat situation, #6.

Other situations are more literally *extended* in time, such that the problem to be solved – the "goal" of the situation – is reached *only* at the end of a required sequence of intermediate junctures. If the persons do not persist in maintaining the sequence in the face of costs, or are not patient with or committed to their partners, then the goal will not be reached. The best known of such problems is the Investment situation (#13: "Building for the future") in which both partners must commit contributions at each period of time for the potentially larger rewards to be finally realized. Confidence in the "investment" and trust in the partner are clearly important temporal issues that are highlighted in the situation. In contrast, the Delay of Gratification situation (#14: "Resisting temptation") involves forgoing rewards rather than making contributions. It is the classic example of an extended situation where one person is typically unilaterally dependent on the other, and where the self-control/patience of the dependent person is at issue.

Incomplete Information Situations

Incomplete information about the various outcomes for self or other resulting from the different behavioral options might occur in any of the situations we have described to this point. Often outcomes are potentially knowable through generalizations from past experience and effective communication with a partner. While we assume that the given matrix specifies what *will* happen, whether the two persons anticipate the outcomes or not, when a new situation is experienced, the individuals may sometimes not be certain of their outcomes before having to decide on their behavior.

However, there are some types of situations where incomplete information is an essential feature of the situation as it occurs in social life. For instance, in Negotiation situations (#15: "Can we agree on a deal?"), both persons typically have information about their own outcomes, but lack information about their partner's. To deal with the issue of information interdependence, each person must decide on the communication strategies that will be adopted. Further, because such situations are typically "mixed motive," each person must walk a fine line between cooperative (e.g., honesty) and competitive communication procedures (e.g., secrecy).

In the Encounters with Strangers situation (#16: "Lack of information about a partner"), individuals know little about each other and are forced to rely on their expectations about other people more generally, and the rewards they might experience in certain types of situations, in order to decide how to act. That is, sometimes the uncertainty is quite general and the information gaps that must be filled by inference are quite extensive.

Other situations involve incomplete information because of uncertainty about what the *future* holds. For instance, in the Joint Decisions under Uncertainty situation (#17: "Bird in the hand"), both individuals know what outcomes they would experience if they decide to take a *current* option but do not have a clear idea of what "lies around the corner." Thus they might choose to wait and see if future circumstances present them with a better alternative; however, it is often impossible to turn back and take the earlier opportunity once it has been passed up. Such situations may reveal individuals' optimistic or pessimistic expectations about opportunities that are likely to occur in the future.

On the other hand, sometimes one does not have the ability to simply decide to take a set of "safe" current outcomes. Instead, one is forced to deal with the fact of considerable uncertainty in terms of what the future might hold. In the Twists of Fate situation (#18: "Coping with an uncertain future"), individuals must find solutions to the problem of potential dependence on their partner if crises occur where they themselves are greatly in need of help. What can one do to insure that the other will come to one's aid when it is crucial to receive help, that the partner is not simply a "fair-weather friend"? Do close partners need the mutual assurance of a commitment "for better or worse"?

Beyond the Dyad: Three- and N-Person Situations

While the goal of the Atlas is largely to achieve an understanding of dyadic interaction, the logic of our analyses is easily extended to multiple others. We use two examples to demonstrate this. First, we examine the situation involving Third Parties (#19: "Effects of an outsider"), exploring the potential for the presence of someone else on the scene to disrupt the dyadic processes of exchange and coordination described earlier in the Atlas. Second, we examine the classic example of a social dilemma, as defined in the research literature (see Allison et al., 1996). In this situation, participants must choose between maximizing short-term, individual self-interest or acting for the collective good of their larger group. In the N-person PDG (#20: "Tragedy of the commons") that we examine, it is more "profitable" to maximize self-interest, but if everyone does, then the group is ultimately worse off and in peril of not surviving.

Movement from One Situation to Another

The various principles of interdependence theory provide an analytic framework for describing how choices *among* situations are jointly controlled and further, the critical criteria that underlie individuals' preferences among situations. Various authors have contended that selection among potential situations is one of the most diagnostic tasks for distinguishing individuals' personalities (e.g., Snyder & Cantor, 1998). Our analysis of Movement among Situations (Entry #21: "Where do we go from here?") emphasizes approach or avoidance tendencies along the dimensions central to an interdependence perspective, including level of closeness, symmetry of dependence, conflict of interests, exchange or coordination tasks, short- or long-term perspectives, and amount of informational uncertainty. However, our theory also suggests that control over intersituational movement will depend heavily on the particular partner involved, and that the regions of the interpersonal space that are frequented will essentially define the type of relationship that has developed with another.

How Adequate Is Our Coverage?

Our Atlas entries listed in Figure 4.4 are few in number and necessarily scattered over the domain of possibilities. The first four provide anchors for the three dimensions and define the three regions (total interdependence, exchange, and coordination) that outline the universe of symmetrical patterns. Beyond that, the patterns located on the planes provide selective coverage of the possibilities. Excluding Entry #1, Independence (BAC), there is only one situation in the lower range of the interdependence dimension. And with the exceptions of the constant (or zero) sum game, conflicting MJC (#4), the Prisoner's Dilemma (#5), and to a degree, the Threat situation (#6), there are no situations located in the conflicting interests portion of the dimension of covariation of interests. How do we justify such selective coverage of the total domain?

We tended to include situations that have been the focus of researchers of interdependence problems, because we, like they, considered these to be especially worthy of study. It is probably obvious why situations of low interdependence have not been found interesting: "There's not much going on there." Nor have prior investigators focused much on situations of strong conflict of interest, with the notable exceptions of the three mentioned above (zero-sum, Conflicting MJC, and PDG). It seems that the attention of situation researchers has been focused largely on cases of considerable interdependence and with conflict of interests somewhat less important than commonality of interests. These situations define problems in which, in view of the interdependence, meaningful conflict of interest exists but is accompanied by a common interest component that presents opportunities for its resolution.

Thus the mixed motive area is important because it evokes relatively strong *intrapersonal* conflict. Indeed, decision difficulty is why a situation may be referred to as a "dilemma." Further, the solutions reached in these situations are directly linked to functioning, to how well a dyad is able to attain reasonable outcomes that will sustain the relationship. That resolution depends greatly on the persons' responsiveness to their common interests. Such responsiveness and its necessary conditions have been predominant issues in situation research, for example, McClintock's (1972a & 1972b) work on the social person factors (e.g., prosocial, individualistic, and competitive orientations) that affect behavior in the various mixed motive games (see Van Lange & De Dreu, 2001).

Furthermore, research on everyday interpersonal relations has usually assumed that moderate to high levels of interdependence and some conflict of interest underlie various relationship problems (Holmes, 2000). Thus, relationship researchers have often dealt with the phenomena we analyze by studying situations in the mid-ranges of interdependence and correspondence of interest. Consider, for example, the Threat situation with its implications for fairness and loyalty, the Turn-Taking situation with its potential for establishing reciprocity over time, and Hero with its opportunities for sacrifices that benefit one's partner. These comments suggest that our entries cover a large portion of the interdependence domain that is relevant to the interpretation of interpersonal episodes.

As we discussed in chapter 4, the reader is left to judge whether our "named" situations in the 2 × 2 domain are the "best" of their kind, the most prototypical or paradigmatic cases. In Figures 4.1, 4.2, and 4.3 we indicated "variants" in the family of scenarios identified with the key situation by creating shaded areas. We suggested that as one "moves away" from the prototypical case in the three-dimensional space (or in the symmetry assumption), essential properties that are distinct to the situation are lost, resulting in its not posing the same degree of "dilemma" for actors. That is, an identified situation should have counterbalanced forces that create sharper conflicts, both intrapersonally and interpersonally. Thus a "variant" may possess, but not sharply define, a situation's unique properties. In contrast, a "neighboring" situation, such as Martyr with Hero, should provide the opportunity for an actor to reveal distinctive (but related) character qualities. The question of distinctiveness is obviously difficult, and the reader could argue that neighbors such as Martyr, Trust, and Turn Taking deserve their own designation.

Our sampling of response and information conditions is representative more than it is comprehensive. In terms of the sequential-temporal aspects of response conditions, the transition list procedures permit various sequences *within* (i.e., through) each type of situation, and important variants are discussed in each entry. Though there may be exceptions, changes in the sequence of behavior typically serve to "transform" the focal situation into another, usually simpler, situation that is included in the Atlas. Similarly, all of the 2 × 2 situations might have delayed delivery of outcomes, without essentially changing their structure. We chose to focus on the Investment and Delay of Gratification situations because they are the classic examples of problems that afford the expression of individuals' temporal interpersonal motives, such as persistence, self-control, and dependability. These constructs are not easily captured in the simple 2 × 2 structures.

Finally, our selection of situations to sample those involving incomplete information was determined by a logical analysis of *which type* of information remained uncertain. In Negotiation situations, it is information about the partner's outcomes, whereas in Encounters with Strangers, it is information about both own and other's likely outcomes. Then, we added a consideration of *temporal perspective* to our analysis. In the Joint Decisions under Uncertainty situation, current outcomes are known, but future ones are uncertain. In the Twists of Fate situation, it is unclear when and if one will be put in a situation of unilateral dependence on the partner; the quandary is how to establish an accord with a partner that will insure that help will be forthcoming if ever necessary.

Whatever the case, we do not argue that we have identified a list of sufficient and necessary situations that fully specify the geography of situational domains. Other investigators may identify further situational structures using the logic of interdependence theory that are not properly represented in our scheme of things and, indeed, we hope they do. And, of course, they may wish to contend that other theoretical vantage points add important perspectives on situations that are missing in our analysis.

Summary of the Situation Features Described in the 21 Atlas Entries

The Introduction Table presents what is essentially a table of contents of the entries. It lists the 21 situations, along with their numbers and the names we apply to them. For each entry, the next three columns describe the features of its outcome patterns. In some cases (#19 and #21), the entry discusses a variety of outcome patterns (indicated by "various"), and in one case, #16, the outcome pattern is uncertain, as indicated for all three features. The proper description of the features of entries #9 and #10 pose special problems, which are described in section 4.2.2 in the text.

In the interdependence column the degrees are coded according to the location of the situations on that dimension in Figure 2.1. Except for the asymmetric case, the interdependence is mutual. In the Corresponding/Conflicting column, the several situations described as "neither" lie at the middle of the corresponding versus conflicting interests dimension, and the ones described as "mixed" are those in which the two persons have a common interest in attaining or avoiding certain outcomes but a conflicting interest in relation to the other possible outcomes. The situations coded as "both" in the Exchange/Coordination column are ones in which both Partner and Mutual Joint Controls exist.

Response conditions are distinguished by the type of control commonly associated with single episodes of the situation, and for other situations, whether they are studied in extended or iterated form. In some cases, the listed response condition is clearly necessary to describe the situation as

INTRODUCTION TABLE . *The Atlas Entries and Their Features*

Entry No.	Technical Name	Interdependence	Outcome Pattern		Response Conditions	Information Conditions
			Corresponding/ Conflicting	Exchange/ Coordination		
Basic, single-component patterns						
#1	Independence	Zero	Neither	Neither	Irrelevant	Complete
#2	Mutual Partner Control	Total	Neither	Exchange	Various	Various
#3	Corresponding Mutual Joint Control	Total	Corresponding	Coordination	(A then B)	Various
#4	Conflicting Mutual Joint Control	Total	Conflicting	Coordination	Uncertain	Various
Two- and three-component patterns						
#5	Prisoner's Dilemma	Medium to High	Mixed	Exchange	(Simultaneous)	Complete
#6	Threat	Medium	Mixed	Exchange	Uncertain	Complete
#7	Chicken	Total	Mixed	Both	Various	Complete
#8	Hero	Medium to High	Mixed	Coordination	Uncertain	Complete
#9	Conjunctive Problems	Total	Corresponding	Both	Uncertain	Complete
#10	Disjunctive Problems	Total	Corresponding	Both	Irrelevant	Complete
#11	Asymmetric Dependence	Unilateral	Various	Various	Uncertain	Various
Time-extended patterns						
#12	Iterated PD	Medium to High	Mixed	Exchange	Iteration	Complete
#13	Investment	High	Corresponding	Both	Extended	Complete
#14	Delay of Gratification	Unilateral	Neither	Neither	Extended	Complete
Incomplete information situations						
#15	Negotiation	High	Mixed	Both	Various	Partial
#16	Encounters with Strangers	Uncertain	Uncertain	Uncertain	Uncertain	Little
#17	Joint Decisions under Uncertainty	High	Mixed	Both	Extended	Partial
#18	Twists of Fate	High	Corresponding	Exchange	Extended	Little
N-person situations: Beyond the dyad						
#19	Third Parties	Various	Various	Various	Uncertain	Complete
#20	N-person PD	Medium to High	Mixed	Exchange	Iteration	Complete
Movement from one situation to another						
#21	Movement among Situations	Various	Various	Various	Uncertain	Complete

it occurs in normal social life. In certain cases, there is indicated a particularly appropriate response condition (Entry #3) or one used commonly in research on the pattern (Entries #5 and #20). The information conditions describe the degree of information that is typical of everyday instances of a type of situation or that have been provided to subjects in laboratory research.

SINGLE-COMPONENT PATTERNS

Entry #1

Independence

We Go Our Separate Ways

1.1 Examples

Situations characterized by mutual independence are those in which neither individual has preferences or aversions regarding the partner's possible behaviors. For example, two students share a large apartment in which each one has a separate room for sleeping and studying. When they retire to their separate rooms, each may behave as he or she wishes without affecting the other's outcomes or being affected by what the other happens to do. Similarly, estranged partners who "go their own way" and are indifferent to one another's actions are mutually independent. Neither person's actions have any impact, for better or for worse, on the well-being of the other. If neither partner in a close relationship derives any benefits or costs from the other's reading habits, then the partners' choices of reading material illustrate mutual independence. Each partner reads what he or she wishes to read, with no implications for the partner's outcomes. (Of course, research on "social facilitation" [Zajonc & Sales, 1966] suggests that exceptions may occur when the partners' mere presence in the same room affects each other's enjoyment and effort.)

1.2 Conceptual Description

The requirement for the situation of mutual independence is that each person's outcomes are affected *only* by that person's actions and not by what the partner does nor by what the two do as a pair. Because each

Harold Kelley and Caryl Rusbult had primary responsibility for preparation of this entry.

person is affected by his or her actions, we may say that each person's outcomes are determined by "actor control." When that is true for both members of a pair, the mutual independence situation is referred to as "Bilateral Actor Control" (BAC for short), meaning that for both persons (i.e., bilaterally), the outcome variations are controlled by each actor's own behavior.

If the two persons have no effect on each other's outcomes, why do we think of them as being in the same situation? (E.g., why do we, as below, put them in the same outcome matrix?) There are two reasons for doing so: (1) Mutual independence is often a *separate* situation in an ongoing sequence of situations that have some sort of dependence or interdependence between the two persons. (2) It is often necessary to recognize mutual independence as a *component* of a more complex situation.

The first case is illustrated by the two students sharing an apartment. They will often be interdependent, as when they prepare meals in their kitchen, or when they go together to movies. In the course of that relationship, when they go to their separate rooms, to study, relax, or sleep, their independence occurs as a special situation. We consider this aspect of mutual independence in the discussion of interaction sequences below. In the second case, mutual independence is not a separate situation but is an integral part of a complex problem – a part that contributes to that problem's special nature. How mutual independence enters into complex situations was illustrated in chapters 2 and 4.

The two points above explain why we include this case of the absence of dependence in our atlas of interdependence situations. Additionally, we should note that this situation serves to define one of the major reference points in the domain of situations. In the requirement that each person's outcomes are affected only by their own actions, the BAC situation is to be contrasted with those in which *only one* person is affected by the partner (Entry #11) and those in which *both* persons are affected by each other (Entries #2 through #10). The importance of BAC as a reference point in our "geography" of interdependence is shown vividly in Figure 4.4 in chapter 4. There we see that the independence situation defines not only the zero point on the dimension of "degree of interdependence," but also the neutral point on the two dimensions of "covariation of interests" (where simple BAC has no covariation, neither corresponding nor conflicting) and "basis of interdependence" (where simple BAC represents the absence of both coordination and exchange problems). Figure 4.4 also shows the increasing diversity of interdependence situations as the other basic components are combined with it, in increasing ratios. Some consequences of that diversity are discussed below where, in section 1.4.6, we briefly consider the implications of increasing interdependence.

1.3 Variants and Combinations

From the perspective of each person, situations of mutual independence may involve self-gratification (in which the person may experience certain of his or her actions as pleasurable, as in the earlier example of independent reading) or self-inflicted discomfort (in which the person's actions create costs, e.g., from effort, pain, fatigue, as when the two roommates independently apply themselves to their studies). In the matrix in Table E1.1 below (at the end of this entry), the situation is such that each person can benefit himself or herself or not, and in Table E1.2, one person's actions vary his or her outcomes from positive to negative (as between watching a favorite sitcom or studying) whereas the other's actions create negative or neutral outcomes for himself or herself.

As a component of more complex situations, Bilateral Actor Control is an essential element of most of the interesting interdependence problems people face. For example, the Prisoner's Dilemma Game (Entry #5) is one in which each person can markedly benefit the other but, in doing so, reduces his or her own outcomes to some degree. As a consequence, each person may feel a temptation to receive benefit without giving it, so the mutual exchange of benefits is cast in doubt. The problem or dilemma is created by the particular way in which mutual independence (as this entry) exists as an interfering "overlay" on a strong pattern of Mutual Partner Control (as in Entry #2). In another example, mutual independence is superimposed on a strong pattern of corresponding Mutual Joint Control (as in Entry #3). For example, a dating couple might strongly wish to be together on a particular evening (the Corr MJC pattern), but they also have mildly different preferences (the BAC pattern) about which of two things to do. The latter creates a problem. If each takes the action most pleasing to himself or herself, the effect is to preclude their spending the evening together. This sets up a scenario in which one can agree to do what the other prefers and thereby show a bit of altruism. It is from that event that the situation takes it name, "Hero" (Entry #8).

1.4 Interaction Process and Person Factors

It is oxymoronic to speak of "interaction" when the two persons do not affect each other's outcomes. However, mutual independence plays an important role at various junctures in interdependent life. As a state before, during, and after an active relationship, it is much in the minds of the persons and greatly affects their behavior.

1.4.1 *Forming and Ending a Relationship*

Mutual independence is the logical starting point in the development of a relationship, in that it characterizes the pre-relationship state during which neither individual's behavioral choices have any impact on their partner's well-being. Mutual independence is a mixed blessing. The advantages are freedom from control by another person and from having to deal with the conflicting interests common to interdependence. The disadvantages lie in having to forgo the benefits derived from interaction – the pleasures, task accomplishments, shared possessions, and security that an association can make possible. It is not surprising that, torn between those advantages and disadvantages, people are often ambivalent about leaving a state of independence and entering a relationship of interdependence. Eidelson (1980) has studied the implications of this conflict, which he describes as one "between an individual's motives to affiliate with, and at the same time remain independent from, another person" (p. 460). From studies of friendship development among university freshman, he presents evidence that satisfaction with a relationship grows at first, but later takes a brief downturn before moving on to higher levels. This pattern is consistent with the view that the affiliation tendency increases with early interaction (as the relationship yields many rewards and has few restrictions), but then becomes offset temporarily by increasing pressures from the partner to modify behavior and make time commitments. Later, satisfaction increases as the person adjusts to and comes to accept the costs inherent in the relationship.

If mutual independence is the logical starting point of a relationship, it is also the logical end point in the deterioration of a relationship, in that mutual independence characterizes the post-relationship stage during which the partners' behavioral choices no longer have any impact on one another's well-being. In the latter instances, in what are sometimes referred to as "empty shell" relationships, the partners may continue to exist in close proximity, yet feel indifferent about one another's actions. At the point of complete disruption of a relationship, mutual independence may be the end product of a series of mutually frustrating, ineffectual, or unsatisfying interactions. Both persons may regard mutual independence as a desirable solution to those problems, but it is also likely to involve some degree of regret and real or perceived loss. Thus, the ambivalence about forming a relationship often finds its counterpart in ambivalence about ending it.

1.4.2 Privacy

In the dictionary sense of being apart from company and observation, privacy enables a person to be more or less in total control of his or her own outcomes. Two people, each with privacy, are obviously mutually independent. A well-developed theory of privacy is that of Altman (1975). His dialectical view is that the person strives to strike a balance between too little social interaction and too little privacy. People regulate privacy by various means, but prominently by managing the physical environment in ways that create territories over which each one has exclusive control. This territoriality reduces interdependence, through designating chairs, beds, drawers, tools, and so forth, as belonging to and reserved exclusively for oneself. Agreement about such arrangements increases the number of situations of mutual independence a pair will encounter and thereby serves to reduce the frequency of conflicts that may attenuate overall satisfaction with their relationship. For example, a major task of air travel is how to sustain independence from one's neighbors, "staking one's claim" to a portion of the available armrest and overhead bin space, avoiding unwanted interaction and unpleasant noise (e.g., crying babies), and in other respects reducing or eliminating interdependence with one's neighbors.

Altman's dialectical theory obviously has much in common with Eidelson's notion of the conflict between affiliation and autonomy. Furthermore, evidence from Altman and his colleagues' research (Altman & Taylor, 1973) is consistent with one of Eidelson's implications – that early encounters with conflictful interdependence jeopardizes continuation of a relationship. Pairs of sailors, initially unacquainted, were required to live together in isolation for eight uninterrupted days. Those pairs who best tolerated isolation established territories early in the period and then reduced them later on. Apparently, their success in limiting their first interactions to situations of mutual independence or low interdependence enabled them to develop the understandings and strong relationships necessary to survive the stresses of isolation. Altman observes that "territorial behavior [read "mutual independence"] has an important function in regulating social interaction, in easing the stresses of life, in clarifying roles" (1975, p. 143).

1.4.3 *"Time-Out" and Threat*

Mutual independence may sometimes be a temporary state that partners create as "time out" from conflictual interaction. Time-out may be brief or extended in duration. For example, during the course of a conflictual negotiation, the parties may create short-term independence so as to cool off and think things through (e.g., "We're at an impasse so let's take a break and come back to this later"). Alternatively, time-out may involve relatively more extended escape from problematic interaction. For example, close partners may agree to engage in periods of mutually agreed-upon independent action (e.g., "Let's take separate vacations this year"; "Since we have different preferences, let's go our own ways on Friday nights").

The varieties of time-out procedures call attention to the question of how movement from one situation to another is controlled (as in Entry #21). In the earlier-noted examples, the move to mutual independence typically is made bilaterally, by agreement. However, sometimes it is made unilaterally, as when a mother places her child in a playpen and goes about her other business. Although the situation that led to placing the child in a playpen is not one of mutual independence, the new situation becomes so when the child is placed there.

The unilateral move to mutual independence is often used as a threat. One person threatens to spend his or her Friday evenings independently, leaving the partner to make the best of it. Workers call a "strike," unilaterally withdrawing their labor from an employer and forcing both parties to rely on their independent resources. In these cases, the mutual independence is merely one in a sequence of situations. During its existence, the persons are mutually independent, each being solely in control of his or her own outcomes. When one person's level of outcomes from independent activity is poorer than that derived from interdependence, the partner's move or threatened move to mutual independence is a means of putting pressure on the person to make concessions in the area of interdependence.

Time-out as a deprivation has been studied extensively as a means for parents or teachers to modify the behavior of disobedient children. The technique has many variants but generally involves sending a child to a special place with the intention of depriving him or her of positive reinforcement. The child is sometimes sent to a different room, but in other cases, the disciplinarian simply withdraws all attention from the child. The temporary mutual independence is created unilaterally and is imposed for a fixed period of time or until some behavioral criterion is met. Of course, the time-out is not effective as a punishment if, through the child's Actor

Control (e.g., independent resources for pleasurable fantasies or singing to oneself), he or she is able to create as good or better outcomes than those derived from interdependence. Studies of the method suggest that it is a useful aid in treating children with a variety of behavioral problems (Hobbs & Forehand, 1977).

1.4.4 Being Alone: Its Circumstances and Consequences

The empirical literature suggests that people are alone about one-third of the waking hours of each day (Donner, Nash, Csikszentmihalyi, Chalip, & Freeman, 1981; Larson, Csikszentmihalyi, & Graef, 1982; Sorokin & Berger, 1939). Thus, being alone is clearly an important part of our lives. However, time alone occurs for different reasons and has a variety of consequences. Obviously, a person may be alone out of choice or as a result of being exiled or overlooked by potential partners. In the latter case, being alone is rather like "time-out" in that it is externally imposed and deprives one of ordinary satisfactions.

Larson et al. (1982) found that, suggestive of the ego-debilitating effects of the latter circumstances, being alone often depresses one's mood, making one feel "lonely," weaker, less cheerful, and less alert. When, as in these cases, being alone is nonvoluntary, we would expect a person's emotional reactions to reflect how their outcomes compare with those they typically receive or believe others receive from interaction. This idea is supported by research on the interaction correlates of feelings of "loneliness." The sheer frequency of being alone versus with others is only weakly associated with feelings of loneliness. However, when quality of interaction (i.e., its intimacy, pleasantness, amount of disclosure) is taken into account, the feelings of loneliness are fairly accurately predicted by the absence of interaction (Wheeler, Reis, & Nezlek, 1983). Apparently, loneliness is not primarily a matter of being alone (i.e., having little contact); it is more an effect of missing out on enjoyable interaction that fulfills important social motives (Brandstätter, 1983). Like other general evaluations of interpersonal situations, people's reactions to being alone involve comparisons with their real or imagined experiences in alternative situations.

1.4.5 Individual and Cultural Differences

Whether and how strongly people prefer independence to interdependence are reflected in dispositional measures of affiliation and autonomy motives. For example, in the Edwards Personal Preference Schedule (Edwards, 1959), the affiliation items include preferences "to do things for friends" and "to share things with friends." The autonomy items include preferences "to feel free to do what one wants" and "to be independent of others in making decisions." Autonomy motives have come under study in more recent research on clinical couples, illustrated by the "desire for independence" subscale of Christensen's (1987) Relationship Issues Questionnaire. Similarly, the recent study of adult attachment styles suggests that avoidance of closeness is a major component of how people relate to their romantic partners (Brennan, Clark, & Shaver, 1998). These various measures provide reliable distinctions among individuals in their orientations to interdependent life. This is one of many instances in which interpersonal dispositions are revealed in selections made between situations (cf. Entry #21).

Individual differences are also revealed by whether, in situations of low or ambiguous interdependence, people tend to act as if they and others are mutually independent or as if they and others are interdependent. There appear to be substantial differences among cultures in this regard (Markus & Kitiyama, 1991). In "individualistic" cultures, behavior is determined to a relatively greater extent by the individual's own personal goals and desires. That is, many situations of interdependence are treated as if they are ones of mutual independence. In contrast, individuals from "collective" cultures tend to treat more situations as ones of interdependence, taking more account of the impact of their actions on the interests of significant others.

1.4.6 Implications of Increasing Interdependence

As noted earlier in this entry, this situation of zero interdependence provides an anchoring point for our analysis of situations. In Figure 4.4, which displays the distribution of the symmetric 2×2 patterns in the space defined by the three dimensions (degree of interdependence, corresponding vs. conflicting interests, and coordination vs. exchange situations), the case of simple BAC possesses none of those three properties. When either or both of the other simple components, MPC and MJC, are added to BAC, there is an increase in interdependence and the resulting situation has some degree of the other two dimensions. As the shape of the solid in Figure 4.4 shows, with the increasing importance of the MPC and MJC components, the range of possibilities mushrooms in its diversity.

We might think of upward movement in the situational space as a route that a person takes as he or she leaves the privacy of personal quarters and ventures out into the interpersonal world. Alternatively, we might think of that movement as a path that a pair of people follow as they become increasingly "close," as they establish a friendly or working relationship, or as a pair of lovers moves into common quarters and becomes increasingly intimate. With the increase in interdependence, there arises an increasing potential for common interests achieved through exchange and coordination processes, as well as for conflicting interests with the exercise of Partner and Joint Control in their resolution. Furthermore, interdependence brings problems and opportunities associated with the response and information conditions in various situations. These conditions create issues of when to act and what to say, as well as problems of keeping track of the partner's actions and understanding their implicit and explicit communications.

The consequences of an increase in interdependence are varied. *First*, it frequently yields increases in *situation*-relevant attention, cognition, and affect. The more complex a situation is, the more we need to think about it in order to decide how to behave. The types of increased complexity outlined above sound rather difficult to comprehend, so it is reasonable to ask whether people are really aware of such complexities. Granted, few people analyze interpersonal situations using matrices or transition lists. At the same time, recent advances in the natural sciences make it evident that human intelligence is highly interpersonal in character (Tooby & Cosmides, 1992). In describing human intelligence as "interpersonal," we mean that people can identify key features of interaction situations insofar as such features: (a) are relevant to their personal well-being – that is, people can recognize the ways in which their outcomes may be affected by others' actions; and (b) are relevant to others' well-being – that is, people can recognize the ways in which others' outcomes may be affected by their own actions. Moreover, we suggest that such knowledge is relatively abstract, in that: (c) people can recognize that some interaction situations resemble previously encountered situations; and that (d) people respond to interpersonal situations as instances of general patterns rather than perceiving and responding to each situation de novo. Thus, one consequence of increasing interdependence is that people attend to key features of situations with increasing care, recognizing similarities between current situations and previously encountered situations: Each person will want to know "what is this situation all about?" (e.g., "Do I possess the power to unilaterally affect the other's outcomes?"; "Is there potential here for mutual cooperation?").

A *second*, related consequence of increasing interdependence is increased *person*-relevant attention, cognition, and affect. When our well-being is influenced by others' actions, each individual becomes interested in how the other is likely to behave and will devote increased thought to understanding and predicting the other (e.g., Berscheid, Graziano, Monson, & Dermer, 1976; Erber & Fiske, 1984). Each person will want to know "what sort of person is this, and how is this person likely to behave?" Indeed, highly interdependent situations provide rich opportunities for interpreting the meaning of one another's actions. Departures from the pursuit of one's direct, self-interested impulses are important clues as to "what sort of person is this?" If a partner provides me with good outcomes in a situation in which doing so is costly, I can infer that the partner is concerned with my well-being. If a partner behaves in a competitive manner even when the situation provided opportunities for mutual cooperation, I can infer that the partner is competitively oriented. Similarly, highly interdependent situations provide information about the meaning of one's own actions. Thus, self-presentation activities become more prominent with increased interdependence – each person will seek to communicate his or her own abilities, needs, and goals, either honestly or deceptively (e.g., Leary, 1995). Once again, departures from what is dictated by the situation proper are meaningful – departures from the pursuit of one's direct, self-interested impulses provide essential clues about "what sort of person I am."

A *third* consequence of increasing interdependence is an associated increase in the importance of learning- and adaptation-relevant activities. The complexity that frequently accompanies high interdependence means that people encounter more difficulties in their attempts to achieve good outcomes. Situations of total conflict of interests are essentially impossible to "solve." In such situations, people may be reduced to finding the best way to defend themselves or to escape from their interdependence. Situations of perfectly corresponding outcomes pose only the relatively easy problems of coordinating actions. However, most situations a person is likely to encounter are those of some but not perfectly corresponding interests. These make it important that the two arrive at a mutually acceptable course of action – a process that requires learning and using the skills necessary to adapt to each other's needs and inclinations, such as the skills of attribution and self-presentation described above. Relevant skills also involve using communication resources and response conditions to shape the interaction process and share an understanding of its direction and likely outcome. Communication can make explicit the consequences of particular events (e.g., "When you behave that way, it hurts me"; "I would benefit greatly if you were to enact Response A and I were to enact Response B"). Interdependence can also promote efficient use of sequential possibilities inherent in the situation (e.g., "You should go first"; "I promise not to change my behavior, once I act"). And, of course, people may attempt to influence one another's behavior via the use of threats, or via less heavy-handed methods, such as by proposing and explaining a mutually beneficial course of action or by invoking norms or prior commitments.

Implicit in the points above is a *fourth* consequence of increasing interdependence: "Person factors" – the abilities, needs, and goals that are relevant to interaction – become increasingly important. That is, stable "transformational tendencies" are activated. For example, when increases in interdependence are relatively short-term and the interests of the two persons are somewhat at odds (e.g., resources are perceived to be scarce), antisocial dispositions, values, or goals may be activated. People may wish to elevate the self at the expense of others (e.g., they may behave in a competitive manner, or may take pleasure in downward social comparison), or they may experience rivalry and engage in aggressive acts. Such shifts in the representation of self relative to others have been examined in the literatures regarding competition (e.g., McClintock, 1972a & 1972b) and aggression (Geen, 1998). In contrast, when increases in interdependence involve (a) temporally extended interaction in situations with (b) moderately to highly corresponding interests, such increases tend to be accompanied by shifts in self-concept involving movement from "me-ness" to "we-ness." Such shifts in self-representation have been examined in the empirical literatures regarding cohesiveness (e.g., Cota, Evans, Dion, Kilik, & Longman, 1995), self-other merger (e.g., Aron & Aron, 1997), cognitive interdependence (e.g., Agnew, Van Lange, Rusbult, & Langston, 1998), and commitment (e.g., Rusbult, Drigotas, & Verette, 1994). "We-ness" tends to bring with it increased attraction, along with the experience of "linkage" or attachment to the dyad or group. Also, members of cohesive, committed dyads and groups frequently take action to sustain stable membership (e.g., Levine & Thompson, 1996), engage in costly or effortful prosocial acts to benefit the group or dyad (e.g., Batson, 1998), and exert pressure on one another to conform to group- or dyad-relevant roles and norms (e.g., Cialdini & Trost, 1998).

Importantly, people derive "higher order outcomes" from the expression of person factors. The concrete outcomes specified in the *given* situation are augmented by the satisfaction or dissatisfaction derived from the expression of various motives and values, such as those of altruism, competition, the exercise of leadership, patience, and truth telling. Such outcomes are experienced from one's own activities and the underlying motives they plausibly serve. For example, a person may gain the positive outcomes of pride from helping a partner obtain good outcomes or, in a different relationship, from showing oneself to be more courageous than an opponent. And, for example, a person may suffer the negative outcome of guilt from failing to take account of a valued partner's outcomes and, instead, giving priority to one's own interests. Or one may feel shame about the cowardice shown in failing to stand up for one's partner when their rights have been challenged. Similar "higher order" outcomes are often provided by another's actions and the apparent reasons behind them. I may feel pleasure when my partner's actions show his or her concern for my well-being, or when my partner takes an initiative that effectively promotes our joint welfare. Such outcomes may be experienced even in cases where one's own concrete outcomes have not been affected, as when my partner helps another, needy person at some cost to himself or herself, and I draw satisfaction from the display of a generous disposition.

These higher order outcomes derived from the display of person factors play a central role in our most important relationships. Kelley (1979, pp. 163–64) has suggested that a relationship can be defined as "personal" to the degree that its interdependence entails the persons' attitudes and motives and, therefore, involves interdependence in both concrete outcomes and the symbolic and abstract outcomes based on perceptions of those attitudes and motives. Personal relationships are best illustrated by close friendships and love relationships, in which the signs of mutual responsiveness to and caring for one another's needs provide much of the strength of the bonds. In analogy to the "personal friend" or lover, there may also be the "personal enemy" whose behaviors are closely examined for the negative qualities they display, and whose successes and failures occasion, respectively, negative and positive outcomes. My rival's selfish actions may even be an occasion for satisfaction, when they confirm my worst expectations regarding his or her bad character.

Reprise. In short, with increasing interdependence, interpersonal life becomes more complex. Sometimes it is far more rewarding than solitary life, particularly if it exists in positive "personal relationships." But it may also be frustrating and unpleasant, if one becomes trapped in a relationship with a selfish and controlling person (as with the playground "bully), or involved in a personal vendetta with an aggressive rival. In either case, interdependent life is demanding of one's higher mental processes and, often, challenging to one's emotional susceptibilities. We can easily understand why people are often eager to enter into interdependence and frustrated when shunned or rejected by possible partners. We can also understand how people with little interpersonal experience or past failures in interaction find reasons to dread or, even, to avoid becoming interdependent.

1.5 Matrix Representations

Table E1.1. Mutual independence (Bilateral Actor Control, or BAC) in which A's #1 response benefits A (+8 in the upper right corners of the left cells) but has no effect on B's outcomes. Similarly, B's #1 response benefits B (+10 in lower left corners of the upper cells) but has no effect on A's outcomes.

TABLE E1.1

	A	
	a1	a2

		a1	a2
B	b1	+8 (top-right), +10 (bottom-left)	0 (top-right), +10 (bottom-left)
	b2	+8 (top-right), 0 (bottom-left)	0 (top-right), 0 (bottom-left)

Table E1.2. Mutual independence in which A's #1 response has a large positive effect on A's outcomes and A's #2 response, a sizable negative effect – the two responses having no effect on B's outcomes. Person B's #1 response enables B to avoid large negative outcomes and has no effect on A.

TABLE E1.2

	A	
	a1	a2

	a1	a2
	+8 (top-right), 0 (bottom-left)	−6 (top-right), 0 (bottom-left)
	+8 (top-right), −10 (bottom-left)	−6 (top-right), −10 (bottom-left)

Entry #2

Mutual Partner Control

I Scratch Your Back, You Scratch Mine

2.1 Examples

The Mutual Partner Control situation rests on each individual's preferences and aversion regarding the partner's possible behaviors. Each person's concern is "How do my partner's actions affect me, and how do my actions affect him or her?" This situation exists when people can benefit each other or not. For example, colleagues may (or may not) compliment each other's writing style, lovers may (or may not) exchange endearments, and cousins may (or may not) send each other greeting cards at Christmas. This situation also exists when people can harm each other or not. Members of opposing political parties may (or may not) deliver gratuitous insults and young siblings may (or may not) hurtfully poke each other. In each case, each person's choice is whether or not to have a positive or negative effect on the partner's outcomes.

2.2 Conceptual Description

There are two essential requirements for an ideal or "pure" situation of Mutual Partner Control. *First*, the outcome of each individual must be entirely in the hands of the interaction partner. Each individual's well-being is entirely under the control of the partner's actions. The individual can do nothing to enhance or ameliorate the partner's effect. For example, under many circumstances the two siblings can avoid or dodge each other's blows. To consider that as a situation of Mutual Partner Control, we would

Harold Kelley and Caryl Rusbult had primary responsibility for preparation of this entry.

have to imagine their being in some confined space (e.g., the back seat of the family car) where such dodging is not possible. (This illustrates the important general point that interdependence situations depend not only on the persons' abilities and vulnerabilities, but also on the physical circumstances in which they are interacting.) In short, A's effect on B's outcomes is absolute and not contingent on what B does in that setting. In this respect, the situation of Mutual Partner Control is to be contrasted with situations of Mutual Joint Control (Entries #3 and #4) in which a partner's effect is contingent on what the actor does.

The *second* requirement is that although each person's behavior is experienced as pleasurable or aversive by the recipient, it occurs at little or (ideally) no cost or benefit to that person. For example, if two neighbors both have successful vegetable gardens but one has a surplus of eggplant and the other has a surplus of tomatoes, each can give the other an item the other will value without making any sacrifice. Similarly, by loaning books or CDs not currently in use, each friend can benefit the other without cost to oneself. This condition does not preclude the possibility that costs or benefits may be incurred in a subsequent situation. Making an endearing remark to one's lover may yield later benefits and, of course, insults and snide comments are likely to have consequences subsequently. Even within the particular situation, if one makes the insulting remark before the other takes an action, the insult may provoke a counterremark that would not otherwise have been made. However, the requirement here (for "pure" Mutual Partner Control) is that each person's action, whether to benefit or harm, has no immediate *direct* effect on that person's own outcomes. (In this requirement, that a person's own outcomes are not directly affected by what that person does for or to the partner, the Mutual Partner Control situation is to be contrasted with many other situations, the most prominent being the Prisoner's Dilemma [Entry #5] in which benefiting the partner incurs some cost to the self.)

Formally, these two requirements are illustrated by the matrix representations of Mutual Partner Control shown in Tables E2.1 and E2.2 below (at the end of this entry). Those matrices show that A's control over B's outcomes is absolute and can be exercised without affecting A's own outcomes. And the same is true for B's control over A's outcomes.

2.3 Variants and Combinations

The behaviors that yield good or bad outcomes for the partner need not be similar for the two persons. One lover may provide an endearing remark and the other, a pleasurable foot massage. The neighbors exchange goods, one delivering eggplant and the other, tomatoes. In another variant of Mutual Partner Control, one person's options benefit the partner or not, and the partner's options harm the person or not. One sister may (or may not) compliment the other's coiffure and the latter may (or may not) make a snide remark about the first one's dress.

Mutual Partner Control situations may involve various levels of dependence. Each individual's well-being may be only weakly controlled by the partner's actions, in which case, each person is relatively indifferent to what the partner does. In the extreme, the degree of control is so slight that the situation is essentially one of zero dependence. (Compare this situation with Bilateral Actor Control [Entry #1] – pure independence.) Or, each one's well-being may be strongly controlled by the partner, in which case, each is greatly concerned about what the partner does.

Mutual Partner Control may also involve equal or unequal dependence. The two young siblings may be able to hurt each other to about the same degree, but in interaction between a younger and an older brother, the control over pain may be quite asymmetrical, as illustrated in Table E2.2 below and in Entry #11, Asymmetric Dependence.

Despite the simplicity of the Mutual Partner Control situation, it plays a very important role in interdependence, often being a major component of more complex situations. Some of the notable examples are the Prisoner's Dilemma (Entry #5) and the Threat Game (Entry #6).

2.4 Interaction Process and Person Factors

The clearly "desirable" sequences of interaction are those in which (for the case of help vs. not) the two persons give each other benefits and (for the case of hurt vs. not) the two persons abstain from harming each other. In our examples, we have found it natural to refer to an "exchange of endearments" or "exchange of goods." These labels highlight the fact that Mutual Partner Control is the basic element of situations in the broad interpersonal category commonly referred to as "exchange" processes and relationships. Its role in *"exchange"* is to be contrasted with the parallel role of situations of Mutual Joint Control (Entries #3 and #4) as essential elements in the broad category of *"coordination"* processes and relationships.

Situations are linked to patterns of interaction by the particular dispositions and norms that the interdependent persons express through their behavior, but the relevant dispositions and norms depend on the nature of the interdependence afforded by a given situation. For the Mutual Partner Control situation, those factors obviously have to do with helping another person or not, hurting or not, or helping versus hurting. In general, behavior within this situation reflects awareness of one's effects on the partner, and even if the behavior is performed without such awareness, it will often be interpreted by the recipient as involving such awareness. Actions in this situation make salient a person's degree of sensitivity to the partner's needs and vulnerabilities, and a person's willingness to benefit or harm that partner.

Considered in isolation, action that benefits the partner implies a degree of altruism, although that implication is tempered by the fact that the action incurs no cost. Altruism is more clearly indicated in contrasting situations where helping requires some sacrifice (for example, in Entries #5 or #8). Considered in isolation, an action that harms the partner implies a pointless maliciousness, or a wish to cause harm for its own sake, there being no benefit to self.

2.4.1 *Aversive and Beneficial Outcomes*
Although the concept of Mutual Partner Control draws no distinction between positive and negative outcomes, substantial evidence suggests that a given dose of negative outcome has greater impact than the same dose of positive outcome. Baumeister (1999) summarizes a great deal of relevant evidence under the heading that "bad is stronger than good." For example, a partner's destructive actions and transgressions have more impact on a relationship than constructive actions and prosocial acts. From a practical standpoint, then, Partner Control that inflicts harm on the partner may be more consequential, both for the individual and the relationship, than similar levels of Partner Control that benefit the partner.

2.4.2 *"Dominance"*
The circumstances surrounding Mutual Partner Control usually permit A and B to act freely, one or the other doing so first, or both acting at about the same time. Under these circumstances, it is possible for one person, let us say A, to use his or her Partner Control to exert some control over the other's behavior. Assuming also that circumstances permit A to communicate with B, A may say, in effect, "I'm going to wait and see what you do, and then I'll act accordingly, benefiting you if you have helped me but hurting you (or failing to benefit you) if you have hurt or failed to help me." Logically, we can see that if carried out, this combination of threat and promise tends

to transfer control over both persons' outcomes to B. By appropriate action, B can insure that both get benefits or that neither does so.

In using Partner Control in this manner, person A demonstrates the personal disposition known as "dominance." Buss and Craik (1980) obtained many behavioral examples of what undergraduate students regard as evidence of "dominance" and then had those examples judged by other students as to how well they illustrate the concept. Among the examples judged to be the best prototypes of "dominance" were these two:

> "He forbade her to leave the room."
> "She demanded that he run an errand."

It seems clear that these commands imply that the force of some promise or, more particularly, some threat lies behind them. They imply that the person exercising the influence has some Partner Control over the target of the influence and, vice versa, that the person being influenced has Partner Control over the influencer. If "*she* leaves the room" (which may be to the disadvantage of the influencer), *she* will be harmed. If "*he* runs the errand" (which may benefit the influencer), *he* may receive some benefit, but if he fails to run the errand, he will surely receive some harm. Thus, there are clear implications as to the Mutual Partner Control situations in which these kinds of influence events occur.

If there is any doubt about what is implied by the influence attempts described in those sentences, it is eliminated by the use of abstract influence scenarios that make explicit the veiled promise/threat components (Kelley, 1997b). The abstract scenario based logically on Mutual Partner Control interdependence is this:

> "He (she) used threat or promise, implicitly or explicitly, to get the other(s) to do what he (she) wanted them to do."

In short, person A uses Partner Control over B to induce B to use B's Partner Control in a way favorable to A. When items of the type given above from Buss and Craik were judged as to their conformity to this abstract scenario, they were rated very highly. In other words, that scenario is a "prototype" of the kind of influence those items represent. Furthermore, when the abstract scenario itself is rated along with Buss and Craik items for how well they represent "dominance," the scenario receives as high ratings as the best of the Buss and Craik items. Those results are to be contrasted with parallel results for certain other examples from Buss and Craik (e.g., "He assigned roles and got the game going") which can be logically linked to the Mutual Joint Control pattern with corresponding interests (Entry #3). In general, this analysis of contrasting influence events as they are logically based in contrasting situations illustrates the benefits of acquiring familiarity with situational structures. Those structures help us make useful distinctions among the numerous and confusing varieties of interpersonal events.

2.4.3 Social Norms

Just as different situations "bring out" or afford expression to different personal attitudes and values, different situations provide the rationale for different social norms. Turiel (1983) draws a contrast between moral norms and conventional norms, which have distinctly different scenarios of admonition, transgression, and reaction. The distinction between Mutual Partner Control (i.e., "exchange") situations and Mutual Joint Control (i.e., "coordination") situations with common interest provides a rationale for these two types of norms: *Moral* norms are logically relevant and necessary to the former, and *conventional* norms are logically relevant and necessary to the latter. Conventional norms are described in Entry #3, Corresponding Mutual Joint Control, which deals with situations that pose coordination problems. Here, we briefly consider the moral norms.

Moral norms exhort the person to help and not hurt others. Thus, their pertinence to decisions in Mutual Partner Control situations is obvious. In observations of children's interaction on the playground, Turiel and his colleagues (Nucci & Turiel, 1978) were able to identify interactions in which one child transgresses a moral norm, for example, by hitting or taking something from another child, or by not sharing. The observed reaction to this transgression, whether by another child or a teacher, involves invoking the norm, calling attention to the harm done, and delivering or threatening to deliver punishment for further transgression. Turiel's colleagues were able further to show that second graders and even many preschool children have good understanding of moral norms (Turiel, 1983). They know the kinds of behavior prohibited by these norms, they say that those would be wrong even if there were no explicit rules against them, and they understand that the moral norms are applicable everywhere and at all times. In short, they know the difference between these universal or absolute rules for behavior, and the more time- and place-specific rules that define the "conventions" necessary for smooth social transactions.

Here, as in the case of the meaning of the disposition "dominance," our distinctions between situations help us understand the special properties of distinguishable normative systems as well as the beliefs associated with those systems. Turiel writes that "systems of actions are coordinated with systems of thought" (1983, p. 48). He might also have observed that both actions and thoughts are coordinated with and, indeed, derived from situations of interdependence.

2.4.4 *Implicit Accommodation*

Some of the few laboratory studies concerned with pure Mutual Partner Control have revealed the interesting fact that persons in this kind of situation may reach an accommodation through implicit processes, even in the absence of explicit knowledge of their interdependence. The laboratory setting, often described as the "minimal social situation," places a pair of subjects in a Mutual Partner Control situation that occurs on repeated occasions. Placed in separate rooms and without knowledge of each other, each subject has two response options and, after each choice, receives one of two outcomes, either a "point" on a counter or a mild electric shock. Each one's problem, then, is to determine what choices to make in order to avoid the shocks and increase the points. However, a person's choices have no effect on that person's own outcomes. The two rooms are interconnected in a way such that each one's choices determine whether the *partner* receives a shock or a point. They are, without knowing it, in a recurrent situation of simple Mutual Partner Control.

Following earlier work by Sidowski, Wyckoff, and Tabory (1956), Kelley, Thibaut, Radloff, and Mundy (1962) showed that under certain conditions (namely, when the response conditions require them to make their choices at the same time), subjects are able greatly to improve their ability to avoid shock and gain points. This means, of course, that they implicitly learn to benefit and to avoid harming each other – "implicitly" because they do this without becoming aware of each other. The accommodation occurs because each one tends to obey a simple version of the law of reinforcement, repeating their last choice after receiving a point but changing it after a shock. At some point, each has just shocked the other, and each changes to their other response. They then give each other points and they each continue to do so. This research is one of several lines of work showing that mutual accommodation in interdependence situations does not always require full information and explicit communication. (See Kelley, 1968, for other examples.)

2.5 Matrix Representations

Table E2.1. Mutual Partner Control in which A's #1 response benefits B (causing the +8 in the lower left corners of the left cells) but has no effect on A's outcomes (in the upper right corners of each cell). Similarly, B's #1 response benefits A (causing the +10 in upper right corners of the upper cells) but has no effect on B's outcomes (in the lower left corners).

TABLE E2.1

		A	
		a1	a2
B	b1	+10 / +8	+10 / 0
	b2	0 / +8	0 / 0

Table E2.2. Asymmetric Mutual Partner Control in which A's #1 response has a large negative effect on B's outcomes but B's #2 response has only a small negative effect on A's outcomes.

TABLE E2.2

		A	
		a1	a2
B	b1	0 / −10	0 / 0
	b2	−2 / −10	−2 / 0

Entry #3

Corresponding Mutual Joint Control

Getting in Sync

3.1 Examples

Each person's outcomes depend on the joint effect of what the two persons do. Each one is concerned not about their own action or the partner's action, but only about the combination of their two actions. For example, when two friends agree to meet for dinner, the particular restaurant each goes to is less important than that they both go to the same place. When two cars approach each other on a two-lane road, both drivers strongly prefer that both keep to their respective sides, either to the left (as in England) or to the right (as in the United States). Success in attempting to move a heavy piece of furniture without dragging it over the floor requires that one person lift one end and the other person, the other end. When two boys want to practice their baseball skills, it is necessary for one to pitch and the other to bat; other combinations, both pitching or both batting are, to say the least, unsatisfactory.

3.2 Conceptual Description

In each of the above examples, both persons gain benefits and/or avoid harm from the same combinations of behavior. As a consequence, they desire that their behaviors be "coordinated" in some particular way. In the simplest case, each person is indifferent as among the several mutually preferred combinations, so they have a common interest in doing one – any one – of those combinations. In these simple cases it is easy for the

Harold Kelley had primary responsibility for preparation of this entry.

two to agree to produce one of the better combinations (going to the same restaurant, driving to the left, lifting at opposite ends, one pitching while the other bats) and to avoid the less desirable ones.

In their early writings, Thibaut and Kelley (1959) referred to this situation as "mutual behavior control." The rationale was that in this type of situation, if one person overtly takes a particular action or indicates an intention to do so, the other person will adjust his or her behavior accordingly. So each person has the potential, by varying his/her behavior, to induce the other to modify his/her behavior. Inasmuch as each has the potential for control over the other's behavior, the control is mutual. In this Atlas, we refer to this pattern as one of Mutual Joint Control (MJC for short), to describe the fact that each person's outcomes are controlled jointly by the actions of both their own and the partner's actions.

Among the situations that can be described by simple, 2 × 2 outcome matrices, this situation, along with those described in Entries #1, #2, and #4, is one of four basic patterns. The persons' concerns in the present case – with the combinations of their actions – are to be contrasted with their concerns about only their own actions (in Entry #1) or about only their partner's actions (in Entry #2). The shared preferences for certain combinations in the present case are to be contrasted with their conflicting preferences among the various possible combinations that is characteristic of the coordination problem with conflicting interests (Entry #4). As described in chapter 2, those four situations are "basic" in the sense that all the other 2 × 2 patterns of interdependence can be shown to be composed of two or more of these basic patterns, combined in various magnitudes and orientations (Kelley & Thibaut, 1978). Thus, the four constitute the basic elements of 2 × 2 interdependence.

3.3 Variants and Neighbors

As the earlier examples illustrate, coordination problems may require similar actions from the two persons (both going to the same restaurant) or complementary actions (one boy pitches and the other bats). Coordination problems also vary in whether they involve insuring good outcomes (as in meeting for dinner at the same place, illustrated by Table E3.1 below, at the end of this entry) or avoiding bad outcomes (as in using opposite sides of the road to avoid a collision). A variant on the mutual desire to be together in order to have pleasant experiences involves the mutual desire to be apart in order to avoid unpleasant ones (illustrated by Table E3.2 below). For example, a recently divorced man and woman may prefer to go to different coffeehouses in order to avoid embarrassing encounters.

The metaphor of the 10-ton gorilla (who sits wherever he wants) reminds us that the dependence on coordinating with one's partner may be unilateral. Coordination may be more important to one person than to the other. This asymmetry is revealed by the interaction in which the smaller gorilla waits for her 10-ton uncle to locate himself before finding a seat for herself.

The representation of a situation in which such waiting is possible requires locating the outcome controls within a transition list. The list in Table E3.3 below shows a sequential-temporal structure that permits either actor to wait and see what the other one does before acting. The outcomes in the list correspond to those in Table E3.2 where matching actions (a1b1 and a2b2) are to be avoided because they yield negative consequences for both persons. In this list, an action can be taken at any time inasmuch as the "null" responses, aN and bN, permit the designated person to do nothing – to "wait" – at the particular juncture. However, once taken, an action is irrevocable. This structure makes it possible, for example, for person A to wait until B acts and then do the opposite, thereby enabling the negative outcomes to be avoided. If this interaction sequence occurs, it suggests that B exercises a sort of "leadership" and A follows that lead. Even with this flexible structure, there remains a coordination problem for the pair, regarding who acts and who waits.

Mutual Joint Control with corresponding interests has several important "neighbors" in the situational space shown in Figure 4.4 of chapter 4: "Hero" (Entry #8) and "Turn Taking" (also known as the "Battle of the Sexes"). In those and similar cases, the two persons have common interests in which combinations of their actions to avoid but conflicting interests about which of the more desirable combinations to enact. For example, the two boys practicing for baseball may both prefer to bat rather than pitch. They have a shared interest in having one pitch and the other bat, but each may prefer to bat while the other pitches. Taking turns in playing the preferred role in this kind of situation provides a solution to the degree of conflict inherent in it.

3.4 Interaction Process and Person Factors

Although persons in this situation have no conflict of interest, they nevertheless have a "problem," namely, which of the mutually desirable behavior combinations they should enact. Offhand, this problem may seem minor, one that is easily solved. And it usually is. However, it is useful to examine the various ways it is solved. These ways illustrate the wide range of processes and factors relevant to interdependent interaction: reasoning, interaction adjustments, individual dispositions, complementary patterns of dispositions, rules and norms, and institutionalization. Which one or set of these factors enters into the coordination process depends on the novelty of the problem and the circumstances surrounding it.

3.4.1 *Tacit Coordination through Reasoning*

Out of sight or communication with each other and dealing with a novel problem, the two persons may have to make their selections independently. For example, the recently divorced couple, both desiring to avoid meeting, is likely to make their selections independently and without prior information about each other's movements. Under these highly constrained circumstances, a pair may still be able to coordinate by ad hoc reasoning and using their knowledge of each other. (This problem, of how coordination can be achieved tacitly, has been discussed at length by certain philosophers [e.g., by D. K. Lewis, 1969, to understand the conventions of language] and by game theorists [e.g., T. C. Schelling, 1960, to explore possible means of conflict resolution].) For example, a man planning to hike the length of the John Muir Trail in the Sierra Nevadas and unable to carry all the supplies he will need, may make arrangements with his wife to leave a cache of supplies at a particular trail junction along the route. Not knowing the particular physical features at the junction, they can make no specific designation of the cache's location. If the transfer of supplies is to succeed, their problem is to coordinate the independently selected "hiding" location with the similarly selected "seeking" location. (This common interest problem can be contrasted, of course, with the conflicting interest Mutual Joint Control situation, Entry #4, illustrated by the game of "hide-and-seek.") The problem is solved by commonsense reasoning on the part of both the hider and the seeker. At the trail junction, each identifies plausible hiding places – ones that offer concealment from a causal passerby, but that stand out (have a functional salience) as "hiding places" for persons who know of the agreement. That reasoning reduces the number of possible locations considerably. There is likely to be further delimitation by the hiders' and seekers' familiarity with each other: "Where is Bill likely to think is an obvious place to look?" "What is Beth likely to regard as a good place to hide the cache?" The reasoning process analyzes the physical environment with a particular focus on how it is likely to be analyzed by the other person. They make a meta-analysis of each others' thoughts, and may implicitly extend that to a meta-meta-analysis along the lines of "Where will she think I am likely to think she will think to hide it?"

3.4.2 *Interaction Adjustments*

If the two persons are in sight of each other or in other ways can know what each other is beginning to do, they can adjust to each other's behavior. For example, two persons walking in opposite directions along a narrow passage have to coordinate about which sides they will pass on. This sometimes results in a sort of to-and-fro "dance," each dodging back and forth until they settle on a particular combination of their actions. The Mutual Joint Control properties of the situation are vividly revealed in this spontaneous interaction pattern. As it may occur between persons of the opposite sex who are passing on the sidewalk, Sigmund Freud suggested that the pattern reveals implicit sexual desires.

3.4.3 *Interpersonal Dispositions ("Initiative")*

In cases such as that above, one person can exercise a kind of leadership by firmly adopting one behavior and requiring the other to coordinate with it. This is an example of the principle that the corresponding interests, Mutual Behavior Control situation often enables people to show their willingness to take the initiative in interaction. (That, in turn, is an example of the general principle that interdependence situations make it possible for people to express or reveal certain aspects of their social personalities – their dispositions relevant to interpersonal relations. By the same token, interdependence situations can be used diagnostically, to assess individual differences in the particular dispositions each situation can reveal.)

The willingness to take initiative in common interest coordination problems appears to be one component of what is commonly understood by the trait term "dominance." This is shown by research based on Buss and Craik's (1980) study of common conceptions of this trait. They obtained many behavioral examples of what undergraduate students regard as evidence of "dominance" and had those examples judged by other students as to how well they illustrate the concept. Among the examples judged to be the best prototypes of "dominance" were these two:

> "He assigned roles and got the game going."
> "On the auto trip, she decided which direction to take when they got lost."

These items appear to describe an initiative-taking scenario in which one person takes the lead and depends on others to follow his/her example – a scenario indicating the first person's disposition to exercise leadership in achieving a mutually desired coordination. If there is any doubt about what is implied by those examples, it is eliminated by the use of abstract influence scenarios that make explicit the initiative process (Kelley, 1997b). The abstract scenario based logically on common interest, mutual behavior control is this:

> "He (she) acted first, creating a situation where the other(s) had to do what he (she) wanted them to do."

When the two concrete items above, identified by Buss and Craik, were judged as to their conformity to this abstract scenario, they were rated very highly. In other words, the abstract scenario is a "prototype" of the kind of influence those concrete items represent. Furthermore, when the abstract scenario is rated along with the Buss and Craik items for how well they represent "dominance," the scenario receives as high ratings as the most prototypic of Buss and Craik's items. These results are to be contrasted with parallel results for certain other examples from Buss and Craik's study (e.g., "She demanded that he run an errand") which can be linked logically to the Mutual Partner Control pattern (Entry #2) and its implicit use to enforce commands.

Thus, there seem to be two distinguishable components of what we mean in common language when we use the term "dominance." One entails the exercise of Partner Control by way of promise and/or threat, and the other entails assertiveness exercised to expedite commonly desired coordinations. Note that the latter implies a willingness to take responsibility for the success or failure of the coordinated effort.

3.4.4 *Complementary Patterns of Dominance-Submission*

If a pair faces frequent common interest coordination problems of the sort considered here, we might expect their interaction to be most efficient if one person is inclined to be "dominant" (i.e., to quickly take the initiative) and the other to be "submissive" (i.e., to wait and follow the other's lead). With similar tendencies in these respects, we would expect them either to get in each other's way or to get very little accomplished through mutual inactivity. This hypothesis is supported by experimental studies using, for example, a task requiring a high degree of coordination in the control of two model trains running in opposite directions on the same track but with sidings that enable passing (Ghiselli & Lodahl, 1958; Smelser, 1961). A different task, employed by Fry (1965), required two subjects, making repeated independent selections among three options, to learn to match their successive choices. Pairs performing effectively on this task were those having members widely different in their scores on an ascendance-submission scale. Presumably, this difference enabled pairs to avoid a struggle over who should set the pattern of successive selections and who should copy it.

The benefits of this complementarity have also been shown in relationships of longer duration. The difficulties encountered by people who are similarly high on "dominance" are illustrated by Altman and Taylor (1973) in their study of pairs of men forced to live in isolation in confined quarters – clearly, situations of high interdependence with numerous coordination problems. Pairs of men both of whom were high on a measure of desire for control experienced a great deal of conflict initially and then became very territorial, developing living arrangements in which each individual had exclusive use of certain objects and areas. Territoriality is obviously a way of reducing interdependence and thereby eliminating coordination problems.

Winch (1958) advanced the theory that people select each other for marriage on the basis of complementarity in their needs. He suggested, for example, that a person with a strong need to help others will pair off with a person with a strong need to be helped. As Turner (1970) summarizes Winch's evidence, he concludes that the hypothesis is clearly supported only for the type of complementarity considered here, that is, in dominance-deference. Turner interprets this as an indication of the "economy of decision making" achieved when one partner is assertive and the other is receptive.

Like most such broad generalizations, the complementarity hypothesis is undoubtedly limited in its applicability. People in ongoing relationships usually experience not only common interest coordination problems but also most of the other situations described in this Atlas, including ones with conflict of interest and a variety of exchange situations with their potential problems of fairness. This array of situations generally includes many in which the more active or assertive member of the pair will be tempted to pursue his/her own outcomes at the expense of the partner's. So we should not expect the "assertive-receptive" relationships always to show high pair satisfaction and adjustment. This qualification may help explain why, despite the plausibility of Winch's notions, studies of romantic relationships provide far more support for similarity between the partners than for complementarity (Berscheid & Reis, 1998). Only if there are positive attitudes on both sides and/or a preponderance of common interest situations (both the marks of similarity between partners), will a pair composed of a "leader" and "follower" be efficient in dealing with both coordination problems and issues of fairness in exchange.

3.4.5 *Rules and Norms*

Just as contrasting situations afford expression to different interpersonal dispositions, they provide the basis for contrasting norms. As described for Entry #2, Turiel (1983) draws a distinction between moral norms and conventional norms. The rationale for these two types of norms is found in the distinction between Mutual Partner Control situations (Entry #2) and the present situation, Mutual Joint Control with corresponding interests. Moral norms are logically relevant to the former and conventional norms, to the latter.

Moral norms exhort persons to exercise their control over others with consideration of how it affects those others. Moral norms have the same simple message across all the situations to which they are relevant (i.e., those possessing Partner Control): One should help and not hurt others. In contrast, conventional norms have a degree of arbitrariness, as implied by the very term "conventional," which refers to something based on custom or usage. That arbitrariness derives from the fact that common interest MJC situations afford multiple ways of establishing a satisfactory coordination – two ways in our 2 × 2 matrices. If a certain coordination problem occurs repeatedly for a group of people, it is in their mutual interest to develop a rule or norm about the *particular* way in which coordination is to be achieved. Such norms avoid the necessity of depending on ad hoc or tacit modes of coordination or on coordination based on complementarity in personality. The convention for a particular situation designates one of the several coordination solutions as the "proper" one for a particular group of persons. Perhaps this is best illustrated by the rules about which side of the road one should drive on, which illustrates both the arbitrariness (the rule is different in different parts of the world) and the importance of a convention (in eliminating reliance on spur-of-the-moment solutions to the "passing" problem).

In observations of children's interaction on the playground, Turiel and his colleagues (Nucci & Turiel, 1978) were able to identify and distinguish transgressions of both kinds of norms. Transgressions of moral norms, for example, hitting or taking something from another child, were dealt with rather harshly, with the injured child or the teacher delivering or threatening punishment for further transgressions. Transgressions of conventional norms were more benign, involving actions that merely inconvenience or disturb others (e.g., failing properly to line up for returning to

class, talking without raising one's hand) but that are not particularly harmful and often are as unpleasant for the transgressor as for the others. The
response to such transgressions is milder: The deviant child's attention is
drawn to the disorder he/she has created by not properly meshing his/her
actions with those of other pupils, and sometimes the child is ridiculed for
the ignorance or ineptness revealed in the miscoordination.

The researchers were able further to show that the children themselves
have considerable understanding of the distinction between the two
kinds of norms. They know the kinds of behavior prohibited by the moral
norms, they say that those would be wrong even if there were no explicit
rules against them, and they understand that the moral norms are not arbitrary but are applicable everywhere and at all times. In contrast, they know
that the conventional rules are exactly that – "conventional." They can
imagine other groups or places at which the rules are different from the ones
at their school. In short, they know the difference between the universal
rules for good behavior (the moral norms) and the more arbitrary, time- and
place-specific rules that define the "conventions" useful for smooth social
transactions.

3.4.6 *Local Institutionalization*

Children's recognition of the arbitrariness of conventions implies that if
pupils find personal reasons to do so, they will feel some freedom to depart from the conventions. This latitude makes it desirable to have an
"institutionalized" or formal specification and enforcement of the conventions. Of course, moral norms are also "institutionalized," as reflected in
the precepts of the church, the community, and the law. However, being
adapted to the particular coordination problems that arise within a certain
group setting, conventional norms are usually defined and enforced by
the local institutions of that group. In the school yard, the conventions are
largely those defined by the school and the teachers. The teacher is the
one who detects transgressions and enforces the rules. She represents the
institution's "shared" definition of desirable uniformities – in when and
where to line up, rules for speaking in class, and where school yard games
are to be played. In other settings (work groups, athletic teams, etc.), especially those in which there are rapid shifts in the concrete nature of coordination problems, institutionalization takes the form of designated lead-
ers, such as supervisors, coaches, and quarterbacks. Persons in these roles
take the initiative in directing the selection among possible combinations
of actions according to what the momentary concrete problems seem to
demand.

3.4.7 *The Seriousness of Conventional Transgressions*

We all know that the arbitrariness of conventions is reflected in their changes over time and variations from group to group. Clothing fashions come and go, rules of etiquette slowly shift, gender-based conventions shift from generation to generation, and so forth. However, we should not conclude that deviations from conventional norms never have serious consequences. The rules of orderly behavior on the playground do not deal with matters of great consequence, but (to return to the obvious example) rules about driving on the "customary" side of the road do.

In work settings, failures to adhere to coordination conventions may be as important as failures to follow moral norms. This is illustrated by Steiner's (1972) analysis of two types of process loss that occur in work groups. "Process losses occur when (a) organizational [i.e., coordination] problems are not solved in the best possible manner, and/or (b) members of the group are not optimally motivated to employ their resources to create a group outcome" (p. 88). The former reflect deviations from conventions, such as would result from ignorance of the common practices or inattentiveness to their application. The latter reflect deviations from the moral norms of doing one's share and helping others, due to laziness or selfish freeloading. Steiner observes that for tasks requiring complex division and temporal meshing of labor, the losses deriving from malcoordination may be very serious. Obviously, if the stakes are high enough, a person can seriously harm others by failure properly to coordinate with them. In the possible deleterious consequences of their transgressions, conventional and moral norms may not be sharply distinguished. However, they are importantly different in that moral transgressions harm others but, reflecting the mutual interest in coordination, conventional transgressions often harm the actor as well as the others.

3.5 Matrix and Transition List Representations

Table E3.1. Mutual Joint Control in which two persons have a common interest in combinations of similar behavior, a1b1 or a2b2. Both persons can get good outcomes by coordinating their behaviors to produce one of those combinations. Person A, whose outcomes are shown in the upper right corner of each cell, is benefited somewhat more by coordination than is person B. For example, two young people want to spend the evening together in one of their respective apartments rather than separately, and person A is somewhat more desirous of this.

TABLE E3.1

	A	
	a1	a2

B	a1	a2
b1	+10 +5	0 0
b2	0 0	+10 +5

Table E3.2. Mutual behavior control, with a common interest in combinations of different behavior, a1b2 or a2b1. Both persons can avoid negative outcomes by coordinating their behaviors to produce one of those combinations. For example, two persons who find each other's company distasteful have a common desire to have lunch at different tables in the restaurant.

TABLE E3.2

	A	
	a1	a2

B	a1	a2
b1	−10 −10	0 0
b2	0 0	−10 −10

Table E3.3. This sequential-temporal structure permits either person to wait, by selecting the null option (aN or bN), thus permitting the other person to act first. For example, if A waits and B selects the b1 option, the pair is moved to juncture K, where B's initial action is still in effect – it is "irrevocable." At K, A may select a1 (to their mutual detriment), a2 (to their mutual advantage – what A is likely to do knowing what B's action has been), or aN (which returns A to the K juncture to make another selection.

TABLE E3.3 *Representation of a Situation in Which Either Person Can Wait for the Other to Take the First Action*

Junctures	Options	Possible Selections	Outcomes for A	B	Transition to Next Juncture
[J	(a1, a2, aN)	a1b1	−10	−10	X]
[	(b1, b2, bN)	a1b2	0	0	X]
[		a2b1	0	0	X]
[		a2b2	−10	−10	X]
[		aNb1	−	−	K]
[		aNb2	−	−	L]
[		a1bN	−	−	M]
[		a2bN	−	−	N]
[		aNbN	−	−	J]
[K	(a1, a2, aN)	a1b1	−10	−10	X]
[	(b1)	a2b1	0	0	X]
[		aNb1	−	−	K]
[L	(a1, a2, aN)	a1b2	0	0	X]
[	(b2)	a2b2	−10	−10	X]
[		aNb2	−	−	L]
[M	(a1)	a1b1	−10	−10	X]
[	(b1, b2, bN)	a1b2	0	0	X]
[		a1bN	−	−	M]
[N	(a2)	a2b1	0	0	X]
[	(b1, b2, bN)	a2b2	−10	−10	X]
[		a2bN	−	−	N]

Entry #4

Conflicting Mutual Joint Control

Match or Mismatch

4.1 Examples

A younger brother wants to "hang out" with his older brother and be at the same place as the older one, but the older brother finds that the younger one "cramps his style" and prefers not to have the younger one around. So the situation is one of hide and seek, with the older brother doing the hiding and the younger, the seeking. In marriages, situations of this type are sometimes reflected in a general conflict over closeness. One member of the couple wants a close relationship while the partner wants more independence. (Christensen and Heavey [1993] report that in heterosexual pairs, it is usually the woman who wants closeness.)

Athletic competitions, whether they be individual or team contests, involve one situation of this sort after another. The concepts of "offense" and "defense" are based on the distinction between different preferences about being "with" or being "separate from" another person or team: The offense wants to go to a location different from where the defense is located but the defense wants to be where the offense is. The preferences can shift rapidly. For example, in baseball the batter wants to swing where the ball "is" but then wants the ball to travel to where the fielders "aren't." In other words, the batter "defends" the plate (as the coach often instructs the Little Leaguer) but acts offensively in relation to the other team's defense. In boxing, each man shifts from defensive dodging to offensive striking on a moment-by-moment basis.

Harold Kelley had primary responsibility for preparation of this entry.

4.2 Conceptual Description

As in the case of Entry #3 (MJC with corresponding outcomes), each person's outcomes depend on the joint effect of what the two persons do. However, in contrast to that situation, here the two persons have different preferences among the various combinations of their behaviors. In the simplest case, illustrated in Table E4.1 below (at the end of this entry), one person's positive outcomes in each cell are equal to the other person's negative ones. This type of situation is known as a "zero-sum" game because one person's gains equal the other's losses. Structurally, the situation is a "competitive" one. As in the case of the corresponding interest version of MJC (Entry #3), there is a "coordination" problem, but here there is no mutually acceptable "solution" – no basis for agreement about what to do. Like Entry #3, this entry is one of the four basic patterns of interdependence from which all 2 × 2 outcome matrices are derived.

4.3 Variants

The situation may not be a zero-sum game. For example, though opposite in signs, the outcomes in each cell may be unequal in magnitude. This would be true in the example above if the younger brother is less concerned about being with the older one than the latter is about avoiding the younger one.

The situation of coordination with conflicting interests lends itself to many important variants when we employ transition lists to describe the sequential-temporal problems that arise around such coordinations. For example, common in athletic contests are situations that permit an adept person (e.g., a running back in football) to gain an advantage in the coordination by misleading clumsy opponents (e.g., large defensive linemen) as to his intentions by taking a tentative action which induces them to commit theirselves to move in a particular direction which the more agile person then renders irrelevant by quickly reversing his direction.

The problem of interdependent escape from an impending danger is one of many coordination problems that may involve conflicting interests. Assume that the escape route allows only one person to escape at a time and, after some period, it closes down entirely. If that period is brief, only one person may be able to escape. This is shown in Table E4.2 below, where if one person tries to escape while the other one waits, the former avoids the danger, but if both try to escape, neither succeeds (they become jammed in the exit), and if neither tries to escape, the possibility of escape is lost to both.

An extended variant of this situation, which permits both persons to escape, can be represented by the transition list shown in Table E4.5 below. This list describes two successive points in time at which escape is possible. At juncture J, if both wait (awbw) or try to escape (atbt), they waste that moment in time and are moved to juncture K. There the control pattern is identical to that in Table E4.2 below, where if both wait or try to escape, neither does so and both suffer the negative consequences, but if one waits and lets the other try to escape, the latter avoids those consequences. However, at juncture J in this transition list, it is possible for one to escape (e.g., the "awbt" pattern of selections, with A waiting and B trying, permits person B to escape and exit from the situation) while permitting the other person to have a second moment in time which permits escape (e.g., the "awbt" selections move A to juncture L where A has complete control over his or her own outcomes and can escape or not). It should be clear that the situation permits both to escape if they can agree on the *order* in which they should use the escape option. The reader will realize that this "variant" in effect changes the conflicting interest MJC into one with corresponding interests: Both can escape if they can coordinate on one of the two possible orders of using the escape option. In general, the establishment of orderly queues depends on explicit or implicit agreements that establish rules about the sequence in which people will have access to avenues of escape from negative outcomes or to gain positive outcomes. (The reader interested in learning more about transition lists is referred to Kelley, 1984b.)

4.4 Interaction Process and Person Factors

One of the most important prescriptive principles regarding interdependence situations specifies the implications of common versus conflicting interests for the transmission of information. In situations of common interest, persons are well advised to be open, honest, and trusting in their communications, because full and valid information exchange increases the likelihood of solving the common problem. In situations of conflict of interest (as in our present case), they are well advised to do the opposite. Any valid information you provide the other person enables that person to gain at your expense. Most of the varieties of interaction patterns observed in this situation revolve around the control of information, both in its provision and in its acquisition.

4.4.1 Problems of Hiding

In an example given for Entry #3, the helpful wife's problem is to hide the supply cache where her hiking husband will think to look and, then, find it. Here the problem is to hide where the other person won't think to look. In trying to avoid his younger brother, the big brother tries to go to a place that doesn't appear on the younger one's mental map. In the absence of such options, an alternative means of hiding is provided by camouflage. In the family parlor game of "hide the thimble," there is the rule that the thimble must be hidden within a circumscribed area and must be in plain sight. This creates the challenge of finding a place where the thimble blends in with its surroundings. This information control task is handled in nature and military equipment by camouflage, that is, adopting a pattern of coloration that blends in with the typical surroundings.

4.4.2 Misdirection

Rather than withholding information by hiding, one may approach the information control problem by providing misleading information. In dynamic competitive interaction, the person on the "defense" watches closely to see what the other is likely to do. The importance of anticipating the other's move makes the defensive player highly susceptible to small cues (e.g., a movement of the head, or "head fake") and, thus, to being misled or "faked out." The successful offense often begins an action which, once the defense reacts to it, can be adjusted to their reaction. So the "fake" serves both to provide (false) information and gain (credible) information. In the process of adjustment and counteradjustment, the opponents' relative perceptiveness and agility become apparent to the observer.

4.4.3 Lying and Its Detection

As a misleading expression of one's intention, the "fake" is a kind of lie. Thus, like the "fake," the essential purpose of lying is to lead another person to make an adjustment to your behavior which, relative to the adjustment they would make if they knew the truth, is to your advantage and their disadvantage.

When the older brother tells the younger one what he intends to do on a particular occasion, can the younger one tell what the true intention is? Is the truth being told with an expectation it will not be believed, or is the statement a lie told in the hope it will be believed? There has been a great deal of research on detecting lying, though none of it deals with such simple situations as that of the two brothers. The speakers' statements have generally been ones that express their feelings or opinion about some person or issue. (For summaries, see Depaulo, 1994, and DePaulo & Friedman, 1998.) It appears that when presented with a set of videos that show instances of known truthful and untruthful statements, samples of persons from diverse backgrounds and with varying experience are in considerable agreement as to which instances they label as "truth-telling" versus "lying." However, although their judgments correspond to the facts to some degree, over a number of separate studies, the correspondence is almost never very much greater than chance. While there seems to be a general belief that important clues as to lying are to be found in the speaker's face (e.g., to detect deception, people prefer to interact face-to-face rather than on the telephone), this appears not to be true. Spotting lying is no better than chance when the viewers have access only to the face and, further, combinations of face with other information (speech, body) produce less accuracy than combinations of information in which no facial cues are available. In careful analyses of video and audio tapes, researchers have identified certain cues that are valid indicators of lying (e.g., dilation of the pupils of the eyes, blinking, pitch of the voice) but those are probably not available to the unaided and naïve observer. People seem to believe that failure to look one in the eye is an indication of lying, but that is not confirmed by the close analyses.

Are there individual differences in the ability to lie successfully? The most notable result here concerns experienced salespersons whose false and true statements, recorded on video tapes, cannot be distinguished by samples of undergraduate students who are able to discriminate with some accuracy among the statements made by inexperienced "liars." Apparently, experience counts in this ability. The situation of the salesperson is an interesting one to speculate about. We would expect the conflict of interest between a customer and a salesperson to encourage mutual deception – lies told by the seller (in the reasons they give for a purchase), but also lies told by the customer (in the reasons they give for refusing to purchase). So customers have reason to be suspicious of salespersons (as, noted below, they are), and salespersons should have opportunities not only to hone their skills at deceit (which they apparently do) but also, often being the targets of lies, opportunities to become good detectors of the deceits their customers commonly practice (for which, as yet, there is no evidence).

Are there consistent individual differences in ability to spot a lie? In general, the evidence for such differences is weak but, again, there is some evidence of the benefits of experience. There seems to be an enhanced ability to detect a lie told by someone with whom you are familiar, for example, members of your own culture; a speaker for whom you've been trained, in an experimental procedure, to make the "truth-falsity" distinction. Attractive persons seem to be especially skillful in spotting lies told to another attractive person. This again calls our attention to the interaction settings in which persons have experience with lies and truth. Once more we may invoke the notion that conflict of interest gives rise to mutual deceit. The attractive person is likely often to experience the situation described in this entry – a setting in which he or she is frequently subjected to ingratiating misrepresentations by persons seeking to be close to him or her but from whom the attractive person desires to maintain distance. Experience in this situation may account for attractive persons' skill at detecting lies but also their ability under high motivation to tell convincing lies. Lies are useful to an attractive person in gracefully fending off unwanted "advances."

Our Atlas's focus on situations also encourages us to wonder about the situational determinants of lying (e.g., conflict of interest) and the detection of that conflict. The research reveals a strong tendency for experimental subjects to assume that what a person is saying is true. This suggests that people generally assume there to be some commonality of interest between themselves and a speaker – a situation in which truth telling is appropriate. Not surprisingly, that generalized trust does not extend to relationships in which there are typically clear conflicts of interests, as in dealing with salespeople.

One situational variable in deception research has been the importance to the speaker of succeeding in lying. Relating this variable to our Atlas situations, it constitutes a variation in the speaker's dependence on the listener, that is, in how important a successful lie may be. One might argue that success will be enhanced by a strong desire to succeed in a lie but, contrariwise, one might argue that the desire to succeed will interfere with controlling the "leakage" of clues that give away a lie's falsehood. In general, the latter idea seems to be supported. The lies told by persons who are more highly motivated to get away with their lies are more likely to be revealed in their nonverbal behavior. There's an irony here when a lie of great importance is told in a close relationship. On the one hand, the liar is more likely to be caught and, on the other hand, a lie of great importance, once detected, is highly disruptive of the relationship (McCornack & Levine, 1990). Realization of that possibility may encourage people in close relationships to be honest with each other, and that may be reflected in the fact that intimate partners believe that lies will not occur in their interaction.

4.4.4 *Simultaneous (Independent) Selections*

Inasmuch as two persons in a conflicting interest situation such as this one have the same information problems (of concealing, dissembling, not believing), they sometimes create circumstances in which each must act without any information about the other's intention. In a sense, they implicitly collude to maintain a level playing field as far as information is concerned. In the extreme case, each conceals his or her preparation for the ultimate action until some external circumstance (time deadline, intervention of a third party) requires both to act and to do so independently. Simultaneous and independent selections are incorporated by explicit agreement in many recreational games, as illustrated by the school yard game of "scissors, paper, stone" in which scissors "cut" paper, paper "covers" stone, and stone "breaks" scissors. The matrix for this game is shown in Table E4.3 below. If the two persons' selections match, neither scores, but with different choices, one always "beats" the other, depending on the properties of the three objects described above. The game is fair in its informational aspects because the rules require the two players to make and reveal their selections simultaneously. They are reduced to "guessing" what the other will do on any occasion.

In war, opposite sides sometimes have such poor intelligence about each other that they come to junctures where, in effect, they have to make simultaneous, independent decisions. Some of the recommendations from game theory were developed with these circumstances in mind. Consider the matrix in Table E4.4, which describes a three-option situation with a strong component of Mutual Behavior Control. Because it is a zero-sum game, the matrix presents only A's outcomes. (B's outcomes are the same in each cell but with opposite algebraic signs; A's interests here are to act to maximize the value in the matrix and B's interests are to minimize the value.)

Assuming that the two find it necessary to make independent decisions in this situation, what rules might they use? One rule is to look for a "sure thing," that is, an option that is better than or as good as the other two no matter what the partner selects. Because of the MBC component in Table E4.4, neither person has a "sure thing." Another rule suggested by game theory as possibly applicable here is to select an option that will "maximize your security level" (Luce & Raiffa, 1957). Given the fact that your outcomes will be greatly affected by the opponent's actions about which you can have no advance warning, the idea is to protect yourself against the worst that the other person can do to you. For A, this principle requires identifying an outcome that is highest in its row (the variance in which A controls) and lowest in its column (the variance in which B controls). Following that rule leads A to select a2 which guarantees a gain of at least 4. Making a similar analysis, B is led to select his option b2, which guarantees a loss no worse than 4. Thus, in maximizing their respective security levels, the two persons in this particular situation are led to the a2b2 pair. This pair is a sort of implicit "solution" to the problem because it serves both parties' interests in protecting themselves. This does not necessarily mean that they will share this concern about "security" and make the appropriate selections. The logic of game theory merely reveals that for purposes of providing maximal security against the opponent, both persons can do so at the a2b2 pair.

We may note that there is no need to conceal one's intention to select an option that maximizes one's security level. Having that intention requires setting a sort of minimal "level of aspiration" for the interaction, perhaps guided by the person's resolve to disregard outcomes he/she cannot control. A's intention to select a2 needs not be concealed from B because A in effect says, "I'll settle for the outcomes in the a2 column so go ahead and do your worst to me." It is interesting further to note that A's security orientation imposes on B a similar orientation, whether B prefers it or not.

A pair of behaviors that provides the security level is referred to as a "saddle point," inasmuch as when plotted in a three-dimensional space, the higher values above and below it and the lower values on either side of it create a 3-D figure resembling a "saddle." Not all zero-sum situations have saddle points. And even for those that do, a study by Lieberman (1962) suggests that people do not immediately seize upon their benefits. His pairs made repeated independent selections for a 3×3 zero-sum game (similar to the matrix in Table E4.4) and, for the most part, only settled down on the saddle point after a large number of trials. It seems likely that they initially tried to outguess or outwit their partners, in attempts to gain better outcomes than those that maximize one's security level.

4.4.5 Gambling and Feeling Lucky

A simple example of a gambling game is Entry #4 as it occurs in the matching of coins. The matrix in Table E4.1 can apply to the game of matching nickels in which B gains the partner's nickel if they match (both heads or both tails) and A wins B's nickel if they fail to match. When played as a gambling game, each person tosses his/her coin and they then reveal the results simultaneously.

As is true for all the situations in this Atlas, people approach gambling situations in different ways. For example, there are consistent individual differences in people's beliefs in their own luck. Some feel that they "consistently have good luck" and others believe that "luck" (a good outcome) is random. (Few people think they are unlucky.) These differences in beliefs have an interesting effect on reactions to an initial experience of success in a gambling situation. Those who feel lucky act as if they are on a "lucky streak" and become more confident about their future success. Those who do not believe in luck tend to show the opposite effect, becoming less confident after the initial success. The latter may be taken as an example of the "gambler's fallacy" – the belief that a good outcome in a chance situation is more likely to be followed by a bad outcome on the next occasion (Darke & Freedman, 1997).

4.4.6 Guessing Games and Trying to Outguess a Partner

The situation in the matrix in Table E4.1 can also represent a guessing game in which, rather than tossing the coins, both persons privately place their coins on the table and then reveal which sides are showing. Can person A predict what B is likely to do and, therefore, gain an edge in the guessing game? The literature provides no direct evidence on this point, but we do know a good deal about guessing behavior from the extensive literature on probability learning (Bower & Hilgard, 1981). In the standard procedure, a subject guesses or predicts, over a series of occasions, which of two lights on an apparatus will go on next. The lights are generally programmed to occur randomly although not equally often. For example, regardless of the subject's guess, one light may go on 20% of the time and the other, 80% of the time. In this case, if the subject assumes that the order of lights is random, logically he/she can maximize the overall number of correct guesses by always predicting the more frequent event. However, many studies have shown that subjects do not make their guesses in this "rational" manner. Instead, they tend to match the frequency of their selections to the relative frequency of the lights. So in the case above, they tend to predict the more frequent light about 80% of the time. The pattern of their guesses and their introspective reports suggest why. They do not take the sequence of lights to be random. Rather, they search for order in the sequence. As a consequence, their sequence of guesses reveals the above-mentioned "gambler's fallacy": for example, after a succession of lights appears on the left, they predict the next light will be on the right. And they are sensitive to chance patterns (e.g., LLRLLR...) and use them as bases for their guesses. In short, they treat the sequence-generating apparatus as if it must be producing an orderly coherent pattern of events.

If people treat experimental apparatus (whatever that means to them!) in these terms, they must surely have the same tendency in making their guesses about another person's actions – the tendency to assume that the sequence of actions is characterized by order and patterning. But then we have an interesting puzzle about how the interaction between two guessers will play out. In the course of a series of interactions, A may detect (or think he or she detects) a pattern in B's selections and try to take advantage of it. In doing so, A is likely to generate a related pattern (perhaps a mirror image pattern) which B may then detect. In this manner, a chance pattern in B's string may become reflected in a planned pattern in A's string, which then, B detects and reflects in his or her planned pattern. But as each person's selections become more strongly under thoughtful control, they tend to become more predictable, and this is a property neither person will wish to sustain in their succession of guesses.

4.5 Matrix and Transition List Representations

Table E4.1. Mutual Joint Control pattern with conflicting outcomes. A "zero-sum" game inasmuch as the two persons' outcomes in each cell total to zero.

TABLE E4.1

		A	
		a1	a2
B	b1	−5 +5	+5 −5
	b2	+5 −5	−5 +5

Table E4.2. A situation of interdependent escape from (i.e., avoidance of) negative outcomes. The situation affords an opportunity for only one of the pair successfully to avoid those outcomes. If one waits and lets the other "try" to escape, the latter succeeds. If both wait or both try to escape, both incur the negative consequences. This situation provides only one opportunity for escape and, in that regard, is to be contrasted with the transition list in Table E4.5 which provides two opportunities.

TABLE E4.2

		A	
		Wait	Try
		−10 (top) / −10 (bottom)	0 (top) / −10 (bottom)
B	Wait		
	Try	−10 (top) / 0 (bottom)	−10 (top) / −10 (bottom)

Table E4.3. The game of "paper, scissors, stone" – a simple guessing game in which two persons simultaneously show one of the three hand signals that signify paper (hand flat with palm down), scissors (hand with two

TABLE E4.3

		A		
		Sc.	Pa.	St.
	Sc.	0 / 0	−1 / +1	+1 / −1
B	Pa.	+1 / −1	0 / 0	−1 / +1
	St.	−1 / +1	+1 / −1	0 / 0

fingers extended), or stone (clenched fist). If different signals are shown, one always "wins" over the other, as shown by the outcomes in the matrix, which reflect the rules that "paper covers stone, scissors cut paper, and stone breaks scissors."

Table E4.4. Zero-sum game: The outcomes shown are those of person A, so B's outcomes in each cell are equal but opposite in sign. The outcome pattern permits A to satisfy the "maximin" criterion of maximizing the least amount A can gain. This is accomplished by option a2 which includes the highest value in its row and the lowest value in its column, namely, the outcome of 4. A's choice of a2 maximizes the worst outcome that B can cause A to obtain.

TABLE E4.4

		A		
		a1	a2	a3
	b1	8	5	−2
B	b2	3	4	3
	b3	−2	5	8

Transition List in Table E4.5. The situation provides two opportunities for avoiding the negative outcomes, at each one of which only one of the two persons can escape the danger. Each of the two junctures permits an escape only if one person waits while the other "tries" (i.e., the awbt or atbw combinations of options). Mutual waiting or mutual trying wastes the moment for possible escape provided at each juncture. Escape by both is possible if one waits and the other leaves at J, which moves the former to a situation of independent control over escaping. For example, "aw, bt" enables B to exit and moves A to juncture L where A can escape at will.

TABLE E4.5 *Transition List for Situation That Provides Two Successive Occasions for Interdependent Escape*

Junctures	Options	Possible Selections	Outcomes for A	B	Transition to Next Juncture
[J	(aw, at)	awbw	–	–	K]
[	(bw, bt)	awbt	–	0*	L/X**]
[		atbw	0*	–	X/M]
[		atbt	–	–	K]
[K	(aw, at)	awbw	–10	–10	X]
[	(bw, bt)	awbt	–10	0	X]
[		atbw	0	–10	X]
[		atbt	–10	–10	X]
[L	(aw, at)	aw–	–10	–	X]
[	(–, –)	at–	0	–	X]
[M	(–, –)	–bw	–	–10	X]
[	(bw, bt)	–bt	–	0	X]

* The outcome of zero represents the attainment of safety, i.e., relief from the threatening danger.
** L/X indicates that person A is moved to juncture L and person B exits, to safety.

TWO- AND THREE-COMPONENT PATTERNS

Entry #5

The Prisoner's Dilemma

Me versus We

5.1 Examples

Perhaps the best-known interdependence situation is the Prisoner's Dilemma, a situation that derives its name from the classic anecdote about two prisoners who were accused of robbing a bank. In this anecdote, described in Luce and Raiffa (1957), the district attorney, unable to prove that they were guilty, created a dilemma in an attempt to motivate the prisoners to confess to the crime. The prisoners were put in separate rooms, where each prisoner was to make a choice: to confess or not to confess.

The district attorney sought to make confessing tempting to the prisoners by creating a situation in which the sentence was determined not only by their own confessing or not but also by the fellow prisoner's confessing or not. Yet irrespective of the fellow prisoner's choice, the choice to confess yielded a better outcome (or less worse outcome) than did the choice not to confess. Specifically, when the other confessed, confessing yielded "only" an 8-year sentence, whereas not confessing yielded a 10-year sentence. And when the other did not confess, confessing yielded only a 3-month sentence, whereas not confessing yielded a 1-year sentence. So, from this perspective, it seems rational for each prisoner to confess to the crime. However, the crux of the dilemma is that the outcome following from both confessing (an 8-year sentence) is worse than the outcome following from both not confessing (a 1-year sentence). Thus, if both prisoners were completely trusting of each other and strongly committed to supporting or helping each other, neither would confess,

Paul A. M. Van Lange had primary responsibility for preparation of this entry.

despite the district attorney's attempt to make confessing attractive. (The four possible sentences following from both prisoners' choices are derived from Luce and Raiffa [1957]; some other sources report slightly different sentences.)

This *classic* Prisoner's Dilemma describes a situation in which the prisoners were to make their choices simultaneously, irrevocably (i.e., they could not "undo" or take back their choices), and therefore *independently* of one another. The independence of their choices was also insured by putting the prisoners in separate cells, thereby excluding any possibility for communication relevant to the choices they were going to make. In doing so, the district attorney created a rather uncommon situation, because people are usually able to interact in ways that permit them to respond to each other's behavior or communicate about their choices.

Nevertheless, some situations we encounter in real life resemble aspects of the classic Prisoner's Dilemma. For example, it occasionally may be tempting to prepare less than fully for a working meeting with a partner in order to save time and energy for another activity that is more pressing or interesting. Yet the meeting would be more fruitful if both you and the partner invest time and effort and prepare well for the meeting. More generally, the Prisoner's Dilemma represents *exchange* situations, which in the real world often occur under response conditions that make possible alternating choices and/or revocable choices. An example is the exchange of baseball cards, or cards of well-known soccer players, by which two children can, at little cost, provide each other with the card the other desires very much (e.g., the last card that completes one's set of cards). In that sense, the single-trial Prisoner's Dilemma represents the situation in which people "do business," exchanging money, products, or services that are more desirable to the other than to the self. The single-trial Prisoner's Dilemma may also operate at the *N*-person level, involving more than two individuals (see *N*-Person Prisoner's Dilemma, Entry #20). For example, the problem of littering in public places may be analyzed as an *N*-person Prisoner's Dilemma. Most of us enjoy clean public places like parks and sports stadiums, but we often find litter in such places, indicating that it is somewhat tempting to the self to litter although such behavior is undesirable to the collective. Most of the examples discussed so far illustrate the Prisoner's Dilemma but do not perfectly match the features of a single-trial Prisoner's Dilemma, because there usually is a history and/or future of interaction that accompanies working meetings or exchanges of products (e.g., baseball cards). As such, single-trial "interactions" are more common in our dealings with relative strangers rather than partners, friends, or acquaintances.

We should note, however, that the importance of the single-trial Prisoner's Dilemma, especially in its classic form (involving simultaneous and irrevocable choice), derives not so much from its occurrence in the real world, but from the fact that this situation represents an important *motivational dilemma*. It contrasts the motivations of competition (i.e., enhancement of relative advantage) and individualism (i.e., enhancement of own outcomes) *with* cooperative motivation (i.e., enhancement of joint outcomes) and altruism (i.e., enhancement of partner's outcomes). And, as we illustrate later, the single-trial Prisoner's Dilemma has evoked several programs of research, which center on the determinants of cooperative motivation versus self-interested motivation.

5.2 Conceptual Description

The Prisoner's Dilemma is often characterized in terms of cooperative and noncooperative choices, and defined by the conflict between self-interest and joint interest. A person is always better off making a noncooperative choice, irrespective of the partner's choice (i.e., self-interest); the noncooperative choice is therefore often described in terms of *individual rationality*. However, both individuals are better off when both make a cooperative choice than when both make a noncooperative choice (i.e., joint interest). The cooperative choice is therefore often described in terms of *collective rationality*. Hence, the Prisoner's Dilemma represents a situation in which individually rational actions (i.e., choosing what is good for oneself) leads to collective irrationality, as both individuals could have done better if they both had made a cooperative choice.

Frequently, Prisoner's Dilemmas may arise when John has something to offer that David cannot (or can only to a lesser extent) provide for himself, whereas David has something to offer that John cannot (or can only to a lesser extent) provide for himself (e.g., giving each other things that are more precious to the other person than to the self). Hence, the Prisoner's Dilemma involves a high degree of Mutual Partner Control (MPC), and somewhat less Bilateral Actor Control (BAC). In other words, outcomes are more strongly influenced by the partner's choice than by the person's own choice. (The Prisoner's Dilemma involves little or no Mutual Joint Control [MJC]. That is, the Prisoner's Dilemma represents an exchange situation, where dependence primarily derives from unilateral control by the partner).

Prisoner's Dilemmas reflect a pronounced conflict between one's own interest (e.g., not giving yields no loss) and the partner's interest (e.g., receiving yields a great benefit). As such, the two components that underlie the Prisoner's Dilemma – Bilateral Actor Control and Mutual Partner Control – are combined in a discordant orientation with each other. Thus, the Prisoner's Dilemma confronts an individual with a dilemma between two options: (a) to pursue good outcomes for oneself at a *major* cost to the other, or (b) to pursue good outcomes for the other at a *smaller* cost to oneself. (We should note, however, that Prisoner's Dilemmas can vary quite considerably in the degree to which own and other's outcomes are conflicting.)

5.3 Variants and Neighbors

5.3.1 *Neighbors of the Classic Prisoner's Dilemma*

Two neighbors of the Prisoner's Dilemma are Chicken (described in Entry #7) and Trust (also sometimes referred to as Assurance, a situation that is not described in this Atlas). A matrix representation of a single-trial Prisoner's Dilemma is given in Table E5.1 below (at the end of this entry), and matrix representations of Chicken and Trust are given in Table E5.2, panels A and B, respectively. Chicken and Trust differ from the Prisoner's Dilemma in that these situations involve very little or no Bilateral Actor Control (BAC). Instead, the two essential components of Chicken and Trust are Mutual Partner Control (MPC) and Mutual Joint Control (MJC). This implies that in these situations, unlike in the Prisoner's Dilemma, a person is *not* always better off making a noncooperative choice. In both Chicken and Trust, the noncooperative choice does not represent individual rationality, because it depends on the other's choice whether a cooperative choice or a noncooperative choice by the person himself or herself yields the better outcomes.

The similarity between Chicken, Trust, and the Prisoner's Dilemma is that all three situations involve collective rationality: Cooperative behavior by both individuals yields greater outcomes than does noncooperative behavior by both individuals. Specifically, the best (Trust) or second best (Chicken, Prisoner's Dilemma) possible outcome is obtained if both make a cooperative choice, whereas the third best (Trust, Prisoner's Dilemma) or worst (Chicken) possible outcome is obtained if both make a noncooperative choice.

In the Prisoner's Dilemma, tendencies toward cooperation are challenged by both greed (i.e., the appetitive pressure of obtaining the best possible outcome by making a noncooperative choice) and fear (i.e., the aversive pressure of avoiding the worst possible outcome by making a noncooperative choice; Coombs, 1973). In Chicken, cooperation is challenged by greed, whereas in Trust, cooperation is challenged by fear. Thus, in a sense, the Prisoner's Dilemma "combines" Chicken and Trust, representing a stronger conflict of interest, involving both fear and greed. Consistent with this analysis, research has revealed that individuals exhibit greater levels of cooperation in Trust and Chicken than in the Prisoner's Dilemma (Liebrand, Wilke, Vogel, & Wolters, 1986).

Because the Trust situation is not discussed in a separate entry in this Atlas, it is appropriate to discuss it a bit more fully here. In Trust the best outcome is obtained when both individuals make a cooperative choice. At the same time, cooperation is risky because if the other makes a noncooperative choice, cooperation yields the worst outcome. The Trust situation is sometimes described as resembling features of the relationship between the United States and the Soviet Union during the cold war, whereby disarming represents the cooperative choice and arming the noncooperative choice (e.g., Hamburger, 1979). To jointly disarm was clearly the best solution for both countries, yet being the only one to disarm makes one terribly vulnerable, because it may yield the worst possible outcome. Thus, both countries may have armed for a long time because they failed to trust one another, believing that the other party was seeking relative advantage and therefore was to be considered very threatening. As another example, two athletes want to be involved in a fair contest, in that neither one takes drugs to promote his or her performance. However, if one athlete suspects that the other might take drugs, it would perhaps be best to take drugs as well to minimize the odds of losing due to unfair disadvantages (Liebrand et al., 1986).

With these examples in mind, it becomes understandable that individuals do not necessarily cooperate in the Trust situation, despite the fact that mutual cooperation yields the best outcome. There are two important reasons why individuals may fail to make a cooperative choice. First, a noncooperative choice could derive from a lack of trust that the other is going to make a cooperative choice. That is, individuals seek to avoid the worst possible outcome by making a noncooperative choice (i.e., fear). Second, a noncooperative choice could derive from competitive motivation, seeking to maximize relative advantage over the other (rather than simply maximizing outcomes for self in an "absolute" manner). Thus, one "should" make a cooperative choice (a) if one trusts that the other is not competitively motivated, *and* (b) if one is not competitively motivated himself or herself.

5.3.2 *Variants of the Classic Prisoner's Dilemma*

The Prisoner's Dilemma may take a variety of forms. First, while the classic Prisoner's Dilemma involves negative outcomes (varying from no sentence to a 10-year sentence), the Prisoner's Dilemma may also involve positive outcomes or negative and positive outcomes. The distinction between positive and negative outcomes, or the presentation of outcomes as positive or negative, is obviously relevant to psychological processes involving the framing of gains and losses, and the processing of positive versus negative information (e.g., Higgins, 1998; Peeters & Czapinski, 1990; Tversky & Kahneman, 1974).

Second, Prisoner's Dilemmas may also differ in the degree to which the choices impact individuals' outcomes (i.e., level of importance; cf. Van Lange, 1994). The two prisoners were faced with very important outcomes, which varied from no sentence at all to a ten-year sentence. Of course, in our everyday interactions, the stakes are often not that high, especially in regard to our interactions with relative strangers.

Third, the decisions in Prisoner's Dilemmas need not always concern "black or white" issues, but may entail choices that differ in degree of cooperativeness. Patterns of exchange may often occur in a graduated form, where individuals decide, for example, how much they are willing to give up to benefit the other. For example, one may decide to help the other by devoting a couple of hours rather than the entire day to help a friend complete a task. Such graduated (or gray) Prisoner's Dilemmas are important from a psychological perspective, because these dilemmas permit a moderately cooperative choice. For example, when people find it difficult to make a decision, they may solve it by making a moderately cooperative choice.

5.3.3 *Extensions of the Classic Prisoner's Dilemma*

When choices are simultaneous and irrevocable in a single-trial Prisoner's Dilemma, and when communication is not permitted, there is no basis for influencing the partner's choice in one way or another. This is to be contrasted with the Iterated Prisoner's Dilemma, in which a present choice may be guided by the result of past interactions (e.g., retaliation, forgiveness) or aimed at shaping the partner's future choices in a manner consistent with one's long-term interaction goals (see Iterated Prisoner's Dilemma, Entry #12). Also, unlike the classic Prisoner's Dilemma, single-trial Prisoner's Dilemmas involving alternating choice (rather than simultaneous choice), or revocable choice (rather than irrevocable choice) allow individuals to influence the other's behavior.

In Prisoner's Dilemmas involving *alternating* choice, either one can act, irrevocably, before the other. In such situations, it is likely that the one acting first will be making a choice while recognizing that the partner is probably going to respond to this choice in one way or another. For example, setting out to help someone with a task may elicit exchange (or reciprocal help), whereas not helping is unlikely to motivate the other to help you.

In Prisoner's Dilemmas involving *revocable* choice, there is a strong basis for both making promises and using threat. For example, one can communicate a strategy of "conditional cooperation," by making a cooperative choice and undoing this choice when the other makes a noncooperative choice. Of course, in such revocable situations threats and promises are implicit "in the structure" and often need not be actually used for cooperation to occur. One may argue that revocability often takes its form in the implicit or explicit use of communication in everyday life situations. For example, individuals may communicate intended choice in several ways (verbally and nonverbally) before making their definite, binding choice.

Generally, single-trial Prisoner's Dilemmas involving successive choice and/or revocable choice permit social-communicative mechanisms that reduce uncertainty and fear on the part of one or both individuals. Therefore, mutual cooperation is often higher in these situations (e.g., in a situation involving revocable choices) than in the classic Prisoner's Dilemma involving simultaneous and irrevocable choice (Daniels, 1967; for evidence in an Iterated Prisoner's Dilemma, see Insko et al., 1998).

5.4 Interaction Patterns and Person Factors

The classic Prisoner's Dilemma (involving simultaneous and irrevocable choice) represents a situation in which a choice cannot be motivated by considerations regarding past behavior or future behavior. Hence, the motivations underlying choices in a classic Prisoner's Dilemma should be "free" from tactics or strategies. What remains is a *motivational dilemma*, representing a contrast between altruism and cooperation on the one hand, and individualism and competition on the other. Yet the motivational structure of the Prisoner's Dilemma is still ambiguous, in that at least two orientations could underlie a cooperative choice (i.e., altruism and cooperation) and at least two orientations could underlie a noncooperative choice (i.e., individualism and competition).

5.4.1 Interpersonal Dispositions

Researchers have designed instruments for assessing interpersonal dispositions, such as cooperation, individualism, and competition, using single-trial Prisoner's Dilemmas and related structures for presenting choices that affect the outcomes for self and outcomes for other (i.e., using so-called decomposed games; Messick & McClintock, 1968; Pruitt, 1970). A frequently used instrument for assessing such *social value orientations* is the Triple-Dominance Measure of Social Values (Van Lange, Otten, De Bruin, & Joireman, 1997; see also earlier research by Kuhlman & Marshello, 1975). In this measure, people are asked to make choices which influence the "outcomes" for self and another person. The outcomes are presented in terms of points said to be valuable to self and the other, and the other person is described as someone they do not know and that they will never knowingly meet in the future (in an effort to exclude the role of considerations relevant to the future interactions).

An example of a decomposed game is the choice among three options:

(1) *Option A*: 480 points for self and 80 points for other;
(2) *Option B*: 540 points for self and 280 points for other; and
(3) *Option C*: 480 points for self and 480 points for other.

In this example, option A represents the competitive choice (i.e., yielding greatest outcomes for self relative to the other); option B, the individualistic choice (i.e., yielding greatest absolute outcomes for self), and option C, the prosocial choice (i.e., yielding greatest joint outcomes and greatest equality in outcomes). In research using this instrument, most individuals are classified as prosocial (about 60%), followed by individualistic (about 25%), and only a small minority is classified as competitive (about 15%). Of course, these percentages might differ as a function of the sample. For example, there is evidence that prosocial motivation is more prevalent among people raised in cultures characterized by high levels of collectivism, interpersonal closeness, and interdependence (Madsen & Lancy, 1981; McClintock,

1974). Moreover, the percentages of prosocials increase – and those of individualists and competitors decrease – with increasing age. And prosocial motivation is more prevalent among individuals raised in large, rather than small, families and especially in families that include many daughters (Van Lange et al., 1997).

Differences among prosocial, individualistic, and competitive orientations are strongly related to behavior in a single-trial Prisoner's Dilemma, beliefs regarding others' social value orientations, as well as to interactions in Iterated Prisoner's Dilemmas (see Entry #12). Moreover, such findings extend to behavior outside of the laboratory. For example, relative to individualists and competitors, prosocials are more prone to help others, to make donations to noble causes, and the three orientations are relevant to understanding the specific motivations underlying willingness to sacrifice in ongoing close relationships (e.g., McClintock & Allison, 1989; Van Lange, Agnew, Harinck, & Steemers, 1997). Moreover, roommates and friends rate prosocials, individualists, and competitors differently in terms of "what they are like" (Bem & Lord, 1979). Such evidence indicates that the orientations, assessed by measures involving "decompositions" of the classic Prisoner's Dilemma and related choice situations, are relevant to our understanding of patterns of interaction in many situations.

5.4.2 *Beliefs and Impressions*

As noted earlier, because there is no history or future of interaction, the single-trial Prisoner's Dilemma speaks more to our dealings with relative strangers than to our interactions with friends and close partners. Hence, in such situations, one's beliefs regarding the probable behavior of the other are important, and such beliefs or expectations tend to go hand in hand with one's own tendencies to behave cooperatively or noncooperatively (Kuhlman & Wimberley, 1976; Yamagishi & Sato, 1986). To some degree such beliefs may (a) implicitly be derived from one's own interpersonal dispositions (e.g., "Why would the other behave differently from me?" Dawes, McTavish, & Shaklee, 1977), (b) serve to rationalize or justify one's own choice (e.g., "I did not make a cooperative choice, because I thought the other would not either"; Messé & Sivacek, 1979), and (c) guide one's own behavior (e.g., through anticipated reciprocity; "I think the other is going to cooperate, so I do the same"; Van Lange, 1999).

Clearly, in the absence of any history of interaction, beliefs regarding the other's behavior may not be held with great confidence, and may be influenced by impressions that we have formed about others. For example, perceptions of partner's honesty and trustworthiness are important determinants of expectations of partner's choice and own choice, even in the context of other forms of impressions, and even when such impressions are formed on the basis of very specific behaviors (Van Lange & Kuhlman, 1994). This is perhaps not too surprising because fruitful exchange will only be obtained if both the self and the partner behave cooperatively: That is, for making a cooperative choice, one needs to pursue cooperative goals *and* believe that the partner will make a cooperative choice (cf. Goal/Expectation Theory [Pruitt & Kimmel, 1977]; for a further discussion, see Iterated Prisoner's Dilemma, Entry #12). It is interesting that, for some impressions, the translation of an impression of the partner to a specific expectation regarding the partner's choice shows that different people make something different of the same single-trial Prisoner's Dilemma. For example, prosocials tend to believe that intelligent partners are more likely to make a cooperative choice than unintelligent partners are, whereas individualists and competitors tend to believe the opposite: Only unintelligent partners make a cooperative choice (Van Lange & Kuhlman, 1994).

Of course, information directly relevant to another person's trustworthiness, intelligence, or competence is often not available – for example, when interacting with strangers. Under such circumstances, people may derive impressions of trustworthiness from global characteristics of the other (i.e., "category information" stereotypes), from specific nonverbal signals or behavior (e.g., blushing), or from information that people receive from others (e.g., through gossip). New lines of research focusing on reputation and "image scoring" focus on intriguing questions such as whether people tend to behave more cooperatively to people who have been more generous to others in earlier interactions (e.g., Wedekind & Milinski, 2000). In this regard, it is interesting to note that people do have some capacity to tell cooperators from noncooperators. As a case in point, Frank, Gilovich, and Regan (1993) conducted an experiment in which a small group of strangers were put together in a room for half an hour, after which they were asked to predict which of their fellow participants would make a cooperative choice and which would make a noncooperative choice in a single-trial Prisoner's Dilemma. It appeared that participants did considerably better than chance in predicting a stranger's behavior in this dilemma, suggesting that a brief period of getting-to-know-each-other may help people to tell cooperators from noncooperators.

5.4.3 *Strength of Self-Interest*

Because the classic Prisoner's Dilemma represents a motivational dilemma, some researchers have employed it to address the fundamental issue of whether people may be willing to make a cooperative choice, in the absence of several (although not all) self-serving goals such as reputational, self-presentational, or reciprocal concerns. Hence, researchers have designed situations in which the participants are strangers who make a single and anonymous choice for relatively large amounts of money, and interaction among the participants is prevented before and after the experiment. Several studies have revealed that, under such conditions, a substantial number of people make a cooperative choice (for a review, see Caporeal, Dawes, Orbell, & Van de Kragt, 1990). Also, in a different program of research, it has been demonstrated that feelings of empathy provide a powerful motivation to make a cooperative choice in single-trial Prisoner's Dilemmas, even if the other has just made a noncooperative choice (in a single-trial Prisoner's Dilemma with alternating choice; Batson & Ahmad, 2000). Like the literature about social value orientation, such evidence conflicts with the assumption of rational self-interest that stands at the basis of much theory in the social and behavioral sciences. That is, concern with the well-being of others, or at least the motivation not to harm others, can be quite strong, even in situations in which strategic, selfish intent could not underlie such generous forms of behavior.

5.4.4 *Social Norms*

To some degree, the motivations relevant to the single-trial Prisoner's Dilemma may also be influenced by social norms, which often take the form of *moral* norms. The Prisoner's Dilemma gives rise to moral principles by virtue of the fact that the pursuit of self-interest is in direct conflict with rules for moral conduct, which unambiguously dictate making a benevolent choice at a smaller cost to self. For example, many societies have developed strong norms for our interpersonal dealings in public situations. As described by Dawes (1980), many of us would not steal, even if we knew for sure that we would be able to get away with it, and many of us feel a norm to reciprocate favors from others (Gouldner, 1960). Examples of such general norms or principles are "do unto others as you would have them do unto you," "do what is best for all," "do no harm," or simply "be nice" (e.g., Batson, 1998).

Motivations and norms may also differ for the classic Prisoner's Dilemma and the Prisoner's Dilemma involving alternating and/or revocable choice. For example, single-trial Prisoner's Dilemmas involving alternating choice (rather than simultaneous choice) evoke the norm of reciprocity: Behave cooperatively if the other cooperated; behave noncooperatively if the other did not cooperate. Although the norm of reciprocity may not operate in each situation, it is striking that this norm is so ubiquitous, shaping behavior in so many contexts and situations. For example, business people often tend to use the norm of reciprocity by giving favors and discounts to the customer, hoping to receive a "favor" in return from which the sellers can profit considerably (Cialdini, 1993). And even very young children have "learned" to respond benevolently to a benevolent choice by another child (e.g., Eisenberg & Mussen, 1989).

Motivation and norms may play a somewhat different role in single-trial Prisoner's Dilemmas involving revocable choice. One may argue that revocability often takes its form in implicit or explicit use of communication in everyday life situations. For example, individuals may communicate intended cooperation in several ways (verbally and nonverbally) before making their definite, binding choice. Clearly, social norms dictate that one should meet the promises made, which has been referred to as the commitment norm (cf. Kerr & Kaufman-Gilliland, 1994; Orbell, Van de Kragt, & Dawes, 1988). But communication may also take the form of threat, in which the noncooperative choice is communicated as an intended punishment if the partner makes a noncooperative choice. Because the single-trial Prisoner's Dilemma with revocable choice allows for threat and promises, revocability should enhance the likelihood of obtaining mutual cooperation. This idea is supported in research by Dawes et al. (1977), which demonstrated that individuals are more likely to make a cooperative choice if they are able to communicate their intentions prior to making their choice.

5.5 Matrix Representations

Table E5.1. The matrix in Table E5.1 represents a single-trial Prisoner's Dilemma, whereby option 1 presents the cooperative choice (i.e., giving help), and option 2 the noncooperative choice (i.e., not giving help), for both person A (a1, a2) and person B (b1, b2). When the two persons provide help to one another in solving some computer problems, their outcomes are quite good (+5), and they are much better than when they fail to help one another (0). When an individual receives help but does not give help, his or her outcomes are very good (+10). This latter situation yields the worst outcomes to the partner who only gives help but does not receive any help (−5). As the reader will see, the impact of a partner's choice on a person's own outcomes is large. Irrespective of the one's own choice, the individual's outcomes are 10 outcome-units higher when the partner gives help, rather than fails to give help. This represents the benefits of helping to the other: *Mutual Partner Control* (MPC). The impact of an individual's choice on his or her own outcomes is relatively small. Irrespective of the partner's choice, the individual's own outcomes are 5 outcome-units higher when the individual does not give help rather than does. This represents the costs of helping for oneself: *Bilateral Actor Control* (BAC). In this example, MPC is twice as large as BAC. We also see that MPC and BAC are combined in a "discordant" orientation toward each other. Relative to not helping, helping enhances the outcomes for the partner but diminishes one's own outcomes. The Prisoner's Dilemma therefore represents a situation involving relatively strong levels of conflicting interests. Interests are not completely conflicting because both individuals' outcomes are greater when they do help one another than when they do not.

TABLE E5.1. *Matrix Representation of the Single-Trial Prisoner's Dilemma*

		A	
		a1	a2
B	b1	+5 / +5	+10 / −5
	b2	−5 / +10	0 / 0

Table E5.2. In contrast, the Chicken and Trust situations primarily include Mutual Partner Control (MPC) and Mutual Joint Control (MJC), and no or very little Bilateral Actor Control (BAC). The matrix in panel A of Table

E5.2 (at the end of this entry) presents an example of Chicken, in which there is only MPC and MJC (and no BAC). The matrix reveals that the person yields better outcomes if the partner chooses option 1 (i.e., the cooperative choice) rather than option 2 (i.e., the noncooperative choice), both when the person makes a cooperative choice and when the person makes a noncooperative choice. The matrix also reveals a "cross-over interaction," indicating MJC (and the absence of BAC). When the partner makes a cooperative choice, the person is 5 outcome-units better off making a noncooperative choice rather than a cooperative choice. Conversely, when the partner makes a noncooperative choice, the person is 5 outcome-units better off making a cooperative choice rather than a noncooperative choice.

The matrix in panel B of Table E5.2 presents an example of Trust, in which there is, as in Chicken, only MPC and MJC (and no BAC). As in Chicken, the matrix reveals that the person yields better outcomes if the partner chooses option 1 (i.e., the cooperative choice) rather than option 2 (i.e., the noncooperative choice), both when the person makes a cooperative choice and when the person makes a noncooperative choice. As in Chicken, the matrix also reveals a "cross-over interaction," indicating MJC (and the absence of BAC). When the partner makes a cooperative choice, the person is 5 outcome-units better off making a cooperative choice rather than a noncooperative choice. Conversely, when the partner makes a noncooperative choice, the person is 5 outcome-units better off making a noncooperative choice rather than a cooperative choice.

Returning to the Prisoner's Dilemma, it is of interest to note that the outcomes in the Prisoner's Dilemma have been labeled in terms of Temptation (T), Reward (R), Punishment (P), and Sucker's (S) payoff (see Rapoport & Chammah, 1965a & 1965b). T represents the *Temptation* to choose noncooperatively in the hope of getting the best possible outcomes; R represents the *Reward* associated with mutual cooperation; P represents the *Punishment* associated with mutual noncooperation; and S represents the so-called *"Sucker's payoff,"* which is a result of choosing cooperatively while the partner chooses noncooperatively. The structure of the Prisoner's Dilemma is then defined by the following order (from best outcomes to worst outcomes): $T > R > P > S$. (The structure of Chicken is defined by $T > R > S > P$, whereby Temptation yields the best possible outcome, but the Sucker's payoff does not yield the worst possible outcome. The structure of Trust is defined by $R > T > P > S$, whereby Temptation does not yield the best possible outcome, while the Sucker's payoff does yield the worst possible outcome.)

TABLE E5.2. *Matrix Representations of Chicken (Panel A) and Trust (Panel B)*

(a) Chicken Situation

A

	a1	a2
b1	+5 +5	+10 0
b2	0 +10	−5 −5

B is shown at the left spanning the b1/b2 rows.

(b) Trust Situation

A

	a1	a2
b1	+10 +10	+5 −5
b2	−5 +5	0 0

B is shown at the left spanning the b1/b2 rows.

Entry #6

Threat

Trading Loyalty for Justice

6.1 Examples

In this situation, one person has control over how the outcomes resulting from the pair's joint activities are divided between them. If that person exploits his or her power, taking for himself or herself the lion's share of those outcomes, the partner's only (ultimate) recourse is to refuse to continue in the joint activities. For example, when an older and younger brother play "cops and robbers," the older one may be able to determine the enjoyment each gets from the game by assigning the roles and controlling who gets to use the available toys. However, neither will gain any satisfaction from the game unless both play. If the older boy takes the choice roles and the preferred equipment, the younger boy must either accept the unfair allocation or threaten to refuse to play the game with enthusiasm or to continue it at all. It is the weaker person's "threat" in this scenario from which this situation takes its name. In general, this situation gives rise to the problem of managing an exchange of "justice" for "loyalty," one partner's just allocations being made in return for the other partner's loyalty in supporting their joint activities.

The structure and dynamics of this situation are common in various types of relationships and settings. For instance, a supervisor may have the power to determine how important job resources, such as office space and funds for computing, are split between her and a subordinate. To the extent the latter is productive and contributes importantly to the success of their work, the supervisor is well advised to act fairly in distributing the

John Holmes had primary responsibility for preparation of this entry.

resources so as to maintain the continued loyalty of her worker and avoid any threats on his part to quit. In the financial affairs of a traditional marriage, a husband may "control the purse strings," deciding what portion of the family's income each spouse has at their disposal. In the face of his inequitable treatment, the wife's recourse is to lodge complaints, backed up by the threat of leaving the relationship or, less drastically, of withdrawing her cooperation from the joint activities he values. A running back in football may essentially control the amount of publicity and attention the other players receive. If his personal success depends heavily on the hard work and "unselfishness" of his blockers, in order to maintain a cohesive team he may do what he can to insure that his teammates are accorded a fair share of the credit and praise.

6.2 Conceptual Description

The first requirement of this situation is that both persons be dependent on the other's decision to act in a rewarding way. Thus, each individual's "fate" or well-being is directly controlled by the other. Each has the power simply to benefit the other or not. Further, the Mutual Control has the potential to yield positive outcomes for both persons. In the representation in Table E6.1 below (at the end of this entry), this is shown by the Mutual Partner Control (MPC) matrix on the left.

The second feature of this situation is the fact that person B's personal preferences (Actor Control) favor behaving in a way (by the b1 action) that benefits person A, but A's preferences favor behaving in a way (by the a2 action) that is inconsistent with benefiting B. As the matrices show, the Threat game results from a particular combination of the MPC and BAC (Bilateral Actor Control) matrices (elsewhere described as situations #2 and #1, respectively). It can be seen that B's b1 action benefits both A and B but A's a1 action benefits B whereas the a2 action benefits A's self.

The consequence of this combination is that it is personally costly for B not to cooperate by going along and continuing to help create the mutual benefits. However, A is tempted to act in a way that gives a larger outcome to himself or herself and a relatively smaller one to B. Viewing the pattern as a whole, person B controls whether the pair has good outcomes by the decision to continue a mutually beneficial arrangement. Given that B is "loyal" in this regard, person A is cast in the role of "allocator," controlling the allocation of those outcomes in various ways. For instance, A might engage in a type of turn taking where their relative outcomes become balanced out over time. In the absence of this sort of fair treatment, person B is potentially cast in the role of "threatener," confronting the uncomfortable decision about whether to threaten not to cooperate with the current arrangements. It is costly for B to carry out the threat because while it withdraws outcomes from A, it also goes against B's own interests. Yet, both persons have an interest in resolving the "justice for loyalty" issue, so B has some leverage, both practical and moral, in the situation.

6.3 Variants

6.3.1 *Ultimatum Games*

Experimental economists believe the structure of the Threat situation characterizes the circumstances that occur when a monopolist sets prices (or wages) in a free marketplace (see Thaler, 1992, pp. 21–35). Game theorists created "Ultimatum Games" to study behavior in such situations. An Ultimatum Game might involve asking one person to divide up a sum of money, say $10, between himself or herself and a stranger. The other person, the recipient, can either accept what is offered or reject the offer, in which case they both receive nothing. In terms of the pricing metaphor, the monopolist says, "If you want the product, this is the price. Take it or leave it."

Game theory prescriptions for strategic decisions assume that individuals are rational and that they will pursue self-interested goals. Thus, in the Ultimatum Game allocators should make offers approaching zero, and recipients should accept all positive offers, even the smallest unit that can be offered. However, the Ultimatum Game has fascinated economists because experimental findings suggest that the modal offer of allocators is close to 50%, with a mean offer around 37% to 40%. As Thaler puts it, "the utility function clearly has non-monetary arguments," and "game theory seems of little use in predicting actual economic behavior in such studies" (p. 23). He notes that the generous offers imply that allocators have developed a "a taste for fairness" (p. 25).

Of course, the Ultimatum Game is still a situation of interdependence, and the other possibility is that the allocator is concerned that the recipient will view a low offer as insulting and unjust and reject it, however "irrational" that may be. Such worries could lead allocators to try to envision an amount that would meet or exceed the recipients' standard for being "treated fairly."

The Ultimatum Game is essentially identical to the Threat situation in basic matrix structure. However, our conceptual description of the Threat situation emphasizes the possibility of encountering the situation on repeated occasions. That is, our description focuses on trading justice for "loyalty," implying a *continued* willingness by the recipient to cooperate and conclude agreements that create mutual benefits over a period of time. Thus our description of the situation as one involving the issue of justice versus loyalty is not particularly apt in the one-trial version of the Ultimatum Game with strangers.

Other research in the Ultimatum Game tradition has presented participants with "multistage" games (Thaler, 1992), where decisions are repeated anywhere between two and five times. However, these studies have typically had participants *reverse roles* after each game, which changes the structure of the situation rather considerably to one where tit-for-tat strategies are relevant and "threats" would imply threatened punishment through Mutual Partner Control (see Entry #12).

Interestingly, one of the main examples Thaler (1992) presents to illustrate price theory in economics closely follows the logic of the Threat Game that we have emphasized, with repeated encounters where the roles of allocator and recipient are *not* reversed. He describes the dilemma faced by a merchant who owns a hotel and is setting room rates for a homecoming weekend in a college town. The enormous excess demand for rooms that weekend might allow him to double his normal rate. According to Thaler, his reasonable concern, at least from a psychological standpoint, is whether his regular customers would react angrily and label him a "gouger" if he raised his rates on that weekend to charge "what the market would bear." Thus his worry about how an allocation decision would affect his "regular business" is essentially a question of finding a price that is sufficiently fair to secure the "loyalty" of his customers.

6.3.2 *Varying Temptation and Dependency*
As described previously, person A's circumstances create the potential for *A's unjust behavior* toward B and person B's circumstances create the potential for *B's resistance to A's unjust behavior*. Variants of the Threat situation occur when one or both of these factors is reduced in magnitude, person A's being less tempted to be unfair and/or person B's being less able to challenge any unfairness. A comparison of these variants is made in the work of Thibaut and Faucheux, described below.

When the person in control of allocations, A, gives in to the temptation to exploit the partner, our focus falls on the ability of B, the potential threatener, effectively to press for justice. Crucially important are B's Partner

Control over A and how B affects his/her own outcomes by exercising that control. In the earlier example, if the younger brother (B) doesn't really care much about playing the game with the older one (A), B's threat to leave will be credible and its effect will depend on how much the older one will lose by cessation of the game. On the other hand, if B's own preferences to stay in the "game" with A are strong, B's threat is unlikely to be effective. As Thibaut and Kelley (1959) observe, B may have strong Partner Control over A but that power is not readily "useable" if the costs B has to bear in its exercise are high. We might, however, expect its use ultimately, when the exploitation is so extreme and unrelieved that B becomes willing to bear extreme costs to punish A. Instances of mutually costly and prolonged labor strikes come to mind. Alternatively, B's preferences (to be in rather than out of the "game") may be so strong that the situation is essentially one of Asymmetric Dependence (Entry #11) and B must accept whatever allocation A may choose to give.

6.4 Interaction Process and Person Factors

The Threat situation provides a good example of how situations are linked to patterns of interaction by the personality dispositions and norms that participants bring to them. In this situation, "allocators" are tempted to act selfishly or to demonstrate concerns with fairness. Such concerns may reflect moral norms, personal inclinations toward justice, or motives that are related to the particular relationship (e.g., concern for the partner's welfare). Depending on the behavior of the allocator, a person in the "threatener" role faces different issues. If the allocations seem fair, the person may have little to complain about, although one can imagine some individuals bridling at their position of dependence and wondering how they "got into" this situation. If the allocations are inequitable, then their loyalty in continuing to promote the positive joint outcomes will come into question and this may reflect personality factors (e.g., submissiveness), norms imported into the relationship (e.g., not challenging an authority figure), or fealty to the relationship itself (e.g., commitment in a marriage).

6.4.1 The Development of Contractual Norms
In their experimental work, Thibaut and Faucheux (1965) studied the development of explicit norms by pairs of strangers who interacted in situations that varied in the degree to which they resembled the "pure" version of the Threat situation. The interactions were repeated, and occasionally, the

persons were permitted and encouraged to express their views about their "relationship" and to formulate "contracts" that might solve their problems. Thibaut and Faucheux were interested in determining (a) whether people would discuss and develop norms regarding the "justice for loyalty" trade-off described above and (b) the conditions under which these interactions would occur. They hypothesized that such norms would develop when the situation has *high* potential for A's unjust behavior and *high* potential for B's resistance to such behavior.

The first factor was varied by the degree of conflict of interest that A faced when making allocations between himself and B. With high conflict of interest, there was a strong temptation for A's decisions to be unjust. The second factor was varied by providing the potential threateners with either high or low external alternatives to the central allocation problem. With high alternatives, they could make highly credible threats not to participate in the allocation problem and, therefore, not have to tolerate unfair treatment. In short, there were four experimental conditions, in two of which (those with low potential for A's unjust behavior) the "justice for loyalty" issue would not arise, and in one of which it would arise but, because of B's poor alternatives, there would be little basis for B's demanding and requiring fairness. It was in the fourth condition, with high probability of A's being unfair and B's having a basis for not tolerating unfairness, that Thibaut and Faucheux expected the issue to come up and be resolved by a "justice for loyalty" agreement.

As predicted, persons in the last condition were most likely to express concerns about fairness and loyalty. They were also by far the most likely to develop contractual norms appropriate to the situation, that is, norms dealing with issues of equitable distributions of outcomes, on the one hand, and with loyalty in continuing the relationship, on the other hand. Further, the norms they developed were largely effective, resulting in fairer allocations and fewer instances of the threatener's taking the external alternatives. Thus, the allocators were compensated for inhibiting the unjust use of their power by agreement on the partner's part to eschew the temptation to be "disloyal."

This work illustrates Thibaut and Faucheux's general principle that norms can be viewed as specific adaptations to particular interdependence problems, in this case, problems of fairness and loyalty. Thibaut and Faucheux argue that norms emerge out of actual experiences in dealing, often unsuccessfully at first, with conflict where both individuals have useable power. In the absence of conflict of interest that creates occasions for injustice and/or in the absence of good alternatives that enable targets of injustice to refuse to tolerate it, there are not the experiences that lead people to develop and adhere to rules that resolve the "justice for loyalty" issue. For example, the explicit set of rules developed to govern labor-management disputes suggests that at some point workers believed they were not being treated fairly in terms of dividing the profits of their endeavors, and also that circumstances were such that they could be "disloyal" by going on strike.

6.4.2 Demand/Withdraw Cycles in Close Relationships

The configuration of situational factors in the Threat Game leads us to expect interaction patterns in which one person expresses unhappiness while the other "doesn't want to hear it." The logic is that if an allocator is mildly exploiting the other's loyalty by acting unfairly, it is in the partner's interests to engage in conflictual discussions in order to gain a measure of justice. However, it is in the allocator's interests to avoid entering into a discussion of the matter, finding it better to let the issue go unresolved and to continue to benefit from the current arrangements. Kelley (1979) invoked this Threat Game analysis in interpreting his evidence suggesting that men are more often the avoiders and women are more often the engagers in dealing with relationship issues. This is consistent with the general pattern, noted in many Western cultures, that men tend to control resource allocations.

This conflict pattern of engaging-avoiding has been noted by many observers of marital conflict, and it is particularly evident in distressed couples (Gottman, 1994). Gottman has described the more severe behaviors associated with this pattern as the "Four Horsemen of the Apocalypse." He contends that criticism by one person followed by defensiveness by another or, worse, expressions of contempt by one person met with stonewalling and withdrawal by the other are warning signs of serious problems in the relationship. The two "reactive" types of avoidant behavior are of course most typical of men.

The particular tendency of men to try to avoid issues may work in the short run because women are loath to back up their complaints with threats to terminate an arrangement that might have serious consequences for the relationship. We might also suggest that if forced to deal with the issue, men may try to justify their own superior outcomes by referring to their "important responsibilities and contributions" which are borne on behalf of the pair. Essentially, such justifications are an attempt to redefine justice in terms of equity considerations (benefits tied to contributions) rather than in terms of equality within a relationship. Faced with such claims, under-benefited wives who have weak counterpower with which to threaten the husband may have to rationalize their fate by demeaning the value of what they bring to the relationship (Brehm, 1992). Consistent with this analysis, there is evidence that abused wives who stay with their partners, usually because they perceive poor alternatives, tend to see themselves as bringing little of value to the relationship (Rusbult & Martz, 1995).

In recent years, there has been considerable debate over the origins of the pattern of interaction in which wives are more demanding and critical and husbands withdraw and avoid issues. Gottman and Levenson (1986) have suggested that the physiology of men may be such that they find "hot or negative emotional climates" aversive, so they are reinforced by avoiding them. In this "escape conditioning model," the more women increase the intensity of their demands, the more likely men are to try to escape by avoiding the issues.

Other observers have countered that men's supposed aversion to dealing with emotional issues can be explained by socialization and role pressures and the dispositions that result from them, such as lack of expressiveness (cf., Eagly & Wood, 1999). However, the analysis derived from the Threat situation is rather different from such perspectives that focus on personality. It is basically a social psychological explanation that focuses on the conflicts of interests in the situation itself – the terms of interdependence in a *relationship*. That is, the issues in contention may be such that anyone in the wife's role would be demanding, and in the husband's position, withdrawing. If that is the case, there is no need to resort to explanations involving personality differences between men and women – the situational forces, the rewards and costs, provide sufficient reasons for their behavior.

Christensen and Heavey (1993) explored these alternative views of demand/withdraw cycles. Such cycles occur about a broad range of concrete issues, such as housework, finances, and child care. In these interactions, the wives typically "demand" that an issue be discussed and the husbands typically try to avoid or withdraw from such discussion. Consistent with the logic developed here, Christensen and Heavy argue that husbands in our society usually get a "good deal" in their marriages. Thus it is in their interests to preserve a status quo that serves them well. From a strategic standpoint, they have little to gain and much to lose by engaging in serious discussions with their wives about possible changes in any current inequitable arrangements. In short, husbands are usually a conservative force in a marriage and wives are the "reformers." By necessity, wives are put in the role of the demander as they are faced with unfair allocations.

Christensen and Heavey designed an ingenious set of experiments to test these propositions. They first identified whether a problem in the marriage was "his issue" or "her issue," in terms of whether the husband or the wife was the person wanting changes to occur. They then had the couple discuss one "his issue" and one "her issue," videotaping the interactions so that observers could rate them for evidence of demand/withdraw patterns. (This is a pattern that trained observers can reliably detect.) Across three studies with different methodologies and different topics, the results were almost identical. For the wife's issue, the typical "wife-demand, husband-withdraw" interaction occurred. For the husband's issue, the spouses did not differ in their behavior.

The latter finding might suggest that there are indeed some long-standing gender differences that contribute to the pattern, over and above the situational causes emphasized in the present analysis. However, the authors interpreted this finding in terms of the prior experiences in these marriages: The wives had perhaps shown more deference to the husbands' needs in the past, with greater willingness to listen to and consider their complaints. Thus, husbands had less need to be demanding and a "husband-demand, wife-withdraw" interaction pattern was less likely to develop.

In other studies, Christensen and Heavey found an unexpected association between conflicts over closeness and intimacy, on the one hand, and frequency of demand/withdraw interactions, on the other. This is perhaps not surprising because, as Kelley (1979) argued, wives are likely to take husbands' avoidance of explicit problem discussions as an indication of their general lack of considerateness for them. Thus, if a husband withdraws and stonewalls in the face of complaints about unfair treatment on household tasks, the wife may be angered by more than the concrete costs of doing more than her share. She may now also have complaints about his emotional withdrawal, especially if closeness and intimacy issues are already on the table. Worst of all, she may interpret his withdrawal as evidence that he doesn't "really" care for her. If concerns about caring are "the heart of the matter," her feelings are likely further to fuel the intensity of her demands.

6.4.3 *Superordinate Identification and Justice Concerns*
The Threat Game logic has been applied at a more macro, societal level as well as in dyadic relationships. For instance, Huo, Smith, Tyler, and Lind

(1996) have considered the issue of whether authorities in a diverse, multicultural society can maintain social cohesion and acceptance of certain rules of justice amid competing interests and values. They suggest that weaker-positioned people are more likely to accept the political and judicial system if they *identify* with the superordinate group. Their arguments resonate with the justice for loyalty exchange emphasized in the present analysis. The less powerful engage in "relational evaluations," judging the extent to which representatives of the powerful group, such as authorities, treat them fairly. When people feel they are treated with benevolence, respect, and without bias, these perceptions of procedural justice affirm their status as group members. According to the authors' group-value model, people derive a sense of self-worth from group membership. Thus, being treated fairly makes it safe for them to become attached to the superordinate group if they value identification with it. Justice buys their loyalty.

Studies have focused on political attitudes and evaluations of superordinate-group authority in public sector organizations. The results suggest that as long as people identify strongly with the superordinate group, gaining rewards from being loyal, their concerns will be with relational evaluations of fairness. However, people who identify strongly with a subgroup, but not the superordinate group, are not motivated to maintain cohesive relations. Because being a loyal member would not be rewarding, their concerns will be solely related to achieving favorable outcomes for themselves (rather than having a fair process). Conflicts with authority are likely to escalate. Thus promoting identification with the superordinate group is central to maintaining a cohesive society, even if individuals still identify strongly with their subgroup.

6.5 Matrix Representation

The matrix on the left in Table E6.1 is simple Mutual Partner Control, described in Entry #2. The matrix in the center is simple Bilateral Actor Control, described in Entry #1. The matrix on the right is an example of the Threat Game. It is a combination of the first two, derived by simply adding the outcomes in the two components.

The differentiation between the "allocator" and "threatener" roles in the Threat situation stems from the facts shown in the first two matrices: (1) B's Actor Control is consonant with (and thus encourages) B's Partner Control over A, so B prefers to select b1 which benefits both persons. (2) A's Actor Control is dissonant with (and thus discourages) A's Partner Control over

B, so A prefers the action (a2) that withholds benefits from B. As long as A follows that preference, B is treated unfairly, and B's only recourse is to select b2 which withdraws benefits from both of them.

TABLE E6.1. *Representation of the Threat Situation and Its Components*

	Mutual Partner Control		+	Bilateral Actor Control		=	The Threat Situation	
	A			A			A	
	a1	a2		a1	a2		a1	a2
b1	+6 / +6	+6 / 0	+	0 / +6	+6 / +6	=	+6 / +12	+12 / +6
b2	0 / +6	0 / 0		0 / 0	+6 / 0		0 / +6	+6 / 0

(B labels the rows; in each cell the upper-right value is A's outcome and the lower-left value is B's outcome.)

Entry #7

Chicken

Death before Dishonor

7.1 Examples

The name of this situation is based on a deadly game. In one version, the two contestants – invariably males – drive their cars at high speed, headlong toward each other. The essence of this high-stakes game is to see which contestant has the stronger nerves. The first one to veer off course to avoid a collision loses the test of courage and is branded a "chicken" (i.e., a coward). If both drivers (in a simultaneous moment of sanity) veer off, the contest ends in a draw – somewhat embarrassing but giving neither a justification for accusing the other of less courage. Of course, if neither driver "chickens out," the result is a fatal – and hence, rather hollow – "victory" for both. Another variation on this game – in which the contestants simultaneously drive toward a cliff's edge – was depicted in the film *Rebel without a Cause*.[1]

A similar situation occurs when neighboring countries, seeking something valuable possessed by the other, issue ultimatums threatening war if the other will not yield. If one's neighbor yields, one may gain something of

---

[1] In chapter 3, we noted that the objective, tangible payoffs in such situations can be rather different from the subjective, interpersonal payoffs. To the extent that the costs of "losing" the contest (e.g., to one's personal sense of self) are wholly internalized and subjective, we might conclude that this classic Chicken scenario is not really a "given" situation at all but one transformed by the actors' personal and social values. One could, alternatively, view the social costs of such a loss (e.g., to one's reputation or standing in one's social group) as real aspects of the situation in relation to the psychological facts of the actors' basic needs and aversions and, in that sense, view this Chicken scenario as a "given" situation. In any case, some of the other examples offered here (e.g., the international or environmental examples) seem to be "given" situations – i.e., they require no assumptions of social transformation of basic, psychophysical payoffs.

Norbert Kerr had primary responsibility for preparation of this entry.

real value, but if neither yields and both carry through on their threats, the resulting war is likely to cost both far more than what was sought through the initial threats.

Struggles for dominance in a group can also create a Chicken situation. Imagine an animal group in which the dominant male may mate and feed at will, whereas all other males' mating and feeding behaviors are much more constrained (e.g., they are unable to mate; they may only feed after the dominant male has fed). Further, suppose that when the dominant male dies, a new dominant male is identified through combat between any male pretenders to the position. Persisting in such battles offers the chance of improving one's lot, becoming the dominant animal, but if two contestants persist too long, there is also the chance that both will be wounded or killed, and worse off than had they settled for their subordinate lots.

Later (see Entry #20) we will note that many environmental problems (e.g., overharvesting shared resources) or economic problems (e.g., trade protectionism) have the structure of N-person Prisoner's Dilemma or social dilemma situations, wherein a self-serving, competitive choice *always* results in a better personal outcome. However, many other environmental problems have the Chicken structure. The key difference is that for Chicken, a competitive/risky response only makes sense as long as enough others can safely be assumed to be acting cooperatively/safely; if too many others are going to compete, one is better off acting cooperatively. A concrete example might be two companies that manufacture the same product but, because of different manufacturing processes, dump different pollutants into the river that supplies drinking water to the entire community. Further, suppose that either pollutant by itself would not make the water unsafe to drink, but combining them would. Under these assumptions, if one company installs costly antipollution equipment, the other would probably not, gaining a competitive edge without undue risk to the community's (and their own) health. But if the other refuses to install such equipment, the first one should prefer to install it (assuming that it's preferable to be alive with lower profits than to be just as profitable as one's competitor but with poisoned drinking water).

7.2 Conceptual Description

The essence of the Chicken situation is a choice between a safer choice with relatively middling outcomes and a riskier choice with more extreme outcomes – extremely good if the other makes a safe choice but extremely bad if the other makes the risky choice too. It is only by making the risky choice that one can obtain the highest possible outcome and/or can "beat" the other player (i.e., obtain a better outcome). It is only by making the safe choice that one can, in turn, be "beaten" by the other player. But the consequences of both players making the risky choice are the worst possible for both (unlike the Prisoner's Dilemma situation, see Entries #5, #12, and #20).

In the Chicken situation, if the other acted as if she or he were indifferent between his or her choices, there would be no overall advantage to one of preferring one choice over the other (that is, there is no Bilateral Actor Control [BAC] component to make one choice generally more attractive than the other). So, one cannot understand a preference between the risky versus safe choice simply in terms of the overall, marginal benefit to self of making one choice versus the other. One can, though, make sense of the attractiveness of the risky choice in other terms – such as (a) a willingness or preference to accept risk, (b) a strong preference to do better than the other, or (c) a strong aversion to doing less well than the other (cf. Messick & Thorngate, 1967).

In terms of more elementary situations, Chicken is a combination of two elementary patterns of control: strong Mutual Partner Control (MPC; i.e., each player strongly prefers the other to make the safe choice) plus weak Corresponding Mutual Joint Control (Corr MJC, with discordant orientation; i.e., each weakly prefers that actors make different choices rather than the same choice).

7.3 Variants and Combinations

The simplest Chicken situation is one faced by two players making simultaneous, irrevocable choices. Many variations are possible, of course. There is no inherent limitation on the number of players. For example, instead of two cars driving headlong toward each other, one could envision three (or more) cars all traveling at the same speed and converging on a single point, with each driver facing the choice of whether or not to brake before reaching the point of collision. The generic N-person Chicken Game is represented in the matrix in Table E7.4 below (at the end of this entry). Another variation on the simple two-person situation is one in which two (or more) groups are interdependent. It has been shown (e.g., Bornstein, Budescu, & Zamir, 1997) that the risky/competitive choices are more likely when the contestants in a Chicken situation are groups rather than individuals [somewhat similar to the "discontinuity effect" reported by Insko & Schopler (e.g., 1999) for the Prisoner's Dilemma Situation.][2]

---

[2] Somewhat different dynamics are probably at work in the intergroup Chicken situation and the intergroup Prisoner's Dilemma situation. For example, greater mistrust of the

Sometimes actors choose sequentially, rather than simultaneously. Imagine, for example, in the context of the classic test-of-courage Chicken Game that driver A, who chooses first, must either pull his car over to the side of the road (Safe choice) or lock in an autopilot that commits him to continue to drive ahead (Risky choice), regardless of what driver B might do. As long as B wants to maximize his outcomes (and isn't suicidal), A's choice essentially compels B to make the opposite choice. Thus, the sequential version of the Chicken Game is an example of a "preemption game," because one can, by choosing first and publicly, insure that one wins. What this sequential game gains in certainty and control for the first player, though, it loses as a test of nerve – when the outcomes are preempted and fixed by one player's initial move, that player is no longer taking quite the same risk to choose the "risky" alternative (Kelley & Thibaut, 1978).

The Chicken situation may be confronted repeatedly. This version's Mutual Joint Control (MJC) component gives either player a way of "punishing" a noncooperative partner (by matching the partner's uncooperativeness and reducing the partner's [and, necessarily, one's own] outcomes), thereby creating long-term pressures toward mutual cooperation. In principle, another "solution" to the iterated Chicken situation is turn taking. For example, in the idealized Chicken Game (e.g., see Tables E7.1 and E7.2 below), each player can do just as well by taking turns winning as by both players consistently making the safe choice. Under slightly different conditions,[3] such alternation would actually be more rewarding than joint cooperation. However, when the goal of playing the Chicken Game is to establish dominance (e.g., who's braver, who's stronger, who's more willing to take chances), such turn taking, while insuring high individual and joint returns, might well be seen as pointless by the players.

7.4 Interaction Process and Person Factors

The Chicken situation poses many interesting questions about social interaction. What patterns of interaction are likely to induce some people to enter into or to create such high-stakes contests? Which people are particularly prone to do so, and once in the Chicken situation, to opt for the risky

cooperative intent of groups (vs. individuals) seems partly to underlie the discontinuity effect in the PD situation. However, a similar mistrust in the intergroup Chicken situation should prompt more, not less, cooperation.

[3] This would occur if the importance of the MPC component was greater than that of the MJC component, but less than twice as large.

choice? And what are the stakes that would compel someone to persist in making the competitive, risky choice?

7.4.1 The Culture of Honor

Nisbett, Cohen, and their colleagues (e.g., 1996) shed considerable light on such questions in their analysis of the "culture of honor." They note that certain cultures (e.g., the traditional cultures of the Mediterranean, of many Islamic countries, of the preindustrial herding economies of Scotland and Ireland) view aggressive or violent behavior as justified when one's personal or family honor has been threatened. The concept of honor is a rather diffuse and complex one (cf. Cohen, Vandello, & Rantilla, 1998), but Nisbett and Cohen (1996) suggest that it can encompass both one's personal identity and one's social reputation. In such cultures, if one's (or one's family's) honor (e.g., virtue, strength, toughness, or masculinity) is challenged, one is obligated and justified to defend that honor, often by a demonstration of strength or toughness. They trace the roots of these cultural beliefs to patterns of social and economic organization. For example, they suggest that in contrast to traditional farming economies, which require high levels of cooperation for mutual survival, traditional herding economies reward exploiting one's neighbors (e.g., rustling from neighboring clans) and consequently require vigilant defense from such exploitation. One means of protecting oneself from predation in such an economy is to "adopt a pose of extreme belligerence in the face of confrontation. An insult must be retracted, because to allow it to stand means that one may be too weak to defend oneself. Hence, a constant vigilance concerning one's 'honor,' or reputation for strength, toughness, and personal integrity, is an economic necessity" (Fiske, Kitayama, Markus, & Nisbett, 1998, p. 955). Nisbett and Cohen (1996) suggest that this culture of honor is more prevalent (due to immigration patterns) in the American South and West than elsewhere in the United States, and that this at least partially accounts for regional differences in patterns of violence. For example, rates of homicide committed in the context of arguments among white southern males are four times higher than among white northern males (Nisbett, Polly, & Lang, 1995).

And experimental research has shown that, when insulted, college students raised in the South were – compared to those who grew up in the North – more likely to see their masculinity threatened, be upset, have high testosterone levels, and behave in a more aggressive and dominant manner (Cohen, Nisbett, Bowdle, & Schwarz, 1996). Cohen et al. (1996, Exp. 3) even staged a reenactment of the classic Chicken Game. After being insulted or not by one confederate, the experimental subject had to traverse a hallway

only wide enough for a single person to pass. There he met a second confederate walking in the opposite direction on a collision course. How close
to collision would the subject come before yielding to the second confederate (who was trained not to give way)? Cohen et al. (1996) found that
a prior insult didn't affect northern subjects' behavior. However, a previous insult to honor led southern subjects to come much closer to collision
before giving way.

This analysis suggests that if one's bedrock of self-worth and safety
hinges upon maintaining a reputation for strength and toughness, one
may go to great lengths to defend that reputation if it is challenged in any
way (e.g., a possible verbal insult, an invasion of one's territory). To such
a person, failure to defend one's honor is humiliating and invites further
exploitation. If it is paramount to prove that you are not weak, that you
cannot be "pushed around," then mutual destruction (when the drivers
in the classic Chicken contest crash into one another; when a personal
argument spirals into deadly violence) may be preferable to yielding –
"death before dishonor."

Clearly, it can be dangerous to live in a culture of honor. One means
of avoiding the risks of defenses of honor is to employ norms which are
designed to keep interaction on well-understood and safe grounds (e.g.,
Thibaut & Faucheux, 1965). Thus, Cohen, Vandello, Puente, & Rantilla
(1999) argue, American southerners are more likely to observe traditional
politeness norms and to avoid ambiguous, nonnormative behavior which
might trigger a threat to honor. A consequence is that, compared to north-
erners, southerners are initially less sensitive to cues of possible hostility,
but react more explosively after many such cues accumulate (Cohen et al.,
1999).

7.4.2 Developmental Issues

The preceding analysis suggests that a certain set of values and beliefs
which tie one's sense of self to social dominance make one more likely to
enter into a Chicken situation and once there to act competitively. Such
values and beliefs can be acquired within a culture or subculture through
normal socialization practices. And, of course, they can be inculcated by
more particular parenting practices, modeling, and attachment experiences
(cf. Van Lange et al., 1997).

A corollary of this argument is that actions by others that are seen as
intentional challenges to one's honor are particularly likely to prompt competitive or aggressive behavior. Thus, as children become more capable
of making attributions of intention for others' annoying, frustrating, or

interfering behaviors, they become more likely to see such acts as threats to self-esteem and to react with aggressive counterattacks (Hartup, 1974). There is also evidence (e.g., Dodge, 1985) that older children who acquire a reputation for aggressiveness are prone to interpret ambiguous interaction events (e.g., "he knocked over my puzzle") as intentionally hostile and not as events that pose little threat to the self (e.g., "it was an accident").

7.4.3 *Thoughtful versus Heuristic Choice in the Chicken Situation*

A clear understanding of the structure of the Chicken situation carries a clear prescription for behavior – do the opposite of what your partner is likely to do. So, for example, suppose you just observed James engage in the driver's Chicken Game and saw him yield to his opponent. Now suppose it's your turn to challenge James at the same game. If you understand the game and accept its payoff structure, having such knowledge of James's past behavior should make you more likely to refuse to yield in the game (assuming – and praying – that he will play the game in a consistent way).

On the other hand, a fairly simple and useful behavioral heuristic is "do whatever others do." So, in the preceding scenario, if one simply and heuristically *imitates* James's past behavior, one would be more likely to yield after having seen James do so. Thus, the Chicken situation provides an interesting context within which one can probe the relative reliance on a simple "monkey-see, monkey-do" behavioral heuristic versus the rule required by an accurate understanding of the structure of the situation – namely, "monkey see, monkey do the opposite." Hertel, Neuhof, Theuer, & Kerr (2000) exploited this property of the Chicken situation to show that when contestants were in a good mood (and, hence, likely to act more heuristically, cf. Schwarz & Clore, 1996), they were more likely to imitate the recent actions of their opponent, whereas when they were in a bad mood (and, hence, less likely to rely on behavioral heuristics), they tended more to act opposite to the opponent's recent behavior.

7.4.4 *Spiraling Conflict in Interpersonal Encounters*

As we noted earlier in chapter 3, sometimes people end up facing a Chicken situation after they have "made something" out of another, less confrontational situation. A good example of this is the pattern of interaction that all too frequently leads people to move from settings of mild disagreement or conflict to ones in which "backing down" entails extremely high costs. Luckenbill (1977) found, for example, that every single one of the 70 cases of criminal homicide he analyzed were characterized by a generic pattern of escalating conflict: one person acts in a way that is offensive to the other, the other retaliates, and the escalating conflict is resolved with violence. A key element of these situations was that the conflicts quickly became "character contests," in which one or more contestants perceived direct threats to their "face," reputation, or honor.

Of course, such spiraling conflicts are hardly restricted to interactions ending in violence or murder; they are commonplace in ordinary social interaction. They are likely to begin when one either gives to or receives from a friend or spouse some small, perhaps unintentional injury. For example, the noncooking spouse might casually note to the cooking spouse that the dinner soup is a bit salty. The cook, who may have devoted particular attention to the preparation of the soup, is offended and retaliates (e.g., "Why should I bother when nothing I make pleases you"). Such "complaint–counter complaint" exchanges can quickly escalate, particularly when the basis of conflict shifts from the precipitating event to deeper interpersonal or intrapersonal issues (e.g., to questions of character, motive, or trust; to old, unresolved, "hot" issues for the couple). Such escalations can functionally create a Chicken situation where one has to choose between taking up the challenge of getting in the last (hurtful) word versus swallowing one's pride (and, with luck, breaking the cycle before both parties have gone too far). A transition list representation of such a situation is offered in Table E7.5 below.

Work by several scholars (e.g., Cordova, Jacobson, Gottman, Rushe, & Cox, 1993) has shown that such patterns of unchecked negative reciprocity characterize distressed or violent relationships. Conversely, relationships within which partners accommodate one another early – before the situation escalates into a full-fledged death-before-dishonor one – tend to be more successful (i.e., have more satisfied and committed members) (e.g., Rusbult, Verette, Whitney, Slovik, & Lipkus, 1991).

7.4.5 *Person Factors*
Earlier we suggested that making the risky choice in the Chicken situation could be understood in terms of any of three dispositions: namely, (a) a willingness or preference to accept risk, (b) a strong preference to do better than the other, or (c) a strong aversion to doing less well than the other. We have already touched on cultural and individual differences in the acceptance of a culture of honor, which seems to involve both the second and third of these interpersonal dispositions. Personality traits which appear particularly to reflect the second disposition – the desire to "beat" the other – include a need for dominance and a competitive social value orientation (for the latter, there is a bit of supporting evidence; Liebrand,

Wilke, Vogel, & Wolters, 1986). The traits of impulsivity, risk seeking, thrill seeking, or sensation seeking (e.g., Zuckerman, 1971) all appear relevant to the first of these dispositions. Unfortunately, there is very little research currently available that bears on these conjectures in the Chicken situation.

Sometimes it may be cultural norms which require one to aggressively defend any threat to one's honor. But certain habits of ego defense can also prompt some individuals to react very aggressively to any ego threat. Such habits are captured in the common understanding of a "defensive" personality – habits of experiencing nearly any threat to self as intolerable and of going to sometimes drastic lengths to remove such threats. When pairs of such defensive persons interact, the inflated personal stakes can transform ordinary situations of interdependence into the Chicken situation.

Just who are these defensive persons? One likely candidate is the narcissist. Defining characteristics include grandiose views of the self, an inflated sense of entitlement, and low empathy toward others. Recent work (see Baumeister, Bushman, & Campbell, 2000) demonstrates that narcissists are particularly likely to respond to insults with aggression and that violent felons score particularly high on narcissism. Another candidate is unstable self-esteem; it seems to be individuals with high but unstable self-esteem who are most hostile and angry (Kernis, Granneman, & Barclay, 1989).

7.5 Matrix and Transition List Representations

Table E7.1. A matrix representation of the classic, test-of-courage Chicken Game is provided in Table E7.1. Once they are committed to playing the

TABLE E7.1. *Situational Representation of the Classic Chicken Scenario*

	A	
	Veer	Not
B Veer	−3 / −3	3 / −9
B Not Veer	−9 / 3	−15 / −15

game, the contestants each have two choices, to veer away before crashing or not to veer away. A draw (both contestants making the same choice) results in equal outcomes for both – although the outcomes are far more negative when both stubbornly refuse to veer away (both killed, a utility of −15 in the matrix) than when both do so (and both reveal an embarrassing failure of nerve, a utility of −3 in the matrix). Different choices by the two contestants result in victory for one (a utility of 3 in the matrix) and humiliating defeat for the other (a utility of −9 in the matrix).

Table E7.2. In the preceding example, most of the outcomes are negative (which is why it strikes most people as a rather foolish game to play). However, this is not a defining feature of the Chicken situation – one could also face a choice involving only positive outcomes, such as the situation depicted in Table E7.2 (which presents the matrix of Table E7.1 with all entries increased by 18 units). Here, the outcomes are all positive, but once again, the risky choice carries the possibility of both the greatest and the smallest gain. It seems very probable that such differences in framing – focusing on magnitude of gains or the magnitude of losses or the magnitude of gains versus losses – will alter the subjective utility of the game outcomes (Kahneman & Tversky, 1979).

TABLE E7.2. *Situational Representation of Chicken Situation with Positive Outcomes*

		A	
		Safe	Risky
B	Safe	15 15	21 9
	Risky	9 21	3 3

Table E7.3. The generic Chicken situation is depicted in Table E7.3. Here, the quantity P represents the magnitude of Mutual Partner Control – the change in the other's outcome that is under each player's exclusive control; and X represents the magnitude of Mutual Joint Control – the change in outcome that is determined by joint choice. For Chicken, $P > X$. Kelley and Thibaut (1978) suggest that the most acute choice dilemma is posed for both parties when the ratio of *P*:*X* is 2:1. The basic structure of the situation is unaltered by adding or subtracting a constant value, *C*, from all entries in the generic matrix; so, for example, the matrix of Table E7.1 is obtained when $C = -15$ and the matrix of Table E7.2 when $C = 3$, with $P = 12$ and $X = 6$ for each.

TABLE E7.3. *Situational Representation of a Generic Chicken Situation*

		A	
		Safe	Risky
B	Safe	P P	P+X X
	Risky	X P+X	0 0

Table E7.4. Table E7.4 presents an *N*-person generalization of the Chicken situation. In it, each actor receives *P* for every Safe choice made by another group member, and receives *X* for every instance where a group member makes the opposite choice to his or her own (where, again, $P > X$). Thus,

TABLE E7.4. *Situational Representation of N-Person Generalization of the Generic Chicken Situation*

	Number of other group members choosing Safe				
	0	1			n
Actor's Choice — Safe	(N−1) X	P + (N−2) X	• • •		nP + (N−1−n) X
Actor's Choice — Risky	0	P+X			nP+nX

Note: The tabled entries are the outcome values for an actor in an *N*-person group. Any constant, *C*, could be added to all tabled entries without changing the essential structure of the situation.

in an *N*-person group, if *n* people other than the actor make the Safe choice (and, hence, $N - 1 - n$ make the Risky choice), the actor would receive $nP + (N - 1 - n)X$ if she or he made the Safe choice versus $nP + nX$ if she or he made the Risky choice. Generalizing from the simple two-person case, the Risky choice is maximally attractive when everyone else makes the Safe choice, and as the number of others who make the Safe choice declines, the Risky choice becomes relatively less attractive, such that at some point (viz., when $n = (N - 1)/2$, in this generic case) the Risky and Safe choices provide identical outcomes, and then beyond that point, the Safe choice becomes increasingly more attractive.

Table E7.5. Finally, Table E7.5 shows a transition list representing a conflict spiraling into a Chicken situation. Using our example from section 7.4.4 above, suppose husband A initially chooses between an action which is slightly rewarding to him though potentially punishing to his wife

TABLE E7.5. *Situational Representation of Transition List for Escalation to Chicken*

Junctures	Options	Possible Selections	Outcomes for A and B		Transition to Next Juncture
[J	(a1, a2)	a1b1	+1,	−1	K]
[	(b1, b2)	a1b2	+1,	−1	K]
[		a2b1	−1,	0	X]
[		a2b2	−1,	0	X]
[K	(a1, a2)	a1b1	−2,	+2	L]
[	(b1, b2)	a1b2	0,	−1	X]
[		a2b1	−2,	+2	L]
[		a2b2	0,	−1	X]
[L	(a1, a2)	a1b1	+3,	−3	M]
[	(b1, b2)	a1b2	+3,	−3	M]
[		a2b1	−1,	0	X]
[		a2b2	−1,	0	X]
[M	(a1, a2)	a1b1	−4,	+4	C]
[	(b1, b2)	a1b2	0,	−1	X]
[		a2b1	−4,	+4	C]
[		a2b2	0,	−1	X]
[C	(a1, a2)	a1b1	−10,	−10	X]
[	(b1, b2)	a1b2	+5,	−5	X]
[		a2b1	−5,	+5	X]
[		a2b2	0,	0	X]

(e.g., a1 = I'll show interest in the meal she prepared by analyzing the soup) and an alternative action which is neutral to her but slightly punishing to him (e.g., a2 = I'll say nothing about the salty soup). At this juncture, actor A has unilateral control over both his own and his partner's outcomes. Although a2 is the less personally rewarding choice, it has the merit of avoiding further conflict, because by making the comment, the husband opens the door to higher stakes retaliation by wife B at the next juncture (i.e., at juncture K, where b1 might be "Why do I bother trying to make a nice meal when all you do is complain?" and b2 might be to ignore the original comment). In this example, after four rounds, the conflict has escalated into a situation like Chicken, where either party might choose to "win" the argument by firing off some really hurtful remark (a1 or b1), but if both "take off the gloves" and make this choice, substantial and lasting damage to both will result.

Entry #8

Hero

Let's Do It Your Way

8.1 Examples

Pairs of individuals often face situations in which they have a common interest in coordinating their behaviors, but different preferences for the particular combination of behaviors that will be chosen. Among the varieties of this situation is the one considered here, referred to as "Hero" (for reasons to be explained below). In this particular case, the two persons have a strong mutual desire to coordinate their actions, but also a mild conflict of interest about which particular action to pursue among those necessary for such coordination.

For example, in close relationships partners often place great value on doing certain things together, such as going to movies or jogging together. However, they may differ in their preferences for which movie to see or where to jog. A husband may prefer to see a comedy, and the wife a crime movie. Despite this difference, their primary consideration is their strong, mutual interest in engaging in a shared activity and enjoying each other's company. The issue they face then is not whether to go to a movie together or separately, but rather how to determine whose preferred movie they will attend jointly. In these circumstances, the opportunity exists for one partner to "play the hero" by volunteering to go to the movie the other prefers.

These types of situations are likely to occur frequently in the everyday adjustments and coordinating decisions that friends or partners in close relationships must make. The decisions might involve minor issues of the

John Holmes had primary responsibility for preparation of this entry.

sort above, some of which would be repeatedly encountered and which, therefore, enable a pair to "play fair" and take turns in whose preferences they follow. They might also involve major issues, such as a decision about where to go on vacation, or the choice of where to reside together for a two-career couple whose places of work are widely separated. Decisions such as the latter are not likely to occur often and may be particularly difficult to resolve because the opportunity for turn taking (in whose personal preference is best served) is not readily available.

Coordination problems with a similar overall theme of common interests but somewhat conflicting individual preferences might also involve situations with a shared preference for complementary actions, that is, for each individual doing something different. Co-workers might agree, for instance, that certain jobs are best done individually. However, when it comes to dividing up who does what, they might find that they both prefer to do the same job, leaving them with the dilemma of deciding who will end up doing the less preferred job. As another example, success in moving a heavy piece of furniture requires that one person lift one end and the other person the other end. But both individuals may prefer to lift the one end that has convenient handholds, to avoid lifting with a bent back. Or, in completing household tasks, busy couples may often agree that it is more efficient for each spouse to do separate jobs. Two persons taking the car to the auto shop for repairs or shopping for groceries together may not save much time over one person doing it alone. Thus it is in their shared interest to go their separate ways and each complete one of the necessary tasks. However, if both the husband and the wife would rather do the shopping than go to the garage, their similar personal preferences make it more difficult to decide how to split up the jobs.

8.2 Conceptual Description

In each of the above examples, the major concern is about the particular *combination* of the two persons' actions in concert. Such basic patterns are described as Mutual Joint Control (Entries #3 and #4, depending on whether coordination involves preferences for doing similar or different things). In these coordination situations, each person has the potential, by varying his or her behavior, to induce the other to modify his or her choice. So for instance, if a husband bought a ticket for his favorite type of movie, the wife's motivation to spend time together would lead her to modify her choice and attend it with him, rather than following her initial preference for type of movie (which would now mean going to it alone).

However, the current situation is more complex than the simple coordination problems in Entries #3 and #4. Individuals in the present case also have personal preferences about which activity to do – preferences that interfere with the coordination process. Such personal preferences (Bilateral Actor Control) were discussed in Entry #1 (Independence) as one of the four basic patterns. Thus, in the present situation, individuals' primary motivation is to coordinate their actions, but achieving the desirable combinations is made difficult by their opposing (though secondary) motivation to follow their own personal interests (#1). In the one case (see the matrix in Table E8.1 below, at the end of this entry), their (weaker) preferences for doing different things is incompatible with their (stronger) mutual preference for doing *something together* (Corresponding Mutual Joint Control, #3); in the other case (see the matrix in Table E8.2 below), their common preferences for the same particular behavior or activity is incompatible with the fact that coordination requires that they select different, complementary behaviors (Conflicting Mutual Joint Control, #4).

In this situation, neither person will be satisfied if each simply follows his or her personal inclinations in choosing an activity, because they would then forfeit the opportunity to experience better outcomes from their coordinated preferences. How might the potential stalemate be broken? The situation provides an opportunity for one person to step forward and select the activity that promotes the combination of actions preferred by the partner. Such behavior benefits the person showing the initiative, because it brings the sizable benefits of coordinated action. But to an even greater degree, it benefits the partner because his or her preferred activity or behavior was chosen. This pattern of choices was termed "Hero" by Rapoport and Guyer (1966) to focus attention on this willingness to overcome the pull of personal preferences in order to increase the joint outcomes experienced by the pair, despite the salient fact that the benefits of such initiative are greater for the partner.

8.3 Variants and Neighbors

The coordination goals in Hero may involve either achieving good outcomes or avoiding bad ones. The latter is illustrated by a couple trying to decide how to delegate the unpleasant (for them) tasks of going to the auto shop or shopping for food. Let us assume that both the husband and wife detest discussing their car with the mechanic, and the resulting common preference for doing the grocery shopping (if both must be done) interferes with efficient delegation of the two tasks. In this case, the husband's volunteering to go to the auto shop enables them to avoid having to complete both disliked tasks together. His action is "heroic" in the sense that it reduces the wife's costs more than it reduces his.

The Hero situation has a "close neighbor" in the Martyr situation. As its name suggests, this situation is one that provides an opportunity for a person to act as a "martyr." Like Hero, Martyr involves a common interest coordination problem combined with interfering individual preferences. In Martyr, however, the mutual interest in coordination is relatively weak and the preferences for different activities are strong. As a consequence, if a person wishes to accommodate the partner's preferred coordination, that person has to forgo his or her own strong interests. So if one person takes the lead in going along with the partner's preferred activity, that person will receive poorer outcomes than by simply pursuing his or her own interests alone. Not only does the partner benefit (as in Hero), but those extra benefits come at a direct cost to the person. The personal sacrifice required to bring about the solution that makes the partner happiest is the basis for characterizing the situation as one that offers the opportunity to be a "martyr."

Earlier we noted that if repeatedly encountered, situations that fit the Hero paradigm enable fairness or justice to be served by a simple procedure of taking turns. That procedure makes it possible for each person occasionally to "get his or her way" about the pair's joint activities – whenever it is his or her turn to have the privilege. This solution to the conflict obviously requires that various concrete situations be conceptualized as recurrent instances of this type of problem. Thus we might expect to hear a husband who had played the Hero on recent occasions gently reminding his wife, "Last time we went out to dinner, we went out to *your* favorite place . . . "

Hero is one of several types of problem that provide the opportunity for turn taking. They all possess, as important components, correspondent Mutual Joint Control (Entry #3). A classic example is known as the Battle of the Sexes. Like Hero, people in this situation have a strong common interest in how they coordinate their activities. However, whereas in Hero each person's preferences for his or her *own* behavior interfere with achieving a satisfactory coordination, in Battle of the Sexes, the interference comes from each one's preferences for what the *other* person does. In other words, the interference comes from their Mutual Partner Control (Entry #2). If each one does what the partner desires, they fail to achieve the matching of behavior they mutually prefer. For example, two friends enjoy singing two-part duets – requiring one to sing alto and the other tenor. However, if they both prefer to hear each other's voice in the tenor range, those preferences get in the way of performing the duet. Such conflicts have been labeled, tongue in cheek, as the "Battle of the Sexes," because of the struggle to get the other person to play the role that one prefers.

8.4 Interaction Process and Person Factors

There is a wide range of processes and mechanisms relevant to finding solutions to interdependence problems such as Hero. The interaction process will depend on the extent to which coordination is tacit or based on more open communication, the degree to which individuals are free to take the initiative in selecting one of the options, and the degree to which a current problem is conceptualized as involving only one instance in an interaction sequence extended over time.

8.4.1 Tacit Coordination

Individuals will sometimes confront problems like Hero when circumstances dictate that they must handle them without much, if any, communication, making their choices independently. For instance, a couple who agreed to meet at their favorite restaurant for dinner may realize too late that it wasn't clear whose favorite was intended. Or, after discussing at breakfast that someone must pick up some groceries at the store after work and that the kids must be picked up from school, a busy couple may have forgotten to decide who does what. Under these highly constrained circumstances, a pair may still be able to effectively coordinate by using their knowledge of each other and simple reasoning.

To thoughtfully anticipate and contribute to the combination of actions that will satisfy the shared coordination requirements, a person needs to be able to anticipate what the partner will do. This is not merely a matter of knowing what the partner, other things being equal, would prefer to do. It also requires the person to anticipate whether the partner will use the occasion to be a "hero," that is, to try to create a coordination that the person will prefer. Here we encounter the paradox that a husband and wife, both of whom know the other's preferences and act generously to try to benefit the other, will thwart their coordination interests and go to each other's favorite restaurants. Of course, they may realize the possibility of each other's likely "heroism" and suppress their own, but then they end up simply going to their respective preferred restaurants. Only if one is better informed or better able to think through the metacognition problem ("If I do this, and he/she does that...; but then, what if...") can they dependably achieve one of the coordinative solutions they mutually desire.

The dilemma actually becomes less difficult for the husband if he believes that his wife doesn't really understand his preferences and will follow her own inclinations. That would make the situation more predictable, but it would also put the onus on him to be the one to have to make the adjustment that would result in better outcomes for his wife than for him. The paradox here is that the person with better knowledge of another is sometimes at a comparative disadvantage. In many situations, having greater information than one's partner enables one, if so inclined, to gain better outcomes than the partner. However, in a few situations, including Hero, the better informed partner is, in effect, forced into the position of playing the hero, accurately predicting the other person's choice and adjusting to it in a way that benefits the "ignorant" person.

8.4.2 *Opportunities for Showing Initiative*

Ad lib response conditions, which permit either person to take preemptive action by announcing his or her intentions or by making irrevocable arrangements, make it easy to resolve the coordination problem. When one person exercises a kind of leadership by firmly adopting one behavior, the partner will be motivated to coordinate with it. Of course, such initiative would warrant the label of "hero" only if the person is informed about and correctly anticipates the partner's desires. There is a common temptation to project one's own preferences onto close others (Murray, Holmes & Griffin, 1996a; Thomas, Fletcher, & Lange, 1997), and apparent efforts to "put the partner's wishes first" may sometimes reflect an egocentric interpretation of the situation. For instance, a husband who, without consulting his wife, arranges for them to go together to watch their son's baseball game, rather than to purchase plantings for their garden, may incorrectly assume that his initiative would be especially pleasing to her.

Such misreadings aside, we should not assume that taking the initiative is always motivated by the best of intentions. An assertive approach to Hero's coordination problems may also be used to get one's own way in decisions about joint activities a pair enjoys doing together. Preemptively selecting one's own preferred activity is a way of controlling events that can often be rationalized by the (correct) belief that the partner finds it rewarding when they pursue activities they both find pleasure in sharing. The unfairness of such rationalizations may only become apparent over time.

8.4.3 Repeated Encounters with a Problem

When certain situations are repeatedly encountered over time, individuals may come to conceptualize their interactions as a series of exchanges, rather than dealing with each decision solely on an ad hoc basis. Situations might be categorized as being part of a set of exchanges, as being a general, more extended "problem," on the basis of either concrete similarities (e.g., choosing restaurants) or more abstract ones (e.g., activities we share together). If certain common features of these types of situations lead individuals to construe them as a recurring type of problem, exchanges may lend themselves to taking turns. Earlier, we suggested that this is because situations like Hero typically require that one person receive fewer benefits than the other in order for the dyad to reap the rewards of coordinating their actions. Turn taking may alleviate concerns about immediate inequalities by providing the possibility of equality over a longer period of time.

The expectation of ultimate reciprocation frees individuals from localized concerns about fairness issues and may lead a person to define helpful initiatives in the coordination process as "retrievable investments" (Holmes, 1981; see Entry #18). For instance, such a perspective might encourage co-workers to show initiative and play the "hero" role when it seems appropriate, without concern about their relative lack of benefits at the time. However, individuals may differ in how an "accounting" of the balance of turn taking is estimated, depending on their time perspective and their boundaries for what constitutes "domains" within which alternation should occur. Research on justice in close relationships suggests that, in general, pairs who are more trusting (Holmes & Levinger, 1994) and who adhere to more communal norms (Clark & Mills, 1993) will adopt broader definitions of domains and use looser accounting practices. The implication for turn-taking interactions is that such pairs might be expected to deal more effectively with coordination problems because individuals would be less hesitant to incur the relative costs of "playing the hero."

8.4.4 Interpersonal Dispositions

Situations such as Hero provide the opportunity for individuals to show their willingness to take "forceful" initiatives in social interaction, to take a leadership role by firmly and decisively adopting one course of action that then encourages the partner to coordinate with it. In the description of situation #3, it was noted that the willingness to take initiative in common interest coordination problems appears to be one component of what is commonly understood by the trait term "dominance." (The other component consists of unilateral commands and the use of threats and promises.)

In the Hero situation, assertiveness is exercised in the common interest, though it has somewhat different meanings depending on whether the pre-emptive initiative facilitates decisions that favor the partner's preferences or one's own. The former, the "hero" role, involves a willingness to put the partner's interests somewhat ahead of one's own (though the self still gains considerably from effective coordination). Such prosocial initiative might reflect a more general disposition (that combines both agentic and communal tendencies in social interaction, cf. Wiggins & Trapnell, 1996) or a relationship-specific motive. The latter may involve either a caring attitude (i.e., finding it rewarding to benefit the partner, with little concern about the inequality that results) or a trusting one (i.e., expecting that the partner has a similar attitude and where appropriate, will reciprocate).

Taking the initiative in a way that "puts the partner's wishes first" could result in attributions by the partner that the person is "actively considerate." However, such conclusions are somewhat obscured by the fact that the person does gain concrete benefits from promoting the common interest. And if such actions are conceptualized by the partner as being part of a turn-taking pattern, the person might be viewed as "only doing his or her part" in adhering to rules of fair exchange. In contrast, clearer attributions about a person's motivations can be drawn in situational contexts that more closely resemble the Martyr situation. In that situation (as described above), benefiting the partner is at a direct cost to the self, resulting in poorer personal outcomes than would occur if the person simply followed his or her own interests. Such evidence of self-sacrifice would allow the partner to draw more confident conclusions about the person's altruistic motives (Holmes & Rempel, 1989; Rusbult & Van Lange, 1996).

Of course, the Hero situation also affords the opportunity to assert one's *own* interests relative to a partner's, while still furthering joint goals. Such "competitive" preemptive actions that favor one's own preferences might reflect a simple preference for having one's own way, but also a concern with insuring that the partner does not receive better outcomes than oneself (a concern with justice), or even a desire to do better than the partner (a competitive motivation). Research by Mendolia, Beach and Tesser (1996) suggests that even individuals in happy marriages can be shown to exhibit some competitiveness in decisions regarding domains of shared activities that are important to their personal identities. A tendency to be "controlling" in this way, within the context of decisions that also further common benefits in a relationship, can be distinguished from dominance in the context involving threats and promises only in the service of self-interest.

8.4.5 The Transformation of Motivation in Interdependent Situations

Kelley (1979) reports evidence about individuals' "outcome" ratings in various everyday decisions involving shared activities in close relationships. The results provide a clear example of real life problems that can be described in terms of the pattern of outcomes described by Hero, and they also illustrate some important principles involving the *transformation* of individuals' motivation in interdependent situations. In one example, approximately 100 dating couples were asked to give their reactions to the four possible events in a situation where the partners are deciding on which of two movies to attend on a particular evening. The participants were first asked to consider their own reactions to different combinations of choices of the two movies, attended together or alone, with the assumption that they themselves preferred one movie *but their partners had no preference* between the two. Individuals were asked to rate the four possible events on a scale ranging from unpleasant (-10) to pleasant ($+10$). Then, they were asked to rate how their partners would feel about the four possibilities if the partner preferred one movie *but believed they had no preference*. It can be seen that these two sets of ratings, of how they themselves would feel and of how they think their partners would feel, will include an understanding of their mutual interest in going together but will not take account of any difference in their preferences about where to go.

The average ratings are shown in the matrix in Table E8.3 below. The pattern is very similar to that in Table E8.1. For each person, going together to one's preferred movie is very desirable, going together to the "other" movie is slightly positive, and going to separate movies is quite negative (even if it involves going alone to one's preferred movie). In short, in its simplest form (when the respondents make no assumptions about differences in preferences), the concrete problem of which movie to see conforms to the prototypical Hero situation.

But how is the situation changed when they are aware of and able to take account of differences in their preferred movies? In a subsequent set of ratings, the respondents were asked to give their own reactions and to estimate their partners' reactions to the four combinations in circumstances where each person knows there to be differences in the preferred movies. The results are shown in the matrix in Table E8.4 below. It is clear that one's own outcomes are sharply modified to take account of the *partner's* preferences. Going together to one's own preferred movie dropped in attractiveness (from 8.8 to 5.7), presumably because of knowing that choice was not what the partner most wanted. Further, going together to the non-preferred movie increased noticeably in attractiveness (from 1.1 to 5.2), presumably because that would make the partner happiest. This tendency to take account of the other person's outcomes as well as one's own suggests that individuals are responsive to the *total pattern* of interdependence. The typical respondent in this study is at least somewhat inclined toward "heroism," that is, consideration of their partner.

Essentially, the "given situation" in which they find themselves (Table E8.3: the direct consequences of choices, considering only the self) is modified to take account of the partners' outcomes. The partner's happiness with events affects one's own happiness, resulting in an "effective matrix" (Table E8.4) that more directly controls decisions about behavior. Thus, individuals act as if their interdependence were different from that specified in the given matrix. Kelley and Thibaut (1978) refer to this important phenomenon as the *transformation of motivation*.

It is interesting to note that ratings imputed to the partner show the same transformation effect, *but to a lesser degree*. Going together to the partner's preferred movie is perceived to decline in attractiveness for the partner (from 8.9 to 6.4), and going together to one's own preferred movie is perceived to increase in attractiveness (from 0.1 to 3.7). Comparing those shifts with those reflected in the ratings of own outcomes, it appears that one's partner is judged to be somewhat less responsive to one's own outcomes than one's self is to the partner's outcomes. This asymmetry may reflect an egocentric memory bias (Ross & Sicoly, 1979). Individuals may be more aware of instances in which *they* act counter to self-interest and are responsive to their partners' needs than of instances in which the partner does so. One possible explanation for this difference is that it reflects a self-imposed limitation on communication. A desire to act in a "genuinely considerate way" may inhibit individuals from communicating the fact that they were being responsive to the partner's needs, rather than their own. This pattern of perceptions has significant implications because concern about a partner's lack of responsiveness is a frequent source of attributional conflict in couples (cf., Holmes & Murray, 1996). While there may sometimes be quite legitimate reasons to voice complaints about whether a partner is taking account of one's needs, these studies suggest that the salience of one's own behavior that departs from self-interest may contribute to distortions in estimating who is more responsive to the other's needs.

8.5 Matrix Representations

Tables E8.1 and E8.2. The matrix in Table E8.1 is a matching example of Hero, where a strong mutual desire to do the same activity together (Corresponding Mutual Joint Control, Entry #3) is complicated by differences in the preferred activity (Entry #1). The matrix in Table E8.2 is a complementary example of Hero, where a strong mutual desire to do different things (Conflicting Mutual Joint Control, Entry #4) is complicated by similarity in preferred activity.

TABLE E8.1. *Representation of a Matching Example of Hero*

		Person A	
		a1 (Pref.)	a2 (Not)
b1 (Not)		12 / 8	0 / 0
Person B			
b2 (Pref.)		4 / 4	8 / 12

Strong mutual desire to do same activity is complicated by difference in preferred activity

TABLE E8.2. *Representation of a Complementary Example of Hero*

		Person A	
		a1 (Pref.)	a2 (Not)
b1 (Pref.)		4 / 4	8 / 12
Person B			
b2 (Not)		12 / 8	0 / 0

Strong mutual desire to do different activities is complicated by similarity in preferred activity

Tables E8.3 and E8.4. The matrix in Table E8.3 represents outcomes perceived for self and partner in the "going to the movies" example in Kelley's research, based on the assumption that the partner has no preferred movie. The matrix in Table E8.4 represents the outcomes from the same example when the person believes the partner prefers a different movie from the self.

TABLE E8.3. *Outcomes Estimated for Self and Partner for "Going to the Movies" When Partner Has No Preferences*

		Self	
		Pref.	Not
Partner	Not	+8.8 +0.1	−7.7 −8.0
	Pref.	−5.3 −5.6	+1.1 +8.9

In each case, estimates are made with the assumption that each person prefers one movie but believes the **other person has no preference**

TABLE E8.4. *Outcomes Estimated for Self and Partner for "Going to the Movies" When Partner Prefers Different Movie*

		Self	
		Pref.	Not
Partner	Not	+5.7 +3.7	−7.5 −7.9
	Pref.	−3.9 −4.6	+5.2 +6.4

In each case, estimates are made with the assumption that each person prefers one movie and believes the **other person prefers the other one**

Entry #9

Conjunctive Problems

Together We Can Do It

9.1 Examples

This situation is one in which each and every person must make some collectively "right" or cooperative choice for all to obtain a more valued outcome; even one person's making a collectively "wrong" or uncooperative choice guarantees all receiving a less valued outcome. Such situations arise routinely in both dyadic and group settings. For example, a couple trying to conceive a child cannot succeed if either member is not present (e.g., is constantly traveling on business).

A fairly large class of such situations arises in dyads when either party can withdraw from interaction with the partner and thereby deprive both of its benefits. Examples include instances when either married partner refuses to talk to or withdraws affection from the other, and when either negotiator out of frustration refuses to bargain actively and in good faith. In this sense, maintenance of dyadic relationships has this conjunctive feature – the withdrawal of either member can effectively terminate the relationship.

Decision-making groups operating under a unanimity rule (e.g., most juries) are in Conjunctive situations – lack of assent by any member prevents the group from finishing its work and reaching a decision. And, as Steiner (1972) has observed, performance groups face this situation in group tasks where the group's level of performance is constrained to be no better than that of its least capable or motivated member. For example, a mountain climbing team that is tethered to one another can only advance

Norbert Kerr had primary responsibility for preparation of this entry.

at the pace of its poorest climber. It is not just the volume of traffic that makes freeway commuting so time-consuming – at any given moment, a lane of traffic on the freeway can move no faster than the slowest driver in that lane. Besides physical yoking, as in the preceding two examples, tasks that require careful coordination or matching of responses tend to be conjunctive. If either member of the trapeze act makes a mistake, the act is ruined. Likewise, if either parent carelessly gives 12-year-old Melissa permission to go to the Motley Crue Reunion Tour (without investigating what sort of recreation this is or determining whether his/her spouse has already vetoed it), a parenting blunder will result.

9.2 Conceptual Description

The essential feature of the situation of conjunctive interdependence is that a good result for all requires that every person perform a particular behavior and failure of any single group member to do so is sufficient to produce an undesired outcome for all. Like the Disjunctive situation (see Entry #10), it derives its name from Steiner's (1972) taxonomy of group tasks. In dyadic situations, this translates into high Mutual Joint Control, since inaction by one person renders useless action by the other. Matrix representations of such a situation (see section 9.5, below) exhibit a strong interaction effect wherein the effect of one person's action is strongly attenuated or exaggerated by the action of the other. When such patterns arise in a factorial design, these interactions will routinely be accompanied by significant main effects. Correspondingly, the high level of Mutual Joint Control in this situation will routinely be accompanied by substantial Actor Control and Mutual Partner Control – one simultaneously harms both one's own and the other's fate by performing the "wrong" action.

More formally, as shown earlier (section 4.2.3), conjunctive interdependence in a dyad is the result of combining three of the most basic components, namely, BAC, MPC, and Corr MJC, all concordant with each other. The concordance of the components reveals that there is maximum correspondence between actors' outcomes – the same action that benefits self will also benefit the other and both must make the beneficial choice for either to benefit. The net effect is functionally one of total interdependence – each and every member's cooperation is required to obtain the desired outcome.

In groups larger than dyads, one can identify this situation as a special case of the step-level public good problem (see Entry #20, section 20.3). In the most general case of step-level public goods, there is some "provision point" – some critical level of cooperation (e.g., a certain number of cooperators) required to obtain a public good available to all, providers and nonproviders alike. The situation of conjunctive interdependence arises when that provision point is equal to the size of the group – all must cooperate. A single noncooperator will reduce the group's outcome.

In all our examples, the "wrong" choice by only a single person results in a loss of benefit for all, or, to put it otherwise, "success" requires all members to be correct. In other words, the situation is "conjunctive for success." Logically, we could also think of a situation that is "conjunctive for failure" – failure requires all members to be wrong and the "right" choice by only a single person results in a more positive outcome for all. However, because we usually evaluate groups by their success, the latter kind of situation is more naturally described as one of disjunctive interdependence (see Entry #10). (This is merely to note that the generally accepted distinction between "Conjunctive" and "Disjunctive" situations depends on a widely shared evaluative perspective. If we were betting against a group, and hoping for its failure, our thoughts would focus on whether failure will require all the members to mess up [conjunctive for failure] or only any single member to do so [disjunctive for failure].)

9.3 Neighbors and Variants

Implicit in all of our examples so far is a feature that is not essential to the definition of conjunctive interdependence but is almost always present in interesting real-world instances – namely, there is almost always a cost to the person who makes the "right" choice. So, for example, keeping the lines of communication open and not withdrawing in a relationship (e.g., being attentive when one is tired; overtly expressing affection, even if one doesn't feel particularly affectionate at the moment) is often more costly than simply withdrawing. And there are few group tasks where doing the group's work doesn't entail costs (in time, effort) to the member who does it. Without such costs, this situation would be a relatively simple one – all would be eager to "do the right thing" and simultaneously benefit himself or herself and others. With such costs, the situation becomes a more complex one. Such costs introduce a personal disincentive to making the "right" choice unless one can be very confident that everyone else will do likewise. Hence, real situations of conjunctive interdependence (with costs) will engage to some degree the thorny conflict between what's "right" for self versus for others that lies at the heart of the Prisoner's Dilemma situation (and its variations; see Entries #5, #12, and #20).

(However, there is a difference. If a person doesn't contribute to the common welfare in the PD, they nevertheless gain benefits from others' contributions and even gain their best outcomes from taking advantage of others' goodwill. In Conjunctive situations, a person who fails to contribute saves the costs of doing so but is not benefited by others' contributions and also loses out on the possible benefits of everyone's cooperation. So there is no positive benefit derived from "free riding," and the "dilemma" in the choice between own and common interests is less poignant than in the PD.)

The simplest variant of conjunctive interdependence is a single, noniterated play without possibility of communication or coordination of action. If there are no costs for acting cooperatively (i.e., making the "right" choice; see the matrix in Table E9.1 below, at the end of this entry), then all who understand the situation clearly could be expected to cooperate. In the more typical situation, there are costs for acting cooperatively (see the matrix in Table E9.2 below). Here, without communication, each person must do his or her best to anticipate the other's ability and motivation to do the "right" thing. With communication, interactants generally have a better basis for judging the other's capability or intentions and, hence, can make more sensible (i.e., less risky) choices themselves.

In real dyads or groups, situations of conjunctive interdependence are likely to recur (e.g., the same climbing team scales different mountains; parents must coordinate their parenting decisions on multiple occasions). Although the opportunities for accurately judging others' capabilities and intentions are greater, the risks of mutual incoordination of choice are also increased in such recurrent situations. For example, a previous failure may convince group members that the group lacks the requisite ability or goodwill to achieve universal cooperation. Or retaliation (via noncooperation) by any group member for what is seen as prior, willful noncooperation by one member could condemn the group to continued failure. Or, unreasonably high expectations may be placed on a member who is blamed for a previous group failure.

The more difficult case is the one in which all must choose simultaneously. The case where choice is sequential and there are no costs for cooperating is straightforward – each would try to "do the right thing" (since there would be no clear reason not to do so, even if someone preceding one in the response sequence failed to do so). However, sequential choice when cooperation is costly is a far more uncertain and difficult situation. Someone choosing early would again have to anticipate the likely choices of all who follow and could only be expected to cooperate when she or he is fairly optimistic. Someone choosing later would only cooperate when both (a) she or he was also confident about those who were to follow, and (b) all who preceded him or her had cooperated.

So far we have assumed (implicitly) that the situation is symmetric – the costs (if any) of making the "right" choice are the same for all, as are the benefits of universal cooperation. Often, of course, this is not true. The collective performance context is a good example, where perfect equality in task ability across teammates is quite unusual. In order for such groups to succeed in contexts of conjunctive interdependence, where there is little margin for error, it is the least capable members who must perform especially well, often with greater personal costs (in attention, in effort, in lost opportunities) than their more capable partners.

9.4 Interaction Process and Person Factors

A key psychological feature of the Conjunctive situation is its low margin for error – lack of cooperation, effort, or ability on anyone's part spells collective failure. When cooperation is costly, conditions must be nearly ideal – all can make the "right" response; all are confident that all others will make the "right" response; the costs of risking the "right" response are sufficiently low for all – for the probability of such failure to be low. Among the conditions that are likely to make the situation less than ideal are (a) uncertainty about others' capabilities and intentions, (b) high variance in capabilities (Steiner, 1972), (c) any extraneous factor that could further undermine the link between high collective effort and success (e.g., erratic officiating for a sports team), and (d) increasing group size. This latter factor is especially problematic. As Lorge and Solomon (1955) have shown, even if the probability of individuals making the wrong choice, P, is low, the probability of a group of size N containing at least one such choice rises rapidly with group size (viz., it is equal to $1 - (1 - P)^N$).

9.4.1 Attributions for Collective Failure
Whether collective failure in one Conjunctive situation means continued failure in the same or other such situations is likely to depend upon how group members explain the original failure. Some attributions are less fatal than others. For example, we are less likely to give up – and more likely to take actions to educate or motivate our partner – if we attribute our partner's "wrong" choice to misunderstanding the situation (e.g., we honk to let the driver of the slow moving vehicle know that those behind him

may not want to drive at his leisurely pace), to inadequate effort (e.g., our climbing partner didn't realize that we could go faster and he should set his pace accordingly), or to inadequate coordination (e.g., our trapeze partner is trying, but is not yet skillful enough to time release of the bar accurately). Conversely, other attributions can be lethal for long-term cooperative effort – for example, my partner is simply incapable of performing well; my partner mistrusts my capability or willingness to work/cooperate for the group; my partner evaluates his or her personal costs more highly than any joint gain. Just as there is a strong negativity effect in person perception, a little hard-to-account-for collective failure in a Conjunctive situation is likely to undo widespread and long-standing goodwill and cooperation. One example may be the tendency for dissatisfied married couples (who face many situations of conjunctive interdependence) to make dispositional attributions for their partner's negative behaviors (e.g., Bradbury & Fincham, 1990).

9.4.2 *Group Composition and Cohesiveness*
Issues of group composition and maintenance are particularly salient in situations of conjunctive interdependence. Because collective success depends on universal capability and willingness to act cooperatively, groups which must function in such situations must be particularly careful in the recruitment or selection of members. For example, those wishing to create a competitive volleyball team will take special care that all of their recruits have high skill levels, because even a single "weak link" would make the team far less competitive at this game. And, once such a dyad or group has been formed, its durability is likely to depend upon how well the conditions that are required for collective success can be maintained – universal and high mutual trust and confidence, uniformly high capability or willingness to cooperate, the existence of effective means to detect and quickly remedy instances of individual uncooperativeness. The latter are likely to include careful mutual monitoring of behavior, expectations that lack of cooperation be satisfactorily explained and corrected, and marginalization and eventual exclusion of those who cannot be counted on. Since such ideal conditions will be hard to achieve and maintain, groups facing conjunctive interdependence may be particularly vulnerable to disintegration. Good examples of such vulnerable groups might be bands (where a single lousy musician is sufficient to ruin the group's prospects) or sports teams. In the latter case, there is some evidence that ineffective play and feelings of low responsibility for the team's success are linked to low cohesiveness in sports teams (Widmeyer, Brawley, & Carron, 1992)

9.4.3 The Köhler Effect

Over 70 years ago, Otto Köhler (1926) demonstrated the psychological forces operating on members of groups performing what Hertel, Kerr, & Messé (2000) have termed a yoked-conjunctive task. This is a task in which the members of the group are yoked such that any one person's inability or unwillingness to continue to work necessarily halts all others' work. Köhler's task was a physical persistence task. Individuals or groups performed paced, standing pulley-curls (i.e., repeatedly lifting a weighted bar to the chest and then lowering it) to the point of exhaustion. The weight to be lifted for individuals was 41 kg; the weight to be lifted by a dyad was 82 kg. Moreover, group members all grasped and lifted a single bar; hence, whenever one member reached the point of exhaustion, the remaining member(s) would not be able to continue. Köhler (1926) observed what has been a fairly rare phenomenon in group performance research – a group motivation gain effect. Specifically, he found that in dyads – especially those with moderate discrepancy in members' abilities – the less capable member worked harder when yoked to his more capable partner than when working alone. Contemporary research (Hertel et al., 2000) suggests that when less capable members of the group recognize their indispensability to their partner's and the group's level of performance, they may increase their efforts above normal levels rather than being the one responsible for the group's quitting early.

9.4.4 Complementarity in Close Relationships

Our earlier examples suggest that there are two distinctive bases of conjunctivity. For the dyad, these are (1) a "do versus not" definition of the behavioral options that is applicable to both persons (e.g., contribute to the joint effort vs. not) and (2) a "do X versus do Y" definition of the options, combined with differential abilities of the persons to perform the two (e.g., conceiving a child where only the woman can contribute the egg and only the man can contribute the sperm). In the first case, there is a requirement of cumulative activity and in the second, a requirement of a particular pattern of activity. (It is in the second regard that conjunctive interdependence differs from another close neighbor, corresponding Mutual Joint Control. Without a differentiation between the persons in their ability to perform X and Y, the two persons are interchangeable in their roles, pairing of their respective actions brings success, and the situation is one of "Getting in sync" [see Entry #3].)

Examples of differentiation abound in daily life: a strong person and a weak person hanging a picture that is so heavy the strong one must hold it up while the weak one attaches it to the wall; a soprano and her accompanist, and so on. In close interpersonal relations, Winch (1958) proposed that marriages are most successful if the personalities of the couple are different but complementary. He confirmed his hypothesis for a general dimension he decribes as "assertive" versus "receptive." Turner interprets this as an instance of the general principle of economy of decision making: "The problem of reaching pair decisions is great when either two highly assertive persons or two highly receptive persons are together. A well-accepted relationship of inequality, however, simplifies decision making" (1970, p. 78).

The economy principle implies that there is a sort of meta-situation defined by the roles the persons take in the many simpler situations they encounter that require agreement, whether the PD, corresponding MJC, Hero, Delay of Gratification, or whatever. Viewed in terms of the costs of decision making, this meta-situation is one of conjunctive interdependence: both persons' outcomes are best if, across those simpler situations, one person is able and disposed to be a "leader" and the other is able and disposed to be a "follower." A number of laboratory studies support this conclusion, at least for the simpler tasks involving coordination (see Entry #3). Those tasks are solved most effectively by pairs in which one person is more active and dominant than the other (Kelley & Thibaut, 1959, pp. 27–29). (Incidentally, there is no implication in the above that in heterosexual pairs, the male is always the leader and the female, the follower. The case study of the Littleton family, provided by Hess and Handel [1959], is a compelling example of a family in which the opposite is true.)

9.4.5 *Person Factors*

Because this situation (particularly when the "right" behavior is costly) is a close relative of the Prisoner's Dilemma setting (see section 9.3 above), one would expect those dispositions already identified as particularly relevant to the PD and its variants (i.e., Entries #5, #12, and #20) – social orientations/motives, internalization of moral norms, personalized or depersonalized trust – also to be important in the Conjunctive situation. The latter factor, trust, may be particularly crucial in Conjunctive situations. Any "mistrustful" belief system – e.g., high cynicism; jaundiced assumptions about human nature (Wrightsman, 1992) – should discourage one from entering, cooperating within, and remaining in groups in such situations. Indeed, Orbell and Dawes (1993) suggest this may partially explain the evolution of widespread cooperation – those who are unwilling to depend on others may shun such interdependence, leaving the more trustful to pair up (and pass along their trustful inclinations). Moreover, one's level of self-trust is also quite important – if one's own ability to act cooperatively were in real doubt (e.g., one's sense of self-efficacy for performing the "right" behavior were low; Bandura, 1986), one would be unlikely to strive to cooperate in a Conjunctive situation.

Any interpersonal disposition that makes one hypersensitive to the opinions of others also seems likely to be important in these situations. Group members who've taken risks on the group's behalf are likely to expect their fellows to do likewise and are likely to be rather dissatisfied with those who fail to "hold up their end." Those who find such social disapproval particularly aversive – e.g., those with a high need for approval (Crowne & Marlowe, 1964); those with a particularly high "rejection sensitivity" (Downey, Khouri, & Feldman, 1997); those with an acute sense of social responsibility (Berkowitz, 1972) – can thus be expected to be relatively more cooperative in such situations.

Another individual difference which is particularly important in Conjunctive situations is the availability of quality alternative relationships. This is not usually viewed as a trait or disposition, but it depends on the variety of such factors – e.g., appearance, intelligence, "personality" – that make a person attractive to others. The obvious reason is that a more attractive person is usually able to have better alternatives (e.g., Feingold, 1988). The person who has excellent alternatives to the present group is unlikely to persist in cooperative efforts in the face of group failure in Conjunctive settings – rather, she or he is likely to leave the group. In the era of free agency for professional athletes, it is very difficult to keep superstars on one's team (unless one can surround them with fellow superstars; e.g., the Chicago Bulls of the 90s). On the other hand, we might expect the person with poor alternatives to be as cooperative as possible to prevent the present group from breaking apart.

9.5 Matrix Representations

Table E9.1: Conjunctive Interdependence without Costs. In this situation, if both members of the dyad perform the "right" response (response 1 in the table), both receive a benefit worth +7. However, if either makes the "wrong" response (response 2), this benefit is forgone. In this matrix, providing the benefit to the entire group does not reduce one's own final outcome – that is, there are no costs for doing the right thing.

TABLE E9.1. *Situational Representation of Conjunctive Interdependence without Costs*

	A	
	a1	a2
b1	+7 / +7	0 / 0
b2	0 / 0	0 / 0

Table E9.2: Conjunctive Interdependence with Costs. The matrix in Table E9.2 is a variation on the preceding one. In it, the benefit to each group member of both making the "right" response is +7, but it costs a person +3 to do the right thing. The matrix begins to resemble the two-person Prisoner's Dilemma Game (see Entry #5). The primary difference is that here one cannot obtain a better outcome by free riding on one's partner's cooperative actions; rather, the benefits of cooperation outweigh its costs, but only if the other also cooperates.

TABLE E9.2. *Situational Representation of Conjunctive Interdependence with Costs*

	A	
	a1	a2
b1	+7 / +7	+3 / 0
b2	0 / +3	+3 / +3

Table E9.3: A Step-Level Public Good Problem. Let every member of a five-person group start with a \$3 endowment. If all group members are willing to contribute (and, hence, lose) their endowments, each group member receives a \$7 reward (public good; see the matrix in Table E9.3). This is an N-person generalization of the two-person matrix presented in Table E9.2.

TABLE E9.3. *Situational Representation of a Conjunctive Step-Level Public Goods Situation*

Own Choice	Number of Others Contributing				
	0	1	2	3	4
Contribute	0	0	0	0	7
Not contribute	3	3	3	3	3

Note: Matrix entries are number of dollars that the focal person will receive.

Entry #10

Disjunctive Problems

Either of Us Can Do It

10.1 Examples

This situation is one in which the actions of a single person provide a benefit for all (including himself or herself). Such situations arise routinely both in dyadic and group settings. For example, in marriages or business partnerships, joint obligations (e.g., responding to invitations, paying bills) can be fulfilled equally well by either partner. Likewise, either marriage partner can simultaneously benefit self and the spouse by making a particular "right" choice – for example, both benefit when either cleans the house, quiets the children, or prepares a meal. As Steiner (1972) has observed, performance groups face this situation in group tasks where a single member can effectively do the work of the entire group. For example, a group of students in a chemistry lab may have a single lab assignment requiring a single written report, for which all the students will receive the same grade. In such a case, any single lab-group member could (in principle) complete, write up, and turn in the assignment. Many bystander intervention settings (cf. Latané & Darley, 1970) also have this structure. Often only one bystander needs to act (e.g., give or seek help) in order to "solve" the problem confronting the group of bystanders (i.e., deal with the emergency).

10.2 Conceptual Description

The essential feature of the situation of disjunctive interdependence is that an act or choice of any single group member is sufficient to determine a

Norbert Kerr had primary responsibility for preparation of this entry.

desired outcome for all. (It derives its name from Steiner's [1972] taxonomy of group tasks in which he identified a *disjunctive group task* as one at which the group could potentially perform as well as the most capable member of the group [e.g., an intellectual problem which a group can and should be able to solve if it contains at least one member who can solve the problem].) In dyadic situations, this translates into high Mutual Joint Control, because action by one person obviates action by the other. Matrix representations of such a situation (see section 10.5 below) exhibit a strong "three-versus-one" interaction pattern. Such statistical interactions will routinely be accompanied by significant main effects. Correspondingly, the Mutual Joint Control in this situation will be accompanied by Actor and Partner Control – one can simultaneously guarantee both one's own and the other's fate by performing the needed, sufficing action.

More formally, as shown earlier (see chapter 4, section 4.2.3) disjunctive interdependence in a dyad is the result of combining three of the most basic components, namely, BAC, MPC, and Corr MJC, all with equal weight but with the latter discordant with the prior two components – that is, since only one right response is sufficient, each dyad member prefers, all else being equal, that they make different choices. The concordance of the BAC and MPC components reveals that there is fairly high correspondence between actors' outcomes – the same action that benefits self will also benefit the other. The net effect is functionally one of zero interdependence – one can insure the desired outcome solely by his or her own choice.

In groups larger than dyads, one can identify this situation with a variant of the step-level public good problem (see Entry #20, section 20.3). In the most general case of step-level public goods, there is some *provision point* – some critical level of cooperation (e.g., number of cooperators) required to obtain a public good available to all, providers and nonproviders alike. The situation of disjunctive interdependence arises when that provision point is 1 – a single cooperator. (For this reason, this situation has also been referred to as the "volunteer's dilemma"; Murninghan, Kim, & Metzger, 1993).

Implicit in all of our examples so far is a feature that is not essential to the definition of disjunctive interdependence but is almost always present in interesting real-world instances – namely, there is almost always a "cost" to the person who makes the "right" choice. So, for example, there is nearly always a cost (if only an opportunity cost) paid by the spouse who cleans the house, quiets the children, prepares a meal, and so on, that is not paid by the other spouse. As Latané & Darley (1970) have pointed out, potentially there are high costs to the bystander who intervenes in an emergency (the good Samaritan is at the very least inconvenienced and can fare far worse – e.g., be embroiled in others' problems, detained by authorities, dragged into court). And there are few group tasks where doing the group's work doesn't entail costs (in time, effort) to the member who does it.

Without such costs, this situation would be a relatively simple one – all would be eager to "do the right thing" and simultaneously benefit himself or herself and others. With such costs, the situation becomes a much more complex one. Such costs introduce a personal disincentive to making the "right" choice, and they introduce the essential conflict between what's "right" for self versus what's "right" for others that lies at the heart of the Prisoner's Dilemma situation (and its variations; see Entries #5, #12, and #20). The situation becomes one in which there is genuine interdependence – one has opportunities to reap the benefits of another's costly actions without entailing costs oneself.

The examples we have used also all suggest that the "right" choice by only a single person results in a benefit for all. In principle, we might also conceive of a corresponding situation in which the "wrong" choice by only a single person results in a negative outcome for all. However, the latter situation is more easily conceptualized as a situation of conjunctive interdependence (see Entry #9). Here, we will identify the situation of disjunctive interdependence with settings in which a single "right" choice is sufficient to obtain a valued benefit for all, and identify the situation of conjunctive interdependence with settings in which universal "right" choices are necessary to obtain a valued benefit for all.

10.3 Variants and Combinations

The variant best beloved by scholars is, predictably, probably the most difficult for the interactants – a single, noniterated play without possibility of communication or coordination of action. With communication, interactants might find some way of compensating the single person who makes the costly "right" choice or at least find a sensible procedure to select that person (e.g., drawing straws; determining if the cost is relatively smaller for someone). Less useful as a research crucible, but more common in everyday life, are cases in which the situation of disjunctive interdependence arises recurrently (e.g., the family dinner must be prepared every night) or in which there are multiple such situations (e.g., the children must be attended to as well), usually with the opportunity for communication and coordination of choice.

Similarly, the most studied case is the one in which all must choose simultaneously. The case in which choice is sequential is straightforward in principle – the first to choose would "do the right thing" if it could be done with little or no cost; the last to choose would probably do so in the (more common) situation in which it is costly (cf. Suleiman, Rapoport, & Budescu, 1996).

So far we have assumed (implicitly) that the situation is symmetric – the costs of making the "right" choice are the same for all, as are the benefits. Often, of course, this is not true. Particularly in the iterated or multiple-situation cases, such differences in cost provide a means of deciding who should provide the public good (e.g., the strongest bystander ought to be the one to break up a fight; the spouse who least minds doing meal cleanup would take on that responsibility) or of arranging sensible trade-offs (e.g., Ozzie doesn't mind taking care of the car, Harriet prefers to take care of the house).

We noted previously that groups potentially perform at the level of their most capable or motivated member for disjunctive tasks. If we rank order group members with respect to their individual potential productivities (which will, in turn, depend upon their individual abilities and levels of motivation), it is also possible to conceive tasks at which the group's potential is defined by the second (or third, or fourth, or . . .) most capable member (Steiner, 1972). For example, one of the (arbitrary) ways in which we could determine the winner of a multiteam cross-country running meet would be to define each team's score as the time of its second fastest finisher. Another good example would be an N-person organization (a church) in which the number of task roles (m) to be filled (e.g., board members, ushers, acolytes, etc.) is smaller than the number of candidates (n), that is, $m < n$. Under the (unlikely) assumption that every member could take on every task role, we could consider this organization's potential productivity to be limited by the mth most capable member. Although it is possible to imagine and even to find group tasks which have this intermediate structure, the more common and interesting situations are those defined by the anchors of the dimension we have been discussing, namely, Disjunctive and (in Entry #9) Conjunctive situations.

10.4 Interaction Process and Person Factors

The structurally most simple situation (viz., simultaneous, irrevocable choice in a noniterated symmetric situation) is very vulnerable to free riding – all but one benefiting as a result of the one's costly action. This risk grows as the size of the group increases. Latané and Darley's (1970) classic work demonstrates how felt responsibility for intervening in a bystander emergency is increasingly diffused as the size of the group of bystanders increases. This temptation to free ride becomes even more irresistible when choice is anonymous (e.g., Harkins & Petty, 1982), where one can free ride with less chance of discovery and, hence, less guilt (as well as less of an opportunity for any side payments, like gratitude or public approbation).

The risk of guilt (as well as other interesting interaction dynamics) is likely to stem from a couple of factors: moral obligations to accept the responsibility for the group's welfare (e.g., Berkowitz, 1972) and the equity considerations inherent in most situations of disjunctive interdependence. The latter suggests that one person doing more for the group but receiving no more than the rest of the group is bound to be seen as inequitable (particularly by the one carrying the group's load). In recurrent, iterated situations, one obvious solution is turn taking. Similarly, as noted previously, dyad or group members can trade off responsibilities for different disjunctive tasks. It appears that there are some situations in which a benefit is sufficiently attractive to induce one person to carry the others (Williams & Karau, 1991), but there are also clear indications that such an inequitable "sucker's" role can be very aversive (e.g., Kerr, 1983). Perceived equity can be maintained or restored in a number of ways: via direct action (e.g., refusing to do the group's work; leaving the group), reevaluations of utilities (e.g., the sucker subjectively minimizing the cost or maximizing the benefit to himself or herself), or normative loopholes (e.g., seeing the other as incapable and hence as not responsible [cf. Kerr, 1983] or as absolved from responsibility through role requirements, as with a parent who "carries" his or her capable adult child). Indeed, it is precisely when dyads or groups face such situations that well-defined and accepted roles insure that vital group benefits are provided without the uncertainty and conflict of a perpetual struggle for both rewarding and fair outcomes (Thibaut & Kelley, 1959).

10.4.1 *Motivation Losses at Disjunctive Group Tasks*

As suggested previously, the group task performance situations most vulnerable to motivation losses are disjunctive group tasks with nonidentifiable member contributions (e.g., an intellective problem-solving task where a single response is submitted for the entire group). Not only does this situation invite undetectable free riding on others' contributions (if one believes that others can and will do the group's work), and/or stubborn refusal to work (if one believes that others who could contribute are inequitably profiting from one's own work; Kerr, 1983), it is also a situation in which nonidentifiability can directly reduce the incentives for high effort (and/or disincentives for low effort) (Williams, Harkins, & Latané, 1981). As a consequence, groups working at such tasks sometimes effectively perform no better than we might expect of a much smaller group or even of an individual performer (Bray, Kerr, & Atkin, 1978).

As noted earlier, a close cousin to a purely disjunctive group task is one in which the number of capable group members can exceed the number of essential roles or subtasks. Wicker (1979) characterizes such situations as "overmanned" (or, in less sexist language, "overstaffed"). Such a situation seems to lead not only to the kind of task motivation loss alluded to above, but also to (a) other forms of motivation loss (e.g., members feeling unimportant, unneeded, unwilling to assist others, and uninvolved in the group's work; cf. Wicker, 1979) and possibly (b) coordination loss (e.g., the coordination of individual efforts in terms of timing and efficient task division becomes more difficult in overstaffed situations).

10.4.2 *Biases in Perceived Contributions*
Egocentric processes of perception and memory can further complicate social interaction in settings of disjunctive interdependence. As noted earlier, when we think that we are doing more than others in a group or in a relationship but are not being rewarded more than others, withdrawing one's effort or even one's membership can be a way of avoiding the inequitable "sucker's" role (cf. Kerr, 1983). This suggests, for example, that the spouse who does more is, all else being equal, more likely to feel exploited and dissatisfied with the relationship than the spouse who does less. Unfortunately, as Ross & Sicoly (1979) have shown, each person in the relationship or group is likely to exaggerate his or her own contributions relative to what others perceive (probably because it is easier to remember what we have done than what others have done).

10.4.3 *Attention for Equality in Contribution in Relationships*
Disjunctive Interdependence situations clearly tend to challenge individuals' feelings of fairness and justice. And, as described above, the fact that it is easier to remember our own contributions than others' contributions may make things even more difficult. How do people deal with such (perceived) realities of underbenefit (and overbenefit)? It seems to depend to some degree on the type of relationship we are in.

The distinction between communal and exchange relationships (Clark & Mills, 1991) is relevant to the relative emphasis one places on responding to one's partner's needs versus insuring justice and strict reciprocity. As demonstrated in several studies, people in communal relationships (e.g., in some close friendships, intimate relationships) do not necessarily keep track of own and other's contributions, that is, do not keep score (or at least do so substantially less than people in exchange relationships [e.g., in relationships between distal colleagues, business partners]). Moreover, in communal relationships, people may develop idealized perceptions of their partner, perhaps in part to justify violations of equity and fairness (Murray, Holmes, & Griffin, 1996a & 1996b), and may foster certain unrealistic beliefs (for example, that their partner's willingness to sacrifice is greater than their own willingness to sacrifice; Van Lange, Agnew, Harinck, & Steemers, 1997). It is plausible that people in communal relationships tend to take an extended time perspective; that is, to suspend regular and strict equity calculations and instead trust that such inequities tend to balance out in the long run (e.g., Mills & Clark, 1982).

Thus, in exchange relationships, disjunctive interdependence is more likely to raise the specter of each person feeling like she or he does more than his or her "fair share," and a universal vulnerability to feelings of mutual exploitation. This mechanism can have corrosive effects on groups unless group members can correct such perceptual biases (e.g., keep reminding one another of everything each does for the other[s]), or reduce felt inequity through appropriate rationalizations (e.g., subjectively magnifying the value of group membership). But, perhaps the best "strategy" of all is to take a long-term perspective, thereby trusting that inequities tend to balance out in the long run, which is, as noted earlier, more typical of communal relationships.

When people are particularly concerned with equality of contribution, it is also possible that they increase the risk of some coordination loss (Steiner, 1972). Fairness concerns might lead both partners to make a contribution, even though the independent efforts of a single individual would suffice or be more efficient. For example, two or more people preparing dinner might create redundancies, inefficiencies, and poor coordination – or, as the old proverb goes, "too many cooks spoil the broth." This is even more evident in bystander and related helping situations, where it is often the case that the more people who try to help, the less effectively help is delivered (e.g., when too many passersby stop to help at an accident scene, making it more difficult for emergency vehicles to get through).

10.4.4 Person Factors

Because this situation (particularly when the "right" behavior is costly) is a close relative of the Prisoner's Dilemma setting, one would expect those interpersonal dispositions already identified as particularly relevant to the

PD and its variants (see Entries #5, #12, and #20) – social value orientation, internalization of moral norms, personalized or depersonalized trust – also to be important in the present situation. For example, research by Yamagishi and Sato (1986) provides evidence that self-serving tendencies toward free riding tend to underlie noncooperative behavior in Disjunctive situations where the outcomes are determined by the most cooperative member of the group. By contrast, in Conjunctive situations, where the outcomes are determined by the least cooperative member of the group, fear of being exploited tends to motivate noncooperative behavior.

We have suggested that concern with fairness or equity is central to behavior in this situation, and that "doing the right thing" is more likely to occur with those who are less strongly concerned with fairness and reciprocity. The example of communal versus exchange relationships, described in the above section, illustrates this point. It is also possible, of course, that there are stable individual, developmental, or cultural differences in the tendency to adopt this outlook across a variety of relationships. For example, Yamagishi (cf. Yamagishi & Yamagishi, 1994) has provided good empirical evidence that Japanese are generally less trustful than Americans, a cultural disposition that he attributes to heavier reliance on reciprocal obligations in Japanese culture.

Another distinctive feature of the situation of disjunctive interdependence is its efficiency. Proper (although personally costly) action by one person can provide low-cost benefits to many others. At the collective level, the benefit to cost ratio is potentially very high. This suggests that those with a particularly strong concern with the efficiency of action (or who are especially impatient) may, all else being equal, be more willing to "do the right thing," not because it is right (in any social or moral sense) but because of its high efficiency. Similarly, that aspect of "dominance" which reflects the willingness to take initiative in the common interest might well induce one to "do the right thing." In this same vein, Aronoff and Wilson (1985) offer both empirical and theoretical arguments that those most likely to take initiative on the group's behalf (e.g., to assume leadership; to act prosocially) are those with relatively high esteem needs; that is, those with a relatively high need to establish and demonstrate their competence.

Yet another distinctive feature of many Disjunctive situations is the distinctiveness of that group member who does the group's work. Although it can be dangerous or otherwise costly to be the single bystander who intervenes in an emergency, it can also lead to special recognition and attention. This suggests the potential importance of dispositional needs for social attention or recognition, either of the relatively more (e.g., need for approval) or less (e.g., pleasure in martyrdom, narcissism) healthy varieties.

It is also worth noting that research on real-world volunteers implicates a wider range of motives than we have considered thus far. Even activities that appear to be prompted solely by altruistic or social responsibility motives (e.g., volunteering as an AIDS-buddy, donating blood) may also be undertaken to obtain rewards that are personal (e.g., concern with enhancing self-knowledge, self-esteem, or career opportunities) or social (e.g., meeting or making friends, engaging in activities others regard as important) (e.g., Snyder, 1993; Charng, Piliavin, & Callero, 1988). Disjunctive situations require that "somebody's got to do it," but it may not (just) be concern for others or for the group that motivates that somebody.

10.5 Matrix Representations

Table E10.1: Disjunctive Interdependence without Costs. In this situation, if either member of the dyad performs the "right" response (response 1 in Table E10.1), both receive a benefit worth +10. Only if neither makes this response is this benefit forgone. In this situation, providing such a benefit to the entire group does not reduce one's own final outcome – that is, there are no costs for doing the right thing.

TABLE E10.1. *Situational Representation of Disjunctive Interdependence without Costs*

		A		A	
		a1		a2	
b1			+10		+10
		+10		+10	
b2			+10		0
		+10		0	

(B labels the left column group: b1, b2)

Table E10.2: Disjunctive Interdependence with Costs. This situation is a variation on the preceding one. In it, the benefit to all group members of either person making the right response is still +10, but it costs a person +3 to do the right thing. The matrix begins to resemble the two-person Prisoner's Dilemma Game (see Entry #5, section 5.5). The primary difference is that here one does not receive the lowest outcome for "playing the sucker" and carrying an uncooperative partner. There is a high degree of Mutual Joint Control in the Disjunctive situation that is absent in the PDG.

TABLE E10.2. *Situational Representation of Disjunctive Interdependence with Costs*

		A	
		a1	a2
B	b1	+7 / +7	+10 / +7
	b2	+7 / +10	0 / 0

Table E10.3: A Step-Level Public Good Problem. Let every member of a five-person group start with a $3 endowment. If any group member is willing to contribute (and, hence, lose) his or her endowment, each group member receives a $7 reward (public good; see the matrix in Table E10.3). This matrix is an *N*-person generalization of the two-person situation represented in Table E10.2.

TABLE E10.3. *Situational Representation of a Step-Level Public Goods Game with a Provision Point of One*

	Number of Others Contributing				
Own Choice	0	1	2	3	4
Contribute (cooperate)	7	7	7	7	7
Not contribute (defect)	3	10	10	10	10

Entry #11

Asymmetric Dependence

You're the Boss

11.1 Examples

In situations involving asymmetric dependence, one person can influence the well-being of a second person, whereas the second person can exert little or no influence over the well-being of the first. One person holds relatively greater power; the other is relatively more dependent. For example, when a hungry baby cries, the caregiver has the power to reduce the baby's discomfort by feeding her, making the baby smile and coo. When mountain climbers encounter a storm and must descend from a high altitude, the climber in better physical condition has the power to either assist or abandon a fellow climber with frostbite. When one spouse is more in love than the other, the less-involved partner can usually "call the shots," in confident expectation that the more-involved partner will adopt the proposed course of action.

11.2 Conceptual Description

The requirement for asymmetric dependence is that one person's actions play a greater role in determining the outcomes of both individuals. The "power holder" (a) has Actor Control over his or her own outcomes *and* (b) influences the partner's outcomes, exerting Partner Control, Joint Control, or both types of control over the outcomes of the dependent person. In contrast, the "dependent" (a) has little or no Actor Control over his or her own outcomes *and* (b) has little or no influence over the

Caryl Rusbult had primary responsibility for preparation of this entry.

partner's outcomes, exerting neither Partner Control nor Joint Control over the power holder's outcomes.

Note that as across-partner constructs, dependence and power are inextricably related, in that individual dependence is the converse of partner power. That is, a partner is more powerful to the extent that an individual's outcomes are dependent on the actions of the partner. At the same time, as within-individual constructs, dependence and power are independent of one another, in that it is possible for an individual to be simultaneously powerful *and* dependent (or neither powerful nor dependent). When our outcomes are dependent on the actions of a powerful partner *and* the partner's outcomes are equally dependent on our own actions, power and dependence are mutual rather than asymmetric (see Entries #2, #3, and #4). Thus, when we speak of asymmetric dependence, we refer to situations in which one person (the power holder) has low dependence and high power, whereas a second person (the dependent) has high dependence and low power. (Many extant theories of power ultimately miss the mark, in that they fail to distinguish between level of power and mutuality of power. In most contexts in which power is examined, this construct should properly be discussed in terms of both level *and* mutuality.)

There are two pure forms of asymmetric dependence. In the "partner-controlled" form, the power holder exerts complete Partner Control over the dependent's outcomes: The power holder has Actor Control over his or her own outcomes (see Entry #1) and exerts Partner Control over the dependent (see Entry #2); the dependent has no Actor Control and exerts no Partner Control or Joint Control over the power holder. In short, by varying his or her actions, the power holder unilaterally determines the dependent's outcomes. For example, the healthy mountain climber can unilaterally help versus not help a fellow climber with frostbite; the frostbitten climber's fate rests fully in the hands of the healthy climber. Partner-controlled Asymmetric situations typically are experienced as rather direct and "absolute" forms of control, in that the dependent's well-being rests fully in the hands of the power holder.

In the "jointly-controlled" form of asymmetric dependence, the power holder and target jointly determine the dependent's outcomes: The power holder once again has Actor Control, but in this instance exerts Joint Control over the dependent (see Entry #3); the dependent once again has no Actor Control and exerts no Partner Control or Joint Control over the power holder. In short, by varying his or her actions, the power holder makes it desirable for the dependent to vary his or her actions; the joint choices of the two determine the target's outcomes. To enhance his or her personal well-being, the dependent must modify his or her actions contingent on the actions of the power holder. For example, in an interaction between two gorillas, the smaller gorilla has no choice but to scramble about, sitting wherever the alpha gorilla is *not* sitting. Employees who are "in tune" with their employers may enjoy good outcomes as a consequence of attending closely, engaging in perspective taking, and exhibiting other cognitive processes that enhance the predictability of the power holder's actions, thereby enabling them to effectively coordinate with the employer. Jointly-controlled Asymmetric situations typically are experienced as rather indirect and "contingent" forms of control, in that the dependent's well-being rests on coordinating his or her actions with the actions of the power holder.

11.3 Variants and Combinations

In addition to the important distinction between Partner Control versus Joint Control, Asymmetric situations also differ in the extent to which they involve corresponding versus conflicting interests. The implications of conflicting interests differ for partner-controlled and jointly controlled dependence. When dependence is jointly controlled, if the dependent can predict the power holder's behavior or wait to see what course of action the power holder adopts, the dependent can coordinate in such a manner as to obtain relatively good outcomes. Such coordination is possible given both corresponding interests and conflicting interests.

When dependence is partner-controlled, the existence of corresponding versus conflicting interests is more consequential. Given corresponding interests, if the power holder chooses to pursue his or her self-interest, good outcomes are simultaneously produced for the dependent. Given conflicting interests, if the power holder pursues his or her self-interest, poor outcomes are simultaneously produced for the dependent. Thus, when their interests conflict, the dependent's ability to enjoy good outcomes rests entirely on whether the power holder chooses to exercise benevolence, departing from his or her own interests so as to benefit the dependent.

Asymmetric situations also vary in degree of asymmetry. Situations involving *some degree* of asymmetry are more common than *completely* asymmetric dependence. As noted in chapter 4, for virtually all of the situations described in this Atlas, there are variants in which one person's dependence is relatively greater than the other's. For example, in a variant of the Threat Game, the "allocator's" ability to provide an interaction partner with good versus poor outcomes may be less than the "threatener's" ability to remain loyal versus disrupt the relationship (see Entry #6). In a variant of the Prisoner's Dilemma, one person may have relatively greater Actor Control over his or her own well-being, or may have relatively greater Partner Control over the other's well-being (see Entries #5 and #12). When operating under conditions of incomplete information, one partner may have relatively greater control over joint decision making (see Entry #17).

Finally, asymmetric dependence may be chronic or transitory. Some asymmetries rest on relatively stable structural features of dyads or groups, and accordingly can be construed as statelike properties of interdependence. For example, differential power is inherent in the infant-caregiver relationship (caregivers possess greater resources, ability, and the like), such that the roles of power holder and dependent are stable features of the dyad. In contrast, some asymmetries are situationally based and accordingly are more fleeting. For example, over the course of their extended relationship, friends will encounter discrete situations in which one or the other is relatively more dependent: One friend may rely on the other's expertise in installing a new computer program, the other may need assistance in coping with a challenging professional problem. (See Entry #18, Twists of Fate, for a discussion of how partners deal with localized asymmetries in long-term relationships.) Most of the principles outlined in the following pages apply to both chronic and transitory asymmetric dependencies.

11.4 Interaction Process and Person Factors

11.4.1 Bases of Power and Dependence

In understanding the implications of asymmetric dependence, it is appropriate to begin by addressing the bases of asymmetry. Power is derived from several sources. First, the power holder may be in a position to provide the dependent with rewarding outcomes. For example, the power holder may have abilities or expertise that make it possible to assist the dependent, or may be able to provide goods or services that the dependent values (e.g., during travel in foreign countries, your traveling companion may speak languages that you cannot speak). Second, the power holder may be in a position to provide the dependent with poor outcomes, posssessing the wherewithal to cause physical discomfort or pain, or to produce negative emotions such as sadness or embarrassment (e.g., an employer can assign undesirable office or laboratory space, withhold salary increases, or terminate employment).

And third, power may reside in the fact that the power holder has more attractive alternatives than the dependent. The ability to move a partner through a range of outcomes is limited at the lower end by the attractiveness of the partner's alternatives; if the partner suffers outcomes worse than those available in alternative situations, he or she will opt for the alternative (Thibaut & Kelley, 1959). Also, power may rest on the costs of adopting one's alternatives, in that the partner who has less invested in a relationship can more readily move to alternative situations (Rusbult, 1983). Thus, the overall quality of one's alternatives rests on both the attractiveness of alternatives and the ease with which they can be adopted. The person with superior alternatives typically is the power holder. For example, a beautiful woman may have alternative opportunities that are more attractive than those of her less-attractive partner (White, 1980). Unequal alternatives form the structural basis for asymmetric dependence, allowing the woman to unilaterally govern her partner's outcomes (Partner Control) or dictate the course of action with which her partner must coordinate (Joint Control).

Differential power may also derive from relatively less concrete, more symbolic sources (French & Raven, 1959). For example, expert power rests on the dependent's belief that the power holder has superior knowledge; we frequently comply with the requests of experts because we believe the expert can help us attain superior material or nonmaterial outcomes. Power holders may also make use of information power, manipulating available information in such a manner as to make one course of action appear more attractive than alternative courses of action (see Entries #15 through #18 for examples of incomplete information situations). Power may also derive from culture, norms, or social convention. For example, we are more likely to obey the dictates of people who possess legitimate power, which rests on norms regarding acceptable forms, settings, and targets of influence.

Finally, power may rest on the inventiveness with which people utilize the contingencies of interdependence, or the creativity with which they maneuver interaction situations. Several forms of ecological control rest on the power holder's ability to manipulate features of interaction in such a manner as to control the behavior of a target (Jones & Gerard, 1967). For example, power holders may employ roundabout control, placing targets in social or physical environments (e.g., military schools, mental institutions) that are likely to shape their global values and dispositions, thereby modifying their behavioral preferences. Using cue control, power holders present discriminative stimuli that automatically elicit preestablished, habitual behaviors from targets (e.g., feigning in sports and card games, crying "Eeek, a mouse!" on April Fool's Day). And using nondecision making, power holders engage in deliberate inaction in such a manner as to maintain the status quo (e.g., pigeonholing a bill in Congress, failing to release funds for an activity, stonewalling during marital conflict).

11.4.2 *Self-Oriented Behavior by Power Holders*

It is easy to imagine that power holders typically will pursue their personal interests and ignore others' interests. When dependence is partner-controlled, dependents have little or no basis for using threats or promises to induce benevolent behavior, in that decisions regarding power use are in the hands of power holders. Of course, the character of asymmetric interactions is likely to differ considerably depending on whether the situation involves common interests versus conflicting interests. Research by Tjosvold and his colleagues illustrates such differences.

Participants in Tjosvold's research were assigned to serve as managers of Bolt Metals or Ferrous Metals (Tjosvold, 1981; Tjosvold, Johnson, & Johnson, 1984). Bolt had greater resources and earned greater profits; Ferrous had a temporary excess of resources, but the benefits to Ferrous of selling Bolt its resources were greater than the benefits to Bolt of purchasing the resources. In short, managers of Bolt had greater power. Managers of Bolt and Ferrous were asked to negotiate prices in the selling and purchasing of their respective resources. The companies were described as either high or low conflict in conflict of interests. In the high-conflict condition the companies produced the same metals and were in competition, such that the profits of one company represented losses for the other. In the low-conflict condition the companies produced different metals and were part of a larger corporation, such that their profits ultimately were linked.

Given high conflict of interests, power holders behaved in a relatively self-oriented manner, pursuing their own company's interests with little regard for the interests of the low-power company; dependents described power holders as untrustworthy, unresponsive, and not particularly helpful. Given low conflict of interests, power holders exhibited a blend of self- and other-oriented behavior, acting in such a manner as to promote the interests of both their own and the low-power company; dependents described power holders as likable, trustworthy, responsive, and helpful, and experienced less anxiety regarding interaction (Tjosvold, 1981; Tjosvold, Johnson, & Johnson, 1984).

Thus, when we find ourselves in possession of power, if our own interests and others' interests conflict, it is very costly to exhibit benevolence toward dependents, in that for one party to prosper the other must lose.

Forced to choose between benefiting oneself (and harming another) versus benefiting another (and harming oneself), power holders presumably feel that they have little choice but to pursue self-interest. In the absence of powerful social norms or higher order goals favoring benevolence, it is not surprising that power holders frequently behave in a self-oriented manner. Given low conflict of interests, benevolence is not so personally costly, so power holders can better "afford" to exhibit a blend of self- and other-oriented behavior.

11.4.3 *Other-Oriented Behavior by Power Holders*

Even in situations involving conflicting interests, power holders sometimes exhibit other-oriented behavior, promoting others' well-being at some cost to themselves: Many people engage in volunteer work, helping others by contributing their services to charitable organizations; many people support their friends and loved ones, devoting time and effort to provide assistance during times of need; many people intervene in emergency situations, assisting hapless victims while placing themselves at considerable risk; during World War II many people placed their lives in peril in order to shelter Jews and other threatened persons from the Nazis.

When we find ourselves in positions of power relative to needy partners, what motivates us to forgo our direct self-interest and help them? There is ongoing debate about whether the motives underlying prosocial acts are self-oriented versus other-oriented (Batson, 1998). Most social scientists agree that prosocial behavior sometimes is driven by relatively self-oriented motives (albeit motives that extend beyond immediate, gut level self-interest). For example, power holders may behave in a benevolent manner because they want to feel good about themselves, because they wish to be publicly recognized for their generosity, or because they need to relieve personal feelings of discomfort (e.g., horror, shock, alarm; Cialdini et al., 1987). Also, given that power holding may be a localized state in a longer term relationship – that is, given that power holders and dependents may "trade places" over the course of extended involvement – power holders may help others as a means of maximizing their long-term self-interest (see Entry #18). For example, in light of the strength and prevalence of reciprocity norms, power holders may (implicitly or explicitly) recognize that by assisting a partner today, they increase the odds that the partner will provide reciprocal assistance at some time in the future (Axelrod, 1984).

Beyond the variety of self-oriented motives that may underlie helping, prosocial acts may also be guided by relatively other-oriented motives, such as feelings of empathy and caring for others (i.e., genuine concern for the other's well-being; Batson, Duncan, Ackerman, Buckley, & Birch, 1981). Perspective taking also plays a role in promoting helping by power holders, in that simply "standing in another's shoes" – or perceiving circumstances from another person's point of view – increases the probability of helping that person (Arriaga & Rusbult, 1998; Davis & Oathout, 1987). Strong commitment has also been shown to promote prosocial acts, including the willingness to sacrifice one's immediate interests in order to benefit the partner, as well as the tendency to accommodate rather than retaliate when a partner behaves badly (Rusbult, Verette, Whitney, Slovik, & Lipkus, 1991; Van Lange et al., 1997). Tendencies toward power holder benevolence have also been shown to be greater in relationships with greater self-other merger, or a greater blurring of the distinction between self and partner (Aron, Aron, Tudor, & Nelson, 1991), as well as in relatively more communal relationships, or relationships wherein resources are allocated on the basis of each person's needs, irrespective of respective contributions (Clark & Mills, 1979).

11.4.4 *Attention and Cognition in Asymmetric Situations*

Experimental research regarding asymmetric dependence demonstrates that such situations exert reliable effects on attention and cognition (Fiske, 1993). Toward enhancing the predictability and controllability of interaction, dependents attend closely to the behavior of power holders, engage in perspective taking relevant to understanding power holders' intentions, exhibit good memory for power holders' characteristics, and form relatively complex, differentiated, nonstereotypic impressions of power holders' dispositions (Berscheid, Graziano, Monson, & Dermer, 1976; Dépret & Fiske, 1993; Tjosvold & Sagaria, 1978). In contrast, power holders engage in relatively "quick and dirty," undifferentiated processing of information regarding dependents, presumably because the well-being of power holders is not strongly influenced by the actions of dependents.

One might ask what purpose is served by complex and differentiated impression-formation when one is subject to partner-controlled dependence, in that under such circumstances, dependents can do little or nothing to control power holders. We suspect that even when power holder control is rather absolute, dependents nevertheless may seek *some* means of prediction, in that predictable outcomes arguably are less aversive than unpredictable outcomes (e.g., one can "prepare for the worst"). Moreover, the habit of control seeking may be quite robust, emerging even in situations of absolute dependence (e.g., among prisoners in concentration camps; Bettelheim, 1943). At the same time, it seems likely that the sorts of attentional and cognitive phenomena identified in previous research may be more marked for jointly controlled asymmetries (which are relatively more contingent) than for partner-controlled asymmetries (which are relatively more absolute).

11.4.5 Emotional Reactions in Asymmetric Situations

In considering the emotional reactions that accompany asymmetric dependence, it is useful to first address global feelings regarding the roles of power holder and dependent. If an Asymmetric situation involves common interests, the emotional experiences of both people are likely to be relatively benign. What is good for the power holder is likewise good for the dependent, so the exercise of control is unlikely to be particularly problematic for either party (except, perhaps, for the symbolic costs of receiving assistance, as discussed elsewhere in this entry). Indeed, the short-term experience of dependence may sometimes be pleasant, particularly among people who feel momentarily overwhelmed by responsibility or exhausted by the constant exercise of control (Baumeister, 1991).

However, Asymmetric situations do not always involve completely correspondent interests; presumably, power holders and dependents encounter many situations involving at least moderate conflict of interests. When Asymmetric situations involve conflicting interests, emotional reactions are likely to be more complex. Indeed, the empirical literature demonstrates that even in dating relationships and marital relationships – which presumably involve at least some commonality of interests – asymmetric dependence yields characteristic profiles of emotional experience: Dependents experience a mix of negative emotions, including anxiety, insecurity, and mistrust; power holders experience emotions centering on the experience of unwanted responsibility, including guilt, irritation, and resentment (Drigotas, Rusbult, & Verette, 1999).

Emotional reactions arise at two points during interaction, operating both prospectively and retrospectively (Kelley, 1984a). Prospectively, emotions reflect the opportunities and constraints inherent in a given interaction, playing a role in directing behavior with respect to the causal structure of a given situation. Prospective emotions are likely to mirror the uncertainties and complexities of Asymmetric situations. For example, when we find ourselves dependent on others with whom our interests conflict, we may experience prospective emotions such as apprehension ("am I going to be harmed?") or hope ("will my partner exhibit benevolence?"; "can I develop some means of encouraging benevolence?"). When we find outselves in a position to influence others with whom our interests conflict, prospective emotions are likely to reflect the broader considerations that are relevant to interaction, including compassion ("I want to help this person"), anger ("I want to hurt this person"), or resentment ("I don't want to hurt this person, but I must").

Retrospectively, emotions denote a change in personal well-being and serve as summaries of causal factors that are relevant to that change. The most obvious sort of retrospective emotion is outcome based: When an interaction yields good outcomes, recipients experience positive affect; when an interaction yields poor outcomes, recipients experience negative affect. Beyond simple outcome based emotion, people may also experience higher order affect, or emotional reactions related to the dispositions and motives revealed by an actor's behavior. Indeed, Asymmetric situations are powerful affordances, providing relatively unambiguous information about power holders' motives. For example, if a power holder behaves in such a manner as to benefit the dependent even when doing so is antithetical to the power holder's self-interest, the dependent may infer that the power holder is genuinely concerned about the dependent's well-being. Under such circumstances, both dependent and power holder may experience the "added value" of pleasant affect associated with such positive inferences (Holmes, 1981). The "added value" of benevolent behavior under such highly diagnostic circumstances has been shown to form the basis for the emergence of trust (Holmes & Rempel, 1989; Wieselquist, Rusbult, Foster, & Agnew, 1999).

11.4.6 *Attribution and Self-Presentation in Asymmetric Situations*
Asymmetric situations with conflicting interests provide rich opportunities for attribution and self-presentation. As noted earlier, when a power holder forgoes self-interest, exercising Partner Control or Joint Control in such a manner as to benefit a dependent, the power holder provides clear evidence of his or her benevolent motives. The more confidently observers can infer that such behavior is antithetical to self-interest, the stronger the attributions of benevolence (Batson, 1998; Holmes, 1981). Thus, power holders who wish to present themselves in a favorable manner may seek to conceal any personal benefits that accrue from acts of helping, or may seek to emphasize the degree to which self-interest and the interests of dependents conflict. Such impression management is a tricky business, in

that overtly calling attention to one's benevolence typically is regarded as braggardly. (The highest form of benevolence is the private act of generosity or the prosocial act that does not "call attention to itself.")

For dependents, graciously accepting the benevolence of power holders is an equally tricky business. Given the prevalence of reciprocity norms, the recipients of benevolent acts frequently experience resentment or lowered self-esteem, in that benevolent acts may too clearly place the dependent in debt for favors which cannot be repaid. For example, the recipients of help sometimes feel hostile toward those who provide help; welfare recipients perceive that in exchange for assistance, they suffer a humiliating loss of freedom and privacy (Briar, 1966; Gross, Wallston, & Piliavin, 1979). Even among adult siblings who commonly turn to one another for assistance, brothers and sisters frequently feel embarrassed or defensive about seeking help from one another (Searcy & Eisenberg, 1992).

Although the empirical literature reveals evidence of recipient ambivalence in both chronic and transitory Asymmetric situations, the negative consequences of receiving help presumably are greater for chronic asymmetries, where there are only limited opportunities for reciprocity. Moreover, we suspect that the negative consequences of receiving help may be more pronounced for partner-controlled acts of benevolence, whereby the recipient literally receives a "handout" from the power holder. Recipients may experience less ambivalence when helping takes the form of Joint Control, in that when power holders offer a "helping hand" to which the recipient can behaviorally coordinate, assistance should produce less guilt and resentment; in some sense, the recipient can perceive that he or she has "earned" good outcomes. For example, the prototypical Depression Era hobo retained his pride by requesting food in exchange for performing chores.

Thus, a priori, power holders may feel that it would be most generous to offer unilateral, "no strings attached," partner-controlled assistance: Power holders might reason that it would be moralistic or punitive to offer jointly controlled assistance, requiring recipients to perform tasks (or "jump through hoops") to demonstrate their deservingness. But given that partner-controlled assistance may be humiliating for recipients, it might ultimately be more gracious to ask recipients to "earn their way" via jointly controlled assistance. Jointly controlled power holder–dependent relationships were effectively employed in depression era WPA policies, whereby recipients received help in exchange for what was often rather minimal "work," or for "work" for which the power holder had no pressing need (e.g., applying ornamentation to a bridge, producing a work of art). Such programs assisted millions of needy Americans, simultaneously instilling "pride of work" and sustaining recipient self-respect.

11.4.7 *Norms Regarding Power Use in Asymmetric Situations*

In Asymmetric situations involving conflicting interests, dependents are likely to seek some basis for inducing benevolent treatment from power holders. For example, dependents may search for attractive alternatives, they may attempt to reduce or limit their investments in an ongoing interaction, or they may seek some means by which they might influence the power holder's well-being (for good or ill). Any one of these sources of control might be employed as a means of establishing formal or informal agreements encouraging power holders to take the dependent's well-being into consideration. Such agreements sometimes take the form of social norms. For example, to encourage power holder benevolence, dependents may employ what has been termed the "activation of commitments" (Jones & Gerard, 1967), whereby they appeal to prior moral commitments – commitments to normative standards embodied in such unassailable sources as the Ten Commandments, the Constitution, or the marriage vows. Dependents possessing attractive alternatives with which they may threaten a power holder are better able to invoke norms of fairness (Thibaut & Faucheux, 1965; also see Entry #6).

The origins of norms typically can be identified in the situations for which they provide solutions. Thus, it is interesting that many social norms concern the distribution of resources in Asymmetric situations. Some authors have distinguished between (a) contributions-based norms, or rules whereby resources are allocated in a manner commensurate with each person's "deservingness," in recognition of prior (or future) contributions, and (b) need-based norms, or rules whereby resources are allocated on the basis of each person's needs, irrespective of prior (or future) contributions. It has been argued that in relationships involving common long-term interests and asymmetric dependence – for example, in parent-child or teacher-student interactions – the norms guiding behavior are need based rather than contributions based (Clark & Mills, 1979; Deutsch, 1975).

When asymmetry stems from the greater resources of the power holder, a norm such as noblesse oblige may emerge. Specifically, partners may (implicitly or explicitly) adopt a contributions rule whereby the advantaged power holder is held responsible for contributing a greater share to promote the interactants' joint well-being. Norms of this sort may explain why, for example, wealthy people make larger contributions to public television (Murningham & King, 1992; Wit, Wilke, & Oppewal, 1992). Norms such as need-based allocations or noblesse oblige may initially emerge for reasons that yield practical advantages to ongoing dyads or groups, such as enhanced loyalty or increased commitment to shared goals. Over time, such norms may become functionally autonomous, acquiring the power to guide behavior in their own right, independent of the effects of such behavior on personal or collective interests.

As noted earlier, norms sometimes afford power holders the "right" to govern dependents' outcomes or behavior – the right to either uni-laterally dictate the outcomes of dependents (Partner Control) or to take actions that limit dependents' behavioral options, thereby shaping dependents' preferences (Joint Control). For example, norms regarding legitimate power dictate the persons whose outcomes a power holder may influence, the conditions under which such influence is acceptable, and the range of situations to which such influence applies (French & Raven, 1959). Although norms regarding power use frequently dictate benevolent treatment ("never hit a guy when he's down"), norms may also specify the conditions under which purely self-oriented power use is acceptable ("all's fair in love and war").

It should be clear that legitimate power is effective only insofar as tar-gets believe that they are obligated to comply with legitimate authority. Early in life, we learn that it is a good idea to comply with the requests of authority figures because they "know more than us" and/or because they control our outcomes. Later in life, we continue to comply with the wishes of properly constituted authorities, even when it makes little sense to do so. Legitimate power is so compelling that we sometimes comply with illegitimate requests simply because the request is proffered by a per-son with the "trappings" of legitimacy (e.g., a uniform, the title "Doctor"; Bickman, 1974). In a related vein, we sometimes behave as though we are dependent in situations where the "power holder" holds little or no real control over our outcomes. For example, in many studies of obedience, participants exhibit high levels of destructive compliance despite the fact that the authority figure exerts little real influence over their material out-comes (Milgram, 1974). Social convention dictates that the experimenter has "authority" and that participants should "obey," so large numbers of people behave as though they were subject to power holder control.

11.4.8 *Differential Subjective Involvement in Close Relationships*
The empirical literature demonstrates that in ongoing relationships in-volving asymmetric dependence, the "weaker link," or less dependent

partner, is more likely to terminate the relationship (Attridge, Berscheid, & Simpson, 1995; Rusbult, 1983). As noted earlier, the partner who has poorer alternatives (and/or has more invested in the relationship) is vulnerable to the possibility of abandonment. Also, relationships involving asymmetric dependence exhibit poorer adjustment than those involving mutual dependence, being characterized by lower levels of intimacy, companionship, and satisfaction (Drigotas et al., 1999; Witcher, 1999). This association is evident above and beyond the actual level of dependence. That is, asymmetric dependence is problematic in relationships involving both low and high absolute levels of dependence, or in both nonclose *and* close involvements.

What do asymmetric close relationships look like? According to the principle of least interest, "that person is able to dictate the conditions of association whose interest in the continuation of the affair is the least" (Waller, 1938, p. 275). Consistent with this proposition, the empirical literature reveals that the partner who is relatively less involved in a relationship – operationally defined in terms of relative love and commitment – tends to exert greater control over decision making (Safilios-Rothschild, 1976; Scanzoni & Scanzoni, 1981; Sprecher, 1985). Also, the more dependent partner carries the greater burden of interaction costs, in that dependents are more likely to accommodate than retaliate when their partners behave badly, and are more likely to sacrifice their immediate well-being to promote the interests of the partner (Witcher, 1999). In short, an implicit "bargain" is established, whereby the more dependent person defers to the other's wishes to insure that the relationship will persist. Thus, even in close relationships – which presumably involve at least some commonality of interests – asymmetric dependence appears to yield relatively poorer outcomes for dependents than for power holders.

11.4.9 *Differential Resources in Close Relationships*
Asymmetric dependence may not only arise from close partners' differential subjective involvement (their relative love or commitment), but may also rest on differential material resources. For example, one partner may have greater economic resources than the other (salary, inherited wealth), or one partner may possess superior legal or political power (e.g., divorce laws may favor one party; Blood & Wolfe, 1960; Safilios-Rothschild, 1976). Differential resources have been shown to shape a variety of interaction phenomena. For example, in attempting to change one another's opinions, the more dependent partner tends to rely on indirect strategies such as hinting or expressing negative feelings, whereas the more

powerful partner tends to rely on direct strategies such as bargaining, offering logical arguments, or stating desired outcomes (Falbo & Peplau, 1980). During conflicted interaction, the more dependent partner tends to exert pressure for change via requests, criticism, and complaints, whereas the more powerful partner tends to exhibit withdrawal, passive inaction, and stonewalling, thereby avoiding change (Christensen & Heavey, 1990). During the course of everyday communication, the more dependent partner tends to exhibit superior ability at both encoding and decoding nonverbal messages (Sabatelli, Buck, & Dreyer, 1980). And in the context of physically abusive relationships, women are less likely to terminate their relationships to the extent that their economic resources are poorer – for example, to the extent that they have less education and job training, less work experience, and lower earning power (Gelles & Straus, 1988; Rusbult & Martz, 1995).

Asymmetric dependence may sometimes originate in general features of the social environment, such as the availability of suitable alternative mates. The availability of "suitable alternatives" can be operationally defined in terms of sex ratio, or the ratio of men to women in the mating market. Imbalanced sex ratios, or deviations from 1.0, have been argued to "dramatically influence the gender roles of men and women, shape the forms taken by relationships between men and women, and in turn produce changes in family structures and stimulate new kinds of association along gender lines" (Secord, 1983, p. 525). A high sex ratio (more men than women) yields tendencies to place high value on young women, strong norms of commitment, traditional division of labor, and sexual morality; a low sex ratio (fewer men than women) yields sexual libertarianism, tendencies toward brief liaisons, and inclinations on the part of women to establish themselves as independent persons (Guttentag & Secord, 1983).

Note that the consequences of a high sex ratio are not the mirror image of those for a low sex ratio. This lack of symmetry reflects sources of power other than the dyadic power deriving from sexual scarcity. The deviation from what would be expected simply on the basis of supply and demand arguably derives from the fact that in most cultures, men hold greater structural power, or power derived from their economic, political, and legal privileges. Given that men rather consistently possess structural power, (a) when men also possess dyadic power (low sex ratio; women are abundant), they tend to use both sources of power to sustain a pattern of sexual freedom, whereas (b) when women possess dyadic power (high sex ratio; women are scarce), men tend to use their structural power to bring about a pattern whereby they shelter, protect, and isolate their women.

11.4.10 *Asymmetric Dependence in Formal Organizations*

Earlier, we noted that people are more dependent to the extent that they possess poorer alternatives and/or have more invested in a given relationship. This is the case not only in close relationships (as noted earlier), but also in organizational settings: Employees report stronger job commitment and are less likely to quit their jobs to the extent that their work alternatives are poor (e.g., there are few attractive alternative jobs in the region) and to the extent that they have numerous important investments in their jobs (e.g., job-specific training, nonvested retirement programs; Rusbult & Farrell, 1983; Mowday, Porter, & Steers, 1982).

In comparison to their behavior toward less dependent employees, how do employers behave toward relatively more dependent employees? Research regarding allocation behavior demonstrates that employers frequently allocate resources (salary, promotions, and the like) not only (a) on the basis of the equity principle, allocating greater resources to employees with higher performance levels, but also (b) on the basis of employee mobility, allocating greater resources to high-performance employees with greater mobility, or lower dependence on the organization (i.e., superior alternatives, lower investment size; Rusbult, Lowery, Hubbard, Maravankin, & Neises, 1988).

Thus, in comparison to competent employees who are not particularly dependent, equally competent employees who are dependent on their jobs – those who own homes in the area, have school-age children, or are involved in dual-career marriages – tend to receive smaller shares of the available resources. This phenomenon has been termed "rational selective exploitation" in recognition of the facts that (a) it is rational for employers to work toward retaining competent employees and (b) more resources are required to retain independent, potentially mobile employees, *but* (c) this pattern of resource allocation yields deviations from the equity rule and is distressing to employees, even to those who benefit from this pattern of allocation behavior (Rusbult, Campbell, & Price, 1990).

11.4.11 *Asymmetric Dependence and the Self*

Long-term involvement in situations involving asymmetric dependence sometimes changes power holders' and dependents' dispositions. These shifts reflect relatively stable adaptations to the problems and opportunities inherent in asymmetry. Such adaptations come about not only in response to long-term dependence, but also in response to long-term power holding.

Laypeople frequently suggest that power holding "corrupts." This truism presumably implies that long-term power holding yields elevated self-esteem and expectations of deference. By what affective or cognitive mechanisms might such "corruption" come about? Kipnis (1972) addressed this question by asking undergraduates to serve as managers for groups of high school students, instructing them to operate their group at a profitable level by maintaining worker efficiency. Some managers were given high power over their employees, including the right to allocate pay increases or reductions, threaten to fire or actually fire employees, and the like. Other managers were given low power, being forced to rely primarily on legitimate power and persuasion to influence employee performance. In comparison to low power holders, high power holders devalued dependents' performance, attributed dependents' efforts to the power holder's actions rather than to dependents' intrinsic motivation, regarded dependents as objects of manipulation, and, in a variety of other ways, psychologically distanced themselves from dependents. Kipnis's work highlights the potential of asymmetric dependence to yield "corruption" via changes in power holders' perceptions of the self in relation to dependents.

Research regarding the corrupting effects of power holding emphasizes one side of interactions involving asymmetric dependence. What are the consequences of such interactions for dependents? This issue is at the heart of attachment theory, which suggests that the experiences of children (dependents) at the hands of parents (power holders) can exert long-term effects on childrens' perceptions of themselves and others (Bowlby, 1988). Attachment theory focuses on the degree to which caregivers benevolently and sensitively use their power, offering comfort and reassurance when the child is in need and serving as a secure base from which the child can explore. The empirical literature demonstrates that children treated in such a responsive manner develop trusting and secure expectations regarding interactions involving asymmetric dependence (Hazan & Shaver, 1994). To the degree that caregiving is unresponsive or exploitative, children develop anxious and fearful expectations regarding dependence situations, or come to avoid situations in which they need and rely on others.

The effects of long-term asymmetries are also highlighted in theories utilizing constructs such as learned helplessness and locus of control. For example, child-rearing practices that afford children opportunities to manipulate the physical and social environment are argued to yield internal locus of control, or the expectation that one personally controls one's outcomes (Rotter, 1966). Practices that are more heavy-handed and controlling are argued to yield external locus of control, or the expectation that external forces or powerful others control one's outcomes. This difference may rest on the distinction between jointly controlled versus partner-controlled asymmetry: When parent-child interactions involve Joint Control, children learn to coordinate their actions with those of their parents, acquire the capacity to vary their behavior in response to changes in circumstances, and thereby come to believe that they control their own outcomes. When parent-child interactions involve Partner Control, children learn that changes in their own actions do not yield corresponding changes in their outcomes, but rather that their outcomes are controlled by external forces (the parents' actions). Similarly, long-term exposure to uncontrollable aversive stimuli ("Partner" Control) is argued to yield relatively stable patterns of learned helplessness, whereby the individual fails to take action to control the environment even when such control is possible (Seligman, 1975). Such theories emphasize the importance of initiative taking in everyday interaction, highlighting the role of experience with jointly controlled asymmetric dependence in establishing such dispositions.

11.5 Matrix Representations

Table E11.1. In the matrix in Table E11.1, person A (the power holder) has Actor Control over his or her own outcomes and Partner Control over person B's outcomes. Person B (the dependent) has no Actor Control over his or her own outcomes and no Partner Control or Joint Control over person A's outcomes. In this example, person A's interests and person B's interests are in conflict, in that the course of action that is good for person A is precisely that which is bad for person B. Thus, if person A pursues his or her own interests by selecting a2, person B will be harmed; if person A promotes person B's interests by selecting a1, person A will be harmed.

TABLE E11.1. *Situational Representation of Asymmetric Dependence Involving Partner Control and Conflicting Interests*

		A			
		a1		a2	
			−4		+10
	b1				
		+10		−4	
B					
			−4		+10
	b2				
		+10		−4	

Table E11.2. In the matrix in Table E11.2, person A (the power holder) has Actor Control over his or her own outcomes and Joint Control over person B's outcomes. Person B (the dependent) has no Actor Control over his or her own outcomes and no Partner Control or Joint Control over person A's outcomes. This example involves some commonality of interests. To enjoy good outcomes, person B must take action contingent on the choice of person A: If person A pursues his or her own interests by selecting a2, person B must select b2 in order to enjoy moderately good outcomes.

TABLE E11.2. *Situational Representation of Asymmetric Dependence Involving Joint Control and Some Commonality of Interests*

		A	
		a1	a2
b1		-4	$+10$
		$+4$	-4
B			
b2		-4	$+10$
		-4	$+4$

TIME-EXTENDED PATTERNS

Entry #12

Iterated Prisoner's Dilemma

United We Stand, Divided We Fall

12.1 Examples

The single-trial Prisoner's Dilemma, discussed in Entry #5, is defined by the conflict between self-interest ("me") and joint interest ("we"). An individual is always better off choosing a noncooperative option, irrespective of the partner's behavior, even though the cooperative choice is preferable from a dyadic standpoint. Choices in the "classic" case of the single-trial Prisoner's Dilemma, involving simultaneous and irrevocable choice (as in the story from which the situation takes its name), are unlikely to be influenced by past interactions or future goals. In contrast, in Iterated Prisoner's Dilemmas, behavior is likely to be affected by prior interactions and considerations regarding future interactions with the partner. This is true even when the choices at each point are simultaneous and irrevocable. The persons become able to react contingently to each other's prior behaviors and, therefore, to develop strategies for influencing each other's behavior. For example, a person is unlikely to prepare extensively for a joint working meeting if she knows that her colleague has repeatedly slacked off before in past meetings. On the other hand, a person may devote greater time and effort preparing for a joint task when anticipating future shared endeavors in order to motivate the other to enhance her performance in the future.

Iterated Prisoner's Dilemmas are common in everyday life (and are considerably more common than the single-trial Prisoner's Dilemma). For example, friends may help each other with difficult or costly tasks (e.g., moving, preparing for a job interview, figuring out a demanding

Paul A. M. Van Lange had primary responsibility for preparation of this entry.

homework assignment), neighbors may exchange gifts at Christmas time, a worker may stay late to assist a co-worker with a pressing deadline, and a spouse may assume a larger-than-usual share of household chores when his or her partner is otherwise burdened. In contrast to the situations above, which involve helping each other, there are other situations in which individuals are challenged to forgo immediate self-interest by not harming another person. For example, playing loud music may bring about greater costs to one's next-door neighbor than it yields benefits to oneself. Or, on occasions of mutual disclosure of intimate information, two friends have opportunities to listen and withhold criticism rather than take advantage of each other's vulnerabilities.

The common thread in the above situations is that, in each interaction and over time, the dyad's welfare is maximized if both partners behave cooperatively rather than noncooperatively, even though the noncooperative option would enhance each individual's rewards or reduce their costs on each occasion. Iteration implies that the two persons are, objectively, in a continuing "relationship," repeatedly faced with the conflict between self and common interest. Iteration becomes a psychological reality when they recognize the basic similarity among successive situations – that even though they may be diverse in their concrete demands and unevenly distributed over time, they all involve the same essential dilemma.

12.2 Conceptual Description

As discussed in Entry #5, a "Prisoner's Dilemma" exists when two individuals have resources that are relatively more valuable to the partner than to the self. In the iterated case, each interaction situation is identical to the single-trial Prisoner's Dilemma, in that the outcomes are strongly controlled by the partner's behavior and somewhat less strongly controlled by the individual's own actions. That is, both the single-trial Prisoner's Dilemma and each interaction in the Iterated Prisoner's Dilemma are characterized by strong levels of Mutual Partner Control and relatively smaller levels of Bilateral Actor Control. These two components are combined in a discordant orientation toward each other, thus representing a conflict of interest between the actor and the partner. (The resulting outcome matrix is presented in Table E12.1 below, at the end of this entry.)

An important difference between the single-trial and the Iterated Prisoner's Dilemma emerges from the fact that in the iterated version interaction occurs repeatedly: Choices made in each interaction situation can be influenced, often substantially so, by the other's prior and expected future behavior. In part, this is because one's own outcomes from past interactions have been determined by the other's choices. For example, the partner may have failed to provide help when it was needed. Such experiences are likely to influence current decisions about whether or not to provide help. Present choices also tend to be affected by an individual's beliefs about the impact of present behavior on the partner's choices in the future. For example, people are more likely to provide help when they expect that the other will feel motivated to reciprocate later on (Komorita, Hilty, & Parks, 1991).

Because the Iterated Prisoner's Dilemma is characterized by high levels of Mutual Partner Control, an individual's current behavior may be intended primarily to influence the other's subsequent behavior in a manner that will benefit one's long-term goals. For example, a parent wanting a friend to babysit at some time in the future might offer to babysit for the other today (or even several times in the near term). It is highly improbable that one person in an arrangement of this sort will continue to cooperate while the other is repeatedly noncooperative, because, as is evident in the matrix in Table E12.1, those choices yield the worst possible outcome for the cooperating partner (and the best possible outcome for the other). As a consequence, repeated interactions in this situation tend to result in either of two patterns: Both individuals choose to behave cooperatively or both individuals choose to behave noncooperatively (Rapoport & Chammah, 1965a & 1965b).

Where the single-trial Prisoner's Dilemma represents a dilemma between individual and joint outcomes, the iterated version also to some degree represents a dilemma between enhancing short-term versus long-term outcomes. However, this is true only when mutual cooperation is feasible; that is, when both individuals are willing to forgo the best immediate outcome for the self by adopting a strategy of conditional cooperation (i.e., the willingness to act cooperatively if and only if the other does the same). Individuals generally recognize that unilateral noncooperation – exploitation – is a highly unstable pattern over the long run, and is likely to end up creating mutual noncooperation. From this perspective, the Iterated Prisoner's Dilemma has been an exceedingly useful tool for investigating how mutual noncooperation can be avoided or ameliorated. As described below, this seems to be a matter of how the two individuals can adopt a strategy of mutual conditional cooperation. Generally, patterns of cooperative interaction do tend to increase over time in an Iterated Prisoner's Dilemma, indicating the *learning* of cooperation (Rapoport & Chammah, 1965a & 1965b).

12.3 Variants and Neighbors

Iterated Prisoner's Dilemmas may involve positive outcomes, negative outcomes, or both. The "classic" example, that of the two prisoners whose independent decisions affect the lengths of their respective prison sentences, is, of course, a situation with only larger or smaller negative outcomes. But often, Prisoner's Dilemmas represent a mixture of positive and negative outcomes. For example, investing time or energy in helping someone is a personally costly act, which often takes the form of a negative outcome when the partner does not reciprocate, and often takes the form of a positive outcome when the partner does reciprocate.

Prisoner's Dilemma situations also vary in whether the variance in outcomes is small or large, which we earlier referred to as level of importance (see Entry #5). In Prisoner's Dilemmas involving relatively high variance (such as between soldiers in combat), the stakes are obviously very high in each interaction. Related to the level of importance is whether participants in studies of Prisoner's Dilemmas make choices for points (or pennies) or "real dollars." Although several scientists believe that substantial amounts of money are crucial to creating a meaningful experimental context, the empirical evidence is actually inconsistent. In their review of Prisoner's Dilemmas, Komorita and Parks (1994, p. 31) concluded that the majority of studies report no significant difference in the level of cooperation when the stakes (points, pennies, dollars) are varied. These authors do raise the possibility, however, that the effects of motivational differences may be more pronounced when the stakes are high rather than low.

There may also be asymmetries between the two persons in the type and range of outcomes they face. One may be contending with a choice between the lesser of two negative outcomes, whereas the other is choosing between positive outcomes; or, one individual may be faced with very discrepant outcomes, whereas the difference may be slight for the other. Such asymmetries reflect personal differences in one's experience of the resource being exchanged. For example, the time needed to exchange mutual help may be more valuable for one partner than the other (perhaps because of time-management skills or other responsibilities), whereas physical exertion is likely to be less costly to strong than weak individuals. These asymmetries may influence how individuals resolve the Prisoner's Dilemma in each situation. For example, because costs tend to loom larger than gains (Kahneman & Tversky, 1984), the person choosing between two negative outcomes might be less likely to cooperate than the person choosing between two positive outcomes (cf. Brewer & Kramer, 1986). Also, the person with the greater "resources" (e.g., the richer person, the person with greater skill) is likely to make a greater contribution than is the person with smaller resources (Van Dijk & Wilke, 1993).

As noted in Entry #5, Prisoner's Dilemmas need not always concern "black or white" issues, but may take a graduated form entailing choices that differ in degree of cooperativeness (e.g., how much time and energy to devote to helping another person with a particular task). In the context of Iterated Prisoner's Dilemmas, this may serve important communicative purposes. For example, one may behave just a little bit more cooperatively than the partner to communicate not only some generosity, but also the direction in which one wants to move: that is, greater rather than smaller levels of mutual cooperation (see Kollock, 1993). Doing just a little bit more than the partner did for you has been demonstrated to be effective in overcoming the detrimental effects of incidental errors (Van Lange, Ouwerkerk, & Tazelaar, 2002).

Finally, the Iterated Prisoner's Dilemma is relatively closely related to iterated versions of Chicken and Trust. However, relative to the Prisoner's Dilemma, the interests of the two persons involved in Chicken or Trust are less conflicting than in the Prisoner's Dilemma (for a more detailed discussion, see Entry #5).

12.4 Interaction Patterns and Person Factors

We have noted the obvious fact that the Iterated Prisoner's Dilemma differs from the single-trial case in incorporating the effect of historical and future-oriented factors. If the iteration is embedded in a continuing relationship (as our examples have suggested) those factors include the trust the partners have in each other and implicit or explicit norms they have developed over time. When the iteration occurs between strangers, as in the typical laboratory experiment, we have an opportunity to observe at firsthand the emergence of some sort of shared understandings. In fact, in their repeated interactions, even strangers in experiments have an opportunity to develop some sort of "relationship," be it one of mutual trust or one of unremitting uncooperativeness and attempts to exploit each other.

12.4.1 Communication
If communication is possible during the course of repeated encounters (as it usually is), it affords a means of promoting cooperative interaction. The Mutual Partner Control component of the Prisoner's Dilemma provides a

basis for both applying pressure to one's partner and providing positive incentives for their good behavior (see Mutual Partner Control, Entry #2, for a further discussion).

One of the most interesting approaches to the use of communication to establish mutual cooperation in the Prisoner's Dilemma is that of Deutsch (1958). He argued that communication must be designed with an eye to the dynamic factors that underlie a stable cooperative interaction. Specifically, he emphasized a complementarity of cooperative intentions and expectations so that each person should (a) intend to behave cooperatively, and (b) expect cooperative behavior from the other. If there is a departure from that complementarity, a system for restoring it should be activated, taking the form of (c) retaliation that neutralizes a partner's violation, or (d) absolving – forgiving – the partner once the violation ends. As a test of this theory, Loomis (1959) compared the effectiveness in experimental settings of messages incorporating various of those elements: (a) "I will cooperate", (b) "I would like you to cooperate." (c) "If you don't cooperate, then I will choose so that you can't win." And (d) "If you decide to cooperate and make a cooperative choice after not doing so, I will cooperate." In support of Deutsch's theory, Loomis found that a message incorporating all four of those elements was considerably more effective in inducing trust and cooperative choices than no communication or a message incorporating only the first two elements. The application of threat and promise, via the latter elements (c and d, respectively), seems to be important. These principles were subsequently used in designing strategies for building trust and resolving conflict, and for further theorizing (e.g., Graduated and Reciprocated Initiatives in Tension reduction, or GRID; Osgood, 1962; Goal/Expectation Theory; Pruitt & Kimmel, 1977).

In general, as in the single-trial Prisoner's Dilemma, communication prior to the act of choosing between behavioral options enhances cooperation. As suggested above, individuals are able to make promises or threats that increase the likelihood of cooperative interaction. Communication can be considered to be a variant of revocable choice, as discussed in Entry # 5 (Prisoner's Dilemma), in the sense that spontaneous communication allows partners to express their intentions, accompanied by references to the conditions under which they are and are not willing to actually carry out the cooperative choice. Such messages may convey "trust" or "conditional cooperation"; that is, one's willingness to cooperate if the other does the same. At the same time, one cannot be sure whether the "trust" that is communicated will in fact be translated into "deeds." The extant literature suggests that communication often enhances cooperation but that this may not always happen. The credibility of verbal communication is obviously an important issue.

12.4.2 *Reciprocity*

When verbal communication is not possible, individuals may still "communicate" through their behavior. Such forms of behavioral communication are often more effective than verbal communication, because "deeds" (i.e., actually forgoing a tempting noncooperative choice) are more trustworthy and "credible" than "words" (i.e., promising to forgo the tempting noncooperative choice). Consider, for example, the "tit-for-tat" strategy which begins with a cooperative choice and subsequently imitates the partner's previous choice. This strategy has been shown to yield greater outcomes than a 100% cooperative or 100% noncooperative strategy. Following early experiments examining this strategy, Axelrod (1984) organized a computer tournament in which several social and behavioral experts submitted programmed strategies that they believed would, when pitted against other possible programs, produce the highest outcomes. Each strategy then played against (or with) each other strategy. The interesting result was that tit-for-tat yielded far better outcomes for itself than did any of the other strategies.

An important feature accounting for tit-for-tat's effectiveness is its niceness, in that the self is never first to make a noncooperative choice and therefore cannot be perceived as exploitative or aggressive. Tit-for-tat is also effective because it is retaliatory: Noncooperative behavior is responded to with a reciprocal noncooperative action. Furthermore, tit-for-tat is forgiving, in that noncooperative choices by the other in one situation are easily remedied in subsequent situations. Finally, tit-for-tat is also a clear strategy, readily understood by others, and indeed it tends to be experienced as directed toward establishing cooperation.

It is worth noting that tit-for-tat closely parallels the communication designed by Deutsch to promote cooperation (as described above). In both cases, the initial (real or intended) action is a cooperative one, indicating a willingness to cooperate. When the partner acts noncooperatively, the communication is to threaten and the tit-for-tat strategy is to retaliate. And when the partner shifts from noncooperation to cooperation, the communication promises, as the tit-for-tat act demonstrates, to "forgive and forget." In short, both combine a helpful orientation with a firm but contingently forgiving treatment of the partner's misbehavior.

The effectiveness of tit-for-tat in eliciting and maintaining patterns of mutual cooperation has been demonstrated in several experiments (e.g., Komorita et al., 1991; McClintock & Liebrand, 1988). At the same time, it is important to note that tit-for-tat fails to initiate cooperation after there has been a lapse in it. Hence, a limitation of tit-for-tat is that it may give rise to the so-called *echo-effect* (or negative reciprocity; cf. Komorita & Parks, 1995; Pruitt & Kimmel, 1977), interaction patterns whereby the two persons are "trapped" in cycles of noncooperative responses. This limitation is especially important in situations characterized by *noise* – when there are discrepancies between intended and actual outcomes for an interaction partner due to unintended errors (e.g., not being able to respond to an e-mail due to a local network breakdown). In such situations, an unintended error may lead to misunderstanding ("why hasn't he responded to my e-mail?") and eventually a noncooperative response ("I will make him wait as well"), which may instigate the echo-effect. Following some computer simulations (e.g., Axelrod & Dion, 1988; Kollock, 1993), some recent research indicates that some level of generosity might be important in overcoming the detrimental effects of such unintended errors. That is, when unintended errors are likely to occur with some regularity, strict forms of reciprocity will give rise to the echo-effect, which can be prevented or overcome by adding a little generosity to reciprocity: that is, by consistently behaving a little more cooperatively than the other did in the previous interaction (e.g., Van Lange et al., 2002).

Whether people will actually follow generous or "stingy" versions of reciprocity will depend on aspects of themselves, the partner, and the situation. However, it does seem plausible that reciprocal strategies are fairly widespread, especially in comparison to so-called unconditional strategies, which make a cooperative or noncooperative choice, irrespective of the other's choice. As such, reciprocity may also be closely linked to the *learning* of cooperation in Prisoner's Dilemmas. Rapoport and Chammah (1965a & 1965b) not only found an increase in cooperation after repeated interaction, they also found an interesting time-specific pattern. In their 300-interaction trial study, the percentage of cooperative choices in first trial was a little less than 50%, after which there was a decline to about 40% of cooperation. This decline lasted until around trial 30, after which there was a steady increase in cooperation up to about 75%. Importantly, at the beginning of the interactions, most pairs did not make the same choice: One person made a cooperative choice whereas the other made a noncooperative choice. But in the final 25 trials (of the 300 trials in total), the majority of pairs made exactly the same choice. And of these "reciprocal" pairs, most of the pairs had developed a stable pattern of mutual cooperation (76%), and a little less than a quarter had developed a stable pattern of mutual noncooperation (24%). This study suggests that, after a period of decline, many individuals – and pairs – learn to cooperate in Iterated Prisoner's Dilemmas.

12.4.3 *Individual Differences in Goals*

When entering an Iterated Prisoner's Dilemma, individuals may pursue different goals and hold different beliefs regarding others' expected behavior. People who tend to pursue cooperative goals are likely to develop patterns of either cooperative or noncooperative interaction, working cooperatively with cooperative others and noncooperatively with noncooperative others. This reflects the fact, noted above, that individuals pursuing cooperative goals do not continue to make cooperative choices in the absence of any reciprocity. Indeed, individuals pursuing cooperative goals are concerned with enhancing joint outcomes and enhancing equality in outcomes (which is one of the reasons why these individuals are often referred to as "prosocials"; e.g., Van Lange, 1999). In contrast, competitors are unlikely to develop cooperative interaction patterns with any partner, including even those whose preferences are to be cooperative (Kuhlman & Marshello, 1975). This difference has interesting implications. Because they have different experience with others behaving cooperatively as well as others behaving noncooperatively, individuals with prosocial goals develop an understanding that other people are heterogeneous in their orientations to this type of situation. On the other hand, individuals with competitive goals have pretty much the same experience with all their partners. This reflects the fact that, in their efforts to defend themselves against exploitation by competitive partners, individuals with prosocial goals tend rather quickly to become behaviorally similar to those partners (described by Kelley & Stahelski, 1970, as *behavioral assimilation*), but this goes unnoticed by those partners. (The competitive partners fail to notice that their actions elicit what appears to be competitive but is merely defensive behavior.) As a consequence, and in contrast to what happens for prosocials, competitors develop the belief that almost all people are disposed, like themselves, to act competitively.

As Kelley and Stahelski (1970) point out, the above relationship between one's goals and the development of beliefs regarding others' motivations and goals is sustained and reinforced through interaction experiences in Iterated Prisoner's Dilemmas. This process clearly illustrates the notion of a "self-fulfilling prophecy" (Snyder, Tanke, & Berscheid, 1977), in that the competitive individual's goals are, through their own behavior, likely to confirm their preexisting belief that others tend to be noncooperative. Similarly, the heterogeneous beliefs of cooperative individuals are bolstered by the contrasting cooperative versus noncooperative interactions that their own behavior elicits. Of course, as with most self-fulfilling prophecies, the person's observation is accurate, but the analysis of causation is not.

It may be objected that the phenomena of behavioral assimilation and its consequences for the goal-belief pattern (just described) depends on limitations inherent to the Prisoner's Dilemma situation. It does not permit a cooperation oriented person to deal with a competitive partner in any way other than to adopt the very same behavior as the partner's. Why is it not possible for the cooperator to resist the drift toward mutual "competition" without, in doing so, appearing to be competitive? This question was raised by Miller and Holmes (1975) and they answered it by proposing an extended version of the Prisoner's Dilemma shown in the matrix in Table E12.2 below. That situation enables a person not only to cooperate or not, but also (by the a3 or b3 option) to withdraw from the dilemma based interaction. The option to withdraw is important because it allows a person desiring to cooperate to avoid entering into the pattern of mutual noncooperation while neutralizing the partner's efforts to exploit them.

Miller and Holmes showed that individuals who are motivated to behave cooperatively but do not expect a partner to reciprocate are especially likely to choose the self-protective, defensive choice of withdrawal. They also found, as expected, that tendencies toward behavioral assimilation by cooperative individuals and development of homogeneous beliefs by noncooperative individuals are less pronounced when the withdrawal option is available. The matrix in Table E12.2 shows that withdrawal has little direct impact (positive or negative) on one's own and the other's outcomes, but it enables a prosocial person to show their resistance to a competitive partner without becoming (behaviorally) competitive. It is interesting to think about the withdrawal option in relation to tit-for-tat. We remarked earlier that this strategy lacks a means by which a person desiring cooperation can take the lead in initiating it when the pair is locked in a noncooperative exchange (i.e., the echo-effect). The withdrawal option affords a possible site for such initiatives. It affords a "time-out" break in the interaction during which the pair is essentially independent (see Independence, Entry #1). After a break and a "cooling-off" period, it might be appropriate for a cooperative person to reinstate tit-for-tat, again beginning with a cooperative overture and following the strategy's rules thereafter.

It might be expected that cooperative interactions are likely when both partners adopt a cooperative goal. However, this is not necessarily true. As Pruitt and Kimmel (1977; p. 375) state, "the goal of achieving mutual cooperation is insufficient to elicit cooperative behavior. It must be accompanied by an expectation that the other will cooperate." They thereby emphasize the complementarity of intentions and expectations to which Deutsch had earlier called attention (see also Deutsch, 1973). Pruitt and Kimmel note that this principle provides a parsimonious account of many research findings and illustrates the dual importance of cooperative goals and trust in the other's corresponding cooperative goals. Many real-world situations – conflict-resolution among spouses, for example, or labor-management disputes – are impaired when each party fails to recognize the other side's willingness to cooperate, even though both sides intend to cooperate. In such situations, communication – in either a verbal or behavioral form – facilitates coming to believe that the other can be counted on to cooperate. A priori beliefs regarding another's willingness to cooperate reflect interpersonal trust, and a person who makes cooperative choices conveys trustworthiness (Deutsch, 1958; Holmes & Rempel, 1989; Yamagishi, 1988b).

Although goals and expectations regarding the other's behavior are often correlated, in some circumstances an individual willing to cooperate may not expect the other to cooperate. Similarly, a person sometimes may pursue a noncooperative strategy expecting the other to cooperate. One might speculate that such discrepancies are especially likely in asymmetric situations, in which the individuals effectively are faced with different reward-cost alternatives (e.g., when outcome variance is greater for one person than the other or when one's options describe negative outcomes whereas the other's concern positive outcomes). Asymmetric Prisoner's Dilemmas have received little empirical attention, but it is clear that they evoke special norms and motives. For example, norms of justice and social responsibility suggest that relatively advantaged individuals (e.g., those facing low variance among positive alternatives) should be more willing to cooperate, even if they are unsure about the other's (i.e., the "needier" person's) willingness to cooperate (Schopler & Bateson, 1965; Van Dijk & Wilke, 1993). Often in this situation two individuals may agree, implicitly or explicitly, that the person in the more favorable position should contribute more to joint outcomes than the person in the less favorable position. This would appear to be true for many situations, including ones that are not, strictly speaking, Prisoner's dilemmas. For example, after a dinner in a restaurant, the wealthier person tends to be more likely to take care of the tip. Or the more talented person might invest much more time and effort in a joint task than the less talented person.

12.4.4 *Some Key Concepts*

Preferences do not always entirely correspond, and often people are faced with interaction situations that share the features of the Iterated Prisoner's Dilemma. This overview of Prisoner's Dilemmas suggest the importance of at least two broad concepts (see also earlier theorizing by, among others, Deutsch, 1973; Pruitt & Kimmel, 1977). The first key concept could be termed *prosocial motivation* (or cooperative motivation) – the willingness to engage in personally costly actions to enhance good long-term personal outcomes (through exchange or reciprocity) or good long-term joint outcomes. In the context of close relationships, such motivations are addressed in programs of research focusing on pro-relationship motivation and behavior, such as willingness to sacrifice (Van Lange et al., 1997) or specific pro-relationship acts (e.g., accommodation, or willingness to react in a prosocial manner to potentially destructive acts by the partner; Rusbult, Verette, Whitney, Slovik, & Lipkus, 1991). In the context of organizations, such issues are addressed in programs of research focusing on various forms of cooperative behaviors, such as helping colleagues with difficult tasks (cf. organizational citizenship behaviors, Mathieu & Zajac, 1990). From a Prisoner's Dilemma perspective, it is understandable that long-term orientation, feelings of attachment, and the experience of dependence, as embodied by commitment, is a powerful determinant of prosocial motivation.

A second key concept is *trust*. We have seen that trust tends to be a necessary ingredient of stable patterns of cooperative interaction, which holds not only for the Trust situation, described in Entry #5, but also for the Iterated Prisoner's Dilemma. The concept of trust also emphasizes the importance attached to prior interactions, which is a key to understanding future interactions. Several programs of research in the context of close relationships, relationships among colleagues and friends, as well as relations between groups, underline the importance of trust (Holmes & Rempel, 1989; Insko & Schopler, 1998; Kramer & Messick, 1998). Insufficient levels of trust by one or both partners can be quite detrimental to cooperative interaction. Research on adult attachment styles, for example, reveals that relative to trusting, securely attached individuals, those who are not securely attached are less likely to develop stable patterns of mutual cooperation (Gaines, et al., 1997; cf. Hazan & Shaver, 1987).

12.5 Matrix Representations

Table E12.1. The matrix in Table E12.1 represents the situation that exists for each interaction in an Iterated (repeated) Prisoner's Dilemma. On each occasion, each person gains better outcomes from the noncooperative choice (a2 and b2, respectively) than from the cooperative choice, irrespective of the other's choice. Yet if both make these noncooperative choices, they both receive outcomes that are inferior to those obtained when both make a cooperative choice (a1 and b1, respectively). If they make different choices, the person selecting the cooperative option obtains their worst outcome and the person selecting the competitive option gains their best outcome. This possibility undoubtedly appeals to a person who is trying to gain better outcomes than the partner.

TABLE E12.1. *Matrix Representation of an Iterated Prisoner's Dilemma*

	A	
	a1	a2
b1	+5 / +5	+10 / −10
b2	−10 / +10	−5 / −5

(B)

Table E12.2. The matrix in Table E12.2, adapted from Miller and Holmes (1975), represents the same situation as above but with an added option (a3 and b3, respectively) that permits each person to "withdraw" from the dilemma. (For reasons of experimental control, the withdrawal option is associated with different outcomes varying from +1 through +5.) Selecting that option permits a person to avoid interacting within the framework of the dilemma (thereby losing out on the benefits of mutual cooperation but also avoiding possible exploitation of cooperative overtures by an uncooperative partner) and to do so without harming a partner who may have cooperative goals.

TABLE E12.2. *Matrix Representation of an Iterated Prisoner's Dilemma with Withdrawal Option*

		A		
		a1	a2	a3
	b1	+5 / +5	+10 / −10	+2 / +5
B	b2	−10 / +10	−5 / −5	+2 / +2
	b3	+5 / +2	+2 / +2	+1 / +1

Entry #13

Investment

Building for the Future

13.1 Examples

Investment situations are extended situations in which each person, at each of a series of preliminary steps, must make an "investment" in order to move toward a desirable goal. For example, in seeking to establish a sucessful business, the owners proceed through a series of preliminary steps at which they invest time and effort in order to reach their goal. They work evenings and weekends, forgo short-term financial profits, and reinvest early earnings in development activities, including employee training and construction projects. In the situations considered here, those of mutual investment, both owners must engage in these activities. If either loses heart and backs out of the venture, their investments are lost and the company fails. If both persist and jointly work their way through the early steps, making suitable choices and effective investments of time, effort, and resources, they may achieve a desirable goal – a company that will earn substantial profits.

In like manner, the partners in an emerging romantic relationship must work together, making their way through preliminary steps at which they invest a variety of resources in their involvement. They disclose private thoughts and feelings to each other, purchase joint possessions, develop a shared friendship network, spend time becoming acquainted with one another's family members, and exert effort to resolve conflicts involving incompatible preferences. If both partners successfully surmount the preliminary hurdles of their involvement, they may achieve a desirable goal – a

Caryl Rusbult had primary responsibility for preparation of this entry.

committed, trusting relationship in which each partner gratifies the other's needs. Again, the effort must be mutual, and the relationship aborts if either partner fails to persist toward the goal.

13.2 Conceptual Description

The Investment situation is an extended one, consisting of a preliminary series of discrete steps that must be taken if a desirable goal is to be reached. This entry concerns the case of mutual investment in which both people must make a contribution at each step. In its simplest form, the Investment situation is described by a transition list, as illustrated in Table E13.1 below (at the end of this entry). In that list, persons A and B must move through the steps defined by junctures J, K, L, and M to reach the goal at juncture N. At each preliminary step, persons A and B are confronted with a choice between (a) a behavior that leads to the next interaction en route to the desired goal (a1 and b1), versus (b) failing to enact that behavior (a2 or b2), thereby exiting the route to the goal and moving outside the investment situation.

The requirement that the investment be mutual can be seen by the fact that at each step, further movement toward the goal requires that both people select the investment option, the a1b1 pair. The investment at each step is indicated by the negative outcome that each person experiences (the cost incurred) in selecting that option. If either or both people fail to select the investment option at any step, they do not make the next necessary move toward the goal and, instead, leave the Investment situation altogether. In that event, any prior costs they have incurred to that point go for naught.

As illustrated in Table E13.1 below (at the end of this entry), if the interactants make the investments necessary to progress from juncture J to the goal at juncture N, they arrive at a desirable situation. Their interdependence there provides both people with high positive outcomes and they have no conflict of interest among the possible pairs of outcomes. The pair can remain in that situation for an unspecified period of time, as indicated by the recursive transition from N back to itself. They have the opportunity there to recoup the costs they have incurred to reach the goal and to gain positive outcomes in excess of their investment costs.

13.3 Variants and Combinations

13.3.1 *Structure*
There are many variants of the Investment situation. Such situations differ in the number of steps that are necessary to arrive at a goal and in the size

of the required investment outlay relative to the ultimate payoffs. The goal of an investment sequence may be a discrete outcome, or "goal payoff," wherein the interactants simply collect their shares of the dividends and then exit the Investment situation (see the transition list in Table E13.2 at the end of this entry). Alternatively, the goal may be a "goal situation" in which the interactants can remain for an extended period of time (e.g., achieving a succesful ongoing business or long-term relationship; see Table E13.1).

The option that constitutes mutual investment may involve the same versus different behaviors on the part of the interactants, and movement through preliminary steps may rest on either conjunctive or disjunctive control (i.e., movement may transpire only if *both* interactants enact particular behaviors, or may transpire if *either* of the two enacts a particular behavior; see Entries #9 and #10, Conjunctive Problems and Disjunctive Problems, respectively). In addition, it may be necessary for one person to make greater investments than the other, or it may be possible for one person to continue providing the necessary investments should the partner choose to exit the enterprise (see Entry #11, Asymmetric Dependence).

13.3.2 Response Conditions

Investment situations also vary in the response conditions that are present during preliminary steps. For example, when the interactants must respond simultaneously, neither may feel entirely confident that the other will carry through with his or her investment behavior. Under such circumstances, the interactants are likely to rely on communication (promises, threats) to insure continued mutual investment. If the interactants can respond ad lib, the person to make the first investment must take a risk (e.g., disclosing intimately without certainty that the other will reciprocate); the second person can then make his or her investment without undue feelings of vulnerability (and, perhaps, with the perception that reciprocal investment is "owed"). The possibility of revocable investment introduces additional complications, making it possible for people to "test the water" prior to fully committing to an investment sequence, or to "remove themselves" from an unpromising sequence (thereby losing earlier investments but revoking the investment from the present juncture).

13.3.3 Investments May Be Experienced as Costly or Rewarding

In Tables E13.1 and E13.2, we represent investments as costs. There are also cases in which the behaviors enacted in Investment situations may be experienced as rewarding in their own right (represented by positive values at preliminary steps; e.g., outcomes of +2 and +2 for the a1b1 combination). Whereas investments in ongoing relationships such as favors, financial investments, or the provision of emotional support may be experienced as direct costs, investments such as shared recreational activities or mutual disclosure may be experienced as direct rewards. For example, friends who invest time, effort, and material resources in building a log cabin together may find their mutual activities to be pleasurable in and of themselves. Whether a given behavior is experienced as costly or rewarding in its own right, it acts as an investment if it moves the interactants through preliminary steps en route to a desirable goal.

13.3.4 *Investment May Require Forgoing Alternatives*
There are also important instances in which pursuit of a goal requires forgoing alternative activities, in that the appearance of attractive alternatives (more promising ways to spend money, a more attractive or compatible partner for one of the romantic pair) can disrupt the persistent pattern of investment that is necessary to reach a rewarding goal. When preliminary steps present the interactants with tempting alternative situations, they must possess sufficient self-control to forgo the alternatives and persist in single-minded movement toward the goal. (In Entry #14, Delay of Gratification, we focus specifically on phenomena associated with sustaining a goal-directed line of activity in the face of attractive alternatives.)

13.4 **Interaction Process and Person Factors**

When and why do people persist in Investment situations? When and why are they likely to quit? In the following pages we consider some common reasons for persistence. We will see that some causes rest on the objective desirability of a goal, some causes rest on the ways in which investment activities change the consequences of discontinuing the process, and some causes rest on the psychological processes commonly activated by investment behavior.

13.4.1 *Persistence Objectively Warranted by a Goal*
The most obvious reason for initiating and persisting in Investment situations is that doing so "pays off," or is warranted by the objective distribution of costs and rewards (as illustrated in Table E13.1): If one can count on one's partner to behave in a trustworthy manner (to continue providing promised investments) and if one has the resources necessary to make the required investments, the situation offers rich dividends. For example, scientists frequently persist in collaborative research because they believe

that their work will produce important findings. People frequently invest in romantic relationships because they believe that the relationship will yield rich rewards.

13.4.2 Persistence Promoted by Mounting Exit Costs

As people proceed through preliminary steps toward their goal, it sometimes becomes increasingly costly or difficult for them to terminate the sequence (see Table E13.2, where the costs of exit increase from 0 to −6 with movement toward the goal). Sometimes increasing exit costs derive from sources external to the pair. For example, other people may ridicule the investors for undertaking a venture they didn't have the stamina to see to its end, costs may be incurred in disposing of accumulated joint possessions or in dismantling and moving out of shared facilities, or special liquidation costs may be incurred, as in the legal fees required for undoing contractual arrangements or the penalties that financial institutions impose for aborting arrangements with them.

In close relationships, the costs of quitting may increase over time because the investment process directly or indirectly affects the quality of the people who are potentially available as alternative relationship partners. For example, as alternative partners observe the mutual investment process proceed, attractive alternatives may make other arrangements and "take themselves out of the running" (Kelley, 1983). Also, the partners themselves may become less fit for alternative interactions, losing the capacity to enact behaviors that are valued in alternative relationships (e.g., they may "too thoroughly" adapt to their present relationships). As a consequence, as the quality of alternative partners declines, the negative outcomes associated with quitting increase.

The costs of terminating an investment sequence are particularly likely when investments are intrinsic to the investment project or are made in the service of "project building." For example, in the course of building "projects" such as an ongoing business enterprise or a continuing close relationship, partners may create shared understandings, may develop increasing trust in one another, or may develop positive relations with a broader social network (e.g., a favorable public reputation, a valued network of friends). Under such circumstances, exit entails forfeiting all that has been "built" to date and starting from scratch in a new project, such as a new business partnership or a new marriage. Therefore, as mutual investment proceeds, it may become increasingly difficult for the investors to terminate the sequence because the objective consequences of doing so become more negative and/or less positive.

13.4.3 Persistence Given Incomplete Information

Investment situations sometimes are "seductive" because when prospective investors initiate the process, they may not be fully aware of the structure of the situation. Interactants in Investment situations may or may not possess complete information about the number of preliminary steps preceding a goal or about the costs of investment acts and exit options at each step (see Entries #15 through #18, describing incomplete information situations). In a related vein, the payoffs attainable once the goal is reached may or may not remain stable over time. For example, the service or product offered by an organization may rest on an unpredictable market and may rise and fall over the course of preliminary steps, making the prospects and inducements for continued investment volatile and unreliable.

Moreover, assuming that the interactants make all necessary investments to arrive at their goal, the probability that the goal will yield the promised payoffs can vary from a sure thing to something less certain. When attaining the desired goal is less than a sure thing, Investment situations involve risk. For example, when people make telephone calls to obtain important information and are put on hold, they must decide whether to invest time waiting for the other party to return or to hang up and try again later. Even though they recognize that the goal may never be realized, people may persist in waiting situations because: (a) the goal is attractive, even if uncertain (if the other party returns soon, the individual will obtain the desired information more quickly than if he or she hangs up and tries again later); (b) it is reasonable to assume that the longer one waits, the closer one is to the goal (the return of the other party); and (c) the psychological costs of terminating the sequence increase over time (it is more difficult to abandon three minutes invested in waiting than it is to abandon one minute invested in waiting).

The seductive quality of Investment situations with temporally uncertain goals is empirically illustrated by research regarding waiting situations (e.g., Brockner, Bazerman, & Rubin, 1984; Rubin & Brockner, 1975; Staw, 1976, 1981). In the prototypical waiting situation experiment, individuals are given an initial monetary stake that declines over time (i.e., they lose a fixed portion of the stake with each passing minute). To win a monetary jackpot (the desired goal), they must solve a specified number of crossword puzzle problems within a fixed period of time. The problems are difficult and require the use of a resource, a crossword puzzle dictionary. The resource is scarce – individuals must take turns using the dictionary and must wait in line to do so.

In such situations, people frequently continue to wait for the desired resource beyond the point at which they have lost their initial stake. The closer they believe the desired goal is (e.g., the higher their position in queue for use of the resource), the more likely they are to continue waiting (Rubin & Brockner, 1975). We can place a more or less rational interpretation on such behavior, in that the closer one is to the front of the line, the more likely it is that one will gain the jackpot. Yet we can easily imagine other motives that may be especially strong when the goal seems close at hand, such as self-recrimination for giving up, social judgment that one is a "quitter," and simple competitiveness ("The costs be damned, I won't let the others win!").

13.4.4 Persistence When Partners' Goal-Based Outcomes Conflict

The notion that competitiveness may encourage undue persistence calls our attention to those situations in which only one of the investors can fully enjoy the goal, once it is attained. (This contrasts with our paradigmatic situation in which both persons fully enjoy the benefits of the goal.) A priori, it seems unlikely that people would commence investment when the outcomes they pursue cannot be jointly enjoyed. It seems illogical to engage in joint investment toward a goal when only one party can enjoy the ultimate benefits. However, some Investment situations of this type exist. For example, businesses offering similar goods and services may compete with one another for a common market base, and multiple firms may prepare competing proposals for a desirable contract. This type of Investment situation is illustrated by research regarding "both-pay auctions."

In both-pay auctions (Teger, 1980; Tropper, 1972), two people are presented with a set of objects (e.g., a candy bar, a pen) and are asked to state the monetary value they place on each object. Each person is then given a fixed amount of money for bidding on the objects. If they choose to bid more than the amount of money they are initially allocated, they can do so by using their own money. They are not required to bid on any object, and they can keep any money they have remaining at the end of the auction. The auction rules are termed "both-pay" in that both people are required to pay the amount of their highest bids, even though only the highest bidder receives the object on which the two make bids. So only the winner will enjoy the goal, owning the object. Despite the fact that the rules of bidding are stated in advance of the auction, most people bid higher amounts than the value they initially placed on the objects. That is, bidders frequently continue to invest even up to values that exceed the value of the goal.

How does interaction proceed in this situation? Typically, person A makes a low initial bid for the object in the hope of acquiring it at a cost lower than its value (e.g., bidding 15 cents for a $1.00 object). Person B then makes a bid slightly higher than person A's bid, but lower than the value of the object (e.g., bidding 20 cents). Person A, realizing that he or she may lose the desired object, increases the value of the initial bid. The two continue to increase their bids until they reach levels approaching the value of the object (e.g., person B bids $1.00). At this point, person A realizes that he or she will be forced to pay the previous bid (95 cents) and will fail to attain the object, and therefore increases the bid to $1.05, in an effort, perhaps, to insure a smaller net loss (payment of $1.05 for the bid minus the $1.00 value of the object yields a net loss of 5 cents). In response, person B increases his or her bid so as to suffer a smaller net loss. The both-pay auction proceeds in this manner until one person "chickens out," discontinues investment (i.e., abandons bidding), and suffers the costs of terminating the sequence (i.e., pays the cost of the last bid) without attaining the goal.

Thus, once two people begin to invest in the both-pay auction, both typically continue to invest well beyond the point at which it would be rational to exit. The situation is one in which successive investments automatically raise the costs of exiting and place the two in competition about who will bear the greater exit cost. In such situations, people may not fully appreciate the cumulative consequences of a process that begins innocently, as a simple auction. Because the goal is attractive and the cost of initial investment is low, people commence investment via preliminary bids and only later realize the competitive situation at which they finally arrive. Thus, the situation has some properties of a "social trap," insofar as it is difficult to anticipate the ultimate negative consequences of pursuing ordinary positive goals. The difference is that the negative consequences are more disastrous (paying and not getting anything) for one of the people caught in the trap than for the other.

We described the denouement of the both-pay auction as occurring when one person "chickens out." This calls our attention to features that this situation shares with the Chicken situation (see Entry #7): It finally becomes clear that one person must win and the other must lose. This is the upshot of the scenario in Chicken, when one partner challenges the other to a contest of "courage." Thus, the both-pay auction may encourage "irrational" persistence because it finally arouses mutual competitiveness, with the result that the concrete outcomes (money, objects) lose their usual significance and become instead symbolic of the personal characteristics of the investors (their strengths and resources, and their willingness to use them). In short, the objective properties of the situation may be modified by psychological properties, in effect transforming a given situation into a different situation, no longer simply the site of investment but also (or instead) a setting for competition.

13.4.5 *Persistence as a Means of Justifying Prior Investments*

In the examples reviewed thus far we have seen a variety of reasons for persistence in an Investment situation. Some of these reasons include decisions that are well founded, in light of the situation's objective promise or the growing costs of exit. We would describe such decisions as "rational." But we have also seen that persistence may be motivated by other considerations that become relevant as a consequence of the transformation of motivation, such as competitiveness.

One of the most common reasons investors state for persistence is the necessity of recouping the costs of prior investments. In some sorts of investment activity, to quit is to surrender all that has been invested over the course of the investment process. To the extent that an enterprise represents project building there may be some objective basis for such a rationale, in that terminating the investment sequence entails forfeiting all that has been built to date and starting from scratch in a new project.

However, investment counselors will quickly point out that the recouping argument has serious limitations, noting that we should base decisions solely on the relative merits of the options at hand, disregarding prior decisions. This is not to suggest that we should focus solely on current outcomes. If a given stock holds realistic promise of long-term profits, then it makes sense to hold onto the stock and not panic and sell at the first sign of decline. At the same time, if we encounter an alternative course of action that promises greater short- and long-term yields than the current activity, we should drop the current activity and adopt the alternative. We should persist with stock in a particular company only if its market value cannot be put to better use; we should not persist simply by virtue of the fact that we purchased the stock at some time in the past. (Of course, investment counselors often have a vested interest in the selling and buying of their stocks, but we set that fact aside in our present argument.)

It is important to recognize that the argument of recouping one's prior investment has strong intuitive appeal. Such motives are often cast in terms of "sunk costs" and, more psychologically, as a matter of "justifying" prior investments. A sunk cost is a cost incurred toward the goal of attaining a desired outcome. For example, college roommates may make a nonrefundable cash deposit to reserve a cottage at the beach during spring break. Later, they may decide that they would prefer vacationing in the mountains. The roommates nevertheless may persist in their earlier plan to vacation at the beach because doing so psychologically justifies their sunk cost; going to the beach may seem more desirable than it would in the absence of the sunk cost. Although it is not strictly rational for interactants to construe sunk costs in this manner (investment advisors would urge that the options of going to the beach versus going to the mountains should be evaluated in their own right, without regard to the prior action), pursuing a goal that is linked to a sunk cost may be psychologically experienced as a course of action that justifies the prior investment.

The notion of justifying prior investments applies to both small and large investment sequences. For example, although the decision of U.S. military personnel to persist in the Vietnam War may have been based in part on considerations such as national security interests or long-standing political principles (democracy vs. communism), persistence may also have rested partially on the desire to justify prior military losses. Arguably, military advisors continued to invest equipment and the lives of American soldiers in this military action because they believed that if the United States were ultimately to attain the desired goal (winning the war), prior investments toward that goal would be justified (deaths and losses could be construed as investments warranted by circumstances).

The concept of "justifying a past action" means that it is shown to be just, right, or reasonable. This is a common phenomenon in social life. We initiate projects with the intention of completing them and we take responsibility for doing so. Upon their completion, we gain pride in the accomplishment and social kudos for success. On the other hand, failure to complete projects yields self-recrimination and social criticism. When, in extended situations such as the Investment situation, there are interruptions or delays in the process, self-justification becomes aroused as a way to avoid the consequences of possible failure. The recognition that one's decisions in the investment process make one accountable for its failure reveals that quitting the enterprise will make one vulnerable to negative outcomes. Therefore, we refuse to believe that those decisions were mistaken and try to correct the situation through increased persistence.

The justificatory mechanism comes into play to make it difficult to give up the venture. One tries harder, often throws good money after bad, and develops various reasons for persistence ("I'll show them. I'll prove that my original plan was a good one. I'll make it work").

The irony is that the transformed motives that promote our undertaking extensive ventures in the first place (pride, fame) can later turn on us and become the basis for unrealistic continuance of flawed pursuits sustained by self-deceiving justifications. The further irony is that the farther along the investment path we travel, the more there is to justify and, often, the more extreme are the self-deceptions. And, of course, in case of eventual failure, the self-justification often results in deflecting blame away from the self by blaming one's partner, failures of other parties the pair had counted on, or unforeseeable circumstances.

It can be seen that self-justification, like competitiveness in waiting situations and both-pay auctions, affects the dynamics of persistence in ways that are not directly relevant to the outcome structure of the Investment situation. As such, the transformation process produces reasons for persistence that are not described in the basic structure of the situation. Such psychological processes create continued investment for reasons largely unrelated to the direct costs of investment and quitting relative to the direct benefits of the goal. In short, self-justificatory and competitive motives transform the situation from its "objective" structure – the form in which the experimental game is given to participants or in which the economic marketplace defines the investment costs and benefits (its given character) – to a form reflecting how that structure is used to express self-justificatory and competitive motives (its effective, transformed character).

Indeed, it has been argued that persistent investment may sometimes rest wholly on the kinds of psychological processes just described, on processes that are largely unrelated to the objective situation (cf. Becker, 1960; Brickman, Dunkel-Schetter, & Abbey, 1987; Kiesler, 1971). The psychological bases for persistence may include: (a) generalized cultural expectations, or normative injunctions that once one commences investment in a line of activity, it is wrong to desist; and (b) desire to behave in a consistent manner, or the feeling that once one commences investment, it is inconsistent (and therefore distressing) to desist (e.g., Aronson & Mills, 1959). When interactants jointly commence investment, they may also persist due to: (c) interpersonal commitment, or belief that once one commences investment with a partner, to desist would constitute betrayal of the partner. This factor is especially important in close relationships, our next topic.

13.4.6 *Persistence Promoted by Trust and Commitment*

Research regarding investment in close relationships has emphasized two phenomena – trust and commitment. (Of course, trust and commitment are important in all Investment situations, but we examine these phenomena primarily in their relevance to the formation and maintenance of romantic pairs.) When interactants initiate an investment sequence, they must possess some degree of confidence that the desired goal can be attained contingent upon successfully working through the preliminary steps. In mutual Investment situations, once the interactants initiate an investment sequence, they make themselves vulnerable to possible desertion by their partners and, thereby, to the risk of losing their investments (i.e., to losing the fruits of the project to date, or to losing "everything that one has put into a relationship").

Trust facilitates the ability of interactants to confidently pursue a remote goal, single-mindedly suffering direct costs and forgoing tempting alternatives (Holmes, 1981; Holmes & Rempel, 1989). Trust involves uncertainty reduction, or increasing confidence that the partner can be relied upon to uphold prior promises and to be responsive to one's own well-being. Trust is enhanced to the extent that each partner observes the other's willingness to forgo direct self-interest at junctures where those interests are pitted against the interests of the partner or of the relationship (Wieselquist, Rusbult, Foster, & Agnew, 1999). Such situations are likely to be common in investment sequences.

Commitment may also facilitate movement through Investment situations (cf. M. Johnson, 1991; Levinger, 1979; Rusbult, 1983). Commitment reflects intent to persist, psychological attachment to the partner (i.e., concern with his or her well-being), and long-term orientation (i.e., the inclination to consider future implications of present actions). Commitment increases to the extent that people are more dependent on their relationships, or to the extent that (a) satisfaction level is high (past and current experiences in preliminary steps are gratifying), (b) quality of alternatives is poor (past and current alternative situations are unattractive), and (c) past and current investments are sizable (Bui, Peplau, & Hill, 1996; Farrell & Rusbult, 1981; Rusbult, 1983; Simpson, 1987). To the extent that partners are more strongly committed to one another (and/or to pursuit of their shared goal), they are more likely to exert effort and endure cost in order to protect one another's interests and single-mindedly persist in movement toward an investment goal. Thus, via the intervening construct of commitment, prior investment (along with high satisfaction and poor alternatives) begets further investment.

In ongoing relationships, strong commitment has been shown to promote a variety of maintenance mechanisms that facilitate movement toward a remote yet desirable goal (cf. Rusbult & Buunk, 1993). First, commitment enhances the interactants' willingness to control their impulses and depart from their direct self-interest in circumstances of conflict. For example, committed individuals are willing to accommodate rather than retaliate when their partners behave poorly (Rusbult, Verette, Whitney, Slovik, & Lipkus, 1991); they are willing to sacrifice their direct self-interest for the good of the partner and/or in pursuit of the goal (Van Lange et al., 1997); and they are willing to forgive the partner's acts of betrayal (Finkel, Rusbult, Kumashiro, & Hannon, in press). Second, commitment promotes patterns of thinking that support the decision to persist toward a goal: For example, committed individuals exhibit cognitive interdependence, thinking of themselves in terms of "we, us, and our" rather than "I, me, and mine" (Agnew, Van Lange, Rusbult, & Langston, 1998); they are inclined toward positive illusion, placing exceptionally positive evaluation on and being excessively optimistic about interaction events (Murray & Holmes, 1996; Rusbult, Van Lange, Wildschut, Yovetich, & Verette, 2000); and they avoid or derogate tempting alternatives (Miller, 1997; Johnson & Rusbult, 1989).

Trust and commitment influence one another in a reliable feedback loop (Wieselquist et al., 1999). Above, we noted the many ways in which commitment motivates individuals to enact "pro-relationship" behaviors, forgoing their direct self-interest at junctures where those interests are pitted against the interests of the partner or relationship (e.g., accommodation, sacrifice, forgiveness). We also noted that trust is enhanced to the extent that each partner observes the other's willingness to enact such behaviors. Thus, trust is an implicit gauge of the strength of a partner's commitment. In turn, strengthened trust makes people increasingly willing to make themselves vulnerable by becoming more dependent on their partners – they not only become increasingly satisfied, but also become increasingly willing to forgo tempting alternatives and persist in investment activities. Increasing dependence in turn strengthens commitment, which in turn motivates further pro-relationship acts, which in turn strengthens trust, and so on in a congenial, temporally extended, mutual feedback sequence. (Or, alternatively, when things begin to "go south," such processes produce a destructive mutual feedback sequence.) Thus, so long as mutual investment activities proceed smoothly, the very act of mutual investment can strengthen commitment and trust, thereby encouraging continued investment toward a goal.

13.4.7 *Assessment and Locomotion in Investment Situations*

Dispositional differences in assessment and locomotion tendencies may be relevant to understanding behavior in Investment situations. "Assessment" involves the critical evaluation of goals, means, and performance (Kruglanski et al., 2000). If interactants are to effectively make their way through preliminary steps in Investment situations, they must possess sufficient cognitive sophistication to foresee a possible future goal and recognize the specific steps required to achieve that goal. People with strong assessment tendencies may more carefully and accurately scrutinize the efficacy of investment behavior as a route to attaining desirable long-term goals. As a consequence, they may exhibit greater caution about entering into Investment situations, and may be less prone to suffer the sorts of transformation processes that yield "irrational" investment behavior (e.g., competitiveness, desire to save face).

"Locomotion" involves the drives relevant to achieving movement from state to state, including effort expenditure and the application of other resources toward goal attainment (Kruglanski et al., 2000). Investment situations require some degree of self-control, in that interactants sometimes are required to endure short-term costs or forgo desirable alternatives in pursuit of long-term goals. People with strong locomotion tendencies may exhibit greater willpower, exhibiting more single-minded persistence toward desired goals. As a consequence, they may not only pursue investment goals irrespective of short-term costs and tempting alternatives, but may also fall prey to the sorts of transformation processes that result in "irrational" investment (e.g., desire to save face, vulnerability to the trap of sunk costs).

13.4.8 *Promotion and Prevention in Investment Situations*

Individual differences in promotion and prevention focus may also be relevant to understanding behavior in Investment situations. Individuals with strong "promotion focus" are concerned with the pursuit of long-term ideals, goals, and aspirations (Higgins, 1997). Strong promotion focus is argued to emerge out of childrearing practices that emphasize overcoming difficulties and pursuing positive outcomes (Higgins & Silberman, 1998). Therefore, people who are very promotion-oriented may pursue goals in a more single-minded manner, enduring costs and forgoing attractive alternatives en route to achieving long-term investment goals.

Individuals with strong "prevention focus" are concerned with living up to obligations and responsibilities (Higgins, 1997). Strong prevention focus is argued to emerge out of childrearing practices that emphasize security, compliance with societal expectations, and avoiding negative outcomes such as self-recrimination and social criticism (Higgins & Silberman, 1998). Therefore, at least in part, people who are very prevention oriented may be more likely to persist in investment sequences as a means of saving face, demonstrating their trustworthiness, and justifying prior investment activities.

13.4.9 *Self-Control in Investment Situations*
Because Investment situations frequently require willpower, self-control presumably is relevant to understanding persistence in Investment situations. Self-control is argued to rest on both personal dispositions and situational factors. Dispositional self-control describes the relatively stable ability and inclination to exert control over one's immediate impulses. People with high self-control focus on the many broader considerations that may be relevant to action (e.g., long-term goals, the well-being of important interaction partners), inhibiting inclinations to impulsively maximize short-term outcomes. For example, in ongoing close relationships, people with greater dispositional self-control have been shown to more reliably inhibit impulses toward immediately gratifying yet ultimately destructive behaviors such as negative reciprocity and physical violence (Finkel & Campbell, 2001; Finkel & Foshee, 2001).

Self-control also rests on situational factors, in that self-control appears to be a limited resource that is depleted by situational demands across diverse domains. Research regarding performance across differing tasks, each of which draws on a common self-control "pool," reveals that as a consequence of exerting self-control in one domain, self-regulatory resources relevant to other domains become depleted. For example, in comparison to individuals in a no-depletion control condition, those whose self-regulatory resources are temporarily depleted (e.g., by being asked to eat radishes instead of chocolates, perform a task that requires strict attention, or suppress natural emotional responses) exhibit reduced ability to perform tasks requiring further self-control (Baumeister, Bratslavsky, Muraven, & Tice, 1998).

13.4.10 *Security and Insecurity in Investment Situations*
Given that Investment situations make people vulnerable to the possibility of desertion by their interaction partners (and, thereby, to the loss of prior investments), trust is essential to successful movement through investment

sequences. Earlier, we characterized trust as a relationship-specific phenomenon that emerges as a consequence of observing the partner "behave well" in situations involving conflicting interests (i.e., situations pitting the partner's direct self-interest against one's own interests). People may develop rather stable, long-standing inclinations to trust (vs. not trust) others as a consequence of their early childhood experiences. Secure attachment results from childrearing experiences in which adult caregivers reliably attend to the infant's needs (Hazan & Shaver, 1994). Later in life, securely attached individuals tend to be more trusting, or more confident that others can be "counted on" to follow through on commitments and take their interests into consideration. Accordingly, they should be more willing to enter into Investment situations without fear of desertion or exploitation by interaction partners.

In contrast, insecure attachment results from childrearing experiences in which adult caregivers are either unreliable (anxious-ambivalent attachment) or neglectful (avoidant attachment; Hazan & Shaver, 1994). Later in life, long-term Investment situations are likely to be problematic for insecurely attached individuals. Anxious-ambivalent individuals may fervently desire situations involving mutual investment toward a desirable goal, yet are likely to fear the vulnerabilities that such situations entail. Thus, they may be prone toward volatile behavior in Investment situations, overreacting to signs of uncertainty or unreliability on the part of their interaction partners. Avoidant individuals may find the vulnerabilities underlying Investment situations so repellant that they become disinclined to enter into such situations, despite possibilities for exceptionally desirable long-term investment outcomes.

13.4.11 *Functional Purpose of Persistence in Investment Situations*
We have described some simple instances of mutual investment in which the tendency toward continued investment reflects objective features of the given situation, such as the attractiveness of the goal relative to the size of the required investment outlay. In a related vein, we have described investment behavior in project-building endeavors, where continued investment may yield mounting costs of terminating a sequence. When exit entails forfeiting all that has been accomplished to date and working through comparable steps in a new project, it may become increasingly difficult for investors to exit a sequence. In contrast, we have described cases where the transformation of motivation may cause people to engage in persistent investment for relatively more "psychological reasons," in the expression of competitive motives, out of desire to appear consistent, or as a means of justifying prior actions. Thus, reasons for persistent investment sometimes

are to be located in objective features of Investment situations, and sometimes are to be located in a transformed version of the situation reflecting the psychological processes that frequently are activated in such situations.

13.5 Transition List Representations

Table E13.1: Investments by Both Persons Move the Pair toward the Goal of a Mutually Desirable Payoff Situation. If persons A and B are to arrive at a very attractive payoff situation (juncture N), both must behave in such manner as to move through successive preliminary junctures (junctures J, K, L, and M). At each preliminary juncture, each person can make an investment of two units (by enacting a1 and b1, respectively) or can exit the investment situation (a2 and b2). At any

TABLE E13.1. *Investments by Both Persons Move the Pair toward the Goal of a Mutually Desirable Payoff Situation*

Junctures	Options	Possible Selections	Outcomes for A and B		Transition to Next Juncture
J	(a1, a2)	a1b1	−2	−2	K
	(b1, b2)	a1b2	−2	0	X
		a2b1	0	−2	X
		a2b2	0	0	X
K	(a1, a2)	a1b1	−2	−2	L
	(b1, b2)	a1b2	−2	0	X
		a2b1	0	−2	X
		a2b2	0	0	X
L	(a1, a2)	a1b1	−2	−2	M
	(b1, b2)	a1b2	−2	0	X
		a2b1	0	−2	X
		a2b2	0	0	X
M	(a1, a2)	a1b1	−2	−2	N
	(b1, b2)	a1b2	−2	0	X
		a2b1	0	−2	X
		a2b2	0	0	X
N	(a3, a4)	a3b3	+16	+16	N
	(b3, b4)	a3b4	+16	+16	N
		a4b3	+16	+16	N
		a4b4	+16	+16	N

juncture along the way, if either fails to make the necessary payment, they exit the situation, lose payments made up to that point, and lose the possibility of enjoying any payoffs from their investments (lose the opportunity to arrive at juncture N). Only if both make their contributions at each juncture do they move toward the payoff situation offering mutually desirable outcomes (where their investments "mature"). Once they arrive at the final "goal situation," the two can remain there indefinitely (enacting a3 or a4, and b3 or b4, respectively).

Table E13.2: Investments by Both Persons, with Increasing Exit Costs, Move the Pair toward the Goal of Moderately Desirable Mutual Payoffs. If persons A and B are to attain a moderately desirable payoff (juncture N), both must behave in such a manner as to move through successive preliminary junctures (junctures J, K, L, and M). As in the previous example, if the persons are to arrive at the payoff, both must make their contributions

TABLE E13.2. *Investments by Both Persons, with Increasing Exit Costs, Move the Pair toward the Goal of Moderately Desirable Mutual Payoffs*

Junctures	Options	Possible Selections	Outcomes for A and B		Transition to Next Juncture
J	(a1,a2)	a1b1	−2	−2	K
	(b1,b2)	a1b2	−2	0	X
		a2b1	0	−2	X
		a2b2	0	0	X
K	(a1,a2)	a1b1	−2	−2	L
	(b1,b2)	a1b2	−2	−2	X
		a2b1	−2	−2	X
		a2b2	−2	−2	X
L	(a1,a2)	a1b1	−2	−2	M
	(b1,b2)	a1b2	−2	−4	X
		a2b1	−4	−2	X
		a2b2	−4	−4	X
M	(a1,a2)	a1b1	−2	−2	N
	(b1,b2)	a1b2	−2	−6	X
		a2b1	−6	−2	X
		a2b2	−6	−6	X
N	(a3,b3)	a3b3	+8	+8	X

at each juncture; at any juncture, if either decides to exit the situation, both lose payments made up to that point and lose the possibility of a payoff. In this example, the costs of exit increase across junctures, representing increasing costs of terminating the sequence (making it increasingly unlikely that either will exit). If both people continue to the final "goal payoff," they collect their shares of the dividends (their a_3 and b_3 option) and exit the situation.

Entry #14

Delay of Gratification:

Resisting Temptation

14.1 Examples

Mary's father offers her a trip to Disneyland if she earns good grades during the coming year. To earn the prize, Mary must exercise self-control, forgoing activities that she otherwise would love and engaging in activities that are not necessarily fun but will help her do well in school. She may need to cut back on soccer practice in order to spend more time on homework, and may find it necessary to spend some afternoons studying rather than playing with friends. This self-control problem will be less difficult if she places considerably greater value on the trip to Disneyland than on the alternative activities that she must forgo, and to the degree that she can count on her father to deliver on his promise if she indeed earns good grades.

John's cholesterol level is dangerously high. His wife promises to buy him a Jaguar if he radically changes his eating habits and lowers his cholesterol level. To obtain the Jaguar (and avoid the risk of serious health problems), John must carefully plan and prepare meals, forgo the convenience of fast food, and inhibit the impulse to eat many of his favorite foods. He is more likely to be successful if he develops strong intentions to engage in health-related behaviors and identifies strategies to forgo temptation. He may find it helpful to distract himself, bringing to mind "cool" thoughts about high cholesterol foods ("french fries look like a stack of lumber") and inhibiting "hot" thoughts ("french fries are crispy, salty, and delicious").

Caryl Rusbult had primary responsibility for preparation of this entry.

14.2 Conceptual Description

The Delay of Gratification situation is an extended one, consisting of a series of preliminary steps that must be completed if a desirable goal is to be reached. This entry concerns interpersonal delay of gratification, or situations in which person A (Mary's father) presents person B (Mary) with a valued outcome (a trip to Disneyland), the attainment of which requires that B exerts self-control in the face of temptation (to earn good grades, Mary must forgo fun activities). Thus, the essence of this situation is an individual's goal-directed restraint in the face of temptation, combined with the need to trust the interaction partner to "deliver on the promise" when the goal is attained. The simplest form of delay of gratification can be described by a transition list, as displayed in Table E14.1 below (at the end of this entry).

A pure Delay of Gratification situation has three features. First, at each preliminary step, person B must choose between (a) an immediately available but moderately valued outcome (playing with friends now), versus (b) an undesirable outcome (studying now) that must be endured to continue moving toward a highly valued but remote goal (Disneyland later; at junctures J, K, and L, person B must choose b1 [+1] rather than b2 [0] in order to move toward juncture M). Second, control over movement toward the goal rests in the hands of person B, indicated by the fact that at each preliminary step, movement toward the goal requires that person B choose the less attractive b2 option (Mary exercises Actor Control over movement through junctures). Failure to exhibit self-control aborts the route to the goal (yields exit [X], which takes the pair to an unspecified location outside this situation). Third, control of the remote goal rests in the hands of person A (at juncture M, Mary's father exercises Partner Control over Mary's trip to Disneyland); when persons A and B arrive at the goal, person A has complete Partner Control over delivering the highly valued outcome, indicated by the fact that at juncture M, person A must choose a1 if person B is to enjoy the valued outcome (+10 vs. 0). In Table E14.1 below the valued outcome is a one-time event. Following person A's choice and person B's consumption of the valued outcome, the situation is at an end.

Some instances of delay of gratification are not strictly "interpersonal," in that control over delivery of the remote outcome rests in the hands of an external, nonhuman agent. For example, when the remote goal is to earn a high score on the GRE and no one offers the individual a "carrot" for excellent performance, the individual exercises self-control in pursuit of a task-administered outcome. Such instances can be described in terms of "task interdependence" rather than "interpersonal interdependence" (Thibaut & Kelley, 1959). Most principles outlined below apply to both types of delay situation, in that both types require willpower and sacrifice, the exercise of which is facilitated by variables such as trust in the person/mechanism who is to deliver the remote outcome, "cool" mental transformations of the remote outcome, strong commitment to the remote goal, and the like.

14.3 Variants and Combinations

Delay of Gratification situations come in many forms, varying in the number of steps preceding the desired goal, whether self-control involves forgoing benefit or enduring cost, in the magnitude of outcomes at preliminary steps and at the remote goal, and in the probability that upon arriving at the goal the anticipated outcomes will be forthcoming. Also, Delay situations may involve either corresponding or conflicting interests for the involved parties, and correspondence of interests may differ for preliminary steps and remote goal. Moreover, such situations may include two partners who exercise mutual self-control toward a goal to be delivered by a third party (the partners may mutually function as "B," with the third party functioning as "A"). The following paragraphs review several of these and other common variants.

14.3.1 Variations in Number and Complexity of
Preliminary Junctures

Delay of Gratification situations differ in the number and complexity of the preliminary steps during which the individual must exercise self-control in order to attain a remote goal. For example, safe sex arguably involves relatively simple preliminary steps: Partners must obtain a condom in advance of sexual intercourse and must delay intercourse briefly in order to make use of the condom. (The fact that large numbers of people do not engage in safe sex testifies to the variety of psychological factors that may influence self-regulatory behavior beyond "objective" features of the situation.) In contrast, earning a Ph.D. requires that an individual actively execute rather complex goal-directed pursuits over an extended period of time and in the face of numerous obstacles and temptations, engaging in a variety of trade-offs and choices in the pursuit of quite remote benefits.

14.3.2 *Variations in the Magnitude of Benefits and Costs at Preliminary Junctures Relative to the Remote Outcome*

Delay situations also differ in whether the self-regulation problem during preliminary steps entails forgoing a desirable behavior or engaging in an undesirable behavior. Such situations also differ in the magnitude of the benefit that people must forgo (or the cost they must endure) at each step in order to continue moving toward the goal. More to the point, Delay situations differ in the magnitude of the remote outcome in relation to the temptations available during preliminary steps. In general, the more attractive the remote goal is in relation to the immediately available outcomes that must be resisted, the greater the probability of self-control.

14.3.3 *Variations in Certainty of Outcomes upon Arrival at the Goal*

Delay situations also differ in the extent to which receipt of the remote outcome is a "sure thing." Sometimes delivery of the remote outcome is guaranteed. For example, when an employer offers his employees a bonus for every new client they bring to the firm, delivery of the remote outcome may be guaranteed by a legal contract or by a financial arrangement whereby bonus funds are automatically deposited in deserving employees' accounts. But frequently, people do not know with absolute certainty that the remote outcome will be delivered once the goal is reached. Under such circumstances they may wish to increase the probability that their self-regulatory activities are not for naught. For example, a wife may offer her husband dinner at the best restaurant in town if he quits smoking for a month. To maximize the odds that his wife does not conveniently "forget" her promise, he may insist that they make a reservation at the restaurant one month in advance. To insure that she does not renege on the deal, he may further insist that she place funds for the dinner in a bank account to which neither person has access until the end of the month.

14.3.4 *Variations in Knowledge of Each Person's Choices and Outcomes*

Partners may or may not possess complete knowledge of one another's choices and outcomes (see Entries #15 through #18, examples of incomplete information situations). Although person A presumably knows whether and when person B reaches the goal (it must be possible to monitor arrival at the remote juncture), person A may possess unreliable information regarding B's actions at preliminary steps. For example, it may be possible for B to "cheat," falsely claiming to have engaged in required self-regulatory behaviors. Also, person B may only partially achieve the remote goal (Mary's grades may only improve slightly), in which case person A must decide whether no-reward or partial-reward is in order (a trip to Tom and Jerry's rather than Disneyland?).

Moreover, person B may or may not possess full knowledge of person A's options and outcomes. In Table E14.1, B is aware that A has no vested interest in the situation: In preliminary situations as well as at the remote goal, person A's outcomes for all possible joint choices are known to be 0. A situation of incomplete knowledge would be indicated by substituting ?s for 0s in A's designated outcomes, indicating that person B has incomplete information about where person A's interests lie. For example, in negotiation situations, each person has rather complete knowledge of his or her own outcomes for all possible forms of agreement, but frequently has little knowledge of outcomes for the party with whom he or she is negotiating (see Entry #15). In like manner, children typically possess full knowledge of their own outcomes for the options of studying versus playing, but frequently possess little knowledge of the effects of their choices on parents.

14.3.5 Variations in Person A's Vested Interests

In Table E14.1 person A has no vested interest in person B's choices. The transition list in Table E14.2 (at the end of this entry) illustrates a situation which in many respects parallels the transition list in Table E14.1: To achieve a valued remote outcome, person B must move through preliminary steps, and at each step B must choose the less valued b2 rather than the more valued b1. When the goal is reached, person A controls whether B receives the valued outcome. The difference is that in Table E14.2, the interests of A and B to some degree conflict. At each preliminary step, the mildly tempting b1 yields a small cost for A, whereas the mildly distasteful b2 yields a small reward for A (i.e., A would prefer that B exercise self-control). Once they arrive at the goal, A's choice of a1 would yield very good outcomes for B at a small cost to A, whereas A's choice of a2 would yield a small cost for B but very good outcomes for A (i.e., one but not both will benefit from B's earlier self-control). The uncertainty for person B arises from the question of whether person A will ultimately follow through on the promise or break his or her word. For example, a "con man" may lure a trusting target into making numerous financial sacrifices toward some promised remote outcome (owning the Brooklyn Bridge), only to betray the target when the goal is at hand.

14.4 Interaction Process and Person Factors

When and why do people persist in Delay of Gratification situations, exerting self-control and refusing to give in to temptation? Under what circumstances do people continue to pursue goals in the face of seemingly endless obstacles? Why do people exhibit the persistence required to stick with a difficult task over relatively long periods and to resist the temptations of easy shortcuts? Some bases for persistence can be explained as rational reactions to "objective" features of the situation, whereas other bases for persistence rest on relatively more "psychological" causes.

14.4.1 Relative Desirability of Immediate and Delayed Outcomes

We illustrate the effects of several objective situational features on rational choice behavior using research from a "Choice to Delay" paradigm, which requires children to choose between a small immediate reward and a larger reward to be gained by waiting (e.g., 25 cents today vs. 40 cents one month later). When the delayed reward and the immediately available reward are relatively close in attractiveness, fewer children exhibit delay of gratification than when the delayed reward is substantially more attractive than the small but immediately available reward (Mischel, Shoda, & Rodriguez, 1989).

But even when the delayed reward is substantially more attractive than the immediate reward, some children (and some adults) choose the smaller immediate reward. Why? From a strictly logical point of view, why is it that people do not consistently choose large rewards over small rewards irrespective of whether the reward is immediate or delayed? Research examining the expected value of immediate versus delayed rewards among both children and adults reveals that in part, the value of a delayed reward is reduced in comparison to an immediate reward because delay of reward involves some cost; arguably, waiting per se objectively is costly (Mischel, Grusec, & Masters, 1969).

14.4.2 Certainty regarding the Association between Behavior and Outcomes

It is possible that people sometimes choose a smaller immediate reward over a larger delayed reward because they do not perceive a reliable link between behavior during preliminary steps and later rewards. Indeed, when it is nearly certain that the delayed reward will be delivered – for example, when the experimenter tells participants that she will "definitely be back" at the designated time to deliver the reward – more people exhibit delay of gratification, choosing a large delayed reward over a small immediate reward (Mischel & Grusec, 1967). When there is a lower probability that the delayed reward will be delivered – for example, when the experimenter indicates that the probability is "about fifty-fifty" – fewer people exhibit delay of gratification.

Thus, to effectively regulate our behavior we must feel confident that there is a reliable link between earlier behavior and later outcomes. "Just world" beliefs embody such confidence, representing the conviction that the world "is a just and orderly place where people usually get what they deserve" (Lerner & Miller, 1978, p. 1030). The empirical literature reveals that people with a stronger belief in a just world exhibit more persistent effort toward self-improvement; such beliefs are predictive of tolerance for delayed reward, sustained focus on long-term goals, pursuit of such goals through sanctioned means, and persistent investment toward remote goals (Hafer, 2000; Hafer & Olson, 1993; Long & Lerner, 1974). Uncertainty that good actions will yield good outcomes leads people to succumb to temptation, pursue goals through socially disapproved means (cheating), or opt for easy shortcuts.

14.4.3 *Monitoring Movement toward Remote Goals*

Assuming that long-term goals are more attractive than immediate temptations, and assuming that we feel confident of the association between earlier behavior and later outcomes, it becomes important to consider how we monitor progress toward our goals. How do we "direct" ourselves in situations involving delay of gratification, moving through preliminary steps in pursuit of long-term goals? What sorts of cognitive activities accompany effective self-control?

Research regarding adult self-regulation stresses the importance of feedback processes in promoting effective movement toward goals. Adopting an expectancy-value perspective, Carver and Scheier (1982) propose that people engage in a continual process of establishing goals and intentions, adjusting patterns of behavior in such a manner as to match those values. People use informational feedback ("where am I in relation to my goal?") as a guide to evaluate their progress, experiencing positive affect in response to greater velocity and acceleration in progress toward goals (i.e., in response to discrepancy reduction; Carver, Lawrence, & Scheier, 1996; Carver & Scheier, 1990).

Models of the self also play a role in directing movement toward personal goals (Markus & Nurius, 1986). Some work distinguishes between two components of the self: (a) the ideal self, which is oriented toward goals and aspirations; and (b) the ought self, which is oriented toward duties and responsibilities (Higgins, 1987). Discrepancies between one's current state and remote but valued goals (as embodied in ideal and ought selves) yield characteristic emotional reactions. Discrepancies between the actual self and the ideal self yield dejection-related emotions, including sadness and disappointment; discrepancies between the actual self and the ought self yield agitation-related emotions, including fear and anxiety (Moretti & Higgins, 1990). The strength and character of emotional reactions direct and motivate later self-regulatory activity. For example, Mary may feel disappointed when she performs poorly on an exam (high actual-ideal discrepancy); the greater her disappointment, the more likely she is to study in preparation for future exams.

14.4.4 *Insufficient or Depleted Self-Regulatory Resources*
Irrespective of the attractiveness of our long-term goals, and irrespective of the effectiveness with which we monitor our progress toward those goals, we will not reach our goals unless we can control the impulse to seek immediate gratification. Resisting such temptation requires willpower, or self-control. Although it seems tautological to note that people sometimes choose small immediate rewards over large delayed rewards because they have insufficient self-control, levels of self-control *do* differ across individuals and across situations.

Dispositional self-control describes the relatively stable inclination to exert control over one's immediate impulses. People with high self-control focus on the many broader considerations that may be relevant to action (e.g., the desirability of remote goals, the relevance of one's actions for important partners), inhibiting the impulse to pursue immediate rewards. For example, in romantic relationships, people with greater self-control more reliably inhibit impulses toward immediately gratifying yet ultimately destructive behaviors such as negative reciprocity and physical violence (Finkel & Campbell, 2001; Finkel & Foshee, 2001). Thus, self-control is a key component of transformation of motivation, in that this construct embodies the inclination to forgo immediate self-interest, instead behaving in such a manner as to promote the broader interests that are relevant to behavior in a given situation.

The self-control construct becomes particularly interesting when we recognize that this variable is not only a personal disposition, but is also influenced by situational factors. That is, self-control appears to function as a limited resource that can be depleted by situational demands across diverse domains. Research regarding performance across a variety of tasks, each of which arguably draws on a common self-control "pool," reveals that as a consequence of exerting self-control in one domain, self-regulatory resources relevant to other domains are reduced. For example, compared to individuals in a no-depletion control condition, those whose self-regulatory resources are temporarily depleted (e.g., by being asked to eat radishes instead of chocolates, perform a task that requires strict attention, or suppress natural emotional responses) exhibit reduced ability to perform tasks requiring further self-control (Baumeister, Bratslavsky, Muraven, & Tice, 1998). Thus, Delay of Gratification situations become more challenging during periods when we pursue multiple remote goals, each of which requires the exercise of self-control.

14.4.5 Distraction from Tempting Immediate Outcomes

Even without self-control, we may be able to resist the temptation of immediately available rewards if we can somehow ignore them. Some work regarding the psychological processes underlying delay of gratification examines the effects of distraction using a "Duration of Delay" paradigm. Children are shown two rewards (a marshmallow and a pretzel) and are asked to specify which they prefer. The experimenter leaves the room, telling children that if they patiently wait until she returns, they will receive the more preferred reward. If children do not want to wait, they can ring a bell and the experimenter will return; however, in this case the child will receive the less preferred reward. Duration of delay prior to ringing the bell measures delay of gratification.

The most straightforward finding in this tradition is that children find it very difficult to resist temptation when the valued reward is "right under their noses." Children are better able to resist (i.e., they exhibit longer durations prior to ringing the bell) when rewards are hidden under the table than when they are physically visible (Mischel, Ebbesen, & Raskoff-Zeiss, 1972; Moore, Mischel, & Zeiss, 1976). The perceptual salience of temptation also influences the ability to delay gratification. Children in a "reward focus" condition were instructed to actively think about rewards while waiting for the experimenter to return ("think about the marshmallow and pretzel"). In comparison to children who received instructions designed to actively distract them from temptation, those in the reward focus condition exhibited greater tendencies to succumb to temptation (Mischel et al., 1972).

The manner in which children perceptually represent temptation also plays a role in shaping delay of gratification. For example, children in a "see-picture" condition were instructed to form a mental picture of the rewards while waiting ("make a color picture of the marshmallow and pretzel"); children in a "see-real" condition were instructed to form a vivid mental image of the rewards ("close your eyes, take the picture of the marshmallow and pretzel and make it real; pretend that you can see them"). In comparison to children in the see-real condition, those in the see-picture condition exhibited greater delay prior to succumbing to temptation. Thus, to the degree that people can form symbolic representations of temptation, delay of gratification is strengthened. Indeed, in facilitating self-control, the manner in which children perceptually represent temptation is more powerful than the actual presence versus absence of the tempting rewards (Moore et al., 1976).

In like manner, adults deal with temptation by increasing their distance from tempting alternatives, distracting themselves, and avoiding see-real confrontation with the source of their temptation. For example, romantic partners may find that they occasionally experience attraction to alternative partners. They may deal with this problem by distancing themselves from alternatives (behaving in a cool manner, not flirting), by calling to mind distracting thoughts when in the presence of temptation ("think about sexually transmitted diseases"), or by creating symbolic barriers between themselves and tempting alternatives (wearing a wedding ring; Kelley, 1983). Also, romantic partners appear to (consciously or unconsciously) avoid problematic see-real conditions by perceptually avoiding tempting alternatives – by literally spending fewer milliseconds attending to the object of their temptation (Miller, 1997). Finally, close partners exercise self-control by cognitively derogating tempting alternatives, evaluating alternatives more negatively to the degree that the alternative "objectively" is more attractive ("he's great looking, but I bet he's stupid"; Johnson & Rusbult, 1989; Simpson, Gangestad, & Lerma, 1990).

We more vigorously employ these mechanisms for resisting temptation to the extent that we are more fervently committed to a given goal. Specifically, the tendency to perceptually avoid and cognitively derogate tempting alternatives is more robust among people who are strongly committed to their relationships – that is, among people for whom the remote goal (sustaining the current relationship) is more valuable (Miller, 1997; Johnson & Rusbult, 1989). Thus, commitment to a goal encourages psychological transformations that promote effective self-regulation. Following such transformation, delay of gratification becomes a simpler situation – one in which persisting toward the goal is easy, involving the choice between a relatively unappealing (and/or not particularly salient) immediate reward versus an attractive delayed reward.

14.4.6 *Enhancing the Desirability of Remote Goals*

We may achieve increased self-control not only by reducing the attractiveness and salience of immediately available outcomes, but also by enhancing the desirability of remote goals. Research regarding positive illusion suggests that when we are strongly motivated to exercise self-restraint toward attaining a remote goal, we may perceptually enhance the attractiveness of the goal. Indeed, people's thoughts about themselves and their long-term goals are more positive than a strictly veridical view of the world can support, and such positively biased thoughts appear to serve a functional purpose, sustaining constructive, goal-directed behavior in the face of challenges (Taylor & Brown, 1988).

For most people, close relationships are an important long-term "project." In thinking about our relationships, we rather reliably (a) translate our partner's faults into virtues, developing beliefs about our partners that are more positive than our partners' beliefs about themselves, and (b) exhibit downward social comparison, developing beliefs about our relationships that are more positive (and less negative) than our beliefs about others' relationships (Murray, Holmes, & Griffin, 1996a; Rusbult, Van Lange, Wildschut, Yovetich, & Verette, 2000). In addition to exhibiting unrealistically positive evaluations of our relationships, we are also inclined toward exaggerated belief in control and unrealistic optimism regarding the future of our relationships (Murray & Holmes, 1997; Martz et al., 1998). These transformations, too, should promote single-minded pursuit of remote goals, helping us sustain conviction in the face of temptation and doubt (Rusbult et al., 2000; Taylor, 1983).

14.4.7 *Mental Transformations That Promote Delay of Gratification*

A good deal of work regarding the psychological processes underlying self-control has examined cognitive transformations of the Delay situation, identifying mental representations that transform the situation in such a manner as to promote self-control. Using the Duration of Delay paradigm, children in a "consume strategy" condition were instructed to focus their attention on the consumability qualities of the objects for which they were waiting ("think about how crunchy and salty the pretzels taste"); children in a "transform strategy" condition were instructed to cognitively transform the desired reward ("think about the pretzels as tree trunks"). In comparison to children who received consume instructions, those in the transform condition exhibited greater delay prior to succumbing to temptation (Mischel & Baker, 1975).

These types of cognitive activity have been characterized in terms of "hot" (consumability) versus "cool" (cognitively transformed) ideation. Many empirical studies support the claim that hot representations of the delay situation cause people to focus exclusively on immediate self-interest ("I want it badly and I want it now"). Given hot representations, it is simply too difficult to take account of the broader considerations that may be relevant to action. These studies pay testimony to the power of cool mental transformation of the situation in helping people control their impulses, exercising self-control toward achieving important long-term goals (Mischel, Cantor, & Feldman, 1996; Mischel et al., 1989; for a review, see Metcalfe & Mischel, 1999).

14.4.8 Trust in Interaction Partners

Thus far, we have focused on the structure of the Delay situation and person B's place in that situation. We have considered the reward structure of Delay situations, the ways in which people monitor their movement through such situations, and the ways in which immediate and remote goals are cognitively represented. Although some portion of the tendency to opt for small immediate reward rather than large delayed reward can be explained by variables of this sort, it seems likely that interpersonal variables account for some of the observed variance. Why so?

Interpersonal Delay situations entail risk, in that partners may not reliably live up to the promise to deliver rewards contingent upon goal attainment. Such risk is particularly acute to the extent that Delay situations involve conflicting interests. For example, if Mary's father needs to make a business trip during the scheduled trip to Disneyland, will he follow through on his promise to Mary or renege on the deal? People may sometimes choose small immediate reward rather than large delayed reward because they do not trust the interaction partner to deliver the delayed reward.

Relevant to this point, Mischel's first published research regarding delay of gratification used the Choice to Delay paradigm to examine self-imposed delay among Black and East Indian children on the island of Trinidad (Mischel, 1958). This research revealed lower tendencies toward delay of gratification among Black children than among East Indian children. Typically, these findings have been explained in terms of differential trust (Banks, McQuater, Anthony, & Ward, 1992): In comparison to Black children, East Indian children may have found it easier to trust a Caucasian experimenter to deliver the delayed reward, experiencing greater confidence in the probability that the reward was forthcoming. In support of this trust-based interpretation, Stickland (1972) observed greater tendencies toward delay of gratification among Black children when the experimenter promising the delayed reward was Black than when the experimenter was Caucasian. This interpretation is also compatible with empirical work including experimental manipulations of trust (Mahrer, 1956; Mischel, 1963).

What forms the basis for trust in a partner? Holmes and Rempel (1989) propose that we develop increased trust in specific partners as a consequence of observing those persons "behave well" in diagonstic situations, or as a result of observing them benevolently depart from their immediate interests in order to promote our welfare. Consistent with this claim, research regarding ongoing relationships reveals that we come to trust our partners when we observe them enact diagnostic behaviors such as accommodation and sacrifice – behaviors which are not in the partner's immediate interests, but which promote couple well-being (Wieselquist, Rusbult, Foster, & Agnew, 1999). As we become increasingly trusting – or increasingly certain of a given partner's benevolent motives – we become increasingly willing to "place ourselves in the partner's hands" in situations involving vulnerability. With increased confidence that the partner indeed will deliver promised rewards, it becomes easier for us to defer immediate gratification in pursuit of long-term goals.

14.4.9 Dispositional Trust in Interaction Partners

In addition to experiencing greater or lesser trust in specific partners, we may develop relatively stable expectations regarding the trustworthiness of "people in general." Attachment theory suggests that people develop stable inclinations to trust (vs. not trust) interaction partners as a result of their early childhood experiences. Secure attachment results from childrearing experiences in which adult caregivers reliably attend to the infant's needs (Hazan & Shaver, 1994). Later in life, securely attached people tend to be more confident that others can be relied upon to follow through on their commitments, and they accordingly should be more willing to enter into interpersonal delay situations without fear of exploitation or betrayal by their partners.

In contrast, insecure attachment results from childrearing experiences in which adult caregivers are either unreliable (anxious-ambivalent attachment) or neglectful (avoidant attachment; Hazan & Shaver, 1994). Later in life, interpersonal delay situations are likely to be problematic for insecure people. Anxious-ambivalent individuals may fervently desire situations in which others reward them for achieving long-term goals, yet are likely to fear the vulnerabilities that such situations entail (e.g., they may overreact to signs of unreliability). Avoidant individuals may find the vulnerabilities underlying interpersonal Delay situations so repellant that they become disinclined to enter into such situations, despite possibilities for desirable long-term outcomes. Consistent with this line of reasoning, toddlers who display evidence of secure attachment and trust in their mothers exhibit greater ability to delay gratification at age 5 (Sethi, Mischel, Aber, Shoda, & Rodriguez, 2000).

14.4.10 Commitment to Interaction Partners

Many delay of gratification situations arise in response to the needs inherent in ongoing relationships, in that when close partners encounter problematic interdependence situations, the "easy" response frequently is destructive. For example, when Susan's partner says something rude to her, her immediate impulse may be to respond in an equally rude manner. When her partner wants to move to a part of the country that she dislikes, her impulse may be to say "hell no." Indeed, children's tendencies toward delay of gratification predict interpersonal adjustment 20 years later, with poorer delay of gratification predicting later aggressive behavior and peer rejection (Ayduk et al., 2000).

Thus, impulsive interpersonal acts appear to be harmful to interpersonal relations. Indeed, work regarding adult relationships demonstrates that couple well-being is enhanced to the extent that partners control their impulses toward immediately gratifying yet ultimately destructive behaviors, instead enacting constructive, "pro-relationship" behaviors such as (a) accommodating rather than retaliating when a partner behaves badly, (b) sacrificing one's immediate preferences to promote the partner's well-being, and (c) controlling the impulse toward vengeance following betrayal, instead behaving in a forgiving manner (Finkel, Rusbult, Kumashiro, & Hannon, in press; Rusbult, Verette, Whitney, Slovik, & Lipkus, 1991; Van Lange et al., 1997).

Beyond stable tendencies toward delay of gratification, what predicts the inclination to engage in costly but necessary "relationship-regulation" acts? We suggest that the answer is increased interdependence, as manifested in subjective commitment. Commitment reflects intent to persist in a relationship, psychological attachment to the partner, and long-term orientation (Rusbult, 1983). Commitment increases to the extent that people are more dependent on their partners, or to the extent that (a) satisfaction level is high, (b) quality of alternatives is poor, and (c) many important investments are linked to the relationship (Bui, Peplau, & Hill, 1996; Rusbult, 1983). The empirical literature reveals that to the extent that partners are committed to one another, they are more likely to exert effort and endure cost toward sustaining the relationship, exhibiting relationship-regulation behaviors such as accommodation, sacrifice, and forgiveness (for a review, see Rusbult, Olsen, Davis, & Hannon, 2001).

14.4.11 *Group Discussion and Commitment to Group Goals*
Frequently, Delay of Gratification situations involve remote goals that are shared by multiple persons. Thus, the tendency to persist toward remote but valued social outcomes may be encouraged by interpersonal communication that enhances commitment to shared long-term goals. Indeed, the empirical literature demonstrates that group discussion reliably promotes constructive, cooperative behavior in social dilemmas, or Delay situations in which widespread pursuit of immediate self-gratification leads to long-term collective disaster (e.g., destroying the environment, increasing budget deficits). Discussion promotes cooperative behavior (self-control in pursuit of remote collective goals) even when people's behavior cannot be scrutinized and there is no opportunity for social sanctions, and even when group members cannot coordinate their behavior in such a manner as to yield efficient sharing of the remote goal, once attained; also, the effect does not rest on "general benevolence norms" or the humanizing of fellow group members (for a review, see Dawes, Van de Kragt, & Orbell, 1990).

Recent research examined reasons for the effect of communication using a step-level public goods task – a task that embodies the conflict between pursuit of a small immediate reward for oneself versus a large delayed reward for the group. A manipulation of communication (face-to-face communication with group members vs. listening to another group's discussion) revealed that communication reliably promoted cooperation (Kerr & Kaufman-Gilliland, 1994). The effect of communication was not attributable to enhanced group identity. Rather, communication promoted cooperation because it increased commitment to honoring cooperative agreements. Thus, even when it is tempting to "free ride" on other group members, and even when there is little chance of detection and censure for noncooperation, one important motive for pursuing shared goals appears to be "conscience, including the dictate to do what one has committed oneself to do" (p. 527). Communication produces a transformation of the social dilemma into a new situation in which one's self-respect is at issue, thereby promoting one's inclination to exercise self-control toward shared remote goals.

14.4.12 Developmental Changes in Self-Regulatory Behavior

People can be taught to adopt self-regulatory behaviors that promote the exercise of self-control in the pursuit of long-term goals. One of the most fundamental rules of self-regulation is that delay is easier when rewards are not in view. Even when people are physically confronted with rewards, the ability to resist temptation is greater to the extent that people adopt strategies to promote delay, such as enhancing the desirability of remote goals. Also, mental representations that focus attention on hot, consumability features of rewards impede effective self-regulation, whereas mental transformations that focus attention on cool, abstract features of rewards promote effective self-regulation.

When do we develop the ability to understand and spontaneously adopt strategies and transformations that promote delay of gratification? Very young children (4-year-olds) appear to produce self-defeating problems for themselves by actively creating tempting situations – they choose situations in which rewards are in full view without recognizing that they will be unable to make use of strategies to overcome temptation. By the age of 6 children appear to understand and make use of two basic forms of self-regulation: cover rather than expose the rewards, and engage in distracting activities while waiting. Around the age of 12 children come to recognize that hot, consumability ideation will impede self-regulation, whereas cool, abstract representations will promote effective self-regulation (Mischel & Mischel, 1983; Mischel et al., 1989). Such findings suggest a hierarchy of psychological mechanisms for self-control, proceeding from physical manipulation of the environment to attentional strategies to, finally, relatively abstract, rule-based transformations of the situation.

14.5 Transition List Representations

Table E14.1: Person B's Choices Lead the Pair to a Potentially Desirable Goal for B, and Person A Has No Vested Interests. If persons A and B are to arrive at a situation in which a valued outcome is available to person B (juncture M), person B must behave in such a manner as to move through successive preliminary junctures (junctures J, K, and L). At each preliminary juncture, person B must suffer an undesirable outcome (b2) rather than enjoying a moderately desirable outcome (b1).

At any juncture, if B fails to exercise Actor Control by forgoing a small immediate reward, both persons exit the situation. If B exercises restraint at each juncture and the two arrive at the remote goal, person A exercises Partner Control over whether B receives a valued outcome. Person A's outcomes are not influenced by person B's choices.

TABLE E14.1. *Person B's Choices Lead the Pair to a Potentially Desirable Goal for B, and Person A Has No Vested Interests*

Junctures	Options	Possible Selections	Outcomes for A and B		Transition to Next Juncture
J	(a1, a2)	a1b1	0	+1	X
	(b1, b2)	a1b2	0	0	K
		a2b1	0	+1	X
		a2b2	0	0	K
K	(a1, a2)	a1b1	0	+1	X
	(b1, b2)	a1b2	0	0	L
		a2b1	0	+1	X
		a2b2	0	0	L
L	(a1, a2)	a1b1	0	+1	X
	(b1, b2)	a1b2	0	0	M
		a2b1	0	+1	X
		a2b2	0	0	M
M	(a1, a2)	a1	0	+10	X
	(b1)	a2	0	0	X

Table E14.2: Person B's Choices Lead the Pair to a Potentially Desirable Goal for B, and Person A's and Person B's Outcomes Are Noncorrespondent. If persons A and B are to arrive at a situation in which a valued outcome is available to person B (juncture M), person B must behave in such a manner as to move through successive preliminary junctures (junctures J, K, and L). If the persons are to arrive at that juncture, person B must exercise restraint by forgoing a small immediate reward and suffering small costs. Also, if B exercises restraint and the two arrive at the remote goal, person A exercises Partner Control over whether B receives a valued outcome. In this example, the interests of persons A and B conflict. During preliminary steps, person B's choice of a small immediate reward yields poor outcomes for person A, and B's choice

TABLE E14.2. *Person B's Choices Lead the Pair to a Potentially Desirable Goal for B, and Person A's and Person B's Outcomes are Noncorrespondent*

Junctures	Options	Possible Selections	Outcomes for A and B		Transition to Next Juncture
J	(a1, a2)	a1b1	−1	+1	X
	(b1, b2)	a1b2	+1	−1	K
		a2b1	−1	+1	X
		a2b2	+1	−1	K
K	(a1, a2)	a1b1	−1	+1	X
	(b1, b2)	a1b2	+1	−1	L
		a2b1	−1	+1	X
		a2b2	+1	−1	L
L	(a1, a2)	a1b1	−1	+1	X
	(b1, b2)	a1b2	+1	−1	M
		a2b1	−1	+1	X
		a2b2	+1	−1	M
M	(a1, a2)	a1	−1	+10	X
	(b1)	a2	+10	−1	X

of a small immediate cost yields good outcomes for A (i.e., A would prefer that B exercise self-control, yielding movement toward the goal). If the two arrive at the remote goal, person A's choice of a1 would yield very good outcomes for B at a small cost to A, whereas person A's choice of a2 would yield a small cost for B but very good outcomes for A (i.e., one but not both will benefit from B's earlier self-control).

INCOMPLETE INFORMATION SITUATIONS

Entry #15

Negotiation

Can We Agree on a Deal?

15.1 Examples

The prototypical example of this situation is the encounter of buyer and seller whenever there is no fixed selling price (i.e., "haggling" is permitted or even expected). In the United States, most new and nearly all used car purchases can involve some negotiation of a mutually acceptable price. Although negotiation examples that involve economic conflicts (e.g., union contract negotiations; trade negotiations) or political conflicts (e.g., recent attempts to negotiate issues of land and sovereignty between Israelis and Palestinians) probably come to mind first, many common interpersonal situations permit some degree of negotiation. For example, husbands and wives may negotiate a division of financial and domestic responsibilities, neighbors may work out arrangements arising from their proximity (e.g., how late parties may end, how freely children and pets may wander), or roommates may settle any number of living arrangements (e.g., who gets which bedroom, whether food will be shared, who cleans what when). As these examples illustrate, a negotiation need not be focused on a single choice dimension (e.g., selling price), but can involve multiple issues, as when a divorcing couple negotiates division of property, child custody, visitation, and child support as part of a comprehensive divorce agreement.

15.2 Conceptual Description

For ease of presentation, let us assume negotiation between two parties. Such Negotiation situations are ones with the following properties:

Norbert Kerr had primary responsibility for preparation of this entry.

(a) There is a set of pairs of outcomes (e.g., deals; settlements), any one of which may be selected by mutual agreement of the parties. In many instances, these outcomes are tangible ones – money, land, natural resources, and so on. However, they need not be; people can negotiate anything they value, including services, rights, responsibilities, time, access, favors, or esteem. (b) There is a separately specified pair of outcomes (the "status quo" or the CL_{alt} outcomes) that represent the consequences of failure to reach agreement. (c) There are both conflicting interests (the parties' preferences among possible deals are not perfectly correlated) but at least some common interest (i.e., at least some possible deals are preferable to failing to reach an agreement; otherwise, there would be no reason to negotiate). (d) And finally, the parties can communicate, even if only to make successive offers. Another typical, although perhaps not defining, feature of Negotiation situations is that each party possesses only part of the information about the other's preferences. A typical Negotiation situation is one in which each party knows his or her own outcomes for all possible agreements as well as for failure to agree, but has only vague ideas about those same outcomes for the other party.

The third requirement (for "mixed motives") is met by most of the interdependence situations identified in this book. Thus, when the other requirements could be met, these other mixed motive situations could become negotiation situations. So, for example, if the police would permit it, the two prisoners of the Prisoner's Dilemma Game could meet and negotiate their joint actions in response to the prosecutor's offers, perhaps leaving the standard, no-communication version of the PDG as the "no agreement" default. And, although it would take much of the drama out of the encounter, the teenage gladiators who meet in an automotive Chicken match might negotiate in advance on just how close they could get before they each swerve (providing each with some snatch of honor and a chance to live to clash another day).

Although the potential for negotiation is, at least in principle, associated with nearly all of the situations we consider in this book, we have not treated negotiation as simply a variant of many other situations but rather as a distinct situation of its own. This is partly because certain required conditions – namely, the opportunity to discuss and coordinate choices and the existence of no-agreement outcomes – are routinely absent in the generic versions of these other interdependence situations. Moreover, there are interesting and common behavioral patterns and affordances that arise in most if not all Negotiation situations, regardless of the precise nature of interdependence.

One such defining feature of Negotiation situations is the existence of a no-agreement or "status quo" set of outcomes. In many of the other situations, we have presumed that each actor must make a choice. In many experimental simulations of these situations, participants are required to do so. However, in fact, in many of these situations, particularly their real-world versions, one potential action is inaction – simply to maintain the status quo. To be sure, there may be costs associated with this "choice"; e.g., the new car shopper must get by with his old vehicle and the seller must bear the costs of keeping an unsold vehicle on the lot. As noted above, in Negotiation situations this status quo is less rewarding than at least some of the outcomes potentially available in the interdependence situation – if this were not true, there would be little incentive to negotiate. However, most negotiators proceed with a keen awareness that until they strike a bargain, they have (or are stuck with) a default, status quo outcome.

15.3 Variants and Combinations

The simplest Negotiation situation is one with a single focal issue (e.g., price) and very few (a minimum of two) choice alternatives. A primitive example would be a situation in which a father and prospective bridegroom negotiate whether the bride's mandatory dowry will be one or two cows (and where the marriage cannot occur unless agreement is reached). More commonly, of course, there are many possible alternatives (e.g., when dowries can be paid in some finely denominated resource like money), providing a range of possible bargaining solutions (Schelling, 1960).

The simplest – yet a common – pattern of interdependence within which negotiation occurs is one of noncorrespondent Mutual Joint Control (see Entry #4). For example, in many purchasing situations, there is a constant amount of a single resource (e.g., dollars to be spent), and one party's gain (e.g., a drop in selling price) insures the other party's equivalent loss (e.g., a drop in profit to the seller; see Table E15.2 below, at the end of this entry). We may contrast such simple, pure conflict "zero-sum" or "constant sum" situations with more complex mixed motive situations, in which there may be more than one issue to be settled and negotiator's interests are at least partially correspondent. For example, in a labor negotiation, both the employer and the union may have correspondent interests in certain issues, like maximizing on-the-job safety (although perhaps for very different reasons – to maintain production or avoid expensive medical costs for the employer; to avoid personal injuries for the employees). Or, different parties may attach different importance to different issues. For example, the issue of labor costs may be of paramount importance to the employer, whereas job security may be most important to the employees (see, for example, Table E15.3, below). In such settings, which appear to be quite common (cf. Deutsch, 1973), some agreements yield higher joint gain than others. For example, even though the employees might prefer to have both high wages and high job security, they might gain more on the latter issue by yielding somewhat on the former issue.

If both parties knew each other's payoff tables for all issues, it would, in principle, be easy to identify and agree upon the optimal, so-called *integrative* solution, one which wastes no resources and is impossible to improve upon from the perspective of both parties. In practice, it is often very hard to either recognize or achieve such integrative solutions. One reason is that there may less than complete knowledge of all parties' utilities. Most commonly this would entail partial or total ignorance about other parties' payoffs, but it could also entail some ignorance about one's own payoffs (e.g., an ex-wife's denial that one of her motives in divorce negotiations was spite, to punish her ex-husband). Another reason is that parties frequently fail to recognize that their interests coincide on certain issues (Thompson & Hrebec, 1996). This can result from many negotiators mistakenly holding a *fixed-pie perception* (Thompson & Hastie, 1991), assuming that their interests are always and perfectly opposed, and thereby failing to recognize possibilities – e.g., of trade-offs on different issues, of expanding the pie – that could result in a better solution for all.

15.4 Interaction Process and Person Factors

Negotiation settings involve interpersonal communication, extended in time, between parties with both shared and discordant interests. Hence, many (nearly any) social psychological processes can be involved in the interaction patterns that develop in this relatively complex setting, including impression management and formation, attribution, problem solving, social influence, and reliance on social roles and norms. Here, we shall focus on just a few of the patterns of interaction that have been documented in the extensive negotiation and bargaining literature (see, Pruitt & Carnevale, 1993, or Pruitt, 1998, for comprehensive reviews).

15.4.1 *Starting Assumptions*

Like many extended interaction settings, the course of negotiation is strongly guided by what the parties bring to the setting. Among the initial negotiator assumptions that tend to make the process more contentious (i.e., result in larger initial demands, smaller concessions, and slower progress) are high expectations and aspirations (either held oneself or presumed to be held by one's constituency), overconfidence, and framing the issues in terms of possible losses (rather than possible gains). Likewise, negotiators are less likely to find creative or integrative solutions if they enter negotiations with fixed-pie assumptions or believe that the parties are in conflict on all issues. Likewise, negotiators who believe they have more power, who mistrust or have a negative relationship with the other side, are more likely to be contentious and less likely to obtain mutually optimal agreements. Finally, such contentious and ineffective negotiations are more likely when one sees one's relationship with the opponent as temporary, rather than one that is continuing.

15.4.2 *Actions and Reactions*

Negotiation typically is a process of exchange – of offers and reactions to offers. Hence, a key factor in the process of a negotiator's behavior is the behavior of the other party. Pruitt (1998) suggests that there are two basic forms of reaction – matching (wherein one imitates the opponent's behavior) and compensating or mismatching (wherein one does the "opposite" of one's opponent, e.g., yields when the partner is inflexible). These two patterns of reaction tend to emerge at different points in the process. Compensation is more common at the beginning of negotiation, apparently because one tries to insure that one's initial offers fall close enough to one's opponent's offers to be seen as realistic. Matching becomes more likely during the middle part of the negotiation process – rigidity is met with rigidity, and concessions with concessions, although there is also a self-serving tendency to undermatch (i.e., to reciprocate an opponent's concession with a somewhat smaller concession; Pruitt, 1998). When negotiation is contentious, such matching can thwart the process, with negative behavior breeding matching negative behavior and costly stalemate. Because of time pressures, fatigue, and the desire to reach an agreement, compensation is likely to reemerge near the end of negotiation.

15.4.3 *Norms in Negotiation*

Social norms are particularly likely to emerge and to guide behavior within settings with high levels of conflict (Thibaut & Kelley, 1959), such as Negotiation settings. Prominent among the norms with special applicability to Negotiation settings are (a) distributive justice or fairness norms, such as equality or equity, (b) social exchange norms, such as the turn taking and reciprocity norms (which can also prescribe matching concessions during negotiation), and (c) special, "good faith" bargaining norms (e.g., concessions should not later be retracted; direct negotiations should be attempted before relying on outside parties; ad hominem attacks should be avoided). As far as being functional for concluding negotiations, such norms can be two-edged swords. If the parties both see a norm as applicable and also have a common evaluation of the information required to actually apply the norm, it can be a powerful tool for reaching agreement. On the other hand, different parties may see different norms as applicable and may either lack or disagree about the information required to apply the norm. For example, even if parties agree that concessions should be equal, they may not agree on the values of one another's concessions. In such instances, it may be very difficult to make progress in negotiation, in part because the application of a norm or rule seen as "fair" or "just" can arouse strong emotions and rigidity.

15.4.4 *Learning*

Some negotiation strategies work better than others (cf. Thompson, 1998). When negotiation is not a one-shot affair, but repeated with the same or different parties, this creates the opportunity to learn and apply strategies that were relatively more successful in old negotiations to new negotiations. For example, setting high initial offers and making few concessions tend to be associated with more favorable final outcomes. Thus, relatively more experienced negotiators appear more likely to set their initial offers higher (Kelley, 1966) and to make fewer concessions (Thompson, 1990).

15.4.5 *Negotiation Strategies*

The patterns of interaction during negotiation depend strongly upon the negotiation strategies the parties adopt. The simple act of mirroring or matching one's opponent's actions (e.g., concessions), sometimes termed the "tit-for-tat" strategy, is a common strategy. It can, as noted above, lead to impasse but, when leavened with certain modifications (being slow both to retaliate and to forgive exploitative behavior; making concessions to break impasses), it can promote mutual concessions and good outcomes.

One set of strategies is characterized by a negotiator focusing on particular issues, cues, or outcomes in some systematic way. Certain norms (e.g., striving for equal outcomes or equal concessions) could illustrate such focused strategies. Another example would be labor negotiators who plan to settle issues one at a time, rather than simultaneously working on all issues. Patterns of offers and counteroffers can illuminate the underlying strategies negotiators are using. A good example is the development of the *systematic concessions model* (e.g., Kelley & Schenitzki, 1972). That model holds that a negotiator sets an overall profit goal and then tries any and all offers or proposals which would satisfy that goal. If none of those proposals is acceptable to the other side, then the negotiator lowers his or her profit goal a bit and tries all new proposals that meet this revised goal. The set of options is likely to be enlarged through this process of gradually lowering goals and eventually some overlap in mutually acceptable options can be achieved (particularly when the situation has high "integrative potential," e.g., where some issues are important to one party but relatively unimportant to the other, see section 15.3 above).

An ever-present problem in Negotiation situations (as well as other situations of interdependence where communication is permitted) is what (if any) information to share with one's partner. In purely cooperative situations, it is highly desirable to be open, honest, and trusting. In purely competitive situations, the opposite is true – don't show your hand; if you do, do so in a misleading way; and, knowing that the partner is under the same pressures, don't trust what he or she communicates. The Negotiation situation, by definition, requires communication in a mixed motive situation, posing the problem of how to balance the conflicting communication strategies or "rules." There is some evidence (Kelley, 1966) that such information dilemmas in negotiation are resolved tacitly, as a by-product of the process of offer-counteroffer (e.g., following the systematic concessions model – starting high, making concessions slowly, exploring multiple packages, etc.). One tends to move from initial distrust to more trust, giving some information when the other gives some, extracting information by multiple testing at each level, and so forth. Such a process permits a negotiator to gain a feeling of walking an appropriate line between the two undesirable extremes that are appropriate, respectively, in purely cooperative and purely competitive situations.

A running theme throughout this book is that the relative concern one has for one's own versus the other's welfare – either as a stable personal outlook or as a viewpoint shaped by situational factors – can determine one's behavioral choices and the course of interpersonal interaction. This theme is nowhere more important than in Negotiation settings, within which the self-other emphasis can not only explain how one's degree of concern for the other guy's welfare can effectively transform one situation (with few mutually acceptable solutions) into another (with many more viable solutions) but can also color and direct the many social processes that are involved in negotiation (e.g., attribution; risk-taking; interpersonal attraction). This theme has been most fully developed in Pruitt and Carnevale's (1993) *dual concern model* of negotiation. They suggest that four generic negotiation styles or strategies correspond to the cells of a simple 2 × 2 table, where the factors are concern for self (high vs. low) and concern for the other (high vs. low) (see Table E15.1).

TABLE E15.1. *The Dual-Concern Model*

		Concern for others	
		Low	High
Concern for self	High	Contending	Problem solving
	Low	Inaction	Yielding

High self-concern paired with low other-concern tends to lead to "Contending," attempting to get the other party to concede (via persuasion, threats, and the like). High other-concern paired with low self-concern tends to lead to "Yielding," giving in to the other party's demands. The early stages of romantic relationships, when each party is eager to accommodate and be accepted by the other, are often characterized by a mutual willingness to yield. Low self-concern and low other-concern tend to lead to "Inaction," for example, stalling, slow concession making, avoiding or quitting negotiation. Finally, high self- and high other-concern tends to lead to "Problem solving," that is, trying to discover or create mutually satisfactory solutions. These strategies are not exhaustive, of course; there are other strategies that combine these extremes. For example, "compromise" as a generic strategy seems to involve both looking for good joint solutions and some degree of yielding. Pruitt and Carnevale (1993) show that the effects of many variables (e.g., having to satisfy a demanding constituency, emphasizing potential losses vs. potential gains) on behavior in negotiation can be analyzed and understood through the mediating effects of self- and other-concern.

15.4.6 Person Factors

There also appear to be stable individual differences in preferred or typical methods of resolving disputes. Multidimensional scaling of lists of such methods (e.g., van de Vliert, 1990) has revealed a two-dimensional solution quite consistent with the two-dimensional, "self- versus other-concern" space theorized by the dual concern model. Thus, for example, there is a cluster of methods in the "southwest" quadrant (corresponding to the low self-/ low other-concern region of the dual concern model; see Table E15.1) which could be characterized as "inaction" (e.g., avoidance, separation, withholding); there is another cluster in the "southeast" corner (high self-/ low other-concern; see Table E15.1) that could fairly be identified as "contending" (e.g., physical force, verbal force, confrontational discussion); and so forth. Earlier (e.g. in Entries #5 and #12) we noted that measures of social motivation or social orientation can be used to assess the stable degree of concern one has for self versus others in mixed motive settings. The preceding discussion of the dual concern model suggests that such social motives should predict how a person tends to negotiate. Hence, we would expect yielding to be relatively more common among those (few) with altruistic social motives, contending to be more common among those with competitive social motives, and problem solving to be more common among those with cooperative social motives. There is some evidence (e.g., de Dreu & Van Lange, 1995) that the latter group is more willing to make lower demands, to concede more, and to see the other party in more positive terms than relatively less prosocial individuals (although the picture appears to become more complicated when different combinations of parties' social motives are considered; cf. Olekalns & Smith, 1999).

Similarly, stable individual differences in attribution or social perception should make certain forms of negotiation more likely. To illustrate, it has been shown that those with higher levels of interpersonal trust are more willing to share information and are more able to reach agreement in negotiation (Lindskold & Han, 1988) (see section 15.4.5, above, on the generic dilemma of information sharing).

15.5 Matrix Representations

Table E15.2. A simple constant-sum negotiation issue is represented in Table E15.2. Suppose it costs an auto manufacturer $15,000 to make and sell a car, which it then list-prices for $20,000. Let's further suppose that the car is worth at least $15,000 to a buyer who has $20,000 to spend and would like to buy a new car, but for as little as possible. If the only issue that could be negotiated was the car's price, the left side of the matrix in Table E15.2 might represent the effect of agreement on any particular price on the seller's and buyer's profits. Notice that failure to agree is represented as a loss for both parties; the seller has to sell cars to stay in business and the buyer needs new/better transportation. As noted earlier, in most negotiations there is less than complete information available to the parties. This could be represented (as introduced in chapter 3) by indicating that each party only knows his or her own outcomes with certainty, as in the right side of the matrix in Table E15.2. To simplify presentation, we will not use the question mark notation; this (lack of) information condition will be assumed in all of the example matrices presented below.

TABLE E15.2. *Situational Representation of Simple, One-Issue Negotiation*

Price	Seller's Profit	Buyer's Profit	Outcomes Known to Seller*	Outcomes Known to Buyer*
20,000	5,000	0	5000,?	?,0
19,500	4,500	500	4500,?	?,500
19,000	4,000	1,000	4000,?	?,1000
18,500	3,500	1,500	3500,?	?,1500
18,000	3,000	2,000	3000,?	?,2000
17,500	2,500	2,500	2500,?	?,2500
17,000	2,000	3,000	2000,?	?,3000
16,500	1,500	3,500	1500,?	?,3500
16,000	1,000	4,000	1000,?	?,4000
15,500	500	4,500	500,?	?,4500
15,000	0	5,000	0,?	?,5000
No-sale	−250	−200	−250,?	?,−200

* Outcome pairs represent (seller, buyer) outcomes.

Table E15.3. A more complex but more realistic bargaining situation is represented in Table E15.3 below, summarizing a labor-management negotiation over a new labor contract. There are three issues to be settled: wages, pensions, and benefits. There are three alternatives for each of these issues, denoted in the table by the letters A, B, and C; earlier letters are options preferred by management, while later options are preferred by labor. These options define 27 possible contracts, namely, (alternative A for Wages, alternative A for Pensions, alternative A for Benefits) = (A_W,A_P,A_B), (A_W,A_P,B_B), ... , (C_W,C_P,C_B). The net benefit to each party of each possible contract is just the sum of entries in the table (denoted in millions of dollars). So, for example, the net benefit to the employees of agreeing to (A_W,A_P, B_B) is just \$.78M ($= .10 + .60 + .08$), while this contract would be worth \$9.93M ($= 1.7 + 8.2 + .03$) to the employers. In addition, there is always the option of reaching no agreement, which in the present example is worth \$1.3M to the employees (perhaps the strike fund is large enough to provide this level of earnings until all employees find new jobs or the current contract is extended by court order) and \$1.6M to the employers (e.g., the expected profit with hiring "replacement workers" minus the expected costs of legal expenses). Inspection of the table reveals that there is not perfect inverse symmetry in the payoff tables for management and labor. The wages issue is a constant sum one, but the others are not. The pension issue is very important to management but relatively less important to labor. The final issue, benefits, is more important to the employees. The first thing one can see is that many potential agreements are simply out of the question because they provide one or the other party with outcomes worse than reaching no agreement at all, namely, (A_W,A_P,A_B), (A_W,A_P, B_B), (A_W,B_P,A_B), and (A_W,B_P,B_B) for labor, all of which are worse than the no-contract outcome; any agreement involving C_P for management; and (A_W,C_P,A_B) and (A_W,C_P,B_B) for both parties. This example is high in integrative potential, which would be unrealized if the parties held to inaccurate assumptions (e.g., fixed-pie perception) or relied on certain ineffective negotiation strategies (e.g., if they settled on a middling alternative for every issue, which would result in (B_W,B_P,B_B), a suboptimal agreement for both parties). The optimal, integrative solution is (C_W,A_P,C_B), which yields \$5.01M for labor and \$8.32M for management; in each case, these outcomes are not much worse than the parties' ideal solutions – (A_W,A_P,A_B) worth \$10.03M to management and (C_W,C_P,C_B) worth \$5.21M to labor – and no alternative contract can improve upon the parties' joint outcome.

TABLE E15.3. *Situational Representation of*
Three-Issue Negotiation

Option	Wages	Pensions	Benefits
	Total Value to Employees		
A	0.10	0.60	0.01
B	0.90	0.70	0.08
C	1.70	0.80	2.71
No contract		1.30	
	Total Value to Employer		
A	1.70	8.20	0.13
B	0.90	3.40	0.03
C	0.10	1.00	0.02
No contract		1.60	

Note: Numbers denote millions of dollars.

Table E15.4. A much more complex situation is presented in Table E15.4 below (adapted from Kelley & Schenitzki, 1972). Suppose the seller is a truck manufacturer and the buyer is a car exporter who wants to resell trucks abroad. Further, suppose that various factors (e.g., economies of scale for manufacturing; storage and shipping costs for exporting) result in a profit table for the negotiators like Table E15.4 (a blank entry means that no profit could be earned and so no such agreement would be acceptable to a party). Within any particular agreed upon quantity, the situation is a constant sum game – lowering the price reduces the seller's profits exactly the same amount that it raises the buyer's. However, it can be shown (although it is not apparent upon simple inspection) that the total profit available to the pair is nonmonotonically related to quantity, such that the greatest joint profit occurs if the cars are sold in lots of nine. Thus, regardless of the price that the negotiators settle on, they're both better off by trading in lots of nine than some other quantity. This illustrates a negotiation setting in which there is an issue (viz., quantity) for which the traders have a common interest, but which is non-obvious, even if the negotiators did possess one another's profit tables.

In the illustrations provided thus far, we have implicitly assumed that negotiators simply wrangle over alternative deals (defined by the table/ matrix of outcome values) and either agree on one or fail to reach agreement. Actual negotiations, however, are usually more complex. The value of the no-agreement option may change as the negotiation progresses; for example, every day that a strike continues costs both management and labor, so that the value of no agreement drops as a strike wears on. Or, if negotiators see certain norms as fair (and the violation of those norms as costly), the value of one alternative may depend upon the other party's most recent offer; for example, if one side has just made a concession, it may be particularly unwilling to accept any new proposal which doesn't involve some kind of concession from the other side. Representing and analyzing the dynamics of such more complex, extended-in-time negotiations require more complex representations of negotiation (such as the transition lists introduced in chapter 3).

TABLE E15.4. *Situational Representation of Complex Negotiation Problem*

Manufacturer's/Seller's Profit Table					Buyer's/Exporter's Profit Table			
	Quantity					Quantity		
Price	8	9	10	11	Price	8	9	10	11
24,000	119,000	135,000	143,000	143,000	24,000				
22,000	105,000	117,000	121,000	117,000	22,000				
20,000	91,000	99,000	99,000	91,000	20,000	12,000	9,000	3,300	
18,000	77,000	81,000	77,000	65,000	18,000	26,000	27,000	25,300	22,100
16,000	63,000	63,000	55,000	39,000	16,000	40,000	45,000	47,300	48,100
14,000	49,000	45,000	33,000	13,000	14,000	54,000	63,000	69,300	74,100
12,000	35,000	27,000	11,000		12,000	68,000	81,000	91,300	100,100
10,000	21,000	9,000			10,000	82,000	99,000	113,300	126,100

Entry #16

Encounters with Strangers

Lack of Information about a Partner

16.1 Examples

Two strangers on a train or plane become interdependent because they are seated next to each other, share an armrest, are able to interrupt each other's reading or thoughts by talking, the one in the aisle seat is required to get up to enable the person at the window seat to go to the lavatory, and so forth.

On the first day of classes, two new college students in a Freshman math class are made interdependent by being assigned to work on a particular problem together.

Two research subjects, not known to each other, are scheduled for a Prisoner's Dilemma experiment in which the outcome matrix is fully specified. Or, they may be in an "unstructured" situation, left alone together on the pretext of waiting for separate interview rooms to become available, but covertly observed and recorded.

In dozens of studies in child development, an infant, either alone or accompanied by its mother, is confronted with a stranger who moves into various degrees of proximity to the child or says or does various things to it.

16.2 Conceptual Description

We describe this as "*encounters* with strangers" in order to refer to both the "situation" and the "persons." This entry is appropriate for our Atlas of

Harold Kelley had primary responsibility for preparation of this entry.

situations because, as explained below, each person's lack of information about the unkown partner almost inevitably results in some lack of information about the situation. Thus, the situations for these encounters are located in the "incomplete information" portion of the domain of interdependence situations.

We recall that the situation depends on both the environmental or physical circumstances and various simple properties of the two persons – their needs and abilities. In certain of the "stranger" situations, the environmental conditions are fairly clear as to the options available to each person (e.g., the actions involved in enabling the person with the window seat on an airplane to gain access to the aisle). In other stranger situations, such as those in waiting room settings, the range of behavioral options defined by the environment situation are less clear, allowing talking, reading, sleeping, pacing, maintaining distance, and so forth. Thus the strangers may not even know what situation is likely to develop, as one or both of them select certain options (speaking, selecting seats, raising conversational topics, etc.) from among the many that are available.

Whether the behavioral *options* are clear or diffuse, there is further uncertainty about how the various possible individual and joint actions will affect each person's *outcomes*. For the case of adjoining airplane seats, these will depend on the needs of the person in the window seat to gain access to the aisle, how that person's clumsiness in doing so may create discomfort for the partner, and so forth. In the waiting room, the outcomes to the two persons will depend on their needs (to read, think, maintain distance, reduce anxiety, etc.) in relation to what they choose to do.

Beyond incomplete information about the individual factors that determine the behavioral options and outcomes in the "given" *situation*, there is little information about the partner's *"person factors"* (considerateness, generosity, dominance, etc.) relevant to whatever situation may develop. In the airplane, a person may wonder what the partner will "make" of the concrete problem of using the common armrest. Will it be treated as a situation of fair sharing, or as an issue of dominance, that is, who gets to "hog" the armrest? In the waiting room, there may be similar problems of coordinating activities, sharing the newest magazine, or hitting on a conversation topic of mutual interest versus one person's egocentric monologue.

16.3 Variants and Neighbors

We can locate various situations according to three informational factors:

(1) *information* about the concrete situation, that is, about the available options and their effects, individually and jointly, on each person's outcomes;

(2) *information* about each person's interpersonal dispositions, such as cooperativeness, or tendency to dominate;

(3) each person's *expectations* that are relevant to the situation and person factors in (1) and (2). The importance of expectations in this list is found in the ways they supplement or fill gaps in the explicit information described in (1) and (2) ... ways described more fully below.

The variants of the Strangers' Encounter are ones with varying patterns of the explicit information. For example, in classical research on the Prisoner's Dilemma (Entry #5), two persons with no prior acquaintance or contact make independent decisions in the PD matrix which has been fully revealed to them. There are no mysteries about their options and their concrete outcomes. However, they do not have information about the interpersonal dispositions – their "social orientations" – that govern whether they will be cooperative, competitive, or individualistic. Once they understand the outcome structure of this pattern of outcome interdependence, most people have expectations that serve, to a degree, to supply the missing information. Specifically, they have beliefs about people in general – whether they are cooperative, competitive, and so forth. For example, cooperative people expect others to be cooperative, and as a consequence, themselves make cooperative choices and continue to do so until the partner's behavior disconfirms that expectation. In brief, in the classic PD study, the persons are provided with explicit information about the situation, have no information about each other's dispositions, and often have expectations that supply the latter.

A contrasting informational variant is that of the strangers in the waiting room, where there is little explicit information about either the concrete situation or the other person's interpersonal dispositions. However, from prior experience in such settings, many people have expectations about both factors. The physical circumstances and lack of concrete tasks lead one to expect that interdependence may never become very great and, therefore, that person factors are not likely to be very important. They are also likely to expect that behavior will be governed by widely shared norms of "good" or "polite" behavior. (Norms and expectations are closely linked, inasmuch as norms entail *both* expectations about others' behavior *and* meta-expectations, that is, expectations about others' expectations for one's own behavior.)

A more stressful variant of the last case, with little situational and dispositional information, is the social setting requiring interaction with strangers who may be evaluating you, but in which, because of its novelty, you have few expectation based guidelines for behavior. This is illustrated by the situations Forgas (1976) found to be ones in which people report feeling ill-at-ease and not knowing how to behave. For Oxford undergraduates, these included "meeting new people at a sherry party in college" and "getting acquainted with a new person during dinner in hall."

The patterns of outcome interdependence with strangers include many of the situations described elsewhere in this Atlas. For example, the pair may be free to interact or not, that is, in whether or not to enter into some degree of interdependence with each other (cf. Entry #21). Once they choose or are compelled to become interdependent, that interdependence may include any of the patterns of control described in other Atlas entries. For example, Mutual Joint Control with conflict of interest (Entry #4) is illustrated by the problem of coordination in using the single armrest between the two tourist-class seats on the airplane. There are many common interest coordination problems (Entry #3) with strangers in daily life, including some with high stakes, as in passing at high speeds on a narrow highway. Encounters with strangers that involve exchange or sharing of some resource (Entry #5) occur when, like the Freshmen in the math class, we are required to work with a stranger on a task involving mutual help. Sharing and taking turns as a means of sharing (the "Turn-Taking Game," sometimes referred to as the Battle of the Sexes) occur when, for example, strangers find themselves waiting in a room with inadequate facilities (too few chairs, too few magazines).

Expectations. As preceding examples illustrate, expectations play a very important role in strangers' interactions, providing cognitive content that supplements the given information. In the air travelers' example, expectations based on evidence about the physical situation (paired airplane seats) and the other person's simple characteristics (size, probable needs inferred from age and gender) affect a person's understanding of the concrete situation. Expectations about the partner's "dispositions" (based on demeanor, dress, and broad stereotypes of people who fly tourist class) affect anticipations of how that person will play out the concrete problems. Those expectations will be stronger and more relevant for persons with extensive flying experience. The youngster flying for the first time may have to rely on expectations derived from similar situations (riding the school bus). One general point here is that, as a consequence of the role that expectations play in filling information gaps, we rarely encounter a completely "strange" circumstance. As adults, our expectations relevant to interdependence patterns and varieties of behavior common to each are quite extensive and usually serve to supply much of the information we need. Furthermore, those expectations we happen to share with our associates provide the basis for *interpersonal norms*, which include guidelines useful in interaction with strangers, for example, rules for avoiding conflict, maintaining appropriate distance, and so forth. With such norms at hand, we usually need not feel that we "don't know how to behave."

Expectations play a role similar to that of the other "person factors," such as considerateness, dominance, and fairness, in that they change the "given" situation into a different one. In effect, they modify the information parameters of the problem the person confronts. At the same time, the useful role of expectations introduces another kind of "person factor." It is generally unwise to rely wholly on expectations as a basis for behavior in encounters with strangers. However, as in the case of other "person factors," there are individual differences in this reliance. Those differences are revealed by measures of "need for closure" (e.g., Webster & Kruglanski, 1994), which distinguish (1) persons who make decisions on the basis of expectations elicited by initial information from (2) persons who act more cautiously and pursue the strategies of information gathering made possible by the situation (through its flexible response conditions, iteration, extension in time, etc.). The incomplete information property of situations affords the expression of individual differences in this and other generalized information-processing tendencies, such as optimism-pessimism or trust-distrust.

16.4 Interaction Process and Person Factors

The huge research literature using strangers' encounters gives us great latitude as to the particular phenomena to be considered here. In the examples that follow, our discussions of *interaction* will emphasize the strangers' gathering and exchange of information and our discussions of *person factors* will emphasize individual differences in reactions to strangeness. As in the other entries, our implicit task will be to identify what interaction sequences and person factors are afforded or more or less required by these situations of great informational ambiguity.

16.4.1 *The Infant and Strangers: Inhibition and Shyness*
Perhaps the most important person factor revealed in the Strangers' Encounter is "shyness," which refers to timidity, inhibition, anxiety, and

avoidance of unknown others. Because it is viewed as an important factor in social development, there have been dozens of developmental studies of shyness in infants. The research has revealed much about infants' interaction with strangers and the consistency over time of individual differences in shy behavior. Our focus will be on how infants seem to cope with the uncertainties they face with a stranger.

The more or less standard test situation is one in which a 4- to 9-month-old infant, accompanied by its mother, is faced with a strange woman, who either sits quietly or approaches the child in some standardized way. Some work (e.g., that described by Kagan, Snidman, & Arcus, 1998) distinguishes infants according to the degree of their fearfulness – fretting or crying, staying close to its mother, maintaining distance from the stranger, and refusing to respond to requests by the stranger. Kagan's major purpose was to obtain evidence about the consistency over the first 5 years of life in whether children are inhibited or uninhibited in their reactions to strangers. The results were mixed, but there was enough consistency for Kagan to suggest that early reactivity is a "temperamental disposition" that has some persistence.

An interesting early study by Wiehe (described in Lewin [1935, 1951]) dealt in detail with the physical parameters of the encounter. Wiehe observed that infants become more inhibited and avoidant with increasing proximity to a stranger. But he also noted that this effect is weaker when the child is behind the stranger (where the child cannot be seen) rather then in front. Lewin conceptualized these results as revealing the adult's "powerfield" – a field that extends most strongly in front of the adult and, like a magnetic field, becomes weaker with distance from its source.

In general, the results of this work can be interpreted as showing that infants avoid becoming dependent upon or interdependent with a stranger. By staying close to the mother, they maintain a source of power that is dependably supportive of their own welfare. By maintaining distance from the stranger, though less so when behind the stranger and out of her sight, infants are able to gain information (closely watching the stranger is common) while avoiding coming under her "power." Infants also seem to know that entering into coordinated interaction with the stranger (through responding to her invitations and requests) may move them into interdependence with her. In short, infants seem to want to learn as much as possible about the stranger while, at the same time, avoiding coming under her control.

However, as noted in Kagan's work, there are individual differences in infant shyness. In a study by Ricard and Gouin-Decarie (1993), the mother was present and the (young female) stranger was passive, making no overtures but only responding to the child's initiatives. About half of the 9-month-old infants not only looked at, smiled at, and vocalized to the stranger, but moved near her. However, in other respects, those "bold" infants behaved much like their "shy" counterparts who never approached the stranger. Both sets visually focused intently on the stranger, seemed more interested in her than in the mother (indicated by the glances and smiles they directed to the two adults), and even appeared to treat the stranger as a "target that must be smiled at." Also, distance was important for both bold and shy infants, the difference being only in "the pace at which they performed the same kind of distal familiarization" (p. 145). Even the bold ones approached only after studying the stranger from a distance.

Ricard and Gouin-Decarie conclude that the bold and shy infants are more alike than different in their "familiarization" with the passive stranger. Their results are consistent with other developmental evidence that early reactions to strangers are not simply matters of more or less fear. Rather, they reflect two competing sets of feelings and behaviors – affiliation and approach on the one hand and fear and avoidance on the other. Viewed in this light, the authors suggest that under the benign conditions in their study (few of their infants displayed fear), the 9-month-old infant's interaction with a stranger reflects an affiliative strategy made possible by their level of cognitive development. At about that age, infants develop an understanding of "persons" as special objects in their world – as autonomous agents, largely self-governed, and not to be treated in the ways inanimate objects are. So "persons" are not to be touched or manipulated, but rather, they are to be smiled at, looked at, and communicated with from a distance. Interaction with strangers at a distance is necessary *before* closer contact can be established. Overt avoidance behavior that is interpreted as fear may not be such, but instead, may be part of an affiliative strategy that is appropriate in moving from unfamiliarity to familiarity with a person.

The infant's concepts of appropriate paths to familiarity undoubtedly also apply to the stranger who, rather than being passive, comes close to and interacts with them. An example is provided by Mangelsdorf's study (1992) of reactions to strangers by 6-, 12-, and 18-month-old infants. The negative reactions of the youngest sample were increased by the stranger's touching and lack of positive affect (failing to smile and laugh). The negative reactions of the two older samples were little affected by those aspects of the stranger's unilateral behavior, but were affected by complex features of the stranger's *interaction* with them. The older children reacted favorably to an interaction pattern characterized by the stranger's being sensitive to the child's signals, meshing tempos with the child and avoiding abrupt actions, and allowing the child to exercise control of the interaction. Mangelsdorf observes that this developmental difference corresponds to the transition, made around the end of the first year, *"from* affect based primarily on the intensity or arousing qualities of stimulation *to* affect based on the appraisal of the meaning of stimulation" (p. 204, italics added).

An interdependence interpretation of Mangeldorf's observations would draw a distinction between simpler and more complex patterns of interdependence and their associated interaction patterns. The stranger's *Unilateral* Partner Control and dispositions to use it in a negative manner (as in invading the child's personal space by touching it and withholding signs of friendliness) are threatening to the younger child. However, for the older child, more important is the feeling of being treated as a "person," through being involved in a situation of *Mutual* Joint Control with an adult who coordinates with the child and permits it to exercise initiative ("agency"). The first seems to be a simpler concept, one more readily acquired, and the second, a more sophisticated concept, likely to require the greater cognitive abilities that develop somewhat later in infancy.

We might consider those infant tendencies and skills in relation to the practical problem of teaching older children to resist the lures of a stranger (e.g., so as to avoid being abducted). One program of training preschoolers for this purpose (Holcombe, Wolery, & Katzenmeyer, 1995) teaches them to respond to strangers' lures ("Want to go for a ride in my car?" "Would you like to see my puppy?") by (1) moving away from the stranger and toward a teacher or parent, (2) saying "No. I have to ask my teacher/parent," and (3) reporting the occurrence to the teacher or parent. This training obviously capitalizes on the earlier tendencies to maintain distance from the stranger and to seek the protective dependence of a friendly person. However, as we're sure the designers of these programs know, there are a number of possible complications, including these: (1) Some small children tend to freeze or become motionless, particularly when a strange person becomes too "familiar" by coming close, touching them, or staring at them. (2) Looking at the stranger for the important reason of keeping track of what they are doing makes one vulnerable to their influence. (Remember when the other driver at an intersection bluffed you into giving them the undeserved right-of-way by obviously *not* looking at you?) (3) Speaking to the stranger, even to say "No," has a similar effect but also draws one into a level of interaction that is strongly governed by norms of politeness – norms that restrain us from being unduly abrupt. (Remember the twinge of guilt you felt the first several times you said "No" to the telephone caller who was politely but insistently selling something?) Perhaps relevant to this last point, Holcombe et al. (1995) report that the preschoolers seem to acquire and maintain the "walk away" rule better than the "Say 'No'" rule. In general, the child's untutored reactions to strangers provide some protection from strangers' lures, and, as the research suggests, those reactions can be improved through explicit training.

16.4.2 *Adults' Dependence on Strangers: Selective Information Processing*

Although we usually pay little attention to strangers, we obviously do more so when we are in or about to enter situations of interdependence with them. The general notion is that we observe strangers and try to understand the causes of their actions when circumstances of interdependence require us to exercise control in our interactions with them.

That principle was demonstrated by Berscheid, Graziano, Monson, and Dermer (1976). Students interested in meeting persons of the opposite sex were given the opportunity to observe videotapes of three such persons, all strangers to the students, discussing dating. Each student was designated to go on a date with a particular one of the three, but due to limitations of the video system, was able to view only one of them at a time. There was a clear tendency for the students to spend most of their time watching the individual with whom they were scheduled to interact. The results also suggested that the students used the information they gained to construct "coherent" conceptions of the future partners, as indicated by the fact that for those targets, more extreme ratings were also made with greater confidence. Such more precise and crystallized perceptions would presumably provide the observer with a greater degree of confidence about being able to predict and exercise some control over the future interaction.

The effects on attention of anticipated interdependence with a stranger were studied further by Fiske and her colleagues. The hypothesis was that anticipated interdependence motivates paying attention to the stranger in order to form accurate impressions of them. The research method, described in Erber and Fiske (1984), paired a subject with a particular stranger for joint work on a task requiring creativity and yielding a prize to the best team. In a noninterdependent condition, similar prizes were promised for the best individual work. In an initial exchange of information about themselves, the subject was led to have certain expectations about the partner's probable competence on the upcoming task. Then, the subject was given time to examine a number of evaluative statements about the stranger's competence, made by persons familiar with the stranger. Half of the statements were consistent with the prior information and half were inconsistent, permitting measures to be taken of the time a subject spent looking at the consistent versus inconsistent information.

In line with their reasoning that anticipated interdependence arouses a need for accuracy, the investigators found that the subjects anticipating interdependence spent more time looking at the inconsistent information, presumably because that is where additional useful information is to be found. In subsequent work (Ruscher & Fiske, 1990), the same effect was found when subjects expected to *compete* with the stranger. People are motivated to "size up" not only their future co-workers but also their future competition.

In the work of Fiske and her colleagues, there are strong indications that the interdependence motivated picture of the stranger is painted in dispositional terms, with special reference to stable person properties relevant to the forthcoming interdependent activities. Those properties include not only task skills (e.g., "cleverness") but also attitude and motivation factors more uniquely relevant to productive interaction (e.g., "conscientious" and "motivation to work").

16.4.3 *Interaction between Strangers: The Waiting Room Situation*

The rationale for assessing personality by studying the interaction between strangers is simple: The effects of any prior relationship between the persons are eliminated so the observed behavior is determined by the two persons' personalities and the observable course of their present interaction. This point is illustrated by Ickes's program of research (1982) on the expression of personality in "unstructured" interaction between strangers. Two persons, who have not previously met and are selected on the basis of their personal characteristics or personality test scores, appear for an experiment. On a plausible pretext, they are left alone for 5 minutes to wait for the experiment to begin. During this time together in a small, minimally furnished room, videotapes are covertly made of their interaction, for subsequent coding. Ickes has used this procedure to identify interaction differences between persons differing in birth order, gender, ethnicity, and various personality measures (e.g., self-monitoring, locus of control, sex-role orientation). The research has confirmed expected differences and revealed individual and pair effects not previously identified. For example, pairs of women sit closer together and orient their bodies more toward each other than do pairs of men. Male pairs who both have high external locus of control scores talk to and look at each other more than do pairs with high internal scores. Those and many other comparisons support Ickes's conclusion that dispositional influences on social behavior "are strong, internally consistent, and generally replicable" (p. 327).

Ickes's rationale for developing what he calls the "unstructured situation" follows from what he and other psychologists take to be the likely reason for the low "validity" correlations between paper-and-paper personality measures and observed behavior in real-world and laboratory situations. The argument is that such situations are usually too "strong," directing attention to external cues and causing them to be used to guide behavior (the extreme case being when the cues imply that some behaviors are more "appropriate" then others). That reasoning leads to the conclusion that personality measures will yield higher validity correlations if they are compared with behavior in unstructured situations, where people are forced to depend more on their internal dispositions. It is not entirely clear that Ickes's results confirm this expectation as to the magnitude of test-behavior correlations, but it is clear that the unstructured situation permits him to identify behavior and interaction patterns distinctively associated with a variety of individual differences.

The versatility of Ickes's procedure, in its sensitivity to a variety of personal qualities, is quite impressive. But is it properly described as "unstructured"? The theory used in this Atlas repeatedly calls our attention to the *essential logical relation between situations and the expression of individual differences*, a logic expressed by the concept of "affordance": A situation affords the expression of a particular person factor only if, among its various options and their consequences, there is a distinctive way in which the factor can be freely acted upon. Applying this logic to Ickes's "unstructured" situation and its apparent flexibility in giving expression to an array of personality factors, it would appear that, far from being *un*structured, the situation is *multiply* structured. That is to say that Ickes's results require us to conclude that among its many behavioral options (e.g., talk or not, look or not, initiate or not, move close or not, coordinate or not, assume an open vs. closed posture), his situation must afford ones that permit expressing individual differences in locus of control, birth order, sex role orientation, and so forth. Indeed, rather than considering the situation to be "unstructured," we should probably think of it as "hyperstructured," affording persons with many different social tendencies unique opportunities to express themselves.

These comments are not meant to belittle the value of Ickes's work. The great utility of research conducted in the situation he has created cannot be gainsaid. Our comments are meant merely to suggest that his critique of the usual "validation" situations should not be directed at their "structure," but rather, at what are often referred to as "demand characteristics," meaning informational cues as to social expectations that tend to force behavior into normative channels. Such cues do, indeed, inhibit the expression of individual differences in tendencies relevant to social interaction. The ideal situation for studying individual differences is one without demand characteristics, that is, with few cues as to expectations, and that is exactly what Ickes has created. However (and this is the point to be emphasized), it must be one that has "structure" in the sense that it affords different interpersonal consequences for different behavior. Otherwise, the personal factors that underlie selections on the basis of such behavior-consequence links cannot be distinguished.

16.4.4 Interaction between Strangers: Self-Disclosure

A hypothesis derived from Simmel's (1950) classic commentary on strangers is expressed in the "stranger on the train" phenomena. Contrasting the "stranger" with the "group member," Simmel observes that "the stranger is more impartial; the member is more understanding" (p. 216).

With the objectivity of the stranger is connected the phenomenon chiefly (but not exclusively) true of the stranger who moves on. This is the fact that he often receives the most surprising openness – confidences which would be carefully withheld from a more closely related person. (p. 404)

The hypothesis is that strangers' encounters which have a clearly limited time frame (as in the case of two strangers sharing a compartment on a train) make it possible to reveal one's secrets without fear of retribution and with expectation of an objective rather than partial reception.

The research bearing on this hypothesis is found in studies of "self-disclosure." Subjects are given opportunities (often in an exchange of confidences with another subject – who, sometimes, is a programmed confederate) to reveal personal feelings or intimate facts about themselves. Consistent with the "stranger on the train" hypothesis, there is some evidence of spontaneous revelations made to strangers (Cozby, 1973, p. 84) and of suppression of disclosure by the prospect of future interaction – when the encounter is with a stranger who is not "moving on" (Rubin, 1975).

The more striking and consistent finding is that there is greater willingness to reciprocate the intimate disclosures of a stranger than those of a close friend (e.g., Derlega, Wilson, & Chaikin, 1976). This result is variously explained (1) by the greater safety in revealing intimacies to a stranger who initiates disclosure, (2) by the operation of a conversational norm that applies to polite interaction with a stranger, and (3) by a desire to reciprocate the trust and liking that seem to be shown by the stranger's intimate disclosure.

The last interpretation suggests that mutual self-disclosure is important in the early development of close relationships, and this is now widely accepted (e.g., Collins & Miller, 1994; Berscheid & Reis, 1998). However, this does not imply that reciprocal disclosure necessarily continues throughout the course of a relationship. Once a mutuality of trust is established, close friends feel little obligation *immediately* to respond to the partner's disclosure with one of their own. Indeed, one of the norms common in close relationships is the "communal" norm. In contrast to the "exchange" norm that requires one to respond to a partner's positive actions immediately and in kind, the communal norm requires responding to the partner's needs, whenever they may arise. So a close associate's disclosure, say, of a problem, is not likely to result in one's own immediate similar disclosure, but rather, in a "helping" session in which one tries to console and advise him or her about the problem he or she has just revealed. That is done with the understanding that any problem one later reveals will receive similar attention.

16.4.5 Interaction between Friends versus between Strangers

Researchers (e.g., Ickes, 1982) sometimes study the interplay between strangers as a way to assess individual differences in interaction without the observations being contaminated by preexisting patterns of pair behavior. Here, we consider comparisons between friends' and strangers' interaction made for the explicit purpose of revealing the preexisting patterns that are characteristic of ongoing relationships.

Interdependence concepts suggest that there are two essential differences between the bases of our interactions with friends (close associates, spouses, etc.) and strangers: We are *more interdependent* with friends and that interdependence has a particular *past and future*. Those two factors have different but interrelated consequences:

(1) With greater interdependence, there comes greater variability in the range both of outcomes possibly to be derived from interaction and of the possible incidence of extremes of common versus conflicting interests (cf. the "inverted pyramid" shown in Figure 4.4 in chapter 4). Our continued associations are generally sustained because they yield good outcomes,

so close associations usually entail greater benefits. But also, due to the almost inevitable conflicts of interest, they also entail greater possibilities of poor outcomes and unfair allocations.

(2) The greater time span of our close associations provides opportunities for developing shared understandings, agreements about which social norms are applicable to the interaction, and, importantly, mutual engagement of the attitudes and values by which symbolic outcomes (pride, shame, pity, etc.) and self-reward systems govern interaction. Those outcomes and rewards also increase the range of satisfaction-dissatisfaction possible from close associates – for example, the pleasure from receiving their help versus the disappointment when they fail to give it.

The comparison between our interactions with friends and with strangers enables us to see the consequences of the two factors above. There are some surprises here. It is obvious that we help friends more than strangers and that friends help us more than they help strangers. We keep closer track of our friends' needs (Clark, Mills, & Corcoran, 1989) and tend to provide them with larger shares of joint resources (Aron, Aron, Tudor, & Nelson, 1991). We also place friends under greater obligation to help us. When they do so, we feel less grateful (than when receiving comparable help from strangers), but when they fail to help us, we are more resentful (Bar-Tal, Bar-Zohar, Greenberg, & Hermon, 1977).

The lengthy time span of our interaction with close associates means that "help" often takes account of past issues, ongoing problems, and future possibilities. When a close partner discloses something they'd like to change, we're inclined to deal with it as a problem to be solved, so we interpret its causes, advise remedies, and sometimes use the occasion to try to change the partner in ways we wish for. A similar disclosure from a stranger is met only with polite attention and some empathy (Barker & Lemle, 1987), perhaps as a disclosure merely to be reciprocated. In simple conversation with a spouse (as compared with a stranger of the opposite sex), we are, of course, more likely to discuss "spouse-like" topics, and in those discussions we may become presumptuous, directive, and controlling. That contrasts with the unassuming, acquiescent, and attentive style we adopt toward strangers (Premo & Stiles, 1983). That comparison is "confounded," of course, by differences in the degrees of interdependence – the outcomes and conflict involved – for the friends' and strangers' discussions. But those differences are not mere "confounds" – they are essential ways in which the situations underlying the two kinds of discussions differ.

Gottman (1979) summarized some of these effects as reflecting a contrast between "history and no-history groups." He concludes that "human behavior in marriages and families is generally less positive and less polite than it is with strangers" (p. 53, italics omitted). We would add to that a contrast between "future and no-future groups." Thus, we would emphasize the obligations we feel toward friends and the orientation to problem solving revealed in spousal conversations. Considering all the facts, we would draw a somewhat broader conclusion: We tend to treat our close associates *both better and worse* than we treat strangers.

Entry #17

Joint Decisions under Uncertainty

Bird in the Hand

17.1 Examples

Evan and Lori are headed down the interstate on a long car trip. Nightfall is nearing, they have been driving for some time, and both are beginning to get hungry. Approaching an exit, they notice a billboard proclaiming the easy accessibility of Dorothy's Country Kitchen, site of the finest home cooking in the state. "Dorothy's" seems appealing but they hesitate, having doubts about how good this restaurant really is, and whether a better one might appear if they went on. Neither Evan nor Lori has traveled down this particular road before so the decision to stop now or continue onward must be made in the absence of specific information about this restaurant or the availability of others within reasonable driving distance. If they choose to go on, they may not find another restaurant as good as Dorothy's (and it would not be reasonable to backtrack). How do they decide what to do?

A university tenure committee must decide whether to grant tenure to one of its faculty. This faculty member has an above average but not outstanding record. Some members of the tenure committee feel confident that the department could hire someone better were they to conduct a national search; others feel that new hires are always risky and that the department would be served better by retaining a faculty member with known-to-be-adequate, albeit less-than-stellar, qualities. Do they grant this individual tenure or do they search for a new colleague?

Harry Reis had primary responsibility for preparation of this entry.

Jean and Joe are contestants on Monty Hall's famous game show of the 1960s and 1970s, "Let's Make A Deal."[1] They have loved this show for a long time and have invested a great deal of effort and energy to get there. The game typically proceeds with the host selecting contestants from the audience and immediately trading some unusual item they had brought with them (perhaps a silly hat) for a modest but significant prize (perhaps $1,000). Contestants are then given the opportunity to redeem this prize for whatever is hidden behind curtain number one, curtain number two, or curtain number three. Usually, one of the curtains hides a substantial prize (a new automobile, perhaps) whereas another curtain conceals a booby prize (a year's worth of breakfast cereal, perhaps). Often, there are repeated choices, with contestants offered the chance to give up a substantial prize already won for a chance at something exceptional. All the while, the audience is screaming for Jean and Joe to keep their current prize or to gamble on one or another of the curtains. Jean and Joe covet a chance at the concealed large prize but they fear exchanging the prize already in hand for what may be a booby prize. Their decision must be made quickly, under the pressure of public scrutiny. What do they choose?

17.2 Conceptual Description

As these two examples show, dyads and groups sometimes must make irreversible decisions about whether to stay in a current situation or to pursue the possibility of better outcomes without clear information about the actual availability of such outcomes. In the dyadic case, the dyad has in its grasp outcomes that are at least minimally acceptable to one or both partners, but the possibility exists that by forgoing the current outcomes and continuing onward, even more favorable outcomes may be attained. However, because their expectations are at best educated conjectures, the partners acknowledge that the future may yield poorer outcomes than the present holds. Thus, the dyad's decision represents a choice made with substantial (if not total) uncertainty between the promise of greater rewards in the future weighed against the risk of lesser rewards. Folklore suggests that "a bird in the hand is worth two in the bush," but this adage represents only one possible solution to the dilemma inherent in this situation.

---

[1] In the actual show, contestants participated as individuals although they sometimes sought guidance from partners seated in the audience. For the sake of this example, we describe contestants participating as a couple.

Dyads may encounter this situation in many life circumstances. For example, the decision to stay in one's current relationship, house, job, or city, or to move to a new, potentially more promising but also potentially less satisfying, alternative is often made with incomplete information, with consequences for both partners. The irreversibility of these choices is an important facet of the situation. Such choices would of course be far simpler if it were possible to move to the future location, try it out, and then either accept it or return to the original circumstances. But when choices are irreversible and founded on at best limited data, future outcomes must be estimated from a variety of factors: generalizations from past experiences in similar situations, feedback from others, social comparisons, and personal dispositions such as optimism-pessimism and preferences for risk taking versus security. The known outcomes may be compared (implicitly or explicitly) with the comparison level (CL) to determine their acceptability. The anticipated future outcomes reflect the outcomes perceived to be available outside the current situation.

Central to the interdependence features of this situation is the necessity for joint actions. Of the two stages inherent in this situation – assessment of alternatives and resolution of conflicting preferences – the latter more clearly involves questions of interdependence. Although each partner may individually prefer to stay put or to speculate, because they must act together, their decision will have consequences for both. Often, then, resolution may reflect not merely the weighing of options but more so the adoption of a decision rule for reconciling their conflicting preferences. For example, in the restaurant example, a couple might elect to continue on only if both partners were so inclined. Or, they may continue on if either one preferred to do so. Alternatively, partners might assign the decision about whether to stay or proceed to the hungrier person or to the one who had better hunches about roadside restaurants. Some of these possibilities are discussed below.

One possible pattern is represented schematically in Table E17.1A below (at the end of this entry). At juncture J, the two partners present their views on the decision. In a sense, they vote, either to "stay" at the present restaurant or to "go" down the road to the next one. Their choice is between dining at the available and at least mildly favorable option (indicated by K, where their dining, a_3b_3, will yield a positive outcome value of $+1$) and rejecting it in favor of going to an alternative location where their dining (a_4b_4 at juncture L) will yield an uncertain but possibly larger reward value. That the actual future outcome is unknown is reflected in the designation of these outcomes with question marks. The rule by which their views about staying versus going on are converted into action is shown by the pattern of transitions at juncture J: If either of them votes to stay, that is what the pair does, by moving to K. This pattern of control over the dyad's movement, only one of several possible patterns, may reflect a shared "decision rule" – an important topic to which we return later.

In their discussion, the partners' preferences will reflect their respective subjective estimates of the most likely outcomes, as listed in the table of possible alternative situations (see Table E17.1B, at the end of this entry).[2] This table includes four possible situations the partners can imagine encountering, were they to move forward. Their construals of the several possible outcomes at L are denoted by the letters L_1 through L_4. Each possible situation has an incentive value and a probability of occurrence. "Subjective expected values" may be calculated as the product of the incentive value of a given outcome multiplied by the perceived probability of that outcome's occurrence, as motivational and decision theories commonly do to represent construals of the various behavioral options imaginable in a given situation (Atkinson, 1964; Edwards, 1954). Of course the list of possibilities that may be encountered in such situations is in principle unlimited; the table consists of four alternatives for simplicity.

Because the participants lack the knowledge necessary to make an informed selection – choosing to move on might land them in any or none of these four imagined possibilities – their preferences reflect the desirability of each imagined alternative (for example, a pit barbecue restaurant situated at the next highway exit) weighted by the assumed probability of this alternative actually occurring. The fact that our travelers know that better restaurants exist would have little influence on their decision making if they believed that there were no such restaurants on this highway. It is apparent that A may be described as optimistic because the more desirable outcomes, L_1 and L_2, (signified by their outcome values of 9 and 5, respectively) are imagined to be relatively likely (3 and 4 chances out of 10, respectively), whereas B is pessimistic, anticipating that the less desirable outcomes, L_3 and L_4, are more likely. Thus, partner A expects moving on to produce a better outcome than exists in the current situation (i.e., averaging across the four possible eventualities, moving on has a subjective expected value of 3.5 versus the outcome value of the known situation, 1) whereas B envisions a greater likelihood of poorer outcomes (subjective

---

[2] We use the device of listing subjective expected values in a separate table to be clear that these values are not part of the given (or objectively defined) situation, but rather represent the individuals' subjective impressions of future possibilities.

expected value of -1.1 versus 1).[3] Of course it need not be the case that the partners evaluate each imagined situation identically. Whether subjective expected values are the same or different depends on both components of the equation, evaluation and probability.

As depicted in Table E17.1B, neither partner has a vested interest. Both evaluate the current situation equivalently, and both rate the culinary desirability of each hypothetical restaurant that might be encountered identically. They differ only in the perceived likelihood of that hypothetical restaurant appearing. Thus, any divergence of their expected values (and resultant personal preferences) reflects the process of "filling in the blanks" in the face of indeterminate information, rather than differences in how known alternatives would be evaluated.

Dyads will differ in the nature of control over the choice at juncture J (see also Entry #21). Because of the ambiguity inherent in uncertain outcomes, "bird in the hand" may be particularly revealing of relationship-specific norms – how partners respond to each other's needs and preferences. This is not an issue given correspondence of interest – when both are optimistic or both are pessimistic – but conflicting interests require reconciliation for a joint decision to be made. Unilateral or absolute control is one possibility, in which one partner determines the dyad's decision, irrespective of the other's preferences (see Asymmetric Dependence, Entry #11). Also likely is the possibility that dyads adopt particular decision rules to control the reconciliation process. It can be seen in Table E17.1A that if either partner wishes to accept the existing, minimally acceptable outcome, the dyad will stay put; in other words, both must agree to abandon the status quo and the more pessimistic member's preference is likely to be binding.

Of course other decision rules are also possible. For example, their rule may be to discuss and "vote" on an issue until they agree. As shown in Table E17.2 below (at the end of this entry), the transition list indicates that if they disagree, the pair remains at juncture J for further discussion and expression of preferences. The simple fact that dyads can and do select among various decision rules underscores a central theoretical point: that there is more to understanding interdependent behavior than the mere preference for larger immediate outcome values.

Inherent in the logic of this situation is the use of an optimizing strategy: comparing outcomes readily at hand with the expected value of what the

---

[3] Although we have assumed no direct cost from forgoing the available option, in reality pursuing an unknown alternative may entail costs associated with uncertainty and unfulfilled needs, such as hunger in the restaurant example.

future may hold. Thus partners should prefer to move on if they anticipate improving their outcomes whereas they should stay put if movement
seems likely to diminish their outcomes. An alternative strategy involves
satisficing (March & Simon, 1958; Simon, 1990), whereby partners are concerned only with the discovery and selection of a minimally acceptable alternative (eating in a "good enough" restaurant). By satisficing, the actors
in Tables E17.1A and E17.1B would accept the available and known option
because its perceived rewards apparently exceed each one's comparison
level, allowing them to complete the task of finding a place to eat efficiently
and satisfyingly (albeit not optimally so). Satisficing is particularly likely
when the perceived marginal improvement of pursuing better alternatives
is small or ambiguous, and when time, information, and mental resources
are limited (Gigerenzer & Goldstein, 1996), as may often be the case in Bird
in the Hand situations.

17.3 Neighbors and Variants

Bird in the Hand involves interactive decision making with incomplete information, in that neither partner can know what the available alternative
outcomes are. A contrasting case is Negotiation (Entry #15) in which each
person knows what outcomes he or she will receive from the various possible combinations (i.e., either reaching or failing to reach an agreement),
but not necessarily the comparable outcomes for his or her partner. For
this reason, in Bird in the Hand, the process of decision control is necessarily more ambiguous, involving personal preferences for the known
contrasted with the possibility of gain weighed against the risk of loss. In
Negotiation, because partners have reasonably well-founded assessments
of their respective choices, behavior tends to more closely reflect the actual
value of their alternatives. Furthermore, in Negotiation situations, partners often enact strategies to obtain information possessed by the other
but hidden from themselves (e.g., spying, reading nonverbals, co-opting
third parties). Thus, these two situations differ primarily in the location
(and hence obtainability) of information.[4]

---

[4] One explanation for the so-called discontinuity effect – the tendency of groups to make
more competitive choices than individuals do – is the greater fear of exploitation that
groups engender compared to individuals (e.g., Insko, Schopler, Hoyle, Dardis, & Graetz,
1990). This seems more like the Negotiation situation than Bird in the Hand because group
members have a reasonable idea how their own entity intends to behave; only the other
entity's behavior is uncertain. Of course the future is never known with certainty; these
situations differ primarily in the degree of confidence about future prospects.

Another situation resembling Bird in the Hand in certain respects is Delay of Gratification (Entry #14). In that situation, individuals forgo immediately available but moderately valued outcomes to pursue a later but more highly valued outcome. The distinction is that in the present case, partners have at best educated hunches about the actual availability of the various potential outcomes that might be encountered, whereas in Delay of Gratification belief in a particular contingent sequence – "if outcome X is forgone now, then better outcome Y will result later" – is usually based on reasonably sound information. Thus degree of uncertainty plays a relatively smaller role in the decision to defer gratification, relative to the comparative value of in-hand versus later-won rewards. In contrast, in Bird in the Hand, multiple outcomes are possible, and relative probability assessments are key.

A second difference between these situations concerns the possibility of diminished outcomes. In the worst of circumstances, Delay of Gratification involves the failure to attain either the earlier, modest reward or the sought-after greater reward. In Bird in the Hand, because the decision to proceed is irreversible, subsequent junctures may be somewhat and perhaps even decidedly more negative than the original juncture was. For example, after passing up Dorothy's Country Kitchen in the hope of something better, Evan and Lori, our highway travelers, may encounter nothing but unpalatable fast-food restaurants while their hunger mounts.

Bird in the Hand differs from Encounters with Strangers (Entry #16), another of the situations involving incomplete information, in an important respect. In both, partners have inadequate information from which to evaluate the concrete situation and its alternatives; however, in Bird in the Hand person factors (i.e., the partner's tendency to cooperate, domineer, be cranky, etc.) are well-known whereas in Stranger the partner's dispositions are essentially unknown. This difference implies that behavior in the former situation will be relatively more revealing about dispositions and relationship-specific norms than in the latter situation. That is, because available information provides little basis for deciding, resolution of the partners' conflicting individual preferences is likely to reflect conditions of their relationship. For example, a caring attitude may be expressed in the act of setting aside personal preference in favor of a partner's desire. It is important to recognize that although both situations may reveal individual differences, only Bird in the Hand is likely to reveal relationship norms and habitual patterns of interaction. This is because interaction in ongoing relationships involves historically grounded expectations about the partner's behavior and response as well as consideration of possible future consequences. With strangers, there is no past to recollect and the future tends to matter little (unless, of course, the initial meeting develops into acquaintanceship).

Bird in the Hand differs from another situation involving the predicament of an uncertain future, Twists of Fate (Entry #18), which describes one partner's unilateral dependence on the other partner for needed outcomes (as when one individual asks another for a loan without the assurance of repayment) and in which there is nonsimultaneous exchange of outcomes (i.e., a loan is made at one time but repaid later). In contrast, the dependence in Bird in the Hand tends to be bilateral and simultaneous – both partners' outcomes will be determined at once by their joint decision. Although the partners in Bird in the Hand may have differential and/or asymmetric access to information, as discussed below, the desire to make the best of limited information in reaching a joint decision would likely foster open communication. Twists of Fate, in contrast, provides ample opportunities for either party, but especially the supplicant, to deceive the other or withhold information. As such, expectations about and attributions for the other's trustworthiness are likely to be more influential in the latter situation.

17.4 Interaction Processes and Person Factors

The influence that relationship partners exert on each other may be particularly evident in the Bird in the Hand situation, characterized as it is by the need to make irrevocable decisions with important consequences for both individuals on the basis of minimal information. Embedded in this process is a series of questions: On what basis do partners base their assessments about the relative likelihood of the various anticipated but essentially unknown situations that may appear "down the road?" Upon whose judgments do they rely for which types of decisions? And, how is control over the dyad's movement divided between the individuals?

17.4.1 *Choice of a Decision Rule*

Because decisions are made jointly, dyads must reconcile competing preferences (when they exist) about whether to accept available outcomes or to pursue an uncertain but potentially preferable future. The process of developing decision rules can be constructive or destructive for couples, involving choices between coordination and exchange, and between symmetry and asymmetry (see Entry #11, Asymmetric Dependence). For example, the decision depicted in Table E17.1A is controlled by the more pessimistic partner, inasmuch as either partner's preference to stay put is conclusive; in other words, both must consent in order to pursue the risky, uncertain future. In view of the priority typically assigned to averting losses over acquiring gains (discussed below), this conservative pattern seems more likely to the extent that the current situation is relatively favorable and the potential losses are great. A dual-career couple might decide not to accept new jobs in a different city unless the new positions were expected to be strongly advantageous to both.

Decision rules, which may be formal and explicit or informal and implicit, may be understood in two ways. Some research examines the consequences of different rules for collective choice (e.g., comparison of unanimity and non-unanimity rules in jury decisions; see Miller, 1989). More relevant to the present discussion is the observation that these rules may be informative as to the partners' orientation toward each other and their relationship. For example, a long-standing program of research by Clark, Mills, and their colleagues (e.g., Clark & Chrisman, 1994; Mills & Clark, 1994) indicates that partners in close or communal relationships tend to use a need-based rule – providing outcomes according to the partner's need – whereas acquaintances are more likely to use an equity rule – providing outcomes commensurate with inputs. In the Bird in the Hand situation, this implies designating decision control to the needier partner (e.g., whoever is hungrier). On the other hand, a dominant partner may decide what to do without considering a submissive partner's wishes. After a touchdown, a football coach decides whether to attempt a one- or two-point play without regard to the players' preferences (and without knowing whether or not the play will succeed). In both cases, the enacted decision rule illuminates the prevailing relationship norm.

Implicit in much of this discussion is the assumption of symmetry of informational interdependence – that is, that partners have more or less equivalent access to relevant information. This need not be the case, of course. Joint decisions often must be made in the face of uncertainty when groups members have different, usually specialized, expertise. Research by Stasser and his colleagues has examined conditions under which shared (i.e., possessed by all group members) and unshared (i.e., possessed by one or more persons, but not the entire group) information tends to influence group decisions. Across a variety of measures and discussion formats, their experiments show that shared information tends to be overrepresented in group discussions, decision processes, and memory (e.g., Stasser, 1999;

Stasser, Stewart, & Wittenbaum, 1995; Stasser & Titus, 1985). Thus, it is implied that in the Bird in the Hand situation, asymmetrically held information may not influence decisions to the extent that a rational analysis would suggest.

An important and common exception to this generalization vests decision control in the more knowledgeable partner. This occurs, for example, when information asymmetry reflects specialization in one or another type of information or judgment. The research cited above by Stasser and his colleagues shows that groups often defer to experts (i.e., persons possessing unshared information) when their expertise is explicitly identified and when group discussion is structured to bring out such information. In fact, work groups are often designed to take advantage of distributed expertise (Moreland, Argote, & Krishnan, 1996). Likewise, friends and romantic dyads may seek to optimize their performance on certain tasks by allocating responsibility for particular roles or decisions to the individual with greater expertise in that domain, as shown in Wegner, Erber, and Raymond's (1991) description of "transactive memory" systems. (In that research, college student couples performed better on a memory task when each partner spontaneously took responsibility for memorizing information in categories with which he or she was naturally more familiar. Couples performed worse when categories were randomly assigned by the experimenters, thereby disregarding the partners' natural areas of expertise.) Thus, decisions about where to stop for dinner might be delegated to the partner with more insight about highway dining possibilities. Assignments of this sort may be made on the basis of expertise, vested interest (i.e., allowing the needier partner to decide), experience (i.e., when one partner has made such choices successfully in the past), or perhaps just feeling lucky.

Rather than enacting formal decision rules, dyads often do so informally, through persuasive communication. The ambiguity of information about the future places a premium on the ability to convince a partner that one's personal prognostication is more plausible. For example, positions that are extreme in the socially valued direction are more likely to prevail, as is suggested by the phenomenon of group polarization – in fact, the presence of several individuals in a group advocating a risky decision may under certain circumstances lead the group to adopt even riskier alternatives than any of the individuals had previously favored (Myers & Lamm, 1976). Receptiveness to persuasion also matters: In one study of married couples, the person with the wider preference latitude (that is, the partner who defines more of the available choices as acceptable, as indicated by positive entries in the value columns of Table E17.1B) tended to be more persuadable (Schopler, Hoyle, Dotson, & Marshall, 1988). We further speculate that in Bird in the Hand situations, partners with lesser power within the relationship or who see the other's preference as less objectionable would be more likely to concede.

Finally, the nature of the discussion process that leads to a particular decision rule may also be important. As described in Entry #16 (Encounters with Strangers), partners typically are more satisfied with and likely to accept decisions that follow from procedures perceived to be fair – in this instance, the opportunity for both partners to voice a preference and have it considered openly and respectfully by the other (Tyler, 1990). This process of communication and responsive listening is widely considered to be essential to constructive conflict resolution, especially in marriage (e.g., Christensen & Walcyznski, 1997).

17.4.2 Decisions to Enter/Stay in a Relationship

The decision to enter and then to continue a relationship with a particular partner often follows the pattern of the Bird in the Hand situation. Imagine Jane and Pablo, who have been dating for some time and are considering marriage. Although both find the relationship moderately satisfying, neither feels that the relationship is perfect. Deciding whether or not to commit to marriage requires comparing their current situation to the perceived likelihood of establishing a more satisfying relationship with alternative partners. Because most people engage in one romantic relationship at a time, their future prospects are necessarily speculative, requiring each partner to choose between the known, somewhat positive relationship and the uncertain possibility of a better relationship with someone else, recognizing that better alternatives may not appear. This choice is likely to reflect the sort of subjective assessments that are represented in Table E17.1B, incorporating social comparisons, prior experiences, and other person factors. Decisions of this sort are common not only in the initiation of romantic relationships but also in decisions about dissolution and divorce.

In most cases, romantic relationships are formed (and continued, when a decision about possible termination must be made) only when both individuals decide to accept the other. In other words, the desire by either partner to exit the relationship is usually sufficient to cause its termination. Typically, the partner who is less dependent on the relationship – that is, the one who evaluates the current situation as relatively less favorable than available alternatives and who has less invested in the relationship – has greater influence in determining whether it continues. Existing research shows that when partners perceive that better opportunities for satisfying important needs are available to them outside of an existing relationship, breakups are more likely (Drigotas & Rusbult, 1992; South & Lloyd, 1995). On the other hand, derogation of alternatives (i.e., assigning potential alternative partners a lower subjective expected value [SEV]) is one psychological mechanism for bolstering the sense of security in an ongoing relationship given an uncertain future (Rusbult, 1983).

This aspect of transition control – assessing the favorability of one relationship (whether real or imagined) against possible alternatives – may help explain the well-known and well-documented *matching hypothesis*, which proposes that romantic partners tend to be approximately matched in terms of their social assets (e.g., attractiveness, popularity; Walster, Walster & Berscheid, 1978). Although often attributed to people's desire to bond with similar others, a simulation study by Kalick and Hamilton (1986) suggests that de facto matching may result even when the preference is for more desirable partners, inasmuch as the most desirable individuals are likely to pair off with each other, leaving individuals of lesser social desirability no option but to pair off among themselves.[5] Presumably, then, individuals possessing greater assets would decline to enter relationships with others of lesser social capital, because they anticipate acceptance by more desirable others. Similarly, anticipated rejection, which presumably incorporates prior feedback about one's relative social position, may lead people to shun potential higher status partners (e.g., Shanteau & Nagy, 1979).

17.4.3 Loss/Gain Focus

Other things being equal, people tend to be more attuned to the prospect of loss than to the potential for gain. Research on prospect theory (Kahneman & Tversky, 1984) indicates that decision making tends to focus relatively more on the possibility of loss than on the chance of gain, even when the outcomes have identical expected value. This conservative principle is implied in the adage for which this situation is named, "a bird in the hand is worth two in the bush," in the sense that the possible loss of a single bird is proposed to outweigh the potential of gaining an additional bird. Among several suggested explanations for this phenomenon is the greater evolutionary significance of losses relative to gains. Threats to existing circumstances may have had more immediate and direct adaptive consequences for the individual's survival and welfare than opportunities

---

[5] A simple classroom demonstration of this effect is described by Ellis and Kelley (1999).

for profit. Guaranteeing one's safety, in other words, may matter more in adaptive terms than enhancing one's resources.

Higgins (1998) and his colleagues have identified several important differences between adopting a loss-avoidance or a gain-attainment focus for self-regulation, labeled as prevention and promotion, respectively. With a prevention focus, people aim primarily to insure against errors of commission and to preserve their current outcomes. On the other hand, a promotion focus engenders sensitivity to the possibility for gains and a desire to capitalize on opportunities that arise. Promotion and prevention orientations are systematically related to the manner in which people approach decision-making tasks, as well as to their emotional reactions. The application of this research in the present situation seems clear: A prevention focus should maximize tendencies to live with the current circumstances, assuming they surpass some minimally acceptable threshold, whereas a promotion focus should increase the likelihood of forgoing the current juncture in the hope of attaining better outcomes later.

Numerous situational and person factors make promotion and prevention more or less likely. Irrevocability of a dyad's choice is one such factor – revocable decisions diminish the risks associated with a promotion focus, allowing partners to return to their prior circumstances should the new situation prove less desirable. Irrevocable decisions, especially when the stakes are high, may also influence the choice of a decision rule, inasmuch as both partners will need to live with the outcomes of their decision (e.g., a happily married couple might decide to become parents only if both desired to do so). Time pressures may also influence the focus on potential gains or losses; for example, the need for quick decisions may encourage people to stay with acceptable, albeit potentially suboptimal, options (Kruglanski & Webster, 1996). Both components of the SEVs of Table E17.1B are important. It seems unlikely, for example, that a person would elect to undergo very risky elective surgery for a comparatively small improvement in life quality, just as it would seem unlikely that one would have such surgery with a low probability for success. Among dispositional factors that would influence the choice between sticking with known, acceptable outcomes and an indeterminate possibility of better outcomes are sensation seeking (which fosters risk taking for the prospect of novel and intense experiences; Zuckerman, 1994), the relative dominance of reward-approaching and punishment-avoiding motives (e.g., Elliot, 1997; Gable, Reis, & Elliot, 2000; Gray, 1990), and attachment insecurity (i.e., the preference for proximity to a secure base).

The relative focus on losses and gains is relevant to the interdependence aspects of Bird in the Hand situations in another way. When the decision to pursue an uncertain future results in poorer outcomes than had been available, partners may experience feelings of regret. As Gilovich and Medvec (1994) have demonstrated, short-term regrets tend to focus on errors of commission – actions that ended up badly. Over the long term, however, regrets tend to focus on errors of omission – things that one failed to do. Exiting the transition list at a point with relatively low outcomes invites this latter form of regret (e.g., "we should've looked for a better restaurant"). In some cases, anticipation of either form of regret may impel one choice or the other. That is, accepting the certain but lower outcome precludes commission-based regret, whereas risking the unsure future precludes regrets about not having tried to do better. In the dyadic context, regret may engender recrimination ("I told you so"), particularly when later events reveal that the partner's preferences were incorrect. In certain circumstances, the more optimistic partner might acquiesce out of the desire to avoid possible recriminations.

Recrimination is, of course, an attributional process, and it seems likely that the seemingly ubiquitous tendency to seek after-the-fact explanations for events would be enhanced in situations where ambiguity at the time of decision is eventually resolved one way or the other. Within marriage, the role of attributions has been studied extensively (see Bradbury & Fincham, 1990, for a review), in part because the process of "blaming" may contribute directly to the long-term success and stability of a marriage.[6] A common finding is that, other things being equal, spouses in dissatisfied couples more readily blame each other for negative outcomes and occurrences than satisfied spouses do. This pattern suggests motivational possibilities contributing to the choice of a dyadic decision rule. For example, Lori might yield to Evan's desire to dine at Dorothy's to gain the attributional upper hand: Not only does she avoid the likelihood of blame should her preference prove unsuccessful, but she also can fault Evan if the meal at Dorothy's turns out to be unpalatable.

17.4.4 Person Factors

The relative paucity of concrete information in this situation creates an opportunity for personality effects to be revealed. As discussed in chapter 3, the impact of individual differences will be most evident in situations

---

[6] Of course the causes and consequences of blaming are also important in most ongoing dyads and groups.

that permit (but do not mandate) expression of those factors. The two stages involved in Bird in the Hand, assessment and resolution, tap different types of dispositions. As already discussed, the resolution stage affords expression of interpersonal dispositions relevant to coordination and control, such as dominance, generosity, and need for control. Individual differences local to a particular relationship may also be important (e.g., faith in a partner's judgment). The informational uncertainty inherent in Bird in the Hand suggests that the former stage, assessment, is particularly likely to reveal the influence of individual differences relevant to estimating with little objective guidance the likelihood of good and bad outcomes. Optimism-pessimism is one such individual difference variable.

Optimism describes a general tendency to expect that future outcomes will be relatively positive, whereas pessimism refers to a more negative expectancy about future outcomes (Scheier & Carver, 1993). Considerable research suggests that all other things being equal, people tend to evaluate their future prospects relatively more favorably than is objectively warranted, across such domains as health, relationships, and academic success (e.g., Taylor & Brown, 1988; Weinstein, 1980). Over and above this general tendency, there are stable individual differences in dispositional optimism (Scheier, Carver, & Bridges, 1994). Of course these dispositions may be situation specific as well, such as when people "feel lucky" at the casino or decide to be adventurous in picking a mountain to climb.

Compared to dispositional pessimists, dispositional optimists tend to be healthier and happier and fare better in various activities. For example, in one study optimistic men recovered more quickly and more fully from coronary artery bypass graft surgery (Scheier et al., 1989). Other studies have shown that optimism about a relationship's future predicts greater commitment (Martz et al., 1998), higher levels of satisfaction and stability one year later (Murray & Holmes, 1997), and greater longevity for long-distance relationships (Helgeson, 1994). It is believed that these effects are caused by the different coping patterns associated with optimism and pessimism. Optimistic expectations lead people to adopt more adaptive coping strategies: for example, focusing directly on problem solving, putting problems in perspective, persistence, and making the best of difficult situations, all of which may facilitate positive movement toward a goal. On the other hand, pessimistic expectations tend to induce resignation, avoidance, and acceptance of the status quo, strategies that often hinder development. Of course these results refer to situations in which optimistic coping is likely to facilitate positive outcomes. Unrealistic optimism, a tendency to deny realistic risks, is associated with an unwillingness to engage in appropriate protective behaviors (e.g., practicing unsafe sex) and potentially poorer outcomes (e.g., Davidson & Prkachin, 1997).

In the typical Bird in the Hand situation, because the partners have little if any objective basis on which to generate expectations, it seems likely that dispositional tendencies to anticipate relatively better or worse future outcomes would be important. A pessimistic outlook suggests that future opportunities are unlikely to improve one's situation over the minimally acceptable present, and thus encourages exiting the situation selection process at a relatively less rewarding juncture, insuring realization of existing outcomes but precluding the possibility of better ones. In many life circumstances, of course, better outcomes may accrue from active pursuit of uncertain but potentially rewarding opportunities.

The necessity for making decisions about an uncertain future inherent in Bird in the Hand also highlights the impact of person factors relevant to information processing. One such factor that has received considerable research is the "need for closure," described as a sense of personal urgency to obtain and then maintain a sense of mental closure in uncertain circumstances (Kruglanski & Webster, 1996). Persons relatively high in the need for closure tend to accept minimally satisfactory decisions sooner and tend to be less thorough in their consideration of potential alternatives, similar to the "satisficing" strategy discussed earlier in this entry. A somewhat similar trait described by Sorrentino and his colleagues (Sorrentino, Holmes, Hanna, & Sharp, 1995; Sorrentino, Roney, & Hanna, 1992) distinguishes between uncertainty-oriented and certainty-oriented individuals. Given uncertainty, the former tend to seek clarity by attempting to master unknown features of the situation whereas the latter prefer to adhere to those features that are already known. In dyadic relationships, trust tends to be highest among certainty-oriented individuals, in part reflecting their emphasis on known qualities of the status quo. Both of these person factors are made salient by the central dilemma inherent in this situation: choosing between tangible, available, and acceptable outcomes and an indeterminate future. High-need-for-closure and certainty-oriented individuals seem likely to find the status quo relatively more desirable, whereas low-need-for-closure and uncertainty-oriented persons would be more likely to wish to explore potentially greater future prospects. Just how dyads whose members differ in these information-processing tendencies would go about reconciling discrepancies highlights the important role played by coordination in information processing in interpersonal situations.

17.5 Transition List Representations

TABLE E17.1A. *Transition List Representing Joint Decision Making with Uncertainty about Alternative Situations with Conjunctive Control over the Decision to Go On*

Junctures	Options	Possible Selections	Outcomes for A and B		Transition to Next Juncture
[J	(a1-Stay; a2 -Go)	a1b1	−,	−	K]
[	(b1-Stay; b2 -Go)	a1b2	−,	−	K]
[		a2b1	−,	−	K]
[		a2b2	−,	−	L]
[K	(a3, b3)	a3b3	+1,	+1	X]
[L	(a4, b4)	a4b4	?,	?	X]

TABLE E17.1B. *Dyad Members' Perceptions of Possible Alternative Situations*

Possible Situation	Partner A		Partner B		Partner A SEV	Partner B SEV
	Probability*	Value	Probability*	Value		
L_1	.3	9	.1	9	2.7	0.9
L_2	.4	5	.2	5	2.0	1.0
L_3	.2	−3	.4	−3	−0.6	−1.2
L_4	.1	−6	.3	−6	−0.6	−1.8
					3.5	−1.1

* Probability refers to the partner's estimate of the likelihood of occurrence of each of four possible situations. Value refers to the reward value for the partner of each situation were it to occur. The SEV (subjective expected value) for each partner is the summed product of these estimates.

TABLE E17.2. *Transition List Representing Joint Decision Making with Agreement Required for Any Decision*

Junctures	Options	Possible Selections	Outcomes for A and B		Transition to Next Juncture
[J	(a1-Stay; a2 -Go)	a1b1	−,	−	K]
[	(b1-Stay; b2 -Go)	a1b2	−,	−	J]
[		a2b1	−,	−	J]
[		a2b2	−,	−	L]
[K	(a3, b3)	a3b3	+1,	+1	X]
[L	(a4, b4)	a4b4	?,	?	X]

Entry #18

Twists of Fate

Coping with an Uncertain Future

18.1 Examples

Mike learns that the company where he has worked for 9 years is downsizing in his division and that he is losing his job. His supervisor explains that Mike and his colleagues have become outmoded in their computer skills since the advent of new software and that it is cheaper for the company to hire a smaller number of new people rather than to retrain them. This sudden and unexpected turn of events leaves Mike feeling very dependent on his wife Susan for both financial help and emotional support while he updates his computer knowledge. He feels quite vulnerable because Susan is very secure in her job and it is not at all clear that circumstances would ever turn around in a way that would permit him to reciprocate the help he now needs. He comforts himself with the thought that Susan values him and will be willing to help in his time of need. After all, her vow was to care for him, "for better or for worse." Despite Mike's hopes, what factors are likely to influence Susan's decision about whether to honor this pledge and provide costly support to him over an uncertain period of time?

In a different context, Brian and Jason have been close friends for over 10 years and have enjoyed a lot of good times together. The past 6 months have been extremely difficult for Jason. First his marriage ended and he had to make the many adjustments involved in adapting to a single life. Then he discovered that he had prostate cancer and would have to undergo a long regimen of radiation therapy. The treatment center was over 50 miles away and he was warned that the daily treatments would be very fatiguing.

John Holmes had primary responsibility for preparation of this entry.

Jason feels that he could cope with the radiation and keep up his job if Brian would take some time off work and drive him to the health center. However, he knows that this is a lot to ask of Brian. Worst of all, what if the treatment isn't fully successful in restoring his health and he never has the opportunity to return such a favor when Brian is in a position of needing help? Jason finds himself preoccupied with the issue of whether he can risk asking his friend for help: Will Brian prove to be only a "fair-weather friend"? And if Brian helps, will Jason feel permanently indebted to him?

18.2 Conceptual Description

18.2.1 The Basic Situation

The Twists of Fate situation is in fact a very simple one, though the solution to the dilemma it presents may be quite complex. The situation describes a set of circumstances in which one partner in a relationship might unexpectedly find himself or herself in a position of extreme unilateral dependence on the other for costly help. The negative, even catastrophic events that might lead to such variability in degree of need are likely to be somewhat rare and unpredictable. Nevertheless, the vicissitudes of life are such that circumstances can indeed occur in which individuals find themselves in serious need of a friend's or partner's support or help. Twists of Fate involving ill health, personal problems, job stress or loss, an unpredictably hostile environment, the death of close kin, and so on cannot typically be fully anticipated or controlled. Further, reversals of fortune, and thus times of unilateral dependence on a partner for costly help, are not likely to follow a predictable path where partners can simply take turns responding to each other's needs.

Consequently, individuals face dilemmas about requiring and providing costly assistance in circumstances that do not guarantee that opportunities for achieving fair and equal exchange will occur. Thus, the question concerns the particular conditions in a relationship, or the personal attributes of the person giving or needing help, that would influence the potential helper's decision to provide benefits under such circumstances of uncertainty.

The transition list in Table E18.1 below (at the end of this entry) represents these circumstances more formally. It describes the general situation in which *either* of two friends or intimates could find that a twist of fate (f1 or f2) results in a situation of relatively extreme unilateral dependence (K or L) where serious help is needed from the other. The ?? symbols indicate that information is missing as to what event will occur. This uncertainty, as well as the relatively small chance of either event occurring during some period of time, is noted by the low probability value $p = .10$ for each of f1 and f2. Examining one such possibility, "fate" might create circumstances (f1) at juncture J such that A finds that B is in serious need of help at juncture K. This unilateral dependence involves B being subject to extreme Partner Control by A, having to rely on his or her "good intentions" and prosocial motivations (see Entry #11).

In our initial example, when Mike unexpectedly lost his job, he became unilaterally dependent on Susan's financial and emotional support while he retrained and searched for new work. For Susan (A) to benefit Mike (B) and provide much needed help (+50) by selecting a1, Susan will experience a large direct cost (−20) and perhaps a smaller indirect cost from forfeiting enjoyment of another activity a2 (i.e., a possible Actor effect of +5). In more tangible terms, Susan would bear the direct cost of being responsible for supporting Mike financially and for having his concerns become temporarily paramount in their relationship. Also, by supporting Mike, Susan suffers the indirect costs of not taking planned extra time off work and of spending less time sharing activities with other friends.

The critical feature of this overall extended situation is that person A (Susan) cannot be confident (after helping, in returning to juncture J) that twists of fate will result in subsequent situations of unequal need that would permit turn-taking possibilities where the roles are reversed and person B (Mike) could *reciprocate* the favor. That is, there is no guarantee in dealing with the predicament of an uncertain future that juncture L will occur in a timely fashion and permit a "fair" balancing of exchange. Indeed, the chances of that occurring in the next period of time are somewhat small, $p = .10$. Juncture K, in which B is again in need of help, might occur instead, either because a problem such as ill health continues, or because a new problem arises. Or, of course, the chances are high ($p = .80$) that situations of serious unilateral dependence will not occur at all. Thus, from A's perspective, the decision is, "Should I help or not?" in a situation in which B is in serious need of support and there is no assurance that such benefits will be reciprocated. From B's point of view, the question is, "Can I count on A to help under these uncertain circumstances?"

18.2.2 *An Evolutionary Perspective: The Banker's Paradox*
Evolutionary theorists suggest that for our hunter-gatherer ancestors, this recurrent predicament constituted an important adaptive problem (Tooby & Cosmides, 1996). Illness, injury, bad luck in foraging, physical

or environmental challenges, or the inability to resist attack alone might all have posed reversals of fortune that could affect individuals' survival. Thus the ability to attract assistance during such sudden and unanticipated reversals of welfare would have important selective consequences.

The evolutionary perspective helps us understand why the solution to this problem is complex. Natural selection would seem to favor decision rules that cause others to desert you just when your need for help was greatest, because you are then most likely to be seen as a costly liability. Indeed, Tooby and Cosmides (1996) illustrate the dilemma by describing what they have called the *Banker's Paradox*. As they tell it,

> Bankers have a limited amount of money, and must choose whom to invest in. Each choice is a gamble: taken together, they must ultimately yield a net profit or the banker will go out of business. This set of incentives leads to a common complaint about the banking system: that bankers will only loan money to individuals who do not need it. The harsh irony of the Banker's Paradox is this: just when individuals need money most desperately, they are also the poorest credit risks and, therefore, the least likely to be selected to receive a loan. (p. 131)

Robert Frost made the same point more cryptically: "A bank is a place where they lend you an umbrella in fair weather and ask for it back when it begins to rain." Thus the problem that individuals face when they are in the banker's shoes is whether to help someone who is at least temporarily a credit risk, a person who may not be able to pay back the "loan." Conversely, if individuals are in the shoes of the person needing help, the concern is whether there is something about them in particular that would encourage the banker to take a chance and provide support. The interpersonal processes functionally "designed" to deal with this dilemma are the focus of this entry.

18.3 Variants and Neighbors

18.3.1 *Turn-Taking Situations*
A neighboring situation involves circumstances in which the occurrence of more "everyday" negative events results in variations of modest, or at least less extreme, unilateral dependence. These more "ordinary" variations in degree of need result in far more frequent instances in which one person needs help and are thus more likely to statistically "even out" over time. Such circumstances present more opportunities for shifting the "needy" and "helper" roles and achieving some sort of overall balance or fairness in exchange over an extended period of time.

Table E18.2 below presents the transition list for a Turn-Taking situation. The amount of help needed by the unilaterally dependent person in this situation is depicted as more modest (+15) than in the Twists of Fate situation (+50) in Table E18.1. Further, the more frequent, everyday variation of such needs is represented by a transition list in which the chances of f1 and f2 each occurring during any period of time are high (p = .45). (Over long periods of time, the cumulative probability of both events occurring would be extremely high, say, 90%.) Thus, once K has occurred, it is likely that the *opportunity* would then be available to reverse the helper and recipient roles at juncture L at some later point in time, and so on.

Such situations permit a rough balancing over time of instances in which one partner could benefit most from help, so that turn-taking opportunities occur. Essentially, the list describes a reality where fate is obliging in allowing the possibility (though not the necessity) of "fair" exchange. For example, in more normal circumstances when Mike had not lost his job, he might have asked Susan to take up the slack in household duties that resulted from his encountering a very busy time at work. Susan might have helped with the expectation that Mike would return the favor in kind, or help her in some other, comparable way at a later point in time.

The distinction between the Twists of Fate situation and the Turn-Taking situation involving the potential for reciprocation over time may sometimes be difficult to make, both for scientists and the individuals actually involved. Consequently, the uncertain future, Twists of Fate situation in Table E18.1 could be *incorrectly construed* by person A as the Turn-Taking situation depicted in Table E18.2. That is, once juncture K has occurred, juncture L could be *seen* as more likely to occur in the future, reflecting a type of Gambler's Fallacy, Optimism (see Entry #17), or a Belief in a Just World (Lerner, 1980). As we will see later, the given situation would then have been transformed in subtle, but important, ways.

18.3.2 *Variants of Turn-Taking Situations*

Reciprocation or turn taking is obviously an important mechanism for dealing with any situation where one person receives clearly superior benefits at a particular point in time. In earlier Entries we noted that *turn taking* involving reciprocated solutions or tit-for-tat norms is a common means of preserving equity and fairness across recurring situations where asymmetrical outcomes may occur in localized circumstances (see for instance, the Threat situation, Entry #6, or joint control problems such as the Hero situation, Entry #8).

18.4 Interaction Processes and Person Factors

The important general question raised by the two neighboring situations described in this Entry is how individuals deal with imbalances in outcomes in localized circumstances within the extended, longer term context of their relationships. We suggest that the answer to this question is different depending on which situation is being considered. The adaptational processes contributing to finding a solution to the Twists of Fate problem, involving more extreme and infrequent unilateral dependence, will require the development of mutual agreements involving "communal norms" (cf. Clark & Mills, 1979). Communal norms are rules specifying that each person responds noncontingently to the other's needs as they occur, with no expectation of reciprocation. In contrast, the processes contributing to coping with the Turn-Taking situation involving more everyday, modest imbalances in need will require the development of rules of reciprocity in exchange. Benefits would be given with the expectation of receiving a comparable benefit in return. Each set of processes or "solutions" relevant to the different situations will be considered in turn.

18.4.1 *Coping with Twists of Fate behind a "Veil of Ignorance"*
It is usually not clear as a relationship begins and two people become more interdependent which person is more likely to find himself or herself unilaterally dependent on the partner for help. As the term "twists of fate" implies, such occasions are difficult if not impossible to predict given an uncertain future. Thus the solutions for dealing with this problem will often be developed in ignorance of knowing whether one would on average be a net provider or net recipient of help. Approaching the Twists of Fate situation behind such a *"veil of ignorance"* (Rawls, 1971), you could imagine unexpectedly finding *yourself* in the more dependent role. Facing that prospect, you would certainly feel safer and more secure knowing that a partner would respond unconditionally to your needs and take care of you. But of course, the downside of agreeing to a communal norm is that you might end up in the net provider role, providing costly help without expectation of repayment.

In this regard, the philosopher John Rawls (1971) has argued that fair decision-making rules are most likely to be developed when individuals are informed of the nature of justice dilemmas but do not know what their own position will be within them. As an example of this principle, Thibaut and Walker (1975) demonstrated empirically that rules for adjudicating legal cases achieved under a veil of ignorance were most likely to be judged as fair to both parties. Following this logic, when people negotiate the "rules" for dealing with Twists of Fate behind a veil of ignorance, they are likely to be able to agree on useful and mutually satisfying commitments to follow communal norms.

Thus in the face of uncertainty about what the future holds, people are likely to *hedge their bets* and forge an agreement where each partner is committed to responding to the other's needs as they occur. In essence, when future prospects are risky, it pays to pool the risks. In this sense, such a *mutually advantageous* agreement represents a type of *security insurance*. Agreements featuring mutual loyalty and commitment to the relationship serve the desire for a sense of felt security in the face of uncertainty, quelling considerations of shorter term self-interest. Thus the understanding, often made explicit in ceremonies, is that a relationship is "for better or for worse," that friends or intimates can be counted on to "be there" for someone in a time of serious need. A "true friend" can be depended on in good times and bad times, for richer or for poorer ("a friend in need is a friend indeed..."). We will deal later with the important issue of what conditions result in a person feeling secure that such agreements will be honored in times of great need.

18.4.2 Coping with Everyday Imbalances in Exchange through Reciprocation

In contrast to this way of thinking, individuals might choose to help, not because they are straightforwardly responding to their partners' needs, but because there are opportunities in a situation for *reciprocation* by the partner that permit fair and equal exchange to be ultimately achieved over a period of time. Responding to this *different* situation, they might help now with the clear expectation that the partner will respond in kind in the future. The terms of such quid pro quo exchanges may be more elastic in close relationships, involving a long line of credit and considerable flexibility in deciding on an "equivalent" benefit (Holmes, 1981). Nevertheless, helping may still be instrumental to eliciting later, improved benefits for oneself, so that exchange is at least implicitly (sometimes quite explicitly) contingent on expected returns (Batson, 1993).

18.4.3 Communal and Exchange Relationships

The contrasting rules or norms that might develop to deal with the two different situations analyzed above are very similar to those proposed by Clark and Mills (1979) to govern the giving and receiving of benefits in interpersonal relationships. To use their terminology, in an *exchange* "relationship," benefits are given with the expectation of reciprocity, of receiving a comparable benefit in return. The quid pro quo of the marketplace is the dominant rule. In contrast, in a *communal* "relationship," benefits are given in response to needs as they occur, or to demonstrate a general concern for the other person, with no expectation of repayment.

From the point of view of the present analysis, the two different rules could be solutions to different *problems*, one involving coping with unpredictable and potentially quite significant examples of unilateral dependence, the other dealing with more common exchanges where turn taking or reciprocation provide a solution to temporarily unbalanced "accounts." Further, we surmise that solutions to *both* problems must be developed in most long-term, adult close relationships (though not in relationships of unequal dependence, such as parent and child). Thus there is no reason that the two rules could not coexist within a single relationship, to varying degrees and with varying "weights." From our perspective then, it is more appropriate to use such terms as "communal" and "exchange" in reference to rules or norms for behavior in certain situations rather than for describing types of *relationships* per se (as do Clark and Mills, 1979, and Fiske, 1992). People in particular kinds of relationships might indeed experience a situational "profile" with a heavier weighting of one type of situation, but their "relationship" can then be partly defined by specifying the situational "mix."

The distinction we make between the two situations also seems relevant to an important debate in the literature on close relationships. Batson (1993) has criticized the ideas of Clark and Mills, suggesting that the psychological difference between the two types of "relationships" is less than is imagined. From our perspective, his point may relate to the *actual* similarity between the two situations – they are indeed "neighbors" in the space of interpersonal problems. Further, as we discussed previously, people may often misconstrue Twists of Fate circumstances as Turn-Taking situations.

The crux of Batson's argument is that there is too strong an assumption in Clark and Mills's work that individuals in communal relationships have altruistic motives, rather than instrumental ones. He contends that even in "communal" relationships, benefits are often bestowed with an eye to gaining reciprocal self-benefits, including having one's own needs met in return and having a rewarding relationship. He suggests that exchange principles are still present in communal relationships, but the reciprocity is less explicit and can occur over extended periods of time. Further, benefits will not always be exchanged in kind, but instead may vary in type so long as they are comparable in terms of value. Basically, he suggests that although the exchange process in long-term, close relationships may be more subtle, Clark and Mills have not made a compelling case that reciprocity principles are not still operating.

Part of Batson's criticism rests on his concerns about how Clark and Mills have often operationally represented the term "communal." In many of their experiments, they try to manipulate the *desire* for a certain type of relationship. For instance, a typical procedure to create an "exchange-relationship" condition involves undergraduate males learning that an attractive young woman, with whom they expect to work closely on a task, is married and thus "unavailable" in terms of forming a closer relationship. In the "communal-relationship" condition, the young woman is single, a transfer student who is eager to meet new friends. Using this paradigm, the authors found that participants in the exchange condition working on a joint task together with the young married woman liked her more when she reciprocated their help and less when her request for help was not linked to a promise of repayment. Conversely, in the communal condition, reciprocated helping by the "available" young woman actually *decreased* liking for her, presumably because her actions could be seen as rejecting the possibility of a communal relationship. However, noncontingent requests for help on her part, which indicate a desire to follow communal rules, resulted in increased liking for her (Clark & Mills, 1979).

At a conceptual level, the latter results do not seem consistent with Batson's focus on instrumental, reciprocity concerns as the critical motivation in relationships. However, Batson had concerns as to whether responses in such experimental situations tell us anything about real, ongoing communal versus exchange relationships. Indeed, Clark and Mills (1993) acknowledge that there are real differences between the two settings. However, they believe it is noteworthy that participants who want to make a good impression and perhaps start a relationship with the "available" young woman take care to follow the *rules* of communal relationships (whatever their motivation for doing so). The rules are apparently so well known that they provide a "language" that clearly communicates one's intentions. Clark and Mills (1993) also point out that the results in studies using the "desired relationship" manipulation directly parallel the results obtained in their studies when behavior toward close friends versus strangers is compared.

In addition, the authors have provided evidence that individuals in communal relationships typically have little concern with later reciprocation.

For instance, Clark (1984) showed that individuals desiring a communal relationship avoided keeping track of the other's inputs on a joint task, even when the other had no way of knowing whether they were doing so. In contrast, individuals desiring an exchange relationship were more likely to monitor the other's inputs. Clark, Mills, and Corcoran (1989) demonstrated a similar pattern comparing the behavior of close friends and strangers. When the other person was making substantial contributions to the joint task, individuals actually monitored inputs more closely if the other were a stranger than a friend. In contrast, they monitored more carefully when friends might need help. These results suggest that responding to needs is foremost among friends, not keeping a balanced set of books. Of course, even impressive results such as these do not demonstrate the extent to which individuals are willing to follow a truly communal rule when the real-life costs are more substantial, the basis for the Twists of Fate situation.

Different Adaptations to Different Situations. There are no easy answers in the debate between Clark and Mills and Batson over whether communal rules are followed for truly "altruistic" reasons or, instead, for motivations that are "ultimately" self-serving. Kelley and Thibaut (1985) reacted to similar earlier discussions about the nature of altruism by arguing that excessive cynicism "will result if 'altruism' can exist only if there is some form not explainable *in any way* by 'self-interests'" (p. 31). Even helping behavior governed by innate altruistic impulses might not qualify, on the grounds that it serves the actor's genetic "interests" (see also Pinker, 1997, p. 401). Kelley and Thibaut contend that while historically and developmentally some form of self-interest probably underlies most prosocial tendencies, that would not preclude the possibility that contemporaneously, prosocial behavior might reflect a direct, functionally autonomous concern for another person's interests. Further, such genuinely altruistic impulses can *coexist* with thoughts of ultimate gain and reciprocity without the existence of the latter rendering the former somehow counterfeit. From this point of view, altruism is best viewed as a matter of degree rather than as a categorical construct.

It is perhaps ironic that Batson argues that "communal" forms of behavior are actually brought about by rules or strategies involving "enlightened self-interest" that maintain long-term reciprocity, *rather* than by truly "altruistic" motivations. This is because reciprocity itself has been seen by some theorists as an important adaptational route for the evolution of "altruistic" interpersonal tendencies (along with kin-selected altruism). Among others, Tooby and Cosmides (1996) contend that the mutual provisioning of benefits in dyads, based on cooperative, tit-for-tat sequences of contingent favors in situations like that in Table E18.2, could certainly have evolutionary roots. "Reciprocal altruism" might develop because of the likely selection benefits reciprocity provides to dyads through "gains in trade," that is, through mutual profit.

However, consistent with theorizing in social psychology (e.g., Clark & Mills, 1979; Holmes, 1981), Tooby and Cosmides argue that "such narrow exchange contingency does not capture the phenomenology or indeed the phenomenon of friendship" (p. 131). They suggest that people report experiencing a spontaneous pleasure when they can help close others, without any expectation of reciprocation. Further, explicit linkage between favors is often taken as a sign of a lack of friendship, as Clark and Mills have indeed shown. Instead, Tooby and Cosmides propose a further form of altruism that developed from individuals being forced to deal with the predicament of an uncertain future and sudden twists of fate.

As we observed earlier, the "design features" or adaptational processes that contribute to the solution to this problem involve mutual adherence to rules involving responding to each other's needs as they occur without efforts to maintain a fair balance of exchange, or what Clark and Mills have called communal norms. The critical point, made both in our analysis and by Tooby and Cosmides, is that rules involving communal responding versus long-term exchange reciprocity may have developed as *solutions* or adaptations to quite *different* problems in the first place, problems described abstractly in Tables E18.1 and E18.2, respectively. Thus from this perspective, Batson would sometimes be right, sometimes wrong in interpreting the cause of individuals' apparently costly sacrifices in helping partners in times of need as reflecting expectations of reciprocity.

While evolutionary theorists might contend that distinct genetic forms of altruism would have developed to deal with these different circumstances, the social psychological perspective of interdependence theory would simply suggest that even contemporaneously, the solutions are functional in dealing with the two types of problems. As an example of this logic, people should be driven to develop communal sharing rules in domains of their environment in which they are subject to the whims of fate. Pinker (1997, pp. 505–06) provides the compelling example of a study of a Paraguayan tribe that hunts game and gathers plant foods. While hunting is unpredictable and largely a matter of luck, foraging for food is more a matter of effort. As predicted, communal sharing of meat occurred throughout the band, apparently as a solution to the problem of substantial *uncertainty* in success in hunting. In contrast, equity rules of exchange applied to other foods, with communal sharing only taking place in the nuclear family.

18.4.4 *The Modern Reality?*

In modern times people probably live in environments that are far more predictable, controllable, and safe than those inhabited by their ancestors. If modern life is less volatile, there is less need for solutions to deal with unpredictable fates and reversals of fortune. Situations with *opportunities* for balanced, fair exchange, at least over longer periods of time, may be more predominant. Despite this, sudden twists of fate still occur, leaving individuals dependent on close others for help and support during times involving ill health, job stress, and adjustment, family problems including child care, personal problems, and so on. Further, evolutionary theorists would argue that the legacy of earlier adaptations in harsher environments would remain, leaving people motivated to place great value on "faithful friends" as a type of insurance against the whims of fate.

The paradox of modern living then is that while individuals still need others to rely on when the going gets tough, there are fewer opportunities for distinguishing "fair-weather friends" from genuine ones (Buss, 2000; Tooby & Cosmides, 1996). Periods of personal trouble in which costly help is needed are potentially clarifying, providing diagnostic situations for confidently assessing friends' "deep engagement," to use Tooby and Cosmides' evocative phrase. These authors suggest that the result of these changes is that individuals may "feel hungry for the confident sensation of deep social connectedness" that people who live in environments that force deep mutual interdependence typically enjoy (p. 135).

18.4.5 *The Role of Beliefs*

Of course, individuals' adjustments in their relationships will depend not only on the actual situations they face, but also on how they *construe* the nature of these situations. As noted earlier, the differences between the situations depicted in Tables E18.1 and E18.2 hinge importantly on whether "fate" will be kind, even-handed, and predictable, or harsh, unfair, and unpredictable. Thus individuals' *beliefs* about "the fates" become extremely important in the types of arrangements they consider necessary. For instance, individuals can reduce their general sense of vulnerability about what life will hold, and thus their dependence on the quality of their connections to others, by believing that because "life is fair" and they are essentially "good people," misfortune will not strike them (i.e., a Belief in a Just World; Lerner, 1980). Life gives you what you "deserve."

Lerner argues that the very basis of the Protestant ethic is a "personal contract" that individuals develop with themselves, a belief that if they work hard and are virtuous now, their just desserts will be forthcoming: "Good things will happen to good people." Zuckerman, Siegelbaum, & Williams (1977) provide the delightful example of individuals with strong beliefs in a just world performing more good deeds before final exams than after them, presumably to impress the "fates" as to their deservingness of good outcomes. The point is that those who emphasize the predictability of rewards in our society for anyone willing to put in the work are likely to oppose communal norms and, in fact, to see them as a threat to their own deserved personal outcomes (Lerner, 1980). In contrast, individuals who see the fates as random, who believe that, "There but for the grace of God go I," are most likely to value communal norms and a sense of connection to others.

Most generally, the psychological threat of having to cope with unpredictable future reversals of fortune might underlie people's strong need for "belief" in a religious sense, in the existence of strong and friendly forces, which, if we relate properly to them, will protect us from the fates. Thibaut (1965) suggested that a "coalition" with such powerful agencies of control is essentially formed against the vicissitudes of a harsh environment. A person's confidence in the coalition, that the powerful other is "on his or her side," depends on continuing efforts to maintain and improve his or her relationship with the powerful agency. In some religions, individuals try to persuade God of their worth by expressions of faith, in others, by their good works and sacrifices in face of tests of their virtue.

Similarly, Pepitone and Saffiotti (1997) provide cross-cultural evidence that individuals often cope with the issue of ultimate justice by believing that there is a dynamic moral order in the universe that influences outcomes so that they are proportional to the moral worth of the persons to whom they happen. With such forces on one's side, one becomes less dependent on the good will of faithful friends in insuring one's future security. However, such beliefs may also free the person from thinking about being repaid after helping others: In many religions, the "afterlife" is a means of insuring that any good deeds that were not compensated in the mortal life will receive appropriate "recognition" later. Ultimately, justice will prevail.

18.4.6 *The Basis of Mutual Assurance Associations*

In our discussion to this point, we have argued that having a partner who will follow the communal rule of responding to your needs as they occur will offer safety in the face of an uncertain future. While that is certainly true, the claim is a somewhat empty one in that it does not deal with the important question of *exactly why* a partner might make a costly sacrifice for you with no assurance of reciprocation.

The most obvious answer to the question is that the most secure mutual provisioning is one guaranteed by *mutual love*. In many modern societies, "love" is the common label for the motivational basis of mutual assurance associations. Love has been shown to be a combination of both caring and needing (Berscheid & Reis, 1998; Steck, Levitan, McLane, & Kelley, 1982). When love is mutual, each person's need is met with the other's caring, so an implicit (often explicit) contract of mutual assurance is established. Further, each person's "needing" reflects and is evidence of the value of the partner to the person, which, when apparent to the partner, assures the partner that the person's caring is secure. Interestingly, discussions of the communal norm apparently have not focused on the role of mutual love in considering people's adherence to the rule.

Another motivational basis for following communal norms is a person's *commitment* to maintaining the partner's welfare. One view of commitment is that it reflects a person's investments in and satisfaction with a relationship, as well as the overall attraction to it *compared* to other alternative relationships (Rusbult & Van Lange, 1996). Other forms of commitment involve a sense of duty or obligation, or what Lydon, Pierce, and O'Regan (1997) have called "moral commitment." However, there is evidence that individuals feel most secure when they believe that their partners are committed to them by an emotion, an emotion we call romantic love, rather than simply by the benefits they provide or by the extent to which their partners are "stuck" with them (Pinker, 1997, p. 418). Indeed, a belief that a partner's motivation to remain with you is "intrinsic," beyond rational reasons relating to your instrumental "mate-value," appears to be most predictive of trust in a partner's love and willingness to make sacrifices for you (Rempel, Holmes & Zanna, 1985).

However, in contrast to this logic, in some cultures commitments may be less a "private pledge" of the sort discussed above than a type of public "contract." Because stable bonds may have potential benefits to the group as a whole, marriage contracts may be enforced by kinfolk, religious institutions, or the community. These external sources thus serve the crucial third party role of providing the "assurance" that the marriage will indeed be "for better or for worse."

The Banker's Paradox: Becoming Irreplaceable. This logic brings us back to the conundrum that we earlier referred to as the Banker's Paradox. As Tooby and Cosmides (1996) put it, when individuals need help most desperately, other things being equal, they are also the poorest credit risks and, therefore, the least likely to be selected to receive a loan. The question the authors pose in terms of the banker metaphor is what might make some people more attractive investments than others? What adaptational mechanisms might contribute to individuals' ability to overcome this obstacle and attract help?

Tooby and Cosmides suggest that a key factor is the degree to which the "banker" regards the potential recipient as someone who is not easily replaceable, who has a unique package of valued attributes that are regarded as indispensable and not readily found in others. Investing a lot in "rescuing" such a person and helping him or her out of difficulty would then restore a valued relationship and secure the important benefits that person can provide in the future. Thus "selection pressures" should favor individuals adopting decision rules to invest in and show *loyalty* to a friend or partner to the extent that they view the person needing help as irreplaceable and possessing uniquely valuable qualities. If the assistance and benefits that someone provides are easily supplied by others, then that person is "substitutable" and extremely vulnerable to desertion.

If this logic is correct, then evolutionary pressures should lead to adaptations where humans are very concerned about and keep track of how they are valued by others. Critically, being regarded as "special" becomes the basis for a secure sense of "belonging" or social connectedness that would insure help in the face of reversals in welfare. Individuals should develop "an appetite to be recognized and valued for . . . their exceptional attributes," to use Tooby and Cosmides's words (p. 139). They should cultivate special skills and attributes and choose friends or groups who most value their particular qualities. Put most generally, there should be a general motivation for achieving unique status as a means of insuring your own security in the face of an uncertain future. Further, because the primary risk is a social circle devoid of partners who are deeply engaged with you, adaptations should be designed specifically to recognize and respond to signs of waning affections (Tooby & Cosmides, 1996).

Baumeister and Leary (1995) have similarly argued for a universal need for "belonging" as a hedge against life's risks. Leary extends this argument in a very interesting way, suggesting that feelings of self-worth or *self-esteem* are essentially just summaries of experiences of acceptance or rejection by others, and in consequence, low self-esteem (both acute and chronic) indicates a need for approval and for more secure interpersonal connections (Leary, Tambor, Terdal, & Downs, 1995). According to the authors' logic, a sense of "self-esteem" exists only because it is a useful mechanism for securing social acceptance and inclusion, which are seen as having been critical for survival in our evolutionary history. Self-esteem is a useful mechanism because it serves as a gauge or *"sociometer"* that monitors interpersonal acceptance. Accordingly, feelings of self-doubt alert individuals to the possibility of social rejection and trigger compensatory behaviors designed to restore a sense of connection.

A Dependency-Regulation Model. From their analysis of the logic of the Banker's Paradox, Tooby and Cosmides reached two important conclusions, principles that are also consistent with our analysis of the Twists of Fate situation. First, individuals should be centrally concerned with whether they are valued and deemed "irreplaceable." Second, each individual should be thought of as having a very limited number of "friendship niches," with the goal to fill each "slot" with persons who value the individual's welfare. If an individual feels excessive uncertainty about a partner's regard, the individual would presumably look to other alternatives and reduce his or her dependence on the relationship in question. In terms of the Twists of Fate logic, the mutual assurance pact must indeed be *mutual*, or an individual would risk being abandoned in a time of great need. Consequently, allowing oneself to be dependent on and attached to a partner who did not fully reciprocate one's feelings would leave one extremely vulnerable to the whims of fate.

Consistent with these ideas, interdependence theorists have proposed a *dependency-regulation model*, arguing that individuals regulate feelings of closeness (and thus dependence) with respect to their sense of security, not letting themselves feel fully in love until they feel confident in their partners' reciprocated regard and affections. Thus, individuals will only risk dependence on another if they trust the other's basic motivation to be responsive to their needs (Berscheid & Fei, 1977; Holmes & Rempel, 1989). These dynamics are also consistent with Bowlby's (1982) model of *general* attachment processes. He contended that individuals regulate feelings of attachment in a self-protective fashion, not allowing a strong bond to form if the proximate goal of *felt security* has not been realized.

There is strong evidence in support of the dependency-regulation principle. For instance, Murray, Holmes, and Griffin (2000) studied how individuals believed they were regarded in their close relationships and whether such inferences are accurate or not. They asked both partners in dating and married relationships to describe themselves, their partners, and how they believed their partners saw them (i.e., meta-perceptions of *perceived regard*, traditionally labeled "reflected appraisals") on a wide variety of traits and qualities. They found that individuals who felt less well regarded defensively perceived less value in their relationships, disengaging from them and evaluating their partners less positively in return, both concurrently and longitudinally. In a further study, Murray, Holmes, Griffin, Bellavia, and Rose (2001) found that both dating and married individuals who were uncertain about and less trusting of their partners' caring and love tended to self-protectively report that they were less attached to their partners and were less dependent on the relationship as an important part of their identity.

As we will discuss later, the dynamics of the dependency-regulation model seem to apply whether individuals' perceptions about their partners' feelings are accurate or not. Nonetheless, they are certainly evident when concerns about being valued reflect the "reality" of a partner's feelings. That is, the dynamics, on average, seem "functional" in helping individuals adapt to real risks in their relationships. For instance, Murray et al. (2001) found that accurate perceptions of a partner's love governed individuals' reciprocal love for the partner. Also, in a recent longitudinal study, Wieselquist, Rusbult, Foster, and Agnew (1999) demonstrated that individuals' trust in a partner was reasonably calibrated to the partner's actual level of commitment. Moreover, a longitudinal analysis showed that a sense of trust allowed individuals to risk increased dependence, fostering greater commitment over time. The authors conclude that individuals' trust and commitment fit together in a pattern of "mutual cyclical growth." Conversely, a lack of trust in a partner's caring inhibits the development of commitment.

A Caveat: A Miscalibrated Sociometer? Leary et al. (1995) implied that the "sociometer" of self-esteem will be a reasonably accurate representation of the regard with which a person is actually held, that in large part, individuals understand how they are viewed by others. In contrast, attachment theory and symbolic interactionist perspectives (see Kenny, 1994, for a review) contend that individuals develop *expectations* about how they are viewed by others that give rise to errors in their understanding of how they are regarded in current relationships.

To explore this issue, Murray, Holmes, and Griffin (2000) examined the extent to which individuals' perceptions of their partners' regard were accurately calibrated to the partners' *actual* regard. They found that individuals acted like naïve realists, assuming that their partners saw them just as they saw themselves. Critically, low self-esteem (LSE) target individuals believed their partners held them in low regard, when in fact, there was little evidence that partners' actual regard was tied to the targets' self-esteem. Thus LSE individuals *incorrectly* believed that they were not much valued by their partners; in turn, they reacted defensively, distancing themselves from their relationships and evaluating their partners more negatively. Moreover, these insecurities about a partner's feelings strongly mediated the relation between low self-esteem and low satisfaction with the relationship, providing an explanation for this widely reported finding.

Such inaccurate, but nonetheless self-verifying perceptions of a partner's regard on particular traits need not compromise perceptions of a partner's love, however (Swann, Hixon, & De La Ronde, 1992). Individuals may believe their partners love them despite their faults. And earlier we argued that *perceived love* may be most critical to individuals' beliefs that their partners will respond to their needs in a crisis. Nevertheless, if individuals try to logically account for their partner's love, perceiving that they are held in low regard would make it harder to construct confident inferences that a partner truly cares for them. Consistent with the latter argument, Murray et al. (2001) found that individuals troubled by self-doubt indeed dramatically underestimated their partners' love. Thus, self-doubts turned into *unwarranted* relationship insecurities about *both* a partner's regard and affections.

18.4.7 No Bright Line between Situations

This analysis suggests that *trust* in a partner's caring is centrally important in dealing with the anticipation of predicaments brought on by twists of fate. Is the implication then that trust is less critical in situations involving reciprocal exchange? To a certain extent, yes. There is less onus on trust if a fair balance of exchange can be consistently insured through such strategies as turn taking and tit-for-tat sequences, as research in experimental "games" with strangers has demonstrated (see Entry #16). However, efficient exchange that best satisfies the joint interests of a pair in a close relationship requires quite loose accounting rules, permitting inequalities in exchange to occur over longer periods of time to allow the exchange process to be responsive to variations in each person's needs. Thus a strong sense of trust in a partner would facilitate "gains in trade" and more efficient exchanges. Further, if the partner is seen as motivated to be fair, it would also reduce the costs of monitoring events and maintaining "account books" on the balance of exchange. (For discussion of these issues, see Holmes, 1981). Consequently, the role of trust in these two situations differs as a matter of degree rather than in kind.

18.4.8 A Pact of Mutual Responsiveness

The current analysis underlines the fact that commitments to respond to important needs as they occur in a relationship must be mutual, involving a pact that acknowledges mutual dependence. As noted earlier, such pacts of mutual loyalty typically form under "a veil of ignorance" where neither person knows whether he or she will be a net provider or recipient of help. That is, their sense of risk and vulnerability is mutual and requires a joint solution. Moreover, Tooby and Cosmides argue that perceiving a partner's positive regard reinforces dyadic solidarity – believing that a partner values you implies that he or she feels a stake in your welfare, a fact that in itself makes the partner valuable to you in return.

This reasoning expands on social psychological explanations for the long-recognized phenomenon of *reciprocal attraction*. As Berscheid and Reis (1998) point out in their recent review of the field, virtually all attraction theorists have viewed another's expression of esteem as a valuable reward the recipient is likely to reciprocate. Indeed, even similarity-attraction effects have been interpreted as due to expected liking by others who are similar in various ways. Perceived liking by another has been seen as "rewarding" because it validates the self, and because it reduces concerns about conflict and increases confidence in mutually rewarding interactions. Though these explanations are undoubtedly important, the current analysis emphasizes the critical link between perceiving that a partner values you and the relationship and his or her willingness to provide costly help and support to you in times of unexpected reversals of fortune.

18.5 Transition List Representations

Table E18.1: The Twists of Fate Situation. The transition list in Table E18.1 represents the "veil of ignorance" situation in which *either* of two friends or intimates could find that a twist of fate (f1 or f2) results in a situation of relatively extreme unilateral dependence (K or L) where serious help is needed from the other. The ?? symbols indicate that information is missing as to what event will occur. This uncertainty, as well as the relatively small chance of either event occurring during a particular period of time, is noted by the low probability value p = .10 for each of f1 and f2. Examining one such possibility, "fate" might create circumstances (f1) at juncture J such that A finds that B is in serious need of help at juncture K. For A to benefit B and provide much needed help (+50) by selecting a1, A will experience a direct cost (−20) and perhaps an indirect cost of forfeiting enjoyment of another activity a2 (i.e., a possible Actor effect of +5).

The unique and critical feature of this overall extended situation is that A cannot be confident (after helping, in returning to juncture J) that twists of fate will result in subsequent situations of unequal need involving turn-taking possibilities where the roles are reversed and B could *reciprocate* the favor. That is, there is no guarantee in dealing with the predicament of an uncertain future that juncture L will occur in a timely fashion that would permit a "fair" balancing of exchange. Juncture K, in which B is in further need of help, might occur instead, or, most likely, situations of serious unilateral dependence may not occur again at all. Thus, from A's perspective, the decision is, "Should I help or not?" in a situation where B is in serious need of support and there is no assurance that such benefits will be reciprocated. From B's point of view, the question is, "Can I count on A to help under these uncertain circumstances?

TABLE E18.1. *A Transition List Representation of the Twists of Fate Situation*

Junctures	Options	Possible Selections	Outcomes for A and B		Transition to Next Juncture
J	Fate	f1 ?? (p = .10)*	−,	−	K
	(f1, f2, f3)	f2 ?? (p = .10)	−,	−	L
		f3 ?? (p = .80)	−,	−	J
K	(a1, a2)	a1b1	−20,	+50	J
	(b1, b2)	a1b2	−20,	+50	J
		a2b1	+5,	−50	J
		a2b2	+5,	−50	J
L	(a1, a2)	a1b1	+50,	−20	J
	(b1, b2)	a1b2	−50,	+5	J
		a2b1	+50,	−20	J
		a2b2	−50,	+5	J

*The ?? symbols indicate missing information about which events will occur. The notation p = .10 indicates a 10% chance of occurrence of the event during a particular period of time.

Table E18.2: The Turn-Taking Situation. Table E18.2 presents the transition list for a Turn-Taking situation. The amount of help needed by the unilaterally dependent person in this situation is depicted as more modest (+15) than in the Twists of Fate situation (+50) in Table E18.1. Further, the more frequent, everyday variation of such needs is represented by a transition list in which the chances of f1 and f2 occurring during a particular period of time are quite high (p = .45). Thus, once K has occurred, it is likely that the *opportunity* would then be available to reverse the helper and recipient roles at juncture L at some later point in time, and so on.

TABLE E18.2. *A Transition List Representation of an Extended Situation That Permits Turn Taking*

Junctures	Options	Possible Selections	Outcomes for A and B		Transition to Next Juncture
J	Fate	f1 ?? (p = .45)*	−,	−	K
	(f1, f2, f3)	f2 ?? (p = .45)	−,	−	L
		f3 ?? (p = .10)	−,	−	J
K	(a1, a2)	a1b1	−5,	+15	J
	(b1, b2)	a1b2	−5,	+15	J
		a2b1	+2,	−15	J
		a2b2	+2,	−15	J
L	(a1, a2)	a1b1	+15,	−5	J
	(b1, b2)	a1b2	−15,	+2	J
		a2b1	+15,	−5	J
		a2b2	−15,	+2	J

*The ?? symbols indicate missing information about which events will occur. The notation p = .45 indicates a 45% chance of occurrence of the event during a particular period of time.

N-PERSON SITUATIONS

Entry #19

Third Parties

Effects of an Outsider

19.1 Examples

There are many situations in which a third person is involved in a problem with a dyad. For example, when the dyad lacks information necessary for an important decision, a third person may appear who is able to provide it. As an instance of Entry #17 (Joint Decisions under Uncertainty), a couple in a strange city is not sure whether to enter the restaurant immediately before them or to try to find a better one among possibilities further down the street – along which they cannot see very far. A local resident passes by and they ask his opinion.

A family therapist helps a feuding couple find mutually satisfying coordination solutions to the problems of meshing their conflicting schedules and increasing their periods of relaxation together for romantic interludes. Two drivers arrive simultaneously at an intersection with four-way stop signs and are uncertain as to who should proceed first. They are aided in this coordination problem by a policeman, who signals for one to wait and the other to go ahead.

Two sisters are in strong disagreement about what they should wear to school on the first day. They turn to their older sister and each tries to get her to support their particular preference. Or, they may be quarreling about the use of the bathroom they share. Their mother intervenes, clearly states the value the family places on harmony and fairness, and suggests that they take turns.

Harold Kelley had primary responsibility for preparation of this entry.

Two young people are enjoying themselves on the dance floor, practicing their recently learned dance steps. An older fellow, who has been showing off his dancing skills, comes over and asks if he can "cut in."

Art and Bob are trying to complete their collections of baseball trading cards. Art has an extra X card which Bob needs, but Bob's extra Y card is one Art already has. So they cannot work out a trade. However, Carl comes along with the extra Z that Art needs and Carl, himself, needs Bob's extra Y card. A three-way circle of "giving" is easily arranged, with Art giving X to Bob who gives Y to Carl who gives to Z Art.

19.2 Conceptual Analysis

As the examples suggest, a third person can affect any or all of the several features that distinguish the entries in this Atlas, including the pair's behavioral options, their possible outcomes and its pattern, and their response and information conditions. The stranger's advice increases their information, the fancy dancer's request to "cut in" provides new alternatives and possible outcomes, and the policeman's directions change their response conditions (from ad lib to "A, then B"), and so forth. The mother's statement of "family values" may change the attitudes the sisters bring to their dispute and motivate them to transform the situation from one of self-interests to one of equity and fairness.

It is probably not necessary to point out that the large number of possible dyadic situations implied by chapter 2's distinctions is dwarfed by the great variety of possible triadic situations. That difference is apparent when we shift from 2×2 outcome patterns to $2 \times 2 \times 2$ patterns (the minimal patterns for a triad) and consider distinguishing those patterns by partitioning the variance in the outcomes by analysis of variance. In place of the three possible sources of variance in each person's outcomes, there are seven. Thus, in the dyad, A's outcomes may have Actor's, Partner's, and Joint sources of variance, but in the triad, A's outcomes may have Actor's, Partner B's, and Partner C's sources, along with $A \times B$'s, $A \times C$'s, and $B \times C$'s two-way Joint sources *and* an $A \times B \times C$'s three-way Joint source of variance.

After a brief effort in the direction of characterizing the many possible patterns, Kelley and Thibaut (1978) simplified the task by limiting their discussion to certain triadic patterns that illustrate various unique phenomena. These included one situation in which the third person invokes social norms that promote resolving conflict (as in the example of the mother's exhortations to the quarreling sisters) and another in which the third party makes possible an indirect exchange between A and B (as in the trading card example). Although there are many such instances of facilitation, our topics below will generally emphasize the negative effects the third person may have.

19.3 Interaction Patterns and Person Factors

Of the many available topics, we have selected for inclusion three for which there is a research literature and which require a consideration of dyadic versus triadic interaction for their interpretation. For the most part, these are cases in which the third person has an antagonistic or disruptive relation to a focal dyad, so the three topics have much in common theoretically.

19.3.1 Coalitions: "Three" Becomes "Two against One"

Coalition Games. There is an extensive literature based on experimental games in which outcomes are gained through coalition formation. The simplest situation involves three participants, any two of whom can form a coalition to the exclusion of the third. The game specifies the outcomes that each possible coalition stands to gain as well as the outcomes that each person will receive if excluded from a coalition. In the typical procedure, a participant indicates which of the others he or she wants to pair with and a proposed division of the spoils available to that pair. When a proposal is mutually acceptable, the members of the pair receive the agreed-upon outcomes and the excluded person gets some alternative value, often nothing. In an example game, it is specified that the AB pair will gain 100 points; the AC pair, 80 points; the BC pair, 60 points; and the person left out of a coalition, 0 points.

One of the more successful theories applied to this kind of situation is Komorita's "equal excess model" (1979). It assumes that people select partners with whom they will generate the largest joint outcomes, so in the above example, A and B will select each other. In negotiating a division of their coalition's outcomes, each one sets a personal goal that assumes he and the partner will first each take from the coalition outcomes an amount they would get in their best alternatives and then divide equally the excess that is left over. In the example, from the AB coalition's 100 points, A will take out the 40 points available as his half in the alternative (AC) coalition, and B will take out the 30 points similarly available to him in the BC coalition. Then they will divide the 30 points that are left over, each taking 15 points, yielding a total of 55 for A and 45 for B, and, of course, C, being excluded gets 0 points.

There is evidence supporting Komorita's model, with respect both to the most likely coalition and the division the partners will negotiate. It can be seen that the model assumes that in the negotiation, each person takes account of his or her respective alternatives but also applies a fairness rule in dividing up the excess outcomes the coalition provides.

In the experiments, the three participants often repeat the coalition-negotiation process for a number of trials, retaining their respective possible outcome values throughout. One interesting finding is that the frequency of the possible coalitions changes over trials. This reflects the growing discontent of the excluded person and his or her ability to induce defections from the initial coalition. Komorita's theory takes account of this process and predicts (what has been observed) that there is a tendency in later trials for the three coalitions to occur equally often. In the example above, as subject C is repeatedly excluded, rather than be completely left out, he drastically lowers his expectations and offers B a lion's share of the BC coalition's outcomes. As B is induced to form the coalition with C, then A must reduce his demands and become a more generous coalition partner. After many iterations of negotiations and choices, there develops some equilibrium among the three possible coalitions.

These "coalition" games can be quite complex. With experience in them, people learn how things go and how to think ahead to next steps. In iterated form, the logic of dealing with each occasion and partner separately must be replaced with an understanding of special arrangements necessitated by how that partner may subsequently be influenced by the third party. The three are part of a dynamic system in which the initially excluded individual may eventually gain partners through making great sacrifices.

The explicit and neat numerical structure of these games has encouraged mathematically minded researchers such as Komorita to develop formal models to predict the results. However, there are complications. In their review, Komorita and Parks (1995) observe that the various theories of coalition formation vary in their assumptions about people's motives for forming a coalition – whether "to maximize control over other members, maximize status in the group, maximize similarity of attitudes and values, or minimize conflict among its members. However, the majority of theories assume that the parties are motivated to maximize some external reward, such as money or points" (p. 188). The problem, of course, is that this latter assumption is not always true. For example, if permitted to, some triads forgo pursuing their individual interests in favor of developing a "grand coalition" that includes all players. It is difficult to understand this behavior solely in terms of "external" rewards.

From the theoretical perspective in this Atlas, the notion of "external" rewards, as contrasted to "internal" rewards (such as those derived from treating one's business partner fairly), is a familiar one. Our parallel distinction is between the "given" situation, with its outcome structure defined by the "external rewards," and the "effective" situation, with its structure reflecting the particular motives (competitiveness, altruism, fairness, etc.) evoked within a particular relationship (i.e., "internal" to it) and acting to "transform" the given situation. The coalition situation obviously lends itself to the expression of different motives, as Komorita and Parks's list illustrates. And in its iterations, it also provides information about partners and their interpersonal dispositions, which often induce changes in a person's motivation.

In this research, and particularly in that conducted in the growing field of "experimental economics," there is an interesting attempt to avoid the problems of individual differences in how the game's outcomes are (we would say) "transformed." Wanting to apply theoretical models that assume the subjects are uniformly motivated by a motivation to maximize the outcomes specified in the game, some researchers try to make that assumption come true. They do so by offering very sizable concrete rewards (e.g., amounts of money) in the hope that the subjects will then not be able to control their greed and adopt any other motivation, that is, that their preferences will be brought into perfect alignment with the game's numbers. This apparently doesn't work very well. The experimental economist Roth observes that "these designs may sometimes fail to control subjects' preferences, because subjects may in fact also be concerned with the payoffs of other subjects" (1995, p. 80). From the perspective expressed in chapter 3, we are not surprised. There we saw that interdependent persons are often responsive to the overall pattern of outcomes, including not only their own but those of their partners as well. They focus on broader goals than self-interest and may gain symbolic outcomes from achieving those goals. So increasing the concrete stakes in a game is not an assured way of inducing altruists or, for that matter, competitors to become solely focused on their own outcomes. Indeed, the higher stakes increase the situation's opportunities to display genuine altruism and gain its derivative satisfactions and may, therefore, have an effect opposite the intended one.

Coalitions in Ongoing Relationships. As in one of our initial examples, members of a dyad who are in conflict sometimes try to draw a third person into their debates. The purpose may be to be able to influence that person's outcome control over the initial partner, or to get an opinion or informational support for a contentious matter about which one is in an argument with the initial partner. So the "coalition" may be based on informational control and interdependence. And it may be fleeting or become a relatively stable part of the triadic structure.

In research on families, drawing a third person into a conflict is often referred to as "triangulation." In their study of young married couples and their 5-year-old children, Lindahl, Clements, and Markman (1997) observed each couple as, in the child's presence, they discussed a major problem in their relationship. Observations were made of each parent's "triangulating" or involving the child in the discussion, as by "asking the child's opinion to settle a source of disagreement or detouring the marital discussion by focusing on the child's behavior" (p. 143). The couple's interaction had been observed in a similar discussion before the birth of the child. The investigators were interested in whether prebirth measures of a couple's problems in handling conflict (specifically, their tendency to generate an escalation of negative affect) would predict the present interaction. The strongest result was that earlier evidence of negative escalations was predictive of the husband's tendency to "triangulate" the child into the present marital conflict.

Earlier, Minuchin (1974) had suggested that such involvement of the child is often used by parents to detour around their own problems or divert attention from them. Considered in this light, Lindahl et al.'s result brings to mind the evidence presented in Entry #6 (the Threat Game) about the demand-withdraw pattern. In discussions of marital problems, wives tend to make demands (for change, rights, etc.) but their husbands tend to withdraw from or avoid the discussion. The Lindahl et al. result suggests that in the presence of their child, the husband has an additional strategy for shifting the focus of the interaction, namely, bringing the child into the discussion, either as an ally or as a scapegoat.

In their conflicts, members of a couple may also seek allies from among third persons outside their family. Klein and Milardo (2000) studied the outsiders, whether friends or family members, from whom members of dating couples expect to receive support or criticism for their respective views about a particular recent conflict (e.g., about spending money, or how much time to spend together). Not surprisingly, support is expected more from one's own friends and kin than from those of the partner. So the external network of the couple makes it possible for disagreement simply to be expanded beyond the pair, as each one recruits an ally from the separate sets of third persons they judge to be likely supporters rather than critics. One of the most consistent findings is that for these young daters, third persons from the *family* networks are expected to provide both approval and disapproval, whereas third persons from the *friendship* ties are expected mainly to provide approval. This probably reflects the fact that friends are chosen (often, because they are understanding and sympathetic) whereas one has little choice in the matter of who is "family."

Does expected support from outsiders affect a person's feelings that his or her position in the conflict is appropriate and reasonable and, therefore, predict the extent to which he or she will push for it and try to get his or her way? For both the young men and women in the sample, the greater the number of perceived supporters, the stronger their beliefs about the legitimacy of their own positions. And for men, the absence of critics had the same effect. Klein and Milardo's evidence provides some modest support for the further idea that perceived support versus criticism from outsiders affects how hard a person will push for his or her position versus adjust to the partner's view. The strongest results were for the women: Those who claimed support from their own networks of family and friends reported more contentiousness during the conflict and less willingness to compromise, and the same was true for those who claimed support from their partner's networks. So these data suggest how the available third parties may affect the conflict process within a dyad, encouraging conflict rather than accommodation.

19.3.2 *Third Party Interventions in Dyadic Conflict*

Formal Procedures. Frequently, a third person comes to a pair of disputants for the explicit purpose of helping them settle their conflict. In such instances, the third person almost always lacks important information about the two sides of the dispute (e.g., what the two persons view as important issues and their positions on them). So, the third party must make initial efforts to gather and evaluate such information. Then, if the third party has sufficient influence over the two, there may be the further step of using that influence to influence their actions. The latter step is illustrated by the parent who instructs two siblings in what they must do, or by the local justice of the peace who acts to settle a dispute between two neighbors.

In their influential work on "procedural justice," Thibaut and Walker (1975) made an experimental comparison of two formal informational procedures used in courtrooms, before a third party, the judge, who has the final say about what is to be done: (1) *Adversarial procedure*: Each person's evidence is presented to the judge by lawyers who are selected by the person they represent and who are directed to present the most favorable possible case for their respective clients. (2) *Inquisitorial procedure*: All the evidence from both sides is presented by a single lawyer selected by the judge and directed to present both sides' evidence. In both procedures, after hearing the evidence, the judge renders a judgment.

In comparing these two procedures, Thibaut and Walker took steps to insure that the same information was presented under each and that the judge's decision randomly favored either one side or the other. The important result: Independently of whether the judgment favored or disfavored the disputants, they were more satisfied with the adversarial procedure and considered it to have been more fair. In other words, a procedure that appeared more certain to give consideration to a disputant's side of the issue was itself a source of satisfaction with the process of that decision.

Similar results from a number of experiments led Thibaut and Walker to the important concept of "procedural justice": the perceived justice of a dispute settlement process – its perceived fairness – depends greatly on the informational procedure involved and not merely on the outcome. "Justice" is not merely a matter of fair allocation of *outcomes*, but is also a matter of fair distribution of *information*.[1]

Various explanations can be offered for that phenomenon. As Lind and Tyler (1988) point out, receiving a fair presentation of one's side of a problem may be valued because it is assumed to insure that, in the long run, outcome decisions will be fair. In other words, procedural justice may be instrumental to distributive justice. But, as Lind and Tyler further argue, the "just" procedure may also be valued in its own right, independently of any beliefs about its long-term effects on outcomes. Procedural justice, like other facets of fairness, is likely to be a group value instilled through socialization and, like other such values, followed for its own sake, without respect to its effect on concrete outcomes.

In this Atlas, we emphasize the outcomes that people gain from the values expressed by their own and others' behavior in various situations.

---

[1] The Thibaut and Walker work is important in showing the subjective benefits of procedural justice, namely, the feelings of fairness that may result independently of the final judgment. However, those results should not be taken as a basis for an unqualified endorsement of adversarial procedures in our courts or other dispute settlement settings. The interested reader is referred to Lind and Tyler (1988, pp. 112–23) for an overview of the possible problems with adversarial procedures, including flaws in the information presented, the costs of frivolous law suits, and possible disadvantages for plaintiffs who cannot employ the best attorneys.

For example, a wife experiences a rewarding glow of pride when she prepares a special delicacy for her husband and he recognizes her effort with a warm compliment. The concept of "procedural justice" implies that, in a similar way, people experience positive outcomes when their status and rights are recognized by others, and in disputes, such recognition apparently begins with "hearing their side of the 'story.'" Thus, the evidence for "procedural justice" motives suggests that people "transform" the initial stage of the dispute settlement process from one of mere information exchange to one in which the procedure by which that exchange is accomplished yields symbolic outcomes to the disputants.

Informal Procedures. In contrast to the formalized intervention between disputants illustrated by courtroom procedures, there are also frequent informal interventions by third parties in the settlement of everyday dyadic disputes. These include instances in which managers intervene between employees, parents, between their children, police, between husbands and wives, and students, between their friends. Here we consider the results of one of the most thorough studies of informal conflict intervention, reported by Sheppard, Blumenfeld-Jones, and Roth (1989).

Through questionnaires and intensive interviews with persons drawn into the third-party role, they distinguished the forms informal interventions take and some of the determinants of the form in particular instances. Though initially strongly influenced by Thibaut and Walker's distinction between control of information and control of outcomes, Sheppard and his associates soon found that informal interventions usually involve more stages and occur in more forms than envisioned by the inquisitorial-adversarial dichotomy. As we will see, some of the major differences derive from the fact that the third party is usually interdependent with the pair of disputants and is also in a position to be aware of and take account of the ongoing interdependence between them.

Some of the third party procedures are those that characterize mediation or therapeutic intervention – feeling out the parties' emotional states, clarifying their feelings and arguments, defining what is in dispute, and so forth. Although such procedures characterize only a minority of informal interventions, they are more likely if the dispute is complex and important, if it involves underlying "personality clashes," and if the disputants are highly interdependent in their ongoing activities. Those circumstances evoke the third party's concerns about the disputants' satisfaction with and commitment to the eventual resolution of the conflict. The implication is that the dispute may revolve around differences between the disputants that are not primarily about concrete actions and outcomes but involve the negative symbolic outcomes the pair create for each other – outcomes relating to status, fairness, loyalty, honesty, and so on. The circumstance of their continuing interdependence makes it necessary, if at all possible, to deal with the underlying "personality" issues, and not merely with the current concrete ("presenting") problem.

But the third party often needs to make a quick resolution of the issue. For example, they may be dependent on their superiors who will not tolerate their spending time with "therapeutic" procedures. So if the third party has the authority to do so, he or she may be inclined simply to specify a solution to the problem. The evidence from Sheppard and his colleagues suggests that this involves gathering facts and then making what the third party thinks is a fair decision, without thought of the pair's subsequent satisfaction or commitment to the solution. Such intervention is often accompanied by an interpretation of the dispute in terms of right and wrong: based on the rules or norms that apply to the dispute, one party is right and the other is wrong. In general, possessing authority, third parties most often act like adjudicators rather than as mediators. Their authority interferes with the kind of problem diagnosis and clarification necessary for serving as a neutral intermediary and dealing with the deeper issues of personality conflicts. Whether for matters of their own convenience or their responsibilities to yet higher authorities, the third party tends to move directly to a judgment of right and wrong, and to specify a solution on that basis.

From that brief sketch, we can see the network of dependencies and interdependencies in which the dyadic dispute conflict is embedded. The members of the dyad themselves are interdependent in the person factors they bring to their interactions about concrete tasks. As a mediator, the third party should be responsive to that interdependence, but in view of his or her own competing activities and interdependence with yet other persons, the third party may be inclined simply to come down in favor of one disputant or, in some cases, to try to make the dispute go away by simply telling the pair to stop their quarreling.

19.3.3 *Jealousy: Its Basis in Intimacy*

Third parties may have a quite different type of influence on an interdependent dyad than any we have described above. Here, we consider how their presence may threaten the unique intimacy that a dyad has developed and thus result in feelings of jealousy on the part of one member of the pair. We present the hypothesis that jealousy is rooted in intimacy. This idea is suggested by the writings of the German sociologist Georg Simmel (published in translation by Kurt Wolff, 1950). In the course of developing an understanding of groups and larger social structures, Simmel gave considerable thought to comparisons between the dyad and the triad. His comments include these:

> No matter how close a triad may be, there is always the occasion on which two of the three members regard the third as an intruder. The reasons may be the mere fact that he shares in certain moods which can unfold in all their intensity and tenderness only when two can meet without distraction: the sensitive union of two is always irritated by the spectator. It may also be noted how extraordinarily difficult and rare it is for three people to attain a really uniform mood – when visiting a museum, for instance, or looking at a landscape – and how much more easily such a mood emerges between two.... This intimacy, which is the tendency of relations between two persons, is the reason why the dyad constitutes the chief seat of jealousy. (p. 135–36)

Jealousy is a complex emotional state that usually includes fear and anger. The classic example is the "love triangle" – two lovers, one of whom fears losing the partner to the third person. The feelings of one member of the dyad may seem to be a rather unusual place to begin the description of a "situation entry." Our problem is to work backward and try to understand the situational circumstances and personal factors that can reasonably be thought to be the necessary antecedents of those feelings and their associated interactions. A special problem arises here from the fact that the prototypical example of jealousy involves the particular concrete activities and outcomes associated with romantic interaction. We will attempt to develop a more abstract view of jealousy by advancing the hypothesis that jealousy and intimacy are closely linked and, therefore, that jealousy occurs in relation to a broad class of interactions that includes but is not limited to sexual episodes – a class that is appropriately described as encompassing "intimate interactions."

In what kind of pair relationship is jealousy likely to be a problem? After all, in the course of social life, pairings come and go, involving now persons A and B, but later, B with C and, perhaps, A with D. People do leave some dyads and enter others, without those shifts occasioning jealousy. The answer, of course, is that the pair relationship subject to jealousy is special in some way. *Our hypothesis is that the dyad in which jealousy may occur has become special through a process of intimate interaction.*

An Interdependence Analysis of Jealousy. Let us consider two partners in a romantic relationship, Jim and Betty. He has come to enjoy high positive outcomes in their interaction – outcomes he believes to be unique or irre-placeable, not obtainable in relationships with alternative partners. Those outcomes will obviously be lost if Betty withdraws from interaction with him or from their relationship altogether. In brief, he is in a situation of dependence and, possibly, worry, and, therefore, is vulnerable to jealousy.

Jim generally assumes that Betty also gains uniquely good outcomes similar to his. But his information (about what only she can directly know) may be vague, and he may be uncertain on that point. The matrix in Table E19.1 below (at the end of this entry) provides a snapshot of the situation as Jim might understand it. On the left, each partner is shown to have the options of staying in their relationship or leaving for an alternative partner. Reflecting Jim's experience of high positive outcomes unique to the ongoing relationship, his outcomes are shown to be very high when he and Betty associate with each other but not otherwise. We place question marks in the locations of Betty's outcomes to represent the fact that he has no direct knowledge of them. That matrix simply represents one of the basic results from jealousy research, that the person prone to jealousy feels dependent on the partner's remaining in the relationship (Bringle & Buunk, 1986; Buunk, 1982).

There are two contrasting ways for Jim to fill in the missing informa-tion in Table E19.1, one way that reflects feelings of security about the relationship (as shown by the upper matrix on the right, where Betty is also getting high outcomes from the relationship) and another way that reflects feelings of insecurity (as shown by the lower matrix, where she will get better outcomes elsewhere). If Jim is prone to jealousy, he will follow the "insecure" route. This is implied by White's research (1981a): The jealousy-prone member of a heterosexual pair is likely to feel inade-quate in the relationship and to judge that he or she is putting more effort into the relationship than the partner is. Both of those judgments reflect clues that encourage his view that the situation is one of unilateral depen-dence in which he has little outcome control over the partner who has great outcome control over him. For example, his "greater effort" can be taken to reflect the well-documented fact (see Kelley, 1979, pp. 44–47) that the less dependent member of a pair has more "say" about what goes on in a relationship. Understanding that phenomenon, Jim's sense of his own greater effort indicates to him that Betty has been able to use his greater dependence to induce him to put great "effort" into the relationship.

At some point, Jim receives further evidence of his greater dependence when he observes (or believes he does) that Betty is attracted to someone else (also found, not surprisingly, to be an important correlate of jealousy;

Buunk & Bringle, 1987). At that point, the third party enters the scene, as a possible disrupter of the special relationship.

Situation versus Person Factors in Jealousy. Inasmuch as the crucial processes in the arousal of jealousy occur in the jealous person's perceptions and thoughts, they may not always be consistent with the facts about the pair's relative dependence and the threat posed by a third party. Are there person factors that make some individuals particularly susceptible to those perceptions and thoughts?

It is not possible in existing research to cleanly separate the jealous person's circumstances (e.g., the reality of his relative dependence and/or the quality of the information the partner provides about that reality – she may be deceiving him) from person factors (e.g., feelings of inadequacy, suspiciousness) that might lead him to an erroneous understanding of those circumstances. It can be said with some confidence that jealousy occurs less often for persons with secure attachment styles, that is, persons comfortable with getting close to and dependent on others and not concerned about being abandoned (Buunk, 1977; Guerrero, 1998; Sharpsteen & Kirkpatrick, 1997). So person factors do seem to play a role. On the other hand, as evidence that the jealous person may often be in touch with the reality of his greater dependence, a number of studies show that the two members of a close relationship tend to agree about who is less dependent and more likely to leave (e.g., Drigotas, Rusbult, & Verette, 1999). Their consensus suggests that the two of them are responding to the same facts about their relative dependence. The same conclusion is suggested by White's results (1980), that the member of a pair whose photograph is rated by independent judges as less physically attractive reports worrying more about the partner's wanting to start a relationship with someone else.

It is reasonable to conclude that jealousy probably involves some mixture of unwarranted concerns about being abandoned and veridical perceptions of one's greater dependence on the relationship.

Intimacy: The Basis for High and Irreplaceable Outcomes. Why might Jim's good outcomes in the relationship with Betty be high and irreplaceable – that is, unique or special to their relationship? After all, other women (at least some, perhaps not all) can provide the sex, companionship, help with housework, and so forth that Betty provides. We must now consider the broad kinds of outcomes people gain from their interactions, along the lines of chapter 3's distinction between concrete and symbolic outcome. Except that now we must extend those distinctions to the special kind of interaction we describe by the term "intimacy." This leads us to recognize that information itself often provides important rewards.

The essential nature of "intimate interaction" is specified in the intimacy model proposed by Reis and Shaver (1988). Intimacy is defined as mutual perceptions of understanding, validation, and caring. The paradigmatic interaction sequence for intimacy consists of one person's self-revealing disclosures to a partner (e.g., Jim to Betty), and her response that leads Jim to feel *understood* (Betty shows that she understands what he has expressed), *validated* (she shows respect for the point of view and/or personal qualities he has revealed), and *cared for* (he feels supported, protected).

A rather detailed description of the process can be drawn from Reis and Patrick (1996). They precede their review of intimacy processes with a similar review of attachment processes. In their justification of that linkage, they point out that the two sets of processes are closely related and have common components. Of the several such components they list, the major one involves the concept of "responsiveness":

> To attachment researchers, responsiveness refers to a caregiver's sensitive, appropriate reactions to an infant's needs and emotional state. Although adult responsiveness differs in several important respects, intimacy also depends on having partners who respond sensitively and appropriately to each other. (p. 525)

From an interdependence theory perspective, the person factor or mechanism of "responsiveness" points to the existence of underlying *coordination problems*. Chapter 2 and Entry #3 of this Atlas describe a situation of behavior coordination, which confronts a pair with a problem of co-ordinating one person's actions with another's, so that both may gain good outcomes. A problem of *information coordination* is closely analogous. If two people are to have the benefits of accurate communication, one person's reply must mesh well with the other's initial comment or question. Understanding is shared when there is such coordination through each person's sensitive and appropriate responsiveness. The point to be emphasized here is that *intimacy is a complex task requiring coordination of information*.

For example, in his intimate interaction with Betty, Jim may reveal something that he has rarely, if ever, revealed before, for example, a "secret" or a personal feeling. In doing so, Jim enters a "risk-taking" situation such as shown in the matrix in Table E19.2 below. His options are to "reveal" or be silent. When he chooses to reveal, Jim is exposed to Betty's support or criticism, with sharply different consequences.[2] Not having been revealed

---

[2] The reader may realize that this situation is more accurately represented by a transition list that specifies that B can make the selection between "support" and "criticize" *only after*

before (thus, likely to be a "sensitive" matter), the secret's or the feeling's revelation may open Jim to criticism or censure – hence, the sizable possible negative outcomes. On the other hand, Jim often stands to gain sizable benefits from Betty's acceptance and support of the revelation. For example, her clearly perceptive understanding of his problem may enable her to help Jim place a favorable interpretation on a recent event that he has construed in a self-derogatory way. Thus, Betty may suggest a causal interpretation of the event that implies that Jim is not a bad person and that others have the same experience. Or, to take another example, from Betty's understanding and validating a creative idea that Jim has never described to anyone before, Jim will have a strong feeling of pride and an increased sense of his uniqueness and value as a special person. Furthermore, in providing support rather than criticism, Betty gives evidence of having his interests at heart, that is, of caring.

Intimate Interaction Concerns Self-Concepts. The examples above reveal what is special about "intimate interaction" and the rewards it may provide. It enables people to develop, clarify, and crystallize their understandings of themselves. The most important questions each person has about him or her self concern whether he or she is socially valuable – worth caring for.[3] The question "Do I have admirable qualities – ones of which I may be proud?" is especially addressed to what, in chapter 3 and this Atlas, we have described as "person factors." These include the qualities of fairness, persistence, competitiveness, honesty, courage, social skills, generosity, and so forth that affect one's interactions with others and make one desirable and successful in interpersonal relations.

Why might a person be uncertain about those qualities in the self? Most people encounter a wide range of interdependence problems – problems defined by varying situations and partners. Adaptation to that variety of problems requires compromises, trade-offs, and adjustments of contradictory impulses to the different problems. Generosity must be balanced against own interests, assertiveness against passivity, honesty against deceit, persistence against quitting, conformity against individuality, and so

---

A's revelation. The example also reveals another important reason for using transition lists: Strictly speaking, the 2 × 2 matrix in Table E 19.2 is not entirely logical inasmuch as person B's options make no sense if A remains silent. That problem is obviated through the use of a transition list in which B's options in response to A can depend on what A's initial action is.

[3] Entry #18, "Twists of Fate," provides a further perspective on the importance of interpersonal acceptance and the derivative processes for monitoring and improving how highly one is valued by others.

on. That necessity of proper balancing among and flexible display of such qualities leaves many individuals confused and uncertain about what, "deep down," they "are really like."

Intimate interaction is one of the most powerful (though not the sole) and dependable means of providing answers to those questions. In his intimate exchanges with Betty, Jim may find tolerance for his inconsistencies – that assertiveness in some situations is admirable, that selfishness or deceit with certain partners in particular settings is not immoral, that an offbeat idea may be merely that but may also be an avenue to some new and worthwhile venture, and so forth. And Betty's responsiveness to Jim – her attention to and validation of his disclosures and her readiness to keep in strict confidence his most "guilty" and vulnerable secrets – distinguishes her as a special person. This type of specialness is reflected in Jim's high degree of dependence on her for important and unique positive outcomes.

Intimacy as a Dyadic Process Subject to Interference by a Third Person. Why does a third person have the potential to interfere with intimate interaction? We emphasized above that intimacy is a complex task requiring coordination of information. Betty's reactions to Jim's revelations must, to some degree, fit with his existing thoughts about himself. That is the meaning of "validation." For properties of his "self" about which Jim is least clear or certain, Betty's interpretations must crystallize and strengthen certain nascent ideas. In general, her "responsiveness" requires that her side of the information exchange process be coordinated in various ways with his. And it goes without saying that the phenomenon about which the process must be coordinated is one of great complexity and subtlety ("subtle," from the Latin *subtilis,* literally, "finely woven").

We are reminded of Simmel's observation about the difficulty of "coordination" ("attaining a really uniform mood") when viewing a museum piece or landscape – surely, phenomena of complexity and subtlety. And we note his insight that the coordination (uniform mood) emerges much more readily between two persons than when a third person is present.[4]

---

[4] In the realm of information coordination, the relation between increasing size of group and the deterioration of coordination probably depends greatly on the complexity or subtlety of the phenomenon at the focus of the coordination process. The text adopts Simmel's implicit view, that for complex phenomena, the deterioration is marked even for the small increase from two to three persons. At the other end of the scale, shared feelings and understandings of *simple* phenomena can readily develop even among large collections of information sharers, as evidenced by the generation of common feelings and perceptions by crowds at political rallies, athletic contests, etc. The shared "subjective veridicality" is achieved by communications and thoughts that focus on simple elements of what in reality may be very complex phenomena – e.g., issues of optimal rates of taxation for various

In short, our explanation of the third person's interference is found in the intricate nature of the information coordination task characteristic of intimate interaction. Given the great complexity of the phenomenon toward which the information coordination is directed, that is, the self, the development and success of the process is easily disrupted by an additional participant.

To illustrate the problem: To be effective, the information coordination process must be carried out carefully, unequivocally, and with the confidant's (e.g., Betty's) attunement to the confider's (e.g., Jim's) disclosures. If we consider the possibility of *two* persons (e.g., Betty and Jane) rather than one playing the role of confidant, there are the obvious problems of how the two will coordinate their feedback with respect to each of the three intimacy components. Betty and Jane may disagree between themselves and even become antagonistic to each other. Their effectiveness will be diluted if their reactions diverge significantly in any respect. Ideally, they must gain closely similar understandings of Jim's subtle and complex problem, stay "on the same page" in their reactions to it, spontaneously develop a convincing consensus in how they express their validation, and provide a unified expression of support.

Several lines of research bear on these matters. From Steiner's review of the effects of group size (1972), we can extract what seem to be the essential facts: (1) For tasks in which two or more persons must mesh their actions, successful coordination becomes less probable the greater the number of people involved. (2) When the actions to be coordinated require effort, there are also motivational problems. Each person tends to feel less responsibility for the success of the coordination and the cumulative efforts decline. (3) In discussions of complex problems and their solutions, as compared with larger groups, dyads have been observed to be especially likely to avoid disagreement and antagonism in favor of gentle and supportive behavior (Bales & Borgatta, 1955). The last result is particularly pertinent to the problem of including a third person in the processes of intimate interaction.

---

income levels, or of responsibility for the events in a scrambled football play that resulted in a penalty. The processes of sloganeering, stereotyping, and simplification involved in such mass information coordinations are, of course, antithetical to the processes essential to attaining the stable and sustainable sense of "self" that we describe as occurring in dyadic intimacy. In seeking that sense, most of us resist being stereotyped or met with simple theories about ourselves, as in comments such as "You're just like your father," or "What can you expect after never having taken school seriously?" Our self-image is validated by detailed information about ourselves that distinguishes us from others and is consistently confirmed as we think and rethink about ourselves during encounters with the shifting demands of life's problems.

Further evidence comes from studies of dyadic disclosure. Is there evidence that, as argued above, rewarding intimacy is unique to dyads? Its "rewardingness" may be assumed if we find people choosing to be intimate under certain conditions. So we venture to answer the question by examining evidence about the interpersonal circumstances under which most voluntary disclosure occurs. We find first that intimate disclosure tends *not* to be a matter of individual differences, with some people simply being more open with others in general. Rather, people are generally selective as to its targets, being willing to disclose intimate matters only to particular others (Miller and Kenny, 1986).

If intimate disclosure occurs with particular others rather than as a general personal tendency, it also seems to occur more in dyads than in triads. This is illustrated by Taylor, DeSoto, and Lieb's experiments (1979). When their undergraduate subjects imagined themselves sometimes with one other person and sometimes with two, they anticipated greater willingness to disclose to the single person, and this was particularly true for topics rated as more intimate. In a second study, recordings were made of conversations in pairs or trios of acquainted college freshman, in each case with instructions to share specific personal experiences. Ratings of the intimacy of the interactions were higher in the dyads than in the triads. Similar results were later reported by Solano and Dunnam (1985), both as to greater willingness to disclose intimate information in dyads and as to greater actual disclosure in "getting acquainted" conversations.

Asymmetry in Dependence on Intimate Interaction. We have now reached the point in our Jim and Betty story at which Jim is gaining very important information-based outcomes from his intimate interaction with Betty. The outcomes are unique to his relationship with Betty, that is, they are ones he has not experienced before and they have been gained in interaction exclusively with her. Under what conditions will that experience translate into worry and, potentially, jealousy about her interaction with other persons? Will the experience imply an asymmetry in their dependence on the relationship?

Intimate interaction is often mutually rewarding, existing as a recurring, two-way process within ongoing adult relationships. Each of the two persons has information to disclose, so over their successive "intimate" interactions, they tend to shift back and forth between the A and B roles shown in the matrix in Table E19.2. This is most apparent in sexual interaction, in which private facts about their bodies, performances, and feelings are revealed almost simultaneously or in a turn-taking sequence, being made available for admiration and understanding that, the intrinsic pleasures of intercourse aside, provide each partner with unique feelings of self-worth. As a pair goes through a series of interactions with some alternation in who assumes the risky (or riskier) role, they have an opportunity to develop an exchange of the rewards to be derived from being understood, validated, and cared for. And as they manage to preserve that exchange by keeping each other's secrets and being dependably understanding, they provide the informational basis for mutual trust in each other's future support.

Under what conditions is intimacy unilaterally rewarding? The answer is found in the relative gains in self-esteem that two partners can attain through it. The evidence noted earlier, that jealousy occurs more often for persons with insecure attachment styles, suggests that asymmetry is to be traced to person factors. In our story, Jim stands to gain high outcomes from successful intimacy with Betty because he has previously lacked independent external (from other people) and/or internal (from his own information resources) bases for a positive and consistent self-image. Those facts imply that he will regard the great gains in self-esteem he has achieved with Betty to be unique to his relationship with her. He is also likely to regard them as irreplaceable through alternative relations. (The important exception here is that from the intimacy with Betty, Jim may have acquired internal resources that support his new self-evaluation, or, perhaps, he has developed communication skills that give him confidence in having productive intimate interaction with other partners.)

In contrast, if Betty began with high self-regard, she is less likely to value their interaction as much as he does. Her initial self-regard implies that she has the internal resources and social skills necessary to maintain it in other relationships. In those differences in person factors are found the bases for their asymmetrical dependence on intimacy with each other. In short, the outcomes from intimacy are very great for Jim and (subjectively) unique to the relationship with Betty, but the parallel outcomes (if any) are less for her and are (subjectively) available with other partners.

The Partner's Intimacy with a Third Person: The Violation of Exclusivity Assumptions. The special nature of intimate interaction, the *improved attitudes toward the self*, and the experiences showing the *safe haven* provided by a trusted partner, all feed into Jim's hopes and expectations that the special relationship is mutually valued and is likely to continue into the future. It is, of course, the threat to the fulfillment of those expectations posed by a third person that provokes Jim's feelings of jealousy. As noted earlier, jealousy develops in anticipation of possible loss of a unique dyadic relationship with an intimate partner through their association with a third party. And, of course, it also develops when that loss becomes a reality. At the point of actual loss, the affective components tend to shift from feelings of anxiety and inadequacy, to feelings of anger, directed at both the prior partner and the third party.

When Betty is known or suspected to interact intimately with a third party and to do so in a way similar to what Jim has experienced, there are several distinct consequences for him. The positive outcomes derived from the intimacy are withdrawn. There is a betrayal of the implicit commitments (made by investments of time and affect) or explicit promises that were made in the course of that intimacy. And probably the most serious consequence is that the authenticity of the information gained from the prior interaction is cast in doubt. Unless Jim has learned how to support a positive self-image by independent information sources (own thoughts, information now gained from other associates), the gains he has made in his view of himself are likely to be lost. When deserted by Betty, Jim is likely to ask himself, "Am I really what I saw myself to be in my intimate relationship with her?" The many reasons for anger create a complex emotional mix, and a not uncommon reaction is violence against the ex-partner and/or third party. (For example, of 306 homicides in Detroit in 1972, 58 were known to be the result of jealousy, according to Daly, Wilson, & Weghorst, 1982.)

A Broad View of Jealousy and Intimacy. We have provided an interdependence analysis that supports Simmel's assertions that intimacy "is the tendency of relations between two persons" which explains why "the dyad constitutes the chief seat of jealousy." Our analysis is intended to extend the understanding of jealousy beyond the particular realm customarily assumed for it. Jealousy is *not* unique to threats relating to sexual relations. Wherever intimate interaction is important in a close dyadic relationship, a real or imagined third party will provide the provocation to the fear, anger, and/or sadness that constitute jealousy. With the birth of their first child, a father who finds himself deprived of the customary intimacies with his wife may be jealous of her attentions to the infant. Two sisters who have regularly exchanged intimacies create the conditions for possible jealousy if one of them enters into similar conversations with a school chum. A patient in psychotherapy who has received attentive and sensitive responses to his dreams and anxieties from a psychotherapist may become jealous when his impression of the uniqueness of their interaction is dispelled by overhearing her similar conversations with another patient. In short, we argue that sexual interaction is but one concrete example of a much broader category of intimate interactions that make a pair vulnerable to jealousy.

Space does not permit us to consider what broader social conditions may promote jealousy. For example, the interpersonal functions served by intimate interaction seem to require, as its "customers and providers," persons indoctrinated in a cultural model that places high value on individuality. Those would be the Jims of the world who need to feel "unique," to be validated as "special," and the Bettys of the world who are able to serve as sensitive confidants. Our argument implies that some such model may be necessary if the "script" of intimate interaction is to find the "actors" for whom its roles seem to be tailored.

19.4 Matrix Representations

Table E19.1. These matrices show the situation in which dependent Jim is uncertain about Betty's dependence on him, and the two contrasting ways Jim may resolve the uncertainty.

TABLE E19.1.

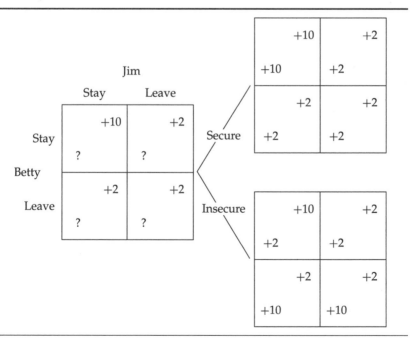

Table E19.2. This matrix shows the risk-taking situation that Jim faces in deciding whether or not to reveal a secret to Betty. It is a situation of incomplete information inasmuch as he does not have a basis for knowing her outcomes from their various actions. Jim's options are to reveal a secret or to remain silent. Betty's options are to support or criticize him.

TABLE E19.2.

	Jim (A)	
	Reveal	Silent
Support	+10	0
	?	?
Betty (B)		
Criticize	−10	0
	?	?

Entry #20

N-Person Prisoner's Dilemma

Tragedy of the Commons

20.1 Examples

This situation is a generalization of the two-person Prisoner's Dilemma situation to more than two persons (hence, it is sometimes called an *N*-person PD or *NPD* situation; its other most common label is a *social dilemma*). As in the Prisoner's Dilemma Game (PDG), each person's concern is whether she or he should make a choice which advantages the self but disadvantages others – in this situation, several others (e.g., all members of a group). For example, the police might give each member of a captured *N*-person criminal gang the same basic choices offered to the two prisoners in the classic PD (e.g., confess and thereby knock 1 year off your own sentence but also thereby add 2 years to every other gang member's sentence). Or, members of a fishing village might choose between maximizing their individual catches (and, hence, profits) versus limiting their catches/profits (but thereby helping to preserve the long-term viability of the fishing grounds upon which this and future generations of the village depend); Hardin's (1968) famous example of the "Tragedy of the Commons" is a very similar social dilemma. Or, members of a group performing some task might choose between working hard (and thereby improving the chances of the group performing well and quickly) or hardly working (and saving themselves effort while still profiting from any group success). In each case, noncooperative behavior brings better outcomes for oneself; but cooperative behavior brings better outcomes to the group as a whole.

Norbert Kerr had primary responsibility for preparation of this entry.

20.2 Conceptual Description

This situation has the same essential conceptual requirements as the basic two-person PD (see Entry #5, section 5.2). As illustrated above, the noncooperative choice yields better outcomes for self than a cooperative choice (Bilateral Actor Control). At the same time, a noncooperative choice yields worse outcomes for the others involved (Mutual Partner Control). The disadvantages of noncooperative behavior for the group as a whole are greater in an absolute sense than the advantages it yields for the individual actor (Partner Control is greater than Actor Control). Thus, like the two-person Prisoner's Dilemma, the N-person Prisoner's Dilemma confronts an individual with the choice of whether to pursue good outcomes for oneself at a major cost to the others involved or to pursue good outcomes for the others at a smaller cost to oneself (i.e., poses a conflict of "me vs. we"). The exchange of benevolent, cooperative behaviors yields greater outcomes for all individuals ("exchange with mutual profit") than does an "exchange" of noncooperative behavior.

Thus, the N-person Prisoner's Dilemma is a generalization of the two-person case to situations involving more than two persons. But the shift from two to N ($N > 2$) persons also brings other important psychological changes (Orbell & Dawes, 1981). First, in the two-person situation, the harm done by a defecting choice falls entirely on the single other. In the NPD, this harm is diffused across and shared by several (sometimes many) others. So, for example, some degree of harm to the fishing grounds is caused by a fisherman maximizing (vs. restraining) the size of his catch. However, when one divides this harm by the total number of others (in this and future generations) harmed, the harm to each other person may rightly be perceived as being quite small (particularly in contrast to the personal benefit of catching all one can). From the group's perspective, the difficult thing about this situation, of course, is that even if the degree that one harms each other group member by defecting is trivial, if enough people defect, the harm (in toto) can be substantial (e.g., the group can destroy the common resource it depends upon; Hardin, 1968).

Second, in the two-person PD, it is impossible to make one's choices anonymously. Each prisoner can easily infer what choice his partner-in-crime has made; that is, by knowing one's own choice (confess vs. not confess) and knowing one's ultimate sentence, the other's choice is evident. However, in the NPD, choices can be (and often are) anonymous. Unless every fisherman can be compelled to report his catch (and there are no devious ways to conceal catches above the ecologically responsible catch limit), there may be no way of telling which particular fishermen are being uncooperative; in fact, it might not be until long after one defects that the consequences of such defection are noticeable to anyone. To the degree that cooperation is motivated by concern with meeting others' normative expectations, we could expect such anonymity to undermine cooperative behavior (cf. Kerr, 1999).

Finally, in the Iterated two-person situation (see Entry #12) one can exercise one's control over the other's outcomes (i.e., use one's Partner Control) to shape the other's behavior (see Entry # 12, section 12.4). However, because the harm done by noncooperation is diffused throughout the entire group in the iterated NPD, one typically cannot do this. Suppose the villagers all agree to catch limits to preserve the commons. Further, suppose a few of the villagers violate the agreement (probably anonymously) and take larger catches. One can retaliate by increasing one's own catches, too, but this ends up punishing everyone, both the guilty (who are overharvesting) and the innocent (who are not). Consequently, compared to the PDG, it is much more difficult to use Partner Control to encourage mutual cooperation in NPDs or social dilemmas.

20.3 Variants and Combinations

The simplest (and a quite common) social dilemma situation is one in which the nature and level of interdependence is the same for each and every member of the group. For example, every fisherman could have the same capacity boat, the same opportunity to fish, the same value placed on each fish caught, and so on. Within this relatively simple situation there are many interesting variations. One distinction is whether noncooperative behavior actively harms the group (reduces others' outcomes) or simply fails to benefit the group (fails to increase others' outcomes). The former type of social dilemma often takes the form of a *resource dilemma*, confronting the individuals with the decision whether or not – and how much – to take from a commonly shared resource. The latter type of social dilemma often takes the form of a *public good dilemma*, confronting individuals with the decision of whether or not – and how much – to contribute to a provision or maintenance of a *public good*.

Problems of providing or maintaining public goods (e.g., public radio, public parks, or an unpolluted, breathable atmosphere) are examples of public good dilemmas. Noncooperative behaviors mean forgoing an opportunity to benefit others. The essence of public goods is that, once provided, they are available to all (even those who did nothing to provide them can enjoy public parks, public radio, and clean air). The essence of the dilemma in providing public goods is that one might be tempted to free ride on others' contributions, enjoying the public good without bearing the cost of providing it, yet universal free riding deprives all in the group of a valued public good. When the public good is some reward for successful group performance, many group performance tasks can also be recognized as types of social dilemmas, in which noncooperation consists of making suboptimal contributions in effort, free riding on the efforts of others (Kerr, 1986).

In some cases, provision of a public good is not a continuous matter (as, e.g., with polluting the atmosphere) but requires some critical level of contributions (as, e.g., school band members raising sufficient money for the public good of a band trip). Such *step-level* public goods problems may present exceptions to the defining rule in Prisoner's/social Dilemmas that one is *always* personally better off defecting, no matter what others do (see section 20.5 below); for example, if the group were exactly one contribution short of providing a valuable public good, cooperation might be both the collectively and personally more rewarding choice.

Problems of preserving shared resources (e.g., fishing grounds, a water supply) are examples of resource dilemmas (sometimes also referred to as *commons dilemmas*, following Hardin's (1968) seminal description of the "tragedy of the commons"). Noncooperative behaviors mean taking something of value and thereby reducing what others may harvest. Such dilemmas often combine problems of social interdependence with problems of temporal traps – situations in which direct (or short-term) interests conflict with long-term interests (see Entries #13 and #14). So, for example, overharvesting fish may both immediately reduce the opportunity for others' catches (social trap) and also hasten the day when the fishing grounds are depleted (temporal trap). Of course, the longer the delay of punishment (or reinforcement), the harder it will be to recognize and respond appropriately to the outcome contingencies of the situation (e.g., Skinner, 1953). This kind of temporal uncertainty can also be compounded by uncertainty about how resilient the environment will be to human choices (i.e., *environmental uncertainty*, e.g., how quickly could fishing grounds recover if all fishing were halted). There is good evidence (e.g., Rapoport, Budescu, Suleiman, & Weg, 1992) that the latter kind of uncertainty reduces cooperation.

Of course, in many actual social dilemma situations, there is likely to be some asymmetry in the group members' preferences and aversions.

For example, compared to a poor person, it is less of a sacrifice for a rich person to contribute toward providing a public good (e.g., supporting a symphony or museum) (cf. Rapoport, Bornstein, & Erev, 1989); likewise, members of that public will usually differ in the value that they place on such public goods. Such asymmetries can introduce a number of complications, such as concerns with whether one's contributions and benefits are equitable (e.g., how much more should the rich pay for benefits available to all?; cf. Van Dijk & Wilke, 1994).

The simple NPG situation can also be a building block for other, somewhat more complex situations. Three examples are:

1) Social dilemmas can themselves be nested. So, for example, members of a fishing village facing the social dilemma of preserving their fishing grounds might also have to decide whether to voluntarily contribute to the public good of a sanctioning system (e.g., fishing inspectors), designed to identify and fine those who exceed catch limits (Yamagishi & Sato, 1986).

2) Rather than a simple contrast between personal and collective interest, a situation may pose conflicts between different levels of a hierarchically nested set of groups (Wit & Kerr, 1992). Most academicians have been in situations (e.g., hiring decisions) in which personal interests, departmental interests, and university interests could not simultaneously be maximized.

3) A situation may simultaneously involve both social dilemmas and intergroup competition (Rapoport & Bornstein, 1987). Competitive team sports provide a good illustration – team members may have to decide how much effort to contribute toward the team's performance, when the team which performs best obtains some valued reward (e.g., a championship).

20.4 Interaction Process and Person Factors

Behavioral choice in the social dilemma situation can be analyzed as a response to a number of different motives. The most obvious are the twin motives of narrow self-interest (or *greed*) and a desire to avoid exploitation at the hands of others (or *fear*). Other salient motives include a) the desire to manage the common resource or welfare efficiently, b) the desire to benefit others, c) the impulse to do what others do (i.e., be guided by *descriptive norms*), and d) the motive to comply with salient *prescriptive* or *injunctive norms* (Cialdini, Reno, & Kalgren, 1990). Each of these motives can shape and guide the course of social interaction. Although there has been a considerable amount of research done on behavior in social dilemma situations (see Komorita & Parks, 1994, for a good overview), much of it fails to probe social interaction patterns. Many studies have focused on one-shot, noniterated games. And even in those studies where repeated choices are made, the experimental constraints nearly always severely limit the scope of interaction. For example, the modal experimental paradigm employs ad hoc, temporary groups of strangers, allows no verbal interaction between group members, and provides individuals with no or preprogrammed feedback of others' choices. Nevertheless, one can identify a number of interesting patterns of interaction likely to arise in these situations (beyond those already considered in two-person PD situations, see Entries #5 and #12).

20.4.1 *Identification with One's Group*
Social identity theory has stressed the importance that our group memberships take in defining and bolstering our sense of self. In her work in this area, Brewer (e.g., Kramer & Brewer, 1984) has suggested that with stronger identification with one's group comes a blurring of the distinction between personal and collective welfare. Of course, if one derives some personal benefit from other group members' benefits, one begins to transform the social dilemma situation from one in which personal and collective interests conflict to one in which they coincide. Brewer and her colleagues have shown that temporary situational factors which induce a stronger sense of collective identity (e.g., having a shared fate) produce a greater willingness to act cooperatively.

In many actual, real-world social dilemma situations, the groups involved are likely to be well established, cohesive ones in which there already is a strong sense of shared social identity. What's missing in the social psychological research literature is work focusing on how this shared social identity is shaped through group interaction. One might speculate that a history of positive interaction experiences, particularly in situations that promote people's willingness to "be a valuable group member" (such as in social dilemmas), can contribute to the development of shared social identity. For example, the verbal reports of participants after encountering a social dilemma reveal that mutual cooperation is associated with positive feelings toward one another, whereas incidents of free riding and exploitation are associated with negative feelings toward one another (Dawes, 1980).

20.4.2 *Prescriptive Norms in Social Dilemmas*

As we have noted repeatedly in this Atlas, social norms offer one means of regulating interaction in contexts of interdependence, particularly in situations characterized by Mutual Partner Control (like social dilemmas). A fair amount of research now documents the importance of two such norms in social dilemmas – the commitment norm and the reciprocity norm.

When the structure of a social dilemma is well understood, the desirability of mutual cooperation – versus either exploitation by some or universal defection – is evident. One means of translating this understanding into action is through mutual voluntary commitments/promises to cooperate. A well established finding of the social dilemma literature is that allowing group members to discuss the dilemma encourages cooperation. Research by a number of scholars (e.g., Kerr & Kaufman-Gilliland, 1994; Orbell, Van de Kragt, & Dawes, 1988) now suggests that such discussion results in group members making and feeling bound by commitments to cooperate with one another. What's not well understood, at present, is what exactly is required during interaction to bind (and, subsequently, to release) people from such a commitment norm.

When a cooperative act is seen as such (and not as an act of stupidity or a strategy to lure another into a position where she or he can be exploited), the reciprocity norm provides another means of getting to mutual cooperation. At least part of the power of a tit-for-tat strategy (always do what one's partner did on the last trial) to encourage cooperation in one's partner in the iterated two-person situation (Axelrod, 1984) may lie in its harnessing of this norm (see Entry # 12, section 12.4). Its power is somewhat diffused, though, in the NPD because cooperative or uncooperative acts often cannot be "targeted" at just one other group member (who's cooperativeness or uncooperativeness one wishes to reciprocate). Nevertheless, recent theoretical and empirical work suggests that cooperation may be reciprocated even in such diffuse social dilemma situations (e.g., Komorita & Parks, 1999).

Another interesting direction for research on norms in social dilemmas is the way in which cooperation-encouraging norms evolve over long periods of interaction. There is relatively little empirical work on this question, but computational modeling is beginning to be used (e.g., Liebrand & Messick, 1996) to try to identify models of social interaction (including social interaction norms) which can explain the indisputable fact that people routinely cooperate at high rates in many real-world social dilemmas (contrary to the predictions of basic game theory).

20.4.3 Entering and Exiting Situations of Interdependence

A common feature of social interaction is that one usually gets to choose which dyadic or group relationships one enters or leaves. It seems likely that people will remain in relationships where (most or enough) others act cooperatively but will leave relationships where they feel exploited. Unfortunately, almost none of the social dilemma literature has focused on situations where group members have this discretion.

There are a few notable and interesting exceptions (also see Entry #21, Movement among Situations). Orbell and Dawes (1993) have shown that if one assumes that others will act as one acts (sometimes as a result of a "false consensus" effect), we could expect those who are chronic defectors to avoid entering into interdependent situations with one another (since they would anticipate mutual defection), but those who are chronic cooperators to more willingly enter into such situations. Dawes and Orbell suggest that this mechanism may be sufficient to explain the evolution of cooperative groups.

In some contexts of interdependence, one may not have complete discretion about whether to enter or remain. A largely unexplored empirical issue is how groups regulate their memberships to solve social dilemmas. In this vein, some work (e.g., Kerr, 1999) has begun to show that the threat of exclusion by other group members who can learn one's history of choices in the social dilemma can lead group members to cooperate more.

20.4.4 Person Factors

Kelley (1997b) suggests that we can consider interpersonal dispositions to be stable tendencies to employ certain decision rules in contexts of social interdependence (among other contexts). He also suggests a few (viz., five) generic choice points that routinely arise in contexts of interdependence. Here we will briefly consider examples of how such dispositions can be engaged at two such generic choice points in social dilemmas.

Outcome Rules. The most obvious (and thoroughly researched) decision rules are those that govern the value placed on own versus other outcomes at the point of behavioral choice. As noted earlier (Entry # 5, section 5.4), it is possible to identify people who chronically place some nontrivial value on others' welfare (so-called cooperators, prosocials, or Js for Joint benefit), those who place relatively no value on anyone else's welfare but their own (individualists or Os for Own benefit), and even those who place a negative value on others' welfare relative to their own (competitors or Rs for Relative benefit), and incorporate such values into behavioral decision rules. Clearly, those with cooperative social motives are more prone to cooperate in social dilemmas than are those with individualistic or competitive motives (e.g., Liebrand & van Run, 1985), yet – unlike competitors – individualists may be cooperative when doing so is seen as serving their long-term personal welfare. Unlike many laboratory situations, interactions in the real world are often characterized by a future of interactions, in which the interaction partners are able to reciprocate noncooperation (or to engage in retaliation). Under such circumstances, individualists are likely to cooperate, especially when they experience strong dependence on such others (Van Lange, Agnew, Harinck, & Steemers, 1997).

Information Rules. At various points in interaction, one may employ certain decision rules to provide and acquire information about others. A relatively simple such rule is one manifested by individuals possessing *depersonalized trust* in others. In situations in which one has no or ambiguous information about others' intentions, people with high (low) trust may assume the best (worst) about others' intentions, and act accordingly. For example, Messick et al. (1983) showed that when feedback indicated that a shared resource pool was being exhausted, those high in trust responded by reducing their own consumption, whereas those low in trust increased their harvesting, trying to get what they could while something still remained. This suggests that those high in trust assumed that others, like them, would recognize and respond to the need for mutual sacrifice to save the commons.

Liebrand, Van Lange, and their colleagues have shown similar information-acquisition/interpretation rules linked to social orientations. Those with competitive social motives not only place a lower value on others' welfare (an outcome rule), but are more likely to interpret cooperative behavior by others as indicative of weakness (Liebrand, Jansen, Rijken, & Suhre, 1986) or stupidity (Van Lange, Liebrand, & Kuhlman, 1990) than those with cooperative motives. The latter, by contrast, tend to attach stronger moral significance to others' level of cooperation (Liebrand et al., 1986). Also, prosocials base their expectations regarding others' cooperative or noncooperative behavior more on morality and less on intelligence. Individualists and competitors base their expectations more on perceived intelligence, expecting cooperation from unintelligent others and noncooperation from intelligent others (Van Lange & Kuhlman, 1994).

20.5 Matrix Representations

It is not possible to represent the NPD using the same simple 2×2 matrix which we have heretofore used to represent dyadic interdependence.

However, for symmetric situations (same benefits and costs for every group member), one can do so with a slightly different matrix representation which presents the outcome for a focal person as a function of his or her own choice and the combined choices of the rest of the group.

Table E20.1. The matrix presented in Table E20.1 summarizes a five-person analogue of the two-person PD situation. No matter what others do, refusing to confess (i.e., cooperating with other gang members) adds a year to one's own sentence, whereas confessing (i.e., defecting) adds 2 years to every other gang member's sentence. Confessing is personally rational, yet universal defection leads to a much worse outcome (7 years in prison) than universal cooperation (1 year in prison).

TABLE E20.1. *Situational Representation of an N-Person Prisoner's Dilemma*

| | Number of Other Gang Members Confessing | | | | |
Own Choice	0	1	2	3	4
Not confess (cooperate)	−1	−3	−5	−7	−8
Confess (defect)	0	−2	−4	−6	−7

Note: Matrix entries are number of years that the focal person must spend in prison (hence, the negative sign).

Table E20.2. Table E20.2 shows a matrix representation of a common experimental social dilemma, the Give Some Game. Suppose one can keep or contribute one's $2 endowment. If contributed, it is quadrupled to create a larger public good which is split equally among all five members of the group. Again, refusing to cooperate results in better personal outcomes, no matter what others do, but universal defection leads to a much poorer outcome ($2) than universal cooperation ($6.40).

TABLE E20.2. *Situational Representation of a Give Some Game*

| | Number of Others Contributing | | | | |
Own Choice	0	1	2	3	4
Contribute (cooperate)	0	1.60	3.20	4.80	6.40
Keep (defect)	2	3.60	5.20	6.80	8.40

Note: Matrix entries are number of dollars that the focal person will receive.

Table E20.3. Table E20.3 shows a step-level public good problem. Again, every member of a five-person group has a $2 endowment. If three or more group members contribute (and, hence, lose) their endowments, each group member receives a $4 reward (public good).

TABLE E20.3. *Situational Representation of a Step-Level Public Good Problem*

Own Choice	Number of Others Contributing				
	0	1	2	3	4
Contribute (cooperate)	0	0	4	4	4
Not contribute (defect)	2	2	2	6	6

Note: Matrix entries are number of dollars that the focal person will receive.

Graphical Representations. One may also represent social dilemmas graphically. Figures E20.1, E20.2, and E20.3 provide graphical analogues of the previous three matrix examples. Note that for the "pure" social dilemmas (Figures E20.1 and E20.2), defection always results in better outcomes than cooperation, no matter what others are doing. In the step-level situation (Figure E20.3), this is usually but not always true. Other two- or N-person interdependence situations can be recognized as similar variations on the social dilemma graph (Liebrand, 1983). By changing the rules slightly in our Give Some Game (Table E20.2), it can be converted into an N-person analogue of other two-person situations of interest. For example, suppose that every contributor in the old Give Some Game received a $4 prize, but she or he received only a 30% share of the public good. In such a case, the Give Some situation of Figure E20.2 would become the N-person Chicken situation (see Entry #7) of Figure E20.4 (see Liebrand, 1983). Or, alternatively, suppose that those who contributed to the public good would get a bonus of 25% of their share of the public good. In such a case, the Give Some situation of Figure E20.2 would become the N-person Assurance or Trust situation of Figure E20.5. As one can see, in contrast to the social dilemma situation, the lines cross over each other in the latter situations, such that cooperation (contributing) leads to better rewards when most others refuse to cooperate (the Chicken situation, see Fig. E20.4) or when others agree to cooperate (the Trust situation, see Fig. E20.5).

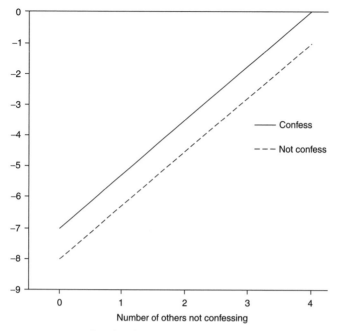

FIGURE E20.1. Graphical representation of Table E20.1, N-person Prisoner's Dilemma

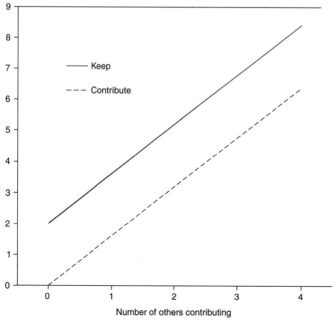

FIGURE E20.2. Graphical representation of Table E20.2, N-person Give Some Game

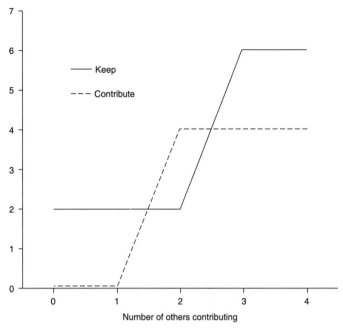

FIGURE E20.3. Graphical representation of Table E20.3, a step-level public good problem

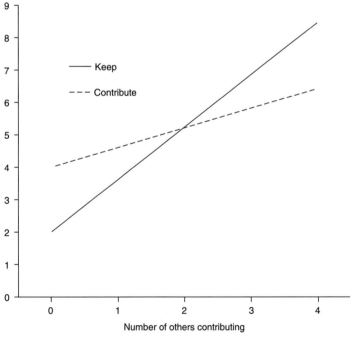

FIGURE E20.4. Graphical representation of an N-person Chicken Game

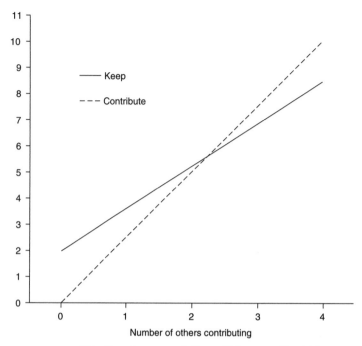

FIGURE E20.5. Situational representation of *N*-person Trust/Assurance Game

MOVEMENT FROM ONE SITUATION
TO ANOTHER

Entry #21

Movement among Situations

Where Do We Go from Here?

21.1 Examples

Interpersonal life is not limited to responding to situations. Social interactions and relationships also unfold through movement among situations, or *situation selection*, which involves the choice to enter another situation or to change an existing situation in a significant manner. Choosing to enter another situation, or to change an existing situation, brings the individual, the interaction partner, or the pair (or even an entire group) to situations that are "new" (i.e., different from the previous situation) in terms of outcomes, options, or both.

Whether to attend a party, visit parents-in-law, or sit close or not so close to a colleague at a dinner party are examples of situation selections that involve entering (or avoiding) a new situation. Also, individuals may choose to interact in "cooperative situations," when, for example, they seek out each other's company (e.g., "let's have a beer"), or "competitive situations," when, for example, they seek out a situation in which to compare their strength or ability (e.g., "let's play a game of chess"). These examples illustrate situation selections in which an individual actively seeks to enter a particular situation. However, situation selections are also revealed in changing a situation, such as, for example, stopping work on a joint project, changing the topic of conversation during dinner, or leaving a party early.

The reader will note that the above examples illustrate fairly explicit forms of situation selections. However, situation selections can also take more implicit forms, including various nonverbal behaviors, such as

Paul A. M. Van Lange had primary responsibility for preparation of this entry.

gazing, tone of voice, and smiling. For example, seeking eye contact, perhaps coupled with smiling, are subtle forms of behavior by which individuals select a situation permitting the initiation of a conversation.

21.2 Conceptual Description

As indicated by the question that appears in the title of this chapter ("Where do we go from here?"), the question of where the actor, the partner, or the two-as-pair might be going is pertinent to our understanding of situation selection: the *where-to-go* question. Additionally, there is the question of who controls where the two are going: the *who-controls* question. That is, who determines (or controls) the situation selections; the actor, the partner, or the actor-and-partner together. These two questions will be discussed in the following sections, as well as the general importance of situation selection.

21.2.1 *Which Situations May Be Selected: Where Do We Go from Here?*
In principle, people may be able to go to any of the situations discussed in this Atlas. It is useful to characterize such movement in terms of the "dimensions" that underlie the "geography" of the situations discussed in this Atlas. Similar to going north or south, east or west, situation selections can be understood in terms of shifts in (a) degree of interdependence, (b) mutuality of dependence, (c) covariation of interests, and (d) basis of dependence.

One fundamental dimension relevant to the situational space in which people move is *degree of interdependence*. That is, individuals may move from situations involving independence (see Entry #1) to the many different situations involving interdependence. Increasing levels of commitment, closeness, and intimacy seem to be some of the concepts that individuals may use to characterize their movement to increasing interdependence. For example, we may initiate disclosing private information with very good, trusting friends, but may not initiate, or may not respond favorably to, such self-disclosures by less good friends. Related to the degree of interdependence is *mutuality of dependence*. Individuals may sometimes wish to select or create situations in which they are less dependent on the other than vice versa. For example, a friend might propose that he will drive so as to avoid dependence on his or her friend's driving ability.

People may also seek out situations that vary in terms of *covariation of interests*, such as the "cooperative" and "competitive" situations described at the beginning of this entry. "Seeking company" was described as an example of selecting a situation of correspondent interest, and "seeking to play a game of chess" was described as an example of selecting a situation of conflicting interest. Sometimes, individuals may actively seek to change a situation so that the interests of the two (or more) individuals are less conflicting (or more correspondent). For example, two "old friends" may change a "competitive" topic of conversation (e.g., how much money they make in their jobs) into a more "cooperative" topic (e.g., the great time they had together at college).

Relevant to *basis of dependence*, sometimes individuals may seek out or avoid situations characterized by strong levels of Joint Control and turn them into ones in which the partners are unilaterally dependent. For example, after observing that it is rather difficult to work together on a joint task – one of the partners is a morning person, the other is an evening person – they might sharply define different subtasks and work on them individually at their own pace and preferred time. A situation characterized by strong Mutual Joint Control, challenging their abilities to coordinate, is replaced with a situation characterized by greater levels of strong Mutual Partner Control.

Situation selections may also involve choices among situations that differ in the degree to which these situations extend over time (i.e., the *"time-extendedness"* of situations). For example, people may commit themselves to a long-term collaborative project or to a relatively short-term project. And within the context of ongoing close relationships, there is substantial variability in the degree to which individuals commit themselves to a long-term relationship, which is closely associated with tendencies toward investing in that relationship (Rusbult, 1983). It is also interesting to consider situation selections from an *informational* point of view. Sometimes people seek out new, adventurous situations, as part of a process of "getting to know each other more." Examples are raising some conversational topics as a further exploration of a new relationship, or a survival weekend for a work team to examine how well members of the team can work together in various contexts outside of the work setting. Sometimes people seek out situations that are a little "cloudy," or attributionally ambiguous for others, allowing them to hide some aspects of themselves (e.g., not-so-good intentions, a lack of skill). For example, one might avoid several "deeper" conversation topics so as to hide some inclinations or tendencies that would not reflect favorably on oneself, the interaction partner, or their relationship. Or one might adopt one of several strategies, including self-handicapping (i.e., sabotaging one's own performances to provide excuses for subsequent failures; Berglas & Jones, 1978) to hide an imperfection of themselves, the partner, or the relationship.

21.2.2 *Control over Situation Selections: Who Controls Where We Are Going?*

But who controls the movement from one situation to another? Similar to the distinctions among Actor Control, Partner Control, and Joint Control as three sources of outcome control (see chapter 2), such movement could be controlled by the actor, the partner, or the actor-and-partner together. (Of course, the selection of situation is also sometimes "externally" controlled, i.e., controlled by the environment or fate. For example, one sees a colleague when doing grocery shopping and now faces the situation of whether or not to initiate a brief conversation. Or, it just so happens that husband and wife like or do not like the same piece of furniture that they come upon when shopping. We will not address the topic of external control here, but simply confine our attention to the interpersonal forms of control. It is of interest to note here that a good number of situations are externally controlled; cf. Emmons & Diener, 1986).

Actor Control and Partner Control of movement involve unilateral control, which exists when the individual or the partner is in the position to unilaterally determine where they will go. Some examples can be found in "asymmetrical" relationships, in which one of the two partners typically takes the lead by virtue of some basic person factors (i.e., one person has greater knowledge or experience in that interaction-relevant domain) or social person factors (e.g., one person has a strong aversion to following and a strong desire to taking the lead). For example, a parent often determines for a child the toys at a playground with which the child can or cannot play; the project manager initiates a discussion in a team about how to coordinate some public relations activities. But, of course, unilateral control also occurs in more "symmetrical" relationships. For example, whether to stay late at work or whether to phone one's partner during a trip are decisions that are by and large unilaterally controlled, yet have implications about whether the couple will soon talk to each other. And, finally, several of the more "subtle" situation selections that we mentioned earlier (e.g., various nonverbal behaviors) tend to be taken (or at least initiated) unilaterally.

Joint Control reflects the interaction effect of the actor (self) and partner in determining where they will go, individually or collectively. One important form of Joint Control is when either partner can veto a situation selection. Such is the case, for example, when a new project will be initiated if and only if both partners agree to participate in it. Joint Control is very common in relationships and groups. For example, where to have a vacation is often decided on the basis of conjunctive Joint Control, in which either person can veto a proposal. Similarly, in contexts of group decision making, decisions may be reached following the rules of "majority vote" or "unanimity," whereby the majority or all have to agree before there is "green light" to go for it (e.g., the appointment of new leader, the implementation of a new strategy, or the production of a new product).

21.2.3 *The Importance of Situation Selection*
The idea that actors select different situations has received relatively little attention in the history of psychology. Although classic writings by, for example, Lewin (1935, 1936/1966) and Festinger (1950) involve concepts such as movement and locomotion, this work focused on understanding movement and change within a particular situation, rather than movement among situations. The topic has received somewhat greater attention in the past decades (e.g., Emmons, Diener, & Larson, 1986; Mischel, 1999; Snyder & Ickes, 1985). More recently, Snyder and Cantor (1998) provide a functionalist analysis of several issues relevant to selecting situations. They conceptualize the interplay of features of situations and features of persons in terms of *reciprocal influence*, arguing that situations influence individuals *and* that individuals influence situations through selecting them.

It is interesting to speculate about why the phenomenon of situation selection has received (relatively) little attention. A *first* reason may be that the experimental approach has led researchers to focus on how individuals respond to different experimental situations or conditions, rather than on why and how individuals select their own situations (or conditions). Given that the experimental approach has been dominant in psychological research, it becomes understandable that situation selection is considered a threat to the validity of our empirical studies (i.e., it violates random assignment of participants to conditions) rather than an important topic for empirical investigation (cf. Snyder & Ickes, 1985).

A *second* reason is that the tools used to represent situation selection activities were considered to be rather awkward. As a case in point, Heider (1958; p. 14) considered Lewin's (1935) topological psychology, in which movement was argued to be a central process, to be "cumbersome" and "inadequate" in analyzing and understanding interpersonal phenomena. Nevertheless, there is good reason to believe that issues relevant to situation selection will receive greater empirical attention in future research. One largely theoretical reason is that if one seeks to understand social interaction sequences in dyads and groups, it becomes crucially important to examine the goals with which individuals might enter or avoid situations. A largely methodological reason is that our research methodology and statistics have become more sophisticated, increasingly allowing us to examine issues that have to do with the flow (or dynamics) of interaction. For example, we have witnessed a growth in research focusing on ongoing interactions in relationships, which is promoted by new methodologies (e.g., the Rochester Interaction Record; Reis & Wheeler, 1991) and statistical tools (e.g., the Social Relations Model; Kenny & La Voie, 1984). Other examples are the development of new dynamic paradigms for the study of cooperation and competition in dyads and small groups, such as simulations of various types of social dilemmas involving change (e.g., resource dilemmas, social traps; e.g., Messick & Brewer, 1983) and actions other than cooperation and competition that can be taken to resolve social dilemmas (e.g., withdrawal, choosing among varying levels of interdependence, possibilities for excluding others from the group; e.g., Kerr, 1999; Orbell, Schwartz-Shea, & Simmons, 1984; Van Lange & Visser, 1999; Yamagishi, 1988a).

The importance of situation selection has been recognized explicitly in Kelley's (1984b) transition list approach. This approach, which is briefly described in chapter 3, represents patterns of interdependence in terms of both options and outcomes, as well as in terms of the sequences and timing of behavior and interactions. As such, the transition list approach provides conceptual tools by which situation selection and related behaviors can be described. The transition list can be used to describe not only the various situations described in this Atlas, including the more complex, time-extended situations, but also the two topics that we discussed in the previous sections of this chapter: (a) the *where-to-go* question: Where might the actor, the partner, or the two-as-pair be going, and (b) the *who-controls* question: Who determines or controls the situation selection (i.e., the actor, the partner, or the actor-and-partner together).

21.3 Variants and Neighbors

It is virtually impossible to discuss "neighbors," because situation selection represents a very broad class of situations, including single-, two-, and three-component patterns, time-extended patterns, incomplete information situations, and N-person situations. Nevertheless, it is useful to briefly outline some variants of situation selection. In analyzing such situations, it is useful first to deal with the where-to-go question (and then later address the who-controls question). In principle, one could move in any of the several "directions" implied by the dimensions discussed in this Atlas. In reality, of course, an individual's degrees of freedom may be importantly constrained by various basic person factors, such as having insufficient skill or resources so that some options for movement are not available. For example, when Mary comes home exhausted, it may be nearly impossible for her to initiate a very lively conversation with John.

The situation of Movement among Situations may be very complex, but it need not be so. For example, whether to initiate a brief chat with a colleague in the corridor of a university building, whether to phone one's partner during a brief business trip, or whether to smile at one's neighbor is not necessarily complex. Also, whether to leave early from a party when not feeling well is a situation defined by very clear options (leaving early or not) and very clear outcomes (not leaving while feeling sick is obviously very unattractive). Thus, several situation selections may be relatively simple in terms of options and outcomes. In fact, some of these selections (e.g., nonverbal behaviors) are made almost continuously when one is around other people.

One unique quality of situation selection is that the pair will enter another situation. The possibility of entering some situations may bring about considerable uncertainty, which may derive from the fact that the individual has acquired very little experience with that situation, or the individual has no experience with the partner-in-that-situation. For example, it is easy to imagine that risk averse individuals wish to avoid some new situations, or that individuals who are uncertain about their relationship do not wish to explore several new situations with one's partner (e.g., after a couple of weeks of dating, one may not yet be ready for meeting the partner's parents). Given the potentially large levels of uncertainty that could be linked to the situation of Movement among Situations, this situation is somewhat similar to Joint Decisions under Uncertainty (see Entry #17), which is characterized by incomplete information.

Also, for some important situation selections, the outcomes may not only be somewhat uncertain, they may also extend over a relatively long period of time and may be reversible or irreversible. The choice to have sexual intercourse without adequate protection is an obvious example of a situation selection with far-reaching, rather uncertain, "delayed," and somewhat irreversible consequences. As such, this situation sometimes is related to other "time-extended situations" in which the dimension of time is essential (e.g., Iterated Prisoner's Dilemma, Investment, Delay of Gratification, see Entries #12, #13 and #14). Such far-reaching consequences may not always be clear at the time one is faced with these options.

21.4 Interaction and Person Factors

The situations that individuals select, and whether these selections are controlled by the actor, the partner, or the actor-and-partner, are important to our understanding of social interactions. We first suggest that the questions of "where-to-go" and "who-controls" are important to understanding *personality processes*, including how personality differences may influence situation selections, and how personality development may be shaped by situation selections. Next, we discuss how situation selections may underlie *relationship processes*, including the formation and development of relationships, and how such selections may determine patterns of interaction in the context of ongoing relationships.

21.4.1 Personality Processes

In this Atlas, we use the term "personality" quite broadly, representing forces (e.g., motives, ability, goals, orientations) that reside within the individual and that may, or may not, be stable across situations or over time. Many of the situation selections we engage in ourselves, or observe in others, may be guided by *basic person factors*. For example, when one happens not to feel very well, one may have a substantially weaker motivation or ability to explore – and become actively involved – in new situations (e.g., one is less likely to invite friends over for dinner; one may be less likely to discuss important issues with a partner). Some situation selections may not even be considered when one lacks important resources (e.g., skill, money, or energy) that are essential to a particular situation selection. For example, a couple may not (even) consider the possibility of paying a joint visit to a particular foreign country, because one of them has a fear of flying, they cannot really afford it, or they find traveling too tiring. Thus, many situation selections are motivated or guided by basic person factors.

Situation selections are also guided by *social person factors*, such as, for example, fairness, affiliation, competition, control, dominance, honesty, trust, and optimism. The need for affiliation, for example, is positively correlated with the time spent in social rather than individual recreations (Diener, Larson, & Emmons, 1984; Emmons et al., 1986). As another example, relative to individuals who are more self-centered in their orientation, individuals with prosocial orientation are more likely to volunteer (as well as to volunteer a greater number of hours) as a participant in psychology experiments if their university would indeed benefit from such activities (McClintock & Allison, 1989).

Why Does Personality Affect Situation Selection? Many of the examples used to illustrate the link between personality and situation selection are consistent with a simple model that assumes congruence between the goals one seeks to attain and the selection of situations that afford the pursuit of those goals. Such goal-based models of situation selection should "explain" many situation selections. An illustrative example may be derived from Snyder and Gangestad's (1982) research on self-monitoring, that is, differences in the degree to which one is sensitive to the demands of social situations. Individuals scoring high on self-monitoring tend to behave in accordance with the demands of social situations, whereas those scoring low on self-monitoring behave in ways that express their internal attitudes and dispositions. These differences are also reflected in situation selection activities. Unlike high self-monitors, low self-monitors tend not to enter situations that are incongruent with their personal beliefs, values, and attitudes (Snyder & Gangestad, 1982).

As another example, whether to ask permission to cut into the queue in order to copy five pages on the copying machine has a relatively simple goal structure. The goal to do things efficiently should be particularly salient to an impatient person who would be more likely to ask for this favor than a more relaxed person. Also, some differences in psychological states (e.g., whether or not one is in a hurry because of a very tight external deadline), rather than "stable traits," may be closely associated with situation selections.

People sometimes identify goals "in a situation" even when these goals are not so evident to others. For example, a competitively oriented person may define even a fairly "cooperative situation" as one in which one can only win or lose, thus requiring strength and competence (cf. Liebrand, Jansen, Rijken, & Suhre, 1986). As another example, in his research on the self-evaluation maintenance model, Tesser (1988) found that male siblings sometimes have a desire to compete with each other even when the situation does not directly call for competition (for a similar discussion, see Chicken, Entry #7).

Decisions to leave a particular situation are often a consequence of the degree to which one is able to satisfy one's primary interaction goals in that situation. For example, many individuals will be strongly motivated to move out of a situation when one is unable to attain good outcomes for one's self (cf. Miller & Holmes, 1975). Recently, Van Lange and Visser (1999) extended the stay versus leave decision to choices among situations that differed in the degree of interdependence. They observed that prosocials, individualists, and competitors selected situations of high interdependence when they repeatedly found that they were able to satisfy their interaction goals in those situations. This finding was observed irrespective of whether their goals focused on enhancing collective outcomes (and equality in outcomes), own outcomes, or relative advantage over others. A particularly noteworthy finding was that, unlike prosocials and individualists, competitors selected situations of *low* interdependence when they interacted with another person who followed the tit-for-tat strategy. Because the tit-for-tat strategy reciprocates both cooperation and noncooperation, one cannot beat a partner who employs it. Therefore, competitors facing such partners could not achieve their interaction goals. Thus, moving to lower rather than higher levels of interdependence with tit-for-tat partners became attractive to them. Incidentally, this finding suggests an important benefit of the tit-for-tat strategy: namely, its ability to drive away those who are oriented toward obtaining greater outcomes than others, while "attracting" those who are willing to behave cooperatively.

The Importance of Situation Selection to Understanding Personality. Efforts devoted to enhance our understanding of the link between personality and situation selection are important for at least three general reasons. *First*, there may be interesting asymmetries between the "active" (situation selection) and "passive" sides of personality differences. Personality traits may to some degree differ from one another insofar as some are conceptually more strongly linked to situation selections, whereas other personality traits are more strongly linked to responding to situations. For example, sensation seeking, which centers on the seeking of arousal-provoking situations, the seeking of excitement, and the seeking of change and unpredictability (Zuckerman, 1974, 1978), is conceptually strongly linked to situation selection. A less obvious possibility is dispositional optimism (Scheier & Carver, 1987), with optimists being more likely to enter new situations and change existing situations than pessimists. Another, though related, example may be the fifth dimension of the Big Five, often labeled culture or intelligence, which centers on openness to new experiences, motivation to learn, and flexibility in thinking. In contrast, traits such as "field-dependence" and "authoritarianism" (Adorno, Frenkel-Brunswik, Levinson, & Sanford, 1950) might be more strongly linked to responding to situations.

Second, insofar as personality differences influence the selection of situations, the further development of that personality should be influenced by those selections. Research by Caspi and his colleagues (Caspi & Bem, 1990; Caspi, Elder, & Bem, 1988) suggests that the situations that individuals encounter in their lives can exert important influences on their behavior, which in turn may shape their personalities. For example, it is easy to imagine that, relative to individualistic and competitive individuals, prosocial people are more likely to select situations in which they can help and support others (e.g., becoming a nurse), which may then reinforce their prosocial orientations. Similarly, shy children may avoid certain social situations, which in turn may not help them to overcome their shyness (Caspi et al., 1988). Given that interaction is a function of two individuals *and* the situation, it should be clear that interaction experiences, and the learning from such experiences, should be powerfully influenced by the kinds of situations in which individuals finds themselves, including ones that they selected themselves. If shy children tend to avoid, for example, Encounters with Strangers (see Entry #16), then they may be less likely to learn norms, conventions, and etiquette, the mastery of which makes one comfortable in such encounters.

Third, failure to take into account the possibility that people select situations can yield an incomplete understanding of a particular phenomenon in real life. To illustrate: in the debate regarding media influences on aggressive behavior, there are several experiments, using random assignment procedures, which provide good evidence in support of the claim that exposure to aggressive films and movies can cause aggressive behavior. But, at the same time, research also reveals that, in real life, there is a self-selection process in such exposure. Relative to individuals who are less prone to be aggressive, aggression-prone individuals are more likely to attend films and movies that contain aggressive behavior (Black & Bevan, 1992). Thus, violence in the mass media seems to bring about aggression, but only in those who are predisposed to expose themselves to such films and movies.

21.4.2 Relationship Processes

Situation selection represents activities that are important to interaction patterns that unfold in the context of dyads and small groups. Below, we seek to illustrate situation selection (a) in the course of relationship formation, and (b) in ongoing relationships.

Situation Selection in the Course of Relationship Formation. The processes preceding relationship formation seem appropriately captured by dilemmas of independence versus interdependence, that is, dilemmas of autonomy versus closeness. These "dilemmas" tend to center on deliberations about avoiding versus approaching situations with greater stakes and interdependence. For example, Gottman (1983) describes patterns of avoidance versus approach between previously unacquainted preschool children. These children tended to engage in an alternation between increasing and decreasing the closeness of their play. Specifically, they moved from side-by-side activities in which the risk of conflict is low, to interactive play characterized by greater risk but considered more interesting, and then back again to the more independent side-by-side play.

Similarly, early stages of relationship development tend to be characterized by the conflict between retaining one's autonomy versus increasing closeness (e.g., Eidelson, 1980). Typically, ambivalence regarding closeness tends to be pronounced at first, after which it tends to decline when the couple moves to greater levels of mutual commitment. One might argue that the exchange of intimacy involves risk and uncertainty which, when fruitfully solved, may yield a foundation for enhanced trust and commitment. For example, in the process of getting to know each other, young couples may raise topics of conversation that are quite personal, which may be a source of commitment and love as well as a source of embarrassment, disagreement, and conflict. As such, it is plausible that, at early stages of relationship development, partners may alternate between selecting situations characterized by closeness and interdependence versus selecting situations characterized by autonomy and independence.

Obviously, various basic and social person factors may be related to situation selection at early stages of a relationship. As to basic person factors: One person may be (largely) unable to spend much time with the partner because of a very hectic period at work. Or if two new partners are together, one of them may find it difficult, due to a lack of skill or experience, to enhance the levels of comfort and intimacy. As to social person factors, one might think of differences in trust and attachment. Much previous research on adult attachment styles focuses on the three-category typology involving (a) secure attachment (enjoyment of closeness and confidence in partner's responsiveness), (b) ambivalent attachment (strong desire for closeness but lack of confidence in partner's responsiveness), and (c) avoidant attachment (no strong desire for closeness and lack of confidence in partner's responsiveness; Hazan & Shaver, 1987). Relative to the other two attachment styles, when individuals with an anxious/ambivalent attachment style enter a new relationship, they should experience pronounced levels of ambivalence about selecting situations with high interdependence, because they desire intimacy and closeness but are not very trusting of others.

Many examples illustrate that people seek varying levels of interdependence and closeness on the basis of global impressions of another person. In hiring colleagues, choosing friends, initiating relationships, we avoid other individuals whom we do not trust and avoid places where they might "hang out" (e.g., "this is not my kind of bar"). Often, such situation selections are based on initial impressions of the other, which may influence, for example, how many seats away an individual wants to sit from another person (consider, for example, the so-called seating procedure that has been used in previous research as a specific behavioral measure of closeness; e.g., Pleban & Tesser, 1981; for an example in research on stereotyping, see Macrae, Bodenhausen, Milne, & Jetten, 1994).

Initial impressions may play a key role in the formation of a more enduring relationship. The "selection" of a partner can be understood in terms of situation selection, in that one seeks greater levels of interdependence and closeness with a person to whom one is attracted. The issues focusing on attraction, mating, or partner selection have received considerable attention, and the main conclusion is that people are more attracted to similar others than to dissimilar others (Byrne, 1969) and more "repulsed" by dissimilar others than by similar others (Rosenbaum, 1986). A nice example is described by Buss (1987), who asked participants to express their preferences regarding a dating partner on several bipolar adjectives that assessed the Big Five dimensions of personality: agreeableness, extraversion, conscientiousness, emotional stability, and openness/intelligence. The results revealed for each dimension a significantly positive correlation between their own scores and preferences regarding a potential partner's score. These correlations were significant when their "own scores" were measured using self-reports *and* using partner-reports, that is, judgments of their preferred partner by their actual dating partners.

Situation Selection in Ongoing Relationships. In the context of ongoing relationships, individuals continuously select situations. As noted earlier, one important "dimension" is degree of interdependence, representing level of commitment, closeness, and intimacy. For example, disclosing important information about the self and sharing secrets illustrate how individuals may (or may not) enhance levels of interdependence. Self-disclosure, for example, may be rooted in personality variables (e.g., attachment style; Mikulincer & Nachshon, 1991), as well as in patterns of interactions that are shaped in the context of the relationship

(Reis & Shaver, 1988; for a recent illustration on the sharing of secrets, see Finkenauer & Hazam, 2000). Typically, by engaging in strong levels of self-disclosure, one communicates trust in the partner, who in turn tends to reciprocate such disclosures. Hence, self-disclosure can be largely understood in terms of enhancing interdependence, a pattern of interaction that is often initiated by one partner and reciprocated by the other.

Relationships provide many occasions for exchanging various psychological benefits. One important situation that is selected by one partner is the seeking of psychological support, enabling the other to give or not to give that support. This situation has been examined in research by Simpson, Rholes, and Nelligan (1992). Dating couples were videotaped for 5 minutes in a waiting room while the women waited to participate in an activity known to provoke anxiety in most people. The women had previously been shown the room in which they would "participate" – a darkened, windowless room that looked like an isolation chamber and contained psychophysiological equipment. Nothing had been revealed to the men about this stressful situation. Prior to the experimental sessions, Simpson et al. assessed the attachment styles of both women and men. Independent observers rated each partner's behavior on several dimensions, which included global impressions and specific behavior.

The results revealed that for women with a secure attachment style, there was a positive association between seeking emotional support from their dating friend and the degree to which they were fearful: Stress caused securely attached women to seek support (e.g., openly discussing their anxiety with their partner, seeking contact with the partner). For those with an avoidant attachment style, there was a negative association between seeking emotional support and the degree to which they were fearful: Stress caused women with an avoidant attachment style to "pull back" from their partner. The results also revealed that for men with a secure attachment style there was a positive association between observed fear in the woman and the amount of support given her: The woman's stress led these men to give support. Conversely, for men with an avoidant attachment style, there was a negative association between the woman's observed fear and the amount of support given her: The woman's stress led these men "to move away from her."

The Simpson et al. (1992) study illustrates that one needs to know both persons' tendencies (adult attachment styles, in this example) in order to understand their interactions. In general terms: The support-giving situation is instigated by a woman who is fearful about the upcoming situation but secure about her relationship with her partner. Then, the sought emotional support is provided by a partner who is also secure about their relationship. Thus, in this study, by selecting situations and responding to such selections, both partners shape their interactions and the outcomes following from such interactions (e.g., whether the need for support and understanding is fulfilled).

Situation selections can also be directly relevant to the junctures between one's existing relationship and the possibility of entering a new one. As a case in point, Johnson and Rusbult (1989, Study 2) examined individuals' ratings of a fictitious, opposite-sex applicant for a campus-based computer dating service. Participants were presented with a photo of an applicant, along with some fictitious personal information about the applicant. Using pre-test ratings of the applicant's photo, the physical attractiveness of the applicant was systematically manipulated. Among several dependent measures, Johnson and Rusbult asked participants "Do you want to go on a date with X?" Not surprisingly, results revealed that participants were more likely to "go for a date" when the applicant was very attractive. More importantly, individuals who were more strongly committed to their own relationship, were far less likely to go for a date when the applicant was very attractive than were individuals who were only weakly committed to their relationship. Such influences of differences in commitment were weaker when the applicant was moderately attractive or relatively unattractive. Thus, individuals with strong commitment may be relatively more likely to avoid situations in which they might meet attractive alternative partners. Other dependent measures (e.g., ratings of alternative partner) revealed evidence consistent with the hypothesized "derogation-of-alternatives" phenomenon among individuals with strong commitment to their current relationship. That is, the impact of commitment on various evaluations of the alternative partner was especially pronounced when confronted with highly attractive alternative partners.

Several situation selections in ongoing relationships tend to involve Joint Control. Where to go for a vacation, whether or not to visit parents-in-law, or how to spend a Saturday night seem to be situation selections that are a result of such control. Research suggests that many consumer decisions are a result of Joint Control. For example, the actual buying of a certain piece of furniture is influenced by how each partner feels about that particular piece of furniture and, ultimately, both need to agree before they will buy it. Such forms of Joint Control seem to be even more pronounced in happy than in unhappy couples (e.g., Wagner, Kirchler, & Brandstatter, 1984). Complementary lines of research not only support this conclusion, but also suggest the complex form of Joint Control that exists in family contexts involving children. Children tend to take a very active role in certain decisions and, at least in the context of family and peers, they tend to favor decisions procedures characterized by consensus rather than procedures characterized by majority rule or authority control (Helwig & Kim, 1999).

We close by outlining the nature of the association between personality processes and relationship processes. It is clearly important to realize that the personalities of the individuals involved in a relationship are important determinants of interaction processes that take place in that relationship. However, just as personalities influence relationships, so may relationships influence personality processes. Relationships form the powerful interpersonal contexts in which personality may persist or change. On this point, there is intriguing evidence indicating that individuals who select partners who are similar to themselves exhibit greater temporal stability in their dispositions than do individuals who select partners who are somewhat less similar to themselves (Caspi & Herbener, 1990). Thus, situation selection is relevant to understanding not only relationship development and processes, but also personality development (continuity and change) in the context of relationships.

21.5 Transition List Representation

Because individuals can move to any of the situations described in this Atlas, the situation of Movement among Situations can vary from relatively straightforward and simple to very complex. For illustrative purposes, we discuss a fairly simple situation of Movement among Situations and represent it in terms of a transition list (see Table E21.1).

The situation represents possible movement from Independence to Corresponding Mutual Joint Control. In list L, the two persons are independent because their own outcomes are completely controlled by themselves. That is, irrespective of the choice made by the other person, choosing option 1 always yields positive outcomes (+2), whereas option 2 yields negative outcomes (−2). This holds for both person A and person B. Thus, from this perspective, they are likely to choose option 1. However, this also means that they will remain in the situation of Independence, whereas the overall situation affords moving to a situation of Corresponding Mutual Joint Control (list M).

Both individuals will move to list M, if one is, or both are, willing to make the personally costly choice for option 2. That is, as can be seen in list L, if either person A or person B, or both, choose option 2, they will move to a situation of Corresponding Mutual Joint Control. In that latter situation, both individuals should make the same choice (either option 1 or option 2), and they will both receive very good outcomes. That is, matching is quite rewarding (+4) whereas mismatching is somewhat costly (−2).

The movement from Independence to Corresponding Mutual Joint Control (at a cost to at least one person) generally resembles situations in which one individual has to engage in a personally costly behavior to bring both partners to an interdependent situation which affords very good outcomes for both individuals. For example, one or both partners could do some "preparatory work" (e.g., getting information about the most recent movies that one could rent) for a joint activity that both find very enjoyable. Once they have that information, they could match their preferences (e.g., choosing either to watch together a movie they both like very much – "Movie 1" or "Movie 2" – or to get both movies and watch them separately). This situation may in fact also arise in the context of relationship formation: Examples are to invest a little in getting to know another person so as to initiate a fruitful collaboration, to form a mutually gratifying friendship, or to simply be able to engage in activities that both regard as very enjoyable. Finally, we should note that more complex examples of Movement among Situations are easy to generate. The above situation could become more complex if, for example, the two persons could easily move back and forth between Independence and Corresponding Mutual Joint Control, or if the two persons could move among more than just two situations.

TABLE E21.1. *Situational Representation of Movement from Independence (List L) to Corresponding Mutual Joint Control (List M)*

Lists	Options	Possible Selections	Outcomes for A and B		Transition to Next List
L	(a1, a2)	a1b1	+2,	+2	X
	(b1, b2)	a1b2	+2,	−2	M
		a2b1	−2,	+2	M
		a2b2	−2,	−2	M
M	(a1, a2)	a1b1	+4,	+4	X
	(b1, b2)	a1b2	−2,	−2	X
		a2b1	−2,	−2	X
		a2b2	+4,	+4	X

PART THREE

EPILOGUE

The front of the dust jacket of this book is decorated with an early map of the world, titled *Charta Cosmographica, Cum Ventorum Propria Natura Et Operatione* (*A Cosmographical Map with Special Consideration of the Nature and Operation of the Winds,*[1] also reproduced here as Figure E.1). This map was produced by Gemma Frisius in 1544 for inclusion in a very early atlas, Peter Apain's *Cosmographicus Liber.* Quite apart from its cartographic content, Frisius's map is a beautiful, fanciful work, filled with clouds, heroic figures, strange land and sea creatures, and numerous "windheads" blowing lustily. Noteworthy in this regard are the three grisly windheads at the bottom of the map who express the then-widespread belief that plague was carried by winds from the south.

Of course, compared to a modern world map, Frisius's early map manifests many gross inaccuracies. The continent of North America is reduced to a narrow sliver, to the west of which lies a narrow Pacific Ocean and then a barren Asian mainland. Caribbean islands like Hispanola and Cuba, first discovered by Columbus only about 50 years earlier, are given exaggerated prominence. Distances are often distorted (e.g., between the British Isles and the North American coast). And certain large land masses, like Australia and Japan, are missing altogether.

On the other hand, even this very early map contains much accurate and useful information. The actual shapes, sizes, and locations of Africa, Eurasia, and South America are roughly captured. In the region that the mapmaker and his contemporaries knew best (western Europe), the level

[1] Thanks to Pat Laughlin for providing a translation from the Latin.

Norbert Kerr had primary responsibility for preparation of the epilogue.

FIGURE E.1

of detail is very good; for example, one can easily find the Mediterranean islands of Cyprus, Crete, Sicily, Sardinia, and Corsica. And even in recently discovered lands, much is conveyed. For example, in northwestern South America one can find Peru, land of the Incas, and also, on the eastern, Brazilian coast, dangerous lands reputedly inhabited by "Canibales." Likewise, with a careful look, one can find such important landmarks as the Isthmus of Panama, the River Nile, the Himalayas, and the Equator. Thus, although this early map was far from perfectly accurate, the navigators, traders, colonizers, and explorers of the day probably found it a very useful tool.

It has been less than 50 years since Thibaut and Kelley (1959) first began to systematically explore the domain of social interdependence. It should not surprise us, then, if future generations of scholars eventually conclude that the mapping of interpersonal situations presented in this Atlas – like Frisius's early map of the physical world – contains many inaccuracies and omissions. In this epilogue, we briefly discuss some of our hunches about possible flaws, in the hope that they will be useful to future explorers. We also outline some empirical and theoretical explorations which could contribute to more accurate and comprehensive atlases in the future.

Terra Incognita

Frisius and other early cartographers realized that there were many unexplored territories in their world, *terra incognita*. In the *Charta Cosmographica*, for example, one sees far less detail in places like the interior of South America, northern Asia, the Arctic (Frisius's *Zona Frigida*), and the compressed North American continent (*Baccaleorum* for Frisius) than in places like Europe and North Africa. The former places were, for Europeans of the 16th century, remote, inaccessible, or rarely traversed.

In much the same way, in preparing this Atlas, we have tended to "stick to the coasts" – to the most accessible and fully explored interdependence situations. For example, most of our situations have been defined and illustrated for dyads with relatively uncomplicated response and information conditions. Most of the situations we have presented are very limited in time or focus on brief slices of what are likely to involve much more extended interactions. The behavioral explorers of our day (e.g., social psychologists, sociologists, and other behavioral scientists) have sensibly looked in these more accessible, more easily observed contexts first. Only occasionally have they (or we, e.g., for the N-person PD or the Delay of

Gratification situations) ventured into the tangled jungles of the "interior" (e.g., with group interdependence, lengthy interaction sequences, or uncertain futures). Are there unique or distinctive new situations to be identified in that interior? Undoubtedly so. We expect, though, that they may often be recognized and understood as variations or combinations of the simple situations we focus on here, much as Frisius and his fellow cartographers probably expected newly explored lands to contain many of the same basic features (rivers, plains, mountains, etc.) with which they were already familiar.

In this Atlas we have identified 21 prototypical situations (or broad classes of situations, like Encounters with Strangers or Third Parties). In all such taxonomic enterprises, one faces the challenge of where to draw the lines – which differences to pay attention to and which differences to ignore. Of course, cartographers face the same dilemma: Should Europe be considered a separate continent or just part of a single Eurasian continent? Should political, cultural, linguistic, tribal, topological, or any of several other distinctions be used to carve up the world? In preparing this Atlas, we have struggled with similar questions. Should every possible combination of the basic components identified in chapters 3 and 4 be distinguished as a unique situation? Which combinations are best considered fundamental and which simply variations on those more fundamental ones? The preceding chapters represent our resolution of such questions, but we readily acknowledge that there are other defensible ways in which to carve up the world of social interdependence (cf. Bugental, 2000; Fiske, 1992). Our taxonomy is grounded in the theoretical logic and language of interdependence theory. Alternative taxonomies might be based upon different theories or perhaps upon less "logical" foundations – for example, intuitively appealing differences among situations. However, we believe (or at least hope) that alternative taxonomies will end up being consistent with our core working assumption: that in interpersonal life, we encounter only a finite (and hopefully, reasonably small) number of generic situations, characterized by objective and distinctive features, affording the expression of certain basic personal dispositions, and engendering distinctive patterns of interpersonal behavior.

On the "Reality" of Situations

In the first few chapters of the Atlas, we developed our conception of "the situation." An important aspect of that conception is that situations are "real," that they have an existence and effects that are, to some degree, distinct and independent of our more behaviorally proximal, subjective construals of them. As noted in chapter 1, this position swims against some strong currents in contemporary psychology. One such current would give explanatory priority (or even supremacy) to the personal and subjective *meanings* actors give to situations (e.g., Ross & Nisbett, 1991). Another, more extreme, postmodernist position would hold that situations can never be known in any objective sense, and that any understanding of them must of necessity be constructed and wholly subjective.

Such issues quickly tend to suck us into philosophical quicksand that we would rather avoid. Rather than debate such thorny ontological questions, we recall instead Samuel Johnson's reaction to Bishop George Berkeley's antimaterialist doctrine that everything material was an illusion that really existed only in the mind of God. Boswell wrote:

After we came out of the church, we stood talking for some time together of Bishop Berkeley's ingenious sophistry to prove the non-existence of matter, and that everything in the universe is merely ideal. I observed that though we are satisfied his doctrine is not true, it is impossible to refute it. I shall never forget the alacrity with which Johnson answered, striking his foot with mighty force against a large stone, till he rebounded from it, "I refute it thus." (Boswell, 1799/1961, p. 333)

Our reply to those who question the reality of situations with social interdependence is similar. We have defined and illustrated a number of basic social situations that we (and, we expect, most readers) encounter with some regularity. Those encounters produce noticeable, regular patterns of thought and action – we "rebound from" these situations in distinctive and regular ways that convince us that there is, indeed, something real there and that something is the pattern of interdependence that exists between actors and its consequences for their social interaction. If we have done a sufficiently good job of describing the situations and common reactions to them, the reader may come to share our conviction that the situations we identify are, in most important regards, as real as Sam Johnson's stone.

New Expeditions

Much of the data that Frisius and his contemporaries used to construct their maps was based on the records brought back to Europe by explorers and traders. Their expeditions were usually motivated by hopes of profit or conquest and rarely conducted solely for the sake of geographical knowledge. Having completed our Atlas, we can envision a number of scientific research expeditions that could add appreciably to our store of knowledge about situations of interdependence.

One difference between a simple map and an atlas is that the latter provides all sorts of additional information besides the shape, size, and location of land and sea – information such as population, rainfall, vegetation, language, and so forth. A glaring deficiency of this Atlas is that although we have proposed a set of basic situations, we have presented little information about how common each of those situations is – how often do we find ourselves facing a Chicken situation, the pure Mutual Partner Control situation, and so on? A research expedition to acquire such information would be interesting and valuable. For example, we envision training respondents to recognize each of the 21 basic situations and then randomly sampling the interpersonal situations they encounter daily (e.g., using a suitably modified version of the Rochester Interaction Record; Reis & Wheeler, 1991; cf. Pemberton, Insko, & Schopler, 1996) to distinguish between relatively rare and more commonplace interdependence situations.[2]

Such an exploration would be useful to estimate the "population" of each situation and also to better understand just who chronically inhabits each one. For example, Nisbett and Cohen's work (e.g., Nisbett & Cohen, 1996) led us to speculate in Entry #7 that persons reared in a culture of honor or those high in narcissism are relatively more likely than others to find themselves facing Chicken situations. Also, it seems likely that each situation is relatively prone to be faced by people with certain combinations of age, sex, culture, and personality (cf. Miller & Holmes, 1975, for the Prisoner's Dilemma). It also seems probable that some situations are more likely than others to arise in particular stages of relationships. For example, we have speculated that the beginnings of relationships tend to involve situations of relatively low interdependence, while well-established relationships tend to be characterized by higher levels of interdependence. Such questions might be answered by research expeditions that supplemented the simple tallying of situations

---

[2] Of course, we should not assume that the importance of situations (e.g., for personality development, for defining relationships) is determined solely by their frequency. At times, very rare events may turn out to be the most important ones. For example, infrequent events – like marriage proposals or our children's births – may be far more memorable and influential on our lives than more common, ordinary events – like brushing our teeth or sleeping. Similarly, certain relatively rare situations (e.g., a harrowing, character-defining test of courage in a Chicken situation) may have much more impact on our lives than more common ones (e.g., everyday situations of simple coordination and exchange).

with careful descriptions of the interactants and the nature of their relationships.

Travelers commonly use an atlas to plan their route of travel – how does one get from one place to another? An atlas will tell us, for instance, whether one can travel directly between two countries or whether one must traverse through a third country en route. We have, for the most part, considered each basic situation in isolation, without worrying whether occupation of one situation affects our chances of entering another (Entry #21 on Movement among Situations is a notable exception to this rule). It is possible, but not necessarily the case, for example, that people tend to move between situations that are neighbors in the three-dimensional conceptual space presented in chapter 4 (see Figure 4.1). We envision a longitudinal research expedition that samples situational occupancy and that utilizes time-series analysis to address this intriguing question.

It is a curiosity of standard atlases that the political boundaries – the boundaries used to demarcate the multicolored regions of a map – fail to identify the more salient, recognizable features of the societies and human groups that inhabit those regions. Korea is a good example. The language, traditions, social norms, topography, values, and so forth, of North and South Korea differ in few essential respects. The 48th parallel is a largely arbitrary, political line of demarcation, an accident of history. Another example – highlighted by the Gulf War of the early 1990s – is the land and culture of the Kurds, which sprawls across the borders of Turkey, Iran, and Iraq but is invisible on most maps. Although interdependence theory has led us to certain distinctions among various situations, we have too little solid evidence to conclude with confidence that these situations are psychologically distinct. Ultimately, this is an empirical question. The relevant "expedition" would require the close comparison of situations that our analysis identified as neighbors (e.g., those that lie close to one another in the three-dimensional space described in chapter 4). Are the usual behavioral responses to such neighboring situations sufficiently different to justify distinguishing them from each other? Might we find that certain conceptual features (e.g., covariation in interests) more reliably distinguish perceptual or behavioral reactions to situations than others, much as certain physical features (e.g., land masses and bodies of water) are more salient for cartographers than others are (e.g., type of vegetation). Or, should we conclude that, despite genuine conceptual differences (like the genuine political differences that underlie national borders), it is more accurate and informative to treat some of our situations as functionally equivalent?

The Atlas as a Theoretical Tool

Standard geographic atlases are typically used as tools to accomplish practical tasks – to locate a city, to plan a route, or to estimate distance. As noted previously, this Atlas is also intended to help solve very practical problems – e.g., to understand and reduce conflict in relationships, to facilitate better group performance, to promote collectively responsible use of shared resources, and so forth. But, in addition, this Atlas is intended to be useful as a theoretical tool – to provide a set of concepts and abstract principles that can fruitfully direct the search for and organization of knowledge about social interaction.

Only time will tell just how useful a theoretical tool the Atlas will turn out to be. However, this epilogue provides us with a good opportunity for identifying some of the ways we hope and expect the Atlas to be used. Good scientific theories should serve several functions. First, they bring order and coherence to existing observations. It is noteworthy that relatively little of the varied research discussed in the Atlas's individual entries was undertaken primarily to test the core theoretical ideas underlying the Atlas (viz., interdependence theory and the importance of the situation for social interaction). Yet this very diverse collection of results could be presented together here in the Atlas with some degree of coherence, illustrating the validity and explanatory utility of those core theoretical ideas.

A second function of scientific theory is to direct the search for new knowledge – to help identify the most interesting questions, to tell us where to look and what to look for. Each of the Atlas's entries has, to varying degrees, pointed to new research questions, questions that arise organically from attention to the nature and implications of the situation. One extensive and persuasive example is the interdependence analysis of jealousy in Entry #19, Third Parties. There have been many useful and empirically fruitful theoretical perspectives on jealousy, emphasizing, for example, the self (e.g., Salovey & Rodin, 1991), emotions (e.g., Salovey & Rodin, 1986), cognitions (e.g., White, 1981a & 1981b), social comparison (e.g., DeSteno & Salovey, 1996), attachment (e.g., Sharpsteen & Kirkpatrick, 1997), and human evolution (Buss, Larsen, Westen, & Semelroth, 1992). But one gets a rather novel perspective on this complex phenomenon by tracing its situational roots to the effects of informational interdependence in intimate relationships. As the presentation in Entry #19 shows, this theoretical perspective raises a number of novel questions for research on jealousy – for example, what is the role of the actual or perceived uniqueness of the relationship? What effects do the exchanges between intimate partners have on each partner's sense of self and, consequently, vulnerability to jealousy? How asymmetric is the dependence of the partners on each other when jealousy arises? How is jealousy related to the difficulties of coordinating information exchange in a three- versus two-person group? What is the role of mutual disclosure (both in the present and in prior relationships) on the etiology of jealousy? Many of these questions (and many others besides) might not be recognized as relevant to the study of jealousy without the theoretical tools suggested by interdependence theory.

Of course, there is nothing unique about jealousy in this regard. If the proper study of social psychology is interaction (Kelley, 2000), and if the starting point for an understanding of interaction is the situation within which interaction emerges and proceeds, then the study of all social psychological phenomena, from the most molecular processes of social cognition to the most complex functioning of organizations, can likewise profit from the diligent application of those same theoretical tools.

Tools of the Atlas Trade

Early European cartographers relied on limited geographic information – many areas of the globe had never been visited by European explorers (e.g., Australia). Moreover, early cartographers were limited by the tools available to them, which included not only the physical tools of their trade (e.g., tools of navigation and surveying) but also the conceptual tools of their trade. These conceptual tools have evolved over the centuries. For example, after Columbus, mapmakers had to move from the relatively easy task of representing a flat world on a two-dimensional grid to more complex representations that projected a spherical globe onto a flat surface. Similarly, progress in producing a more complete and accurate Atlas will depend, in part, on refining our conceptual tools.

The conceptual tool on which we have relied most heavily is interdependence theory (IT). We hope to have demonstrated to the reader the utility of contemporary IT for identifying and analyzing interdependence situations. But, like the early mapmakers who could only dream of gaining the eagle's perspective with hot-air balloons, much less the modern-day satellite, we can envision developments of IT that would enhance its utility. For example, chapter 4 showed how most of these 21 situations are simple combinations of two (of three) more basic components. Nearly all these combinations can be located on the planes of a three-dimensional solid (see Figure 4.4). But combining all three basic components (i.e., creating new situations which lie within the solid in Figure 4.4) makes possible many other situations, of which we have only considered the conjunctive and disjunctive situations. Penetrating the solid and charting its interior will undoubtedly be a significant advance for IT.

The transition list notation, introduced by Kelley (1984b), extended IT from static, one-choice situations to extended interactions. Although transition lists have proven to be useful descriptive tools, IT has yet to develop a systematic framework for organizing and categorizing possible transition lists (at least no framework as systematic as the component analysis of outcome interdependence, presented in chapters 2–4). Progress in this area could easily expand and refine the list of basic situations that extend in time (of which only a few are included in this Atlas, viz., the Investment, Delay of Gratification, and Joint Decision under Uncertainty situations).

IT explicitly acknowledges the importance of any situation's response and information conditions and has identified a few important varieties of these conditions. In our Atlas, we have noted how many basic situations of outcome interdependence might change as response and information conditions change, but in only a few instances (e.g., the Iterated PD, Delay of Gratification, and Investment for response conditions; the Strangers and Twists of Fate situations for information conditions, and Negotiation and Bird in the Hand for both) have we used response or information conditions to define a new situation. An important area for development of IT is expanding the vocabulary of response and (especially) information conditions, and then determining which combinations of outcome interdependence, response, and information conditions result in behaviorally equivalent situations.

Future Atlases of Interdependence Situations?

As new data and new tools accumulated, the inaccurate and incomplete maps and atlases of the 16th century were revised and improved, so that by the middle of the 18th century, world maps were nearly as good as those available today, at the beginning of the 21st century. The early atlases were useful enough to motivate their regular improvement. Whether there will be future atlases of interpersonal situations will likewise depend upon how useful this first effort proves to be. We would not be surprised if scholars of human interaction, whether in the next decade or the next century, conclude that there are more (perhaps many more) or perhaps fewer than the 21 basic situations we have identified in this Atlas. For our part, we will be content if this first Atlas of interpersonal situations eventually proves to have done as good and as useful a job of capturing the true shape of the world of human interaction as Frisius's early map captured the true shape of the physical world. More immediately, we will be content if you, the user of this Atlas, find that it helps you navigate your way around the complex world of human interaction.

References

Adorno, T. W., Frenkel-Brunswik, E., Levinson, D. J., & Sanford, R. N. (1950). *The authoritarian personality*. New York: Harper and Row.

Agnew, C. R., Van Lange, P. A. M., Rusbult, C. E., & Langston, C. A. (1998). Cognitive interdependence: Commitment and the mental representation of close relationships. *Journal of Personality and Social Psychology, 74,* 939–954.

Allison, S., Beggan, J., & Midgely, E. (1996). The quest for "similar instances" and "simultaneous possibilities": Metaphors in social dilemma research. *Journal of Personality and Social Psychology, 71,* 479–497.

Altman, I. (1975). *The environment and social behavior*. Monterey, CA: Brooks/Cole Publishing Co.

Altman, I., & Taylor, D. A. (1973). *Social penetration: The development of interpersonal relations*. New York: Holt, Rinehart and Winston.

Aron, A., & Aron, E. N. (1997). Self-expansion motivation and including other in the self. In S. Duck (Ed.), *Handbook of personal relationships: Theory, research and interventions* (2nd ed.; pp. 251–270). New York: Wiley & Sons.

Aron, A., Aron, E. N., Tudor, M., & Nelson, G. (1991). Close relationships as including other in the self. *Journal of Personality and Social Psychology, 60,* 241–253.

Aronoff, J., & Wilson, J. P. (1985). *Personality and the social process*. Hillsdale, NJ: Erlbaum.

Aronson, E., & Mills, J. (1959). The effect of severity of initiation on liking for a group. *Journal of Abnormal and Social Psychology, 59,* 179–181.

Arriaga, X. B., & Rusbult, C. E. (1998). Standing in my partner's shoes: Partner perspective-taking and reactions to accommodative dilemmas. *Personality and Social Psychology Bulletin, 9,* 927–948.

Asch, S. E. (1952). *Social psychology*. New York: Prentice Hall.

Atkinson, J. W. (1964). *An introduction to motivation*. Princeton, NJ: Van Nostrand.

Attridge, M., Berscheid, E., & Simpson, J. A. (1995). Predicting relationship stability from both partners versus one. *Journal of Personality and Social Psychology, 69,* 254–268.

Axelrod, R. (1984). *The evolution of cooperation*. New York: Basic Books.

Axelrod, R., & Dion, D. (1988). The further evolution of cooperation. *Science, 242,* 1385–1390.

Ayduk, O., Mendoza-Denton, R., Mischel, W., Downey, G., Peake, P. K., & Rodriguez, M. (2000). Regulating the interpersonal self: Strategic self-regulation for coping with rejection sensitivity. *Journal of Personality and Social Psychology, 79,* 776–792.

Bales, R. F., & Borgatta, E. F. (1955). Size of group as a factor in the interaction profile. In E. P. Hare, E. F. Borgatta, & R. F. Bales (Eds.), *Small groups: Studies in social interaction* (pp. 495–512). New York: Knopf.

Bandura, A. (1986). *Social foundations of thought and action: A social cognitive theory.* Englewood Cliffs, NJ: Prentice-Hall.

Banks, W. C., McQuater, G. V., Anthony, J. R., & Ward, W. E. (1992). Delayed gratification in blacks: A critical review. In A. K. Burlew, W. C. Banks, H. P. McAdoo, & D. A. Y. Azibo (Eds.), *African American psychology: Theory, research and practice* (pp. 330–345). Newbury Park, CA: Sage.

Barker, C., & Lemle, R. (1987). Informal helping in partner and stranger dyads. *Journal of Marriage and the Family, 49,* 541–547.

Barone, D. F. P. (1999). *The problem of interaction in experimental social psychology: An historical inquiry.* Paper presented at the meeting of Cheiron, International Society of the History of the Behavioral and Social Sciences, Ottawa, Canada, June, 1999.

Bar-Tal, D., Bar-Zohar, Y., Greenberg, M. S., & Hermon, M. (1977). Reciprocity behavior in the relationship between donor and recipient and between harm-doer and victim. *Sociometry, 40,* 293–298.

Batson, C. D. (1993). Communal and exchange relationships: What is the difference? *Personality and Social Psychology Bulletin, 19,* 677–683.

Batson, C. D. (1998). Altruism and prosocial behavior. In D. T. Gilbert, S. T. Fiske, & G. Lindzey (Eds.), *The handbook of social psychology* (4th ed.; Vol. 2, pp. 282–316). Boston: McGraw-Hill.

Batson, C. D., & Ahmad, N. (2000). Empathy-induced altruism in a prisoner's dilemma II: What if the target of empathy has defected? *European Journal of Social Psychology, 31,* 25–36.

Batson, C. D., Duncan, B. D., Ackerman, P., Buckley, T., & Birch, K. (1981). Is empathic emotion a source of altruistic motivation? *Journal of Personality and Social Psychology, 40,* 290–302.

Baumeister, R. F. (1991). *Escaping the self: Alcoholism, spirituality, masochism, and other flights from the burden of selfhood.* New York: Basic Books.

Baumeister, R. F., Bratslavsky, E., Finkenauer, C., & Vohs, K. D. (in press). Bad is stronger than good. *Review of General Psychology.*

Baumeister, R. F., Bratslavsky, E., Muraven, M., & Tice, D. M. (1998). Ego depletion: Is the active self a limited resource? *Journal of Personality and Social Psychology, 74,* 1252–1265.

Baumeister, R. F., Bushman, B. J., & Campbell, W. K. (2000). Self-esteem, narcissism, and aggression: Does violence result from low self-esteem or from threatened egotism? *Current Directions in Psychological Science, 9,* 26–29.

Baumeister, R. F., & Leary, M. R. (1995). The need to belong: Desire for interpersonal attachments as a fundamental human motivation. *Psychological Bulletin, 117,* 497–529.

Becker, H. S. (1960). Notes on the concept of commitment. *American Journal of Sociology, 66*, 32–40.

Bem, D. J., & Lord, C. G. (1979). Template matching: A proposal for probing the ecological validity of experimental settings in social psychology. *Journal of Personality and Social Psychology, 37*, 833–846.

Berglas, S., & Jones, E. E. (1978). Drug choice as a self-handicapping strategy in response to noncontingent success. *Journal of Personality and Social Psychology, 36*, 405–417.

Berkowitz, L. (1972). Social norms, feelings, and other factors affecting helping and altruism. In L. Berkowitz (Ed.), *Advances in experimental social psychology* (Vol 6., pp. 63–108). New York: Academic Press.

Berscheid, E., & Fei, J. (1977). Romantic love and sexual jealousy. In G. Clanton & L. G. Smith (Eds.), *Jealousy* (pp. 101–109). Englewood Cliffs, NJ: Prentice Hall.

Berscheid, E., Graziano, W., Monson, T., & Dermer, M. (1976). Outcome dependency: Attention, attribution, and attraction. *Journal of Personality and Social Psychology, 34*, 978–989.

Berscheid, E., & Reis, H. T. (1998). Attraction and close relationships. In D. T. Gilbert, S. T. Fiske, & G. Lindzey (Eds.), *The handbook of social psychology* (4th ed.; Vol. 2, pp. 193–281). Boston: McGraw-Hill.

Bettelheim, B. (1943). Individual and mass behavior in extreme situations. *Journal of Abnormal and Social Psychology, 38*, 417–452.

Bickman, L. (1974). The social power of a uniform. *Journal of Applied Social Psychology, 4*, 47–61.

Black, S. L., & Bevan, S. (1992). At the movies with Buss and Durkee: A natural experiment on film violence. *Aggressive Behavior, 18*, 37–45.

Blood, R. O., & Wolfe, D. M. (1960). *Husbands and wives: The dynamics of married living*. New York: Free Press.

Bornstein, G., Budescu, D., & Zamir, S. (1997). Cooperation in intergroup, N-person, and two-person games of chicken. *Journal of Conflict Resolution, 41*, 384–406.

Boswell, J. (1799/1961). *Boswell's life of Johnson*. London: Oxford University Press.

Bower, G. H., & Hilgard, E. R. (1981). *Theories of learning*. Englewood Cliffs, NJ: Prentice-Hall.

Bowlby, J. (1982). *Attachment and loss (Vol. 1: Attachment)*. London: Hogarth Press.

Bowlby, J. (1988). *A secure base: Parent-child attachment and healthy human development*. New York: Basic Books.

Bradbury, T. N., & Fincham, F. D. (1990). Attributions in marriage: Review and critique. *Psychological Bulletin, 107*, 3–33.

Brandstätter, H. (1983). Emotional responses to other persons in everyday life situations. *Journal of Personality and Social Psychology, 45*, 871–883.

Bray, R. M., Kerr, N. L., & Atkin, R. S. (1978). Group size, problem difficulty, and group performance on unitary disjunctive tasks. *Journal of Personality and Social Psychology, 36*, 1224–1240.

Brehm, S. S. (1992). *Intimate relationships*. New York: McGraw-Hill.

Brennan, K. A., Clark, C. L., & Shaver, P. R. (1998). Self-report measurement of adult attachment: An integrative overview. In J. A. Simpson & W. S. Rholes (Eds.), *Attachment theory and close relationships* (pp. 46–76). NY: Guilford Press.

Brewer, M., & Kramer, R. (1986). Choice behavior in social dilemmas: Effects of social identity, group size, and decision framing. *Journal of Personality and Social Psychology, 50,* 543–549.

Briar, S. (1966). *Welfare from below: Recipients' view of the public welfare system.* San Francisco: Chandler.

Brickman, P., Dunkel-Schetter, C., & Abbey, A. (1987). The development of commitment. In P. Brickman (Ed.), *Commitment, conflict, and caring* (pp. 145–221). Englewood Cliffs, NJ: Prentice-Hall.

Bringle, R. G., & Buunk, B. (1986). Examining the causes and consequences of jealousy: Some recent findings and issues. In R. Gilmour & S. Duck (Eds.), *The emerging field of personal relationships* (pp. 225–240). Hillsdale, NJ: Erlbaum.

Brockner, J., Bazerman, M. H., & Rubin, J. Z. (1984). The role of modeling processes in the "knee deep in the big muddy" phenomenon. *Organizational Behavior and Human Performance, 33,* 77–99.

Bugental, D. B. (2000). Acquisition of the algorithms of social life: A domain-based approach. *Psychological Bulletin, 126,* 187–219.

Bui, K. T., Peplau, L. A., & Hill, C. T. (1996). Testing the Rusbult model of relationship commitment and stability in a 15-year study of heterosexual couples. *Personality and Social Psychology Bulletin, 22,* 1244–1257.

Buss, D. M. (1987). Selection, evocation, and manipulation. *Journal of Personality and Social Psychology, 53,* 1214–1221.

Buss, D. M. (2000). The evolution of happiness. *American Psychologist, 55,* 15–23.

Buss, D. M., & Craik, K. H. (1980). The frequency concept of disposition: Dominance and prototypically dominant acts. *Journal of Personality, 48,* 379–392.

Buss, D. M., Larsen, R. J., Westen, D., & Semelroth, J. (1992). Sex differences in jealousy: Evolution, physiology, and psychology. *Psychological Science, 3,* 251–255.

Buunk, B. P. (1977). Personality, birth order and attachment styles as related to various types of jealousy. *Personality and Individual Differences, 23,* 997–1006.

Buunk, B. (1982). Anticipated sexual jealousy: Its relationship to self-esteem, dependency, and reciprocity. *Personality and Social Psychology Bulletin, 8,* 310–316.

Buunk, B., & Bringle, R. G. (1987). Jealousy in love relationships. In D. Perlman & S. Duck (Eds.), *Intimate relationships: Development, dynamics, and deterioration* (pp. 123–147). Newbury Park, CA: Sage.

Byrne, D. (1969). Attitudes and attraction. In L. Berkowitz (Ed.), *Advances in experimental social psychology* (Vol. 4, pp. 36–90). New York: Academic Press.

Cacioppo, J. T., & Berntson, G. G. (1999). The affect system: Architecture and operating characteristics. *Current Directions in Psychological Science, 8,* 133–137.

Cantor, N., Mischel, W., & Schwartz, J. C. (1982). A prototype analysis of psychological situations. *Cognitive Psychology, 14,* 45–77.

Caporael, L. R., Dawes, R. M., Orbell, J. M., & Van de Kragt, A. J. C. (1990). Selfishness examined: Cooperation in the absence of egoistic incentives. *Behavioral and Brain Sciences, 12,* 683–699.

Carver, C. S., Lawrence, J. W., & Scheier, M. F. (1996). A control-process perspective on the origins of affect. In L. L. Martin & A. Tesser (Eds.), *Striving and feeling: Interactions among goals, affect, and self-regulation* (pp. 11–52). Hillsdale, NJ: Lawrence Erlbaum.

Carver, C. S., & Scheier, M. F. (1982). Control theory: A useful conceptual framework for personality-social, clinical, and health psychology. *Psychological Bulletin, 92*, 111–135.

Carver, C. S., & Scheier, M. F. (1990). Origins and functions of positive and negative affect: A control-process view. *Psychological Review, 97*, 19–35.

Caspi, A., & Bem, D. J. (1990). Personality, continuity, and change across the life course. In L. Pervin (Ed.), *Handbook of personality: Theory and research* (pp. 549–575). New York: Guilford Press.

Caspi, A., Elder, G. H., & Bem, D. J. (1988). Moving away from the world: Life course patterns of shy children. *Developmental Psychology, 24*, 824–831.

Caspi, A., & Herbener, E. S. (1990). Continuity and change: Assortative marriage and the consistency of personality in adulthood. *Journal of Personality and Social Psychology, 58*, 250–258.

Charng, H., Piliavin, J., & Callero, P. (1988). Role identity and reasoned action in the prediction of repeated behavior. *Social Psychology Quarterly, 51*, 303–317.

Choi, I., Nisbett, R. E., & Norenzayan, A. (1999). Causal attribution across cultures: Variation and universality. *Psychological Bulletin, 125*, 47–63.

Christensen, A. (1987). Detection of conflict patterns in couples. In K. Halweg & M. J. Goldstein (Eds.), *Understanding major mental disorders: The contribution of family interaction research* (pp. 250–265). New York: Family Process Press.

Christensen, A., & Heavey, C. L. (1990). Gender and social structure in the demand/withdraw pattern of marital conflict. *Journal of Personality and Social Psychology, 59*, 73–81.

Christensen, A., & Heavey, C. L. (1993). Gender differences in marital conflict: The demand/withdraw interaction pattern. In S. Oskamp & M. Costanzo (Eds.), *Gender issues in contemporary society* (pp. 113–141). Newbury Park, CA: Sage.

Christensen, A., & Walczynski, P. T. (1997). Conflict and satisfaction in couples. In R. J. Sternberg & M. Hojjat (Eds.), *Satisfaction in close relationships* (pp. 249–274). New York: Guilford.

Cialdini, R. B. (1993). *Influence: Science and practice.* Boston: Addison Wesley Longman.

Cialdini, R. B., Reno, R. R., & Kalgren, C. A. (1990). A focus theory of normative conduct: Recycling the concept of norms to reduce littering in public places. *Journal of Personality and Social Psychology, 58*, 1015–1026.

Cialdini, R. B., Schaller, M., Houlihan, D., Arps, K., Fulz, J., & Beaman, A. L. (1987). Empathy-based helping: Is it selflessly or selfishly motivated? *Journal of Personality and Social Psychology, 52*, 749–758.

Cialdini, R. B., & Trost, M. R. (1998). Social influence: Social norms, conformity, and compliance. In D. T. Gilbert, S. T. Fiske, & G. Lindzey (Eds.), *The handbook of social psychology* (4th. ed.; Vol. 2, pp. 151–192). Boston: McGraw-Hill.

Clark, M. S. (1984). Record keeping in two types of relationships. *Journal of Personality and Social Psychology, 47*, 549–557.

Clark, M. S., & Chrisman, K. (1994). Resource allocation in intimate relationships: Trying to make sense of a confusing literature. In M. J. Lerner & G. Mikula (Eds.), *Entitlement and the affectional bond: Justice in close relationships* (pp. 65–88). New York: Plenum.

Clark, M. S., & Mills, J. (1979). Interpersonal attraction in exchange and communal relationships. *Journal of Personality and Social Psychology, 37*, 12–24.

Clark, M. S., & Mills, J. (1991). Reactions to and willingness to express emotion in communal and exchange relationships. *Journal of Experimental Social Psychology, 27*, 324–336.

Clark, M. S., & Mills, J. (1993). The difference between communal and exchange relationships: What it is and is not. *Personality and Social Psychology Bulletin, 19*, 684–691.

Clark, M. S., Mills, J. R., & Corcoran, D. M. (1989). Keeping track of needs and inputs of friends and strangers. *Personality and Social Psychology Bulletin, 15*, 533–542.

Cohen, D., Nisbett, R. E., Bowdle, B. F., & Schwarz, N. (1996). Insult, aggression, and the southern culture of honor: An "experimental ethnography." *Journal of Personality and Social Psychology, 70*, 945–960.

Cohen, D., Vandello, J., Puente, S., & Rantilla, A. (1999). "When you call me that, smile!" How norms for politeness, interaction styles, and aggression work together in Southern culture. *Social Psychology Quarterly, 62*, 257–275.

Cohen, D., Vandello, J., & Rantilla, A. (1998). The sacred and the social: Cultures of honor and violence. In P. Gilbert & B. Andrews (Eds.), *Shame: Interpersonal behavior, psychopathology, and culture* (pp. 261–282). New York: Oxford University Press.

Collins, N. L., & Miller, L. C. (1994). Self-disclosure and liking: A meta-analytic review. *Psychological Bulletin, 116*, 457–475.

Coombs, C. A. (1973). A reparameterization of the prisoner's dilemma game. *Behavioral Science, 18*, 424–428.

Cordova, J. V., Jacobson, N. S., Gottman, J. M., Rushe, R., & Cox, G. (1993). Negative reciprocity and communication in couples with a violent husband. *Journal of Abnormal Psychology, 102*, 559–564.

Cosmides, L., & Tooby, J. (1992). Cognitive adaptations for social exchange. In J. H. Barkow, L. Cosmides, & J. Tooby (Eds.), *The adapted mind: Evolutionary psychology and the generation of culture* (pp. 163–228). New York: Oxford University Press.

Cota, A. A., Evans, C. R., Dion, K. L., Kilik, L., & Longman, R. S. (1995). The structure of group cohesion. *Personality and Social Psychology Bulletin, 21*, 572–580.

Cozby, P. C. (1973). Self-disclosure: A literature review. *Psychological Bulletin, 79*, 73–91.

Crowne, D. P., & Marlowe, D. (1964). *The approval motive: Studies in evaluative dependence.* New York: Wiley.

Daly, M., Wilson, M. I., & Weghorst, S. J. (1982). Male sexual jealousy. *Ethology and Sociobiology, 3*, 11–27.

Daniels, F. V. (1967). Communication, incentive, and structural variables in interpersonal exchange and negotiation. *Journal of Experimental Social Psychology, 3*, 47–74.

Darke, P. R., & Freedman, J. L. (1997). Lucky events and beliefs in luck: Paradoxical effects on confidence and risk-taking. *Personality and Social Psychology Bulletin, 23*, 378–388.

Davidson, K., & Prkachin, K. (1997). Optimism and unrealistic optimism have an interacting impact on health-promoting behavior and knowledge changes. *Personality and Social Psychology Bulletin, 23*, 617–625.

Davis, M. H., & Oathout, H. A. (1987). Maintenance of satisfaction in romantic relationships: Empathy and relational competence. *Journal of Personality and Social Psychology, 53*, 397–410.

Dawes, R. M. (1980). Social dilemmas. *Annual Review of Psychology, 31*, 169–193.

Dawes, R. M., McTavish, J., & Shaklee, H. (1977). Behavior, communication, and assumptions about other people's behavior in a commons dilemma situation. *Journal of Personality and Social Psychology, 35*, 1–11.

Dawes, R. M., Van de Kragt, A. J., & Orbell, J. M. (1990). Cooperation for the benefit of us—not me, or my conscience. In J. Mansbridge (Ed.), *Beyond self-interest* (pp. 97–110). Chicago: University of Chicago Press.

de Dreu, C. K. W., & Van Lange, P. A. M. (1995). The impact of social value orientations on negotiator cognition and behavior. *Personality and Social Psychology Bulletin, 21*, 1178–1188.

DePaulo, B. M. (1994). Spotting lies: Can humans learn to do better? *Current Directions in Psychological Science, 3*, 83–86.

DePaulo, B. M., & Friedman, H. S. (1998). Nonverbal communication. In D. T. Gilbert, S. T. Fiske, & G. Lindzey (Eds.). *The handbook of social psychology* (4th ed.; Vol. 2, pp. 3–40). Boston: McGraw-Hill.

Dépret, E. F., & Fiske, S. T. (1993). Social cognition and power: Some cognitive consequences of social structure as a source of control deprivation. In G. Weary, F. Gleicher, & K. Marsh (Eds.), *Control motivation and social cognition* (pp. 176–202). New York: Springer-Verlag.

Derlega, V. J., Wilson, M., & Chaikin, A. L. (1976). Friendship and disclosure reciprocity. *Journal of Personality and Social Psychology, 34*, 578–582.

DeSteno, D. A., & Salovey, P. (1996). Evolutionary origins of sex differences in jealousy? Questioning the "fitness" of the model. *Psychological Science, 7*, 367–372.

Deutsch, M. (1958). Trust and suspicion. *Journal of Conflict Resolution, 2*, 265–279.

Deutsch, M. (1973). *The resolution of conflict.* New Haven: Yale University Press.

Deutsch, M. (1975). Equity, equality, and need: What determines which value will be used as the basis of distributive justice? *Journal of Social Issues, 31*, 137–149.

Diener, E., Larson, R. J., & Emmons, R. A. (1984). Person x situation interactions: Choice of situations and congruence response models. *Journal of Personality and Social Psychology, 47*, 580–592.

Dodge, K. A. (1985). Attributional bias in aggressive children. In P. C. Kendall (Ed.), *Advances in cognitive-behavioral research and therapy* (Vol. 4, pp. 73–110). New York: Academic Press.

Donner, E., Nash, K., Csikszentmihalyi, M., Chalip, L., & Freeman, M. (1981). *Subjective experience in marital interaction.* Paper presented at the meeting of the Society for Experimental Social Psychology, Nashville, TN, November, 1981.

Doob, L. W. (1971). *Patterning of time.* New Haven, CT: Yale University Press.

Downey, G., Khouri, H., & Feldman, S. I. (1997). Early interpersonal trauma and later adjustment: The mediational role of rejection sensitivity. In D. Cicchetti & S. L. Toth (Eds.), *Developmental perspectives on trauma: Theory, research, and intervention* (pp. 85–114). Rochester, NY: University of Rochester Press.

Drigotas, S. M., & Rusbult, C. E. (1992). Should I stay or should I go?: A dependence model of breakups. *Journal of Personality and Social Psychology, 62*, 62–87.

Drigotas, S. M., Rusbult, C. E., & Verette, J. (1999). Level of commitment, mutuality of commitment, and couple well-being. *Personal Relationships, 6,* 389–409.

Eagly, A. H., & Wood, W. (1999). The origins of sex differences in human behavior: Evolved dispositions versus social roles. *American Psychologist, 54,* 409–423.

Edwards, A. (1959). *Edwards personal preference schedule revised manual.* New York: The Psychological Corporation.

Edwards, W. (1954). The theory of decision making. *Psychological Bulletin, 51,* 380–417.

Eidelson, R. J. (1980). Interpersonal satisfaction and level of involvement: A curvilinear relationship. *Journal of Personality and Social Psychology, 39,* 460–470.

Eisenberg, N., & Mussen, P. H. (1989). *The roots of prosocial behavior in children.* Cambridge: Cambridge University Press.

Elliot, A. J. (1997). Integrating the "classic" and "contemporary" approaches to achievement motivation: A hierarchical model of approach and avoidance motivation. In M. Maehr & P. Pintrich (Eds.), *Advances in motivation and achievement* (Vol. 10, pp. 143–179). Greenwich, CT: JAI Press.

Ellis, B., & Kelley, H. H. (1999). The pairing game: A classroom demonstration of the matching hypothesis. *Teaching of Psychology, 26,* 118–121.

Emmons, R. A., & Diener, E. (1986). Situation selection as a moderator of response consistency and stability. *Journal of Personality and Social Psychology, 51,* 1013–1019.

Emmons, R. A., Diener, E., & Larson, R. J. (1986). Choice and avoidance of everyday situations and affect congruence: Two models of reciprocal interactionism. *Journal of Personality and Social Psychology, 51,* 815–826.

Erber, R., & Fiske, S. T. (1984). Outcome dependency and attention to inconsistent information. *Journal of Personality and Social Psychology, 47,* 709–726.

Falbo, T., & Peplau, L. A. (1980). Power strategies in intimate relationships. *Journal of Personality and Social Psychology, 38,* 618–628.

Farrell, D., & Rusbult, C. E. (1981). Exchange variables as predictors of job satisfaction, job commitment, and turnover: The impact of rewards, costs, alternatives, and investments. *Organizational Behavior and Human Performance, 27,* 78–95.

Feingold, A. (1988). Matching for attractivness in romantic partners and same-sex friends: A meta-analysis and theoretical critique. *Psychological Bulletin, 104,* 226–235.

Festinger, L. (1950). Informal social communication. *Psychological Review, 57,* 271–282.

Finkel, E. J., & Campbell, W. K. (2001). Self-control and accommodation in close relationships: An interdependence analysis. *Journal of Personality and Social Psychology, 81,* 263–277.

Finkel, E. J., & Foshee, V. A. (2001). *When we don't abuse our romantic partners: An interdependence analysis emphasizing self-control.* Unpublished manuscript, Carnegie Mellon University, Pittsburgh, PA.

Finkel, E. J., Rusbult, C. E., Kumashiro, M., & Hannon, P. (2002). Dealing with betrayal in close relationships: Does commitment promote forgiveness? *Journal of Personality and Social Psychology.*

Finkenauer, C., & Hazam, H. (2000). Disclosure and secrecy in marriage: Do both contribute to marital satisfaction? *Journal of Social and Personal Relationships, 17,* 245–263.

Fiske, A. P. (1991). *Structures of social life: The four elementary forms of social relationship.* New York: Free Press.

Fiske, A. P. (1992). The four elementary forms of sociality: Framework for a unified theory of social relations. *Psychological Review, 99,* 689–723.

Fiske, A. P., Kitayama, S., Markus, H. R., & Nisbett, R. E. (1998). The cultural matrix of social psychology. In D. T. Gilbert, S. T. Fiske, & G. Lindzey (Eds.), *The handbook of social psychology* (4th ed.; Vol. 2, pp. 915–981). Boston: McGraw-Hill.

Fiske, S. T. (1993). Controlling other people: The impact of power on stereotyping. *American Psychologist, 48,* 621–628.

Forgas, J. P. (1976). The perception of social episodes: Categorical and dimensional representations of two different social milieus. *Journal of Personality and Social Psychology, 34,* 199–209.

Forgas, J. P. (1983a). Episode cognition and personality: A multidimensional analysis. *Journal of Personality, 51,* 34–48.

Forgas, J. P. (1983b). Language, goals and situations. *Journal of Language and Social Psychology, 2,* 267–293.

Frank, R. H., Gilovich, T., & Regan, D. T. (1993). The evolution of one-shot cooperation: An experiment. *Ethology and Sociobiology, 14,* 247–256.

French, J., & Raven, B. (1959). The bases of social power. In D. Cartwright (Ed.), *Studies in social power* (pp. 150–167). Ann Arbor, MI: Institute for Social Research.

Fry, C. L. (1965). Personality and acquisition factors in the development of coordination strategy. *Journal of Personality and Social Psychology, 2,* 403–407.

Gable, S. L., Reis, H. T., & Elliot, A. J. (2000). Behavioral activation and inhibition in everyday life. *Journal of Personality and Social Psychology, 78,* 1135–1149.

Gaines, S. O., Reis, H. T., Summers, S., Rusbult, C. E., Cox, C., Wexler, M. O., Marelich, W., & Kurland, G. J. (1997). Impact of attachment style on reactions to accommodative dilemmas in close relationships. *Personal Relationships, 4,* 93–113.

Gallo, P. S. (1972). Prisoners of our own dilemma? In L. S. Wrightsman, J. O'Connor, & N. J. Baker (Eds.), *Cooperation and competition: Readings on mixed motive games* (pp. 43–49). Belmont, CA: Brooks/Cole.

Geen, R. S. (1998). Aggression and antisocial behavior. In D. T. Gilbert, S. T. Fiske, & G. Lindzey (Eds.), *The handbook of social psychology* (4th. ed.; Vol. 2, pp. 317–356). Boston: McGraw-Hill.

Gelles, R. J., & Straus, M. A. (1988). *Intimate violence.* New York: Simon & Schuster.

Ghiselli, E. E., & Lodahl, T. M. (1958). Patterns of managerial traits and group effectiveness. *Journal of Abnormal and Social Psychology, 57,* 61–66.

Gibson, J. J. (1979). *The ecological approach to visual perception.* Boston, MA: Houghton Mifflin.

Gigerenzer, G., & Goldstein, D. G. (1996). Reasoning the fast and frugal way: Models of bounded rationality. *Psychological Review, 103,* 650–669.

Gilovich, T., & Medvec, V. H. (1994). The temporal pattern to the experience of regret. *Journal of Personality and Social Psychology, 67,* 357–365.

Gottman, J. M. (1979). *Marital interaction.* New York: Academic Press.

Gottman, J. M. (1983). How children become friends. *Monographs of the Society for Research in Child Development, 48,* Series No. 201.

Gottman, J. M. (1994). *Why marriages succeed or fail.* New York: Simon and Schuster.

Gottman, J. M., & Levenson, R. W. (1986). Assessing the role of emotion in marriage. *Behavioral Assessment, 8*, 31–48.

Gottman, J. M., & Notarius, C. I. (2000). Decade review: Observing marital interaction. *Journal of Marriage and the Family, 62*, 927–947.

Gouldner, A. W. (1960). The norm of reciprocity: A preliminary statement. *American Sociological Review, 25*, 161–178.

Gray, J. A. (1990). Brain systems that mediate both emotion and cognition. *Cognition and Emotion, 4*, 269–288.

Gross, A. E., Wallston, B. S., & Piliavin, I. M. (1979). Reactance, attribution, equity, and the help recipient. *Journal of Applied Social Psychology, 9*, 297–313.

Guerrero, L. K. (1998). Attachment-style differences in the experience and expression of romantic jealousy. *Personal Relationships, 5*, 273–291.

Guttentag, M., & Secord, P. F. (1983). *Too many women? The sex ratio question*. Beverly Hills, CA: Sage.

Hafer, C. L. (2000). Investment in long-term goals and commitment to just means drive the need to believe in a just world. *Personality and Social Psychology Bulletin, 26*, 1059–1073.

Hafer, C. L., & Olson, J. M. (1993). Beliefs in a just world, discontent, and assertive actions by working women. *Personality and Social Psychology Bulletin, 19*, 30–38.

Hamburger, H. (1979). *Games as models of social phenomena*. San Francisco: W. H. Freeman and Company.

Hardin, G. (1968). The tragedy of the commons. *Science, 162*, 1243–1248.

Harkins, S., & Petty, R. E. (1982). Effects of task difficulty and task uniqueness on social loafing. *Journal of Personality and Social Psychology, 43*, 1214–1230.

Hartup, W. W. (1974). Aggression in childhood: Developmental perspectives. *American Psychologist, 29*, 336–341.

Haslam, N. (1994). Categories of social relationship. *Cognition, 53*, 59–90.

Hazan, C., & Shaver, P. R. (1987). Romantic love conceptualized as an attachment process. *Journal of Personality and Social Psychology, 52*, 511–524.

Hazan, C., & Shaver, P. R. (1994). Attachment as an organizational framework for research on close relationships. *Psychological Inquiry, 5*, 1–22.

Heider, F. (1958). *The psychology of interpersonal relations*. Hillsdale, NJ: Lawrence Erlbaum.

Helgeson, V. S. (1994). Long-distance relationships: Sex differences in adjustment and breakup. *Personality and Social Psychology Bulletin, 20*, 254–265.

Helwig, C. C., & Kim, S. (1999). Children's evaluations of decision-making procedures in peer, family, and school contexts. *Child Development, 70*, 502–512.

Hertel, G., Kerr, N. L., & Messé, L. A. (2000). Motivation gains in performance groups: Paradigmatic and theoretical developments on the Koehler effect. *Journal of Personality and Social Psychology, 79*, 580–601.

Hertel, G., Neuhof, J., Theuer, T., & Kerr, N. L. (2000). Mood effects on cooperation in small groups: Does positive mood simply lead to more cooperation? *Cognition and Emotion, 14*, 441–472.

Hess, R. D., & Handel, G. (1959). *Family worlds*. Chicago, IL: University of Chicago Press.

Higgins, E. T. (1987). Self-discrepancy: A theory relating self and affect. *Psychological Review, 94,* 319–340.

Higgins, E. T. (1997). Beyond pleasure and pain. *American Psychologist, 52,* 1280–1300.

Higgins, E. T. (1998). Promotion and prevention: Regulatory focus as a motivational principle. In M. Zanna (Ed.), *Advances in experimental social psychology* (Vol. 30, pp. 1–46). New York: Academic Press.

Higgins, E. T., & Silberman, I. (1998). Development of regulatory focus: Promotion and prevention as ways of living. In J. Heckhausen & C. S. Dweck (Eds.), *Motivation and self-regulation across the life span* (pp. 78–113). New York: Cambridge.

Hinde, R. A. (1997). *Relationships: A dialectical perspective.* East Sussex, England: Psychology Press.

Hobbs, S. A., & Forehand, R. (1977). Important parameters in the use of timeout with children: A re-examination. *Journal of Behavior Therapy and Experimental Psychiatry, 8,* 365–370.

Holcombe, A., Wolery, M., & Katzenmeyer, J. (1995). Teaching preschoolers to avoid abduction by strangers: Evaluation of maintenance strategies. *Journal of Child and Family Studies, 4,* 177–191.

Holmes, J. G. (1981). The exchange process in close relationships: Microbehavior and macromotives. In M. J. Lerner and S. C. Lerner (Eds.), *The justice motive in social behavior* (pp. 261–284). New York: Plenum.

Holmes, J. G. (2000). Social relationships: The nature and function of relational schemas. *European Journal of Social Psychology, 30,* 447–495.

Holmes, J. G., & Levinger, G. (1994). Paradoxical effects of closeness in relationships on perceptions of justice: An interdependence theory perspective. In M. J. Lerner & G. Mikula (Eds.), *Justice in close relationships: Entitlement and the affectional bond* (pp. 149–173). New York: Plenum Press.

Holmes, J. G., & Rempel, J. K. (1989). Trust in close relationships. In C. Hendrick (Ed.), *Review of personality and social psychology* (Vol. 10, pp. 187–219). Newbury Park, CA: Sage.

Huo, Y., Smith, H., Tyler, T. R., & Lind, A. (1996). Superordinate identification, subgroup identification, and justice concerns. *Psychological Science, 7,* 40–45.

Ickes, W. (1982). A basic paradigm for the study of personality, roles, and social behavior. In W. Ickes & E. S. Knowles (Eds.), *Personality, roles, and social behavior* (pp. 305–341). New York: Springer-Verlag.

Insko, C. A., & Schopler, J. (1998). Differential distrust of groups and individuals. In C. Sedikides, J. Schopler, & C. A. Insko (Eds.), *Intergroup cognition and intergroup behavior* (pp. 75–107). Mahwah, NJ: Erlbaum.

Insko, C. A., Schopler, J., Hoyle, R. H., Dardis, G. J., & Graetz, K. A. (1990). Individual-group discontinuity as a function of fear and greed. *Journal of Personality and Social Psychology, 58,* 68–79.

Insko, C. A., Schopler, J., Pemberton, M. B., Wieselquist, J., McIlraith, S. A., Currey, D. P., & Gaertner, L. (1998). Long-term outcome maximization and the reduction of interindividual-intergroup discontinuity. *Journal of Personality and Social Psychology, 75,* 695–710.

James, J. (1953). The distribution of free-forming small group size. *American Sociological Review, 18,* 569–570.

Johnson, D. J., & Rusbult, C. E. (1989). Resisting temptation: Devaluation of alternative partners as a means of maintaining commitment in close relationships. *Journal of Personality and Social Psychology, 57*, 967–980.

Johnson, M. P. (1991). Commitment to personal relationships. In W. H. Jones & D. W. Perlman (Eds.), *Advances in personal relationships* (Vol. 3, pp. 117–143). London: Jessica Kingsley.

Jones, E. E., & Gerard, H. B. (1967). *Foundations of social psychology*. New York: Wiley.

Jones, E. E., & Nisbett, R. E. (1971). The actor and the observer: Divergent perceptions of the causes of behavior. In E. E. Jones, D. E. Kanouse, H. H. Kelley, R. E. Nisbett, S. Valins, & B. Weiner (Eds.), *Attribution: Perceiving the causes of behavior* (pp. 79–94). New York: General Learning Press.

Kagan, J., Snidman, N., & Arcus, D. (1998). Childhood derivatives of high and low reactivity in infancy. *Child Development, 69*, 1483–1493.

Kahneman, D., & Tversky, A. (1979). Prospect theory: An analysis of decision under risk. *Econometrica, 47*, 263–292.

Kahneman, D., & Tversky, A. (1984). Choices, values, and frames. *American Psychologist, 39*, 341–350.

Kalick, S. M., & Hamilton, T. E. (1986). The matching hypothesis reexamined. *Journal of Personality and Social Psychology, 51*, 673–682.

Kelley, H. H. (1966). A classroom study of the dilemmas in interpersonal negotiations. In K. Archibald (Ed.), *Strategic interaction and conflict* (pp. 49–73). Berkeley, CA: University of California Press.

Kelley, H. H. (1968). Interpersonal accommodation. *American Psychologist, 23*, 399–410.

Kelley, H. H. (1979). *Personal relationships: Their structures and processes*. Hillsdale, NJ: Erlbaum.

Kelley, H. H. (1983). Love and commitment. In H. H. Kelley, E. Berscheid, A. Christensen, J. H. Harvey, T. L. Huston, G. Levinger, E. McClintock, L. A. Peplau, & D. R. Peterson (Eds.), *Close relationships* (pp. 265–314). New York: W. H. Freeman.

Kelley, H. H. (1984a). Affect in interpersonal relations. In P. Shaver (Ed.), *Review of personality and social psychology* (Vol. 5, pp. 89–115). Newbury Park, CA: Sage.

Kelley, H. H. (1984b). The theoretical description of interdependence by means of transition lists. *Journal of Personality and Social Psychology, 47*, 956–982.

Kelley, H. H. (1997a). Expanding the analysis of social orientations by reference to the sequential-temporal structure of situations. *European Journal of Social Psychology, 27*, 373–404.

Kelley, H. H. (1997b). The "stimulus field" for interpersonal phenomena: The source of language and thought about interpersonal events. *Personality and Social Psychology Review, 1*, 140–169.

Kelley, H. H. (2000). The proper study of social psychology. *Social Psychology Quarterly, 63*, 3–15.

Kelley, H. H., Berscheid, E., Christensen, A., Harvey, J. H., Huston, T. L., Levinger, G., McClintock, E., Peplau, L. A., & Peterson, D. R. (1983). *Close relationships*. New York: Freeman.

Kelley, H. H., & Schenitzki, D. P. (1972). Bargaining. In C. McClintock (Ed.), *Experimental social psychology* (pp. 298–337). New York: Holt.

Kelley, H. H., & Stahelski, A. J. (1970). Social interaction basis of cooperators' and competitors' beliefs about others. *Journal of Personality and Social Psychology, 16,* 66–91.

Kelley, H. H., & Thibaut, J. W. (1959). *Group problem solving.* In G. Lindzey & E. Aronson (Eds.), *Handbook of social psychology* (2nd ed.; Vol. 4, pp. 1–101). Reading, MA: Addison-Wesley.

Kelley, H. H., & Thibaut, J. W. (1978). *Interpersonal relations: A theory of interdependence.* New York: Wiley.

Kelley, H. H., & Thibaut, J. W. (1985). Self-interest, science and cynicism. *Journal of Social and Clinical Psychology, 3,* 26–32.

Kelley, H. H., Thibaut, J. W., Radloff, R., & Mundy, D. (1962). The development of cooperation in the "minimal social situation." *Psychological Monographs, 74* (19, Whole No. 538).

Kenny, D. A. (1994). *Interpersonal perception: A social relations analysis.* New York: Guilford.

Kenny, D. A., & La Voie, L. (1984). The social relations model. In L. Berkowitz (Ed.), *Advances in experimental social psychology* (Vol. 18, pp. 141–182). Orlando, FL: Academic Press.

Kenny, D. A., Mohr, C. D., & Levesque, M. J. (2001). A social relations variance partitioning of dyadic behavior. *Psychological Bulletin, 127,* 128–141.

Kenrick, D. T., & Trost, M. R. (1997). Evolutionary approaches to relationships. In S. Duck (Ed.), *Handbook of personal relationships: Theory, research, and interventions* (2nd ed.; pp. 151–177). Chichester, England: John Wiley & Sons.

Kernis, M. H., Grannemann, B. D., & Barclay, L. C. (1989). Stability and level of self-esteem as predictors of anger arousal and hostility. *Journal of Personality and Social Psychology, 56,* 1013–1022.

Kerr, N. L. (1983). Motivation losses in task-performing groups: A social dilemma analysis. *Journal of Personality and Social Psychology, 45,* 819–828.

Kerr, N. L. (1986). Motivational choices in task groups: A paradigm for social dilemma research. In H. Wilke, D. Messick, & C. Rutte (Eds.), *Experimental social dilemmas* (pp. 1–27). Frankfurt am Main: Lang GmbH.

Kerr, N. L. (1999). Anonymity and social control in social dilemmas. In M. Foddy, M. Smithson, S. Schneider, & M. Hogg (Eds.), *Resolving social dilemmas: Dynamic, structural and intergroup aspects* (pp. 103–119). Philadelphia: Psychology Press.

Kerr, N. L., & Kaufman-Gilliland, C. M. (1994). Communication, commitment, and cooperation in social dilemmas. *Journal of Personality and Social Psychology, 66,* 513–529.

Kiesler, C. A. (1971). *The psychology of commitment: Experiments linking behavior to belief.* New York: Academic Press.

King, G. A., & Sorrentino, R. M. (1983). Psychological dimensions of goal-oriented interdependence situations. *Journal of Personality and Social Psychology, 44,* 140–162.

Kipnis, D. (1972). Does power corrupt? *Journal of Personality and Social Psychology, 24,* 33–41.

Klein, R. C. A., & Milardo, R. M. (2000). The social context of couple conflict: Support and criticism from informal third parties. *Journal of Social and Personal Relationships, 17,* 618–637.

Köhler, O. (1926). Kraftleistungen bei Einzel- und Gruppenabeit [Physical performance in individual and group situations]. *Industrielle Psychotechnik, 3,* 274–282.

Kollock, P. (1993). "An eye for an eye leaves everyone blind": Cooperation and accounting systems. *American Sociological Review, 58,* 768–786.

Komorita, S. S. (1979). An equal excess model of coalition formation. *Behavioral Science, 24,* 369–381.

Komorita, S. S., Hilty, J. A., & Parks, C. D. (1991). Reciprocity and cooperation in social dilemmas. *Journal of Conflict Resolution, 35,* 699–705.

Komorita, S. S., & Parks, C. D. (1994). *Social dilemmas.* Madison, WI: Brown and Benchmark.

Komorita, S. S., & Parks, C. D. (1995). Interpersonal relations: Mixed-motive interaction. *Annual Review of Psychology, 46,* 183–207.

Komorita, S. S., & Parks, C. D. (1999). Reciprocity and cooperation in social dilemmas: Review and future directions. In D. V. Budescu & I. Erev (Eds.), *Games and human behavior: Essays in honor of Amnon Rapoport* (pp. 315–330). Mahway, NJ: Erlbaum.

Kramer, R. M., & Brewer, M. (1984). Effects of group identity on resource use in a simulated commons dilemma. *Journal of Personality and Social Psychology, 46,* 1044–1057.

Kramer, R. M., & Messick, D. M. (1998). Getting by with a little help from our enemies: Collective paranoia and its role in intergroup relations. In C. Sedikides, J. Schopler, & C. A. Insko (Eds.), *Intergroup cognition and intergroup behavior* (pp. 233–256). London: Lawrence Erlbaum.

Kruglanski, A. W., Thompson, E. P., Higgins, E. T., Atash, M. N., Pierro, A., Shah, J. Y., & Spiegel, S. (2000). To "do the right thing" or "just do it": Locomotion and assessment as distinct self-regulatory imperatives. *Journal of Personality and Social Psychology, 79,* 793–815.

Kruglanski, A., & Webster, D. M. (1996). Motivated closing of the mind: "Seizing" and "freezing." *Psychological Review, 103,* 263–283.

Kuhlman, D. M., & Marshello, A. F. J. (1975). Individual differences in game motivation as moderators of preprogrammed strategic effects in prisoner's dilemma. *Journal of Personality and Social Psychology, 32,* 922–931.

Kuhlman, D. M., & Wimberley, D. C. (1976). Expectation of choice behavior held by cooperators, competitors, and individualists across four classes of experimental games. *Journal of Personality and Social Psychology, 34,* 69–81.

Larson, R., Csikszentmihalyi, M., & Graef, R. (1982). Time alone in daily experience: Loneliness or renewal? In L. A. Peplau & D. Perlman (Eds.), *Loneliness: A sourcebook of current theory, research, and therapy* (pp. 40–53). New York, NY: Wiley-Interscience.

Latané, B., & Darley, J. (1970). *The unresponsive bystander.* New York: Appleton-Century Crofts.

Leary, M. R. (1995). *Self-presentation: Impression management and interpersonal behavior.* Madison, WI: Brown & Benchmark.

Leary, M. R., Tambor, E. S., Terdal, S. K., & Downs, D. L. (1995). Self-esteem as an interpersonal monitor: The sociometer hypothesis. *Journal of Personality and Social Psychology, 68,* 518–530.

Lerner, M. J. (1980). *The belief in a just world: A fundamental delusion*. New York: Plenum Press.

Lerner, M. J., & Miller, D. T. (1978). Just world research and the attribution process: Looking back and ahead. *Psychological Bulletin, 85*, 1030–1051.

Levine, J. M., & Thompson, L. (1996). Conflict in groups. In E. T. Higgins & A. W. Kruglanski (Eds.), *Social psychology: Handbook of basic principles* (pp. 745–776). New York: Guilford.

Levinger, G. (1979). A social exchange view on the dissolution of pair relationships. In R. L. Burgess & T. L. Huston (Eds.), *Social exchange in developing relationships* (pp. 169–193). New York: Academic Press.

Lewin, K. (1935). *A dynamic theory of personality*. New York: McGraw-Hill.

Lewin, K. (1948). *Resolving social conflicts*. New York: Harper.

Lewin, K. (1951). *Field theory in social science*. New York: Harper.

Lewin, K. (1966). *Principles of topological psychology* (F. Heider & G. Heider, Trans.). New York: McGraw-Hill. (Original work: Lewin, K. [1936]. *Principles of topological psychology*. New York: McGraw-Hill.)

Lewis, D. K. (1969). *Convention: A philosophical study*. Cambridge, MA: Harvard University Press.

Lieberman, B. (1962). Experimental studies of conflict in some two-person and three-person games. In J. H. Criswell, H. Solomon, & P. Suppes (Eds.), *Mathematical methods in small group processes* (pp. 203–220). Stanford, CA: Stanford University Press.

Liebrand, W. B. G. (1983). A classification of social dilemma games. *Simulation and Games, 14*, 123–138.

Liebrand, W. B. G., Jansen, R. W. T. L., Rijken, V. M., & Suhre, C. J. M. (1986). Might over morality: Social values and the perception of other players in experimental games. *Journal of Experimental Social Psychology, 22*, 203–215.

Liebrand, W. B. G., & Messick, D. M. (1996). Computer simulation of cooperative decision making. In W. Liebrand & D. Messick (Eds.), *Frontiers in social dilemma research* (pp. 215–234). Berlin: Springer-Verlag.

Liebrand, W., & van Run, G. J. (1985). The effects of social motives on behavior in social dilemmas in two cultures. *Journal of Experimental Social Psychology, 21*, 86–102.

Liebrand, W. B., Wilke, H. A., Vogel, R., & Wolters, F. J. (1986). Value orientation and conformity: A study using three types of social dilemma games. *Journal of Conflict Resolution, 30*, 77–97.

Lind, E. A., & Tyler, T. R. (1988). *The social psychology of procedural justice*. New York: Plenum Press.

Lindahl, K. M., Clements, M., & Markman, H. (1997). Predicting marital and parent functioning in dyads and triads: A longitudinal investigation of marital processes. *Journal of Family Psychology, 11*, 139–151.

Lindskold, S., & Han, G. (1988). GRIT as a foundation for integrative bargaining. *Personality and Social Psychology Bulletin, 14*, 335–345.

Long, G. T., & Lerner, M. J. (1974). Deserving the "personal contract" and altruistic behavior by children. *Journal of Personality and Social Psychology, 29*, 551–556.

Loomis, J. L. (1959). Communication and the development of trust. *Human Relations, 12,* 305–315.

Lorge, I., & Solomon, H. (1955). Two models of group behavior in the solution of eureka-type problems. *Psychometrika, 20,* 139–148.

Luce, E. D., & Raiffa, H. (1957). *Games and decisions: Introduction and critical survey.* New York: Wiley.

Luckenbill, D. F. (1977). Criminal homicide as a situated transaction. *Social Problems, 25,* 176–186.

Lydon, J., Pierce, T., & O'Regan, S. (1997). Coping with moral commitment to long-distance dating relationships. *Journal of Personality and Social Psychology, 73,* 104–113.

Macrae, C. N., Bodenhausen, G. V., Milne, A. B., & Jetten, J. (1994). Out of mind but back in sight: Stereotypes on the rebound. *Journal of Personality and Social Psychology, 67,* 808–817.

Madsen, M. C., & Lancy, D. F. (1981). Cooperative and competitive behavior: Experiments related to ethnic identity and urbanization in Papua New Guinea. *Journal of Cross-Cultural Psychology, 12,* 389–408.

Magnusson, D. (1971). An analysis of situational determinants. *Perceptual and Motor Skills, 32,* 851–867.

Mahrer, A. R. (1956). The role of expectancy in delayed reinforcement. *Journal of Experimental Psychology, 52,* 101–105.

Mangelsdorf, S. C. (1992). Developmental changes in infant-stranger interaction. *Infant Behavior and Development, 15,* 191–208.

March, J. G., & Simon, H. A. (1958). *Organizations.* New York: John Wiley and Sons.

Markus, H., & Kitiyama, S. (1991). Culture and the self: Implications for cognition, emotion, and motivation. *Psychological Review, 98,* 224–253.

Markus, H., & Nurius, P. (1986). Possible selves. *American Psychologist, 41,* 954–969.

Martz, J. M., Verette, J., Arriaga, X. B., Slovik, L. F., Cox, C. L., & Rusbult, C. E. (1998). Positive illusion in close relationships. *Personal Relationships, 5,* 159–181.

Mathieu, J. E., & Zajac, D. M. (1990). A review and meta-analysis of the antecedents, correlates, and consequences of organizational commitment. *Psychological Bulletin, 108,* 171–194.

McClintock, C. G. (1972a). Game behavior and social motivation in interpersonal settings. In C. G. McClintock (Ed.), *Experimental social psychology* (pp. 271–297). New York: Holt, Rinehart, and Winston.

McClintock, C. G. (1972b). Social motivation – a set of propositions. *Behavioral Science, 17,* 438–454.

McClintock, C. G. (1974). Development of social motives in Anglo-American and Mexican-American children. *Journal of Personality and Social Psychology, 29,* 348–354.

McClintock, C. G., & Allison, S. T. (1989). Social value orientation and helping behavior. *Journal of Applied Social Psychology, 19,* 353–362.

McClintock, C. G., & Liebrand, W. B. G. (1988). The role of interdependence structure, individual value orientation and other's strategy in social decision making: A transformational analysis. *Journal of Personality and Social Psychology, 55,* 396–409.

McCornack, S. A., & Levine, T. R. (1990). When lies are uncovered: Emotional and relational outcomes of discovered deception. *Communication Monographs, 57*, 119–138.

Mehrabian, A., & Russell, J. A. (1974). *An approach to environmental psychology.* Cambridge, MA: MIT Press.

Mendolia, M., Beach, S., & Tesser, A. (1996). The relationship between marital interaction behaviors and affective reactions to one's own and one's spouse's self-evaluation needs. *Personal Relationships, 3*, 279–292.

Messé, L. A., & Sivacek, J. M. (1979). Predictions of other's responses in a mixed-motive game: Self-justification or false consensus? *Journal of Personality and Social Psychology, 37*, 602–607.

Messick, D., & Brewer, M. B. (1983). Solving social dilemmas: A review. In L. Wheeler & P. Shaver (Eds.), *Review of personality and social psychology* (Vol. 4, pp. 11–44). Newbury Park, CA: Sage.

Messick, D. M., & McClintock, C. G. (1968). Motivational basis of choice in experimental games. *Journal of Experimental Social Psychology, 4*, 1–25.

Messick, D. M., & Thorngate, W. B. (1967). Relative gain maximization in experimental games. *Journal of Experimental Social Psychology, 3*, 85–101.

Messick, D. M., Wilke, H., Brewer, M., Kramer, R., Zemke, P., & Lui, L. (1983). Individual adaptations and structural change as solutions to social dilemmas. *Journal of Personality and Social Psychology, 44*, 294–309.

Metcalfe, J., & Mischel, W. (1999). A hot/cool system analysis of delay of gratification. *Psychological Review, 106*, 3–19.

Mikulincer, M., & Nachshon, O. (1991). Attachment styles and patterns of self-disclosure. *Journal of Personality and Social Psychology, 61*, 321–331.

Milgram, S. (1974). *Obedience to authority: An experimental view.* New York: Harper & Row.

Miller, C. E. (1989). The social psychological consequences of decision rules. In P. Paulus (Ed.), *Psychology of group influence* (2nd ed.; pp. 327–355). Hillsdale, NJ: Erlbaum.

Miller, D. T. (1999). The norm of self-interest. *American Psychologist, 54*, 1053–1060.

Miller, D. T., & Holmes, J. G. (1975). The role of situational restrictiveness on self-fulfilling prophecies: A theoretical and empirical extension of Kelley and Stahelski's triangle hypothesis. *Journal of Personality and Social Psychology, 31*, 661–673.

Miller, L. C., & Kenny, D. A. (1986). Reciprocity of self-disclosure at the individual and dyadic levels: A social relations analysis. *Journal of Personality and Social Psychology, 50*, 713–719.

Miller, R. S. (1997). Inattentive and contented: Relationship commitment and attention to alternatives. *Journal of Personality and Social Psychology, 73*, 758–766.

Mills, J., & Clark, M. S. (1982). Communal and exchange relationships. In L. Wheeler (Ed.), *Review of personality and social psychology* (Vol. 3, pp. 121–144). Newbury Park, CA: Sage.

Mills, J., & Clark, M. S. (1994). Communal and exchange relationships: Controversies and research. In R. Erber & R. Gilmour (Eds.), *Theoretical frameworks for personal relationships* (pp. 29–42). Hillsdale, NJ: Erlbaum.

Minuchin, S. (1974). *Families and family therapy.* Cambridge, MA: Harvard University Press.

Mischel, H. (1963). *Trust and delay of gratification*. Unpublished doctoral dissertation, Harvard University.

Mischel, H. N., & Mischel, W. (1983). The development of children's knowledge of self-control strategies. *Child Development, 54,* 603–619.

Mischel, W. (1958). Preference for delayed reinforcement: An experimental study of a cultural observation. *Journal of Abnormal and Social Psychology, 56,* 57–61.

Mischel, W. (1999). *Introduction to personality*. Orlando, FL: Harcourt Brace College.

Mischel, W., & Baker, N. (1975). Cognitive appraisals and transformations in delay behavior. *Journal of Personality and Social Psychology, 31,* 254–261.

Mischel, W., Cantor, N., & Feldman, S. (1996). Principles of self-regulation: The nature of willpower and self-control. In E. T. Higgins & A. Kruglanski (Eds.), *Social psychology: Handbook of basic principles* (pp. 329–360). New York: Guilford.

Mischel, W., Ebbesen, E. B., & Raskoff-Zeiss, A. (1972). Cognitive and attentional mechanisms in delay of gratification. *Journal of Personality and Social Psychology, 21,* 204–218.

Mischel, W., & Grusec, J. (1967). Waiting for rewards and punishments: Effects of time and probability on choice. *Journal of Personality and Social Psychology, 5,* 24–31.

Mischel, W., Grusec, J., & Masters, J. C. (1969). Effects of expected delay time on the subjective value of rewards and punishments. *Journal of Personality and Social Psychology, 11,* 363–373.

Mischel, W., & Shoda, Y. (1995). A cognitive-affective system theory of personality: Reconceptualizing situations, dispositions, dynamics, and invariance in personality structure. *Psychological Review, 102,* 246–268.

Mischel, W., Shoda, Y., & Rodriguez, M. L. (1989). Delay of gratification in children. *Science, 244,* 933–938.

Moore, B., Mischel, W., & Zeiss, A. (1976). Comparative effects of the reward stimulus and its cognitive representation in voluntary delay. *Journal of Personality and Social Psychology, 34,* 419–424.

Moreland, R. L., Argote, L., & Krishnan, R. (1996). Socially shared cognition at work: Transactive memory and group performance. In J. L. Nye & A. M. Brower (Eds.), *What's social about social cognition: Research on socially shared cognition in small groups* (pp. 57–84). Thousand Oaks, CA: Sage.

Moretti, M. M., & Higgins, E. T. (1990). Relating self-discrepancy to self-esteem: The contribution of discrepancy beyond actual-self ratings. *Journal of Experimental Social Psychology, 26,* 108–123.

Mowday, R. T., Porter, L. W., & Steers, R. M. (1982). *Employee-organization linkages*. New York: Academic Press.

Murningham, J. K., Kim, J., & Metzger, A. R. (1993). The volunteer dilemma. *Administrative Science Quarterly, 38,* 515–538.

Murningham, J. K., & King, T. R. (1992). The effects of leverage and payoffs on cooperative behavior in asymmetric dilemmas. In W. B. G. Liebrand, D. M. Messick, & H. A. M. Wilke (Eds.), *Social dilemmas: Theoretical issues and research findings* (pp. 163–182). New York: Pergamon.

Murray, S. L., & Holmes, J. G. (1996). The construction of relationship realities. In G. J. O. Fletcher & J. Fitness (Eds.), *Knowledge structures in close relationships: A social psychological approach* (pp. 91–120). Mahwah, NJ: Erlbaum.

Murray, S., & Holmes, J. G. (1997). A leap of faith? Positive illusions in romantic relationships. *Personality and Social Psychology Bulletin, 23,* 586–604.

Murray, S. L., Holmes, J. G., & Griffin, D. W. (1996a). The benefits of positive illusions: Idealization and the construction of satisfaction in close relationships. *Journal of Personality and Social Psychology, 70,* 79–98.

Murray, S. L., Holmes, J. G., & Griffin, D. W. (1996b). The self-fulfilling nature of positive illusions in romantic relationships: Love is not blind, but prescient. *Journal of Personality and Social Psychology, 71,* 1155–1180.

Murray, S. L., Holmes, J. G., & Griffin, D. W. (2000). Self-esteem and the quest for felt security: How perceived regard regulates attachment processes. *Journal of Personality and Social Psychology, 78,* 478–498.

Murray, S. L., Holmes, J. G., Griffin, D. W., Bellavia, G., & Rose, P. (2001). The mismeasure of love: How self-doubt contaminates relationship beliefs. *Personality and Social Psychology Bulletin, 27,* 423–436.

Murtha, T. C., Kanfer, R., & Ackerman, P. L. (1996). Toward an interactionist taxonomy of personality and situations: An integrative situational-dispositional representation of personality traits. *Journal of Personality and Social Psychology, 71,* 193–207.

Myers, D. G., & Lamm, H. (1976). The group polarization phenomenon. *Psychological Bulletin, 83,* 602–627.

Nisbett, R. E., & Cohen, D. (1996). *Culture of honor: The psychology of violence in the South.* Boulder, CO: Westview Press.

Nisbett, R. E., Polly, G., & Lang, S. (1995). Homicide and U.S. regional culture. In R. B. Ruback & N. A. Weiner (Eds.), *Interpersonal violent behaviors: Social and cultural aspects* (pp. 135–151). New York: Springer.

Nisbett, R. E., & Ross, L. (1991). *The person and the situation: Perspectives of social psychology.* New York: McGraw-Hill.

Nucci, L. P., & Turiel, E. (1978). Social interactions and the development of social concepts in preschool children. *Child Development, 49,* 400–407.

Olekalns, M., & Smith, P. L. (1999). Social value orientations and strategy choices in competitive negotiations. *Personality and Social Psychology Bulletin, 25,* 657–668.

Orbell, J., & Dawes, R. (1981). Social dilemmas. In G. Stephenson & J. H. Davis (Eds.), *Progress in applied social psychology* (pp. 37–65). Chichester: Wiley.

Orbell, J., & Dawes, R. (1993). Social welfare, cooperators' advantage, and the option of not playing the game. *American Sociological Review, 58,* 787–800.

Orbell, J. M., Schwartz-Shea, P., & Simmons, R. T. (1984). Do cooperators exit more readily than defectors? *American Political Science Review, 78,* 147–162.

Orbell, J. M., Van de Kragt, A. J. C., & Dawes, R. M. (1988). Explaining discussion-induced cooperation. *Journal of Personality and Social Psychology, 54,* 811–819.

Osgood, C. E. (1962). *An alternative to war or surrender.* Urbana, IL: University of Illinois Press.

Osgood, C. E., Suci, G. J., & Tannenbaum, P. H. (1957). *The measurement of meaning.* Urbana, IL: University of Illinois Press.

Peeters, G., & Czapinski, J. (1990). Positive-negative asymmetry in evaluations: The distinction between affective and informational negativity effects. In W. Stroebe &

M. Hewstone (Eds.), *European review of social psychology* (Vol. 1, pp. 33–60). New York: Wiley.

Pemberton, M. B., Insko, C. A., & Schopler, J. (1996). Memory for and experience of differential competitive behavior of individuals and groups. *Journal of Personality and Social Psychology, 71*, 953–966.

Pepitone, A., & Saffiotti, L. (1997). The selectivity of nonmaterial beliefs in interpreting life events. *European Journal of Social Psychology, 27*, 23–35.

Pervin, L. A. (1976). A free-response description approach to the analysis of person-situation interaction. *Journal of Personality and Social Psychology, 34*, 465–474.

Pervin, L. A. (1978). Definitions, measurements, and classifications of stimuli, situations, and environments. *Human Ecology, 6*, 71–105.

Pinker, S. (1997). *How the mind works*. New York: Norton.

Pleban, R., & Tesser, A. (1981). The effects of relevance and quality of other's performance on interpersonal closeness. *Social Psychology Quarterly, 44*, 278–285.

Premo, B. E., & Stiles, W. B. (1983). Familiarity in verbal interactions of married couples versus strangers. *Journal of Social and Clinical Psychology, 1*, 209–230.

Pruitt, D. G. (1970). Motivational processes in the decomposed prisoner's dilemma game. *Journal of Personality and Social Psychology, 14*, 227–238.

Pruitt, D. G. (1998). Social conflict. In D. Gilbert, S. Fiske, & G. Lindzey (Eds.), *The handbook of social psychology* (4th ed.; Vol. 2, pp. 470–503). Boston: McGraw-Hill.

Pruitt, D. G., & Carnevale, P. J. (1993). *Negotiation in social conflict*. Pacific Grove, CA: Brooks/Cole.

Pruitt, D. G., & Kimmel, M. J. (1977). Twenty years of experimental gaming: Critique, synthesis, and suggestions for the future. *Annual Review of Psychology, 28*, 363–392.

Rapoport, A., & Bornstein, G. (1987). Intergroup competition for the provision of binary public goods. *Psychological Review, 94*, 291–299.

Rapoport, A., Bornstein, G., & Erev, I. (1989). Intergroup competition for public goods: Effects of unequal resources and relative group size. *Journal of Personality and Social Psychology, 56*, 748–756.

Rapoport, A., Budescu, D. V., Suleiman, R., & Weg, E. (1992). Social dilemmas with uniformly distributed resources. In W. Liebrand, D. Messick, & H. Wilke (Eds.), *Social dilemmas: Theoretical issues and research findings* (pp. 43–57). Elmsford, NY: Pergamon Press.

Rapoport, A., & Chammah, A. M. (1965a). *Prisoner's dilemma: A study in conflict and cooperation*. Ann Arbor: University of Michigan Press.

Rapoport, A., & Chammah, A. M. (1965b). Sex differences in factors contributing to the level of cooperation in the prisoner's dilemma game. *Journal of Personality and Social Psychology, 2*, 831–838.

Rapoport, A., & Guyer, M. (1966). A taxonomy of 2 × 2 games. *General Systems, 11*, 203–214.

Rawls, J. (1971). *A theory of justice*. Cambridge, MA: Belknap Press of Harvard University Press.

Reis, H. T., Collins, W. A., & Berscheid, E. (2000). The relationship context of human behavior and development. *Psychological Bulletin, 126*, 844–872.

Reis, H. T., & Patrick, B. C. (1996). Attachment and intimacy: Component processes. In E. T. Higgins & A. Kruglanski (Eds.), *Social psychology: Handbook of basic principles* (pp. 523–563). New York: Guilford.

Reis, H. T., & Shaver, P. (1988). Intimacy as an interpersonal process. In S. W. Duck (Ed.), *Handbook of personal relationships: Theory, research, and interventions* (pp. 367–389). Chichester, England: Wiley.

Reis, H. T., & Wheeler, L. (1991). Studying social interaction with the Rochester Interaction Record. In M. Zanna & L. Berkowitz (Ed.), *Advances in experimental social psychology* (Vol. 24, pp. 269–318). New York: Academic Press.

Rempel, J. K., Holmes, J. G., & Zanna, M. P. (1985). Trust in close relationships. *Journal of Personality and Social Psychology, 49,* 95–112.

Ricard, M., & Gouin-Decarie, T. (1993). Distance-maintaining in infants' reaction to an adult stranger. *Social Development, 2,* 145–164.

Rosch, E., (1988). Principles of categorization. In A. M. Collins & E. E. Smith (Eds.), *Readings in cognitive science: A perspective from psychology and artificial intelligence* (pp. 312–322). San Mateo, CA: Morgan Kaufmann, Inc.

Rosch, E., Mervis, C. B., Gray, W., Johnson, D., & Boyes-Braem, P. (1976). Basic objects in natural categories. *Cognitive Psychology, 8,* 382–439.

Rosenbaum, M. E. (1986). The repulsion hypothesis: On the nondevelopment of relationships. *Journal of Personality and Social Psychology, 51,* 1156–1166.

Ross, L., & Nisbett, R. E. (1991). *The person and the situation: Perspectives of social psychology.* New York: McGraw-Hill.

Ross, M., & Sicoly, F. (1979). Egocentric biases in availability and attribution. *Journal of Personality and Social Psychology, 37,* 322–336.

Roth, A. E. (1995). Introduction to experimental economics. In J. H. Kagel & A. E. Roth (Eds.), *The handbook of experimental economics* (pp. 3–109). Princeton, NJ: Princeton University Press.

Rotter, J. B. (1966). Generalized expectancies for internal versus external control of reinforcement. *Psychological Monographs, 80* (Whole No. 609).

Rozin, P. (2001). Social psychology and science: Some lessons from Solomon Asch. *Personality and Social Psychology Review, 5,* 2–14.

Rubin, J. Z., & Brockner, J. (1975). Factors affecting entrapment in waiting situations: The Rosencrantz and Guildenstern effect. *Journal of Personality and Social Psychology, 31,* 1054–1063.

Rubin, Z. (1975). Disclosing oneself to a stranger: Reciprocity and its limits. *Journal of Experimental Social Psychology, 11,* 233–260.

Rubin, Z., & Peplau, L. A. (1975). Who believes in a just world? *Journal of Social Issues, 31,* 65–89.

Rusbult, C. E. (1983). A longitudinal test of the investment model: The development (and deterioration) of satisfaction and commitment in heterosexual involvements. *Journal of Personality and Social Psychology, 45,* 101–117.

Rusbult, C. E., & Buunk, B. P. (1993). Commitment processes in close relationships: An interdependence analysis. *Journal of Social and Personal Relationships, 10,* 175–204.

Rusbult, C. E., Campbell, M. A., & Price, M. E. (1990). Rational selective exploitation and distress: Employee reactions to performance-based and mobility-based reward allocations. *Journal of Personality and Social Psychology, 59,* 487–500.

Rusbult, C. E., Drigotas, S. M., & Verette, J. (1994). The investment model: An interdependence analysis of commitment processes and relationship maintenance phenomena. In D. J. Canary & L. Stafford (Eds.), *Communication and relational maintenance* (pp. 115–139). San Diego, CA: Academic Press.

Rusbult, C. E., & Farrell, D. (1983). A longitudinal test of the investment model: The impact on job satisfaction, job commitment, and turnover of variations in rewards, costs, alternatives, and investments. *Journal of Applied Psychology, 68,* 429–438.

Rusbult, C. E., Lowery, D., Hubbard, M., Maravankin, O. J., & Neises, M. (1988). Impact of employee mobility and employee performance on the allocation of rewards under conditions of constraint. *Journal of Personality and Social Psychology, 54,* 605–615.

Rusbult, C. E., & Martz, J. M. (1995). Remaining in an abusive relationship: An investment model analysis of nonvoluntary commitment. *Personality and Social Psychology Bulletin, 21,* 558–571.

Rusbult, C. E., Olsen, N., Davis, J. L., & Hannon, P. (2001). Commitment and relationship maintenance mechanisms. In J. H. Harvey & A. Wenzel (Eds.), *Close romantic relationships: Maintenance and enhancement* (pp. 87–113). Mahwah, NJ: Erlbaum.

Rusbult, C. E., & Van Lange, P. A. M. (1996). Interdependence processes. In E. T. Higgins & A. Kruglanski (Eds.), *Social psychology: Handbook of basic principles* (pp. 564–596). New York: Guilford.

Rusbult, C. E., Van Lange, P. A. M., Wildschut, T., Yovetich, N. A., & Verette, J. (2000). Perceived superiority in close relationships: Why it exists and persists. *Journal of Personality and Social Psychology, 79,* 521–545.

Rusbult, C. E., Verette, J., Whitney, G. A., Slovik, L. F., & Lipkus, I. (1991). Accommodation processes in close relationships: Theory and preliminary empirical evidence. *Journal of Personality and Social Psychology, 60,* 53–78.

Ruscher, J. B., & Fiske, S. T. (1990). Interpersonal competition can cause individuating processes. *Journal of Personality and Social Psychology, 58,* 832–843.

Sabatelli, R. M., Buck, R., & Dreyer, A. (1980). Communication via facial cues in intimate dyads. *Personality and Social Psychology Bulletin, 6,* 242–247.

Safilios-Rothschild, C. (1976). A macro- and micro-examination of family power and love: An exchange model. *Journal of Marriage and the Family, 38,* 355–362.

Salovey, P., & Rodin, J. (1986). Differentiation of social-comparison jealousy and romantic jealousy. *Journal of Personality and Social Psychology, 50,* 1100–1112.

Salovey, P., & Rodin, J. (1991). Provoking jealousy and envy: Domain relevance and self-esteem threat. *Journal of Social and Clinical Psychology, 10,* 395–413.

Scanzoni, L. D., & Scanzoni, J. (1981). *Men, women and change* (2nd ed.). New York: McGraw-Hill.

Scheier, M. F., & Carver, C. S. (1987). Dispositional optimism and physical well-being: The influence of generalized outcome expectancies on health. *Journal of Personality, 55,* 169–210.

Scheier, M. F., & Carver, C. S. (1993). On the power of positive thinking: The benefits of being optimistic. *Current Directions in Psychological Science, 2,* 26–30.

Scheier, M. F., Carver, C. S., & Bridges, M. W. (1994). Distinguishing optimism from neuroticism (and trait anxiety, self-mastery, and self-esteem): A reevaluation of the Life Orientation Test. *Journal of Personality and Social Psychology, 67,* 1063–1078.

Scheier, M. F., Matthews, K. A., Owens, J. F., Magovern, Sr., J. G., Lefebvre, R., Abbott, R. C., & Carver, C. S. (1989). Dispositional optimism and recovery from coronary artery bypass graft surgery: The beneficial effects of optimism on physical and psychological well-being. *Journal of Personality and Social Psychology, 57,* 1024–1040.

Schelling, T. C. (1960). *The strategy of conflict.* Cambridge, MA: Harvard University Press.

Schopler, J., & Bateson, N. (1965). The power of dependence. *Journal of Personality and Social Psychology, 2,* 247–254.

Schopler, J., Hoyle, R. H., Dotson, K., & Marshall, J. (1988). *Husband/wife differences in the determinants of marital adjustment: The role of individual preference latitudes.* Unpublished manuscript, University of North Carolina, Chapel Hill, NC.

Schwarz, N., & Clore, G. L. (1996). Feelings and phenomenal experiences. In E. T. Higgins & A. Kruglanski (Eds.), *Social psychology: Handbook of basic principles* (pp. 433–465). New York: Guilford.

Searcy, E., & Eisenberg, N. (1992). Defensiveness in response to aid from a sibling. *Journal of Personality and Social Psychology, 62,* 422–433.

Secord, P. F. (1983). Imbalanced sex ratios: The social consequences. *Personality and Social Psychology Bulletin, 9,* 525–543.

Seligman, M. E. P. (1975). *Helplessness: On depression, development and death.* San Francisco: W. H. Freeman.

Sethi, A., Mischel, W., Aber, J. L., Shoda, Y., & Rodriguez, M. L. (2000). The role of strategic attention deployment in development of self-regulation: Predicting preschoolers' delay of gratification from mother-toddler interactions. *Developmental Psychology, 36,* 767–777.

Shanteau, J., & Nagy, G. F. (1979). Probability of acceptance in dating choice. *Journal of Personality and Social Psychology, 37,* 522–533.

Sharpsteen, D. J., & Kirkpatrick, L. A. (1997). Romantic jealousy and adult romantic attachment. *Journal of Personality and Social Psychology, 72,* 627–640.

Shaver, P. R., Belsky, J., & Brennan, K. A. (2000). The adult attachment interview and self-reports of romantic attachment: Associations across domains and methods. *Personal Relationships, 7,* 25–43.

Sheppard, B. H., Blumenfeld-Jones, K., & Roth, J. (1989). Informal thirdpartyship: Studies of everyday conflict intervention. In K. Kressel, D. G. Pruitt, & Associates (Eds.) *Mediation Research* (pp. 166–189). San Franciso: Jossey-Bass.

Shoda, Y., Mischel, W., & Wright, J. C. (1993). The role of situational demands and cognitive competencies in behavior organization and personality coherence. *Journal of Personality and Social Psychology, 65,* 1023–1035.

Shoda, Y., Mischel, W., & Wright, J. C. (1994). Intra-individual stability in the organization and patterning of behavior: Incorporating psychological situations into the idiographic analysis of personality. *Journal of Personality and Social Psychology, 67,* 674–687.

Sidowski, J. B., Wyckoff, L. B., & Tabory, L. (1956). The influence of reinforcement and punishment in a minimal social situation. *Journal of Abnormal and Social Psychology, 52*, 115–119.

Simmel, G. (1950). *The sociology of Georg Simmel.* Translated, edited and with an introduction by K. H. Wolff. Glencoe, IL: The Free Press.

Simon, H. A. (1990). Alternative visions of rationality. In P. K. Moser (Ed.), *Rationality in action: Contemporary approaches* (pp. 189–204). New York: Cambridge University Press.

Simpson, J. A. (1987). The dissolution of romantic relationships: Factors involved in relationship stability and emotional distress. *Journal of Personality and Social Psychology, 53*, 683–692.

Simpson, J. A., Gangestad, S. W., & Lerma, M. (1990). Perception of physical attractiveness: Mechanisms involved in the maintenance of romantic relationships. *Journal of Personality and Social Psychology, 59*, 1192–1201.

Simpson, J. A., Rholes, W. S., & Nelligan, J. S. (1992). Support seeking and support giving within couples in an anxiety-provoking situation: The role of attachment styles. *Journal of Personality and Social Psychology, 62*, 434–446.

Skinner, B. F. (1953). *Science and human behavior.* New York: Macmillan.

Smelser, W. T. (1961). Dominance as a factor in achievement and perception in co-operative problem solving interactions. *Journal of Abnormal and Social Psychology, 62*, 535–542.

Snyder, M. (1993). Basic research and practical problems: The promise of a "functional" personality and social psychology. *Personality and Social Psychology Bulletin, 19*, 251–264.

Snyder, M., & Cantor, N. (1998). Understanding personality and social behavior: A functionalist strategy. In D. T. Gilbert, S. T. Fiske, & G. Lindzey (Eds.), *The handbook of social psychology* (4th ed.; Vol. 1, pp. 635–679). Boston: McGraw-Hill.

Snyder, M., & Gangestad, S. (1982). Choosing social situations: Two investigations of self-monitoring processes. *Journal of Personality and Social Psychology, 43*, 123–135.

Snyder, M., & Ickes, W. (1985). Personality and social behavior. In G. Lindzey & E. Aronson (Eds.), *The handbook of social psychology* (pp. 883–947). New York: Random House.

Snyder, M., Tanke, E. D., & Berscheid, E. (1977). Social perception and interpersonal behavior. *Journal of Personality and Social Psychology, 35*, 656–666.

Solano, C. H., & Dunnam, M. (1985). Two's company: Self-disclosure and reciprocity in triads versus dyads. *Social Psychology Quarterly, 48*, 183–187.

Sorokin, P. A., & Berger, C. Q. (1939). *Time-budgets of human behavior.* Cambridge, MA: Harvard University Press.

Sorrentino, R. M., Holmes, J. G., Hanna, S. E., & Sharp, A. (1995). Uncertainty orientation and trust in close relationships: Individual differences in cognitive styles. *Journal of Personality and Social Psychology, 68*, 314–327.

Sorrentino, R. M., Roney, C. J. R, & Hanna, S. E. (1992). Uncertainty orientation. In C. P. Smith & J. W. Atkinson (Eds.), *Motivation and personality: Handbook of thematic content analysis* (pp. 419–427). New York: Cambridge University Press.

South, S. J., & Lloyd, K. M. (1995). Spousal alternatives and marital dissolution. *American Sociological Review, 60*, 21–35.

Sprecher, S. (1985). Sex differences in bases of power in dating relationships. *Sex Roles, 12*, 449–462.

Stasser, G. (1999). The uncertain role of unshared information in collective choice. In L. L. Thompson & J. M. Levine (Eds.), *Shared cognition in organizations: The management of knowledge* (pp. 49–69). Mahwah, NJ: Erlbaum.

Stasser, G., Stewart, D. D., & Wittenbaum, G. M. (1995). Expert roles and information exchange during discussion: The importance of knowing who knows what. *Journal of Experimental Social Psychology, 3*, 244–265.

Stasser, G., & Titus, W. (1985). Pooling of unshared information in group decision making: Biased information sampling during discussion. *Journal of Personality and Social Psychology, 48*, 1467–1478.

Staw, B. M. (1976). Knee-deep in the big muddy: A study of escalating commitment to a chosen course of action. *Organizational Behavior and Human Performance, 16*, 27–44.

Staw, B. M. (1981). The escalation of commitment to a course of action. *Academy of Management Review, 6*, 577–587.

Steck, L., Levitan, D., McLane, D., & Kelley, H. H. (1982). Care, need, and conceptions of love. *Journal of Personality and Social Psychology, 43*, 481–491.

Steiner, I. D. (1972). *Group process and productivity*. New York: Academic Press.

Steiner, I. D. (1986). Paradigms and groups. In L. Berkowitz (Ed.), *Advances in experimental social psychology* (Vol. 19, pp. 251–289). Orlando, FL: Academic Press.

Stickland, B. R. (1972). Delay of gratification as a function of race of the experimenter. *Journal of Personality and Social Psychology, 22*, 108–112.

Suleiman, R., Rapoport, A., & Budescu, D. (1996). Fixed position and property rights in sequential resource dilemmas under uncertainty. *Acta Psychologia, 93*, 229–246.

Swann, W., Hixon, J., & De La Ronde, C. (1992). Embracing the "bitter truth": Negative self-concepts and marital commitment. *Psychological Science, 3*, 118–121.

Taylor, R. B., De Soto, C. B., & Lieb, R. (1979). Sharing secrets: Disclosure and discretion in dyads and triads. *Journal of Personality and Social Psychology, 37*, 1196–1203.

Taylor, S. E. (1983). Adjustment to threatening events: A theory of cognitive adaptation. *American Psychologist, 38*, 1161–1173.

Taylor, S. E., & Brown, J. D. (1988). Illusion and well-being: A social psychological perspective on mental health. *Psychological Bulletin, 103*, 193–210.

Teger, A. I. (1980). *Too much invested to quit*. New York: Pergamon.

Tesser, A. (1988). Toward a self-evaluation maintenance model of social behavior. In L. Berkowitz (Ed.), *Advances in experimental social psychology* (Vol. 21, pp. 181–227). San Diego, CA, Academic Press.

Thaler, R. H. (1992). *The winner's curse: Paradoxes and anomalies of economic life*. New York: The Free Press.

Thibaut, J. W. (1965). The motivational effects of social dependence on a powerful agency of control. In W. Cooper, H. Leavitt, & M. Shelly (Eds.), *New perspectives in organization research* (pp. 87–96). New York: Wiley.

Thibaut, J. W., & Faucheux, C. (1965). The development of contractual norms in a bargaining situation under two types of stress. *Journal of Experimental Social Psychology, 1,* 87–102.

Thibaut, J. W., & Kelley, H. H. (1959). *The social psychology of groups.* New York: Wiley.

Thibaut, J., & Walker, L. (1975). *Procedural justice: A psychological analysis.* Hillsdale, NJ: Erlbaum.

Thomas, G., Fletcher, G. J. O., & Lange, C. (1997). On-line empathic accuracy in marital interaction. *Journal of Personality and Social Psychology, 72,* 839–850.

Thompson, L. L. (1990). The influence of experience on negotiation performance. *Journal of Experimental Social Psychology, 26,* 528–544.

Thompson, L. L. (1998). *The mind and heart of the negotiator.* Upper Saddle River, NJ: Prentice Hall.

Thompson, L. L., & Hastie, R. (1991). Social perception in negotiation. *Organizational Behavior and Human Decision Processes, 47,* 98–123.

Thompson, L. L., & Hrebec, D. (1996). Lose-lose agreements in interdependent decision making. *Psychological Bulletin, 120,* 396–409.

Tidwell, M. C. O., Reis, H. T., & Shaver, P. R. (1996). Attachment, attractiveness, and social interaction: A diary study. *Journal of Personality and Social Psychology, 71,* 729–745.

Tjosvold, D. (1981). Unequal power relationships within a cooperative or competitive context. *Journal of Applied Social Psychology, 11,* 137–150.

Tjosvold, D., Johnson, D. W., & Johnson, R. (1984). Influence strategy, perspective-taking, and relationships between high- and low-power individuals in cooperative and competitive contexts. *Journal of Psychology, 116,* 187–202.

Tjosvold, D., & Sagaria, S. D. (1978). Effects of relative power on cognitive perspective-taking. *Personality and Social Psychology Bulletin, 4,* 256–259.

Tooby, J., & Cosmides, L. (1992). The psychological foundations of culture. In J. H. Barkow, L. Cosmides, & J. Tooby (Eds.), *The adapted mind: Evolutionary psychology and the generation of culture* (pp. 119–136). New York: Oxford University Press.

Tooby, J., & Cosmides, L. (1996). Friendship and the banker's paradox: Other pathways to the evolution of adaptations for altruism. *Proceedings of the British Academy, 88,* 119–143.

Tropper, R. (1972). The consequences of investment in the process of conflict. *Journal of Conflict Resolution, 16,* 97–98.

Turiel, E. (1983). *The development of social knowledge: Morality and convention.* Cambridge, England: Cambridge University Press.

Turner, R. H. (1970). *Family interaction.* New York: Wiley.

Tversky, A., & Kahneman, D. (1974). Judgments under uncertainty: Heuristics and biases. *Science, 185,* 1124–1131.

Tyler, T. (1990). *Why people obey the law: Procedural justice, legitimacy, and compliance.* New Haven, CT: Yale University Press.

Van de Vliert, E. (1990). Positive effects of conflict: A field assessment. *International Journal of Conflict Management, 1,* 69–80.

Van Dijk, E., & Wilke, H. A. M. (1993). Differential interests, equity, and public good provision. *Journal of Experimental Social Psychology, 29,* 1–16.

Van Dijk, E., & Wilke, H. A. M. (1994). Asymmetry of wealth and public good provision. *Social Psychology Quarterly, 57*, 352–359.

Van Lange, P. A. M. (1994). Toward more locomotion in experimental games. In U. Schulz, W. Albers, & U. Mueller (Eds.), *Social dilemmas and cooperation* (pp. 25–43). New York: Springer.

Van Lange, P. A. M. (1999). The pursuit of joint outcomes and equality in outcomes: An integrative model of social value orientation. *Journal of Personality and Social Psychology, 77*, 337–349.

Van Lange, P. A. M., Agnew, C. R., Harinck, F., & Steemers, G. E. M. (1997). From game theory to real life: How social value orientation affects willingness to sacrifice in ongoing close relationships. *Journal of Personality and Social Psychology, 73*, 1330–1344.

Van Lange, P. A. M., & De Dreu, C. K. (2001). Social interaction: Cooperation and competition. In M. Hewstone & W. Stroebe (Eds.), *Introduction to social psychology* (pp. 341–369). Oxford: Blackwell.

Van Lange, P. A. M., & Kuhlman, D. M. (1994). Social value orientations and impressions of a partner's honesty and intelligence: A test of the might versus morality effect. *Journal of Personality and Social Psychology, 67*, 126–141.

Van Lange, P. A. M., Liebrand, W. B. G., & Kuhlman, M. (1990). Causal attribution of choice behavior in three *n*-person prisoner's dilemmas. *Journal of Experimental Social Psychology, 26*, 34–48.

Van Lange, P. A. M., Otten, W., De Bruin, E. M. N., & Joireman, J. A. (1997). Development of prosocial, individualistic, and competitive orientations: Theory and preliminary evidence. *Journal of Personality and Social Psychology, 73*, 733–746.

Van Lange, P. A. M., Ouwerkerk, J. W., & Tazelaar, M. J. A. (2002). How to overcome the detrimental effects of noise in social interaction: The benefits of generosity. *Journal of Personality and Social Psychology, 82*, 768–780.

Van Lange, P. A. M., Rusbult, C. E., Drigotas, S. M., Arriaga, X. B., Witcher, B. S., & Cox, C. L. (1997). Willingness to sacrifice in close relationships. *Journal of Personality and Social Psychology, 72*, 1373–1395.

Van Lange, P. A. M., & Visser, K. (1999). Locomotion in social dilemmas: How we adapt to cooperative, tit-for-tat, and noncooperative partners. *Journal of Personality and Social Psychology, 77*, 762–773.

Wagner, W., Kirchler, E., & Brandstatter, H. (1984). Marital relationships and purchasing decisions: To buy or not to buy, that is the question. *Journal of Economic Psychology, 5*, 139–157.

Waller, W. (1938). *The family: A dynamic interpretation*. New York: Dryden.

Walster, E., Walster, G. W., & Berscheid, E. (1978). *Equity: Theory and research*. Boston: Allyn and Bacon.

Webster, D. M., & Kruglanski, A. W. (1994). Individual differences in need for closure. *Journal of Personality and Social Psychology, 67*, 1049–1062.

Wedekind, C., & Milinski, M. (2000). Cooperation through image scoring in humans. *Science, 288*, 850–852.

Wegner, D. M., Erber, R., & Raymond, P. (1991). Transactive memory in close relationships. *Journal of Personality and Social Psychology, 61*, 923–929.

Weinstein, N. D. (1980). Unrealistic optimism about future life events. *Journal of Personality and Social Psychology, 39*, 806–820.

Wheeler, L., & Nezlek, J. (1977). Sex differences in social participation. *Journal of Personality and Social Psychology, 35*, 742–754.

Wheeler, L., Reis, H. T., & Nezlek, J. (1983). Loneliness, social interaction, and sex roles. *Journal of Personality and Social Psychology, 49*, 129–147.

White, G. L. (1980). Physical attractiveness and courtship progress. *Journal of Personality and Social Psychology, 39*, 660–668.

White, G. L. (1981a). A model of romantic jealousy. *Motivation and Emotion, 5*, 295–310.

White, G. L. (1981b). Some correlates of romantic jealousy. *Journal of Personality, 49*, 129–147.

Wicker, A. (1979). *An introduction to ecological psychology*. Pacific Grove, CA: Brooks/Cole.

Widmeyer, W. N., Brawley, L. R., & Carron, A. V. (1992). Group dynamics in sports. In T. S. Horn (Ed.), *Advances in sport psychology* (pp. 163–180). Champaign, IL: Human Kinetics Publishers.

Wieselquist, J., Rusbult, C. E., Foster, C. A., & Agnew, C. R. (1999). Commitment, pro-relationship behavior, and trust in close relationships. *Journal of Personality and Social Psychology, 77*, 942–966.

Wiggins, J. S., & Trapnell, P. D. (1996). A dyadic-interactional perspective on the five-factor model. In J. S. Wiggins (Ed.), *The five-factor model of personality: Theoretical perspectives* (pp. 88–162). New York: Guilford Press.

Williams, K. D., Harkins, S., & Latané, B. (1981). Identifiability as a deterrent to social loafing: Two cheering experiments. *Journal of Personality and Social Psychology, 40*, 303–311.

Williams, K. D., & Karau, S. J. (1991). Social loafing and social compensation: The effects of expectations of co-worker performance. *Journal of Personality and Social Psychology, 61*, 570–581.

Winch, R. F. (1958). *Mate-selection: A study of complementary needs*. New York: Harper & Row.

Wish, M., Deutsch, M., & Kaplan, S. J. (1976). Perceived dimensions of interpersonal relations. *Journal of Personality and Social Psychology, 33*, 409–420.

Wish, M. & Kaplan, S. J. (1977). Toward an implicit theory of interpersonal communication. *Social Psychology Quarterly, 40*, 234–246.

Wit, A., & Kerr, N. L. (1992). *Social categorization and cooperation in nested social dilemmas*. Paper presented at the Joint Meeting of the European Association of Experimental Social Psychology and the Society of Experimental Social Psychology, Leuven/Louvain-la-Neuve, Belgium, July, 1992.

Wit, A., Wilke, H. A. M., & Oppewal, H. (1992). Fairness in asymmetric social dilemmas. In W. B. G. Liebrand, D. M. Messick, & H. A. M. Wilke (Eds.), *Social dilemmas: Theoretical issues and research findings* (pp. 183–197). New York: Pergamon.

Witcher, B. S. (1999). *The effects of power on relationships and on individuals*. Unpublished dissertation, University of North Carolina at Chapel Hill, Chapel Hill, NC.

Wrightsman, L. S. (1992). *Assumptions about human nature: Implications for researchers and practitioners*. Newbury Park, CA: Sage.

Yamagishi, T. (1988a). Exit from the group as an individualistic solution to the free-rider problem in the United States and Japan. *Journal of Experimental Social Psychology, 24*, 530–542.

Yamagishi, T. (1988b). The provision of a sanctioning system in the United States and Japan. *Social Psychology Quarterly, 51*, 264–270.

Yamagishi, T., & Sato, K. (1986). Motivational bases of the public goods problem. *Journal of Personality and Social Psychology, 50*, 67–73.

Yamagishi, T., & Yamagishi, M. (1994). Trust and commitment in the United States and Japan. *Motivation and Emotion, 18*, 129–166.

Zajonc, R. B. (1998). As quoted in the *APA Monitor* (September, 1998). Washington, DC: APA.

Zajonc, R. B. (1999). One hundred years of rationality assumptions in social psychology. In A. Rodrigues & R. V. Levine (Eds.), *Reflections on 100 years of experimental social psychology* (pp. 200–214). New York: Basic Books.

Zajonc, R. B., & Sales, S. M. (1966). Social facilitation of dominant and subordinate responses. *Journal of Experimental Social Psychology, 2*, 160–168.

Zuckerman, M. (1971). Dimensions of sensation seeking. *Journal of Consulting and Clinical Psychology, 36*, 42–52.

Zuckerman, M. (1974). The sensation seeking motive. In B. Maher (Ed.), *Progress in experimental personality research* (Vol. 7, pp. 79–148). New York: Academic Press.

Zuckerman, M. (1978). Sensation-seeking. In H. London & J. E. Exner, Jr. (Eds.), *Dimensions of personality* (pp. 487–559). New York: Wiley.

Zuckerman, M. (1994). *Behavioral expressions and biosocial bases of sensation seeking.* New York: Cambridge University Press.

Zuckerman, M., Siegelbaum, H., & Williams, R. (1977). Predicting helping behavior: Willingness and ascription of responsibility. *Journal of Applied Social Psychology, 7*, 295–299.

Author Index

Subject Index

abstract categories, of situations, 25, 38, 39, 41

actor control: and asymmetric dependence, 250; and mutual independence situation, 130; and outcome controls, 35–6, 37, 42–3. *See also* Bilateral Actor Control; joint control; Mutual Joint control; Mutual Partner Control

adaptation, and increasing interdependence, 138–9. *See also* evolutionary theory

ad lib conditions, 53, 55

adversarial procedure, 399–400

affect, interdependence and situation-relevant versus person-relevant, 137–8. *See also* emotional reactions

affiliation, and mutual independence situations, 132

affordance: and social person factors, 74; and unstructured versus structured situations, 348

allocation and allocators, and Threat situation, 193, 194, 196, 197, 201

alternatives: and asymmetric dependence, 253; and Delay of Gratification, 313; and Investment situation, 288; and Prisoner's Dilemma, 182–4. *See also* Movement among situations

altruism: and Mutual Partner Control, 145; and Prisoner's Dilemma, 179; and Twists of Fate, 379–80

analysis of variance, 33, 34–5, 36–7, 39–41

assertiveness, and Hero situation, 223

assertive-receptive relationships, 156

assessment, and locomotion in Investment situations, 298

Assurance Game, and *N*-person Prisoner's Dilemma, 425, 428

asymmetric dependence: conceptual description of, 249–51; examples of, 249; matrix representations of, 266–7; and outcome controls, 42; and patterns of interdependence, 47–9; and selection between situations, 66; and three-component patterns, 95–101; variants and combinations of, 251–2. *See also* dependence

atlas: and future research on interdependence situations, 458–9; metaphor of, 17; organization of, 16; situational analysis and concept of, 11–15; as theoretical tool, 456–8

attachment theory: and asymmetric dependence, 265; and Delay of Gratification, 316–17; intimacy and concept of responsiveness, 406; and Investment situation, 300; and Iterated Prisoner's Dilemma, 283; and Movement among Situations, 66, 442–3, 444

attention: and asymmetric dependence, 256–7; interdependence and situation-relevant versus person-relevant, 137–8

attraction, and situation selection in relationships, 443. *See also* physical attractiveness; reciprocal attraction

attribution: and asymmetric dependence, 258–60; and Conjunctive situations, 232–3

authoritarianism, and Movement among Situations, 440

autonomy, and mutual independence, 135–6

avoidant behavior, and conflict patterns in close relationships, 198–9